SAGE Publishing: Our Story

At SAGE, we mean business. We believe in creating evidence-based, cutting-edge content that helps you prepare your students to succeed in today's ever-changing business world. We strive to provide you with the tools you need to develop the next generation of leaders, managers, and entrepreneurs.

- We invest in the right AUTHORS who distill research findings and industry ideas into practical applications.

- We keep our prices AFFORDABLE and provide multiple FORMAT OPTIONS for students.

- We remain permanently independent and fiercely committed to QUALITY CONTENT and INNOVATIVE RESOURCES.

D0780780

Human Resource Information Systems

Fifth Edition

To my wife, Kelley, and my daughters, Rachel and Katherine – R. D. J.

To my wife, Lisa, my daughter Melanie, and son Bryce—you have inspired me and kept me anchored –K. D. C

To my wife, Barbara, and my sons Sean, Colin, and Timothy, and especially to my granddaughter, Isabella – M. J. K.

Human Resource Information Systems

Fifth Edition

Editors

Richard D. Johnson

Washington State University

Kevin D. Carlson

Virginia Tech

Michael J. Kavanagh

University at Albany, State University of New York

Los Angeles | London | New Delhi
Singapore | Washington DC | Melbourne

FOR INFORMATION:

SAGE Publications, Inc.
2455 Teller Road
Thousand Oaks, California 91320
E-mail: order@sagepub.com

SAGE Publications Ltd.
1 Oliver's Yard
55 City Road
London EC1Y 1SP
United Kingdom

SAGE Publications India Pvt. Ltd.
B 1/I 1 Mohan Cooperative
Industrial Area
Mathura Road, New Delhi 110 044
India

SAGE Publications Asia-Pacific Pte. Ltd.
18 Cross Street #10-10/11/12
China Square Central
Singapore 048423

Library of Congress Cataloging-in-Publication Data

Names: Johnson, Richard David editor, Kevin D. Carlson editor, Kavanagh, Michael J., editor.

Title: Human resource information systems / editors, Richard D. Johnson, Washington State University, Kevin D. Carlson, Virginia Tech, Michael J. Kavanagh, University at Albany, State University of New York.

Description: Fifth Edition. | Thousand Oaks : SAGE Publications, Inc, 2020. | Revised edition of Human resource information systems, [2018] | Includes bibliographical references. | Summary: "Human Resource Information Systems: Basics, Applications, and Future Directions is a one-of-a-kind book that provides a thorough introduction to the field of Human Resource Information Systems (HRIS) and shows how organizations today can leverage HRIS to make better people decisions and manage talent more effectively. Unlike other texts that overwhelm students with technical information and jargon, this revised Fifth Edition offers a balanced approach in dealing with HR issues and IT/IS issues by drawing from experts in both areas. It includes the latest research and developments in the areas of HRIS justification strategies, HR technology, big data, and artificial intelligence"– Provided by publisher.

Identifiers: LCCN 2020025063 | ISBN 9781544396743 (paperback) | ISBN 9781544396767 (epub) | ISBN 9781544396750 (epub) | ISBN 9781544396774 (ebook)

Subjects: LCSH: Personnel management–Information technology. | Personnel management—Data processing.

Classification: LCC HF5549.5.D37 H86 2020 | DDC 658.300285–dc23

LC record available at https://lccn.loc.gov/2020025063

This book is printed on acid-free paper.

Acquisitions Editor: Maggie Stanley
Sponsoring Editor: Lauren Gobell
Production Editor: Astha Jaiswal
Copy Editor: Kim Husaband
Typesetter: Hurix Digital
Indexer: Integra
Cover Designer: Candice Harman
Marketing Manager: Sarah Panella

20 21 22 23 24 10 9 8 7 6 5 4 3 2 1

BRIEF CONTENTS

DETAILED CONTENTS

PART III • HUMAN RESOURCE INFORMATION SYSTEMS APPLICATIONS   149

Chapter 7 • HR Administration and HRIS   150

By Linda C. Isenhour and Christopher J. Hartwell

Chapter 14 • HR Metrics and Workforce Analytics 359

By Kevin D. Carlson and Michael J. Kavanagh

PREFACE

As we move into the fifth edition of the book, we once again start with a quote from *Good to Great* by Jim Collins. In the book, he notes that "Great vision without great people is irrelevant." In a sense, this quote gets at the heart of human resources . . . attracting, hiring, motivating, training, and retaining the best people for your organization. However, to be truly successful in this mission, it is becoming critical that organizations leverage investments in technology to support all aspects of human resources management. In this fifth edition of *Human Resource Information Systems: Basics, Applications, and Future Directions*, we continue to focus on the idea of using technology to ensure that organizations can attract, hire, and retain the best talent while also meeting decision-making needs of managers and best supporting an HR strategy that aligns with that of the organization.

The fifth edition of this book has several goals. First, we want to update the text to reflect the current use of technology in organizations. The core HRIS, although still the center of any HR technology investments, is no longer the only technology supporting HR. New technologies such as mobile devices, social media, and artificial intelligence (AI) are driving changes in how organizations deploy technology in HR. Second, we wish to continue to improve the usefulness of the text for faculty and students. Third, we continue with our goals of presenting a broad-based perspective on HRIS, one that includes a focus developing and implementing these systems, an understanding of how these systems impact the practice of HR across several functions, and finally a discussion of the ongoing developments in these systems (e.g., metrics, social media, international HRM, AI). Although there have been several books on HRIS published, most authors have focused only on one aspect or dimension of the HRIS field, for example, on e-HRM, Web-based HR, or the strategic deployment of HRIS in a global context.

In the preface to the first edition of this book, we noted that Kavanagh et al. (1990) stated that "among the most significant changes in the field of human resources management in the past decade has been the use of computers to develop what have become known as human resource information systems (HRIS)" (p. v). Although this statement is now 30 years old, it is important to remember that the introduction of computers to the field of HRM during the 1980s and early 1990s was a *revolutionary* change. That is, paper systems in file cabinets were replaced by HRIS on mainframes and PCs. To keep up with these technological changes in HRM, companies were forced to adapt to remain competitive, even though it was quite expensive. Although we have previously suggested that the changes since the early 1990s were evolutionary, in the past decade, we have entered another period of revolutionary change. No longer are companies purchasing a HRIS, customizing it to fit their needs, and installing it locally. Instead, today organizations are moving to cloud computing, where they "rent" space to maintain their data and rely on the vendors to manage and support the system. In addition, HR is taking advantage of systems outside of organizational control, such as Twitter, Facebook, Instagram, YouTube, and more to support employees throughout the employment life cycle. Finally, companies are embracing AI to support better decision making, to automate processes, and to improve business operations. Thus, HR must develop policies to address this vastly different environment, in which jobs are rapidly changing and much of the data supporting "people" decisions are accessed remotely and often are stored on systems not under the direct control of the organization.

Along with these changes in technology, a revolution has come to the practice of human resources. By adopting software to support HR functioning, HR now has more information on employees and can use this understanding to better attract candidates, hire better employees, and more effectively manage them. In other words, these changes have meant that there have been significant advances in the use of people resources in managerial decisions. Thus, the role of HRM has evolved so that it is increasingly viewed as a strategic partner in the organization. In addition, the role of an HR professional is changing, and the most successful HR professionals will have both HR expertise and a knowledge of and appreciation for how a variety of technology tools can support "people practices" within HR and within the firm.

What do these changes mean for the new learner with a background in HRM or IT who is trying to understand the HRIS field? Although it may be tempting to think that the optimal approach is to train students on the latest HRIS software and the latest trends in HRIS, in reality, this would be like starting with Chapter 17 of this book and then proceeding backward through the book. Unfortunately, many people do, in fact, focus on learning the actual software tool itself (e.g., the HRIS) and the technological advances in HRIS without understanding the basics first. The approach we take in this book, and one we recommend, is to start with an understanding of the *evolutional* changes to technology and how these changes have transformed HR practices (e.g., how HRM moved from using paper records in file cabinets to the computerization of the HR function) and how this interplay between technology and human resources has changed and will continue to change the field of HRIS. Only after understanding these changes will the learner be able to effectively understand how advances in technology can help their organization manage their HR function more effectively.

NEW ASPECTS OF THE FIFTH EDITION

As we do in each edition of the text, we have made substantial revisions in response to feedback from adopters and by advances in the field of HRIS. Consistent with the previous version of the text, we have four main parts to the book:

- Human Resource Information Systems (HRIS)

- Managing HRIS Implementations

- Electronic Human Resource Management (eHRM)

- Advanced HRIS Applications and Future Trends

In our first section, we discuss the modern HRIS, strategic considerations in HRIS adoption and use, and the key IT architectures and people who interact with the HRIS. Chapter 1 continues to evolve as technology evolves, with the goal of more clearly describing how technology is transforming human resources. It further defines what an HRIS is, discusses how an HRIS contributes to HR functioning, and briefly touches the advantages and risks of using HRIS. We have a new Chapter 12, "Strategic Considerations in HRIS," written by Huub Ruël and Tanya Bondarouk. Although understanding the process of developing and using an HRIS's important, any adoption decision must be undertaken in light of HR's strategy. In Chapter 12, the authors discuss the strategic considerations when adopting HRIS and how an HRIS can support HR and organizational strategy.

In our second section, Managing HRIS Implementations, we focus on the development and implementation of a HRIS in an organizational setting. Chapter 6 has been updated with current thinking on justifying HRIS investments, examining different justification strategies, and exemplar calculations that can demonstrate how benefits and costs of HRIS implementation can be estimated. These estimates are useful for guiding decisions about investment choices but also in identifying potential contingencies that may need to be managed during implementation to maximize returns.

Section 3 focuses on eHRM, or the management and delivery of HR functionality enabled by technology. In this section, each chapter focuses on a major functional area of human resources (e.g., recruitment, selection, training, etc.) and discusses how technology is changing its practice. In addition, these chapters bring in some of the latest research-based recommendations for using HR technology. In Chapter 7, we welcome aboard Christopher Hartwell, who adds his expertise to the discussion of HR administration.

The final section of our book focuses on advanced HRIS topics. The chapters in this section continue to evolve. Chapter 14 has been updated to bring out the use of big data, AI, and the importance of the decision-making processes to metrics. Andrew Johnson has joined Stephanie Black in a substantial rewrite of the chapter on the role of social media in HR (Chapter 16). This is an important and timely topic, as many organizations are embracing social media despite the potential risks involved. Finally, Chapter 17 has been updated with a discussion of the latest trends in HR and HRIS that will shape the future of the field, including blockchain and artificial intelligence.

As with the fourth edition, we include a number of "industry briefs" in which industry leaders briefly discuss the importance of the chapter's topic and how it plays out in their firm or industry. Continued positive feedback has contributed to our decision to retain our "HRIS in Action" feature. We did these things to improve the text as a learning and teaching tool—we wanted the text and each chapter within it to present a complete learning experience. Thus, we also continued the consistent structure across all chapters that was introduced in the previous edition. Chapters contain, in the following order: (1) an editors' note, (2) chapter objectives, (3) an industry brief (where included), (4) chapter content, (5) chapter summary, (6) a list of key terms, (7) chapter discussion questions, and (8) a case with student discussion questions. This internal *consistency* for each chapter was established by emphasizing the same chapter learning points for the chapter objectives, chapter summary, key terms, and chapter discussion questions. We felt that this within-chapter consistency would aid the learning process of the students and aid the faculty in identifying the important content of each chapter. Likewise, the websites and additional readings in the appendix have been expanded because of recent changes in the field. In determining to make these changes in the book, the coeditors worked to make this a textbook they would personally be comfortable using to teach their HRIS courses.

FIFTH EDITION SUMMARY

In summary, in this fifth edition, we have described the major advances in the field of HRIS and the relation of HRIS to managerial decision making while, at the same time, exploring the basic concepts of developing, implementing, and maintaining an HRIS. The book represents the intersection of the best thinking and concepts from the two fields of HRM and IT. It was the early intersection of these two fields that changed the role of HR in organizations from record keeper to strategic partner. After introducing the basic concepts of an HRIS combined with new approaches to the operation of HRM in the organization, we then proceed to the more advanced and evolutionary technical changes. The basic philosophy of this book is that the integration or harmonization of technology with people management in an HRIS will create a distinct competitive advantage for organizations. We hope that you, the reader, gain this understanding and that you enjoy this book.

TEACHING RESOURCES

This text includes an array of instructor teaching materials designed to save you time and to help you keep students engaged. To learn more, visit sagepub.com or contact your SAGE representative at sagepub.com/findmyrep.

ACKNOWLEDGMENTS

Undertaking a book like this cannot be done without the contribution of many individuals. Each of you have our thanks, for without you, this book would not be as successful as it has been. First to both the new and returning authors of the chapters . . . THANK YOU! For some of you, this is your Fifth time, and we greatly appreciate all the time and effort you have placed into your chapters each and every time. We know how difficult it is to write a chapter for an edited book, particularly when the editors have defined the philosophy and approach used.

As we regularly do, we again thank Dianna Stone of the University at Albany, SUNY, Virginia Tech, and the University of New Mexico, who has helped us identify potential authors, provided feedback on the book, and co-authored a chapter on privacy and security. Our thanks go to the professionals in the International Association for Human Resource Information Management (IHRIM) and the Society for Human Resource Management (SHRM) who patiently listened and responded to our ideas regarding this book. We would also like to thank Lauren Gobell and Maggie Stanley for their guidance and help in keeping us focused and on track, as well as for their suggestions for resolving technical issues we encountered in writing the book. Finally, we would like to thank copyeditor Kim Husband and Astha Jaiswal for correcting our grammar as needed, finding missing keywords, and finding those mistyped words and grammatical errors that were done by gremlins.

SAGE Publishing gratefully acknowledges the following reviewers for their kind assistance:

Syed Adeel Ahmed, *Xavier University of Louisiana*

Mesut Akdere, *University of Wisconsin-Milwaukee*

Yvonne Barry, *John Tyler Community College*

Kristen Irey Esquire PHR, *Peirce College*

Dan Farrell, *Western Michigan University*

Ray Gibney, *Penn State Harrisburg*

Jonathan Halbesleben, *University of Alabama*

Heidi Helgren, *Delta College*

Tarona Lee, *Baruch College*

Gery Markova, *Wichita State University*

Marc S. Miller, *New York University*

Frank J. Mueller, *Oakland City University*

Jan Mason Rauk, *University of Idaho*

Joel Rudin, *Rowan University*

Azlineer Sarip, *Universiti Teknologi Malaysia*

M. Shane Tomblin, *Marshall University*

Surette Wärnich, *University of South Africa*

Lee Whiteman, *La Roche College*

You will notice that we have made some changes to the editors of the textbook. First, Mickey Kavanagh has stepped back from his active involvement in the book and has headed into retirement. Although we don't know if we should be jealous or excited for him, we do know that we need to provide a heartfelt "thank you" to Mickey. This book reflects Mickey's vision and his deep and long connection to HRIS. Without his hard work and dedication to its success, we would not be here in the fifth edition. For this, Mickey, we say Thank You and best of luck in your new endeavors! Finally, we would like to thank our families, who provided the support we needed when frustration and writer's block crept in!

Richard D. Johnson, Kevin D. Carlson, and Michael J. Kavanagh

HUMAN RESOURCE INFORMATION SYSTEMS (HRIS)

1

THE EVOLUTION OF HRM AND HRIS

Richard D. Johnson and Kevin D. Carlson

EDITORS' NOTE

The purpose of this chapter is to introduce the field of human resource information systems (HRIS), which lies at the intersection of human resource management (HRM) and information technology (IT). A central focus of this chapter is the use of data from the HRIS in support of managerial decision making. The chapter starts with a brief discussion of HRIS and electronic human resource management (eHRM). The history of the field of HRM and the impact of information technology on HRM is covered, as well as the advent of using a human resource information system and the subsequent effects on both HR and IT professionals. The chapter will also discuss the role of an HRIS within this broader organization environment, particularly its alignment with HR and organizational goals. This first chapter lays the groundwork for the remainder of this book, and, consequently, it is important to understand thoroughly the concepts and ideas presented. This chapter contains definitions for several terms in common use in the HRM, IT, and HRIS fields. (Note that a glossary defining these terms is also provided at the back of this book.) The central themes of this book in terms of the development, implementation, and use of an HRIS will also be discussed. A brief overview of the major sections of the book will be presented here as well, one discussing how each chapter is an integral part of the entire field of HRIS. Finally, you should note that the key terms used in this chapter are in bold and contained in a section after the chapter summary. The pattern of sections for this chapter will be consistent for all chapters of this book.

CHAPTER OBJECTIVES

After completing this chapter, you should be able to

- Describe three types of HR activities
- Explain the purpose and nature of an HRIS

- Describe the differences between eHRM and HRIS
- Explain the value and risks associated with the use of a HRIS
- Describe the historical evolution of HRM, including the changing role of the human resources (HR) professional
- Discuss the evolution of the technology of HRIS
- Discuss how the data from an HRIS can assist organizational decision making
- Understand how HRM and HRIS fit within a comprehensive model of organizational functioning in global business environments

HRIS IN ACTION

Situation Description

To illustrate the importance and use of HRIS in contemporary HR departments, this vignette examines the typical memoranda that may appear in the inbox of HR professionals and managers. Assume you are the HR director of a medium-sized organization that primarily maintains and uses manual HR records and systems. This morning, your inbox contains the following memos that *require immediate action.*

Memo 1: A note from the legal department indicates that some female staff members have filed an employment discrimination complaint with the local government agency responsible for the enforcement of equal opportunity employment. The female staff members allege that, for the past 10 years, they have been passed over for promotion because they are women. In order to respond to this allegation, the legal department requires historical data on the promotions of both males and females for the past 10 years for all jobs in the company broken down by department. It also needs the training records for all managers involved in personnel actions, such as promotions, to ascertain whether they have received training in equal employment provisions, especially in terms of unfair gender discrimination.

Memo 2: The second item is a complaint from employees working in a remote location of the company, about 150 miles away. The employees are complaining that their pay slips are not reaching them on time and that they are finding it difficult to get timely and accurate information on the most recent leave and benefits policies of the company.

Memo 3: A letter from the marketing manager states that he has not received any updated information on the status of his request, made three months ago, to recruit a new salesperson. The failure to recruit and hire a new salesperson has had a negative effect on the overall sales of the company's products over the past quarter.

(*Continued*)

(Continued)

Memo 4: A letter from the HR professional in charge of the southwest regional office says that she is swamped with HR administrative work, particularly personnel transactions on employees. As a result, she has not been able to meet employees in her region to describe and begin to implement the recent Employee Engagement Initiative as required by corporate headquarters.

Memo 5: A note from one of the production managers indicates that he has received a resignation letter from a highly regarded production engineer. She is resigning because she has not received the training on new technology that she was promised when hired. She notes that most of the other production engineers have attended this training program and have had very positive reactions to it.

Memo 6: A strongly worded note from the director of finance asks the HR department to justify the increasing costs associated with its operation. The note indicates that the HR director needs to develop a business plan for the overall operation of the HR department to include business plans for all the HR programs, such as recruiting and training. Further, the finance director indicates that unless the business cases can demonstrate a positive cost-benefit ratio, the budget for the HR department will be reduced, which will lead to reductions in the HR department professional staff.

As the HR director, your first thought may be to resign, since searching for the information required by these memos in the manual records on employees will require several days if not weeks to complete. However, you have just returned from a professional conference sponsored by the Society for Human Resources Management (SHRM) and remember how an HRIS may be what you need! As this chapter and the ones that follow will illustrate, an HRIS enables an HR department to streamline its activities and the demands placed on it by automating the HR data and processes necessary for the management of the human capital of the organization. This automation helps develop the capabilities to produce information and reports on the requests contained in the memos in the vignette, and these reports will facilitate efficient and effective managerial decision making. While an HRIS cannot make the judgment calls in terms of whom to recruit or promote, it can certainly facilitate better inputting, integration, and use of employee data, which will reduce the administrative burden of keeping detailed records and should aid and enhance decisions about strategic directions.

Need for an HRIS in Decision Situations

If you read the memos again, you will recognize that each one has a request for human resource management (HRM) information that will be used in a decision situation. The information requested in Memo 1 will help the legal department determine the company's potential liability in a workplace gender discrimination situation. This information may help to determine whether the company should decide to rectify the situation in terms of an informal settlement with the female staff members or to defend the company's promotion procedures as valid—in court if necessary. The information required in Memo 2 may help the HR department decide to change its payroll procedures as well as its distribution of benefits information to remote company locations. The information needed to respond to Memo 3 will impact decisions by the HR department to change recruitment and selection programs. The response to Memo 4 clearly suggests the need for the acquisition of an HRIS. The information required to answer Memo 5 may help in decisions regarding the revision of recruiting and training procedures, especially for new engineers. The information that would be provided in response to Memo 6 will help decide the future of the HR department. As you go through this book, look at information on the capabilities of various human resource information systems, trying to find an HRIS that would allow you (as the HR director) to respond to each of the six memos in one day.

INTRODUCTION

It's kind of fun to do the impossible.

—Walt Disney

What do you think is keeping CEOs up at night? Although you might think that it may be issues such as increasing stock price and market share, navigating and surviving in a globally competitive environment, or government regulation, according to a recent *Harvard Business Review* article (Groysberg & Connolly, 2015), the most-often mentioned concerns are talent related. CEOs are worried about hiring the right individuals and how to properly develop, promote, and retain top talent.

To maintain a competitive advantage in the marketplace, firms need to balance their physical, organizational, and human resources to achieve, profit, and survive. Leading management thinkers (Porter, 1990; Drucker, Dyson, Handy, Saffo, & Senge, 1997) argue that **human resource management (HRM)** will be the most critical and most challenging area for organizations in the 21st century. The most effective and well-respected companies today have innovative and valuable people practices. These organizations know that human resources (HR) cannot afford to simply focus on completing day-to-day activities, but instead they should focus on outcomes and capabilities that align with the broader organizational goals (Ulrich, Younger, & Brockbank, 2008).

But to do this, they need timely and accurate information on current employees and potential employees. The ability of organizations to do this has been greatly enhanced through the use of human resource information systems (HRIS). A basic assumption behind this book is that the effective management of employee information for decision makers will be the critical process that helps a firm maximize the use of its human resources and maintain competitiveness in its market.

HR ACTIVITIES

The goals of human resources are to attract, motivate, develop, and retain employees. Typical HR responsibilities involve things such as record keeping, recruiting, selection, training, performance management, employee relations, and compensation. Within each functional area, activities can be classified as transactional, traditional, or transformational (Wright, McMahan, Snell, & Gerhart, 1998). **Transactional activities** involve day-to-day transactions such as record keeping—for example, entering payroll information, tracking employee status changes, and the administration of employee benefits. These activities are the costliest and most time-consuming activities that HR undertakes. Despite the advances in technology, most HR departments still spend a majority of their time on them. **Traditional activities** involve HR programs such as planning, recruiting, selection, training, compensation, and performance management. HR departments spend about 15% to 30% of their time on these activities. Traditional activities can have strategic value for the organization if their results or outcomes are consistent with the strategic goals of the organization. **Transformational activities** are those activities that add value to the organization—for example, cultural or organizational change, structural realignment, strategic redirection, and increasing innovation. Because of the time and effort to complete transactional and traditional activities, HR departments typically spend only 5% to 15% of their time on transformational activities.

One of the major purposes of the design, development, and implementation of an HRIS is to reduce the amount of time HR employees must spend on transactional activities, allowing the staff to spend more time on traditional and transformational activities. This notion of using technology to improve transactional activities and accomplish them more efficiently is the central theme of this book and provides one of the primary justifications for a computer-based system. In later chapters that discuss various HR programs such as selection and training, we will see how a computer-based system can aid in both traditional and transformational activities to make them consistent with the strategic goals of the organization.

TECHNOLOGY AND HUMAN RESOURCES

What Is an HRIS?

Since the 1940s, technology has been used to support HR processing. In fact, the earliest organizational systems were built to support payroll processing due to increasing tax regulations. But, despite its early start, the complexity and data intensiveness of the HRM function has led to it being one of the last management functions to be automated (Bussler & Davis, 2001/2002). This fact does not mean that an HRIS is not important; it just indicates the difficulty of developing and implementing systems in HR compared with other business functions—for example, accounting and supply chain systems. Only recently has HR embraced the use of technology, with estimates suggesting that now nearly all large organizations have implemented systems to support HR processes and functions (CedarCrestone, 2014). These systems can support activities such as online applications, Internet-based selection testing, management of employee information, support of training, succession planning, and more. Together, these systems are broadly referred to as human resource information systems (HRIS). A sample employee home screen for an HRIS is shown in Figure 1.1

An HRIS is an information system that is focused on supporting HR functions and activities, as well as broader organizational "people" processes. A more formalized definition of a HRIS is a system used to acquire, store, manipulate, analyze, retrieve, and distribute information regarding an organization's human resources to support HRM

FIGURE 1.1   ■   SuccessFactors Employee Home Screen

and managerial decisions. An HRIS is not simply computer hardware and associated HR-related software. In addition to hardware and software, it also includes people, forms, policies and procedures, and data. The major difference between a traditional information system and an HRIS is that the HRIS contains data about people in the organization and can become both the face of HR and the initial system with which new employees interact with the firm. This difference is particularly important, because an HRIS is often one of the first systems with which individuals will interact when considering working for a firm. It can also affect who will accept job offers and who is promoted, and can even affect who remains with an organization. Inaccurate data within an HRIS can stigmatize employees, and employee privacy concerns regarding how and where applicant and employee data are used can affect the organization's reputation.

It is important to note that an information system does not have to include computers. Many small businesses *still* utilize paper-based systems (e.g., stored in files or folders), because historically, the expense of implementing a HRIS was beyond their financial capabilities. Thus, if you work for a small organization, you may find that much of the information in HR is paper based. However, the expense and time associated with paper means that most organizations will invest in technology to support HR. As organizations choose to implement a HRIS, the paper-based systems become the basis upon which the new HRIS is evaluated. For the purpose of this book, however, we will use the term "HRIS" to refer to a computerized system designed to manage the company's HR.

There are three main ways that a HRIS can add value to HR and the organization. First, they automate HR processes to conduct transactional activities more efficiently. Second, by providing accurate and timely information to the HR personnel and managers, an HRIS can help them make better decisions. Finally, by providing new forms of information, HRIS can help HR more fully support the strategic mission of the firm. For example, HR can provide better information used to support planning for needed employees in a merger, to identify potential discrimination problems in hiring, or to evaluate the effectiveness of programs, policies, or practices (Dulebohn & Johnson, 2013).

eHRM and HRIS

The implementation of an HRIS provides HR with the opportunity to update and change their processes so that they are technology enabled. This technology-enabled collection of HR processes has been called **electronic human resource management (eHRM)** and reflects a new way of "doing" HR. eHRM uses **information technology (IT)**, particularly the Web, as the central component of delivering efficient and effective HR services. This can be best seen through the words of Gueutal and Stone (2005): "Things will look a bit different here. No longer will you deal with an HR professional. . . . The HR portal will take care of you" (p. xv). Essentially, technology becomes the nerve center for disseminating, connecting, and conducting human resources (Strohmeier, 2007). Organizations embracing an eHRM approach don't simply utilize technology in the support of human resources but instead see technology as enabling the HR function to be done differently by modifying "information flows, social interaction patterns, and communication processes" (Stone & Lukaszewski, 2009, p. 136). It has also been defined as the "implementation and delivery of HR functionality enabled by a HRIS that connects employees, applicants, managers, and the decisions they make" (Johnson, Lukaszewski, & Stone, 2016, p. 536).

Whereas eHRM is a way of conducting HR, the HRIS is the technology through which eHRM is enabled. An HRIS can include technologies such as databases, small functional systems focused on a single HR application (e.g., performance management), or a large-scale, integrated **enterprise resource planning (ERP)** system and Web-based applications. Today, an HRIS may even incorporate smartphones to allow employees to access data remotely and social networking tools to support employee social connections. Another way of looking at the differences between eHRM and HRIS is that eHRM tends to focus on how HR functionality is delivered, and an HRIS focuses on the systems and technology underlying the design and acquisition of systems supporting the move to eHRM.

The Value and Risks of HRIS

A HRIS can add value to HR in many ways. Advantages of using a HRIS include

- providing a comprehensive information picture as a single, integrated database; this enables organizations to provide structural connectivity across units and activities and to increase the speed of information transactions (Lengnick-Hall & Lengnick-Hall, 2006);

- increasing competitiveness by improving HR operations and management processes;

- improved timeliness and quality of decision making;

- streamlining and enhancing the efficiency and effectiveness of HR administrative functions;
- shifting the focus of HR from the processing of transactions to strategic HRM;
- improving employee satisfaction by delivering HR services more quickly and accurately.

In addition, the implementation of a HRIS can lead to dramatic cost and time savings, including:

- Reduction of salary planning cycle by over 50% (Gherson & Jackson, 2001);
- Reduction of 25% in HR staffing headcount when implementing self-service (Gueutal & Falbe, 2005);
- Reduction of 25% in recruiting cycle time (Cober, Brown, Blumenthal, Doverspike, & Levy, 2000);
- Reduction of recruitment costs by up to 95% (Cober et al., 2000);
- Training cost reductions of 40% to 60% with e-learning (Gill, 2000).

However, the technology alone will not improve HR outcomes. The ability of firms to harness the potential of HRIS depends on a variety of factors, such as

- the size of the organization, with large firms generally reaping greater benefits;
- the amount of top management support and commitment;
- the availability of resources (time, money, and personnel);
- the HR philosophy of the company as well as its vision, organizational culture, structure, and systems;
- managerial competence in cross-functional decision making, employee involvement, and coaching;
- the ability and motivation of employees in adopting change, such as increased automation across and between functions (Ngai & Wat, 2004).

The implementation of a HRIS does not come without risks though. As with any information system, there are potential dysfunctional impacts that may occur when a HRIS is implemented (Johnson & Stone, 2019). These include:

- management by computer and substitution of technology for human judgment—managers may begin to base performance evaluations exclusively on the data captured by the HRIS. Thus, soft-skill behaviors such as teamwork and customer service may not be fully considered.
- privacy concerns—employees and applicants may feel that their data are being accessed and used by those internal and external to the organization.

- system rigidity and lack of flexibility—standardization of HR processes can benefit the organization, but some systems may not allow for the inevitable exceptions that arise and as the HR legal environment changes.

- employee stress and resistance to the use of electronic performance monitoring.

- performance reduction in complex tasks when performance monitoring systems are used.

EVOLUTION OF HRM AND HRIS

To fully understand the current state of HR technology and its role in organizations, it is important to understand both the evolution of HR and the evolution of technologies supporting HR. The historical analysis that follows will demonstrate the growing importance of employees from being just one of the replaceable parts in organizations in the 20th-century industrial economy to being a key source of sustainable competitive advantage in the 21st-century knowledge economy. This means examining the evolution of HRM intertwined with developments in IT and describing how IT has played an increasing role in HRM. This historical analysis will show how the role of HRM in the firm has changed over time from primarily being concerned with routine transactional activities and the utilization of simple, inflexible systems to the support of more strategic activities through the use of flexible, mobile, and web-deployed systems. This evolution is illustrated in Figure 1.2

FIGURE 1.2 ■ Historical Evolution of HRM and HRIS	
Early Systems **Mid-20th Century**	**Emerging Systems** **21st Century**
HR Role	*HR Role*
Employee Advocate	Strategic Management Partner
Maintain Accurate Employee Records	Evidence-Based HR
Legal Compliance	HR Data Supports Strategic Decision Making
React to Organizational Change	External Focus: Serve "Customers"
Internal Focus: Serve Employees	Legal Compliance
System Characteristics	*System Characteristics*
Inflexible	Flexible
"Islands of Technology"	Mobile
Batch Processing	Web-Deployed
Focused on Employee Record Keeping	Integrated With Organizational System
	Real-Time Processing
	Focused on Information Sharing

and will become evident as we trace the historical evolution of HRM in terms of five broad phases of the historical development of industry in the United States. For more information on this historical development, we encourage readers to consult Johnson et al. (2016).

Pre–World War II

Prior to World War II, the personnel function (the precursor of human resources management) was primarily involved in clerical record keeping of employee information. During this period, the prevailing management philosophy was called **scientific management**. The central thrust of scientific management was to maximize employee productivity. It was thought that there was *one best way* to do any work, and this best way was determined through time-and-motion studies that investigated the most efficient use of human capabilities in the production process. Then the work could be divided into pieces, and the number of tasks to be completed by a worker during an average workday could be computed. These findings formed the basis of piece-rate pay systems, which were viewed as the most efficient way to motivate employees at that time.

At this point in history, there was limited government influence in employment relations; consequently, employment terms, practices, and conditions were left to the owners of the firm. As a result, abuses such as child labor and unsafe working conditions were common. Some employers set up labor welfare and administration departments to look after the interests of workers by maintaining records on health and safety as well as recording hours worked and payroll. Of course, at this time, paper records were kept, and we can still see paper-record HR systems in many smaller firms today.

Post–World War II (1945–1960)

The mobilization and utilization of labor during the war had a great impact on the development of the personnel function. Managers realized that employee productivity and motivation had a significant impact on the profitability of the firm. The human relations movement after the war emphasized that employees were motivated not just by money but also by social and psychological factors, such as receiving recognition for work accomplished or for the achievement of work goals.

Due to the need for the classification of large numbers of individuals in military service during the war, systematic efforts began to classify workers around occupational categories to improve recruitment and selection procedures. The central aspect of these classification systems was the **job description**, which listed the tasks, duties, and responsibilities of any individual who held the job in question. These job description classification systems could also be used to design appropriate compensation programs, evaluate individual employee performance, and provide a basis for termination.

Because of the abusive worker practices prior to the war, employees started forming trade unions, which played an important role in bargaining for better employment terms and conditions. Significant numbers of employment laws enacted in the United States allowed the establishment of labor unions and defined their scope in relationship with management. Thus, personnel departments had to assume considerably more record keeping and reporting to governmental agencies. Because of these trends, the personnel department had to establish specialist divisions, such as recruitment, labor relations, training and benefits, and government relations.

With its changing and expanding role, the typical personnel department started keeping increasing numbers and types of employee records, and computer technology began to emerge as a possible way to store and retrieve employee information. In some cases, in the defense industry, **job analysis** and classification data were inputted into computers to better understand, plan, and use employee skills. For example, the U.S. Air Force conducted a thorough and systematic job analysis and classification through its Air Force Human Resources Laboratory (AFHRL), which resulted in a comprehensive occupational structure. The AFHRL collected data from thousands in jobs within the Air Force, and, using a computer software program called the Comprehensive Occupational Data Analysis Program (CODAP), it was able to establish more accurately a job description classification system for Air Force jobs.

During this time, large firms began investing in technology to keep track of payroll, but due to the complexity and expense of computers, only the largest organizations, such as GE, could afford to develop these systems in house. In addition, companies such as ADP were founded as payroll outsourcers and used mainframe computers to support payroll processing.

With increasing legislation on employment relations and employee unionization, industrial relations became one of the main foci of the personnel department. Union–management bargaining over employment contracts dominated the activity of the department, and these negotiations were not computer based. Record keeping was still done manually despite the growing use of computerized data processing in other departments, such as accounts and materials management. What resulted was an initial reluctance among personnel departments to acquire and use computer technology for their programs. This had a long-term effect in many firms when it came to adopting advancements in computer technology, even though the technology got cheaper and easier to use.

Social Issues Era (1963–1980)

This period witnessed an unprecedented increase in the amount of labor legislation in the United States, legislation that governed various parts of the employment relationship, such as the prohibition of discriminatory practices, the promotion of occupational health and safety, the provision of retirement benefits, and tax regulation. As a result, the personnel department was burdened with the additional responsibility of legislative compliance that required collection, analysis, and reporting of voluminous data to statutory authorities. For example, to demonstrate that there was no unfair discrimination in employment practices, a personnel department had to diligently collect, analyze, and store data pertaining to *all* employment functions, such as recruitment, training, compensation, and benefits. To avoid the threat of punitive damages for noncompliance, it had to ensure that the data were comprehensive, accurate, and up to date, which made it essential to automate the data collection, analysis, and report-generation process. As you go through the chapters of this book, these varying laws and government guidelines will be covered within the specific HR topics.

It was about this time that personnel departments were beginning to be called human resources departments and the field of human resource management was born. The increasing need to comply with numerous employee protection laws or suffer significant monetary penalties made senior managers aware of the importance of HRM. In other words, HRM practices were starting to affect the "bottom line" of the firms, so there was a significant growth of HR departments.

Additionally, computer technology had advanced to the point that it could deliver better productivity at lower costs, and organizations were using it more widely. The decreasing costs of computer technology versus the increasing costs of employee compensation and benefits made the acquisition of an HRIS a necessary business decision. As a result, there was an increasing demand for HR to adopt computer technology to process employee information more effectively and efficiently. These technology developments and increased vendor activity led to the development of a comprehensive **management information system (MIS)** for HRM (e.g., an HRIS). In addition, early forms of integrated systems were being developed by SAP, the precursor to the modern ERP. But interestingly, HR was still slow in adopting computer technology. Thus, the major issue at this time in the historical development of HRIS was not the need for increased capabilities of technology but how to best implement it.

Cost-Effectiveness Era (1980 to the Early 1990s)

With increasing competition from emerging European and Asian economies, the U.S. and other multinational firms increased their focus on cost reduction through automation and other productivity improvement measures. In HR, administrative burdens intensified with the need to fulfill a growing number of legislative requirements, while the overall functional focus shifted from employee administration to employee development and involvement. To improve effectiveness and efficiency in service delivery through cost reduction and value-added services, the HR departments came under pressure to harness technology that was becoming cheaper and more powerful.

In addition, there was a growing realization within management that people costs were a very significant part of a company's budget. Some companies estimated that personnel costs were as much as 80% of their operating costs. As a result, there was a growing demand on the HRM function to cost justify their employee programs and services. In one of the first books to address this growing need to cost justify the HRM function, Cascio (1984) indicates that the language of business is dollars and cents, and HR managers need to realize this fact. But the challenge facing HR was that most leaders were not thinking like business managers (Fitz-enz, 1980).

Technology was becoming more cost effective, and an increasing number of organizations were increasingly able to afford using them. In addition, organizations began networking computers together, and the development of microcomputers (e.g., PCs) allowed organizations to leverage the power of both the mainframe and local computer to support HR operations. This allowed managers and employees to have HR information directly available on their workstations. This approach to computing was called client-server computing. Specifically, client-server computing supported the processing and use of both HR data on the mainframe computer as well as on the local personal computer of an employee. Organizations could now distribute employee information to multiple locations throughout the organization, providing more current information to managers in support of their personnel decisions. An early leader in this space was PeopleSoft, which developed one of the first and most popular HRISs during this time.

Although as noted earlier, the prevailing management thinking regarding the use of computers in HR was not that their use would result in a reduction in the number of employees needed in HR departments but that employee activities and time could be shifted from transactional record keeping to more transformational activities that would add value to the organization. This change in the function of HRM could then be clearly measured in terms of cost-benefit ratios to the bottom line of the company.

ERPs and Strategic HRM (1990 to 2010)

The economic landscape underwent radical changes throughout the 1990s with increasing globalization, technological breakthroughs (particularly Internet-enabled Web services), and hyper competition. **Business process reengineering** exercises became more common and frequent, resulting in several initiatives, such as the rightsizing of employee numbers, reducing the layers of management, reducing the bureaucracy of organizational structures, creating autonomous work teams, and outsourcing. Firms today realize that innovative and creative employees hold the key to organizational knowledge and provide a sustainable competitive advantage because, unlike other resources, intellectual capital is difficult for competitors to imitate.

Accordingly, the people management function became strategic and was geared to attract, retain, and engage talent. These developments led to the creation of the **HR balanced scorecard** (Becker, Huselid, & Ulrich, 2001; Huselid, Becker, & Beatty, 2005), as well as to added emphasis on the **return on investment (ROI)** of the HR function and its programs (Cascio, 2000; Fitz-enz, 2000, 2002). With the growing importance and recognition of people and people management in contemporary organizations, **strategic human resource management (strategic HRM)** became critically important in management thinking and practice. Human resources and the intellectual capital of employees were increasingly viewed as strategic assets and a competitive advantage in improving organizational performance (Becker & Huselid, 2006). Organizations became more aware that there was not one best way to strategically deploy HR resources. Thus, researchers increasingly emphasized the **"best-fit" approach to strategic HRM** as opposed to the **"best-practice" approach to strategic HRM**. They argued that it was "the fit between the HR architecture and the strategic capabilities and business processes that implement strategy that is the basis of HR's contribution to competitive advantage" (Becker & Huselid, 2006, p. 899).

A good example of the importance of HR and the information provided by an HRIS can be found in the **human resources planning (HRP)** function. HRP is primarily concerned with forecasting the need for additional employees in the future and the availability of those employees either inside or external to the company. Imagine, for example, that a company is considering a strategic decision to expand by establishing a production facility in a new location. Using the data from an HRIS, HRP can provide estimates of whether there are enough internal employees or individuals in the external labor market of the new location available with the necessary skills to staff the new facility.

Another critical characteristic of strategic HRM is the adoption and use of **HR metrics** (Cascio, 2000; Lawler & Mohrman, 2003). Most functional departments of an organization have utilized metrics for decades due to the nature of their business transactions. For example, the marketing department has set sales goals, and the effectiveness metric that is used is the percentage of sales relative to the goal. But for HR, the focus on the measurement of the cost effectiveness of programs is relatively recent. Despite the recent utilization of metrics, their use continues to grow and has deepened as organizations seek to compete globally.

During this time frame, the technology supporting HR also underwent a dramatic transformation. In the late 1990s, software vendors began developing (ERP) systems. Industry leaders in this area were PeopleSoft, SAP and Oracle. Other vendors focused on one-specific HR function (such as time and attendance, online recruiting, or payroll). This approach where the organization would purchase the best system for each functional area became known as best of breed. Some industry leaders who chose this approach were Kronos for time and attendance, ADP for payroll, and Taleo for online recruiting.

"The Cloud" and Mobile Technologies (2010—present)

Within the last few years, we have seen an additional shift in HR, and much of this has been technology and regulation dependent. In 2010, the **Patient Protection and Affordable Care Act** was passed, and with it, a host of new healthcare regulations were placed on organizations. In addition, several new data requirements were needed by organizations to ensure compliance with this act. Thus, the data needs for organizations continue to grow.

In addition, the technology supporting HR continues to evolve. Rather than the traditional ERP, organizations are increasingly moving to cloud-based HR systems that are accessible over mobile devices and leverage the capabilities of machine learning, social networking, and Web 2.0 tools. This creates new hurdles for HR professionals as they learn to navigate new technologies and the distribution of data across devices and architectures, some of which are internally controlled by HR and others outside of organizational control (e.g., Twitter, Facebook, Instagram, etc.).

Ultimately, as we will see in the ensuing chapters, although technology is a key enabler of Strategic HRM, it is not simply the "best" technology and "best" strategy that leads to competitive advantage but rather the fit between the environmental realities, technology, and strategic practices that lead to competitive advantage.

HRIS WITHIN THE BROADER ORGANIZATION AND ENVIRONMENT

Beyond supporting and providing data for human resources, an effectively designed HRIS must also interface with individuals and systems within the broader organization and organizational environment. The data centrality of the HRIS is pictured in Figure 1.3. Several aspects of this model are critical. First, this model is a framework to use in reading, organizing, and understanding the information given in this book. At the core is the HRIS. The next layer focuses on the human resources environment and the major components of that environment (e.g., HR programs). Outside of this figure represents the organizational environment and its components. Outside the organizational environment is the global business environment, which directly influences the organizational environment and indirectly affects the HR environment. Each of these layers mutually influence each other and together can impact the development and implementation of the HRIS. For example, differing labor laws across countries mean that different HR policies may be implemented and may affect the type of data collected by the HRIS and reported to regulatory agencies in different companies. The figure also indicates the interrelatedness between the strategic management system; the strategic HRM system; and the performance, business, and HR goals that are generated during the strategic planning process.

Second, this is a systems model; that is, it is organic and can change over time, as the environment changes (e.g., the increasing focus on unfair discrimination in society and in the workforce will affect the HR environment and will, in turn, affect the organizational and global business environments). Third, the HRIS and the HR program evaluation results, in terms of HR metrics and benefit-cost results (value added and return on investment—ROI), are in continual interaction. This emphasis is consistent with current thinking in the HRM field (Cascio, 2000; Fitz-enz, 2000, 2002) and the creation of the HR workforce scorecard (Becker et al., 2001; Huselid et al., 2005). Finally, as will be

FIGURE 1.3 ■ **Overview of an HRIS Embedded in Organizational and Global Business Environments**

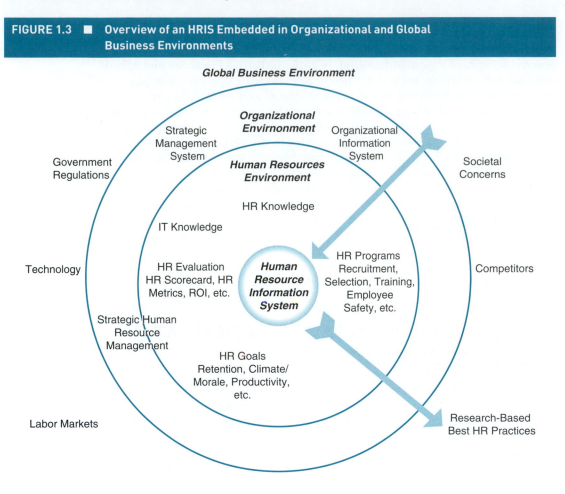

emphasized throughout this book, the *alignment* between the global business environment, the strategic management system, the strategic HR management system, the business goals, the HR goals, and the HR programs is critical to the organization's maintenance of its competitiveness in the market (Evans & Davis, 2005; Huselid, Jackson, & Schuler, 1997).

THEMES OF THE BOOK

The *overall theme* of this book is that the HR and IT operate jointly with HR processes and people to provide accurate and timely information in support of HR and operational and strategic managerial decision making. The book itself is broken into four major themes, each with a different focus

- Part I—System aspects of HRIS. In this section, you will learn about databases and the different technical and design considerations underlying HRIS.

- Part II—Implementation of the HRIS. In this section, you will learn about the systems development process, change management, assessing the feasibility of a HRIS, and how to implement one.

- Part III—eHRM. In this section, you will learn about how technology has transformed the administration of HR as well as how it has transformed the various functions of HR.

- Part IV—Advanced HRIS topics. In this section, you will learn about advanced topics such as including international considerations in HRIS, workforce analytics, privacy and security, and social media. It concludes with a look forward to the future of HRIS and the cutting-edge technologies that will influence it.

Summary

The primary purpose of this chapter was to introduce the field of human resource information systems (HRIS) to readers. The field of HRIS has evolved greatly from just automating simple HR transactions such as cutting a payroll check to one of assisting HR in becoming a strategic partner with the organization. The result of this is that HRISs have evolved from simple mainframe systems with limited capabilities to large-scale integrated, mobile systems that support social networking capabilities. In addition, the use of HRIS has allowed HR to rethink how HR functionality is deployed, leading to an eHRM approach. The distinction between HRIS and eHRM was explained to help the reader avoid confusing these terms when they appear in the remainder of the book. Additionally, the role of HRIS within the broader organization and environment and its mutually influencing role were discussed. Finally, the chapter briefly discussed four major themes covered within the book. This chapter therefore serves as an introduction to the field of HRIS and serves as a foundation for the sections and chapters that follow.

Key Terms

"best-fit" approach to strategic HRM 14
"best-practice" approach to strategic HRM 14
business process reengineering 14
electronic human resource management (eHRM) 8
enterprise resource planning (ERP) 8
HR balanced scorecard 14

HR metrics 14
human resource management (HRM) 5
human resources planning (HRP) 14
information technology (IT) 8
job analysis 12
job description 11
management information system (MIS) 13

Patient Protection and Affordable Care Act 15
return on investment (ROI) 14
scientific management 11
strategic human resource management (strategic HRM) 14
traditional HR activities 6
transactional HR activities 6
transformational HR activities 6

Discussion Questions

1. What are the factors that changed the primary role of HRM from a caretaker of records to a strategic partner?

2. Describe the historical evolution of HRM and HRIS in terms of the changing role of HRM and the influence of computer technology on HRM.

3. What is required for the effective management of human resources in a firm to gain a competitive advantage in the marketplace?

4. Describe the emergence of strategic HRM and the influence of computer technology.

   What are some of the approaches used in HRM to facilitate the use of strategic HRM in a firm's business strategy?

5. How does technology help deliver transactional, traditional, and transformational HR activities more efficiently and effectively?

6. Justify the need for an HRIS.

7. Describe and differentiate the major types of information systems.

Case Study: Position Description and Specification for an HRIS Administrator

One way to assess the nature and importance of a specific function or position in an organization is to examine the job description and job specifications for this position, as they tell us what activities, duties, and tasks are involved in the job as well as what knowledge, skills, and abilities (KSA) are required to perform the job. The following is an actual advertisement for an HRIS administrator. A large corporation placed this ad in the "Job Central" section of the Internet site for the International Association for Human Resources Information Management[1] (http://www.ihrim.org).

HRIS Administrator

Job Level: Senior (5+ Years), Full time
Reports to: Senior Director of Human Resources Operations

Position Summary

MOMIRI, LLC is an Alabama Native Owned Corporation, providing shared services to the MOMIRI family of companies and planning and incubating the next generation of companies serving federal and commercial customers. MOMIRI companies offer core expertise in telecommunications, information technology, product development, major program management, open-source software, construction management, facility operations, and operations support. MOMIRI companies realize that quality personnel are the key to our success. An excellent benefits package, professional working environment, and outstanding leaders are all keys to retaining top professionals.

Primary Function

The incumbent will serve as a key member of the HR Support Services department and provide professional human resources support in specific functions or disciplines to management and staff for the MOMIRI family of companies. This position is viewed as going to a midlevel professional who assists management and staff with HR programs at the tactical level and performs all essential duties and responsibilities at the direction of the Manager of HR Operations.

Essential Duties and Responsibilities

- Provides technical assistance to senior-level HR staff and management on several HR programs to include employee relations, compensation, EEO compliance, company policies and procedures, disability programs (STD, LTD, FMLA, ADA), federal and state employment laws, and personnel actions as needed.

- Supports and maintains the Human Resources Information System (HRIS) in addition to other systems supported by the management of enterprise applications.

- Serves as technical point of contact for assigned functional areas and assists subject matter experts with ensuring data integrity, testing of system changes, report writing, and analyzing data flows for process improvement opportunities.

- Supports HRIS and other enterprise systems' upgrades, patches, testing, and other technical projects as assigned.

- Recommends process/customer service improvements, innovative solutions, policy changes, and/or major variations from established policy.

- Serves as key systems liaison with other departments and process stakeholders (e.g., Payroll).

- Writes, maintains, and supports a variety of reports or queries utilizing appropriate reporting tools. Assists in development of standard reports for ongoing customer needs.

- Maintains data integrity in ATS, HRIS, and other enterprise systems by running queries and analyzing and fully auditing data across all HR departments.

- Conducts new hire in-processing to include systems training for new employees and entering new employee information in Costpoint.

- Conducts termination out-processing to include entering employee separation information in Costpoint and reporting attrition data.

- Develops user procedures, guidelines, and documentation for HR-related systems. Trains system users on new processes/functionality.

- Provides HR tools and resources for management and staff to accomplish their goals and objectives.

- Processes personnel actions (hires, terminations, pay and title changes, promotions, employment status, etc.) to include entering data into HRIS.

- Assists with special HR-related projects and provides training to other staff members as required.

- Performs other duties as assigned.

Requirements

Specialized Knowledge and Skills

- Experience working with a multiple-site workforce.

- Working knowledge of federal and state employment laws and related acts.

- Advanced- to expert-level computer skills.

- Excellent verbal and written communication and presentation skills.

- Great interpersonal skills.

- Strong time-management and prioritization skills.

Qualifications

- Bachelor's degree in HR and/or equivalent professional experience.

- 3–5 years of technical HRIS experience in professional HR environment.

- Self-directed, highly responsive, and detail oriented.

- Ability to maintain absolute confidentiality in all business matters.

- Government contracting experience is a plus.

Case Study Questions

1. How does this position help the HR function become a strategic partner of the organization?

2. From the position description, identify the traditional, transactional, and transformational HR activities that this position is involved with.

3. Using the key responsibilities identified for this position, explain why and how the HRIS function plays a pivotal role in the organizational model as described in this chapter.

2

SYSTEMS CONSIDERATIONS IN THE DESIGN OF AN HRIS

Planning for Implementation

Michael D. Bedell and Michael L. Canniff

EDITORS' NOTE

This chapter focuses on the HRIS as one large information system. It starts with a brief discussion of the various stakeholders who must be considered during the design and implementation of a new HRIS. Next, it turns to a discussion of the various hardware and software architectures that organizations may consider when implementing an HRIS. This discussion traces the history of HRIS from early mainframe systems to today's integrated, mobile, and cloud-based systems. An important consideration for all organizations is whether to select the best software package from different vendors for each functional area of HR (e.g., best of breed) or to select a system that integrates all the functions within one large software package. The chapter touches on how organizations would integrate these best-of-breed solutions so that they integrate as seamlessly as possible. This chapter focuses more on the key technology and processes underlying HRIS implementation.

CHAPTER OBJECTIVES

After completing this chapter, you should be able to

- Understand the different types of users or customers of the implemented HRIS and their different data needs
- Discuss the differences between the five general hardware architectures that are presented, from "dinosaur" to "cloud computing" to "bring your own device"

- Discuss, very generally, the main concepts of hardware and database security
- Discuss the "best of breed" approach to HRIS acquisition and the various options available for each functional area of HR
- Develop an understanding of the general steps and factors that affect system implementation
- Understand the pros and cons of implementing a changeover from one software system to another

INDUSTRY BRIEF
JIM PASCARELL, PRESIDENT, INTEGRA OPTICS

Designing and implementing a Human Resource Information System is one of those initiatives that every organization encounters, yet most of the individuals within an organization usually have little or no experience in going through the process. This, combined with the continuous evolution of technology, puts organizations in the precarious spot of trying to figure out the best approach to successfully choosing and implementing a solution that provides the organization with all of the necessary value added benefits yet manages the risk of a potential failed implementation.

Organizations, whether they are commercial, education, or public sector, that have had the most success follow a design methodology that is centered on people, process, and technology. Those of us that have spent a great deal of our careers designing and implementing these systems have learned, sometimes through trial and error, that the planning and design of the system arguably play the most critical part in determining success. Common characteristics shared by organizations that have been and are most successful are as follows:

Commitment—A frequently used word that is only proven to be true by actions. Defining and understanding what the system needs to provide so that it can be an enabler for the organization and used as a competitive differentiator.

Proper Resource Allocation—Having your best and brightest be part of the design, participating throughout the lifecycle of an implementation. Insight is critical to avoid sloppy design, and it is worth the sacrifice to dedicate some of the most knowledgeable resources in the organization. The cost of not doing this will be paid later on due to rework and changes.

Understanding of Technology—Designing a system that will evolve along with technology, not one that will be restricted as technology changes. Too many organizations design systems that are somewhat outdated in a short period of time. This is primarily caused by the lack of understanding as to what the capabilities of the technology are and how they can help the system continue to be enhanced. I unfortunately have been part of many projects where once a system was "live" and operational, it almost immediately needed to be "upgraded" due to improper design up front.

Clear and Realistic Expectations—Once set, these expectations need to be constantly communicated to all stakeholders. This provides a common bond and keeps everyone focused on what needs to be accomplished.

Acceptance of Change—Through education and training, acceptance defeats resistance. Too many organizations choose the right technology yet fail to allocate the proper attention to change management.

Over 25 years of working and assisting with many diverse organizations as they design their HRIS, the most successful have truly understood and successfully managed these points. Through dedication and perseverance, these organizations have become leaders in their industries by using all of the benefits a properly designed HRIS can provide. As we continue into the digital age with access to more data faster than we could have ever imagined, it has never been more important for organizations to "get it right" when it comes to designing their HRIS.

HRIS IN ACTION

A billion-dollar retailer with more than 4,000 stores finds that it cannot move fast enough to beat out the competition. The organization's senior management arrives at the conclusion that it would be easier to achieve the strategic goals enumerated by the board of directors if the various organizational functions would share information. Shared information would enable them to develop and deploy new actions and tactics more quickly. The CEO and president have therefore ordered the major functions to update their information systems immediately so that data sharing is possible. The senior vice presidents (SVPs) of accounting and human resources immediately conclude that the only solution is to decide jointly on an **enterprise resource planning (ERP)** product. An ERP software application is a set of integrated database applications or modules that carry out the most common business functions, including human resources, general ledger, accounts payable, accounts receivable, order management, inventory control, and customer relationship management (see www.erpsupersite.com). To speed the installation along, the SVPs decide on a rapid-implementation methodology that a company down the street used. The goal is to have the new systems operational in nine months.

Shortly after this decision has been made, the SVP of HR calls you into his office and tells you that you will be management sponsor for this project. You have to decide on everything. You sit back in your nice office and think:

What's the problem with this scenario? It shouldn't be difficult to select a vendor and then borrow the methodology from down the street. It worked for them; it should work for us! We'll call a few vendors in the morning and find out about cost, time frame, and implementation methods. In the meantime, I should find out a little more about how to do this and who will be using the ERP. I remember from my information systems class in college that this is a reasonable first step when it comes to buying software.

What do you think your response would be to this inquiry? As you go through this chapter's material, keep this vignette in mind, and see if your answer changes.

INTRODUCTION

There are two ways of implementing a software design; one way is to make it so simple that there are obviously no deficiencies, and the other way is to make it so complicated that there are no obvious deficiencies. The first method is far more difficult.

—*C.A.R. Hoare, James Martin*

Professor of Computing, Wolfson College

Successful implementation is the central goal of every HRIS project, and it begins with a comprehensive design for the system. As the steps in the system development process are covered in this chapter, the foundation knowledge that is critical to the implementation process will be emphasized. Only by understanding the users/customers of the HRIS, the technical possibilities, the software solution parameters, and the systems implementation process can we increase the probability that the completed software installation will adequately meet the needs of the **human resource management (HRM)** function and the organization. The chapter will begin by identifying the potential users and the kind of information that the HRIS will be managing and storing to facilitate decision making. The chapter will next discuss the technical infrastructure, how the technical infrastructure has evolved, and the many choices that the organization must make. After the technology is discussed, the systems implementation process will be presented.

Those who have participated in a system implementation will tell you that success is the result of careful planning, a dedicated team, top-management support, and an awareness of potential pitfalls. These same people will also tell you that the implementation process provides a host of opportunities to reengineer and systematically improve HR processes to reflect best HRM practices. These opportunities should not be ignored, as they can benefit the organization as much as implementing the software will. Finally, the **implementation team** members will tell you that getting the system up and running was the most intense six months, year, or two years of their work life but that they learned a lot, and every moment of the experience was worth the time.

There are four things that should be remembered throughout the chapter:

1. It is important to keep in mind the customer of the data, the process, and the decisions that will be made.

2. Everything about HRM is a system of processes designed to support the achievement of strategic organizational goals. The HRIS, in turn, supports and helps manage these HR processes.

3. An HRIS implementation done poorly will result in an HRIS that fails to meet the needs of the HR function.

4. Successful implementation requires careful attention to every step in the system design process. However, done well, the implementation process is full of opportunities to improve the organization and processes. More consistent processes will contribute to enhanced organizational performance.

HRIS CUSTOMERS/USERS: DATA IMPORTANCE

Individuals who will be using the HRIS can be split into two general groups: employees and nonemployees. The employee category includes

- managers who rely on the HRIS and the data analyzed by the analyst or power user to make decisions;

- analysts or power users who use the HRIS to evaluate potential decision choices and opportunities;

- technical staff who are responsible for providing a system that is usable and up to date for each user or clerical employees who largely engage in data entry; and

- employees who use the HRIS on a self-service basis to obtain personal information, for example, to look up paycheck information, to make choices about benefits during open enrollment, or to see how much vacation time they have available.

The nonemployee group includes potential employees, suppliers, and partners. Potential employees are those who might log in via a Web portal to search for and apply for a position. Suppliers and partners are organizations that interface with the HR function for a variety of purposes, from recruiting to benefits administration and payroll.

Employees

Managers

The managers referred to within this section may have a variety of titles: manager, director, vice president, and even CEO. What they all have in common is that their primary HRIS need is to have real-time access to accurate data that facilitate decision making with regard to their people (Miller, 1998). The HRIS provides the manager with data for performance management, recruiting and retention, team management, project management, and employee development (Fein, 2001). The HRIS must also provide the information necessary to help the functional manager make decisions that will contribute to the achievement of the unit's strategic goals and objectives (Hendrickson, 2003). Easy access to accurate employee data enables the manager for each employee to view and engage in employee life cycle changes such as salary decisions, job requisitions, hiring, disciplinary action, promotions, and training program enrollment (Walker, 2001; Zampetti & Adamson, 2001).

Many HRIS products provide real-time reporting and screen-based historical information that can provide managers with information about their employees or their functional units. There are also several third-party software products available that provide managers with almost continuous data about the status of their unit and the organization—much as a dashboard on a car provides immediate information. The analysis of more complex situations is beyond the capabilities of many of these reporting and query tools. To facilitate decision making on complex issues, the manager, before making a decision, usually relies on the analyst or power user to complete some type of analysis.

Analysts (Power Users)

The **analysts or power users** are perhaps the most demanding users of the HRIS. The primary role of the analyst is to acquire as much relevant data as possible, examine it, and provide reasonable alternatives with appropriate supporting information to facilitate the decision process of the manager. The analyst is referred to as a power user because this person accesses more areas of the HRIS than almost any other user. Analysts must be proficient with reporting and query tools. Analysts must also understand the process used to collect the data, how new data are verified, and how the HRIS and the employee life cycle interact. They also need to understand the data definitions in terms of what data exist, the structure of the data, and what data fields are up to date and complete. Some HRISs also provide tools that the analyst can use to model scenarios or perform "what-if" analyses on questions of interest.

As an example, a recruiting analyst might be asked to provide a short list of potential internal candidates for a position that opened in the marketing function of a large retailer. The potential candidates' characteristics of interest are queried and may include (1) when they were last promoted, (2) whether they have engaged in continuous personal-skills development, (3) what their undergraduate degrees were, and (4) whether they have ever expressed any interest in marketing. The analyst would query appropriate tables and develop a list of internal candidates.

Another example might have the HR analyst completing an analysis of corporate headquarters turnover to determine if a particular function or salary issue is the cause of the problem. This information would be drawn from existing reports, ad hoc queries, and available salary information. Data could be compiled into categories by salary, function, gender, or organizational level and examined to determine if the cause of the turnover can be pinpointed and then countered.

Technicians (HRIS Experts)

Technicians (HRIS experts) straddle the boundary of two functions. Their role is to ensure that appropriate HR staff members have all the access, information, and tools necessary to do their jobs. HRIS experts do this by understanding what is needed from an HR-process standpoint and then translating that into technical language so the technical employees—programmers, database administrators, and application administrators—know exactly what to do. When the technical staff is planning to install the latest update and one of the results will be a change in functionality, the HRIS expert must take what the technical staff provides and translate that into language HR users understand so as to indicate how processes and activities might change. For example, if an HR professional required that a new report be generated every other Tuesday, the HRIS expert would learn what data the report requires—perhaps mock the report up with the user—and then explain to the technical people how to make sure that this report is automatically generated on the time schedule.

Clerical Employees

Much like power users, **clerical employees** also spend a significant portion of their day interacting with the HRIS. The difference is one of depth. The clerical employee must understand the process required to enter information into the HRIS and may also need to start the process or generate periodic reports. While clerical staff members in the HR employment department do not generally provide input about whether to hire an individual to a particular position, they bear considerable responsibility for seeing that the new employee gets paid properly. Hiring a new employee requires that someone, for example, a clerical employee, enter the appropriate information into the HRIS—such as the reporting relationship of the new employee as well as his or her benefits, salary, and direct-deposit information.

Organizational Employees

Organizational employees are essentially all the other employees throughout the organization who interact with the HRIS. These employees serve in roles such as bank teller, nurse, machinist, salesperson, and accountant. These employees are not involved in human resources and are not likely to make decisions with HR data, but they may utilize the HRIS to help manage their personal information. Typically, all the employees in the organization may interface with the HRIS through a self-service Web portal or secure employee kiosk, removing the necessity of an HR clerk or staff member assisting with many routine HR record modifications (Walker, 2001). Self-service capabilities encourage employees to manage their personal HR profiles with respect to a variety of functions, such as benefit and retirement plan monitoring or computerized training, in addition to using HRIS-based systems to complete numerous personnel forms (Adamson & Zampetti, 2001; Zampetti & Adamson, 2001). Typical self-service applications are accessible most of the day throughout the week. Employees log on to the system, where their identity is authenticated and verified. Then appropriate change options are offered to the employee based on certain parameters that control the areas where the employee is allowed to make valid alterations to the HRIS—such as personnel data updates, job postings, or desired training enrollments (Adamson & Zampetti, 2001; Zampetti & Adamson, 2001). One fairly large financial-services organization noted that self-service options significantly enabled them to reduce the annual benefits open-enrollment process by reducing the paper documents generated, reducing necessary mailings, and reducing the data that had to be read and entered into the HRIS. Data entry time alone was reduced from six to two weeks (Bedell, 2003b).

Nonemployees

Job Seekers

It is estimated that 70% to 90% of large organizations use online recruitment, and that number continues to increase (Stone, Lukaszewski, & Isenhour, 2005). Online recruiting tends to attract individuals who are well educated, Internet savvy, and searching for higher-level positions (McManus & Ferguson, 2003). Online recruitment also attracts people born since 1980, who have grown up with computers and are therefore comfortable with obtaining information on the Internet (Zusman & Landis, 2002). A successful recruitment website needs to be user friendly and easy to navigate while attracting candidates to apply to an organization by clearly communicating the benefits of joining it.

Typical job seekers have little or no prior information about how to interface with the HRIS and have had nearly zero training opportunities with it. Therefore, the recruiting portal needs to provide ease of use and ease of access to up-to-date job information. The Web form that is used to collect applicant data must also be reliably entered into the appropriate fields within the company's HRIS database. This online recruiting activity will facilitate searches for new employees to fill existing and future positions.

Sourcing Partner Organizations

The partner organizations to HR functions require certain information to complete their tasks. **Sourcing partner organizations** such as Monster.com, Adecco, and most executive recruiting firms require information about vacant positions, including a position description, job specifications, desired candidate competencies, potential salary range, and contact information. The information provided is limited to specific searches for open jobs and is updated as needed.

Business partners that are the recipients of decisions to outsource portions of the HR function (e.g., benefit management firms) or that facilitate process completion on behalf of the employee (e.g., banks) require information that is related to current employees. This requirement increases the need for accurate data, training, and specialized security assurances, as employee information is leaving the organization.

Important Data

As is evident in the previous sections, each customer or user of the HRIS has slightly different needs with regard to what information he or she will be using. Some users simply input data and information, a few simply look at data and information provided in the form of reports, while a few others analyze the data and information to make decisions. What these users all have in common is that all the information is about potential and current employees, with a focus on managing the organization's human capital to improve decision making and help to achieve strategic organizational goals. Specific data from the HRIS database fit into three categories:

1. Information about people, such as biographical information and competencies (knowledge, skills, abilities, and other factors)

2. Information about the organization, such as jobs, positions, job specifications, organizational structure, compensation, employee/labor relations, and legally required data

3. Data that are created as a result of the interaction of the first two categories: for example, individual job history, performance appraisals, and compensation information

HRIS ARCHITECTURE

The "Early Days"

In the early days of human resource applications (just 40 years ago), large "dinosaurs" roamed the IT landscape. These were called mainframe computers and were primarily built by International Business Machines (IBM). These large systems hosted the payroll applications for most enterprises. Users of the mainframe system, which mainly consisted of IT personnel and HRMS administrators, executed large batch processes while directly logged onto the mainframe. Although access to the mainframe could be done via a desktop monitor, no processing was done locally. This architecture is commonly called a single-tier computing system. Everything (user interface, application processing, and data storage) resided on the mainframe and had to be accessed by the client company locally.

Client-Server (Two-Tier) Architecture

During the 1980s, it was discovered that many typical HR functions (such as employee benefits, recruiting, training) did not require such high-powered and expensive processing available on the mainframe computers. With the advent of the personal computer (PC), many of these functions could be re-allocated to the local processing power of the PC. The purpose of the two-tier (client-server) architecture was to spread out low-powered processing capability to the dozens of PCs now being used across the enterprise. High-performance applications such as payroll would still be run in a batch process on the mainframe (or large Unix server). Ease of computer usage was a driving factor to include individuals with lower levels of technology experience. By the end of the decade, HRIS vendors such as PeopleSoft began using the power of PCs and created the **client-server (two-tier) architecture** (see Figure 2.1).

Finally, the HR software application technology could be divorced from the database technology. This separation simplified the HR application and allowed an enterprise to select the most appropriate database management system (DBMS) for their needs. This time period coincided with the maturation of the relational database model. This model standardizes how data is physically stored on the computer and provides standard data access via the Structured Query Language (SQL).

Three-Tier and N-Tier Architecture

From about 1995 to 2010, this division of labor concept has expanded from two-tier into three-tier and finally N-tier architectures. With a **three-tier architecture**, the "back

---

FIGURE 2.1 ■ Two-Tier (Client-Server) Architecture

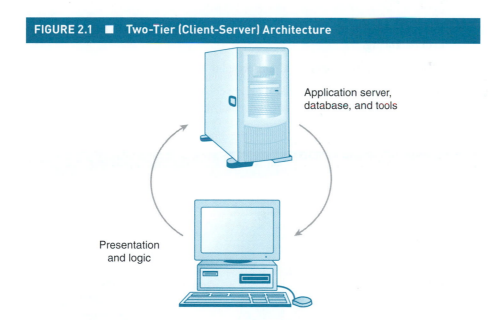

Application server, database, and tools

Presentation and logic

end" servers are divided into two components—the database server and the application server (see Figure 2.2).

The client still managed the user interface, but more demanding processing occurred in the middle—the application server tier. For example, if two recruiters updated the same job position at the same time, a transaction processor would ensure that both updates are committed to the database (if possible). This allowed many simultaneous users to access the central database. There are a couple of drawbacks with both two-tier and three-tier systems. First, there exists a large amount of network traffic or "**bandwidth**" required to execute database transactions between the client and the server. Second, the user interface client needs to be installed (along with database drivers) on every PC that needs to access the HRIS (with a corollary issue being that employees need to be trained on this application). Therefore, HRIS access tended to be limited to employees within the "four walls" of the enterprise (residing within the local area network). Low-bandwidth access, such as Internet dial-up, was impractical.

To truly provide for employee self-service (ESS) portals, the Web browser was adopted to solve these issues. First, the browser created a "thin client" environment as opposed to the "thick client" environment described in the two-tier model. An Internet Web browser comes installed on all major **operating systems** (OS; e.g., Windows, Mac OS, Linux, Android). The browser's user interface has become universal. Therefore, very little employee training is required to use a browser-based application. Finally, a browser works well in a low-bandwidth network environment. So now the typical HRIS application architecture looks like Figure 2.3. A standard Web server, such as Microsoft's Internet Information Server (IIS) or Apache's Web Server, manages **HTML (Hypertext Markup Language)** communication between the browser and the application server. And the application server also issues transactions to the centralized database server. Instead of just limiting ourselves to a four-tier label, this has been labeled **N-tier architecture** for the following reasons:

- It is expandable to multiple Web servers and application servers to handle **load balancing**.

- Web servers can be geographically dispersed to provide worldwide access.

- Additional file servers can be added to save documents, reports, error logs, and employee data, which are generated on a daily basis.

FIGURE 2.2 ■ Three-Tier Architecture

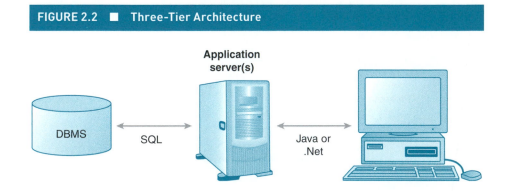

FIGURE 2.3 ■ N-Tier Architecture

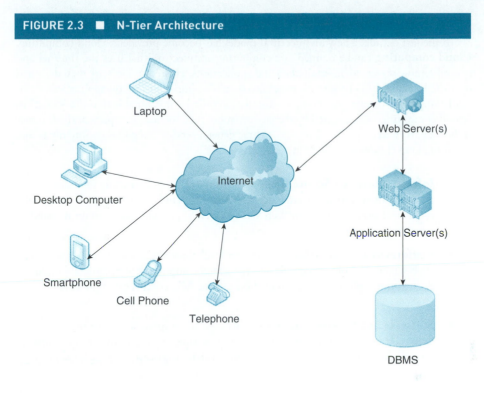

- Multiple print servers or specialized printers can be added as needed. For example, payroll check printing requires a security-enabled toner called MICR to print encoded checks for bank cashing. These check printers can be physically located in a secure environment but connected to the HRIS N-tier architecture like any other printer.

- Additional "process schedulers" can be added to handle large batch jobs such as payroll cycles. These servers offload "heavy" processing from the main application server so that user interaction is not impacted.

The architecture diagram becomes even more complicated when other ERP components are added. For example, when payroll is run, financial-related transactions need to be registered in the company's general ledger (GL) application. Typically, GL exists within the financial/accounting component of large ERP systems from SAP, Oracle, and Microsoft. Therefore, GL transactions must be interfaced between payroll and these systems. So additional application servers and databases enter the picture, depicted in Figure 2.3. So even though the architecture may be more complicated, the logical view of the system remains relatively simple, and this complexity is hidden from the end user. For example, a consultant for a large IT services company can travel throughout the world, work with multiple clients, but still be able to record his or her time and expense reports with a single browser application from any hotel room.

Cloud Computing—Back to the Future?

In the last decade, a new architectural model has become prevalent: cloud computing. **Cloud computing** can be defined as a computing architecture that uses the Internet and central remote servers to maintain data and applications. Hosted services are then delivered over the Internet. Cloud computing technology allows businesses to use applications without having to go through the complex installation process. It is notable that the "cloud" in "cloud computing" was inspired by the cloud symbol that one uses to represent the Internet in flow charts and diagrams. There exist three general service categories commonly recognized in cloud computing. These include:

- **Infrastructure as a Service (IaaS)**—This type of service basically provides access to an operating system (such as Microsoft Windows or Linux) or cluster of connected systems. Amazon Web Services (AWS) provides access to on-demand operating systems.

- **Platform as a Service (PaaS)**—The next level of services include application and Web server technology prebuilt into the leased computer. Enterprises still build out custom applications on top of these servers. Microsoft Azure is an example of PaaS.

- **Software as a Service (SaaS)**—In this case, a complete application is delivered over the Internet. This can be as simple as an e-mail service (think Google Mail) or as complex as the entire HRIS application (e.g., Workday or SAP-Cloud).

The underlying goal with cloud computing is to reduce the resources an organization needs to maintain and run software. To achieve this, a server "cloud," or group of computers is operated off site and accessed through the Internet. In this way, a company can utilize the processing and storage powers of these "clouds" of computers without actually having to own and invest in them. This can reduce software and equipment capital outlays, as the company does not need to keep purchasing new software or hardware to keep pace with technology changes. That investment becomes the responsibility of the vendor offering the cloud computing services. Cloud computing can be sold on demand, by the minute or the hour, and is elastic—meaning that an enterprise can consume as much or as little of a service as it wants at any given time. From an accounting perspective, an enterprise leases a preset amount of computing power over an annual period. This can be budgeted in a similar manner as telephony or electrical expenses. Computing charges then become part of operational budget expense as opposed to large capital investments.

In a sense, cloud computing is a return to the single-tier model of the 1980s. Instead of a single, large mainframe running all of the applications, the Internet is acting as the "supercomputer," providing the application runtime environment. And instead of a "dumb" terminal accessing the mainframe payroll system, the browser now provides the interface to the entire set of human resources applications. In the ancient history of mainframe applications, HR departments had to rely upon corporate data centers to provide high-performing and up-to-date applications. With cloud computing, the burden lies with software vendors such as Oracle, SAP, or Workday to provide the updating. And of course, leveraging the cloud requires solid, high-performance Internet access all of the time.

On-Premise Versus Cloud Computing

Although cloud computing has many benefits, some key differences exist with respect to cloud-computing compared to traditional software delivery approaches. Traditionally, organizations used an on-premise approach to deliver software. With an **on-premise** approach, the purchasing organization (not the vendor) owns the hardware supporting the HRIS and purchases specific licenses for the software. Data for their organization are the only data stored on that instance of the software. . .that is, the software is **single tenant**, and the servers are likely located in-house. Typically, on-premise solutions have a large capital outlay up front when the hardware and software are purchased, as well as ongoing maintenance costs during the life of the system. Given that most software will almost never meet all the organization's needs, and given that the firm's own the license for the software, many organizations choose to customize their on premise solutions. **Customization** refers to enhancing the HRIS with updated software code that is tailored to meet the organization's specific business processes. This code could be separate from the HRIS application or built on top of the platform. Customization is possible because the company owns the software and because only its data are stored on their instance of the software.

Conversely, with cloud-based HRIS, there is minimal up-front capital outlay, because the vendor owns and maintains all the hardware and software. Instead, the organization will pay an ongoing fee annually to access and use the software. In addition, because the hardware and software are owned by the vendor, multiple organizations share the same instance of the software. That is, cloud-computing is **multitenant**, with data from multiple organizations shared on the same instance of the software. Therefore, with cloud computing, organizations cannot customize the software to fully meet their needs. However, they can configure the software to more fully represent their unique environment. **Configuration** can be defined as modifying the HRIS application by turning off or on certain features pre-built into the software, or changing the look and feel of the interface to represent the organization. A simple analogy would be selecting predefined themes or styles in a word-processing document.

Mobile Access

Increasingly, workforces are mobile and work around the clock and around the globe. Most people have mobile devices that have much greater processing speed, power, and memory than even the most powerful computers had, even 20 years ago. In other words, we have the power of a supercomputer in our pockets! Mobile operating systems such as Android and iOS provide an easy to use interface that non-technical people can navigate. Instead of companies forcing mobile devices on their employees, enterprises encourage "bring your own device" (BYOD) policies (see Chapter 17 for more information on BYOD). Employees can then access the HRIS through apps installed on their phones. The majority of HRIS vendors provide apps for user-friendly access to the system. Think of mobile devices as the "thin client" in the N-tier model. Tasks such as approving an expense report, viewing budget data, and managing time cards are easily accomplished on mobile devices (from phones to tablets).

Security Challenges

Security ranks as a top priority for any human resource information system. Cloud service providers now maintain sensitive corporate data (outside of the four walls and possibly in other countries). So when choosing a cloud solution, the evaluation process must include a thorough security analysis. Security needs to be addressed to handle the following situations:

- Exposure of sensitive payroll and benefits data between employees

- Loss of sensitive personnel data outside the enterprise (such as Social Security numbers)

- Unauthorized updates of key data such as salary amounts, stock options (both quantity and dates), etc.

- Sharing of personnel or applicant review comments with unauthorized employees

- Sharing data with external organizations and service providers

There are two auditing standards that cloud service providers should comply with: Statement on Standards for Attestation Engagements #16 (SSAE 16) and ISO 27001. SSAE 16 asserts that a provider meets security process requirements and has been audited. ISO 27001 requires that a provider implement a management and control framework related to security risks. HRIS cloud providers need to pass these certifications on a regular basis. Security for the HRIS is so important that there is an entire chapter that covers this topic in detail. If interested at this point, read Chapter 15 for a comprehensive discussion on HRIS security.

BEST OF BREED

As discussed in the previous section, an HRIS often exists as one of the main parts of an organization's overall ERP solution. However, an HRIS does not need to be a monolithic, or single, all-encompassing, solution. In other words, an organization does not need to purchase one, integrated solution, that supports most, if not all, core HR functions. This section of the chapter addresses the use of multiple HRIS within an organization, each of which supports a very specific HR function (e.g., recruiting, training, talent management, etc.) and the pros and cons of using such an approach. In general, an architecture that combines products from multiple vendors is called **best of breed (BoB)**.

The most well-known example of these BoB architectures comes from the audio industry—surround-sound receivers combined with CD players, DVD players, high-end speakers, and even the occasional retro turntable. All these components "plug and play" with each other to provide the best possible sound experience. This architecture works because of the standards that have been established for decades and that enable different devices to work together. We will see in what follows that BoB software components for an HRIS still need to mature somewhat to reach the capability of the analog audio components. Yet the goal remains the same: deliver the best-possible point solution to meet the business need.

For this synergy to work properly, three conditions need to be present for each software solution:

- First, there should be a perceived need for a specialized solution. For example, if a company expects to receive electronic job applications over the Internet 90% or more of the time, an **optical character recognition (OCR)** program, which scans handwritten or typewritten forms into an electronic format, would not be needed for resume scanning.

- Second, a universally agreed-on set of guidelines for interoperability must exist between applications. This exists at both the syntactical and the semantic levels. The **syntactical level** refers to the base "alphabet" used to describe an interface. For any two applications to communicate, they will need to share data. This data exchange can be done through databases, simple text files (such as Excel), or, increasingly, **XML (eXtensible Markup Language)**. Basically, XML is similar to HTML, which is used in all Internet browsers. XML files can be shared or transmitted between most software applications today. XML presents a structured syntax—an alphabet—to describe any data elements within an HRIS.

- Third, applications need to "speak the same language." Just as the Roman alphabet allows the spelling of words in multiple languages and formats, XML enables data to be described with many different tags. At the **semantic level**, the language needs to map between software applications. An employee's data description may consist of various tagged fields, such as Name, Address, Birth Date, Phone, Title, Location, and so on. If one of the applications does not have most of the same set of XML tags, it will not be able to exchange employee data. As important as the shared data semantics between applications is having analogous business process semantics. For example, a time-keeping system may define a pay period differently from the payroll application that actually prints employee checks.

An HR example would consist of selecting the most robust HR software applications—regardless of vendor—for each need and then using the XML language to move data efficiently among those applications. The HR department might select SilkRoad for talent management (recruiting), Workday for most HR applications and data management, Kronos software for time and labor tracking, ADP software for payroll purposes, and a proprietary vendor product for outsourced HR benefits administration. If all the conditions are met, HRIS applications should be able to interoperate with many point solutions. The following sections provide examples of where best-of-breed solutions are often considered.

Talent Management

The business process to recruit new employees for a company has many BoB opportunities. Large HRIS applications tend to focus on the internal hiring processes of the company—creating and approving job requisitions, saving applicant data, scheduling interviews, capturing interview results, and, finally, hiring the new employee. Yet there exist other software applications to "fine-tune" the hiring process. OCR scanning applications can eliminate the rekeying of applicant data from paper-based resumes, and other applications can perform applicant database searches, post job requisitions directly to Internet job sites, and run applicant background checks. These examples of specific functionality are typically not provided in an HRIS.

Time Collection

Most companies require employees to submit time-keeping data each pay period (e.g., time and attendance). For hourly employees, this typically means using a punch card and time clock to track hours. Some solutions use employee badges with magnetic stripes, thereby enabling employees to clock in and out. Again, most HRIS vendors do not provide the hardware needed to track time. Time-keeping systems will capture the hourly data from various readers throughout a site. Employee scheduling for various shift coverages can be implemented with time collection or planning software. For example, transit districts schedule bus operators to cover a very complex route system throughout the week. Unionized rules force certain break periods and preferences for senior operators. Driver schedules are posted for future pay periods; and actual hours worked, reported sick time, and vacation time are collected for each pay period. Such data will be reviewed each pay period prior to being transmitted to the HRIS payroll application.

Payroll

In some cases, the entire payroll process may be outsourced to another vendor, such as ADP or Paychex. For some enterprises, the cost of maintaining a payroll application and staff in-house may outweigh the benefits of controlling the process. In this case, employee time data, pay rate, and benefit information would be transmitted to the external vendor for processing. This choice of using an outside provider is conceptually the reverse of the typical BoB motivation. The enterprise is not looking for the *best* technical or functional solution but for a provider offering a commodity service at the *lowest* cost. In the case of a large multinational corporation with lots of employee levels, it would probably be prudent to purchase the HRIS payroll application.

Employee Benefits

Each year, most employers present their employees with what is called the benefits open enrollment period, during which signing up for benefits is similar to course enrollment for students each semester. Instead of enrolling in courses, though, employees enroll for major medical, dental, and insurance benefits. For example, employees choose between health care providers such as Kaiser and Blue Cross for their medical insurance. These providers support interfaces with the major HRIS applications so that, as employees log into the enrollment software, they can review offerings tailored to their company's plan. Thus, when

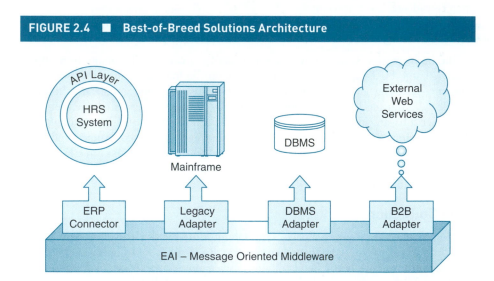

FIGURE 2.4   ■   Best-of-Breed Solutions Architecture

employees select a particular insurance program, they can then transmit enrollment data to the provider through their organization's HRIS.

As one can see in Figure 2.4, BoB solutions introduce additional complexity into the software architecture. This complexity can add IT expense in the form of new software licensing and programming charges. The justification for the added functionality needs to compensate for these additional costs. So a benefit-cost analysis should be performed by the HR function to determine whether the BoB alternative is to be used. Detailed procedures to compute a benefit-cost analysis are covered in Chapter 7.

In summary, BoB options can create a much more powerful solution than a stand-alone HRIS. The BoB alternative also creates system flexibility, as each application can be managed and upgraded independently. Yet this power and flexibility may end up costing the IT department by giving rise to more complex systems administration issues.

PLANNING FOR SYSTEM IMPLEMENTATION

A variety of authors, consultants, and others have discussed implementation methods for information systems. Rampton, Turnbull, and Doran (1999) discuss 13 steps in the implementation process. Jessup and Valacich (1999) divide the implementation of a system into five steps, with a focus on the systems side of the process. Regan and O'Conner (2002) provide eight steps for implementing information systems. Some organizations have proprietary processes that they use for all implementations. Points to remember in regard to system implementation as this section is examined are as follows: (1) this is a process that will take a team of individuals anywhere from 6 weeks to 3 years to complete; (2) a variety of ways to manage this process may be attempted, so long as the key issues are examined and organizational goals for the implementation are achieved; and (3) there is no single definitive approach to be used in all situations.

The first key step is planning. This is an absolutely critical step in any business process and especially in the design of any large-scale software implementation involving multiple-process interfaces. Note that the planning process doesn't guarantee success—rather, it increases the probability that the implementation will be successful. The systematic examination of the following topics provides the organization with the opportunity to see how the implementation will work—to peer into the crystal ball—and identify some contingencies for implementation steps that might not go perfectly. In other words, a robust planning process provides a framework within which the implementation team can proceed, and it provides some decision-making parameters for any unforeseen difficulties that might appear (Bedell, 2003a).

The topics that need to be discussed during the various steps of the planning process include but are not limited to the following:

- Project manager

- Steering committee/project charter

- Implementation team

- Project scope

- Management sponsorship

- Process mapping
- Software implementation
- Customization (vanilla vs. custom)
- Change management
- "Go live"
- Project evaluation
- Potential pitfalls

It is rare that an HRIS will perfectly fit all of a company's business processes. So, as noted earlier, a key architectural decision during implementation is the choice between configuration and customization. However, for the organization to best understand which, if either, approach is optimal, a "fit-gap" analysis should be conducted that systematically works through every process in the HRIS that has been mapped as well as any new processes that have been identified as mission critical. The result is an understanding as to where organizational processes and the software processes mesh (fit) and where they do not (gap). Any gaps that are identified need to be closed either through modifying organizational processes, configuring the HRIS application to perform in a certain manner, or customizing the software. For additional information on analyzing an organization's needs, please read Chapter 3.

Summary

The implementation of an HRIS goes beyond simply placing a new technology into the organization. This chapter focuses on several of the many different organizational, people, and technical issues that must be addressed. The first section considers the important internal and external users or customers of the HRIS and organizational goals. In the second section, four different types of HRIS architectures are enumerated. The evolution of technology, from legacy "dinosaur" systems to contemporary N-tier architectures and cloud computing, has dramatically affected the scope and influence of HRISs in organizations. Therefore, the strengths and weaknesses of each architecture are discussed. Next, a brief overview of mobile HRIS and security is provided to make the reader aware of their importance in any HRIS adoption process. The third section of the chapter discusses the best-of-breed approach to HRIS adoption and the pros and cons of this approach in different functional areas. Finally, the chapter concludes with a general discussion of the steps that organizations might take to plan and implement an HRIS and of the factors that can affect these processes. In summary, organizations that are able to manage the people, processes, and technology involved in an HRIS implementation should be more likely to find that the new HRIS is able to meet their goals more effectively in terms of budget, functionality, and usability.

Key Terms

analysts or power users 26

bandwidth 30

best of breed (BoB) 34

cloud computing 32

configuration 33

customization 33

enterprise resource planning
  (ERP) 23

eXtensible Markup Language
  (XML) 35

human resource management
  (HRM) 24

Hypertext Markup Language
  (HTML) 30

implementation team 24

infrastructure as a service
  (IaaS) 32

load balancing 30

multitenant 33

N-tier architecture 30

on-premise 33

operating systems (OS) 30

optical character recognition
  (OCR) 34

platform as a service
  (PaaS) 32

semantic level 35

single tenant 33

software as a service
  (SaaS) 32

sourcing partner
  organizations 28

syntactical level 35

three-tier architecture 29

two-tier (client-server)
  architecture 29

Discussion Questions

1. Identify the various types of users or customers of an HRIS.

2. What are the three broad categories of data that an HRIS manages?

3. How does network bandwidth affect a two-tier (client-server) architecture?

4. How does an N-tier architecture simplify the IT department's task of maintaining client software?

5. Research https://hropenstandards.org/. How many software vendors are involved with the organization? What are the benefits of open standards?

6. Take a specific industry, say the K–12 education industry. How might HireRight's integration with Oracle's PeopleSoft assist the process of hiring employees such as bus drivers, janitors, or campus security?

7. When might a BoB approach not be the "best" solution for an organization?

Case Study: HRIS in Action Revisited

This case is revisited with some additional information that involves the understanding of the material in this chapter. The additional information will be added to the situation described in the vignette at the beginning of this chapter.

A billion-dollar retailer with more than 4,000 stores finds that it cannot move fast enough to beat the competition. The organization's senior management arrives at the conclusion that it would be easier to achieve the strategic goals enumerated by the board of directors if the various organizational functions would share information. Shared information would enable them to develop and deploy new actions and tactics more quickly. The

CEO and the president have therefore ordered the major functions to immediately update their information systems so that data sharing is possible. The senior vice presidents (SVPs) of accounting and human resources immediately decide that the only solution is to decide jointly on an ERP product. ERP software applications are a set of integrated database applications, or modules, that carry out the most common business functions, including human resources, general ledger, accounts payable, accounts receivable, order management, inventory control, and customer relationship management. To speed the installation along, they will install it using a rapid implementation methodology that a company down the street used. The goal is to have the new systems operational in nine months.

Shortly after this decision is made, the SVP of HR calls you into his office and tells you that you will be management sponsor for this project. You have to decide on everything. You sit back in your nice office and think:

> What's the problem with this scenario? It shouldn't be difficult to select a vendor and then borrow the methodology from down the street. It worked for them; it should work for us! We'll call a few vendors in the morning and find out about cost, time frame, and implementation methods. In the meantime, I should find out a little more about how to do this and who will be using it. I remember from my information systems class in college that this is a reasonable first step when it comes to buying software.

What do you think your response would be to this inquiry? Has your response changed now that you have read this chapter? If so, how?

New Information for the Case: Part 1

After some discussions with department heads from all the departments in the organization, you realize that a large number of people (stakeholders) will be affected by the new systems. Furthermore, you come to realize how important HR data really are to these stakeholders. Based on this information, you think, "Wow, there are far more people who could be potentially using this information system than I expected!" The old textbook and the vendor information should provide a lot to think about.

Using the information from the section of this chapter titled "HRIS Customers/Users: Data Importance," please answer the following questions:

1. Identify some of the customers who would be logical members of the implementation team and explain why.

2. Think through an HR process and sketch out what data are necessary to complete your sample process well. How much history does the organization need to convert to continue functioning?

3. Pick one area of the HR function (e.g., recruiting), and make a list of processes that will need to be mapped and possibly reengineered during this implementation.

New Information for the Case: Part 2

Over the next month, as you continue to obtain information about the design and implementation of the new system, you are still somewhat confused about what to do. Once again, we find you in your office thinking:

> There are so many potential decisions to make with regard to hardware! I wonder what we need to schedule, if we need to buy hardware, and how we should configure the servers to ensure maximum security. And this "bring your own device" stuff is going to drive us nuts! It's time to make another list of questions!

Based on the information in the section of the chapter titled "HRIS Architecture," please respond to the following:

1. Make a list of questions for each of the following individuals: lead hardware technical expert, network manager, and chief software manager.

2. What configuration should the company use? Make a suggestion and support it!

3. Make some recommendations about security and bring your own device.

New Information for the Case: Part 3

As part of your investigation, you have uncovered a system concept called "best of breed." You are in your office again trying to decide what to do, and you think, "Perhaps best of breed might be the easiest and best way to go."

1. Make a recommendation as to whether a BoB option should be chosen or a more standardized option with simpler interfaces between hardware and software should be selected.

2. Think about what the best answer should be when you have to connect your system with accounting and finance. Make a recommendation and support it!

New Information for the Case: Part 4

You have just sat down in your office feeling as if there is way too much to do! Your IS software professional has given you the information from one of the potential vendors about the various steps that need to be taken in implementation of the HRIS. Your immediate reaction is, "Man, am I going to be at work late for the next many months!"

Case Study Questions

Based on the information in this chapter, answer the following questions:

1. Develop the first few steps of the project plan.

2. Discuss the potential political necessities outlined in this section as they relate to this type of implementation.

3. Think about and create a list of steps that make sense for your organization.

4. Is the nine-month rapid-implementation time frame feasible? Or will it just lead to failure?

MANAGING HRIS IMPLEMENTATIONS

PART II

3

THE SYSTEMS DEVELOPMENT LIFE CYCLE AND HRIS NEEDS ANALYSIS

Lisa M. Plantamura and Richard D. Johnson

EDITORS' NOTE

This chapter begins the section of the book focused on managing HRIS implementation—how to determine the needs for an HRIS and how that determination affects the design of the HRIS. The idea that there will be different users of the HRIS with various data and information needs was introduced briefly in Chapter 2. In this chapter, you will see the importance of the initial needs analysis and learn how it is done. In keeping with the holistic nature of HRIS, the systems development life cycle (SDLC) is introduced; however, this chapter focuses heavily on the analysis phase of the SDLC, as the remaining parts, namely, planning, design, implementation, and maintenance, are discussed in subsequent chapters. The authors emphasize that the needs analysis begins the process of HRIS design, but that this analysis is also done continuously throughout the system design process. This notion of continuously updating the needs analysis recognizes the possibility of both organizational and technology changes during the development and implementation of the HRIS. In addition, it is important to complete an accurate and comprehensive needs analysis because this will provide the blueprint for the evaluation of the HRIS after it is implemented.

CHAPTER OBJECTIVES

The learning goals for this chapter are listed here. After completing this chapter, you should be able to:

- Define the systems development life cycle (SDLC)
- Explain how the analysis phase of the SDLC informs the needs analysis process

- Describe the purpose of needs analysis and why it is important
- Outline the main stages of needs analysis
- Identify what is involved in an HRIS needs analysis, including the types of activities performed
- List the typical participants involved in an HRIS needs analysis
- State the key deliverables of an HRIS needs analysis

INDUSTRY BRIEF
DAN STALEY, PARTNER, PwC

A Systems Development Life Cycle ("SDLC") is critical for our consulting practitioners at PwC. First and foremost, SDLC provides everyone—our clients and consultants—a common structure by which to plan and execute the proposed work effort. We generally organize our contracts (statements of work) and associated deliverables / responsible activities around these stages. Secondly, SDLC provides a proven methodology or sequential order for key project activities. Although it seems embarrassingly obvious that one would, of course, *plan* before they *design* or *analyze* before they *implement*, you would be surprised at the temptation to "shoot before aiming" or rush to an answer before fully understanding the question. We see it time and time again when we are engaged to rescue troubled initiatives.

When I bought my first house, a few years after I'd graduated from college, I decided to install my own crown molding throughout. After borrowing my Dad's compound miter saw and buying many planks of molding from the local home supply store, I was eager to make progress. Up the ladder I went for a quick measure of the wall, down and back to the work area to mark the wood with my pencil, and then "buzzzz" went the blade. Back up the ladder and . . . oops . . . I'd cut it too short and with the wrong angle. That piece was ruined. It didn't take me long to learn the importance of the Carpenter's Rule: "measure twice; cut once." The same is true of the

early stages of SDLC. The planning and analysis phases, if shortchanged, are certain to doom whatever you are hoping to construct. Although the excitement is in the implementation phase, it is critical to study the problem first to avoid building something that you or your clients do not need.

A few years ago, a client engaged our Firm to quickly "fix their HR data" and provide an estimate to upgrade their HRMS from their older version to the latest version. The executives were frustrated with the inconsistent and corrupted data in the HR application and needed it fixed yesterday. They also believed that the newer version of the software would help address their issues. They conveyed that they already knew what the data issues were and just needed a few programmers familiar with the application to clean up the data over a few weeks' time. After several conversations, we convinced them that a more thorough root cause analysis was required to truly understand the need. Although the client executives were not thrilled with the delay, the needs analysis ended up saving them from throwing good money after bad.

After several weeks of observing their users entering data, interviews with key business leaders and HR managers, extracting and assessing their data, reviewing and understanding the purpose of their reports and the data critical to running their business, we were able to report our findings. These findings concluded that a

(Continued)

(Continued)

different type of project was needed before any cleanup occurred. We found that HR data entry was decentralized to roughly five different groups, and users were not trained consistently on how and where to enter data. The same data fields were being repurposed in the system and used in a wide variety of ways. Data fields *most* desired by the executive team to run the business did not even exist in the application and wouldn't in the upgraded version either. Instead of "chasing their tail" on never ending data fixes or upgrading immediately, which would not resolve any of their pain points, we suggested that they invest in more systemic changes that would have more immediate and lasting impact. Our recommendations included:

- Change their HR service delivery model—especially around how data is captured and entered (employing ESS, MSS, and a central support group when data must be keyed by HR)

- Update and deliver consistent training for HRIS users entering data

- Add custom fields to the HR data base to capture essential operational data elements not included in the current HRIS

Our team suggested that we clean up (remediate) the current data only *after* the first three items were addressed. This way, we would be confident that it would not immediately be corrupted again a few weeks after we left. Taking the proverbial "step back" to perform a proper needs analysis was critical in this case, as it is most of the time. By "measuring twice," we uncovered issues that the client hadn't seen in their haste to attack the problem originally.

HRIS IN ACTION
FAILING TO PLAN IS PLANNING TO FAIL

A multimedia company planned to offer a special benefits package to a select group of employees. The purpose of the package was to encourage some employees to retire early, which would provide cost savings to the company, as well as meet some of its other needs, such as providing promotional opportunities to help attract and retain younger employees. The special package included granting additional years of service for the purposes of calculating retirement and retiree medical benefits, granting additional age to employees to be used in the calculation of eligibility for early-retirement incentives from the pension plan, and eliminating some portion of the normal reductions in pension plan benefits

for those taking early retirement. The cost of implementing these changes in the existing system for the estimated eligible group of just over 500 employees was prohibitive due to the complex nature of the calculations involved.

The project was in danger of being canceled until a careful needs analysis was done. For 500 employees, did the solution need to be fully automated? Did employees need to be able to model their retirement benefits on the Internet? How much manual work could be relied on to handle the workload? Did the project need to be repeatable?

The answer for the multimedia company was to build a simple solution outside its HRIS using spreadsheet and word merge applications and to couple that simple solution with a high-touch customer service group that was able to respond to the needs of program participants, manage the increased manual paperwork requirements, and perform the interventions into the system to make the components that had to be automated, such as the payment of benefits, function properly. The program that had nearly been canceled was a success, so much so that it was repeated the next year in another company division.

Implementing the changes in the existing HRIS would have been the obvious solution, but creating a one-time solution when it appeared there would be little future need for a complicated implementation was the right choice in this case. Careful, honest, and practical needs analysis made possible what had been impractical due to cost concerns. It should be noted, however, that the HRIS provider recognized the need the multimedia company had expressed and later made a decision to augment its software to include features that would provide greater flexibility for future offerings, meeting a need the provider had not recognized during its own original planning and needs analysis.

INTRODUCTION

For either you know what you are looking for and then there is no problem, or you don't know and then you cannot expect to find anything.

—Plato

This chapter briefly introduces the systems development life cycle (SDLC) and provides readers with an in-depth look at one of its most important phases: analysis. The SDLC focuses on the activities across all aspects of the development project. The second part of the chapter focuses on one specific activity within the analysis phase of the SDLC: needs analysis. **Needs analysis** refers to the process of gathering, prioritizing, and documenting an organization's HR information requirements thoroughly, and it serves as a necessary input for the subsequent design and implementation of an HRIS.

Needs analysis usually takes on a particularly prominent role in the analysis phase of an HRIS development project, prior to significant design and implementation activities. It is important to note, however, that the needs analysis for the HRIS continues through the entire systems development process, because each stage in the process could lead to the identification of new needs for the HRIS. An effective needs analysis can help the organization save costs and reduce headaches in later phases of the development and implementation process. Consider, for example, some of the potential costs of not planning and conducting a thorough needs analysis:

- Users reject an HRIS that fails to provide the functionality they need.

- Vendor software packages are selected based on incomplete, inaccurate, or irrelevant criteria.

- Costly custom systems are developed and built based on arbitrary data.

- Custom additions to the HRIS are required to fill needs after implementation, as these needs were not properly identified during the needs analysis.

- Scope creep occurs because of growth in the goals, functionality, and requirements of the HRIS without adjustments to the time, cost, or resources allocated to the project.

Consequently, needs analysis is not something that HRIS project personnel *choose* to do; it is something they *must* do. The following sections in this chapter provide a road map for conducting a needs analysis. First, we discuss the systems development life cycle.

THE SYSTEMS DEVELOPMENT LIFE CYCLE

The **systems development life cycle (SDLC)** is a formal, multistage process through which information systems are implemented. Specific phases include planning, analysis, design, implementation, and maintenance (Figure 3.1). Just as each organization has a unique culture, so, too, the SDLC is often tailored to the needs of each organization. Some organizations might choose to codify more than 20 phases in their systems development life cycle. However, most scholars and practitioners would agree that the activities outlined in the five-phase SDLC introduced here contain the major system development activities.

This phased approach to system design has multiple advantages. First, it allows the organization to focus on a limited set of issues. Second, it contains many activities within one phase and allows organizations to make "go/no-go" decisions at the end of each phase. If at any time the project is seen as not meeting organizational objectives, it can be terminated, with the work to date providing a baseline for future development (if conditions merit moving forward at a later date).

We encourage readers to take particular note of the dashed lines in Figure 3.1, as they represent the idea that you might find it necessary to revisit previous phases of the life cycle if conditions change or if details are missed. The problem is that, just like climbing a real waterfall, moving back up the life cycle can be costly, challenging, and require significant effort. Just ask salmon how hard it is to swim upstream! Each of the five phases in the SDLC is important, and skipping any specific phase can have a negative impact on the success of your project. Let us consider more closely the SDLC phases depicted in Figure 3.1:

1. *Planning:* The **planning phase** of the SDLC includes both long-range or strategic planning and short-range operational planning. During the planning phase, HR will determine the existing technological and system capabilities and develop a general plan for adapting, upgrading, or changing these plans. In a sense, HR is conducting an analysis of their future human capital strategies and assessing what might need to be done technologically to ensure that these strategies may occur. As this phase is at a strategic level, the planning is very high level and not detailed. At the end of this phase, an organization should have a general idea of the issues it needs to address and may have developed a plan to move forward. It is important to note that, in addition to poor planning, inadequate change management is a significant reason HRIS projects fail. Change management processes should begin during the planning phase to prepare employees for the transformation process that is coming.

2. *Analysis:* It is in the **analysis phase** that an organization's current capabilities are documented, new needs are identified, and the scope of an HRIS is determined. For many projects, this phase can be the most time consuming and important phase of the SDLC. The analysis phase of the SDLC encompasses steps such as reviewing the current system processes, looking for opportunities for improvement, exploring and justifying change, developing requirements for the new system (needs analysis), and prioritizing those needs. At the end of this phase, a formal requirements definition report should be completed and available for use in systems design or vendor evaluation. Because needs analysis is such an integral part of the analysis phase, we devote an entire section of the chapter to it.

3. *Design:* In the **design phase**, the "blueprint" and detailed specifications for the new system are developed and finalized. The final vendor evaluation and selection often occurs during the design phase. (This topic is covered in detail in the next chapter.) Using the results of the needs analysis conducted in the previous SDLC phase, the current human resources processes might be changed and updated to reflect current organizational needs and potentially industry best practices. Organizations have many options in design, and these options are also covered more extensively in the next chapter.

4. *Implementation:* During the **implementation phase**, the HRIS is built, tested, and readied for the actual rollout, or "go live" stage—the point in the SDLC at which the old system is turned off and the new system is put into operation. Two common approaches to switching organizations from their old system to the new system are to either pilot the new HRIS in one location before fully going live or to enable limited functions and then continue to add functionality. There is not one single optimal approach, but instead, the approach used by your organization should reflect your needs and context. Key steps in implementation include coding or configuring modules, system testing, finalizing procedures, converting old data for use in the new system, documentation, and training end users.

FIGURE 3.1 ■ A Typical Systems Development Life Cycle (SDLC)

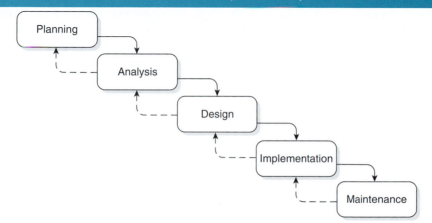

5. *Maintenance:* The SDLC does not end once the go-live date arrives. The **maintenance phase**, sometimes referred to as the "forgotten phase" (Smith, 2001), is the phase in the life of an HRIS during which the primary objective is to prolong its useful life. Maintenance begins immediately when the new system goes live. Consequently, a crucial part of maintenance is the evaluation of the HRIS. Does the HRIS meet the needs of all users as determined earlier in the SDLC? Has the system been accepted by the users? Is the HRIS being used properly? Maintenance serves four main purposes:

   a. **Corrective Maintenance**—There will be times that, despite the best efforts of designers and implementers, something in the system does not work properly and must be fixed (e.g., computer bugs, misinterpreted designs, incorrectly specified designs, or identified needs ignored).

   b. **Adaptive Maintenance**—The human resources environment is always changing and evolving. For example, new government regulations affecting HR practices, such as legislation addressing racial and gender discrimination, can prompt new requirements or alter the old requirements of the system.

   c. **Perfective Maintenance**—The goal of perfective maintenance is to tweak or improve on the existing system. For example, a more efficient routine that speeds up processing times could be developed in the maintenance phase.

   d. **Preventative Maintenance**—Preventative maintenance focuses on the ongoing requirements of maintaining the hardware and software than run the HRIS. Such a maintenance action will prevent future system crashes due to, for example, inadequate hardware.

Having briefly reviewed the SDLC, the remainder of the chapter will focus on needs analysis. Although needs analysis is important throughout the life of a project, it is particularly important early in the project—in the planning and analysis phases.

ANALYSIS

As noted, the analysis phase of the SDLC encompasses multiple steps, including conducting a needs analysis and the writing of a formal requirements definition report. Organizations sometimes skip over analysis, progressing directly to solutions, as people may be influenced by the marketing materials and promises made by software vendors. It is not unheard of for HR representatives, after attending trade shows and viewing potential HRIS solutions, to make a purchasing decision based on what they have seen rather than what their organization really needs.

This phase is particularly important, because unless the requirements are specified in detail, the organization cannot select the best vendor package or design its own system effectively. Regardless of whether it is built or bought, HRIS software is expensive, so the investment made should be in the best system that fits the organization's needs. When an organization does not conduct a proper needs analysis, it might expend considerable effort reworking the solution because it does not meet the organization's needs. In fact, it has been argued that the costs to fix errors increase exponentially through the life cycle. What this means is that a $100 fix during analysis could be a $10,000 fix during the implementation. Additionally, time is wasted, as it takes longer to get to a solution that works for the organization. A proper needs analysis provides the organization with information focused on the essential areas of HR and organizational functioning to be supported by the HRIS. This information is then used to document the functional system requirements. Do not underestimate the importance of analysis. Remember, it is easier (and less expensive!) to fix a problem before the new system is designed rather than after it has been implemented.

NEEDS ANALYSIS

As noted, needs analysis focuses on the process of thoroughly gathering, prioritizing, and documenting an organization's HR information requirements. The first question that you might want to ask is why you would undertake a needs analysis. Essentially, the purpose of needs analysis is to collect and document information related to making changes connected to:

- Current system performance issues;
- The introduction of a new system, application, task, or technology; or
- Any opportunities perceived to benefit the organization.

The process of conducting a needs analysis is systematic, and it should progress in a logical, methodical fashion, as each stage affects those that follow. An effective needs analysis consists of five main stages, as follows, each of which has activities that will be discussed in detail:

1. Needs analysis planning
2. Observation
3. Exploration
4. Evaluation
5. Reporting

Regardless of the type of system desired, all stages should be completed, although more detail might be required when, for example, a system is being built in-house rather than purchased from a vendor.[1] The resulting HRIS will be better formulated, executed, accepted by employees, and used if time and effort are invested in this early phase. At the end of needs analysis, there will be a detailed and prioritized list and description of HR's current and future functional automation support needs.

1. Needs Analysis Planning

During this first stage of the needs analysis process, **needs analysis planning**, the team is assembled and prepares to investigate the current and desired system applications and functions. Once the team is in place, it can begin arranging and conducting a thorough investigation. There are four major activities that need to be completed during this stage. Each is discussed in turn.

Organize the Needs Analysis Team

The needs analysis is generally conducted by a team led by HRIS analysts and involving human resources and information technology staff. The team must work with current systems users and associated constituents and **stakeholders** to identify problems clearly, research possible ways of addressing the problems, and report findings to support a decision on the most appropriate solutions. Several key organizational personnel need to be part of this team. For example, a senior-level manager, preferably with HRIS analysis experience, should be on the team and have overall accountability for needs analysis. In addition, an information technology professional should be included, along with at least one employee who has knowledge of the present HRIS (if there is one) or current HR processes. Finally, for large-scale projects, teams might wish to involve an external consultant. If an outside consultant will be involved in the needs analysis, it is important that he or she be integrated early in the assignment.

In addition to this core project team, a task force of constituents from the functional areas is needed to speak for the stakeholders. This group should include representatives from each area of HR, payroll, and any other areas that might use the HRIS directly (e.g., managers who make personnel decisions) or indirectly. Although these representatives will not be on the core project team, it is good to have a consistent contact from each area for the project. For example, if your HRIS sends data to an outside insurance provider, it is helpful to have someone from the insurance company interviewed to ensure that what they need is available from the new system. Table 3.1 provides a list of several common stakeholders in many large organizations. These people will participate in review and verification of findings, as well as serving as liaisons for their departments or functions. They should support the core team and care about the project.

Determine Management's Role

Next, it is important to determine upper management's role in the needs analysis. If top management support has not already been obtained, getting their active involvement and buy-in of other stakeholders can be difficult. Senior management sponsorship and a visible presence are critical to the success of the project, and mutual respect and honesty will allow the team to acquire the information needed to perform the analysis and make suitable recommendations. This group acts as a steering committee that will guide the team, resolve issues, and set priorities.

Define the Goals

Once the needs analysis team is in place, the next step in planning is to define, clarify, and gain management acceptance on the goals for needs analysis. Goals give focus and provide a standard against which performance and achievement may be measured. Goals help the needs analysis team focus on what it hopes to achieve, how it plans to work, and the anticipated schedule, as well as how the completed needs analysis document will look. In addition to overall systems scope and processes, these goals might also include timing, budget, staffing, and any other factors that could affect system selection, development, implementation, and operations. Like other goals, they should be specific,

TABLE 3.1 ■ Common Organizational Stakeholders	
Human Resources Stakeholders	**Other Internal Stakeholders**
Benefits Administration	Payroll
Compensation	Corporate Security
Diversity Management	Internal Medical and Emergency Services
EEO/Affirmative Action	Auditing
Employment	Legal
Employee Relations	General Ledger
Ethics and Sustainability	Telephone Operators and Directories
Global HR	Mail Room
Health and Safety	Information Technology
HR Consulting	Company Store
Incentive Programs	Community Relations
Labor Relations	Relocation Services
Pension Administration	Corporate Strategy
Profit Sharing	Organizational Subsidiaries
Relocation	
Staffing Management	***External Stakeholders***
Succession Planning	Retirees
HR Technology	Insurance Providers (Medical, Dental, Vision, etc.)
Training and Employee Development	Service Bureaus and Third-Party Processors
Workers' Compensation	Outside Service Providers

measurable, attainable, relevant, and timely (SMART). At this point, the requirements should be expressed in terms of what the system should accomplish rather than how it will work; operational details will be established later in the project.

Determine Tools and Techniques to Be Used

Specific information-gathering tools and techniques should be used when conducting a needs analysis. Each organization and project will require its own combination of observation, exploration, analysis, and reporting approaches. The tools can run the gamut from simple paper-and-pen note taking for smaller projects through complex documentation systems for corporate-wide systems. Whatever the size of the project, it is important to choose tools that are easy to manage and allow the organization to gather the data needed to ensure that it can move into the design mode with accurate and timely data.

It is important to note that, although these tools and techniques assist analysts in examining every indicator, it is also important that the team verify all data and consider each alternative objectively before making any conclusions. In addition to identifying the tools and techniques to be used, it is also important to establish performance standards and criteria to measure the results of the process. This way, stakeholders can be satisfied that the recommendations are based on thorough, rigorous research. We will discuss some of these tools and approaches later in the chapter.

2. Observation

During the **observation** stage, the needs analysis team examines the current systems and processes, forming the basis for later recommendations. At this point, the investigation is at a high level; more detailed data will be gathered later, during the exploration stage. During observation, it is important for the analysts to interact with employees at all levels in the areas that might be affected by the changes. Trends might become apparent, which could be helpful later. Involving employees now provides a great opportunity for them to voice their concerns and for the needs analysis team to better understand the strengths and weaknesses of the current systems and operations. Research has shown that the more involved the users are in the analysis, design, and implementation of new systems, the more successful these systems will be. Involving the users can create a sense of ownership, can lead to more effective communication and idea sharing, and has been shown to relate to more successful systems (Harris & Weistroffer, 2009). The observation stage also consists of multiple steps, each of which is discussed in what follows.

Analyze the Current Situation

This activity begins by assessing the current state of HR systems and processes. Before embarking on the detailed exploration of any new system, analysts must first develop a picture of present HR operations, including any problems and issues in each area or function. As part of this activity, analysts must consider the existing processes and current organizational results and compare these to the organization's expectations for what they anticipate in the future. Once a clear, unbiased understanding of current processes is obtained, this phase continues with a definition of needs. As an example, a tool such as the one shown in Figure 3.2 might be helpful during this stage to help organize the analysis.

Define the Needs

The next step in the observation stage is to define the needs that the new system must meet. The objective of this activity is to determine how those within HR believe their operations should occur, evaluate industry best practices, and begin investigating what changes or updates to the system might be valuable to adopt. As part of this step, organizational policies, procedures, and standards must be considered, along with any regulatory requirements. Essentially, the goal of this activity is to determine what the new system should accomplish.

FIGURE 3.2 ■ Example Preliminary Systems Review Document				
Functional Area	**Task**	**Current Process**	**Desired Process**	**Performance Issues**
Compensation	Performance Reviews			
	Annual Salary Increases			
	Job Analysis			
	Salary Evaluation			
Benefits	Annual Benefits Enrollment			
	Claims Administration			
	Paid Time Off			
Employment	Employment Planning			
	Recruitment			
	Staffing			
Training and Development	Workforce Training			
	Career Development			
	Succession Planning			
	Performance Management			

Identify Performance Gaps

Once the team understands the current operating environment and has gained a strong understanding of the "ideal" operating environment, it can conduct a gap analysis. Comparing the current situation to the desired situation allows the organization to identify and outline any **performance gaps**. These gaps, or areas of mismatch between the existing and required processes, form the basis for developing the systems requirements that are documented during the analysis and reporting stages.

Classify the Data

After the data have been gathered, they need to be organized. It is important to separate the data into categories by function, process, and other groupings that makes sense for your environment. In addition, technical and process systems issues should be separated from other organizational issues. For example, if there are problems with a specific function due to lack of knowledge on how the current process works, this could reflect a training issue rather than a system issue. In addition, the needs analysis team should separate the real problems from symptoms when reviewing the effects of one process on another. For instance, late filings of mandated reports might be considered a problem, but it could actually be a symptom of the real issue, which might be lack of data needed to generate the report. Finally, consider the scope of the issue; does it affect a few employees or the entire management staff?

Determine the Priorities

Using the information given, the team can now set the priorities for the needs that have been identified. The needs might be ranked based on scope, benefit-cost analysis, time to implement, and/or potential impact if ignored. Management will be interested in these assessments when reviewing the results of the preliminary analysis. Before presenting the results to management, it is a good idea to have the task force review priorities to ensure that the assessment is accurate.

Note that both *needs* and *requirements* are strong words in the sense that they imply something that the organization, and therefore the HRIS, *must have*. It is important to recognize that as needs are being identified, a process should be put into place to prioritize them. This ranking will result in a list of needs that fall along a continuum from high-priority or critical needs (e.g., those that definitely will be built into the system) to medium-priority needs, which are likely to be included, to low-priority needs, which may be incorporated if time and resources allow. This is discussed further in the following sections.

Review With Management

When presenting the preliminary findings to management, the analysis team should be prepared to adjust priorities as requested, clarify any remaining questions, and discuss the next phase of the project in order to gain management's continued commitment. It is important to work with management to define the scope, agree on the process, state the desired outcome(s), and establish shared responsibility for the continuation of the project. The team should also ensure that management understands that the full needs analysis takes time to design, develop, and accomplish. How long this will take depends on the complexity of the organization and the number of people working on the analysis. It is crucial *not* to promise more than can be delivered. One of the challenges is that the analysis phase is time consuming and complex, yet HR and management will likely push the team to finish the phase as quickly as possible. Therefore, the analysis team should be prepared to defend the phase and educate stakeholders on what the phase entails and why it should be completed before moving forward. Ultimately, though, management's commitment is essential to fund, staff, and sponsor the next stage. Thus, it is important to receive formal management support and agreement (e.g., memo, contract, etc.) before moving forward.

3. Exploration

The **exploration** stage of the needs analysis process builds on the analysis completed in the observation stage and involves gathering additional and more detailed data regarding HR processes. Remember that the problems must be defined clearly before any suitable solutions can be determined.

Collect the Data

The data collected during exploration provide the foundation for the development of goals that the organization wishes to achieve with the new system. These data also help the organization align its new system with key HR objectives. It is important to keep in mind that the data collected during the needs analysis might be used for other purposes after the system is developed and implemented, so it pays to do a good job now. In other words, good documentation now means fewer problems later! Multiple techniques should be used to collect data for the needs analysis, including interviews, questionnaires, observation, focus groups, and reviews of job descriptions, policies, procedures, and other documentation.

Interviews

The goal of conducting **interviews** is to find representative employees who can communicate the key HR practices and processes to the analysis team effectively so that the team can develop a thorough understanding of current HR operations. A variety of different interview types might be used when conducting a needs analysis. They can run the gamut from completely unstructured interviews, in which a general topic is introduced for discussion and the interviewer lets the interview progress naturally, to highly structured interviews, in which the interviewer asks specific questions in a predetermined order and respondents select from a set of provided answers. An example of a structured interview script/guide is shown in Figure 3.3.

FIGURE 3.3 ■ Interview Guide	
Human Resources Stakeholders	
Interviewee:	
Date:	
Position:	
Function:	
Phone:	
E-mail:	
System/Activity:	
Staffing (FT, PT, Temps, etc.):	

(Continued)

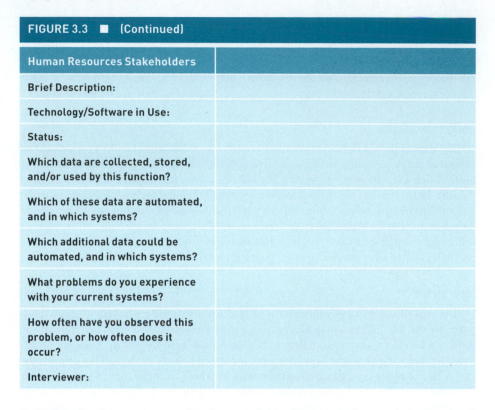

FIGURE 3.3 ■ (Continued)	
Human Resources Stakeholders	
Brief Description:	
Technology/Software in Use:	
Status:	
Which data are collected, stored, and/or used by this function?	
Which of these data are automated, and in which systems?	
Which additional data could be automated, and in which systems?	
What problems do you experience with your current systems?	
How often have you observed this problem, or how often does it occur?	
Interviewer:	

The results of interviews can then be compiled by functional area experts and reviewed by that area's management to make certain that all tasks are covered and represented correctly. Although interviews are time and labor intensive, when conducted well, they can contain the required data needed to assess the system requirements as well as being a rich source of opinions, ideas, and suggestions. It is also important that the interviewer review his or her notes soon after completing the interview to ensure that the information recorded is complete and accurate. The longer you go without writing down and reviewing your notes, the harder it will be to ensure that your notes are accurate.

Questionnaires

Questionnaires are structured data-collection tools that must be designed and implemented carefully in order to obtain usable results. Before the questionnaire is implemented, the purpose and importance of each question should be determined. Time is valuable to everyone, and no question should be included unless it serves a clear purpose that helps the analysts better understand HR data or processes. In addition, from a statistical standpoint, it is important that the questions are reliable and valid so that any analysis of the captured data can be trusted. As you would expect, it is important to design a professional-looking document (or Web survey, if administering the questionnaire online), to use clear instructions, and to focus on developing a document that is easy to use. Before launching the questionnaire to employees, the questionnaire should be tested to ensure that the questions are clear and understandable and that they are collecting the needed data. Finally, throughout the process, it is important to ensure not only that respondents' answers remain confidential but also that the respondents understand that their answers will remain confidential.

As with interviews, questionnaires also have several advantages and disadvantages. For example, one advantage of questionnaires is that they can be distributed to large groups quickly and easily. In addition, questionnaires are much less time consuming than observing or interviewing employees. Questionnaires also lend themselves to easier analysis and can be more convenient for employees (i.e., they can be completed at a time of their choosing). Finally, because questionnaires can be viewed as more anonymous, it increases the likelihood that you will obtain more accurate and honest responses.

Questionnaires do have shortcomings, though. Compared to interviews, questionnaires have much lower response rates. Many employees might not perceive that they have the time to complete them, or they might feel that their responses do not matter. Unlike interviews, questionnaires contain less rich data because there are no opportunities for an interviewer to focus on any nonverbal cues or to engage in follow-up questions as needed. However, questionnaires can sometimes be used to increase employee or management buy-in. People like to have their opinions valued, and interviews can reinforce their feelings of worth. When employees believe that their feelings and perceptions are valued and they are involved in the decision processes, they feel greater ownership in the new system (Wu & Marakas, 2006).

Observation

Another excellent way to gather data regarding HR processes is to observe personnel as they do their jobs. Because observation takes place in the actual work environment, information is obtained within the context in which HR activities occur. Observation is most useful when trying to determine what employees do and in what order. Further, it can be used to identify potential causes of performance issues. Although observation has the advantage of minimizing interruption of routine functions, observers must be skilled in observation and knowledgeable of the process itself.

Prior to observing employees in the work setting, it is important to determine the activity to be studied and to collect and review any documentation available (e.g., mission statements, organization charts, position descriptions, current systems processes, policies, etc.). In addition, try to remain as unobtrusive as possible, take notes for later clarification, and refrain from disturbing the employees' work.

Observation has its limitations, though. First, it is noteworthy that even with a well-trained and effective observer who attempts to remain unobtrusive, his or her presence alone can subtly affect how the employees go about their work (a Hawthorne effect). Second, observation is not as effective for high-level jobs in which the process and outcome of work is not as easily seen. For example, complex tasks that require an employee or manager to make decisions are not easily observed and might require interviewing the employee to fully understand the actual decision-making process. Therefore, observation might be best for simpler tasks, tasks in which data is not as accurately articulated by employees, or tasks for which it may be easy to inadvertently miss key processes using other data collection techniques. Finally, observation is time consuming, particularly when there are many individuals and processes that must be examined.

Focus Groups

Focus groups consist of a small sample of people representing a larger population who gather to discuss a topic; in this case, the topic would relate to the HRIS. Participants are asked for their opinions and attitudes, and the results can help to shape system requirements. Focus groups are important because they can provide the same depth of information as interviews, but they have the added advantage of bringing people together, which can lead to greater and more effective information sharing than if only individual interviews were utilized. Although it can seem challenging to pull together the perfect combination of people at the same time, small discussion groups such as these might uncover needs not previously found and help the analysts identify new requirements. Additionally, today's video-enabled technologies allow online data collection from geographically separated contributors (Kristie, Baird, & Duchesne, 2018). Despite some issues (e.g., technology, skill required to moderate online discussions, effort needed to engage participants), online focus groups can complement face-to-face meetings, keeping users at the core of systems decisions (Stewart & Shamdasani, 2017).

Recommendations for effective focus groups include the following:

- Limit the size of the group to no more than 8 to 12 people.

- Allow sufficient time to cover the material, generally 1 to 2 hours, and keep the meeting focused to make good use of everyone's time. Consider having a moderator assist in this process.

- Before starting the focus group, explain the objectives clearly.

- Encourage group members to speak freely and ensure that everyone participates. An icebreaker exercise can be a great way of opening up group communication.

- Use a variety of group facilitation methods, such as brainstorming, prioritizing, and consensus building to encourage and promote discussion on differences of opinion and to clarify issues.

- Take notes and/or video or audio tape the session so that nothing is lost.

- Thank participants for their time and ideas.

Regardless of the methods chosen, it is critical to develop a concise problem statement that documents the causes of the issues to be resolved and separate facts from opinions. A **problem statement** is a well-defined, succinct description of the known symptoms and issues with current operations, their most-likely causes, and how the proposed system will address these problems. The more precise and measurable a problem statement is, the more it will help to focus the team throughout the project and ultimately solve the problem. Generally, problem statements include three components:

1. A *vision statement* describing the ideal set of processes and technologies that will exist after the system is operational;

2. An *issue statement* explaining the problem using specific issues; and

3. The *method* that will be used to solve the problem.

In developing the problem statements, consideration should be given to those whom the issues affect (individuals, groups, stakeholders, etc.), the boundaries and the impact of the issues, and the risks of not solving them. Additionally, timing and location must be reflected in the problem statement, that is, when and where the issues occur and when they need to be remedied. Further, the reasons the issues need to be resolved should be emphasized. Finally, the problem statement must be written in a way that is clearly measurable and testable to ensure that the new system does solve the stated problem. An appropriate, well-defined problem statement should convince the audience, including management and other stakeholders, of the need to continue the project. Visualizing what could be along with what is and what could happen should provide assurance that a problem does exist and that it can be resolved.

4. Evaluation

Several activities occur during the **evaluation** stage of needs analysis. Once the data have been collected, they must be reviewed and assessed to create a clear picture of the current and desired processes, data sources, and issues. Next, the data should be arranged in a format useful for the next phase of the SDLC: design. Third, the data should be reviewed by the project team to gain additional perspective and encourage suggestions, noting any duplications or omissions. For example, consider whether data must be collected and stored in the new system or if it could be calculated from data already in the system. For instance, if employer-paid life insurance is twice an employee's annual salary, there is no need to store that value in the system, as it can simply be calculated from the existing salary data. In addition, it is important to consider how other areas of business interface with human resources and how HR data might come from and be sent to other systems. As an example, production or sales data may be used by HR as part of a performance appraisal or compensation process, but they would likely be provided from a non-HR module or system.

There are several ways of assessing and analyzing the system data, functions, and processes, and these can be organized in any way that assists in this process. For instance, visual representation of priorities might be displayed in check sheets, graphs, Pareto charts, flowcharts, or data flow diagrams to support and summarize the analysis. When this information is organized, it can then be prioritized according to, for example, the time when it must be present or the level of importance, as shown in what follows. The prioritization method is up to each organization.

Priority	Description
1	Must be present at implementation
2	Must be present within 6 months of implementation
3	Nice to have but not essential
4	Not needed in the near future but might be needed due to environmental changes

Importance	Description
1	Mandatory
2	Strongly desired
3	Nice to have

The result should be an operational depiction of the HR system needs, including a visual representation and descriptive text that lists the particular processing required to support each function. These documents will serve as the primary reference for the remainder of the project, and they also serve as a key communication tool for HR staff, consultants, vendor representatives, and technical staff. Given that no organization has unlimited budget to implement all functionality desired by the organization, prioritizing ensures that the most important functionality will be given first focus. In fact, for many projects, desired functionality will often have to be eliminated because of budget or time constraints.

5. Reporting

The final stage of the needs analysis process, **reporting**, involves preparing a document that summarizes the findings and presents recommendations for the design phase. The final report should include an overview of the current systems and processes, along with a description of how a new system could address the issues and weaknesses with which the function deals. This report should contain the formalized **requirements definition**, the document that lists each of the prioritized requirements for the new system. The requirement definition can include specifications geared toward solving problems identified in the analysis as well as any that focus on new functionality that HR requires in the new system. These requirements should be written in such a way that when the new system is tested, each requirement can be verified as being met.

Although the report can be and often is viewed as a sales presentation to management and other constituents that presents a business justification for continuing the project, it is also a roadmap for moving forward. The report becomes the basis upon which the new system will be designed or purchased. There is no standard format for the requirements report. Instead, the format will depend on the intended audience and corporate and/or information technology reporting standards. A potential outline for the report is shown in Figure 3.4. The written report is generally accompanied by an oral presentation in which stakeholders can ask questions and receive additional information about the project.

FIGURE 3.4 ■ Sample Report Outline

1. Executive Summary

2. Project Background

   2.1. Project Initiation

   2.2. Project Charter

   2.3. Project Scope

   2.4. Project Team

   2.5. Steering Committee

   2.6. Project Schedule

3. Current Systems

   3.1. Description

   3.2. Components and Functions

   3.3. Interfaces

   3.4. Strengths and Weaknesses

4. General Operational Requirements

5. Functional Requirements

    5.1. Function 1

        5.1.1. Function 1 Description

        5.1.2. Function 1 Requirements

    5.2. Function 2

        5.2.1. Function 2 Description

        5.2.2. Function 2 Requirements

    5.3. Etc.

6. Information Technology Requirements

7. Support Requirements

8. Next Steps

9. Appendices

Summary

Organizations faced with the need to update, upgrade, or implement changes to HR processes and to consider new software should follow a formalized, structured process to give them the best chance of success. In this chapter, we briefly introduced this structured process: the systems development life cycle that helps organizations better manage the design and implementation of new or upgraded systems.

The chapter further focuses on the analysis phase of the SDLC, particularly the needs analysis portion of this phase. Needs analysis is designed to help the organization discover the disparity between the organization's present HR system(s) and desired HR systems. The chapter outlines an effective, formal, multistage approach that starts with naming the project team, reviewing current processes and systems, and determining future needs and priorities. The resulting requirements definition can provide the ongoing project team responsible for vendor evaluation and/or system design with a clear picture of what the organization requires and when it must be delivered. It establishes the structure for future phases of this project, as well as a framework for ongoing operations. Needs analysis can, therefore, rightfully be viewed as one of the most critical to the success of the entire project.

Key Terms

adaptive maintenance 50

analysis phase 49

corrective maintenance 50

design phase 49

evaluation 61

exploration 57

focus groups 59

implementation phase 49

interviews 57

Discussion Questions

1. What are some critical success factors for effectively conducting an analysis of HRIS needs?

2. Explain how planning and analysis integrate and inform further steps in the systems development life cycle (SDLC).

3. Compare and contrast the different methods of data collection, explaining the conditions under which each is most effective.

4. Which prioritization method is most useful in establishing the appropriate values for system requirements, and why?

Case Study: Planning the Needs of Other Organizations

If you think a thorough, high-quality needs analysis is daunting on an internal project, imagine if you were an HRIS vendor and your job was to provide a "best of breed" system (see Chapter 2) that meets most of your many different clients' needs. Such an approach makes planning and needs analysis more challenging, because difficult choices must be made as to the functionality that is sufficiently broad to go into a general market package. It is costly to vendors and, indeed might be infeasible, to include functionality that is so specific that only a small portion of a system's client base benefits from the function.

Consider the following hypothetical company, Benefast Partners, which provides a specific market niche HRIS product: benefits administration software. Its challenge: Provide comprehensive benefits administration software that meets the needs of a growing and complex benefits marketplace. According to Davis Hunter, a former employee of Benefast:

"Benefast Partners (name changed to protect confidentiality) was only doing defined benefit pension plans for large employers (20,000 employees). When you focus your business opportunities on *Fortune* 100 companies, it limits your potential for growth to small and midsized markets. Given that there is competition in the market for small, medium, and large clients, there was no real way to expand. We were, however, doing 401(k) retirement plan administration both on our proprietary system, designed and marketed for large employers, and on a purchased platform for smaller companies. We had interest from existing 401(k) clients to take on administration of their defined benefit plans, and we felt we had lost 401(k) business in the past because we didn't offer total retirement outsourcing, just 401(k).

It wasn't possible to charge small employers the kinds of fees necessary to implement their plans on our proprietary system, so our efforts centered on what could be done with the purchased system used for small to midsized 401(k) plans. We quickly determined that the purchased system's defined benefits platform was not sophisticated enough from a calculation standpoint to handle most of the complexity of defined benefit plans, so we decided to use a combination of the purchased system with the calculation engine component for the proprietary system.

We had a lot of needs analysis conversations with our colleagues in another office who were running the project. Given the multiple platforms involved, processing time was a huge concern. We decided to segment the market and serve only those customers who met a fairly stringent set of requirements. Basically, we built a system to serve clients whose plans were easy to administer. In other words,

1. No multiplan clients

2. No retirement modeling

3. No coordination of benefits, for example, no combination of 401(k) and defined benefit plans

4. Limited Web interface

Based on this segmentation, we launched our new product with one of our parent companies (a bank). By the time we had signed our third client, we had already begun to move toward a fairly complex multiplan environment. Our fourth and fifth clients were even more complex. We were

over budget and off schedule on everything, and then we started trying to figure out how to do coordination of benefits. We built a system for plans that were easy to administer—but plans that are easy to administer are few and far between in the marketplace, and those that exist aren't typically managed by organizations shopping for benefits vendors."

Case Study Questions

1. How would you evaluate Benefast Partners' strategy?

2. What changes (if any) would you make?

3. What methods would you employ to ensure that an HRIS package meets the majority of your clients' needs?

Recommended Readings

How to select HRIS software—& defend your planned purchase. (2009, September). *HR Focus, 86*(9), 3–4.

McNamara, C. (n.d.). *Basics of conducting focus groups.* Retrieved from https://managementhelp.org/businessresearch/focus-groups.htm.

Society for Human Resource Management. (2015, August 11). *How to select an HRIS.* Retrieved from https://www.shrm.org/ResourcesAndTools/tools-and-samples/how-to-guides/Pages/how-toselectanhrissystem.aspx

Swedberg, J. (2009). The technological touch. *Credit Union Management*, 32(2), 30–33.

SYSTEM DESIGN AND ACQUISITION

Richard D. Johnson and James H. Dulebohn

EDITORS' NOTE

Building on Chapters 2 and 3, this chapter focuses on the design and acquisition of an HRIS. Thus, the focus of this chapter is on the "design" phase of the systems development life cycle that was introduced in Chapter 3. The authors differentiate between the logical and the physical design of an HRIS as well as emphasize the differences between the data and process views of a computer system. As will be discussed in this chapter, these differences are critical for the effective design of an HRIS that will meet the needs of the various stakeholders of the system, that is, HR and information technology professionals, managers, and employees. Data flow diagramming is discussed as a tool used to analyze and describe the HR processes prior to the actual physical design of the HRIS. In addition, the three choices or options that organizations face when moving into physical design are examined (i.e., do nothing, change processes only, or invest in a new or updated HRIS). All the effort involved in completing an accurate and comprehensive logical and physical design of the HRIS helps ensure that the acquisition of the system will be done properly. The chapter then continues with a discussion of how to develop a request for proposal and how to evaluate proposals received from outside vendors. Finally, the chapter closes with a discussion of how to assess the feasibility of a new system. This last section is a good lead-in to Chapters 6 and 14, which are focused on using HR metrics and analytics to calculate benefit-cost analysis for the acquisition of an HRIS.

CHAPTER OBJECTIVES

After completing this chapter, the reader should be able to

- Understand the difference between the data and process views of a system

- Understand the purpose and components of the data flow diagram (DFD)
- Understand the hierarchy of DFDs and the concept of DFD balancing
- Understand the three choices or options that organizations have when moving into physical design
- Understand the purpose of an RFP and what information should be included in it
- Understand the various criteria used to evaluate vendor proposals
- Describe the various types of feasibility and their purpose in evaluating potential solutions

INDUSTRY BRIEF
JEFFREY D. MILLER, DELOITTE CONSULTING

The world of human resource information systems has shifted over the past decade. Now more than ever, organizations are driving changes in human resources and their associated systems based on business needs. All industries are witnessing increased global competition, which is increasing the need to manage talent and costs of HR services. An increase in generational expansion in the workforce is driving the need to increase focus on employee engagement. These challenges are disruptions. HR has a clear opportunity to lead through the disruptions by focusing its strategy on resolving these issues. Transitions in HR operating models, alignment of policies, and business processes are the key for HR to resolve the HR challenges facing its business.

Through all of the disruption, technology is HR's enabler. Organizations must remember this principle. Whether the organization is investing in a custom portal and related technology, enhancing an existing infrastructure, or implementing a cloud-based solution, the same rule applies: Technology is the enabler not the solution to the business challenges. Using new technology to drive a poorly designed policy or process will result in a bad process, employee experience, and unmet executive-level expectations.

Organizations are changing their HR service delivery model to enable a greater impact in all industries. The focus: adapt the operating model to attend to business issues and movements in the market. This shift requires HR to look at how it operates across many facets, including recruiting, career management, acquisition and divestiture management and how its technology enables the business needs.

The same global competition in the market is propelling changes in talent management. To remain competitive, there is a dramatic shift in the focus on understanding their talent base and aligning the skill growth to expansions and shifts in the market. The right process changes driven by the right information to make decisions related to recruiting, succession planning, and learning are critical to this effort.

The generational shift cannot be ignored. Many organizations are seeing up to four distinct generations resident in their workforces. Each generation has different needs and ways of working professionally and personally. This creates a need for HR and management to be sensitive and adapt the methods of employee engagement in day to day work, performance, provisions for career trajectory and learning. This area is especially sensitive to being overly burdened with technology—relying on exchanges and messaging through technology rather than employing the technology to concentrate and foster conversations.

Selecting the right technical solution for the HR needs is significant. Most applications offered meet the majority of any organization's requirements. The real difference is in how the applications fit in driving the HR objectives and business needs of the organization. The selection and ongoing monitoring are becoming more closely aligned with strategy in many organizations. The selection is not a one-time decision. It is something that must be closely managed. Innovation in HR technology is moving at a staggering pace. This pace will continue. The world of HR technology offers multiple options and investment levels.

For HR to lead through business disruptions, the monitoring and review of technology's fit with HR business objectives must be an ongoing and formalized role in the organization structure. In summary, to have the greatest impact, HR must focus on understanding the true business and market direction of its organization, adapt its processes and policies to contribute to meeting the business needs, and then implement the model and technical solutions that enable the right level of information to enable decisions, employee engagement, cost management, and ease of maintenance.

HRIS IN ACTION

Larson Property Management Company is one of the largest property-management companies in California, with more than 1,000 employees. The company provides a full array of commercial management and development services. These activities include complete management services for commercial office and retail buildings and apartment complexes; the construction, repair, and maintenance of commercial properties; and financial management and billing services for commercial real estate clients. The company has experienced significant expansion over the past 5 years in response to the growth in apartment and commercial construction in southern California, and this expansion has resulted in the need to hire a large number of employees on an ongoing basis to staff its operations.

Larson Property Management has depended on a legacy HRIS to manage its applicant and employee databases. The system runs on a client-server computer system. The system was implemented approximately 10 years ago, prior to the rapid growth of the company and when the organization had fewer than 100 employees. The system's functionality is limited to the storage and retrieval of employee and applicant data. For recruiting purposes, the system requires a clerk to manually enter basic applicant data, the results of the application test, and whether an offer of employment has been made. Prior to this, applicants' files were passed around to those who reviewed the materials and were sometimes misplaced, so trying to locate a particular applicant's file was often a problem. The current HRIS has limited file storage capability for applicant and employee records and currently has reached its storage capacity.

Larson Property Management has decided to replace its legacy HRIS. One application module in the new HRIS that the company wants is a sophisticated applicant-tracking system (ATS). The primary objective of the ATS will be to provide a paperless hiring process. The basic functions of the new system will be managing the requisition and approval of job openings, storing resumes and job applications, and retrieving, through query functions, the names of applicants

(Continued)

(Continued)

who match job requirements, tracking a candidate's progress through the recruiting and selection process, and providing automated reporting functions. The company's managers also want eHRM functionality that includes the Internet posting of job openings through the company's website and external job-posting services, application and resume submission through the Web and through kiosks at various office locations, staff ability to access and use the system remotely through a Web browser, and online resume- and application-scanning capabilities.

Part of the design phase is modeling the processes that will be used in the system for applicant tracking. For Larson Property Management, this modeling will allow the system analysts to design an efficient paperless hiring process.

Case note: As you read this chapter, keep the situation at Larson Property Management in mind. It will be the basis of the case analysis at the end of the chapter.

INTRODUCTION

Never tell people how to do things.
Tell them what to do and they will surprise you with their ingenuity.

—*General George S. Patton (1947/1995)*

The goal of this chapter is to provide a deeper understanding of the process through which an HRIS is designed and acquired. This design and acquisition of an HRIS comprises but one phase in a larger systems development process. As noted in previous chapters, the larger development process is called the **systems development life cycle (SDLC)**. As seen in Chapter 3 (Figure 3.1), the five generic phases of the SDLC are planning, analysis, design, implementation, and maintenance. This chapter focuses on the design phase by discussing briefly the role and features of the structuring of a system's requirements through process system modeling, during which analysts create data flow diagrams (DFDs) to model both the business processes that the system will use to capture, store, manipulate, and distribute data and the options facing the HR department as it moves into design. Next, the vendor–management relationship is covered, including the creation and use of a request for a proposal (RFP), the evaluation of vendor responses, and the choice of a vendor or vendors. Finally, the chapter ends with a discussion of the HRIS feasibility criteria.

DESIGN CONSIDERATIONS DURING THE SYSTEMS DEVELOPMENT LIFE CYCLE

As discussed in previous chapters, the SDLC is a structured set of phases focused on the analysis and design of information systems. The goal of the SDLC is to provide those organizations updating existing systems or designing new ones with a stronger, more structured process to follow. A report by the Standish Group (2004) provides evidence that, as the use of structured development techniques is increasingly practiced, system quality improves. At the same time, this report also found that fewer than 30% of systems projects are successful, and more than 50% go live later than planned and are over budget. Given the wide variety of program needs in the HR department, such as recruiting, selection, training, performance management, and compensation, and the complexity of these needs, the importance of following a structured approach to the development of an HRIS cannot be overstated.

Although each phase in the life cycle is important, the goal of this chapter is to focus specifically on the activities associated with designing the HRIS. The design of the HRIS can occur in two phases: logical and physical design. The design phase is separated into two components because each has a different aim and perspective. The **logical design** of a system focuses on the translation of business requirements into improved business processes, irrespective of any technological implementation. For example, a business requirement for organizations such as Larson Property Management is the acquisition of new employees. HR business processes typically include (1) identifying jobs requiring new employees and approving those jobs; (2) analyzing the requirements of those jobs; (3) posting those positions and recruiting applicants from the labor market; (4) tracking applicants through the recruiting process, (5) selecting from the recruiting pool, through the use of selection tools such as interviews, applicants that best fit the job requirements; and (6) bringing new hires on board and placing them in their jobs. The HR programs associated with these processes are (1) HR planning, (2) job analysis, (3) recruiting, (4) applicant tracking, (5) selection, (6) placement, and (7) record keeping.

Conversely, the focus and goal of **physical design** is determining the most effective means of translating these business processes into a physical system that includes hardware and software. To merge the phases can invite the temptation to focus heavily on the physical aspects of the new system (hardware and software) at the expense of improved business processes. In addition, focusing on the physical aspects of a system can lead to premature decisions and the selection of physical solutions that may not be the most effective ones for the business processes identified.

For example, a new and improved version of software might appear on the market. Imagine that this software is designed to automate and help manage compensation systems based on a combination of base-pay administrative features along with merit modeling, reporting and analysis, and bonus pay plan tools. However, a company purchasing this software because of its elegance may have made a serious error if the company's top management is planning to drop the bonus program in two years as part of the company's new strategic plan. Another example would be the failure to acquire needed software features due to lack of attention on processes. Of course, adequate logical design enables effective physical design. Revisiting the example of Larson Property Management, we can imagine a design scenario related to staffing and the acquisition of new employees in which a thorough and careful analysis of the staffing process (logical design) would permit the company to determine that it needs a particular level of work-flow processing and Web enablement to track applicants and allow the posting of jobs online and online application to posted jobs (physical design).

Logical Design

As discussed in Chapter 3, once an organization has completed the analysis phase of the SDLC, which results in a comprehensive process analysis for the new HRIS, one of the key tasks facing the HR staff and development teams is to model the needs for the new system. There are two ways in which the system can be modeled: the physical model and the logical model. The physical model focuses on the computer technology for the HRIS, that is, on the hardware, software, networking plans, and technical manuals. The strength of this type of model is that it focuses on how the system will actually operate. In turn, this strength also becomes its weakness, because by focusing on the actual way the system will be implemented in terms of technology, analysts and HR staff may be constrained by the current, operational physical model. That is, HR staff members are familiar with the functioning of the current (i.e., legacy) HRIS they are using but, typically, not with the technological aspects of new systems or with the current technology available.

Therefore, system developers like to focus on the essence of the business processes independent of any technological implementation. To do this, logical models of the system are created. Logical models are HRIS models that could be operationalized in multiple ways in terms of the technology. For example, in the logical model, an organization might focus on receiving and processing applicant files. There are several physical ways in which an organization could implement this process. It could use a Web portal in an HRIS, a kiosk at a retail outlet, direct e-mail, or physical mail. The strength of using logical models is that the HR staff and developers can focus specifically on the business processes, policies, and procedures instead of on technology. Marakas (2006) refers to this as "separating the 'what' from the 'how'" (p. 116). By focusing on what the system does or needs to be able to do, the analyst and HR staff will be less likely to be distracted by or to focus on a single technology platform. In turn, they will be more likely to design a stronger solution.

Essentially, a **logical model** is similar to the blueprints for a home or an airplane. It provides the organization with an outline of the key business processes and goals for the system. Then, as the physical system is designed, these are translated into the hardware and software platforms that best fit the business's needs. For an HRIS, there are two types of models created for the system: those focused on the system processes and those focused on the data the system captures.

Two Ways to View an HRIS: Data Versus Process

For any HRIS, the organization must look at the total HR system from two different perspectives: the data perspective and the process perspective.

The **data perspective** focuses on an analysis of what data the organization captures and uses and on the definitions and relationships of the data while ignoring how or where the data are used by the organization. For example, a system whose aim is employee recruiting would need data about the applicants and their knowledge, skills, and abilities (e.g., name, address, degrees received, work experience). The data perspective would focus on the important data to be captured but would not be concerned with how the data are to be used within the organization. In addition, the data perspective focuses on the most efficient and effective way to capture the data to ensure accuracy.

The **process perspective**, conversely, focuses on the business processes and activities in which the organization engages and on how data flow through the HRIS. For example, a recruiting module from this perspective would consider business activities, such as receiving applications, sorting and scanning resumes to determine the interview pool, scheduling interviews, reporting candidate information for legal purposes, and so on but not the data definitions and relationships. The designer would focus on the specific business processes, including the input of the data into the system, the flow of data through the system, and the storage of the data, but not on precisely what data are captured and how they are best organized or stored. Essentially, process modeling uses tools to describe the processes that are carried out by a system.

A key question that the reader might be asking is "Why should I care about these distinctions?" The reason the distinction between the process and data perspectives is important is that each represents a portion of the total HRIS, but neither provides the complete picture. By modeling each separately, the organization is better able to understand and communicate its needs to the technical staff (e.g., the project management team responsible for designing and implementing the HRIS and any external consultants, vendors, or software developers). In addition, while processes may change in the future, data generally represent the most permanent and stable part of a system. For example, employee data from prior systems are often converted into the new HRIS data format and transferred into the new system. This data conversion and migration process is a critical step in the implementation phase, and it provides a bridge and continuity between the legacy system and the new HRIS. This permanency of data and the more dynamic aspect of processes suggest the importance of dealing with each separately.

Over the past three decades, a well-established procedure for modeling information systems has been developed. The procedure is based on a process perspective that uses data flow diagramming. A common aspect of all design methodologies is the use of diagrammatic modeling techniques. While the style of the charting symbols varies, the fundamentals are well established. Our focus in this chapter is on the creation and use of process models.

Logical Process Modeling With Data Flow Diagrams

A **process model** describes and represents the key business processes or activities conducted by the organization, such as applicant tracking. The specific type of process model typically used by organizations is a **data flow diagram (DFD)**. A DFD is a graphical representation of the key business activities and processes in the HR system, the boundaries of this system, the data that flow through the system, and any external individuals or departments that interact with the system.

The focus of a DFD is on the movement of data between external entities (such as a job applicant) and processes (the applicant-tracking process) and between processes and data stores. Kendall and Kendall (2008) argue that DFDs have four distinct advantages over narrative (e.g., written) descriptions:

1. There is freedom from committing to the technical implementation of the system too early.

2. They provide a deeper understanding of the interrelatedness of systems and subsystems.

3. They allow for stronger communication of system knowledge to the employees, since the diagrams are in pictorial form.

4. They ensure a deeper analysis of the proposed system to determine if all business processes have been identified.

A DFD consists of four symbols (see Figure 4.1). These include the entity, the data flow, the process, and the data store. The **entity** represents any external agent (e.g., an individual, department, business, system) that either receives or supplies data to the HR system. For example, in an **applicant-tracking system (ATS)**, a manager could request that a job opening be posted, or an applicant could submit her resume online. In this scenario, both the manager and applicant are entities. Other examples of an entity are a manager inputting merit pay raise information on an employee into the payroll system or the production/

manufacturing system inputting piece-rate production data about the number of products produced by an employee into the payroll system. Similarly, the time-and-labor module, which provides time-card information on employees and their start and end times on work-days, represents an entity for payroll systems. Because entities represent a specific person, place, system, or department, they are labeled with a noun in the DFD.

The **data flow** represents the movement of a single piece of data from point to point through the system (e.g., from process to process, entity to process, or process to data store). As a data flow represents data about a person, place, or thing, it should also be labeled with a noun. The label of a data flow should describe exactly what data are contained in the flow. For example, a data flow labeled "Time Sheet" would represent an employee's time sheet, and the exact data contained in the flow would be precisely defined as part of the diagramming process. Because DFDs describe the key business processes and the flow of data between them, *an important rule to remember is that all data flows must begin or end at a process.*

The third symbol in the DFD represents the **process**. A process represents a business activity or process. The goal of each process is to change or transform inputted data into a useful output (e.g., creating an applicant record, updating an employee record, creating a recruiting yield ratio report, reporting Equal Employment Opportunity Commission data on applicants). Since data are transformed as part of these processes, they should be labeled with action verbs, for example, *calculate*, *send*, *print*, or *verify*.

The final symbol represents the **data store**, in other words, the data at rest in the system or a repository of data. This repository could be a filing cabinet, a file on a desk, a computer file, or a database table. A data store contains data about a person, place, or department and should be labeled with a noun. Examples of data stores include employee files, applicant files, employee records, and customer or current benefits records. Data stores are typically identified with a "D*n*," where D identifies that what is labeled is a data store and *n* is a number reflecting the data store's unique identifier (D1, D2, etc.). The symbols and their use are illustrated in Figure 4.1.

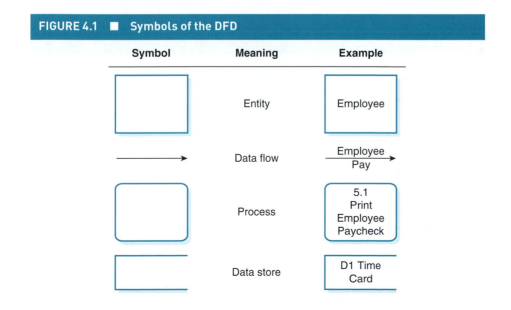

FIGURE 4.1 ■ Symbols of the DFD

Symbol	Meaning	Example
	Entity	Employee
→	Data flow	Employee Pay →
	Process	5.1 Print Employee Paycheck
	Data store	D1 Time Card

Creating and Using the DFD

Most DFDs for integrated business systems are very complex, consisting of hundreds to thousands of processes, data flows, and data stores. If all of these were included on a single diagram, it would make the task of developing and using the DFD too complex. Therefore, DFDs are organized by modeling the individual processes (such as the applicant-tracking process) and components (such as the recruiting module) of an information system. Furthermore, a series of DFDs is created to depict visually increasingly detailed views. The value of this approach is that all individuals involved in the logical design of the system can view the model at their own level of understanding and complexity. Viewing the model provides much better understanding than creating written documents to describe the model and all the processes.

The highest-level DFD developed is called the **context-level diagram**. This diagram describes the full system, its boundaries, the external entities that interact with the system, and the primary data flows between the entities outside the system and the system itself. The context level diagram contains only one HR process, representing the system, data flows, and entities. This process is labeled with the system name and is identified as the context-level diagram. A sample context-level diagram for an ATS is shown in Figure 4.2.

The single HR process in the context-level diagram is then broken into greater detail on the **level 0 diagram** to provide a clearer picture of the HR business process. The level 0 diagram contains the major system processes and the data that flow between them. Each process should be labeled with a verb that reflects the action that the process conducts. In addition, each process is numbered consecutively starting with 1.0 (1.0, 2.0, 3.0, 4.0, etc.). It is important to note at this point that the context-level diagram and the level 0 diagrams should reflect and communicate the same information (see Figure 4.3).

This concept is called the balancing of DFDs. Notice that, although the level 0 diagram shown in Figure 4.3 has more detail than the context-level diagram, it contains

FIGURE 4.2 ■ Context-Level Diagram

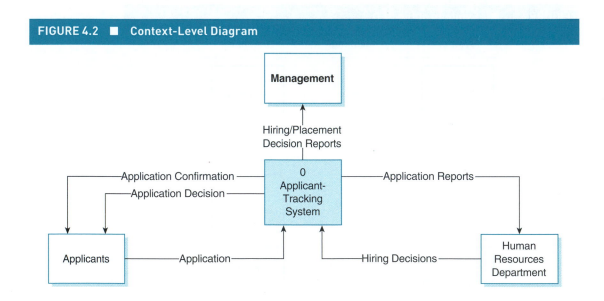

FIGURE 4.3   ■   Level 0 DFD

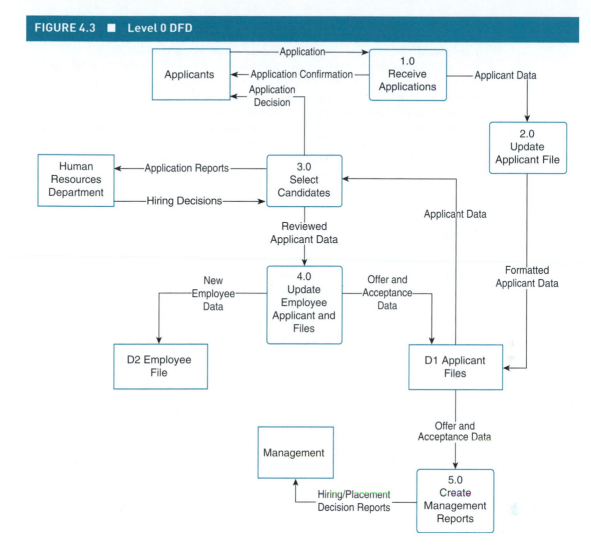

the same inflows and outflows from management, applicants, and human resources. For example, on both levels, the three flows, "Application," "Application Confirmation," and "Application Decision," flow between the Applicant entity and the system in the same way. Balancing DFDs is important because we want to ensure that all individuals are viewing and using the same model of the system. Otherwise, there is the risk that the system will not be designed appropriately.

In the same manner that the context level can be decomposed into a level 0 diagram, the level 0 diagram can be decomposed into *additional-level diagrams.* As with the context-level diagram, the level 0 diagram in Figure 4.3 also hides specific details about all the processing tasks within the HR system. Thus, the next-level diagram (the level 1 diagram) would break down the processes within the level 0 diagram to better portray and help staff to understand the HR processes in the system. This level of detail will, in turn, improve the accuracy of the logical design of the system. The same process of decomposition could occur at successive levels (level 2, level 3, etc.); however, this diagramming becomes a very complex task and is beyond the scope of this book. The DFD is considered complete when it includes all the components necessary for the system being modeled.

The DFD can also be used as a tool for analyzing the current system versus the desired system. In addition, DFDs are often used for business process reengineering, in an effort to improve the system. For example, through the DFD, the analysts designing the ATS for Larson Property Management might discover that data (e.g., rating scores) from a lower-level manager's interview of job candidates currently flow back to the HR department for approval prior to allowing the applicant file to proceed to the next-level manager. Through this analysis, they could find that this step is unnecessary in the new HRIS because the system would use a decision rule, based on the minimum score needed to proceed, to forward the applicant data to the next manager automatically upon an applicant receiving a passing score.

Physical Design

As was discussed in earlier chapters of this book, the acquisition of a system is the culmination of a series of important steps. By this point, the organization should have a strong understanding of its current operations, a set of requirements for the new system, and a new logical model for how it wishes the system to operate. Once the new system has been designed and logical models of the new system have been tested against the business requirements, the organization will move to the physical design phase. The major goal of this phase of the SDLC is to translate the logical model and requirements into a physical system, including all hardware, software, and networking.

Major activities in this phase include (1) determining whether or not there is value in continuing the system design and actual implementation processes, (2) determining hardware and software options and requirements, (3) determining where to obtain the hardware and software (e.g., by in-house development or commercial software purchase), (4) developing an implementation schedule, and (5) working with potential vendors to assess and select software if system software is to be obtained externally. For most organizations, these activities will typically mean that the HR staff specialists (e.g., the recruiting manager) will work closely with HRIS specialists and the internal information technology (IT) staff, as well as with software vendors and any external consultants brought in to help with the physical design of the system. The extent of involvement of these various stakeholders depends on the size, scope, and type of HRIS developed.

During the physical design phase, the HRIS and IT staff will focus heavily on how any new software and hardware will fit within the current **IT architecture**. In addition, IT and HRIS staff will provide technical recommendations on the relative value and cost of building the system internally or purchasing an off-the-shelf package from a commercial vendor. The HR staff will also work with the external vendors to ensure that the focus of the system is on the business requirements and not the technology itself. It is also important at this point to remind the HR staff to be very careful of scope creep, or the growth in project requirements and scope.

Three Choices in Physical Design

The first step in this design phase is to determine how to proceed with physical design. First, the organization has the option of doing nothing. Although this may seem to be counterintuitive because much time and money typically have been spent on the analysis and design process to date, there may be important organizational or environmental reasons for not proceeding. For example, on completion of a thorough analysis and logical redesign of the HR processes, a small organization in the southern United States was faced with a public lawsuit, and it was forced to delay the final design and implementation of the project until this was settled. In other instances, companies have postponed proceeding after learning that a target software vendor was in the process of a major revision of the software product.

The second option is to *make changes to only the HR business processes without implementing new or upgraded technology.* Before any time or money is spent on new technology, it is important that the organization address all proposed business process changes and determine if these processes can be handled using the current HRIS technology. In the book *Good to Great*, Collins (2001) suggests that one important difference between good companies and great companies is that good companies view technology as a solution, whereas great companies see technology as a tool to be used to support great business processes. Furthermore, Brynjolfsson and Hitt (1998) found that organizations were much more likely to increase productivity and performance when they coupled any technology changes with business process changes.

At this point in the process, it can be easy to forget that the goal for the development of the new system should be to use technology to support HR practices, making them more efficient and adding value to the organization; an organization should not get so caught up in the promise of a new technology with industry "best practices" that it ignores actual needs. In HR or IT, although using best practices is desirable, if these practices are not compatible with the specific needs of your organization as identified in the needs analysis, any business process and technical changes are likely to be less effective.

The final option that an organization can choose is to *implement the business process changes along with new or upgraded technology.* There are three basic ways that this can be done: build it, buy it, or outsource the development. Organizations that choose the first approach—to build the technology internally—will take responsibility for the development of the software and hardware. The advantage of this approach is that the organization will control all aspects of the development, including the look and feel and functionality. Using this approach, the organization will be able to write software to meet 100% of the business's requirements. Finally, internally building the software can also provide increased flexibility and creative solutions for the issues within the HR business processes.

There are several shortcomings in building the HR system internally from scratch. First, it can be much more expensive to implement than an off-the-shelf solution. In addition, since it is a unique application, the amount of software testing and the developmental risk are much higher with this approach than for an off-the-shelf system. Further, for this approach to work, the organization must already have or readily be able to obtain the technical, functional, and project management skills necessary to build the system effectively. For most organizations, obtaining what is needed to build the system is a daunting task because software development is generally not part of their **core competency**, and they likely do not have the staff and resources available to complete such an undertaking. Finally, since an HRIS is typically one of at least several core modules that are part of the overall **enterprise resource planning (ERP)** system, building the module in-house often leads to issues and challenges associated with integrating the HRIS with the other core modules, including the data warehouse component used to integrate data as a basis for business intelligence features.

For most organizations, the second approach of buying prepackaged, **commercial off-the-shelf (COTS) software** fits many needs. These systems can range from small, single-function applications costing a few thousand dollars to large-scale ERP software packages costing millions of dollars. The advantage of using this approach to acquiring software is that the systems are well tested and proven and can be purchased and implemented in a short period. For this reason, most of the HR software adopted and used today is COTS. The good news for organizations considering the adoption of a COTS solution is that most business operations are fairly generic, so there are applications available that should meet the majority of the needs of most organizations. The bad news is that even the best system will rarely meet all the specific needs of the organization, with most meeting about 70% of the organization's needs. Thus, organizations choosing to purchase a COTS solution should be prepared either to work with the vendor to customize the system to meet their unique needs or to change their processes to fit with the software (and thereby opt for what is referred to as the "vanilla" approach). As mentioned briefly before, the risk of adapting your business processes to the software is that the business processes supported by the software may be incompatible with the way your organization operates, which can result in increased costs or reduced competitive advantage. In addition, when an organization implements a vendor's upgrade in the future, it will likely be necessary to redo whatever customization was done during the initial implementation.

The final approach to developing the software is to outsource the development to an external company or to obtain access to existing software through an **application service provider (ASP)**. The greatest advantage of outsourcing is that an external software development can bring vast resources, experiences, and technical skills to design a much more effective solution than would otherwise be possible. However, outsourcing the development can be risky. For example, by outsourcing, the firm may expose confidential internal information and business processes to an external organization. Second, outsourcing may not lead to reduced time and expense for the organization, because many of the tasks that would need to be completed if the software were developed in-house would still need to be completed *with* the external software developer.

As can be seen from the previous discussion, there are advantages and disadvantages to each approach for software development. Thus, the decision as to which approach to use will be based on multiple factors and may differ from organization to organization and project to project. In addition, an organization need not rely on a single approach. For most organizations, the solution chosen is often a combination of in-house and external development. The decision regarding which approach to choose is based on a series of factors, including the nature of the business process; the size, technical skills, and project management skills of the software staff; and the development time frame. Table 4.1 contains a matrix of how these different factors may influence the approach chosen.

If the decision is made to purchase and customize COTS or to outsource development, the organization will need to work closely with external software vendors. Thus, vendor selection becomes a very important decision.

ALLIANCE PROGRAMS

To assist organizations that wish to implement a customized solution, most of the major HRIS vendors (e.g., Oracle, SAP, Infor) supplement their mainline enterprise solutions by investing in alliances with other independent software vendors (ISVs). The primary goal of these **alliance programs** is to provide a total solution to make both vendors' products more attractive and effective for their customer base. A secondary goal for the HRIS vendors is to create an "ecosystem" of solutions that can compete more effectively with other HRIS applications. The larger the ecosystem or number of partners in a program, the bigger the footprint the HRIS application will have. A side effect is that the HRIS provider appears to be more "open" from a technical perspective. In fact, Oracle and SAP are actively selling their technical integration capabilities (middleware) alongside their HR applications.

TABLE 4.1 ■ Software Acquisition Strategies

	Development Strategy		
	In-House	**COTS**	**Outsource**
Business need	**Unique**	**Standard**	**Noncore function**
In-house skills	Functional and technical expertise exists	Functional expertise exists	Functional and technical expertise not in-house
Project management skills	Project has skilled and experienced project manager	Project has a manager with experience to coordinate and manage vendor relationship	Project has manager with experience to manage an outsourcing relationship
Time frame	Flexible	Short	Flexible or short

Source: Adapted from Dennis, Wixom, and Roth (2006).

WORKING WITH VENDORS

Although building a new HRIS from scratch with internal resources may be a viable option for some organizations, by far the most common decision is to work with an external vendor to develop or acquire the system. To do this, the HR staff will need to work closely with both the internal IT department and external vendors to ensure that the business process requirements and all technical requirements are presented to the vendor. The first step in this process is to develop a **request for proposal (RFP)**.

An RFP is a document that solicits proposals and bids for proposed work from potential consultants or vendors. An RFP defines the organization's goals and requirements for the new information system. It provides the details that define hardware, software, and services requirements. For the organization, it provides a structured approach that minimizes the chance of omitting important criteria. On return from vendors or consultants, it simplifies the vendor comparison process by providing a format to elicit consistent and complete responses.

The RFP provides an opportunity for the HR department to record systematically what its staff will need the system to do. As part of this process, any remaining implicit assumptions should be made explicit. Basically, the RFP will define what is needed and what is not needed in the system. In addition, the RFP begins the communication process and relationship building with vendors.

Although different factors will determine precisely what should be included in the RFP, experts in the field have argued for the inclusion of a key set of components. Table 4.2 presents an example of these key factors, adapted from recommendations made by the Society for Human Resource Management and the work of Hinojos and Miller (1998).

Table 4.2 is an excellent starting point for developing an RFP, but it should not be taken to include all items that may be required. Those developing an RFP for an organization should keep in mind their unique situation and add or subtract what is included as appropriate for their needs. The information in this table is also very general in nature, and how it is developed will be different for each organization.

TABLE 4.2 ■ Recommended Components of a Request for Proposal

- Data about you

  - Who you are as a business
  - Company name, size, scope, industry, annual sales, locations, etc.
  - Business requirements
  - Required business processes, functionality, and project scope
  - Technical requirements
  - Does it need to work with a particular operating system, existing organization systems, etc.?
  - Delivery time frame needed
  - Is there a desired target implementation date?

- Requested data from vendor

  - Vendor details
  - Company name, size, scope, annual sales, experience, etc.
  - Number of implemented applications
  - System pricing
  - May include license fees, maintenance charges, training costs, implementation costs, and support costs
  - System details
  - Functionality included in the system
  - If customization is necessary, how will this be addressed (timing, delivery, cost, support, etc.)?
  - Supported technology now and in the near future
  - Customer support options
  - Training options
  - Customer references
  - Find out user and organizational experiences with the system.
  - Ask these references for other companies they know using the system to broaden your knowledge (after all, the vendor is likely to provide you with clients who have had positive experiences).
  - Sample contract terms

When developing the RFP, organizations should keep several things in mind. The first recommendation is to *focus on the business requirements*. Given that the system is being considered in association with business process changes, an excellent place to begin the development for the vendor is to review the requirements and logical redesign of the business processes. These should then be communicated to each vendor.

Associated with this requirement, the second recommendation is to *be specific*. After all the effort given to the needs analysis and the redesign of business processes, very specific requirements will be available and should be included in the RFP. It is important to be specific as to your organization's needs, because if you are not specific, you risk allowing the vendors to determine what is included in the final system. Although it is desirable to work with a vendor to develop the final system, it is important that the system be developed to meet your specific business needs not just designed to match the system a vendor has available. Furthermore, an RFP that is too general may not be screened in sufficient detail by the vendor, leading to a product that has too much detail and is too complex and too expensive for the business's needs. The overall objective of the RFP is to have the vendors propose system hardware and software to meet the specific requirements you have identified for your new system.

The third recommendation is to *keep it simple.* One of the temptations in developing an RFP is to include all possible business and technical requirements in it. The problem with including many technical details in the plan is that vendors may review the RFP and screen themselves out because they think they cannot fill the needs outlined in the RFP. For example, it would be important to ask whether a benefits system allows for benefits reports, benefits administration, and so on. Conversely, the RFP would want to stay away from including requirements as to length of fields, types of passwords used, and so on, which do not focus on business needs but instead are focused on technical and physical design issues. Essentially, if something is not important to the HR department and reflective of the business processes modeled in the DFDs, it is best not to include it.

The fourth recommendation is that organizations need to be aware that some *current HR practices will likely differ from the best-practice practices (e.g., workflow and processes) embedded in the HRIS under consideration.* Thus, organizations need to be open to redesigning their HR functions to increase efficiency, match the workflow and processes provided in the new HRIS, and be more consistent with product offerings. As more and more vendors are moving to cloud-based deployment, the alternative of customizing the software to your organizational processes may not be possible, or it may be expensive and inefficient. For example, traditionally, applicant-tracking systems involved only applicants and HR staff in the data input, flow and processes used in applying for and managing the recruitment process. In contrast, newer talent acquisition approaches have adopted more of a shared approach that includes workflow to line managers and other stakeholders who increasingly are involved in recruiting and staffing responsibilities. Thus, during the design phase, the analysis of a vendor response to the RFP provides an opportunity for the project team to rethink its HR processes and consider newer approaches that are reflected in vendor offerings.

The fifth recommendation is to *work closely with the HRIS and IT staff* as the RFP is developed. The professional staff will be responsible for working with the vendor to ensure the smooth installation and maintenance of the HRIS. Therefore, it is important for the HR staff to work closely with the information systems professional staff to make sure that any essential technical considerations are included. For example, if there are existing systems that need to provide information to or receive information from the system, this should be included. In addition, if there is a certain platform (e.g., UNIX, Windows) that the organization has experience with and with which it would like the system to integrate, this too should be included.

Vendor Selection

After the RFPs are sent, the vendors will then evaluate them to determine if they can provide a solution that will fit the specified RFP parameters. If the HR and IT staff have put together a strong RFP, they should get a set of vendors who have a better understanding of the company's specific needs and who can provide a better-tailored response and proposal for the HRIS. After receiving the vendor responses, you will have the opportunity to evaluate the relative strengths and weaknesses of each vendor. To do this, you should consider several things and assess software options according to a number of criteria. These are described in the following sections.

Functionality

As you assess the different vendor responses, it is important to evaluate how fully the functionality of the HRIS meets the HR needs. For example, a software product that meets 70% of the organization's needs will be less desirable than one that meets 98% of its requirements. On the other hand, software that meets 98% of the organization's needs but has no additional functionality may not provide the organization with the opportunity to grow and expand its options in the future, so it may be less attractive than a product that meets 90% of your HR needs but allows for growth over time. It is important that the HRIS implemented today is able to change as the organization grows. Otherwise, within a few years, the organization will have to go through the entire systems development process and purchase or develop an entirely new solution. Finally, an HRIS that will meet your organization's needs with minimal customization for actual use would be more attractive than one requiring significant customization.

IT Architecture and IT Integration

The next issue focuses on the IT architecture for the HRIS. The organization will need to know whether the HRIS will be a stand-alone system, a networked system, a Web-enabled one, or an externally hosted or cloud-based system, etc. In addition, the organization will want to know with what technology or platform the HRIS has been developed (e.g., UNIX, Linux, Windows) and what separate database(s), if any, the HRIS requires. Finally, it is critical to ascertain the extent to which any HRIS will integrate within the broader corporate IT architecture. An HRIS that can more readily interact and communicate with operations, manufacturing, and sales can provide a much stronger return for the company than one that stands as an isolated entity. The easier the integration with the broader IT architecture, the easier it will be to implement and use the system. In today's environment of employee self-service and Web portals, the ability to provide remote access to employees can also be a plus as different systems are considered. Today's cloud-based systems are growing in popularity due to their lower up-front costs, decreased capital hardware expenditures, lower overall costs, rapid implementation and updates, and seamless integration between ERP modules (more information on cloud-based systems is found in Chapter 2) . Finally, if functional HR systems are being considered from multiple vendors, the extent to which they can be integrated rather than requiring middleware and communicate with each other also becomes important.

Price

Although price will ultimately play a very large role in the selection of an HRIS, price should be secondary to the goal of finding a system that meets your process needs. At the same time, price will ultimately determine which system is selected. The ultimate cost of the system will include the visible costs, such as the cost of hardware and software, as well as the less visible costs, such as customization costs, employee training costs, licensing fees (e.g., site licenses, per-seat licenses), upgrade costs, and the cost of system operation and maintenance over time. HRIS costs and benefit-cost analyses are covered in more detail in Chapter 6.

Vendor Longevity and Viability

As with any purchase decision, it is important to evaluate the quality of the vendor itself. The good news is that a number of vendors have been in business for more than 20 years, so vendor longevity is usually not an issue. In today's environment, the viability of vendors can often be assessed through their responsiveness to existing clients and their history

TABLE 4.3 ■ Sample Vendors			
Vendor Name	**Website**	**Twitter**	**Focus**
Infor	www.infor.com	@Infor	ERP
Oracle	www.oracle.com	@OracleHCM	ERP
SAP	www.sap.com	@SAPHCM	ERP
ADP	www.adp.com	@ADP	Core HRIS
Ceridian	www.ceridian.com	@ceridian_US	Core HRIS
SAP SuccessFactors	www.SuccessFactors.com	@successfactors	Core HRIS
Workday	www.workday.com	@Workday	Core HRIS
Ultimate Software	www.ultimatesoftware.com	@UltimateHCM	Core HRIS
OrangeHRM	www.orangeHRM.com	@orangeHRM	Open-Source Core HRIS
Benefitfocus	www.benefitfocus.com	@Benefitfocus	Benefits Management

of providing timely upgrades and increasingly flexible systems. Furthermore, the HRIS vendor marketplace has been undergoing some consolidation as companies seek to better position themselves to provide value-added services across the HR functional spectrum, so the vendor you sign with today may end up merging with another company. A listing of several sample vendors can be found in Table 4.3. In addition, IHRIM provides an online buyers guide for those interested in adopting HR software. (http://www.ihrimpublications .com/Buyers_Guide/BG.php).

ASSESSING SYSTEM FEASIBILITY

At this point in the design process, it is very important that you stop and consider whether the system will work for you. Although the system may meet all the requirements as defined in the requirements document, it still may not be feasible to implement for several reasons. Therefore, it is important to conduct a thorough feasibility assessment of the project. A feasibility assessment should go beyond the traditional economic metrics and should include multiple dimensions, such as technical, operational, human factors, legal, political, and economic.

Technical Feasibility

Technical feasibility focuses on the current technological capabilities of the organization and the technological capabilities required for the implementation of the proposed system. As part of any assessment of technical feasibility, the HR staff must work closely with systems analysts and technical staff to determine whether the current technology can be upgraded to meet the needs of the organization or whether an entirely new technological architecture will be needed to implement the proposed system changes.

Typical questions an organization might ask as part of a technical feasibility assessment are as follows:

1. Do the hardware and software exist to implement this system? Are they practical to obtain?

2. Do we add on or patch the current software or start from scratch?

3. Does our organization have the ability to construct this system?

4. Can we integrate the new system with our current systems?

Operational Feasibility

Operational feasibility focuses on how well the proposed system fits in with the current and future organizational environment. For example, a system, despite meeting technical feasibility criteria, may make such a drastic change in how the organization operates that it may not have a strong chance of being successfully implemented. For example, a series of research studies in information systems has found that the more compatible a system is with an employee's current ways of working, the more likely the employee will be to use the system (Agarwal, 2000). Therefore, when a new system is highly incompatible with current practices, HR staff or designers might seek to change or decrease the scope of the project to reduce these incompatibilities.

In addition, operational feasibility assesses the extent to which the project fits within the overall strategic plans of the HR and IT departments as well as within the organization's overall strategy. Other areas addressed as part of the assessment of operational feasibility include the likelihood of meeting the proposed implementation schedule and delivery date. The HR staff and developers must work together to ensure that the schedule will meet any critical operational deadlines, that resources are sufficient to meet the schedule, and that the schedule takes into account key organization dates (e.g., annual budgeting). The techniques used in project management are very important and will be discussed in detail in Chapter 7.

A second area of operational feasibility focuses on human factors. An assessment of the human-factors feasibility focuses on how the employee uses and works with the system, on the system's usability, and on the training the employee receives. The usability of the system reflects the effectiveness and efficiency of the system to the employee and is often characterized by the usefulness of the system to the employee and the ease with which he or she can use the system. It can reflect how intuitive the interface is to navigate, the effort an employee must put into learning to use the system, and how effective the system is in supporting the employee's work.

Do not underestimate the importance of human factors in determining the operational feasibility and ultimate success of a system. Over the past 20 years, hundreds of studies have found that the usefulness and ease of use of a system play a large role in system use and adoption.[1] In addition, recent research has found that usefulness estimations can be accurately assessed by employees early in the development process but that perceptions of ease of use may evolve as employees gain direct experience with the software (Davis & Venkatesh, 2004). These human-factor considerations will be covered in Chapter 8 in more detail, along with suggestions as to how to solve the acceptability issue.

Typical questions asked as part of the assessment of operational feasibility would include the following:

1. How well does the system fit within our organizational context? Will this make us better?

2. How much will our organization change because of the new business and technical changes?

3. How long will this take to do, and does the schedule fit our business's needs?

4. If we have to squeeze, what might we be able to eliminate?

5. Do we have or can we get the personnel to do this?

6. Can people use the system?

7. What kind of training do we need?

Legal and Political Feasibility

Legal and political issues also play a very important role in assessing the feasibility of an HRIS. The best-designed and -implemented system can end up causing major headaches for the organization if it violates existing laws and regulations. This point is even truer for an HRIS than for many other types of information systems because existing laws and regulations play a larger role in HR than in other core business functions (as will be discussed in Chapter 9). For example, if the HRIS fails to maintain specific employee performance records correctly, legal challenges of wrongful discharges will be more difficult for the company to defend against.

Political feasibility focuses on the political environment of the organization in which the HRIS is being implemented. Issues such as power redistribution involving loss of individual or department control can have major political implications that can affect the effectiveness of the implementation. What is interesting is that political issues can undermine the implementation of a new HRIS more quickly and completely than any technical shortcomings. The challenge here is that while political feasibility may be fairly easy to identify, it can be challenging to effectively address. Individuals who are negatively affected by the implementation of the system (or who perceive themselves to be negatively affected) are likely to undermine, resist, or disrupt its implementation, either overtly or covertly. Thus, it is important to understand and anticipate the political consequences of a system implementation at this point, before implementation is started. Again, these issues are discussed more fully in Chapter 8.

Typical questions asked as part of a **legal and political feasibility** analysis include the following:

1. Does the implementation of this system infringe on existing copyrights?

2. Are we violating any antitrust issues by implementing the system?

3. Do we have contracts with other companies that don't allow use of the new software?

4. Does the system violate any governmental policies?

5. Does the system violate any foreign laws? (This question would be significant for global companies that have operations in multiple countries where different

laws require different practices supporting the capture and use of HR data, for example.)

6. Who is likely to resist the implementation of the system?

7. Who may "win" or "lose" as a result of this implementation?

8. What is the risk of system sabotage?

Economic Feasibility

The final aspect of a feasibility assessment is evaluating **economic feasibility**. The goal of an economic feasibility analysis is to determine whether the costs of developing, implementing, and running the system are worth the benefits derived from its use. To do this, an analyst would identify the appropriate costs and benefits of the HRIS and assign precise values to each. Then these costs and benefits should be subjected to a thorough benefit-cost analysis. As mentioned earlier, Chapter 6 provides comprehensive coverage of how to assess the costs and benefits of an HRIS.

Summary

The goal of this chapter was to discuss the factors that contribute to a more effective system design strategy. First, we discussed how the HR staff and consultants translate the requirements from previous phases of the SDLC into improved logical business processes. We then discussed how these new processes are modeled through logical modeling tools such as the DFD. DFDs are important because they allow the HR staff, consultants, and programmers to have a common model of the system from which to work and because they can be used to identify potential shortcomings not yet identified in the new system. In addition, because DFDs are hierarchical in approach, they allow for the system to be viewed at multiple levels of specificity. This makes them a useful tool for communicating with all relevant actors in the systems development process while also being technical enough to allow developers to best determine how to translate business requirements into the new HRIS. Given that the cost of making changes becomes significantly more expensive once the physical design of the system has been undertaken, it is important that these models be as effective and accurate as possible to avoid system rework.

Third, we discussed the options available for the firm when developing the final physical design for the new system. One option available to firms is not to change their existing practices. Other options include building the software internally or sourcing the software through external vendors. The chapter also briefly outlined the steps of working with a vendor, from the RFP through the selection of the vendor, and it provided several suggestions for getting the most out of the RFP and the vendor selection process. Finally, whatever approach is chosen for the final design, any selected physical system must be assessed as to its feasibility. Although budgeting committees will pay especially close attention to the profitability of the system, we also explained the importance of considering different types of system feasibility. Although this phase of the SDLC can be complex and challenging to manage, we believe that following a structured and disciplined approach such as the one outlined will result in the development or acquisition of a system that is a stronger fit for the organization.

Key Terms

alliance programs 78

applicant-tracking system
(ATS) 72

application service provider
(ASP) 78

commercial off-the-shelf
(COTS) software 77

context-level diagram 74

core competency 77

data flow 73

data flow diagram (DFD) 72

data perspective 71

data store 73

economic feasibility 86

enterprise resource planning
(ERP) 77

entity 72

IT architecture 76

legal and political
feasibility 85

level 0 diagram 74

logical design 70

logical model 71

operational feasibility 84

physical design 70

process 73

process model 72

process perspective 71

request for proposal (RFP) 79

systems development life cycle
(SDLC) 69

technical feasibility 83

Discussion Questions

1. What is the difference between the data view of a system and the process view of a system? Why is this distinction important when designing a new system?

2. Discuss four reasons that a DFD is a stronger tool for supporting system design than a written narrative of the business processes.

3. How do companies use an RFP when sourcing software? What are the key items that should be included in the RFP?

4. If you were advising a firm on developing an RFP, what would be some key suggestions you would make for improving the effectiveness of the RFP?

5. When evaluating vendor offerings, what are the key factors that will help your firm determine the best software product to acquire?

6. Even if a system pays for itself financially, an organization must conduct a thorough feasibility study. What types of feasibility should be assessed, and what information does each type of feasibility assessment provide the organization?

Case Study[2]: Larson Property Management Company

Larson Property Management Company is one of the largest property management companies in California, with more than 1,000 employees. The company provides a full array of commercial management and development services. These activities include complete management services for commercial office and retail buildings and apartment complexes; construction, repair, and maintenance of commercial properties; and financial management and billing services for commercial real estate clients. The company has experienced significant expansion over the past five years in response to the growth in apartment and commercial construction in southern California, and this expansion has resulted in the need to hire a large number of employees on an ongoing basis to staff its operations.

Larson Property Management has depended on a legacy HRIS to manage its applicant and employee databases. The system runs on a client-server computer system. The system was implemented approximately 10 years ago, prior to the company's rapid growth and when it employed fewer than 100 employees. The system's functionality is limited to the storage and retrieval of employee and applicant data. For recruiting purposes, the system requires a clerk to manually enter basic applicant data, the results of the application test, and whether an offer of employment has been made. Prior to this, applicants' files were passed around to those who reviewed the materials and were sometimes misplaced, so trying to locate a particular applicant's file was often a problem. The current HRIS has limited file storage capability for applicant and employee records and currently has reached its storage capacity.

Larson Property Management has decided to replace its legacy HRIS. One application module in the new HRIS that the company wants is a sophisticated applicant-tracking system (ATS). The primary objective of the ATS will be to provide a paperless hiring process. The basic functions of the new system will be managing the requisition and approval of job openings, storing resumes and job applications and retrieving through query functions the names of applicants who match job requirements, tracking a candidate's progress through the recruiting and selection process, and providing automated reporting functions. The company's managers also want an eHRM functionality that includes the Internet posting of job openings through the company's website and external job-posting services, application and resume submission through the Web and through kiosks at various office locations, staff ability to access and use the system remotely through a Web browser, and online resume- and application-scanning capabilities.

Part of the design phase is modeling the processes that will be used in the system for applicant tracking. For Larson Property Management, this modeling will allow the system analysts to design an efficient paperless hiring process.

Larson Property management is well aware that the design stage of the SDLC is critical for the successful implementation of the new ATS. However, there is considerable confusion about how to proceed with this phase. The HR and IT professionals assigned to the ATS committee have been meeting to plan the new system. From their planning and needs analysis, it is clear that a new HRIS application is needed, can save considerable time, and can result in more accurate storage and retrieval of applicant data for benefit-cost and other management reports.

The company has had several vendors provide presentations, with each vendor outlining its particular approach to the design of an ATS. But these presentations were primarily focused on the physical design of the new ATS. The HR and IT committees must now begin the design process, which must be completed in 3 months.

Case Study Questions

1. Based on the material in this chapter, design a 3-month operational plan for the ATS.

   a. In your plan, make certain you differentiate between the logical and physical design of the ATS. Which one should be done first? Which one is more important?

   b. Describe the importance of the data view versus the process view for the design of the new ATS.

   c. Who are the important stakeholders to be considered in the design of the ATS?

   d. How will you determine whether these stakeholders need the information that the new ATS will deliver?

   e. Based on your personal knowledge of recruiting by companies, develop a DFD with at least two levels.

2. Based on the work you have completed for Question 1, provide a brief outline of the RFP that is to be sent to the HRIS vendors.

CHANGE MANAGEMENT AND SYSTEM IMPLEMENTATION

Richard D. Johnson and Michael J. Kavanagh

EDITORS' NOTE

One of the major obstacles in the use of an HRIS is its implementation. The IT and HR literature is filled with stories about the failure to implement well-designed and well-developed computer technology. Although technical challenges will always remain in implementing an HRIS, the major challenge to successful implementation is often more behavioral than technical. In this chapter, the authors examine the important role that change management plays in the implementation of an HRIS. This chapter briefly introduces change management and its role in HRIS implementation. It then introduces the various models of change that can inform HRIS analysts and employees about how to help manage the change management process. The chapter then turns to a discussion of the factors that can impact the success or failure of an implementation. Finally, the authors discuss the various organizational and individual factors that can affect the successful implementation of a new or upgraded HRIS.

CHAPTER OBJECTIVES

After completing this chapter, you should be able to

- Understand the management of change through the perspectives of various change models
- Discuss and compare the various change models
- Discuss the elements important to successful HRIS implementation

- Understand the factors that contribute to HRIS implementation failure
- Discuss the various system conversion approaches
- Discuss the importance of integration of the HRIS with the other systems in the organization

HRIS IN ACTION

The Arizona Department of Administration, Human Resources Division manages the largest human resources system in Arizona. The department administers the state's Human Resources Information Solution (HRIS). The customer base, which includes every state agency, with the exception of the universities, relies on HRIS to accurately pay state employees and manage health insurance coverage. Currently, the HRIS processes information for more than 40,000 employees and the state's annual payroll of $2.5 billion. HRIS is the system that all state employees use to access their pay, leave balances, and W-2 information.[1] The HR Division's early experience with implementing an HRIS provides a good backdrop to the topical coverage in this chapter.

The HR Division initiated a program in 2002 to update its HRIS. According to department estimates, the new HRIS would "produce more than $100 million in cost savings over the next 10 years by automating functions previously performed by administrative staff and [by] reducing turnover due to increased employee satisfaction" (Office of the Auditor General, 2005). The implementation of the new system proceeded in phases: Phase 1 was completed in December 2003 and Phase 2 was supposed to be completed in 2004.

The implementation plan failed to meet planned milestones by a wide margin and in fact exhausted most of the project budget early into Phase 2. With the loss of funding, the HRIS project staff was reduced from 60 to 18 positions. As a result, some state agencies had to rely on in-house systems or manual processes to ensure they had the necessary personnel information processing capabilities.

Compounding this situation was the fact that the implementation team had been slow to address some of the user requests for Phase 1 modifications, some of which were needed to correct programs that did not function properly. The net result of this poor management of the HRIS implementation project was that state agencies had not realized the anticipated efficiency savings from the new system (Office of the Auditor General, 2005).

In 2005, the HR Division considered a new plan to restart the project. Some of the questions the change leadership team was thinking about included: Did they have the right change management competencies to manage this project? What were the likely obstacles that they would face during this next phase of the project—and could they prepare for them in advance? Could they deal with the resistance from some agency managers and users? What mistakes made in the earlier effort could they avoid going forward? And finally, they wondered if the HR Division was ready for this new implementation project—that is, what other steps were needed to ensure that the HRIS project was successful?

We hope to answer many of these questions in this chapter.

INTRODUCTION TO THE MANAGEMENT OF CHANGE

It's not the progress I mind, it's the change I don't like.

—Mark Twain

There is nothing more difficult to take into hand, more perilous to conduct, or more uncertain in its success, than to take the lead in the introduction of a new order of things.

—Niccolò Machiavelli

Statistics measuring the success of systems development efforts are not very encouraging. Inordinate delays, excessive budget overruns, and employee dissatisfaction plague HRIS implementations. "Despite good faith efforts by organizations, analysts, and users, a majority of systems are either abandoned before completion or fail to meet user requirements" (Browne & Rogich, 2001, p. 224). It has been estimated that globally, the problem of IT failures conservatively costs organizations $3 trillion (Krigsman, 2012). One expert in the field noted that, at best, only one-third of these initiatives achieve any success at all (Beer & Nohria, 2000). Even more troubling is the fact that only 13% of completed projects are considered successful by the executives who sponsor them (Lemon, Bowitz, Burn, & Hackney, 2002). A major contributing factor to the failure of these projects is ineffective change management (Schmidt, Lyytinen, Keil, & Cule, 2001).

Successfully introducing an HRIS into an organization requires an effective blend of good technical, organizational, and change management skills, because employees have to adapt to both a technical change and a change in their job requirements and processes. As Lorenzi and Riley (2000) remind us,

> A "technically best" system can be brought to its knees by people who have low psychological ownership in the system and who vigorously resist its implementation. The leader who knows how to manage the organizational impact of information systems can sharply reduce the behavioral resistance to change, including to new technology, to achieve a more rapid and productive introduction of information technology. (p. 116)

Effective change management is a critical core competence that all HR leaders must master. By better understanding the competencies related to managing change, HR professionals can better manage change in their organization and reap the rewards that accrue to successful change initiatives. However, the track record of most change initiatives is poor. Clearly, learning to effectively manage technology change is an important managerial competency. In this chapter, we focus on the change management processes associated with the implementation of a new or upgraded HRIS.

Change Management

Change management (CM) is the systematic process of applying the knowledge, tools, and resources needed to effect change by transforming an organization from its current state to some future desired state (Potts & LaMarsh, 2004). Change is not instantaneous. It requires the organization to focus on three key elements: the current organizational state, a transition, and a future organizational state. Very few people like changes in their lives, particularly when it affects their jobs. Therefore, effective communication with employees regarding the why, how, and benefits of change for the organizational and the employee is important. Successful change requires a "critical mass of people who are committed, are willing to change and will sustain their new behavior to align with the needs of the change" (Miller, 2004, p. 10). Therefore, CM focuses on altering the attitudes and behaviors of employees and can be used on large or small projects. As such, any change model chosen must address the important content, people, and process issues during each phase of the change initiative.

If the change is planned, the process typically is systematic and includes both a vision and a plan to ensure the change activities are on target with respect to cost, time, and expected results. Consider this example. When the catalog retailer Lillian Vernon undertook a major transformation of its IT infrastructure, the initial results proved dismal. What happened was that the change management team—which included the president and the chief information officer (CIO)—failed to take change management seriously. In particular, they overlooked the importance of assessing and managing readiness for change. "Employees resisted mightily, avoiding training and blaming new applications for their frustration. . . . The employees had already made up their minds that the system was not going to work, and they didn't want any part of it" (Paul, 2004, p. 80). The net result was that the company fell short of its ambitious timeline for implementation and missed an opportunity to use the new information system to improve overall performance. Lillian Vernon failed to create a sense of urgency and help the employees understand how the new IT system would benefit them personally. The lesson here is that implementing change goes beyond just installing the physical equipment and system and must consider factors such as employee attitudes and needs and the organization culture and setting.

The Change Management Process: Science and Art

Organizations are in a constant state of change. Some of the forces for change are external, such as the appearance of new technology, while others are internal, such as a decision to downsize the workforce. Regardless of the reason for change, it must be effectively managed, or chaos will occur. The person who is in charge of the change is referred to as a **change agent** or a **change leader**. This change agent can be internal to the organization (e.g., director of HR) or external to the organization (e.g., a consultant).

The process of managing change typically begins with a gap analysis. A **gap analysis** indicates the differences between the current state of affairs in the organization and the desired future state. Sometimes this analysis is done by senior management or the HRIS project team, and sometimes it is done through questionnaires distributed to employees. After the gap analysis has been completed and plans for the change process have been made, the next stage is to begin the implementation of the change. In addition, a major consideration in any change initiative is **resistance to change** from organizational employees. Change is never easy and when faced with change, a natural reaction by employees is to express fear, concerns, struggle, and opposition. This is natural because employees may feel that the technology has been brought in because they were performing poorly, or that perhaps there will be layoffs in the company.

Unfortunately, there is no magic formula or easily prescribed processes to guarantee success to overcome this resistance. The reality is that change is "messy, complicated, and its outcomes are easily swayed by a host of factors that only complicate our ability to ensure success" (Herold & Fedor, 2008, p. xiii).

There is both art and science to managing change. The science of managing change is the framework for diagnosing, planning, and executing change projects. Although some might suggest that applying the "right" change model will ensure success, Lawler and Worley (2006) caution that although designers of the change models "suggest that with the right interventions, most, if not all, organizations can make significant changes. We are not at all sure that this is true" (p. xv). If this were true, then more companies would be successful in executing change initiatives. Notwithstanding the authors' caution, the fate of many change efforts will be worse without a change model to guide change leaders in the process. We discuss several frameworks or models of change in the following section.

The art of managing change is what distinguishes the great from the not so great change agent in making a real difference through the application of the science of change management. It is understanding the culture and behavior of the organization and employees and determining how to best apply change techniques within the organization. Successful change projects require both the application of art and of science.

MODELS OF THE CHANGE PROCESS

In this section, we introduce and describe a general model of the change process and then four specific models of organizational change that have received considerable attention in the change management literature: **Lewin's three-step change model**, Gleicher's **change equation formula**, **Nadler's congruence model**, and **Kotter's eight-stage change model**. Each of the models helps draw our attention to the elements important in the successful management of any HRIS implementation project.

Overview of Organizational Change

Anderson and Anderson (2001) suggest that all change models fall into two categories: frameworks and process models. Frameworks focus mainly on topical areas that change leaders need to pay attention to when executing a change initiative. These models are good planning and diagnostic tools to help in understanding the complexities inherent in organizations and the interdependencies associated with change. Process models are more robust in that they provide more direct guidance on what should be accomplished and in generally what order (Anderson & Anderson, 2001). Just as a roadmap is useful in getting a driver from point A to point B, so also do process models serve as a roadmap and action plan for any transformation effort. "Given the complexity of change, and how to actually get to a new state, a process roadmap is essential" (Anderson & Anderson, 2010, p. 20). Finally, some models can be classified as hybrid, with characteristics of both framework and process models.

Burke (2008) outlines five key reasons why the use of change models is helpful to change leaders:

1. *They categorize information.* With literally thousands of bits of information related to a change initiative, models help categorize the information into manageable compartments.

2. *They enhance understanding.* Given that a change model has a beginning, middle, and end, if problems arise in any of these areas, we can use this information to help diagnose the problem and where action is required.

3. *They help leaders interpret data about the organization.* There is much interdependence with any change effort. As such, a model helps us recognize these linkages and take appropriate action to remedy any problem areas (e.g., structure and strategy).

4. *They provide a common language.* A model helps provide a common language and vocabulary to discuss the change with stakeholders and the change team.

5. *They guide action.* Most importantly, a model helps provide the roadmap mentioned earlier. The sequence of actions and potentially the priority of those actions (depending on the robustness of the model) help guide the change journey and enhances the potential for success.

Leading any change initiative is a complex activity, and one model of change cannot be viewed as superior for all organizations. There is no silver bullet with change. As Schaffer and McCreight (2004) remind us, "because each firm has its own work processes, culture, and competencies, a given change formula may work well in one but fail miserably in the next" (p. 33). The choice of change model to adopt will most likely flow from prior experience or trial and error and be consistent with the culture of the company. In many cases, the adopted model will be a hybrid, with elements taken from more than one of the existing models.

SELECTED CHANGE MODELS

Lewin's Change Model

One of the earliest key contributions to organizational change is Kurt Lewin's three-step change model (see Figure 5.1). Lewin's (1946) framework serves as a general model for understanding planned change and has been used to explain how information systems can be implemented more effectively (Benjamin & Levinson, 1993).

Lewin's change model conceives of change in terms of a modification of the forces that stabilize a system's behavior. In particular, Lewin envisioned a dynamic in which there are two sets of opposing forces—those that are focused on maintaining stability and the status quo and those driving change. When there is a balance between these two opposing forces, we have what Lewin called a state of "quasi-stationary equilibrium." To alter that state and enhance the probability of change, we must decrease the forces that oppose the change while simultaneously increasing the forces for change.

To better understand these forces, we can use a procedure called **force-field analysis**. To develop a force-field analysis, create two columns on a sheet of paper. In one column, list the forces that drive or support a change in an HRIS, and in the other column, list the forces that will inhibit the change. It is helpful to also assign a relative potency or strength to each force listed. By plotting the forces, we can better understand which ones need to be

FIGURE 5.1 ■ Lewin's Three-Step Change Model

strengthened or diminished to bring about change. Lewin suggested that the path of least resistance, that is, modifying those forces maintaining the status quo, would produce less tension and resistance than would increasing the forces for change; thus, the former is a more effective change strategy than the latter.

The key to understanding this approach at the individual level is to see change as a profound, dynamic psychological process (Schein, 1996). This psychological process involves painful unlearning and difficult relearning as one cognitively attempts to restructure one's thoughts, perceptions, feelings, and attitudes. Lewin's Change Model consists of three steps: unfreezing, transition, and refreezing:

Unfreezing

At the outset, every change project requires getting people to change their minds and behavior regarding the old way of doing things and to embrace the new state. Employees need to "see the purpose of the change, agree with it, be supported by rewards and recognition, have the skills to perform the new activities, and see key people modeling the new behavior" (Warhaftig, 2005). This means that the quasi-stationary equilibrium (or status quo) needs to be destabilized (unfrozen) before the old way of doing things can be discarded (unlearned) and new behavior successfully adopted (Burnes, 2004). **Unfreezing** is sometimes accomplished through a process of "psychological disconfirmation." By introducing information that shows discrepancies between behavior desired by organization members and those behaviors currently exhibited, managers can motivate individuals to engage in change activities.

However, the unfreezing process is not easy to accomplish. Schein (1996) argues that three processes are necessary to ready people for and motivate them to change: (1) disconfirmation of the validity of the status quo, (2) the induction of guilt or survival anxiety, and (3) creating psychological safety. For any change to occur, some form of dissatisfaction or frustration with the status quo must be presented. People need to know what drives the need for change, why they should change, and where they are headed. In addition, they should know what will and will not change. They should also know the business rationale for change. Further, managers should help employees understand what's in it for them if they change. Finally, managers should address the rewards or consequences of changing or not changing.

Here, Schein's "survival anxiety" comes into play. Providing a reason for change is not always enough. We also need to convince people that, if they do not change, individual and organizational goals will be frustrated. This is what Kotter (1996) calls creating a **sense of urgency**. Without a sense of urgency, "people won't give that extra effort. . . they won't make needed sacrifices. Instead they will cling to the status quo and resist initiatives from above" (p. 5).

Psychological safety refers to mitigating the anxiety that people feel whenever they are asked to do something different or new. People are concerned about losing their identities, looking dumb, and losing their effectiveness. This anxiety can be a significant restraining force to change. Without sufficient psychological safety present, change leaders will find the road to change filled with more obstacles than they planned on. We can address psychological safety by addressing employee needs. Employees want to know: What must I do differently? What are the new ways I will have to work? How do I learn the new things that I'm going to have to do? Who's going to teach me? Am I capable of making the changes that I will need to make?

Transition

Whereas unfreezing creates the motivation to change, transition focuses on helping change the behavior of employees. **Transition** is "a three-phase process that people go through as they internalize and come to terms with the details of the new situation that the change brings about" (Bridges, p. 3). Not getting everyone through the transition phase puts the outcome of the change project in jeopardy. The transition phase consists of three key stages: ending → neutral zone → new beginnings (pp. 4–5):

1. *Ending:* "Before you can begin something new, you have to end what used to be. You need to identify who is losing what, expect a reaction, and acknowledge the losses openly. Repeat information about what is changing—it will take time to sink in" (Cameron & Green, 2004, p. 108).

2. *Neutral zone:* The step between the old and new way of doing things is a "neutral zone," where people need to make the psychological adjustments necessary to say goodbye to the old and begin to welcome the new. In the neutral zone, people feel disoriented, motivation falls, and anxiety rises. Consensus may break down as attitudes become polarized.

3. *New beginnings:* This final step is about coming out of the transition and making a new beginning. In this stage, people develop new identities, experience new energy, and discover a new sense of purpose that makes the change begin to work.

As Bridges (2003) reminds us, if change agents

don't help people through these three steps in the transition process, even the most wonderful training programs often fall flat. The leaders forget endings and neutral zones (Steps 1 and 2); they try to start with the final stage of the transition. And they can't see what went wrong! (p. 6)

Refreezing

Refreezing, the final step of transition, seeks to stabilize the organization at a new state of equilibrium and to ensure that the new behaviors are relatively safe from regression (Burnes, 2004, p. 986). This often requires changes in the organization's culture and norms, policies, and practices. We address organizational culture in a later section.

Gleicher's Change Equation Formula

When initiating an organizational change project, it's important early on to determine how ready people are to accept and implement the change (Burke, 2002). Gleicher's change equation formula, as modified by Dannemiller and Jacobs (1992), helps us assess this degree of readiness as follows:

$$C = (D \times V \times F) > R,$$

where C is change, D is dissatisfaction with the status quo, V is vision, F is the first steps toward the vision, and R is resistance to change.

If we refer to Lewin's (1946) force-field analysis discussed earlier, D, V, and F are all "forces for change," while R represents the "forces against change." Gleicher's change equation formula provides a simple and straightforward perspective that reveals the possibilities and conditions at work in organizational change. Note that all three forces for change must be active to offset the forces against the change, which are usually manifested as resistance to change from organizational members. The change program must address *dissatisfaction* with the present situation, present a clear *vision* of the future and what is possible, and demonstrate knowledge of the *first steps* necessary to reach the vision. If any one of the three is missing, the product of the equation will tend toward zero, and *resistance to change* will dominate.

In sum, this "change formula is deceptively simple but extremely useful. It can be brought into play at any point in a change process to analyze how things are going. When the formula is shared with all parties involved in the change, it helps to illuminate what various parties need to do to make progress" (Beckhard & Harris, 1987, p. 104).

Nadler's Congruence Model

One of the key steps in understanding and managing change is to first fully understand the dynamics and performance of the organization. Without an understanding of the varied issues affecting performance, successful change may be misdirected by focusing on the symptoms rather than the true causes of a problem. A useful tool that helps change leaders understand the interplay of forces that shape the performance of each organization is Nadler's congruence model (Figure 5.2). The model is based on many years of academic research and practical application in a wide range of companies and industries.

Nadler's congruence model is an organizational performance model that is built on the view that organizations are systems, and only if there is congruence (i.e., "fit") between the various organizational subsystems can we expect changed and improved performance. As reflected in the model, the basic components of any organizational system include *inputs, outputs, and the operating organization.* The operating organization is composed of four components: (1) work activities, (2) the people that do the work, (3) the formal organization, and (4) the informal organization.

This model proposes that effective change management means paying attention to the alignment of all four components. Change agents cannot assume that changing one

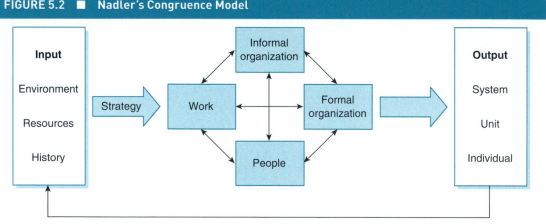

FIGURE 5.2 ■ Nadler's Congruence Model

component will cause the other elements to fall into place (Nadler, 1998). Cameron and Green (2004) use an apt metaphor to highlight this important point:

> Imagine tugging only one part of a child's mobile. The whole mobile wobbles and oscillates for a bit, but eventually all the different components settle down to where they were originally. So it is with organizations. They easily revert to the original mode of operation unless you attend to all four components. (p. 104)

If alignment of each of the components—work, people, structure, and organizational culture—with the others is deficient, then performance will suffer. The greater the fit or congruence, the greater the organization's ability to manage a change process. There are several benefits in using the congruence model (Mercer Delta Consulting, 2003, pp. 10–12).

1. If we use a computer metaphor, at its core, the model depicts both the "hardware" and "software" dimensions of an organization. The hardware represents the strategy, work, and formal organization—how the firm is organized to coordinate, communicate, and motivate the workforce in accomplishing its vision and goals. The software represents the social dimension of the organization—its people and the informal processes (e.g., shared values) that shape the behavior and performance of employees.

2. The model helps us understand the dynamics of change by allowing us to predict the impact of change throughout the organizational system. When leaders conduct a gap analysis to compare results with expectations, it may trigger a review of strategy and a reassessment of what change is needed to achieve stated goals and objectives. This reevaluation may lead to changes in work and formal organization. Unfortunately, at this point, too many change leaders stop without undertaking the difficult but critical task of reshaping the organization's culture to align it with the new strategy.

3. Finally, the model helps change leaders see organizations not as inflexible, static structures but as organic, dynamic sets of people and processes that are interdependent. It helps us recognize that managing real change is a function of several complex dimensions. It provides a useful "mental model" for understanding organizational problems and for enhancing our ability to pinpoint a solution.

Kotter's Process of Leading Change

Kotter's (1996) eight-stage model was developed after studying more than 100 organizations undergoing change. The model offers a process to manage change successfully and avoid the common pitfalls that have beset failed change programs (see Figure 5.3). We can view his approach as a vision for the change process, one that calls attention to its key phases.

The model provides two key lessons. First, the change process goes through a series of phases, *each lasting a considerable period of time.* Second, critical mistakes in any of the phases can have a devastating impact on the momentum of the change process. As can be seen in Figure 5.3, the first four stages coincide with Lewin's "unfreezing" first stage. The next three stages focus on introducing new practices into the organization. Finally, the last

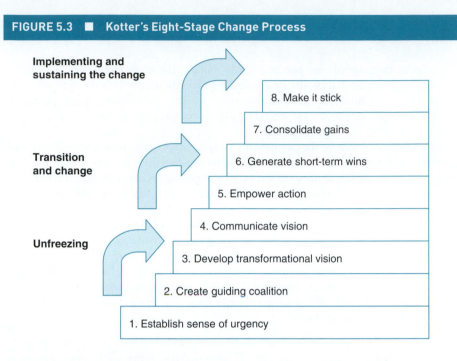

FIGURE 5.3 ■ Kotter's Eight-Stage Change Process

Implementing and sustaining the change

8. Make it stick

7. Consolidate gains

Transition and change

6. Generate short-term wins

5. Empower action

4. Communicate vision

Unfreezing

3. Develop transformational vision

2. Create guiding coalition

1. Establish sense of urgency

stage focuses on grounding the changes in the organizational culture, which coincides with Lewin's third stage, "refreezing."

The model indicates that all the stages should be worked through in order to effect successful change. Skipping a step or getting too far ahead in the change process without a solid base may create problems. Without the follow-through that takes place in the final step, the changes may not stick.

Important Reminders Regarding Change Models

The change models described so far fall under the umbrella of traditional philosophy of change. These approaches generally follow a linear, rational model in which the focus is on controllability under the stewardship of a strong leader or "guiding coalition." Linear change models assume that change involves a number of predictable, reducible steps that can be planned and managed. In other words, the change agent can choose from a menu of formulaic approaches that supposes that organizational change can and should be a controlled and orderly affair. As such, these models appear seductively simple and imply that success is guaranteed if they are followed to the letter. But, as Graetz and Smith (2010) note, there are several shortcomings to these models worth noting.

1. Managers and change agents cannot control organizations the same way that an operator can control a machine made of moving but inanimate parts.

2. The process models often ignore the human factor—treating individuals as automatons rather than active partners in the change process.

3. The models presuppose that employees will respond enthusiastically and uniformly to their leaders' call to arms.

Because the traditional approach to change is concerned with stability and control, what is emphasized in these models is management's singular story about why the change is necessary and ignores the many other distinctive stories unfolding around them in the organization narrative. As a result, the risk is that the principal response by managers may be to *not* listen to but instead silence dissident voices. These risks should be kept in mind as the organization implements any change initiative.

Next, we turn our attention to the factors that contribute to HRIS implementation failures.

WHY DO SYSTEM FAILURES OCCUR?

Increasingly, the failure to successfully implement an HRIS has less to do with technology and more to do with the skills of the change leader and the people and organizational issues related to the change. A review of the change literature has identified a number of key factors beyond the change management processes that contribute to IT system implementation failures (see Figure 5.4). Although no one single factor is the culprit, Lorenzi and Riley (2000) suggest that "a snowball effect is often seen, with a shortcoming in one area leading to subsequent shortcomings in other areas" (p. 117). We have grouped the key factors related to HRIS implementation failures into four main categories: leadership, planning, communication, and training.

FIGURE 5.4 ■ Reasons for IT System Failure	
Leadership	• Lack of executive support
	• Lack of strong leadership and change management skills in project manager
	• Lack of recognition for team's efforts
	• Lack of accountability for implementing the change
Planning	• No clear vision for the change
	• Failure to define a clear and comprehensive project scope
	• Lack of a comprehensive project plan
	• Failure to define fully the functionality of the system
	• Insufficient project staffing; staff turnover and complacency
	• Insufficient project funding
	• Roles and responsibilities not clearly defined or understood by everyone
	• Failure to meet budget and deadlines
	• The change leadership team doesn't include early adopters, resisters, or informal leader
	• Inadequate testing of the system

(Continued)

FIGURE 5.4 ■ (Continued)	
Change management	• Culture and level of readiness for change are not assessed prior to the start of the project
	• Change leaders fail to respect the power of the culture to kill the change
	• No strategies to nurture or grow a new culture
	• The change isn't piloted, so the organization doesn't learn what's needed to support the change
	• Organizational systems and other initiatives aren't aligned with the change
	• End users are not involved in the process
	• Lack of a plan for user resistance/rejection
	• Processes are not reengineered
Communication	• Lack of a comprehensive communication plan
	• Ineffective ongoing communication with all affected stakeholders
	• Failure to customize communications to different audiences
	• People leading the change think that announcing the change is the same as implementing it
Training	• Inadequate or poor-quality training
	• Poor timing of training—too early or too late
	• People are not enabled or encouraged to build new skills
	• Lack of ongoing training

Leadership

Lack of executive and managerial support is one of the main reasons that HRIS implementations fail. Without top management support, organizations lack the funding, approvals, and leadership necessary to implement, integrate, and maintain the system. Individuals given the responsibility to manage the HRIS project are often very knowledgeable in HR or IT, but they cannot lead a major change project effectively unless they possess strong leadership and communication skills. They must be able to communicate clearly, prioritize projects, make tough decisions, manage people effectively, and navigate the political environment (Kandel, 2007). Any successful major change initiative must also be driven by a strong and stable project management team comprised of key executives, department heads, managers, and frontline employees who are committed to the change and who can work together as a team. With respect to leader role and behavior, Higgs and Rowland (2011) identified five broad areas of leadership competency needed in the change process:

1. Creating the case for change

2. Creating structural change

3. Engaging others in the process and building commitment

4. Implementing and sustaining change

5. Facilitating and developing capability

It is also important to highlight that the literature on leadership clearly shows that teams with effective leadership will have significant performance advantages over those that do not (B. Anderson, 2010; Thomas, 1988). Change is not a process that can be simply managed; it needs to be led. Leadership makes a significant difference to chances of achieving change goals (Battilana, Gilmartin, Sengul, Pache, & Alexander, 2010).

Planning

Effective planning is essential to change management. Each successful project has a clearly identified project scope and strategy that outlines key business requirements and project goals. It is important to keep team members on the same page and working toward the same outcome. Additionally, a clearly defined project scope will prevent scope creep from occurring. **Scope creep** is the enlargement of the original project scope as defined in the project charter. Although there may be legitimate reasons for scope changes, such as changing business needs, scope creep can be challenging to control and may have unintended consequences on the change process, the timeline of the project, and its costs. The risk of scope creep is magnified because organizations often begin HRIS implementation projects without a clear definition of the project scope. The project scope must be defined in advance and should identify the project objectives, priorities, goals, and tasks, which will serve as the guiding principles for the team throughout the project's life cycle.

Inadequate funding and staffing further contribute to project failure. Organizations often consider the initial start-up costs for an HRIS project but fail to consider fully the costs of the change management process, of ongoing training, and of the support and maintenance of new systems. Change leaders must look at the big picture and the resources that will be required to implement and maintain the system successfully.

One key resource often overlooked is the adequate staffing of the project. The time requirements needed to manage a project are often severely underestimated. Change leaders make the mistake of thinking that employees can implement a new system by working on this implementation part time while continuing to perform all their regular duties. Although, in smaller organizations, individuals may need to continue with their regular duties, all efforts should be made to have at least some team members dedicated full time to the project. If team members are not fully dedicated, their regular responsibilities will almost always take priority over the project, causing delays and lack of focus.

Communication

Effective communication can make the difference between success and failure of an HRIS implementation project. Leaders who overlook the importance of communicating a consistent change message and vision fuel some of the negative responses (resistance) encountered in managing change (Armenakis & Harris, 2002). No matter what kind of change initiative an organization's leadership may desire, it will not be successful without the support and commitment of a majority of its managers and employees.

Getting employees "unstuck"—that is, getting them to not only embrace the vision but also change their beliefs and thinking to move in the new direction—is a huge communication challenge. Communication can be an effective tool in helping to unfreeze and predispose employees to change (Eccles, 1994).

> If leaders want to change the thinking and actions of others, they must be transparent about their own. If people within the organization don't understand the new thinking or don't agree with it, they will not change their beliefs or make decisions that are aligned with what is desired. (Duck, 2001, p. 28)

For example, the catalog retailer Lillian Vernon encountered huge problems with its IT transformation project when change leaders failed to effectively communicate why the project was necessary and how it would affect each employee specifically. The CIO noted that, instead of focusing on generalized statements about the system making jobs better, "we should have put everyone in a room and said, here is how you fit into this new picture" (Paul, 2004, p. 84). Ultimately, employees didn't know how their jobs had changed and blamed the new system for all the problems.

It is vital that HRIS change leaders develop a communication plan to build awareness and enable understanding throughout the development and implementation process. Having a plan helps mitigate potential barriers by meeting the following objectives (Austin, Adkins, Fox, & Mency, 2010):

- Building awareness and mindshare of the HRIS project, its benefits, importance, and priority

- Creating interest in and energy around participating in the transition to the new HRIS

- Creating confidence that the HRIS project will be marked by open communication and knowledge

- Sustaining interest in the HRIS project throughout the many phases of the project

- Delivering updates on the progress of the project so that employees can contribute to the success of the project and be recognized for it.

Despite the importance of communication, there are a number of barriers to effective communication (Figure 5.5). At their core, these reasons can be summarized as either assuming someone else will take care of communication or that the timing isn't right. As the CIO of Lillian Vernon says, effective communication is characterized by "a few well-placed, well-delivered conversations to the right audience. And then you follow up, again and again" (Paul, 2004, p. 86).

It is clear that communication is critical to the successful implementation of a new HRIS. But what should be communicated? Mercer Delta Consulting (2000) suggests that five key elements should be communicated to employees:

Reason for the change: Answers the question "Why change?" and creates motivation for change. Simply saying that one's job will be better is not sufficient. Employees need to know the business case for the change and how change affects the bottom line.

FIGURE 5.5 ■ Common Reasons Change Leaders Don't Communicate

1. ***They don't need to know yet. We'll tell them when the time comes. It'll just upset them now.*** For every week of upset that you avoid by hiding the truth, you gain a month of bitterness and mistrust. Besides, the grapevine already has the news, so don't imagine that your information is a secret.

2. ***They already know. We announced it. OK, you told them, but it didn't sink in.*** Threatening information is absorbed remarkably slowly. Say it again. And find different ways to say it and different media (large meetings, one-on-ones, memos, a story in the company paper) to say it.

3. ***I told the supervisors. It's their job to tell the rank and file.*** The supervisors are likely to be in transition themselves, and they may not even sufficiently understand the information to convey it accurately. Maybe they're still in denial. Information is poor, so they may not want to share it yet. Don't assume that information trickles down through the organizational strata reliably or in a timely fashion.

4. ***We don't know the details ourselves, so there's no point in saying anything until everything has been decided.*** In the meantime, people can get more and more frightened and resentful. Much better to say what you do know, say that you don't know more, and tell what kind of schedule exists.

Vision of the future: Serves as a starting point and anchor for what we do; answers the question "Change to what?" by providing leadership's vision of the new organization; and creates energy and excitement about the future. We address this factor more deeply later in the chapter.

Plan for getting there: Answers the question "How are we going to change?" and mobilizes people in a common direction. Here, we want to provide the big picture—the agenda, key strategies, and implementation plans.

Believe change is achievable: Answers the question "Is this really possible?" and encourages interest, engagement, and optimism.

Expectations: Answers the question "What can I expect of you and what is expected of me?" and helps people prepare for the change while reducing their uncertainty.

In sum, communication plays a vital role in the success of change programs. It is difficult to engage everyone based on communication alone, however. Ideally, people must participate in the process from beginning to end. If the sentiment is that the change is imposed from the top, then gaining commitment will be tough.

Resistance to Change

At a basic level, when we ask employees to totally change the way they have been working, it can seem like we're asking a basketball team to switch to playing golf. People cannot change their behaviors overnight, "get smarter over the weekend, or 'grow' skills they do not have" (Williams, 2003). Lou Gerstner (2002), former CEO of IBM, aptly noted why employees resist change: "Nobody likes change. Whether you are a senior executive or an entry-level employee, change represents uncertainly and, potentially, pain" (p. 77). It's *natural* for individuals to resist change because they are comfortable with the status quo. One expert suggests that 20% of employees buy in and tend to support and drive a change from the beginning, another 50% are fence-sitters and don't commit, and the remaining 30% tend to take a hard-core stand and oppose the change (Kirschner, 1997).

Another barrier is the tendency for many organizations to develop a comfort level based on their current performance, especially successful organizations. It is easy for successful organizations to become overconfident, complacent, and even a bit arrogant about their success. Managers can develop a myopic view of their company as the center of the competitive universe. It is much easier to hang on to what made you great than to change, which can be costly.

Further, if an organization accumulates a series of failed change initiatives, employees can become burned out and cynical about the change process. When this happens, it's hard to create a feeling of enthusiasm and zeal for the next change, as employees can feel a sense of "initiative overload, change-related chaos, and employee anxiety, cynicism, and burnout" (Abrahamson, 2004, p. 2–3). Before one change program can be brought to fruition and institutionalized, there comes another wave. Soon people become so overwhelmed that they lose track of which change initiative they are working on and why. Employees are no longer motivated to participate in the change, nor do they exhibit the level of commitment necessary for the change program to be a success.

The barriers and pitfalls to change notwithstanding, change leaders must find a way to move beyond the status quo to overcome **employee resistance to change** and motivate employees to make the changes necessary to ensure the successful implementation of the new or upgraded HRIS. This can be made more difficult because every employee may have concerns that can lead him or her to act in a way that undermines the change effort (Baum, 2000).

Employees must understand both emotionally and intellectually why the new system is valuable. Employees' responses to change depend on their understanding of the changing work environment and new system. They want to know why the change is necessary and what the change will look like. Despite the fact that the new HRIS is being implemented to improve the efficiency and effectiveness of HR, fear and resistance to the new system from HR staff will be common and must be anticipated and addressed. HR employees may be concerned about job loss or the new roles, responsibilities, and uncertainty that will result from the change. Employees may be concerned about how the new system may change the relationship between HR and the rest of the organization. Employees may feel that HR is eliminating customer service to cut costs.

This resistance to a technology change can take many different forms. Employees can overtly resist the changes by refusing to make the change or use the new system. They can also overtly sabotage the new system or engage in passive-aggressive resistance, where they outwardly support the system, while working behind the scenes to defeat the systems change (Marakas & Hornik, 1996).

However, despite the listing of resistance to change as a contributor to system failure, resistance can provide important feedback to change leaders.

1. It can unearth potential problems associated with the change. For example, those who are providing the resistance may possess vital details of problems that will arise if the change is made.

2. Those resisting the change often care passionately about the organization, and this passion ignites the resistance. Change leaders may be able to work with these

individuals to refine the change, harnessing their energy to redesign the portion of the plan that could have ultimately derailed the change.

3. Resistance can help narrow the focus and hone the change manager's ability to return to the original focus of the change and help hold them more accountable to the change initiative.

4. Resistance may serve as a conduit for increased communication, participation, and engagement. This increased engagement can potentially deliver greater acceptance and success for the change initiative.

5. Resistance can heighten the awareness of change and can raise its prominence in the organization, extending its life.

Training

Ongoing, effective training is essential in any change management initiative, particularly when new technology and work processes are involved. Successful companies typically provide training in the early stages of the project to reduce uncertainty about the new technology and to generate increased user acceptance (Ruta, 2005). Training is also used in the final stage of "refreezing" because employees obtain a better idea of how to handle the changes. A targeted training plan is one of several change management components that need to be developed as part of any HRIS implementation project. The training plan identifies the key elements and steps necessary for training the various staff on the use of the different components of the HRIS. The plan should include a postassessment tool to measure users' knowledge following the training. A key design feature of the training curriculum will be to ensure employees using the system feel that the learning is valuable to them. Otherwise, the training may not achieve the desired outcomes. The use of training can impact the "transition" and "refreezing" stages. At the beginning of the project, a training plan should be developed. This plan should include a complete assessment of the current skills and future requirements for all who will be affected by the change. We will discuss more about training and its importance in the implementation of the new system later in the chapter.

HRIS IMPLEMENTATION

As discussed in Chapter 3, the implementation phase of the SDLC is the one in which the new system is implemented and goes live. This is also the point in the change management process where new behaviors that fit with the new HRIS must begin to become institutionalized. To most employees who use the system, implementation is the day that they begin to use the system. But implementation actually has a number of important activities that must be completed before the system goes live. In this section, we focus on four specific tasks of particular importance: software testing, data migration, system conversion, and user training.

Software Testing

Another important task to be completed during implementation is software testing. The goal of **software testing** is to verify that the new or upgraded HRIS meets the requirements outlined during analysis and design and to ensure that it does so with as few errors or bugs in the program as possible. Consider an example from payroll. The testing team may work with the HR staff to ensure that the payroll module functions properly, that it avoids double payments or missing payments, and makes sure that checks print.

Data Migration

Data migration (or conversion) involves identifying which data should be migrated, how much historical data should be included in the new system, and the actual process of moving the data from the old system to the new. Decisions must be made in regard to how far back to convert data and how to convert the data from the older system data structures to the new system's data structures. Organizations will also need to determine when and how to convert the data, the time needed to allocate for data conversion, and any implications for data conversion on system downtime.

System Conversion

The third task we will briefly discuss is system conversion. **System conversion** focuses on how the new or upgraded HRIS will be introduced or implemented within the organization. There are four conversion approaches organizations can utilize. In a *direct conversion*, the old HRIS or nontechnical processes are turned off and the new one is turned on. This is the quickest and often the least expensive implementation approach. At the same time, this is the most risky approach. Regardless of training and the change management process, there is an organization-wide learning curve while the users adjust to the new software. In addition, there is no other option if the system has errors or delays. A classic example of the problem with the direct conversion was Hershey Foods' $112 million inventory control and tracking system. A troubled implementation and conversion led to an inability to deliver $100 million of inventory to stores during the Halloween season (Koch, 2002).

In a *parallel conversion*, the new software is turned on for a period of time before the old software is turned off. The time period in question is usually a meaningful business cycle (e.g., a month or a quarter). During this time, both software systems are functioning, receiving input, running reports, and being queried. The positive of a parallel conversion is that enormous testing goes on before the old software disappears. The negatives are that there will have to be dual data entry performed for every task, and there is a risk that employees will try to use the old system processes rather than fully committing to the new system.

In a *pilot conversion*, the new system is implemented in a single pilot location. In large organizations with business units positioned across geographic locations, it may be necessary to use multiple locations as pilot locations during the conversion. The advantages of a piloted approach are that a representative location (or locations) can be selected to test out the new system while minimizing risk. Any needed adjustments can be made to the system before going live across the entire organization.

In a *phased conversion*, the system is brought online through a series of functional components. For example, the organization may wish to turn on the core HRIS first and then bring on recruitment and learning management later. Nestlé USA, the California-based food company, opted for a gradual, phased-in implementation rather than going live all at once. The company started by implementing a new payroll system—first to a small group of 600 employees, then to other business units over time. "By focusing on a small group first, we were able to address many of our interface and reporting needs upfront with a small population of employees. . . . Demonstrating successes and celebrating them along the way reinforced senior management's decision to fund the project, and motivated our team to keep going" (Henson, 1996, p. 5).

Documentation

Ask any developer, engineer, or architect the best time to begin documentation, and they will tell you that documenting processes should begin at the beginning of the project. In fact, the documentation requirements in the SDLC means that work completed in one phase will be documented to support future phases. But the challenge is that documentation is time consuming and is often the last task to be completed, leaving a large amount of documentation work to be completed during implementation.

Most systems, whether developed, purchased, or accessed over the cloud, will have two types of documentation: system documentation and user documentation. System documentation is a record of the design specifications and program code of the HRIS as built. This documentation is important for the system designers and IT staff who maintain the software, because it helps them better understand how to work with the code and the system itself. As the specific design and coding of an HRIS is beyond the scope of this book, we turn to a more relevant form of documentation, user documentation.

User documentation is the documentation that contains the instructions about how the user can interact with and use the HRIS. Although early documentation was paper-based and often stored in a series of volumes in a physical documentation library, today's documentation is mostly online and available to users as they need it. There are typically three types of documentation available to end users:

1. *Context-Specific Reference Documentation*—This form of documentation is focused on helping the end user solve a specific problem or complete a specific task. For example, documentation could provide advice or guidance on how to determine the number of withholdings to claim or could help walk a hiring manager through how to select the appropriate job band or class. As such, this form of documentation should be short and focused.

2. *Manuals*—Manuals provide a guide that walks end users through completing more complex HR tasks such as reviewing and assessing applicants and ranking or conducting and documenting a performance review. Manuals will be longer than reference documentation

3. *Tutorials*—Tutorials are the longest form of documentation and are focused on how to use the major system components. For example, tutorials could focus on the basic operations of the core HR system, the management of the recruitment process, or completing and submitting required government reports.

End User Training

Given the simplicity of apps on our smartphones, HRIS vendors continue to improve the functionality, simplify usability, and enhance the user experience on their systems. The goal is to make these systems as easy to use as the apps on our phone. The challenge is that HR is a very complex and regulated environment, with shifting laws and regulations. Therefore, even the most user-friendly systems will require some form of training. Most vendors of new software will provide training on the new system, and the cost will depend upon the level of training needed for the users.

As noted earlier in the chapter, to determine the amount and type of training needed for users, the organization should complete an analysis of the training needs and follow the recommended phases for effective training (Wexley & Latham, 2002). If possible, this should be done in conjunction with your organization's training professionals. It is important that the training time and cost be included in the project plan, because training has been shown to improve implementation outcomes and user performance (Johnson & Marakas, 2000; Sabherwal, Jeyaraj, & Chowa, 2006).

An effective end-user training plan must also include the following:

- What training will be provided

- When training will be provided for implementation team members and user groups

- Who will provide the training (e.g., vendors, consultants, staff, or others)

- A plan for training new users and addressing turnover issues

- A plan for ongoing training, including advanced skills and refresher training

- A plan for training users in the event of system upgrades or procedural changes

- The resources needed—financial and human—to provide the training

Although some training early in the process is recommended, full training should not be offered until just before the system will be used. One common error is providing too-detailed training too early in the learning process. If training is provided too early, users will not retain the material. An employee may learn how to perform 10 new tasks on the system but may only encounter 5 in a normal workday, 3 over the next year, and 2 in exceptional circumstances. Therefore, by the time the employee has to complete the task in question, the training will have been forgotten. Given this, organizations have found that an effective way of training end-users is through a combination of on-the-job training and self-paced e-learning, providing personalized assistance as required (Dawson & Jones, 2003).

Involving "**power users**," those employees who use the system heavily and who have obtained expertise, can also be an effective training technique. For example, a division of a global petroleum organization utilized a power user concept to diffuse system skills and training and found that as "power users shared their knowledge with other users, knowledge about how to use the system began to permeate the organization" (Jones & Price, 2004, p. 29).

User Acceptance

Ultimately, use of the new HRIS and HR processes represents project success. Organizations cannot simply rely on the strategy of "if you build it, they will come." Change leaders must create user acceptance—otherwise, they risk failure as users choose not to utilize the new system. Research has shown that up to 70% of the functions of new HR systems go untapped because users make the new system do only what the old system did (Roberts, 1998). Several factors have been shown to affect user acceptance. These include:

- Effort expectancy—The expected effort it will take to use the system

- Performance expectancy—The extent to which an employee believes that the HRIS will enhance his or her job performance

- Social influence (subjective norms)—The degree to which users perceive others in the organization to feel that the system is important. In other words, employees are more likely to accept the HRIS if they think doing so will help them fit in and conform to the behavior of others.

- Organizational Support—The extent to which employees believe that the organization is committed and resources are in place to support implementation and use of the system.

To increase the likelihood of employee acceptance of the HRIS, it is important for end users to be involved with and feel ownership of the new system. **Employee participation and involvement** can increase job satisfaction, job performance, systems acceptance, and systems success (cf. Cotton, 1993; Harris & Weistroffer, 2009). Ideally, end users should be brought into the project as early as possible, even as early as defining system requirements. It is also important that users feel that their involvement is providing real value to the system change and that their ideas and opinions are recognized (Greenberg, Fauscette, & Fletcher, 2000). By helping shape the real requirements, users begin to take ownership and a personal stake in the system throughout the development process. The challenge facing organizations is how to involve users without expecting them to add additional hours to their already full schedule.

Informal ambassadors (e.g., gatekeepers), or professional change agents, can help influence the rest of the organization and can make or break the acceptance of a new system. Implementation teams should identify influential individuals and those who have shown an interest in the new HRIS and engage them as informal ambassadors for the change. It is also a good idea to identify the most resistant users and involve them right from the beginning to gain their buy-in (Keener & Fletcher, 2004). Otherwise, they may influence others negatively toward the change.

One of the major obstacles to gaining user acceptance is user reluctance to try out the new system. Some companies have used pilot implementation in one part of the organization to get early reactions and suggestions for modifications. Ensuring that employees use the system when it is not a requirement of their job is more challenging. Offering rewards to encourage user participation in new systems can be very effective. Some examples follow:

- The State of Kentucky offered those who completed an online survey providing feedback on the new system a chance to win a weekend stay at a Kentucky state park (Anheier & Doherty, 2001).

- One organization awarded gift certificates to the first 50 employees who used the system to update their personal information.

- One organization gave employees a $100 bonus for completing their annual benefits enrollment online.

A small investment in rewards such as these can result in increased user comfort and acceptance.

CRITICAL SUCCESS FACTORS IN HRIS IMPLEMENTATION

As you can see, the implementation of a new or upgraded HRIS requires effective change management. In addition, several other factors play a role in ensuring success. Several authors have identified and discussed several of these factors (Ceriello & Freeman, 1991;

Rampton, Turnbull, & Doran, 1999; Walker, 1982). These success factors serve as recommendations for a successful HRIS implementation. Some of these success factors have been mentioned in previous chapters as well as earlier in this chapter. We briefly summarize them here:

1. *Top management support:* Simply stated, the project must have **top management support** at the beginning and throughout implementation and evaluation. Top management (e.g., C-suite members; department or unit heads) must be willing to provide the necessary resources and authority for project success.

2. *Adequate and timely resources:* These resources include not only financial resources but also time and personnel. To successfully implement an HRIS, it is important that enough personnel can devote time to the project to ensure its success. More information on the financial aspects of system implementation, including how to conduct a benefit-cost analysis (BCA), is found in Chapter 6.

3. *Communication:* As noted, everybody involved in and affected by the HRIS project needs to be informed regularly about the goals, progress or lack of it, issues, and challenges throughout the life of the project. This leaves less room for organizational politics, rumor mongering, and misapprehensions.

4. *Organizational culture:* As noted, **organizational culture** can also affect the implementation of an HRIS. Contrast an organization in which change was dictated by management versus one in which there was extensive participation by employees in the change effort.

5. *User involvement:* As indicated in Chapters 2 and 3, user involvement is critical to the effective development and implementation of the HRIS. This ensures that the project is designed and implemented in accordance with user requirements and, therefore, will have a better chance of being accepted.

6. *Project champions:* It is important that your project has a **project champion**. A project champion is an individual or small group that has the authority and status to ensure appropriate resources are applied to the project. Because of the importance of this role, selection of these individuals must be done carefully, and the persons selected should enjoy a good reputation and status in the organization.

7. *Organizational structure:* Typically, the implementation of a new HRIS will require changes in reporting lines of authority as well as changing responsibilities for HR and IT. If the departments are not used to cooperation and collaboration, they will develop a "silo mentality" and will compete against each other, to the detriment of the organization.

8. *Change management:* The assumption that employees will "love" the new system because of its sophisticated features is naive. Selecting a change management approach that fits the organization culture and change needs will enhance the probability of success.

9. *Project control and monitoring:* Trying to execute an HRIS project without a written project plan will lead to failure. Likewise, the project team's failure to communicate project milestones and progress will negatively impact project success.

10. *Cross-integration between business systems:* Poor integration between systems is usually the result of poor communication across functional departments during the development of the HRIS. Without effective communication, the HRIS will be unable to interface with other business systems, such as the financial, operations, or marketing systems. When implementing a new system, do not underestimate the value of understanding what data from the system can be used by other systems or where data from other systems may need to be transferred into the HRIS.

Summary

The aim of this chapter is to deepen your understanding of change management, the implementation process, and the behaviors and organizational factors required for success. To help illuminate the challenges in this effort, this chapter defines change management and the important role effective change management plays in the implementation of any HRIS. The chapter introduces several change models and explains why these are important concepts for today's HR leaders. The evidence is clear that successfully introducing a major HRIS into an organization requires an effective blend of good technical and good organizational skills. Effective management of change is a critical core competence that management and HR leaders must master. By better understanding the competencies needed to manage change, HR professionals can help in the process of change in organizations.

The chapter also discusses the implementation phase of the SDLC, taking particular note of several key implementation activities and factors that affect the success of an information system. Not surprisingly, the majority of these factors are employee and organization focused rather than technically focused. Change leaders must prepare for the inevitable resistance to change and plan to gain user acceptance.

Key Terms

change agent 93

change equation formula 94

change leader 93

change management (CM) 92

data migration 108

employee participation and involvement 111

employee resistance to change 106

force-field analysis 95

gap analysis 93

Kotter's eight-stage change model 94

Lewin's three-step change model 94

Nadler's congruence model 94

organizational culture 112

power users 110

project champion 112

psychological safety 96

refreezing [third step in Lewin's change model] 97

resistance to change 93

scope creep 103

software testing 107

system conversion 108

top management support 112

transition [second step in Lewin's change model] 97

unfreezing [first step in Lewin's change model] 96

user acceptance 110

user documentation 109

Discussion Questions

1. Discuss each of the theoretical change models introduced in this chapter. How can we use them when planning an HRIS implementation to increase our chances of success?

2. Analyze the main reasons for HRIS implementation failure. How can we prevent these from affecting us?

3. Discuss the importance of communication in managing a technology change. What roadblocks might an organization face if it fails to create a good communication plan?

4. If you were asked to develop a training plan for an HRIS implementation, what kinds of things would you include? Why?

5. Discuss the role of culture in HRIS implementation. How might two different organizations with very different cultures approach the same HRIS implementation differently?

6. Create recommendations for an organization that is facing resistance to change from its own HR department. What are some of the likely causes of this resistance? How can they be overcome?

7. Discuss how informal leaders within the organization might be used to increase user acceptance.

Case Study: The Grant Corporation

The Grant Corporation is a financial services firm based in Chicago, Illinois. Its revenue exceeded $1 billion last year, producing a net income of $530 million. It has just over 1,000 employees. Although the organization has been in business for almost 10 years, it has experienced rapid expansion in the past 2 years due to tremendous business growth and a merger with the Enelrad Group, another local firm. Managers have had difficulty keeping up with this growth, especially in the HR department, which has been stretched thin to keep up with staffing needs and other, mainly administrative, duties.

Six months ago, the CEO, Todd Jackson, recognized the need to expand the size and functionality of the HR department and hired Julia Woodland to be its director, reporting directly to him. This was a newly created position, and its incumbent would replace the HR administrator, who had previously reported to the VP of Finance and who decided to retire when the new HR position was announced.

When Woodland was hired, Jackson told her that she would have "free rein" to create a more strategically focused HR department that would be better equipped to handle the organization's needs. She had quite a bit of experience at her previous company and was eager to take on the task.

Although the organization used advanced technology for its business applications, HR was still using a basic payroll processing software program and Excel spreadsheets to track various categories of employee information, including personal data, benefits enrollments, performance evaluation schedules, and compensation. All payroll and benefit information was manually entered into these respective systems, and much of the information had to be entered into multiple spreadsheets when there was a change. The department could not keep up with the information needs—new hires were getting paid incorrectly or not at all. Benefits enrollments were delayed or contained mistakes, and performance evaluations and pay raises were late. The printed employee handbook, benefits binder, and orientation materials were in serious need of updating. In addition, the company had 16 open positions and stacks of resumes everywhere. It was no wonder the HR administrator had decided to retire!

Julia Woodland spent long hours trying to determine what she could do to address the immediate and long-term concerns of her new department. She brought in a temporary employee to help her staff file, process paperwork, and enter data. She focused on hiring two higher-level HR representatives and a payroll clerk. She turned to a staffing agency to help the firm identify candidates for open positions, including those in HR. Finally, she proposed the purchase of an integrated payroll/HRIS that was capable of integrating with the finance department's system as well as with the organization's benefit and 401(k) providers' systems. The proposed software solution also offered the option of a Web-based employee portal, which would allow employees to view information online and change their personal data. Jackson responded favorably and told her to "go ahead and do whatever she needed to do to fix the mess." The next day, Woodland contracted with the HRIS provider.

Woodland spent the next week meeting with her new HRIS vendor representative to discuss the installation and implementation of the system. Because she was so overwhelmed and wanted to get the new system in as quickly as possible, she didn't have time to discuss the project with her staff right away, but she knew that employees

would be excited about the new system and the opportunities it would open up for them as the burden of administrative tasks eased. She closed her door during the meetings so participants could concentrate. She wanted to be able to implement the system by January 1 so that the company's year-end payroll data were accurate and managers could track other data on an annual basis with a full year of data. Since she had been through the process in the past and was familiar with such systems, she figured that she could manage the implementation with the help of IT and her staff as needed. She would make all key decisions to move the project along and meet her deadline.

The current HR staff consisted of an HR assistant and two generalists who seemed to function as clerks and recruiters. They had all been hired at the same time more than 5 years ago, when the HR administrator was the sole member of the department. They were very proud of how they had worked so hard together to build HR and keep up with the increasing demand. They were just getting used to working with Woodland but thought that she was very nice and had high hopes for the improvements and new strategic focus that she would help them implement.

Day by day, the staff watched the vendor representative come and go, along with a parade of candidates sent over by the staffing agency to apply for the new HR positions. They soon began to wonder about all the changes that their new boss was making and what these changes would mean for them. They started making assumptions that had them very concerned.

Woodland contacted the IT director to tell him about the project. He expressed concern over the ability of the server to handle the new system and wondered how they would address firewall issues with the portal. Furthermore, all his staff members were tied up with a critical upgrade to the customer service system, which had caused more than its share of problems. He demanded to know why he and his staff had not been involved sooner and told her that it would be unlikely that they would be able to participate in the implementation or help her meet her deadline. Upset, she called Todd Jackson, who advised her not to worry about it—he would tell them to get it done.

When she contacted Finance to obtain information that the HRIS vendor needed to link the HRIS to that department's system, the finance manager was more than willing to help—but she did not know where to get the system information and did not understand how the information would flow from one system to another. She asked why they couldn't just keep the systems separate and enter the necessary data into the finance system from reports provided by HR. "That's the way we've always done it," she said. "It doesn't take long, and it will be much simpler that way."

In the meantime, morale was declining in HR. Whenever Woodland asked HR employees for information about payroll or their Excel spreadsheets, they seemed uneasy and never provided her with exactly what she was looking for. She didn't understand their antiquated forms or their backward processes but decided she could fix those after the new system was in. Also, it felt like the rest of the company was suddenly treating her differently. They had all made her feel so welcome six months ago when she came on board. Now employees approached her with caution, and managers always seemed abrupt.

Julia Woodland began to wonder if this was the right role for her. Why were things so difficult? She thought that everyone would be thrilled about the new system and its efficiencies and would be eager to help. Was it her problem or theirs?

She thought that perhaps people didn't realize the impact she was making in the organization. She decided to make an announcement about the exciting new system that would help make things more effective and efficient in HR and help the employees simplify their lives as well. She sent out a company-wide e-mail announcing the new payroll/HRIS and outlining its ability to interface with other systems and its Web-portal capabilities. To her disappointment, no one seemed to understand the significance or even pay attention. A few employees asked her if their paychecks would be delayed as a result.

She wondered how she would ever get through this project and what she needed to do to get everyone on board.

Case Study Questions

1. Overall, what did Julia Woodland do right? What could she have done differently?

2. Were the correct people involved in the process? Whom would you have included and why?

3. What errors did Woodland make with her own staff? What impact might these errors have had on the success of the implementation? What should have been done?

4. Discuss the cultural issues involved in this case. Are there things Julia Woodland should have taken into consideration prior to starting the implementation? Why are they important?

5. If you were in Julia Woodland's position, what would you include in your communication plan for the implementation?

6. How can training be used in this case to make the implementation more successful?

7. How can the Grant Corporation increase user acceptance of the system?

8. Discuss the potential benefits of process reengineering in this implementation. What impact might it have had?

9. After the implementation, what steps should the HR department take to ensure proper maintenance and support of the system?

10. What can Julia Woodland do now to "get everyone on board" and increase the likelihood that this implementation will be successful?

6

COST-JUSTIFYING HRIS INVESTMENTS

Kevin D. Carlson and Michael J. Kavanagh

EDITORS' NOTE

Central to the decision to implement a new or improved HRIS will be the benefits and costs of the investment. Like most consumers, HR professionals and managers are frequently awed by new computer-based HR applications and make purchase decisions on the systems' features. However, as discussed in this chapter, without a comprehensive benefit-cost analysis (BCA), such purchases may not yield the desired results. As emphasized by several authors (Cascio, 1987, 1991, 2000; Fitz-enz, 2001; Kavanagh, Gueutal, & Tannenbaum, 1990), the language of business is dollars,[1] not just good feelings about an HRIS investment. The BCA for an HRIS investment needs to be made prior to purchase, early in the system's development life cycle. In fact, a preliminary, estimated BCA of an HRIS investment should be presented to senior management before any detailed work begins. This preliminary estimate should assist senior management in deciding whether the HRIS project should continue. A more detailed analysis can then be made as part of the needs analysis. The information in this chapter provides guidance for making BCA estimates as well as practical advice on how to make the BCA palatable to managerial decision makers. Finally, there is an emphasis on the value of the BCA and its documentation for the management of the project and its implementation.

CHAPTER OBJECTIVES

After completing this chapter, you should be able to

- Explain why a BCA is critical for a successful HRIS project

- Explain the differences between cost reduction and organizational enhancement as strategies for HRIS investments

- Explain how using guidelines for approaches to investment analysis will lead to a better HRIS project

- Identify the various costs and benefits in a BCA of an HRIS investment

- Explain the differences between direct and indirect benefits and costs

- Describe how to estimate costs and benefits, both direct and indirect

- Explain the difference between average employee contribution (AEC) and variance estimates for estimating values in a BCA and understand why the difference between these indices is important for investment analysis

- Define and describe utility analysis as being built by alternate BCAs for different outcomes

- Discuss three common problems that can occur in an HRIS BCA

INDUSTRY BRIEF

HILLARY BROTMAN, DIRECTOR, HURON CONSULTING GROUP

Organizations are increasingly considering "the cloud" as they investigate their next business system investment. The cloud or SaaS (software as a service) is the delivery of services through the internet. In the HRIS space, the three biggest cloud providers are Oracle, Workday, and SAP. With the cloud, an employee would just need internet access to log into the HRIS. Although in many cases this will reduce up-front IT spending, there is still a hard dollar cost in moving to the cloud. These costs include license fees, system integrator implementation costs, and internal costs of backfilling employees assigned to the project. There is also the possibility of adding additional headcount for new roles as a result of the move to the cloud. Justifying these costs becomes a key activity in the process of determining if and when such a move will take place.

Once an organization determines that it wants to move to the cloud, there are two different paths that they can take. It must ask whether it is looking to just move to a new human resource information system (HRIS), or is it looking to move other key corporate functions like finance and accounting and supply chain along with HCM on a single integrated ERP (enterprise resource planning) platform? In both situations, a business case is required. However, the business case for an HCM-only move is much harder to develop.

Why is it harder? There are many reasons, but the primary factor is that for human resources, it is very difficult to quantify hard dollar savings such as reduction in headcount or a reduction in spending based on better data and analytics. So how then can an organization financially justify "the spend" for a new HRIS system? In many instances, organizations have inefficient manual and labor-intensive processes that also produce poor data records. The key points to focus on are (a) how technology will enable the use of industry best practices, (b) the ability to have a system of record with a single data entry point, and (c) the value of the rollout of self-service and mobile capabilities.

When preparing the business case for a new or upgraded system, it is important to consider multiple factors. First, what is the volume of transactions HR receives daily (e.g., paper transactions, phone calls from managers who don't want to fill out paper forms, employee requests for personal data changes, etc.)? Second, assess the current reporting functionality, specifically considering the number of data sources and the level of data manipulation required to complete corporate and regulatory reports. I have had clients tell me that if they ask three people for the same report, they get three different versions of the data.

Once you have the transaction counts, you can begin to document the indirect benefits of the new system. Typically, the main benefits are increased managerial and employee productivity, as they will have the data they need at their fingertips. It will also benefit the HR team, as it will spend less time entering and updating transactional data and have more time for the corporate and strategic initiatives.

Third, it is important to consider the organization's strategic goals. Many of my clients have hiring and retaining top talent as a key strategic goal. Studies have shown that current and potential employees have an expectation that an organization has self-service and mobile capabilities that are intuitive and easy to use. The prime comparison mentioned is the Amazon user experience. There aren't any instructions on how to purchase something on Amazon; it is very intuitive, and people are able to figure it out without training guides, and that is the new expectation of employees and potential employees. When a candidate opens the career site, if the site seems dated, if the application cannot be completed on a mobile device and is not user friendly, they will most likely not apply for a job. They will assume that if the career site doesn't have the latest and greatest technology, the rest of the organization may not have up to date technology either. Although it is possible to assign a hard dollar cost to recruiting an employee, in this case, it is very challenging to assign a hard dollar cost to someone who decides to not even apply. On the other hand, you can assign a hard dollar cost to a termination and determine an annual cost based on the number of terminations in a year.

The final thing to assess is employee engagement and how a change in system may affect engagement (positively or negatively). How happy are your employees? Do they feel that the organization is not putting a high priority on their time due to the inefficient processes and outdated systems? When asked what would make the organization a better place to work, are they saying new, mobile-friendly systems, elimination of paper forms, and an enhanced user experience? In many cases, this is a key component to the decision, as happy employees are more engaged and more productive employees.

In summary, the justification of a new HRIS system needs to include both hard and soft dollar costs. Including the possible hard dollar costs of terminations and new hires may not be enough to justify the investment in a new HRIS. Therefore, it is critical that organizations take the time to look across their business to discover and document the soft (indirect) costs around expected productivity increases, employee morale, strategic initiatives, and employee retention and include these items as part of the justification.

HRIS IN ACTION

An HRIS development and implementation project was being done by FarmforMore,[2] a U.S. manufacturer of farm machinery. FarmforMore has manufacturing operations in the major geographic regions of the United States, although the majority of its plants are situated in the Midwest. Its sales staff is assigned to regions, with sales offices in all major U.S. cities. FarmforMore currently has approximately 28,000 employees. The HRIS project was designed to incorporate computerized applications for 90% of its HR functionality, excluding payroll, which was outsourced to a vendor. The proposal emphasized the benefits of the new HRIS in terms of time saved for HR professionals as well as the timely reports designed for supervisors and managers. According to the project team, the costs, totaling $1.5 million, seemed reasonable considering the potential benefits.

The HRIS project began 2 years ago with a needs analysis and basic design, approval from the CEO, and the selection of the project team and steering committee. The project team was led by the vice president of HRM, and steering groups had representatives from all regions of the country as well as from all major departments—finance, IT, HR, production, marketing, and research and development. A benefit-cost (BCA) analysis was done. The major costs in the proposal were software, implementation costs, and the salaries of the project team's members. However, the project team indicated that time saved by computer-based transactions was the main cost-reduction benefit, estimated to save 14.3 full-time equivalent (FTE) budget lines, which would easily cover the costs of the new HRIS.

About 8 months ago, there was information in a project team interim report that indicated the HRIS project was behind schedule and had some minor cost overruns. There did not seem to be much concern at the time, since even though the project was behind schedule, the project team was certain that the delay was due to developing better working relationships among team members. Plus, it had taken more time to transfer the basic employee information from the old system to the new one.

Two weeks later, the CEO sent a memo to the project team leader, the VP of HRM, to meet with her to determine whether the HRIS project was back on schedule and the cost overruns had been resolved. Unfortunately, the HRM VP reported that the project was now running about 9 months behind schedule and so would need more funding to complete its tasks. This delay meant that the costs of the project had increased by 147%. The HRM VP could not really explain what had happened, since the project team felt it had done a careful BCA. When the CEO looked at the BCA, however, she stated that her college-age son could have done a better job. Since there had been a downturn in national sales as well as profits, the CEO put the HRIS project on hold.

INTRODUCTION

Computers are useless—they can only give you answers.

—Pablo Picasso

In most organizations today, an HRIS provides the primary infrastructure used to deliver HR programs, ensure HR regulatory compliance, and produce the metrics that are used to evaluate not only the HR function but also the contribution of the organization's human resources to the accomplishment of firm-level strategic objectives. **HRIS functionality** continues to evolve and to expand—we no longer see the simple shifting of paper-and-pencil processes to their electronic equivalents but rather new capabilities that leverage the advantages of integrated information systems that are faster and more capable computing technologies. As a result, organizations are faced with new opportunities to extend their investments in HRIS functionality. HRIS functionality refers to the programs or functions—such as recruiting, compensation, and job analysis—that are operational through the HRIS, as well as to the features of these programs that enhance their usability and capacity to affect outcomes. Thus, HRIS functionality could include all HR programs in a fully integrated system or only to a subset of the more important programs, for example, compensation and benefits. HRIS functionality typically varies with organizational size, with larger companies having a greater number of programs or functions in their HRIS configurations than smaller companies.

However, statistics measuring the success of HRIS projects are not very encouraging. The failures of the implementation of systems have been well documented (Standish Group, 2015). Delays in projects and budget overruns as well as user dissatisfaction are some of the most common reasons for the failure of HRIS projects. In fact, the larger the project, the more likely the project is to fail. Systems that are completed generally exceed cost estimates by more than 55% and time estimates by a factor of 2. In addition, only 13% of the systems projects that are completed are considered successful by the executives who sponsor them (Lemon, Bowitz, Burn, & Hackney, 2002). Further, there have been significant failure rates for the implementation of human resource information systems in major corporations that indicate HRIS projects need better planning and cost estimates (Bondarouk & Meijerink, 2010; Dery, Hall, & Wiblen, 2010; Dulebohn, 2010; Grant, Newell, & Kavanagh, 2010; Tansley, 2010). Many of these failures occurred because a **benefit-cost analysis (BCA)** was not done as part of the business case for the justification of the HRIS project.

In the 1990s, BCA played only a limited role in HRIS investment decisions. The pending obsolescence of noncompliant systems in Y2K (year 2000) fueled widespread implementation of new HRIS technology. The result was one of the most concentrated and dramatic shifts in HR practice ever. During this period, purchase decisions were driven by two primary criteria: Did new systems offer the baseline functionality required by the organization in a Y2K-compliant form, and could the systems be delivered and implemented on time (before December 31, 1999)? It was apparent that something had to be done to meet the potential problems of Y2K, and more fine-grained investment analyses would not have affected purchase decisions. Thus, many organizations chose not to invest the time and effort to complete an investment analysis. However, the business landscape has changed today. Many decision makers, some of whom are still waiting to see returns from past IT purchases in terms of successes and failures, are wary of new HRIS investments. Without an event like Y2K driving change, justifying new investments in HRISs will require strong business cases, that is, BCAs.

Justification Strategies for HRIS Investments

Strategies for justifying HRIS investments fall into two categories—*risk avoidance* and *organizational enhancement*. A **risk avoidance strategy** is used when investments are believed to eliminate or mitigate significant future risks faced by the organization, for example, generating reports on whether the gender and racial diversity of employees mirrors levels found in the populations from which the organization recruits. The potential obsolescence of legacy computing systems was a prototypical risk avoidance scenario. For example, in the 1990s, older systems that were not Y2K compliant simply needed to be changed to avoid problems. The need to comply with laws and regulations (e.g., the Equal Employment Opportunity Act) and changes to these laws provide other circumstances in which justification based on risk avoidance is popular. Risk avoidance justifications focus on the magnitude and probability of risks and frequently do not include the extensive investment analyses required by a BCA.

Organizational enhancement strategies, on the other hand, highlight how the effectiveness of the firm will be improved by the addition of a new or improved HRIS—as measured by increases in revenues or reductions in costs. Organizational enhancement justifications are often more challenging to "sell" to decision makers than are risk avoidance justifications, because enhancements do not carry the threat of real loss if no action is taken. Hence, enhancement strategies often fail to create a strong sense of urgency. This situation is supported by research on decision making under risk that consistently demonstrates that, when faced with potential losses, decision makers are willing to accept much greater risk; in other words, they become more risk seeking and willing to make investments to avoid losses than when investment alternatives are framed as gains (Kahneman & Tversky, 1979). Investments justified by organizational enhancements typically are subjected to more intense scrutiny by decision makers.

Evolution of HRIS Justification

Several factors suggest that the next generation of HRIS functionality will be more difficult to justify. In the last two decades, much of the "low-hanging cost-reduction fruit" has already been picked. HRIS implementations have shifted many organizations from administratively intense paper-and-pencil HR processes to electronic transaction processing supported by integrated computer systems. Employee and applicant self-service, online recruitment, electronic payroll processing, and electronic workflow driven by software-embedded business rules have dramatically reduced transaction costs. Employee self-service alone is reported to reduce the cost of many HR transactions by 50% or more. The next wave of HRIS functionality is unlikely to generate comparable reductions in costs, making investment decisions based on further cost reductions more difficult to justify.

Of course, there are still small organizations that use paper-and-pencil systems or HRIS legacy systems that need to be updated. For many of these organizations, particularly those that are growing rapidly, the value of reducing transaction costs will still serve as legitimate justification for adopting or upgrading an HRIS. In addition, these firms may also use a risk avoidance approach to justify the new HRIS—for example, the need for accurate and timely employee records in litigation. However, as will be argued in this chapter, the use of an organizational enhancement approach, which incorporates a combined revenue enhancement and cost reduction strategy, may provide a powerful means of determining the BCA for investment in a new HRIS.

It is therefore less certain that organizations with an operational HRIS will continue to pursue investments in new HRIS functionality aggressively. In fact, underinvestment in HRIS—that is, failing to approve many worthwhile investments—is likely. This underinvestment will not occur because the benefits of new investments in HRIS functionality are too small—in absolute terms, they are still substantial.

Underinvestment in HR functionality is more likely to result from the use of outdated BCA methodologies that emphasize cost reduction and do not adequately recognize the value of organizational enhancements attributable to important new HRIS functionality. HRIS managers will need tools so they can identify the sources of value to the organization that will result from HRIS investments. The field is maturing, and investment analysis tools must mature with it. This chapter examines HRIS benefit-cost dynamics and provides tools and techniques that can be used to conduct and evaluate HRIS BCAs that incorporate organizational enhancement.

Approaches to Investment Analyses Make a Difference: Some Guidelines

As discussed previously, one *must* conduct an investment analysis, frequently referred to as "making the business case" (Mayberry, 2008), for the acquisition of a new or improved HRIS. Usually, there is an HR or HRIS professional with selected team members who form the HRIS project team. This project team, or usually a subset of it, conducts the analyses and can be referred to as the BCA team. The members of this team include senior professionals from the HR and IT departments as well as representatives from other departments who will be affected by the HRIS project. The BCA is one of the first steps in seeking initial approval from senior management for an HRIS project. It is important to recognize that a proper perspective has as much to do with conducting an effective HRIS investment analysis as do the tools and techniques used. Understanding why the analysis is being conducted and understanding the expectations of what is going to be done with the results will influence the judgments made by both the BCA and the entire HRIS project team during the analysis, as well as increase the value of the results produced. It is important that the BCA team be representative of the project management team to ensure the complete involvement of all operational departments and maintain communications between the two teams. In addition, here are several considerations or guidelines that can help the BCA team approach the analysis with an improved likelihood of making the best decision for the organization. These guidelines are contained in Table 6.1. We will briefly cover each of these **BCA guidelines**.

The objective for conducting a BCA is to improve organizational effectiveness.   The primary purpose of each analysis is to make the best decision for the organization. In some instances, the best decision may be not to proceed with an investment. Making an investment should never be the ultimate objective. The desired outcome is to become a more effective organization, not simply *to justify a purchase.*

Be honest with yourself.   The BCA team should enter each analysis with an open mind— not with a solution to justify. It is best to think of the analysis as an investigation devoid of any personal biases. The team needs to come into the decision process without preconceived notions, willing to approach the analysis objectively and willing to accept whatever results the analysis produces. If members of the team have a vested interest in a specific solution, for example, cloud computing or employee self-service portals, biases that influence the analyst toward supporting the desired result can unintentionally be introduced into the analysis. Developing a reputation as an impartial evaluator will increase management decision makers' confidence in analyses done by the BCA team.

Focus on key functionality rather than on specific hardware or software solutions.   Many proposals for a new HRIS have erroneously started by identifying a new software application and then trying to justify how its features and capabilities could benefit the organization. However, it is whether your organization performs more effectively after an HRIS implementation that will determine the success of any HRIS investment. The BCA team must focus on the organization and its process and outcomes (i.e., reduced costs

TABLE 6.1 ■ Guidelines for Successful HRIS Benefit-Cost Analysis (BCA)	
Key	**Description**
The objective is improving organizational effectiveness.	The objective of any HRIS BCA is not to purchase specific hardware or software. The objective is to improve organizational performance.
Be honest with yourself.	Start each analysis with an open mind, not an investment to justify.
Focus on functionality, not products.	The analysis should focus on the improvement in organizational functionality that is to be achieved. Start with that functionality, and let it lead to the product. Don't start with the product and attempt to identify ways to justify its purchase.
Estimate benefits first.	Examine costs only after you have completed the analysis of benefits.
Know your business.	This means really understanding what your business is and how your current processes allow your organization to accomplish its objectives. Understand the dynamics of your current processes and where potential for improvement can be found. Understand organizational politics.
Develop the best estimate possible.	Don't be overly optimistic or conservative. Develop the best estimate you can with the data available to you. This is the core of making the business case.
Separate the development of BCA estimates from questions of how best to package the analysis to justify a final decision.	The questions involved in developing an accurate BCA and attempting to determine how best to justify a choice to organizational decision makers are two separate processes. The latter involves choices about which sources of value should be included in the business case to be presented to decision makers. These are determined by the relative comparisons of costs with the magnitudes and types of revenue sources. Decisions about how to package the analysis for decision makers should be pursued only after a thorough analysis based on best estimates of all benefits and costs has been accomplished.

Source: IHRIM Journal, Volume 8, Issue 1. International Association for Human Resource Information Management.

or increased revenues), identify opportunities to improve effectiveness, and only then look to identify software solutions that provide the desired capabilities. Centering the analysis on a specific software solution shifts the focus of the analysis to the capabilities that solution offers, not necessarily the capabilities that are most needed by the organization. Therefore, the question to be answered is not just whether the system will increase HR functionality but whether the new HRIS will improve organizational effectiveness and fit with the business strategy of the firm.

Examine benefits before you examine costs. This is often difficult to do, but training the BCA team to examine the benefits of a change in HRIS functionality before estimating costs will produce better analyses. Knowing before you conduct the analysis of benefits how much would need to be spent to acquire new functionality can easily lead to an inaccurate BCA. This "backward" approach makes it almost impossible not to consider what level of benefits will be necessary to justify the investment. This approach can cause the team to abort prematurely the process of identifying and analyzing benefits, especially if a single source of benefits appears to be sufficient to guarantee adoption of the HRIS project. It can also encourage "fishing" for questionable benefits when the initially identified benefits may not be enough to justify the HRIS investment.

Know your business. As stated in Table 6.1, this means really understanding the organization's business and how the current processes in all departments allow the organization to accomplish its objectives. Furthermore, it means that the BCA team must understand the dynamics of the current business processes and where potential for improvement exists. Since the BCA team consists of senior representatives from all staff departments affected by the HRIS project, this business knowledge should exist within the team. Obviously, then, the BCA team must have cooperative relationships among its members. Further, it is important that the BCA and PM teams understand the internal politics of the firm.

Develop the best estimate possible. Various methods to achieve this goal are discussed in this chapter. It is also critically important, as mentioned in the previous paragraph, that cooperative relationships exist among members of the BCA team as well as within the PM team. The project team leader must try to reduce or eliminate interdepartmental politics, particularly between the HR and IT departments. Finally, note the advice in Table 6.1 not to be overly optimistic or conservative but to develop the best estimate possible with the available data.

Distinguish between the analysis and the packaging of that analysis for decision makers. The primary purpose of analyzing an HRIS investment is to determine whether and to what extent it will improve your organization. The objective of the analysis should be to provide the "best" possible estimate of the impact of an HRIS investment possible. Developing the estimate should be viewed as separate and distinct from the process of presenting and "selling" the investment opportunity to management decision makers. Decision makers may choose to rely on specific forms of benefit evidence or to adopt conservative assumptions in order to gain approval for the investment. Inappropriate investment decisions may result if overly conservative assumptions in the HRIS investment analysis conducted by the BCA team are compounded by the conservative bias common among decision makers.

HRIS BENEFIT-COST ANALYSIS

A BCA is simply what its name indicates—a comparison of the projected benefits and costs associated with an HRIS investment, which can be depicted using a comparison of benefit and cost dollars or as a ratio with the benefits of the project as the numerator and the costs as the denominator. A cost is any new outlay of cash required for the initial purchase, implementation, or ongoing maintenance of the investment. A benefit is any financial gain resulting from the investment that occurs at any time during the investment's useful life. Benefits include both revenue enhancements and cost reductions.

At its core, the BCA is an analysis of change in the benefit-cost ratio—a comparison of existing levels of outcomes and cost of processes with the projected outcomes and costs associated with the HRIS investment. This comparison means the benefit-cost ratio for the current state must be calculated first. Then the benefit-cost ratio is estimated for the projected HRIS. The *size of the gap between these two benefit-cost ratios* is what will influence the decision to implement a new HRIS or new HR functionality. However, it is important to note that ratios ignore scale, so although increases in the ratio are sought, raw estimates of changes in costs and benefits will be needed to fully understand the investment's impact on the organization.

A common misconception is that conducting a meaningful BCA (and utility analysis) requires financial expertise. Knowing some financial basics, such as discounting, cost of capital, cash flow, **return on investment (ROI)**, **payback period**, net present value, and **internal rate of return (IRR)**, is useful but not required. Organizations differ in the specific financial measures they use to evaluate investments. Organizations may use ROI, IRR, payback period, or other measures alone or in combination. Therefore, it can be useful to seek out an internal adviser to help you package your analysis for the managerial decision-making process used in the organization. Typically, this internal adviser will be someone in the finance or accounting department. However, regardless of the specific financial measures used in the organization, the foundations of all investment analyses, including BCAs, rests on three basic pieces of information: (1) sources of benefits and costs, (2) an estimated dollar value for each benefit and cost item, and (3) the time when the organization will receive each benefit and incur each cost. Developing estimates of these values depend more on an understanding of the business than on financial expertise. The remainder of this chapter will cover how these three basic pieces of information are obtained and used in a BCA.

Identifying Sources of Benefits and Costs

Investments in HRIS functionality differ from more traditional investments because HR is commonly perceived as a source of costs rather than a direct source of revenue (Cascio, 2000). Any impact that HR department activities have on revenues occurs *indirectly* through the effect of HR programs and practices on other units of the organization. For example, a program focused on training retail employees to provide quality customer service is typically a cost ascribed to the HR department; however, its indirect effect of increased sales is classified as revenue for the retail department. Thus, the effects of many HR programs or practices are often described as "soft" or, more appropriately, indirect. As a result, managerial decision makers are justifiably concerned about using indirect benefits to justify spending "hard" dollars, particularly when considering large investments such as a new HRIS. Approving an investment only to find that the expected benefits never materialize is something all decision makers fear. In the absence of obvious risk avoidance justifications and significant reductions in costs from previous HRIS investments, developing expertise in identifying and valuing the direct and indirect benefits derived from HRIS investments is one of the critical challenges that HRIS managers face.

Failing to recognize important sources of benefits or costs is a common problem in HRIS BCA. The HRIS BCA matrix shown in Figure 6.1 can be used to help uncover all

FIGURE 6.1 ■ HRIS Benefit-Cost Analysis Matrix

		Direct (Hard)	Indirect (Soft)
Benefits	Revenue enhancement	New revenue (new sales)	Improvement potential (better decision making)
	Cost reduction	Direct costs (canceled vendor contracts)	Potential costs (saved staff time)
Costs	New implementation costs	Out-of-pocket costs (software, service agreements)	Indirect costs (increased technical support needs)

Source: *IHRIM Journal*, Volume 8, Issue 1. International Association for Human Resource Information Management.

reasonable benefit and cost components in HRIS investment analyses. The HRIS BCA matrix consists of six cells.

The four upper cells (1–4) represent sources of benefits (i.e., direct revenue enhancements, indirect revenue enhancements, direct cost reductions, and indirect cost reductions). The two cells of the bottom row capture costs of implementation (i.e., direct and indirect costs). A simple evaluation of each cell of the HRIS BCA matrix can ensure that important sources of benefits or costs are not overlooked.

Direct Benefits

The four "benefit" cells of the HRIS BCA matrix (Figure 6.1) represent the crossing of two dimensions. The first dimension is the type of benefit—revenue enhancements versus cost reductions. Organizations can enhance revenues by changing employees' job performance. These changes could result in *new revenue* in terms of new sales due to more efficient procedures, for example, those instituted because of a better training program for new employees. Organizations can also reduce costs by changing HR processes or improving the execution of existing processes. HRIS investments often involve both types of effects. For example, an organization with a new HRIS could decide to outsource programs (such as employee recruiting) to vendors who have unique expertise. Investments can also permit the offering of new HR products and services that can increase revenues and enhance profit margins. Thinking about opportunities for cost reductions and revenue enhancements separately allows managers to explore each more fully.

Hard or direct outcomes generally refer to benefits (and costs) (a) that are very likely to occur and (b) whose values are easily estimated. Some examples of **direct benefits** can be seen in Table 6.2, which shows an example of a BCA for an e-learning investment. As can be seen, the organization is considering having e-learning modules created by an external vendor to replace in-house training programs. Direct revenue enhancements include the additional revenue the organization can earn by selling the e-learning modules. Direct cost reductions include expected reductions in the costs associated with delivering training programs, as seen in Table 6.2, for example, reduced travel expenses and reduced facilities costs.

TABLE 6.2 ■ Example of an e-Learning BCA Matrix[1]		
	Direct (Hard)	**Indirect/Contingent (Soft)**
Revenue enhancements	Conducting custom e-learning training module development for other organizations Sales of locally developed learning modules or programs	Better customer service leading to increase in repeat sales A more agile organization able to respond rapidly to market changes Improved training effectiveness through customization and just-in-time delivery = faster learning curve, less lost productivity while waiting for training, and right amount and type of content
Cost reductions	Reduced travel expenses Reduced facilities costs (e.g., for room and equipment rentals and refreshments) Reduced requirements for paper-based training materials and teaching aids Reduced expenses for instructor fees or salary and benefits costs (if internal) Reduced costs for replacement workers if trainees are required to be away from their work	Reduction in turnover and or absenteeism. It is suggested that 41% of employees will look for another job within 12 months due to poor training and education; with good training and education, this percentage drops to 12%. Improved safety (fewer injuries, less lost time, fewer insurance claims, lower workers' compensation costs) Employee time saved
Costs of implementation	Installation support Software purchase or license fee Software installation and initial training support Additional staff: IT administrator, instructional developers, or courseware purchases	Increased use of end-user help desk Lost productivity during conversion to new system

Source: IHRIM Journal, Volume 8, Issue 1. International Association for Human Resource Information Management.

[1]A worked example showing estimates of these values based on the matrix is included on the instructor resource site for this book.

Indirect Benefits

Soft or **indirect benefits**, on the other hand, are often less easily quantified because their occurrence may be less certain or because their value is more difficult to establish. After the HRIS functionality is introduced, indirect revenue enhancements result from improvements in intermediate outcomes that could position the organization to be able to increase revenues. For example, in Table 6.2, e-learning training modules can be used to improve customer service, and potentially sales, by improving the skills of sales employees. Improving managerial leadership could also have an impact on the indirect benefits at the top of Table 6.2 by encouraging employee engagement in the activities that most directly influence organizational effectiveness. Thus, in this example, the intermediate outcomes are the effects of the e-learning training modules that then may lead to the revenue increases. As listed in Table 6.2, these are "Better customer service leading to increases in repeat sales" and "A more agile organization able to respond rapidly to market changes." The e-learning training modules may also affect revenue increase outcomes, by, for example, improving the organization's capacity to attract and retain high-quality employees, achieving a reduction in turnover and absenteeism (see Table 6.2), improving employees' capacity to make decisions, or freeing up time for employees to engage in activities that more directly support the strategic objectives of the organization (see Figure 6.1). Indirect revenue enhancements occur through one or more intermediate outcomes that require some additional activity or condition exists before an increase in revenues is realized. For example, before managers can work on leadership responsibilities and activities that are directly related to strategic company goals, it may be necessary to restructure several departments and provide some in-service training.

Since these benefits are not reported in a dollar metric, current BCAs typically do not include these items in the numeric analysis but will often address them in the narrative discussion supporting the investment. In the e-learning example, better customer service (i.e., service that can lead to increased customer retention and repeat sales) and a more agile organization (i.e., one that can retrain or retool its employees more quickly to respond to rapidly changing markets) are examples of indirect or contingent sources of revenues.

Indirect cost reductions involve those changes that are expected to lead to reduced costs. If we reexamine Figure 6.1, these benefits would fall in box number 4, potential cost reductions through saved staff time, and would include (a) staff time saved that does not lead to reductions in payroll or employee headcount; (b) expected reductions in the amount of or requirements for technical support; (c) expected reductions in absenteeism and turnover; and (d) expected reductions in the time required to bring trainees up to the status of fully functioning employees.

In many instances, time-saving applications are incorrectly projected to result in reductions in employee headcount or FTEs—a direct savings in payroll expenses. More often, though, the deployment of new HRIS functionality results in a new structuring of work that enables the elimination of parts of jobs rather than whole jobs. As a result, the benefit is indirect—a saving of time that can be deployed in other activities rather than a direct saving of the costs of salary and benefits. In the e-learning example, enhancements in training effectiveness are expected to lead to faster learning curves and less time to proficiency. This benefit is expected to result in fewer errors and less rework. Reductions in turnover costs are also anticipated because better-trained employees are expected to have higher satisfaction and remain in their jobs longer. Lower turnover rates for valued employees would have a strong positive effect, allowing the firm to reduce the costs of hiring new employees (see Cascio, 2000). Furthermore, improved access to safety training is also expected to result in less time lost as a result of injuries and reduced insurance claims and workers' compensation costs.

Consequently, because the effects are indirect, analyses of indirect benefits can be challenging. But in many instances, these indirect effects are the real source of benefits for new HRIS functionality. Being able to identify the indirect effects and understand how they are expected to affect costs and revenues is critical to understanding how to justify HRIS investments. An important advantage of understanding how and where indirect benefits are expected to occur is that it allows the organization to plan and manage HRIS implementations in ways that make it more likely for indirect benefits to actually occur. Because these benefits are often contingent on other events, knowing what those events are and managing them as a part of the implementation will likely result in greater organizational impact.

IMPLEMENTATION COSTS

Once benefits have been estimated, the analysis can proceed to estimating the costs of implementation (Table 6.2). In contrast to estimating benefits, cost estimation is often easier to complete because cost data are often readily available and already offered in a dollar metric. In most cases, many sources of **implementation costs** will be direct. **Direct costs** will include but are not limited to (a) costs for the initial purchase and updates of software and any additional hardware and (b) ongoing costs for internal or external systems support. In the e-learning example (Table 6.2), direct costs include the purchase of any new software, hardware, and licenses required to implement the system as well as the cost of the expertise necessary to develop and manage training on this new HRIS.

Indirect costs comprise costs that cannot be known or measured beforehand but may arise in the process of implementing the system. These include the impact of the implementation on the organization, such as lost productivity while the organization completes implementation. This impact includes lost productivity for rank-and-file employees as well as for the HR staff involved in implementation. The e-learning example includes increased use of end-user help desks or other support functions, costs necessary to revamp existing courseware while the organization learns how to use the new system most effectively, and the lost productivity that will occur for any current employees who will be required to take on additional responsibilities associated with the adoption of the new system.

It is important to be thorough in attempting to identify all the sources of costs. If your analysis recognizes some benefit without incorporating an offsetting change in cost, you likely have missed a source of cost in your analysis. For example, organizations that project significant reductions in employee headcounts due to converting paper-and-pencil transactions to electronic systems often failed to recognize the full additional costs that would be required in technical support, training on the new system, or transitioning large numbers of employees out of the organization.

Also, the total costs of implementation will depend on the current state of information system development in the organization. The components of organizational information systems evolve at different speeds across organizations. Knowing the current level of technological evolution of the organization's total information architecture and systems is quite important. These components would include those that are operational within departments concerned with finance, operations, marketing, and information systems, as well as HR. Assessment of these departments' systems should include evaluations of (a) the current state of their computer hardware, software, data, and processes; (b) user sophistication and networking; and (c) telecommunications technology. New HRIS investments may affect all these information systems (IS) components. In any one of these areas, the greater the change required supporting the implementation of the new HR functionality, the more expensive the implementation will be. Total cost will be driven by (a) the scope or size of the HRIS implementation; (b) the amount of customization required; (c) the maturity of the HRIS functionality being considered—the less mature the functionality, the greater the costs of implementation and upgrades are likely to be; and (d) the experience levels of the implementers.

Although early attempts at BCA often grossly underestimated or ignored significant sources of costs, the experiences of organizations over the past decade have provided insights that can be used to do a much better job of recognizing what cost items need to be included in cost analyses. Several sources for determining cost of implementation are available, including organizations that have previously implemented specific packages or functionality, vendors in the HRIS field, and implementation consultants.

TABLE 6.3 ■ Different Approaches to Estimating Benefit Magnitude			
Approach	**Description**	**When to Use It**	**Advantages/Limitations**
Direct estimation	Direct ("gut level") estimates of the relationship of the potential benefits to the estimated costs of engaging in an investment	Best when costs are not large Appropriate when attempting to gain compliance or mitigating extreme risks When substantial direct cost reduction or revenue enhancements exist	Quick and low cost to perform May not provide data that contain enough detail for use in monitoring implementation effectiveness or to perform follow-up analyses Highly dependent on the expertise of the decision maker
Benchmarking	Using benchmark data from other firms to estimate the potential benefits and costs that are likely to result from the purchase of HRIS functionality	Superior to direct estimation when costs are large When the organization either has limited experience or no data concerning the area of functionality	Allows the organization to develop more precise estimates than direct estimation based on the collective experience of other organizations Average estimates of outcomes may not generalize to the target organization
Internal assessment	Analysis based on specific internal assessments of actual costs and likely benefits (e.g., activity-based costing)	When costs are high and benefits are not obviously dramatically larger than costs When the organization has the assessment capabilities in place to gather the appropriate data	Provides the most precise estimates of the baseline costs and current performance of existing processes against which to compare potential improvements May increase both costs and time required to make decisions
Mix and match	Using combinations of these approaches	When different amounts or sources of information are available for different types of costs and benefits (e.g., most likely scenario)	Permits the organization to use the best methods available

Source: IHRIM Journal, Volume 8, Issue 4. International Association for Human Resource Information Management.

ESTIMATING THE VALUE OF INDIRECT BENEFITS

Most HRIS benefit-cost analyses will include some indirect benefits. One of the more difficult tasks in producing an HRIS BCA is estimating the value of these indirect benefits. The difficulty of converting indirect benefit estimates to a dollar metric has limited their role in HR technology investment decisions. To this point, soft benefits are often relegated to the narrative supporting an investment analysis that is otherwise based solely on estimates of direct cost reductions. For good reason, many managers consider these indirect savings cautiously. That does not mean, though, that these benefits are any less important than direct benefits to the organization. In fact, as noted earlier, ignoring them in HRIS investment analysis could result in incorrect or misleading analyses. As a result, we need to adapt the general techniques used to analyze HR technology investments to meet these new requirements.

ESTIMATING INDIRECT BENEFIT MAGNITUDE

Constructing dollar estimates of indirect benefits is challenging, but it can be done. To simplify estimation of the dollar value of indirect benefits and provide a basis for justification, one should break this task into the following three steps: (1) estimating benefit magnitude, (2) mapping benefits to cost or revenue changes, and (3) converting magnitude estimates to dollar values. By separating these steps, we can begin to understand better the factors that influence the value of indirect benefits and, perhaps more important, when these benefits are likely to occur during the HRIS project. Also, since magnitude and value are often driven by different factors, separating these decisions provides a better framework for post-implementation evaluations. Both benefit and value estimates are then open to objective review.

An objective of HRIS BCA is to develop the best-possible estimates of the likely effect of the implementation of new HRIS functionality. Therefore, using a metric that is familiar or comfortable to those developing the estimate of this impact is likely to improve accuracy and, ultimately, make the project easier to manage. For instance, if the new functionality is predicted to reduce turnover (see Figure 6.2), the magnitude of the expected change in "turnover rates" would be estimated first. Then the determination of the dollar value of the differences between the current rate and the expected rate is likely to produce better estimates than if decision makers attempted to estimate the dollar impact of the expected reductions in turnover in a single step. The objective is to choose the metric and measurement procedure that will result in the most accurate estimate possible of the size of the benefit.

Once that metric has been chosen, there are three approaches for estimating **benefit magnitude**: (1) direct estimation, (2) benchmarking, and (3) internal assessment. Which method is the most appropriate depends on the amount of specific information that is available to the organization and the BCA team.

Direct Estimation

Direct estimation is the simplest of the three methods. It is quick and easy to perform. It relies solely on the expertise of analysts or subject matter experts in the BCA team to

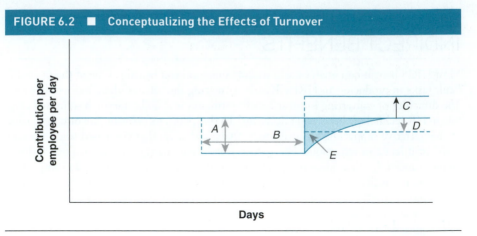

FIGURE 6.2   ■   Conceptualizing the Effects of Turnover

Source: Carlson, K. D. (2004). Estimating the value of the indirect benefits of new HRIS functionality. *IHRIM Journal*, 8(4), 22-28.

Note: A is the average value (contribution) that is lost per day that a given position is left unfilled. B is the number of days that a position remains unfilled. C and D represent the increase or decrease in contribution that occurs if a new hire is more or less effective, respectively, than the employee who left. The gray area noted as E represents the loss of contribution that occurs during the time when a new employee is learning the job.

"estimate" the expected magnitude of the benefit. **Direct estimation** is most appropriate when the scope of the project is small, compliance or risk avoidance is a primary investment justification, the component being estimated is not the primary component of costs or benefits in the analysis, or no other method for estimating benefit magnitude is available. The primary limitation of direct estimation is that the accuracy of the analysis depends on the expertise of the estimator.

When several equally qualified subject matter experts are available, collecting independent estimates from each expert and using the average of these estimates is recommended. In addition, it can be useful to require that experts articulate the rationale for their estimates. Requiring this step not only ensures that experts are thoughtful in the preparation of their estimates but also provides the organization with an analysis of the assumptions or expectations contained in these rationales, which can be used to help improve the accuracy of future estimates.

Benchmarking

Benchmark data on the magnitude of indirect benefits achieved in other firms can be useful. The advantage of **benchmarking** is that it allows an organization to build on the experiences of others. These data can provide evidence that a specific outcome can occur as well as evidence of its potential magnitude. Howes (2002) offers an insightful example on the use of benchmarking data to estimate how much reduction in turnover an organization might expect. In this example, benchmark data about industrywide levels of turnover are used to construct estimates of the potential for improvement in turnover that might be possible for a given organization. If an organization has high turnover relative to industry standards, it has the potential for greater improvement than might be expected for other firms in that industry.

Benchmarking information of various types is becoming more widely available from several sources (e.g., Deloitte, Gartner, Inc., The Hackett Group, PwC Saratoga Benchmarking, Society of Human Resource Management, and Harris Associates—see the websites provided in the Appendix). This chapter contains a reference to HR metrics that can be used in benchmarking (Society of Human Resource Management [SHRM], 2010). Organizations can also conduct their own benchmarking studies to gather specific data from targeted firms, data that may not be readily available from third-party sources. Benchmarking may be preferred over direct estimation for larger projects for which investment risks are greater. Benchmarking is also useful when organizations have limited experience with the targeted functionality of the HRIS project or when there is no access to local data. The primary disadvantage of benchmark data is that the experiences of other organizations may not completely generalize to your firm or business unit.

Internal Assessment

Internal assessment involves the use of a firm's own internal metrics or other forms of the firm's specific data as the basis for estimates. Use of this method requires that the organization has maintained historic records on previous information system projects. Internal assessment can be useful when investment scopes are large and direct estimation or benchmarking suggests that benefits may not be dramatically higher or lower than costs (e.g., less than ± 30%). Internal assessment requires that the organization possesses the capability of gathering data about its own processes, as these data are necessary to support this kind of analysis. An advantage of integrated information systems—systems built on common platforms that permit single instances of data to be used in several applications and the seamless transfer of data between applications—is that the marginal costs of assessments are greatly reduced, permitting cost-effective assessments of a wide range of organizational outcomes. Internal assessments offer the most precise estimates of the costs and performance of existing or newly implemented processes. Internal assessments, though, may be able to provide only a portion of the needed data. That is, an organization may be able to gather accurate data about the outcomes of current processes, but, in order to complete the analysis, it may need to rely on benchmark data from other organizations or obtain direct estimates of the outcomes for new processes.

Even though possessing integrated information systems can reduce the marginal costs of assessments, conducting internal assessments and evaluating the data they produce are not costless activities. As described in Table 6.3, internal assessment provides the most precise estimates of the baseline costs and current performance of existing processes against which to compare potential improvements. However, internal assessments will result in higher costs than direct estimation and, depending on the nature of the assessment, could result in higher decision-support costs than benchmarking. As noted, internal assessment is only possible when the organization has experience with a given form of functionality. It is not possible to assess the effects of new functionality that has not been previously implemented anywhere in the organization.

Each of these three approaches is recapped in Table 6.3. The ideal method for estimating the magnitudes of indirect benefits in most HRIS analyses is to use a combination of these three approaches. This permits each benefit to be estimated using the method that is most appropriate given the availability of data and the investment's cost, risk, and opportunity characteristics. For high-stakes investment decisions, using multiple methods to develop estimates can provide additional insight and increased confidence in the final decision.

MAPPING INDIRECT BENEFITS TO REVENUES AND COSTS

In some instances, the metric of choice may not be one that is easily or unambiguously tied to reductions in costs or increases in revenues. That is, estimating the value of indirect benefits requires that the analyst first be able to articulate how the indirect benefit is linked to an actual reduction in costs or increase in revenues.

Then a Miracle Occurred! The challenge of linking indirect benefits to revenues and costs is not a step that should be taken lightly. In many instances, it can be challenging to articulate exactly the change of events that leads from an investment to changes in the organization's bottom line. This can lead to causal language in investments that identifies the initial links in the sequence, and then jump immediately to argue for the benefits to the organization. These analyses are of the form *A* causes *B* which causes *C* . . . then a miracle occurs . . . and the organization is more profitable. While articulating hypotheses about exactly how the causal change is expected to unfold can be difficult, doing so allows the organization to plan more effectively for success—by adding new metrics at critical junctures to track progress and to identify potential contingencies that must be managed to assure success.

To examine this idea further, let's assume that an indirect benefit of a proposed investment is reduced turnover; and we predict that implementing a new HRIS functionality will result in a reduction in voluntary turnover from 10% to 5% for a targeted group of jobs. Because the effect of turnover on costs and benefits is indirect, we need to understand how reducing turnover is expected to affect an organization's revenues or costs to accurately translate our 5% reduction in turnover to other metrics that are more closely associated with changes in costs and revenues.

Employee turnover is a good example because it affects costs and revenues in several ways, some of which are depicted graphically in Figure 6.2. The departure of an employee can increase costs because it may require the organization to engage in a new recruitment and hiring cycle, and the new employee is likely to require training. But there are other effects as well. For instance, the loss of an employee in a position critical to the day-to-day functioning of the organization will require that efforts be made to cover the work responsibilities in that employee's absence. How an organization chooses to cover those responsibilities will influence the magnitude of the net loss of contribution that results from the vacancy. There will be salary savings for the vacant position, but the cost of temporary hires or of shifting other employees off their primary assignments, not to mention the opportunity costs that result from using less than fully effective temporary or overextended employees, also must be considered. The total loss added by this vacancy is represented in Figure 6.2 by the region $A \times B$—the value of the daily loss of contribution multiplied by the number of days the position remains vacant. Also, as noted in Table 6.2, turnover affects the contribution the organization derives from a position. Perhaps the departing employee was a poor performer and replacing him or her will result in a net gain in average long-term effectiveness for that position (i.e., C in Figure 6.2). Even with training, new hires will most likely require some time on the job before they can become fully effective; their effectiveness will increase as they gain expertise. But during this time, contribution will be less than would have been experienced had there been no turnover in the position (i.e., E in Figure 6.2). Each of these intermediate outcomes can be tied to a specific cost or revenue effect through one or more links.

In this example, a comprehensive estimate of the impact of the expected reduction in turnover is represented by the sum of the estimates of each of these components in Figure 6.2. In some cases, and for specific types of benefits, these relationships may seem quite complex. Do not be discouraged or dissuaded from being thorough. Understanding exactly how these changes are projected to affect the organization may yield important new insights about intermediate outcomes and contingent factors, insights that may put managers in a position to ensure the success of HRIS investments. Understanding which factors are affected by the investment can also aid in further refining magnitude estimates and is essential for estimating value. Cascio (2000) provides a complete list of the costs of voluntary turnover. In addition, there are several metrics important for measuring the effects of turnover, such as "time to fill," "turnover costs," "vacancy costs," and "vacancy rate."

METHODS FOR ESTIMATING THE VALUE OF INDIRECT BENEFITS

Direct revenue enhancements or direct cost reductions are typically estimated in dollars, so their value is provided by the total estimate. Estimates that are developed in other metrics, such as total absenteeism in days lost, must also be converted to dollars. For indirect benefits that can be tied more directly to cost reductions or revenue enhancements (i.e., new products developed or market share increased), the task is somewhat more difficult, but it can be done. It requires estimating the strength of the relationship between the change in intermediate outcomes and changes in revenue or cost (e.g., each new account will generate $50,000 in gross profit annually; reducing scrap by 5% will save $10,000 per month). For other outcomes, such as employee time saved, these conversions are somewhat more difficult to conduct.

For this last category, employee time saved, one method for estimating the value of employee time is average employee contribution (AEC). This method is an alternative to a practice that is *not recommended*—estimating an employee's value as equal to his or her cost to the organization. In nearly all cases, the employee's cost to the organization dramatically underestimates the average employee's contribution. We know that this is true because most organizations are profitable. For an organization to be profitable, each individual in that organization, on average, contributes enough value to compensate for the cost of his or her wages and benefits and for the outlay on the equipment and facilities employed on the job, in addition to covering taxes and accounting for profit. This scenario helps explain why downsizing does not always improve financial results. Downsizing only makes sense when the contribution of the employees eliminated is less than their cost in salary and benefits to the organization.

Average Employee Contribution

In the turnover example discussed earlier, estimating the value lost while a position remains open (i.e., the region represented by the area $A \times B$ in Figure 6.2) requires an estimate of the value of the average daily contribution made by an employee. The average contribution approach argues that the **average employee contribution (AEC)** in an organization is equal to total gross profit divided by the number of employees or full-time equivalents (FTEs). FTEs are the budgeted number of positions for each job in an organization. AEC is not a metric that most organizations track, although a measure of average daily gross margin (i.e., net revenue – cost of goods sold) generated per salesperson would be an example of this type of measure. This is one of the simplest metrics that captures AEC as accurately as is needed for estimating the value of indirect benefits.

$$AEC = (\text{Net revenues} - \text{Cost of goods sold})/\text{No. of employees}$$

By definition, in a profitable organization, this number will be substantially higher than labor costs, which is the sum of total employee pay and benefits. Dividing this number by the number of workdays in a year (i.e., 252) produces an estimate of average daily contribution. Note that in this method, as indicated in the previous equation, contributions attributable to employees are not reduced by the organization's capital expenditures and other non–employee-related expenses—the equipment and tools that aid employees in doing their jobs. The reason is that these tools are used to enhance employee contribution. The tools enhance what employees can do, but they do not generate contribution on their own. That is, if you take away the employees who use the tools and equipment, the contribution goes with them. The tools provide no independent and unique contribution to the organization in the absence of the employee; employees use these tools at work to make themselves more effective.

AEC can be used to estimate the average annual contribution of an organization's employees. Obviously, average contribution can and does differ across jobs. Thus, organizations may want to adjust this number up or down for specific jobs to recognize differences in contribution potential. Jobs that more closely support the organization's mission and offer jobholders broader authority to influence the work of others, and greater autonomy for choosing how and when work will be accomplished, are likely to offer above-average levels of contribution. The advantage of this method is that it establishes a baseline contribution value for each of the different jobs, one that is consistent with the actual financial performance of the organization.

Average contribution estimates, though, provide little guidance in estimating differences in contribution between employees holding the same or similar jobs. This calculation is represented in the turnover example in Figure 6.2 by the difference between the values C and D—the differences in contribution for two different employees who might hold the same position. Differences in contribution can be developed using internal assessment by examining directly the individual employee differences (variance) in the work outcomes produced by a large number of individuals holding equivalent positions. This assessment can be accomplished more readily for jobs when individual production rates can be monitored (i.e., sales, transaction processing, and some manufacturing settings). It is important to understand the difference between AEC and the variance of work outcomes by employees. AEC is the average contribution of work outcomes, and it can be estimated for entire organizations or for individual jobs. So it would be fairly easy to calculate the AEC for sales representatives by week by adding the sales for all representatives and dividing by the number of representatives. However, this does not tell us the range or variance in the weekly sales for the representatives. Some individuals could have done poorly in terms of weekly sales, whereas others could have done quite well. This variance in productivity is very important in the calculation of utility analysis (Boudreau, 1991; Cascio, 1987, 2000; Schmidt & Hunter, 1983), which is beyond the scope of this book.

Numerical Example for Figure 6.2

Cascio (1991, 2000) devotes an entire chapter to "The High Cost of Employee Turnover" and provides some numerical examples for the calculations of employee loss. Cascio also provides both general and specific categories, similar to the ones already discussed, for the costs involved in employee turnover. By using Cascio's categories and numbers, the calculations required in Figure 6.2 will be done. The first general category in Cascio's list, Measuring Separation Costs, measures the following cost items: *the exit interview,* the administrative functions related to termination,[1] and *the cost of replacing employees.*

The interview combines the cost of the interviewer's time both prior to the interview and the time for the interview. This interview also has two other cost factors—the cost of terminating the employee, which is measured by the time required for the interview multiplied by the average daily pay rate for the terminated employee. This value is part of the separation costs, but the time (in days) to replace the employee multiplied by the average daily pay rate for the terminated employee must be added to the interview costs to have a better total cost. Looking at Figure 6.2, this total cost represents a part of *A.* This total cost can also be calculated for a month or a year. If the exit interview process takes 1 hour, 15 minutes for preparation and 45 minutes for the interview, then multiplying by the interviewer's pay rate at $15/hour is one part of determining the value of *A.* The second part of the cost for the exit interview is the cost of the terminating employee's time. If the employee earns $11.80/hour, that is multiplied by .75 (approximate time for the interview) to get costs incurred by the exit interview by the employee. If we add these two costs—$15.00 plus $8.85 ($11.80 times .75), we can calculate the *total costs of the exit interview to be $23.85,* i.e., part of the value for *A* in the figure. If there are 100 turnovers in one year, then the total cost for the exit interviews for the year would be $2,385.00.

The second specific cost category identified by Cascio is the Administrative Functions Related to Termination. This category involves the time required by the HR department in completing the administrative functions multiplied by the average HR employee's pay rate. If the HR employee's average hourly pay is $15.75 and the administrative functions meeting takes two hours, *the total cost for this category is $31.50.* Adding the total cost for the exit interview to this cost means the total cost of terminating one employee is $55.35—$23.85 plus $31.50. This value is another part of *A* in Figure 6.2.

The final specific category identified by Cascio is the separation pay for the terminated employee. If the average daily amount of separation pay by employee, the total in this example *would be $472.00 as the average separation pay per employee terminated*—calculated by multiplying 40 hours/week by $11.80/hour. This value would be the last part of *A* in Figure 6.2. Adding the three costs would be $23.85 + $31.50 + $472.00 = $527.35. The total of Separation Costs would be $527.35. This means the total costs of separation of terminated employees by year would be $52,735 (100 turnovers × $527.35 = $52,735).

The general costs incurred by an organization in replacing a terminated employee are defined as replacement costs. These costs represent *B* in Figure 6.2. The specific cost categories include the following:

1. communication of job availability
2. preemployment administrative functions
3. entrance interviews
4. testing

5. staff meetings

6. travel/moving expenses

7. employment medical exams

8. dissemination of information after hired

As expected, many of these costs involve personnel time by time spent on the activity, both from the HR department as well as managerial time.

Most of the measures of these specific cost categories are common sense, for example, advertising and employment agency fees, costs of tests as well as cost of time for test administration by HR department, and preemployment administrative functions multiplied by a HR professional's time to complete the tasks involved. Thus, it seems that examining most of these costs would not be fruitful. The interested student can check Cascio (1991, 2000) for details from the chapter on the high cost of employee turnover. However, remember that these costs are shown as *B* in Figure 6.2 and represent the number of days that a position is filled.

In addition, new employees can either increase or decrease separation costs due to their effectiveness in their job performance after being hired. Thus, from Figure 6.2, *C* represents a new hire that is more effective in fulfilling the requirements and tasks of his new position than the employee who left; whereas *D* represents a new hire that is less effective in fulfilling the requirements and tasks of the new position than the employee who left. The gray area *E* in Figure 6.2 represents the loss of contribution by the new employee who is learning the job and can be quite variable depending on the individual. That is, some people learn to perform the requirements and tasks of the job faster than others, and this cost would be positive, thus reducing total cost of the termination and replacement. Of course, the slow learner on the job requirements might be terminated, and thus the organization would incur additional termination and replacement costs.

ESTIMATING THE TIMING OF BENEFITS AND COSTS

Once you have identified and valued the sources of benefits and costs associated with an investment in HRIS functionality, the next step of the analysis is to determine when in time each benefit and cost will be incurred during the entire HRIS project. Organizations use this information to estimate the cash outflow and inflows associated with investments. The timing of cash flows is particularly important when costs and benefits occur in different time periods and when the organization's cost of capital is relatively high. This information is critically important in the management of the entire HRIS project.

The task of assigning the benefits and costs to time periods can be accomplished by constructing a simple grid that lists benefit or cost items along one axis and future time periods on the other axis. The number of time periods required will depend on the expected useful life of the investment and the relevant length of time periods (usually years, but months or quarters may be used in some instances). The critical period for most HRIS investments is the first five years. Few organizations are likely to approve HRIS investments with longer payback periods. Furthermore, current rates of development of HRIS functionality and computing systems suggest that most HRIS investments may be functionally obsolete after five years.

The Role of Variance in Estimates

Since the estimates produced for benefit-cost analyses are necessarily based on forecasting future events and may also depend on events outside the control of management, actual outcomes are likely to deviate from those estimated. For example, one may expect an average reduction of 2 hours in transaction processing time. However, the actual amount of reduction will vary depending on the mix of transaction types, operator expertise, and other job requirements and could range from 105 to 135 minutes. *The primary estimate of interest is the overall average expectation.* However, particularly for indirect benefits, it is useful to develop expectations about the range and potential distribution of possible outcomes. Lower- and upper-bound estimates as well as deviations from the average (variance) for magnitude and value estimates are useful auxiliary information that can help convey expectations about potential variability in outcomes.

Variance estimates can be developed by each of the estimation methods described in Table 6.3. For direct estimation, HR and IT professionals could produce estimates of the range and likelihood of various outcome levels. In addition, multiple estimators could be used if two or more equally knowledgeable individuals exist. Each could be instructed to estimate a target value and upper and lower bounds for the estimated expectations, and these could then be averaged to develop overall estimates. Variance estimates for benchmark data from other organizations in the same industry are more difficult to acquire, since most sources only report averages and do not report variance data. In some instances, it may be possible to request the standard deviations associated with each benchmark value from other organizations. However, with internal analysis, variance estimates can be calculated from the archival records of existing HR or IT processes before and after implementation. In all instances, an estimate of the variance of outcomes could then be used to provide a range of the most likely outcomes. However, remember that, in the absence of compelling evidence to the contrary, the best estimate is the one you developed, and that should be the focus of your analysis.

AVOIDING COMMON PROBLEMS

It is not uncommon for HRIS BCA to include an extensive analysis of costs matched with a single source of benefits—typically, an estimate of direct cost reductions. Recognizing only direct cost reductions is problematic for two reasons. First, it ignores HR's more strategic role in improving organizational effectiveness. Online recruitment that results in hiring employees with higher potential and in developing and administering training programs through online tools, for example, is designed to enhance employee job performance and organizational effectiveness—not necessarily to reduce employee headcount. Ignoring these benefits can lead people to dramatically understate the actual value of HRIS investments.

A second problem is that, in many instances, items listed as direct cost reductions are actually indirect cost reductions. Time saved is a prime example. An HRIS will reduce the amount of time required to complete typical HR transactions, but these time savings do not result in actual reductions in overtime or headcount. In these instances, time saved is actually an indirect benefit. Its value depends on how individuals spend the extra time made available to them. As noted in Chapter 1, transactional activities deal mostly with day-to-day record keeping—for example, entering payroll information or employee status changes—and the administration of employee benefits. An HRIS that reduces the time on transactional activities would allow the HR employee to spend more time on traditional or transformational activities (see Chapter 1), both of which can assist the organization in meeting its strategic goals.

Incorrectly recognizing time saved as a direct cost reduction creates the wrong expectation among decision makers. This false expectation can lead to the incorrect perception that an investment did not succeed—no reduction in payroll expenses occurred—when, in fact, the benefits to the organization actually occurred in other forms. This point is illustrated in a BCA completed by the National Institute for Health's Center for Information Technology. This analysis, which does an exceptional job of cost analysis, includes only one source of benefit—employee time saved. In this example, investing in the new system was projected to reduce staff time required by 75%, resulting in a 53% ROI.

Admirably, this organization was required to conduct a postimplementation review within 18 months to examine actual versus estimated costs and benefits and to determine whether use of the new system should be continued. The postimplementation analysis revealed that time saved was only 50%, not 75%. As a result, instead of the expected 53% ROI, the revised ROI was only 6%. One can only wonder what might have happened if the postimplementation review indicated the amount of time saved had been only 45%. In that case, the BCA formulas would have shown a negative ROI. Would this organization have been forced to abandon this new system? Interestingly, in the postimplementation analysis, the evaluators pointed to other benefits to justify the continued use of the new system. However, since they were not included in the original analysis, bringing them into the postimplementation review may have been seen by some as inappropriate. Nevertheless, an indirect benefit, such as the improved employee morale that analysts found in the postimplementation evaluation, would be a powerful indication that the HRIS investment was worthwhile. In addition, employee morale has been directly linked to voluntary turnover, for which costs can be measured.

Third, be sure that value estimates assigned to time saved are reasonable. Many HRIS investments purport to save employee time, making it a common component of an HR technology BCA. When new HRIS functionality will save enough time to make it feasible to reduce the number of employees or reduce overtime expenses, time saved is a source of direct cost reduction. However, more often, HR technology saves time in smaller increments that do not permit direct savings. That is, the amount of time saved does not permit whole positions to be eliminated. In these circumstances, time saved is an indirect benefit. The value of the time saved depends on what value-generating activities employees engage in during the time made available to them. For example, if the implementation of self-service functionality reduces workload but does not lead to headcount reductions, the new functionality might still have tremendous organizational value if those saved hours are used to improve the effectiveness of recruitment efforts or some other value-generating activity, such as the development of a team-training program.

Time saved, though, may not always have value. Consider a situation in which an individual engages in an activity that requires 5 minutes every day, but the application of new HRIS functionality is estimated to cut this time from 5 minutes to 1 minute. What is the value of the 4 minutes saved each day? Generally, larger blocks of time are more easily employed in value-enhancing activities. Consider your own use of time during the day. Could you constructively employ an additional minute of time each day? In most cases, we already have several of these minutes in our schedule that, because of the ebb and flow of daily events, are difficult to use productively. Therefore, it is questionable whether most employees can consistently use short periods of time (i.e., blocks of less than 5 minutes, for instance) productively. Thus, it may be very difficult to generate value for HR technology that is expected to save time but does so in many small increments.

Obviously, knowledge of your organization's business, as noted earlier in this chapter, will be important in identifying potential benefits. Use your own knowledge, but enlist other knowledgeable professionals and managers in this process as well. Individuals in your organization who are currently responsible for HR functionality prior to implementation of the HRIS (i.e., staff engaged in recruiting) or who are downstream customers of these HR products or services are good resources to enlist to identify benefits. They can help fill in the gaps and highlight other sources of benefits that might not be clear to others. Vendors are a second resource. A review of the features and benefits cited by vendors in the relevant HRIS product space can also be used to identify potential sources of benefits. Vendors may also provide case studies that describe the experiences of companies that have implemented their products and the outcomes that were affected in those organizations. Using a combination of these sources can ensure a comprehensive list of the benefits to be gained when new HRIS functionality is developed.

PACKAGING THE ANALYSIS FOR DECISION MAKERS

When you have completed your analysis, you should have (1) data that identify each benefit and cost component examined; (2) estimates of the dollar magnitude of each, including upper and lower bounds; (3) estimates of when the organization will incur each cost and receive each benefit; and (4) documentation justifying each decision you made in developing these values. The importance of documentation has been emphasized in all previous chapters, especially Chapter 5, and will be reemphasized in Chapter 8. After steps 1 to 4 are completed, the next step is to package the analysis for decision makers in your organization. Obviously, this process involves "selling" the analysis to senior management so that it will not be overlooked or minimized. Managerial decision makers prefer well-organized and clear BCAs to help them make their investment decisions.

Packaging the analysis for consideration by decision makers includes deciding what data to include and how the data should be organized. This process should be done with the entire project management (PM) team, since the report must cover the entire HRIS project, not just the investment analysis. A table outlining the value and timing of costs and revenues is likely to be the central focus of the analysis. Some experts encourage limiting the number of sources of benefits presented to decision makers to simplify the presentation and the required justifications. This approach is satisfactory for small projects (e.g., a stand-alone applicant tracking system) but would be inappropriate for a complex HRIS project in which different sources of potential benefits highlight contingencies that may need to be managed during implementation to assure those benefits are captured.

Although being able to make your case on a single page is beneficial, there are several advantages in including all the cost and benefit components that influence the likely outcomes of the investment decision. First, this offers the most complete, best estimate of the value of the investment, thereby giving decision makers the best information to make an appropriate investment decision. Second, it provides the decision maker with a fuller understanding of the investment and of the impact of the investment on the organization. Particularly with respect to indirect benefits, contingent actions taken by managers are likely to influence the extent to which the estimated benefits are achieved. Making decision makers aware of these contingencies can help enlist their assistance in ensuring each investment's future success.

CONCLUSION

Accurately identifying and estimating the value of the benefits and costs of new HRIS functionality will play a critical role in HRIS investment decisions in the foreseeable future. A renewed interest in detailed investment analysis is healthy and should be embraced by analysts and decision makers. In addition to supporting improved investment decisions, detailed BCAs of HRIS investments are also likely to identify implementation contingencies and opportunities that can increase the chances for successful implementations. These analyses also provide the desired organizational targets against which to judge the effectiveness of an investment after implementation.

Summary

The central focus of this chapter has been estimating and understanding the cost effectiveness dynamics of new investments in HRIS, which are assessed by the completion of a benefit-cost analysis (BCA). The calculation of a BCA has become critical for any new investment by an organization, as BCAs are closely linked with strategic goals such as profitability and the survival of the organization. Without an appropriately constructed well-done BCA, managerial decision makers will be much less likely to approve expenditures for new HRIS investments, especially today. In the past, investments in an HRIS were primarily driven by a risk avoidance strategy or by cost reductions made possible by replacing paper-and-pencil or out-of-date systems. Today, organizations frequently rely on organizational enhancement strategies to justify the investment in new HRIS functionality. Organizational enhancement strategies highlight how a firm's effectiveness will be improved by the addition of a new or improved HRIS, as measured in a formal BCA by estimated increases in benefits (e.g., revenues) compared with estimated costs. This requires that we change our approach of cost justifying HRIS to account for these new types of benefits.

This chapter also addressed the importance of adopting an appropriate perspective on the BCA before any numbers are analyzed, and it provided guidelines for successful HRIS BCA (Table 6.1). An organizational enhancement strategy, one that examines both revenue enhancement and cost reduction, was shown to be the appropriate approach for conducting a BCA to justify an HRIS investment in today's organizations. Instructions on how to estimate direct and indirect costs and benefits were covered in detail, with a focus on creating a palatable BCA report for managerial decision makers. The various direct and indirect costs and benefits of an HRIS that go into the BCA have been discussed throughout the chapter, and several are listed in Table 6.2. Identifying the direct and indirect costs and benefits for a BCA must be extensive and complete. Without a comprehensive listing of direct and indirect costs and benefits, it will be impossible to calculate a correct BCA. After this comprehensive list is complete, the next step is to estimate the value of direct and indirect costs and benefits. AEC was examined as one method to assess the indirect benefits of employee time saved by an HRIS investment. This estimating task is done by the HRIS project team, and therefore it is critical that the project team have individuals who can provide significant input to the estimates. Finally, it was argued that in addition to a best estimate of the BCA, potential estimates of the variance in estimates should be used to gain insight into best- and worst-case scenarios. This chapter has provided examples of how to enumerate and then define the value of these estimates (Table 6.2 and Figure 6.1).

Also, the approaches used in the estimation of indirect benefits, as well as the other methods discussed in this chapter for estimating costs and benefits, should be used for the postimplementation evaluation of the HRIS. The three common problems that can occur in a BCA were covered: (1) an extensive analysis of costs matched with a single source of benefits, which typically, is an estimate of direct cost reductions; (2) the listing of items as direct cost reductions that are actually indirect cost reductions (which is a very frequent occurrence); and (3) an unreasonable estimate of the value assigned to time saved or of the effects of time saved on the organization, probably the most common error in developing a BCA. In addition, as recommended in the earlier chapters, the BCA should be documented carefully and completely, as it will be useful in both HRIS project management and HRIS implementation.

Key Terms

average employee contribution (AEC) 137

BCA guidelines 124

benchmarking 134

benefit-cost analysis (BCA) 122

benefit magnitude 133

direct benefits 128

direct costs 131

direct estimation [of benefits] 134

HRIS functionality 121

implementation costs 131

indirect benefits 129

indirect costs 131

internal assessment 135

internal rate of return (IRR) 127

organizational enhancement strategies 123

payback period 127

return on investment (ROI) 127

risk avoidance strategy 122

Discussion Questions

1. How has the use of HRIS evolved over the past 10 years in organizations, and how might this influence an organization's evaluations of additional investments in new or updated HRIS functionality?

2. Why is it important to estimate the benefits to be derived from new HRIS functionality before you estimate the costs? If costs were estimated first, how might this change the analysis?

3. Develop an argument for the implementation of an HRIS using a risk reduction strategy and an organizational enhancement strategy.

4. Organizations have traditionally used "employee time saved" as the primary source of benefits to justify HRIS and other types of information system investments. Why can this be problematic? Give several reasons and relate them to conducting a BCA.

5. How might an organization estimate the direct and indirect benefits of a new HRIS that decreases the time required by employees to complete transactions of the HR department through the implementation of employee self-service by creating employee portals (see Chapter 9) and allows HR employees to work on other projects such as talent management or online recruiting?

6. What makes indirect benefits so difficult to include in a BCA? What techniques might be used?

7. When should benchmarking be preferred to direct estimates of the magnitudes of benefits? When should direct estimates be preferred? Is it appropriate to use both?

8. Why does average employee contribution offer a better estimate of the contribution of individuals to an organization than total compensation (wages, incentives, and benefits)?

9. What are the factors you would have to use in calculating a benefit-cost ratio to support a decision to purchase a new HRIS when the organization already has an HRIS that was acquired 10 years ago? Be sure to mention the factors that would comprise the costs, direct and indirect, and the benefits, direct and indirect, of the current system versus the proposed system.

Case Study: Justifying an HRIS Investment at Investment Associates

Investment Associates, Inc. (IA)[3] started as a small firm in 2001 with four employees plus its owner, Jim Tower. The company specialized in providing financial investment and tax advice to its clients. Jim had brought a substantial number of clients from his private practice, which had become too large for him to handle by himself. His four employees included three colleagues who had some experience in financial investment advice and a administrative assistant. Jim and his three colleagues were all certified public accountants (CPAs), and a considerable portion of the company's business was in tax consultation and the completion of individual and corporate tax returns.

IA was quite successful and, by 2007, had added 42 new employees—financial and tax advisers and additional administrative staff, including an office manager, Marian Sweet. In addition to the office manager's supervisory tasks, Marian had to complete federal and state reports on the employees as required by law.[4] However, Marian was not trained in HRM, and she suggested to Jim that the company needed to hire someone with a background in HRM before they "got into trouble" with the government. Marian was particularly concerned about gender and racial discrimination but did not understand how to apply the provisions of the appropriate laws and guidelines.

In November 2007, IA hired Sylvia Wong, who had an undergraduate degree in psychology and four years' experience in HR. In addition, in December 2007, Jim was negotiating to purchase the financial consulting business of an old friend who was retiring. This purchase would mean the addition of 17 new employees in February or March 2008. Sylvia met with Jim in mid-January 2008 to discuss the growing burden of employee reports and payroll processing, all of which were currently being done using a paper-based HR system. She advised Jim that the company needed an HRIS to process employee records and complete the required government reports. As an example, she stated that, because she had to search through paper copies of all employee files, it took her a full week to complete the Equal Employment Opportunity Report (EEO-1)[5] required by the federal government. Furthermore, based on this report, it appeared that the company could have problems in terms of compliance with several federal laws. She suggested that the company purchase an HRIS to assist with company record keeping and the production of required reports.

Since the company had been using computer-based applications for financial analysis and tax reporting, Jim thought that Sylvia's suggestion to computerize employee records was a good one. However, given his financial background, he wanted Sylvia to develop a business case, including a benefit-cost analysis, for the purchase of an HRIS.

Your task is to help Sylvia justify the purchase of an HRIS.

Case Study Questions

1. What approaches to justifying this investment might Sylvia consider?

2. What are some of the costs and benefits involved in this investment in an HRIS? Which would you be sure to include in your BCA of this project and why?

3. Explain how to estimate costs and benefits, both direct and indirect, in terms that Jim will understand. (Remember, Jim always has his eye on the "bottom line.")

4. Explain how to calculate a BCA to justify the HRIS project. Would you use cost reduction or organizational enhancement (or both) as a strategy for justifying the purchase?

5. What are the three common problems that could occur in your BCA for an HRIS? How would you avoid them?

6. What are some of the ways you can use the HR metrics that would be available after the implementation of an HRIS to justify its purchase?

7. Finally, and most important, explain how variance estimates that can be generated for a BCA would be useful to Jim in the management of his company.

HUMAN RESOURCE INFORMATION SYSTEMS APPLICATIONS

PART III

7

HR ADMINISTRATION AND HRIS

Linda C. Isenhour and Christopher J. Hartwell

EDITORS' NOTE

This chapter begins the third section of the text and introduces the concepts of electronic human resource management (eHRM) more fully. Specifically, it discusses how an HRIS can support HR administrative functioning. It is appropriate to begin a discussion of the eHRM chapters with an introduction to HR administration. The first six chapters of this book explained how to build an HRIS, so, in a sense, these chapters were the building blocks for the HRIS "house." Now the filling of the house begins. In this chapter, the authors introduce how an HRIS can help HR fulfill its administrative role and how it can be used to manage employee data and support required government reporting.

The chapter starts with a discussion of the technology underlying HRIS and its role in supporting data management, data sharing, and employee data privacy. The chapter also introduces the concepts of self-service and discusses how having employees and managers manage their own personal data can be advantageous for the firm. However, any approach to managing data has risks, which are also discussed. The chapter also discusses how and when HR and/or HRIS outsourcing may be appropriate. Finally, the use of an HRIS is also critical for government reporting and compliance with laws and guidelines. Therefore, the chapter closes with a discussion of how an HRIS can support organizations as they supply data in support of a number of these government regulations and laws.

CHAPTER OBJECTIVES

After completing this chapter, you should be able to

- Discuss the complexity of HR administration and the advantages of an HRIS over a "paper-and-pencil" HR operation

- Discuss the advantages of having a service-oriented architecture (SOA) for the HRIS

- Differentiate among the four structural approaches to HR administration service delivery (e.g., self-service portals, shared-service centers, human resource outsourcing, and offshoring)

- Discuss the advantages and disadvantages of each of the four structural approaches to HR administration

- Understand how legal compliance with government mandates is an important part of HRIS functionality and how these mandates add to the complexity of an HRIS in both domestic and multinational organizations

- Discuss the elements important to successful measurement of the strategic alignment of the HR balanced scorecard and how this alignment is related to the strategic alignment of an organization

HRIS IN ACTION

In 2019, Procter & Gamble (P&G) had 97,000 employees in 70 countries. Identifying common measures, improving employee service, and reducing HR administrative costs continued to be strategic imperatives for this global consumer products company committed to ensuring its principles: "Everyone Valued, Everyone Included, Everyone Performing at Their Peak" (Procter & Gamble, 2011; 2019).

Today, the human resource managers at P&G continue to consider a variety of solutions to meet their strategic goals. Should they maintain their decentralized global operation in HRM and use technology such as Internet service portals to improve efficiency? Would the trend toward shared-services centers (SSCs) be better for centralizing operations? How will decisions about outsourcing selected human resource functions be affected by cloud and mobile computing advances? With so many countries and governmental regulations involved, how can P&G achieve sufficient standardization through an HRIS to gain increased savings and still meet its varied responsibilities to such diverse entities? Will its internal customers view the move from decentralized to centralized shared services as meeting their needs? How will such changes be measured from an internal customer satisfaction perspective? Which measures for the various administrative approaches will best align the HR functions with the P&G balanced scorecard strategic goals and objectives?

These are common HRM problems faced by businesses today. This chapter provides a framework to help answer such questions.

INTRODUCTION

Human resources isn't a thing we do. It's the thing that runs our business.

—Steve Wynn

Human resource management (HRM) administration deals with the efficient performance of the transactional activities introduced in Chapter 1. Record keeping, updating policy and informational materials for a self-service portal, generating and disseminating internal reports, complying with governmentally mandated external reporting, and administering labor contracts are all examples of HRM administration associated with managing an organization's workforce. Approximately 65% to 75% of all HR activities are transactional (Wright, McMahan, Snell, & Gerhart, 1998). Human resource information systems (HRIS) are vital tools in managing these increasingly complex transactional requirements. For this reason, it is crucial that the employee record contains accurate and timely data (Kavanagh, Gueutal, & Tannenbaum, 1990; Walker, 1982). The employee database is the repository for all relevant employee information and must be created prior to any other modules (e.g., recruiting and applicant tracking). The approaches and technological techniques described in this chapter ensure that the database, once initially built, remains accurate and up to date.

THE HRIS ENVIRONMENT AND OTHER ASPECTS OF HR ADMINISTRATION

HRIS can assist managers charged with improving the efficiency of HR administration by reducing costs, enhancing the reliability of reporting, improving service to internal customers, and facilitating strategic goal achievement. Information technology facilitates administration in multiple ways. First, an HRIS can help improve data accuracy by (1) reducing the need for multiple inputs, (2) eliminating redundancies in data, and (3) reducing the opportunity for human input errors and associated corrections. In addition, an HRIS, through *relational databases*, speeds the process of building reports with simple query capabilities. Moreover, an HRIS, if properly designed for flexibility, can support differences in reporting mandated by global governmental jurisdictions. Finally, a properly designed HRIS permits secure global distribution of data while providing the desired privacy for employee data, facilitating consideration of alternative methods of consolidating, and improving services to internal customers (Ceriello, 1991; Gueutal & Stone, 2005; Kavanagh, Gueutal, & Tannenbaum, 1990; Osle & Cooper, 2003; Walker, 1982, 1993, 2001).

Administrative issues associated with specific HRM functions as part of the development and implementation of an HRIS have been briefly mentioned in earlier chapters (e.g., recruiting, training, compensating) and will be discussed in more detail in later chapters. However, HR managers face a variety of other administrative requirements in the rapidly evolving HRIS era. The HRM administrative issues highlighted in this chapter include (1) organizational approaches for providing HR in a global economy (i.e., self-service portals, SSCs, outsourcing, offshoring); (2) compliance mandates for record maintenance and report requirements (e.g., **Employer Information Report EEO-1 and Component 2**), which are associated both with government laws in the United States (e.g., **Occupational Safety and Health Act [OSHA]**) and with the labor laws of other countries; and (3) the measurement of HRM contributions to an organization's strategic goals via a balanced scorecard.

HRM ADMINISTRATION AND ORGANIZING APPROACHES

Historically, HR managers operated as adjunct staff to organizations, overseeing the daily transactions associated with hiring, paying, or training employees and reporting on employee issues as required by managers in organizations. As organizations grew more complex, administering these daily transactions also grew more complex. The introduction of mechanization to handle payroll signaled the changing future of HR administration; technology would play an increasingly important role in managing daily employee transactions (Walker, 1982, 1993, 2001).

Today, HRIS capabilities offer considerable support for daily HR transactions and make it possible to move beyond the limited administrative approaches available to the HR managers of the 1950s (PricewaterhouseCoopers, 2006). Modern HR professionals use technology to more effectively support administrative activities and reduce organizational costs while improving data accuracy, employee productivity, and customer service (Bender, 2001; Ulrich, 1997). For example, a recent survey of 1,200 companies worldwide indicated that they planned to increase the use of HR administrative technology to improve one or more of the following: recruiting (25%), onboarding (17%), core HR/TM profile (14%), performance (13%), as well as ESS (9%) and MSS (8%; Sierra-Cedar, 2016). By facilitating more efficient transactional HR processes and allowing for easier access to quantifiable data, HR professionals are able to focus more on adding strategic value to the organization (Marler & Parry, 2016). Moreover, global companies reported that, even with challenging economic conditions, they anticipated growing their technology commitment for strategic human capital talent management, as well as for workforce management, service delivery, and business intelligence. The next section briefly describes the enabling architecture that allows HR administrators to leverage HRIS technology.

Service-Oriented Architecture and eXtensible Markup Language

Service-oriented architecture (SOA) "is a paradigm for organizing and utilizing distributed [computing] capabilities that may be under the control of different ownership domains . . . providing a uniform means to offer, discover, interact with, and use capabilities to produce desired [business] effects" (Organization for the Advancement of Structured Information Systems [OASIS], 2006, p. 8). It is focused on providing overall service that is well defined, self-contained, and context and platform independent; in other words, it is focused on adding value to the organization's business purpose rather than simply adding technological value. In effect, SOA is a collection of internal and external services that can communicate with each other by point-to-point data exchange or through coordination among different services to achieve a business purpose. Figure 7.1 demonstrates the business-driven SOA process (Marks & Bell, 2006).

For example, an HR administration manager in the United States who needs to generate the government-mandated, annual EEO-1 and Component 2 reports cares little about where

FIGURE 7.1   ■   SOA Business-Modeling Process

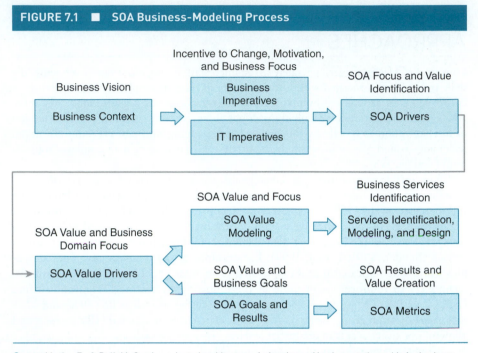

Source: Marks, E., & Bell, M. *Service-oriented architecture: A planning and implementation guide for business and technology.* Wiley, 2006.

the information is stored or which applications, servers, communications technologies, or programming languages are used. Rather, the manager wants easy access to the myriad data necessary to complete the report in a timely manner. SOA focuses on fulfilling that need, moving away from a point-to-point perspective (e.g., HR linked to a single EEO database) to a market perspective of services, reusing data and applications from multiple sources as long as the required service is provided. The principles of SOA include loose coupling, flexibility, autonomy, standards-based computing, reusability, modularity, and services discoverability and optimization. The architectural benefits of SOA include (Campbell & Mohun, 2007).

- IT consolidation opportunities and standards-based integration, using a standards-based approach to integration for IT systems that are very complex and heterogeneous to reduce both cost and complexity over time;

- faster implementation and change management through reuse, modeling, and composite development; and

- improved alignment of business processes and IT implementation.

SOA is enhanced by eXtensible Markup Language (XML). XML combines text and other information about the text, such as its structure, allowing data sharing across different information systems via the Internet. XML underpins SOA such that SOA is ineffective without it. Specifically, XML improves interface technology through platform independence and protocols, such as security and transactions, previously unavailable in interfaces (Erl, 2005). Platform independence refers to software that does not rely on any special features of any single platform (e.g., Windows, UNIX) or, if it does, handles those special features such that it can deal with multiple platforms.

Advantages of XML-Enhanced SOA

Although HR professionals engaged in administration may not make final decisions about the information technology described previously, they need to recognize the benefits associated with having such architecture. For example, Schwartz (2003) reported that Oracle's introduction of HR-XML standards would reduce the requirement to input applicant resumes manually. Therefore, today's use of HR portals for job application receipt and processing, including resume submission, is related directly to this technology. Thus, HRIS capabilities are leveraged dramatically by SOA and XML such that:

- security is improved—this is especially important because of the privacy protection issues associated with HR data and applications;

- performance is enhanced—this aids in reducing transaction costs and increasing customer satisfaction;

- auditing capabilities are added—this supports the growing demand to demonstrate compliance with corporate quality and policy mandates;

- change capabilities are enhanced—this improves reaction time to better meet business-driven change requirements; and

- alternative HR administration structures (e.g., self-service portals, SSCs, outsourcing) are facilitated—this encourages HR managers to consider multiple approaches to meeting the HR administration goals of cost reduction and service improvement (Lublinsky, 2007; Walker, 2001).

The remainder of this section will focus on the four structural approaches to HR administration facilitated by HRIS technology. Each has opened paths to increased efficiency and effectiveness, improved service, and cost controls, possibilities unimagined by HR professionals a decade ago. The four HR administrative approaches—self-service portals, shared-service centers, outsourcing, and offshoring—presented in this chapter are shown in Figure 7.2.

- The **self-service portal** is an electronic access point to an organization's HRM information, such as company policies, benefits schedules, an individual's payroll data, or other records; access may be onsite or remote, and through computers, tablets, or other mobile devices.

- A **shared-service center (SSC)** is a technology-enabled HRM group focused on value creation by providing excellent service to internal customers while reducing costs through increased efficiency and continuous improvement.

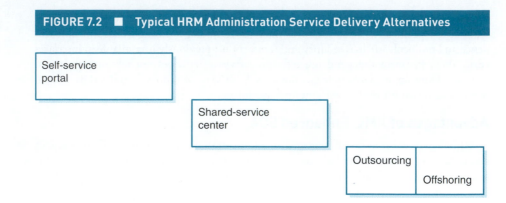

FIGURE 7.2 ■ Typical HRM Administration Service Delivery Alternatives

- **Human resources outsourcing (HRO)** is the practice of contracting with vendors to perform HR services and activities.

- **Offshoring** is an extension of outsourcing that involves contracting with vendors outside a nation's boundaries to effect additional cost savings or gain other benefits over domestic outsourcing alone.

Following a discussion of the theories underpinning these approaches to HR administration, the purpose, advantages, and disadvantages of each will be highlighted. Next, the chapter will examine the different ways in which each alternative approach facilitates the HR administrative reporting mandated by government entities. The chapter concludes with a discussion of how each administrative alternative can be measured to demonstrate the value-added nature of efficient, effective HR administrative functions in support of an organization's strategic goals.

Theory and HR Administration

Barney (1991, 2001) delineated the **resource-based view** of organizations, describing organizations as bundles of resources, identified as physical capital, organizational capital, and human capital. *Physical capital* includes an organization's technology, geographic locations, physical assets (e.g., plants, money), and access to raw material. *Organizational capital* includes its formal reporting structure, its coordinating, planning, and organizing systems, and its internal and external group relationships. *Human capital* includes the experience, capabilities, relationships, and insights of individual employees. Taken together, these resources are combined and managed to determine an organization's *opportunity* to win *sustainable competitive advantage* in the marketplace.

To achieve **sustainable competitive advantage**, a firm's resources, when compared with those of its competitors, must be *valuable, rare, difficult to imitate, and invulnerable to substitutes.* Based on this theory, then, it is likely that innovative combinations of technology (physical capital), organizing systems (organizational capital), and strategic individual knowledge, skills, and abilities may serve to give an organization a strategic position in its marketplace. Thus, alternative HR administrative approaches seek to combine HR technology (e.g., HRIS and Internet) with organizing systems (e.g., self-service portals) and strategic HR knowledge, skills, and abilities (e.g., compensation expertise) to leverage a specific firm's competitive position. It is important to note that this theory suggests that *each* firm in an industry is likely to acquire resources such as human talent to support its *unique* combinations based on its **strategic choices**; it is this unique combination that leads to sustainable competitive advantage. *Merely benchmarking or following trends is unlikely to lead to sustainable competitive positioning for a firm!*

For example, Walmart gained a substantial competitive advantage with its innovative combination of "just-in-time" supply chain management and proprietary technology. This approach linked each Walmart store directly to its suppliers such that the supplier was notified electronically when a product was sold; when a store's predetermined inventory level was reached, the supplier shipped replacement items without any interaction with store managers. This resulted in significant cost savings and improved service with fewer employees. For a time, it appeared that this innovation might lead to a sustainable competitive advantage. However, competitors were able to *imitate* the management supply chain techniques and even improve on the technology to negate the advantage. Walmart's innovation did lead to an advance for the entire industry but did not provide a sustainable advantage for the firm because the innovation could be imitated. Thus, organizations looking to achieve sustainable competitive advantage are more likely to reach that goal through *strategic and unique* combinations of physical, organizational, and human capital than by relying on any one resource.

Transaction cost theory (Coase, 1937; Williamson, 1975) suggests that organizations can choose to purchase the goods and services they need in the competitive marketplace or make those goods and services internally. *Transaction costs* are the expenses associated with an economic transaction, whether internal or external. Managers can compare the "transaction costs" required to purchase products or services, such as contract administration, licenses, and delivery services, from external providers with those incurred in providing the same product or service internally by, for example, using additional personnel, retraining employees, or purchasing hardware and software. Thus, managers can make optimum economic decisions for their organizations. This decision is the classic "make or buy" economic choice facing rational economic actors. Behaving rationally, organizations would make such decisions based on total costs, choosing to "buy" from external providers when total costs were lower and products or services were readily available and choosing to "make" what was needed internally when total costs from external sources were higher or products or services were not readily available. Of course, this example assumes that the make or buy benefits of either choice are straightforward and equal. Typically, however, such decisions are more complex; thus, a benefit-cost analysis should be completed to determine if the organization should make or buy. For example, a small business might elect to buy HR compensation and payroll services from an external provider rather than decide to make its own HR compensation program, which would require purchasing hardware and HRIS software and adding compensation specialists.

General Motors (GM) provides an example of this theory. Amid market pressure to reduce costs as competitors increased their market share at GM's expense, GM elected to divest itself of its fully integrated parts manufacturing functions. GM managers found that "transaction costs" would be reduced if the company standardized automobile parts and purchased them from multiple external providers rather than continuing to manufacture them internally. Transaction costs associated with internal parts production were increasing rapidly in terms of employees' wages, salaries, and benefits and the ongoing maintenance of aging production plants. Thus,

GM spun off its Delphi unit as an independent company. Although Delphi continued to sell to GM, GM no longer relied exclusively on the newly independent company for parts, helping reduce GM's overall corporate costs. Increasing internal transaction costs, coupled with a robust external parts production market, determined GM's strategic "make or buy" choice.

Both resource-based and transaction cost theories can explain the different choices organizations make in their preferences for HR administration approaches. For example, the increasing internal transaction costs of recruiting and hiring employees may lead to the search for an external vendor who specializes in the recruitment and selection of new employees. Organizations may then decide to compare those internal transaction costs and benefits with external transaction costs and benefits from the specialized recruitment and selection providers, leading to outsourcing. Alternatively, strategic concerns about the security of having external providers inadvertently "share" crucial talent-positioning information with competitors, coupled with the decreasing costs of technology, might lead an organization to focus on internal innovation involving physical and organizational resources (e.g., self-service portals coupled with SSCs) to reduce transaction costs, while increasing spending on strategic talent management issues (e.g., hiring, development) to achieve a sustainable competitive position in its industry. Keep these theoretical perspectives in mind as we examine each of the HR administration approaches.

Self-Service Portals and HRIS

The first structural approach to HR administration (Figure 7.2), **employee self-service (ESS)** HR portals, provides an electronic means for a company's employees to access its HR services and information. Such portals provide a single sign-on capability for employees, who can individually complete transactions for their personal data. ESS portals can range from simple intranet websites that allow employees to access static HR policies, such as safety requirements, to sophisticated Internet websites that allow employees to access and change their individual records. For example, adding a new child to an employee's medical benefits can be accomplished anywhere, anytime, and with any type of device (e.g., desktop or mobile) with ESS portals. A sample screenshot of an ESS screen for an address change is found in Figure 7.3, and a partial list of information and services commonly available via ESS portals is given in Table 7.1.

In addition to providing an interface for current employees, ESS portals are also available to prospective employees. For example, individuals who have applied for jobs online through an employer's recruiting website have accessed the ESS portal to complete the application and forward their resumes (Anheier & Doherty, 2001; Gueutal & Falbe, 2005; Walker, 2001). The design of these ESS recruitment portals is particularly important, because their usability can impact the quality and quantity of applicants (Williamson, Lepak, & King, 2003).

Manager self-service (MSS) portals are prevalent in organizations as well. MSS portals are specialized versions of ESS portals designed to allow managers to view extensive information about their subordinates and perform many administrative tasks electronically, including traditional HR functions. For example, in typical MSS applications, managers can complete job requisitions and view resumes of prospective applicants. In addition, managers can view **performance appraisals**, subordinate salaries, productivity, and training histories, and model annual salary increases. However, MSS is not limited to HR functions and may also include budgeting and tracking, reporting, and staff policy and procedure development (Gueutal & Falbe, 2005; Walker, 2001). For example, SAP modules for HR organizations may also include specified employee productivity data used by managers in completing employee evaluations.

FIGURE 7.3 ■ Sample Employee Self-Service Screen

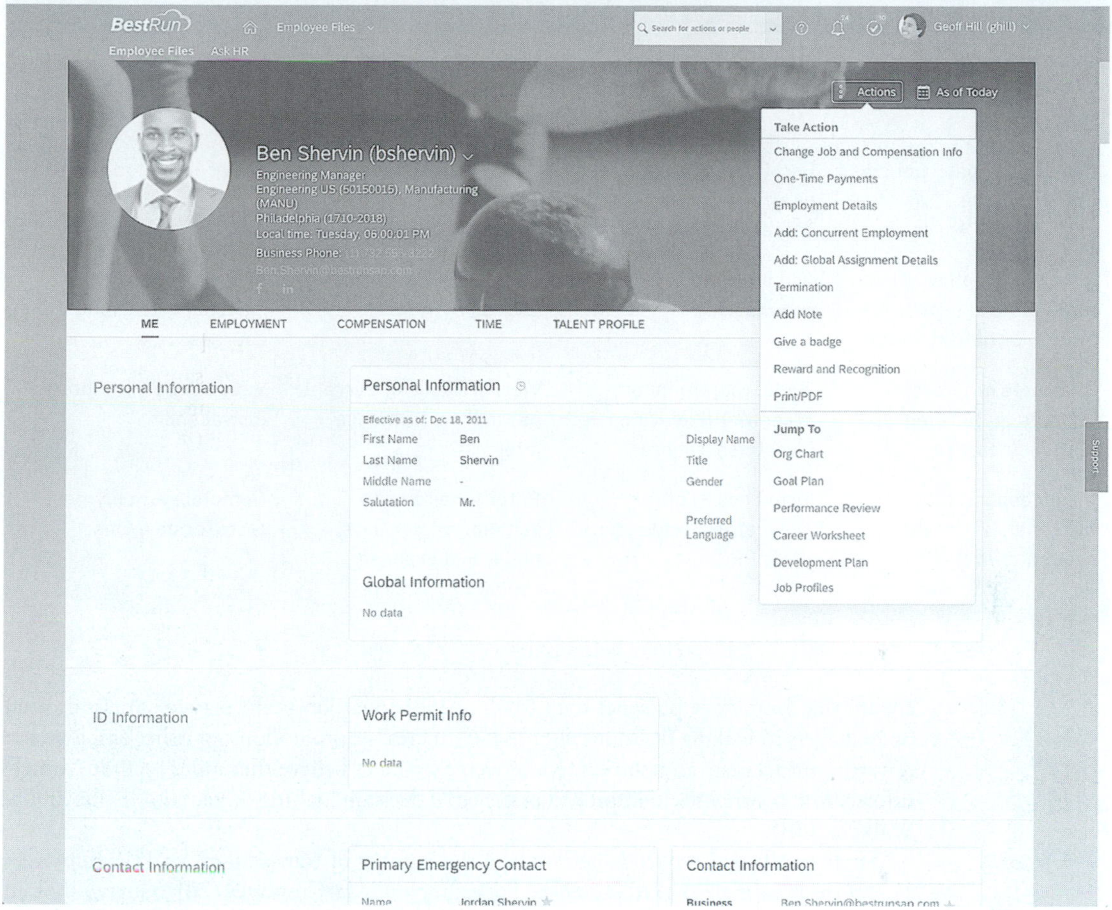

Source: © SuccessFactors, Inc. All Rights Reserved

Advantages of Self-Service Portals for HR Administration

Self-service portals provide several advantages for achieving HR administration goals, including (1) improved speed and quality of service to employees and managers and (2) simplified routine inquiries and changes. Reducing the number of inquiry transactions requiring direct HR staff involvement helps keep information current. For example, with self-service, changes in the doctors and hospitals allowed for each medical plan or status reports on the hiring of a new employee are more likely to be entered into the system as required. Self-service portals also enhance employee satisfaction by permitting employees to control when and where such access activities occur, empowering employees, increasing their productivity, especially for those who travel frequently, and offering privacy for those who prefer to handle such matters without the presence of coworkers. In addition, self-service portals facilitate easy, increased access to HR information, helping employees

TABLE 7.1 ■ Sample Employee Self-Service (ESS) Functionality

Communications	Benefits Services	Personal Data	Development
Review company communications	Research and view plan rules and requirements	Update emergency contact, address, telephone information	Enroll in training courses
Access company policies or procedures	Enroll in cafeteria-style programs (medical, dental, insurance)	Correct errors in personal data (degree, graduation date)	View completed training
Access HR policy manuals and e-mail inquiry or help request	Add or delete dependents	Change W-4 withholding forms	Access internal or external e-learning courses
Complete employee surveys or 360-degree feedback data	Model retirement or access 401(k) savings investment records	View previous or current pay and performance information	View or apply for internal job vacancies
View/respond to personal information requests from HR	Model health plan alternatives' costs (e.g., HMO, PPO)	Enter time reports, vacation or sick days, and travel expense reports	Complete employment tests for new jobs

ensure that important personal data (such as individual job performance appraisals used by managers in making decisions about salary increases, promotions, or other employment rewards) are accurate and current. Moreover, executives believe that more accurate, timely information contributes to improved managerial decision making (Gueutal & Falbe, 2005; Walker, 2001).

Finally, self-service portals help reduce the number of transactions for HR employees and, correspondingly, overall HR costs. For example, CedarCrestone's (2012) survey showed that companies with 500 to 10,000 employees reported that those firms with minimal HR technology served an average of 93 employees per HR staff member. By comparison, organizations with ESS portals served an average of 99 employees per HR staff member, whereas those with MSS portals served an average of 118 employees per HR staff member. Organizations can realize cost savings of 67% to 99% on tasks such as changing employee information, providing current pay and benefit statements, and posting of jobs (Gueutal & Falbe, 2005). Such savings relieve HR specialists of routine transactional work and allow them to focus more on both the traditional and transformational strategic activities described in Chapter 1.

Disadvantages of Self-Service Portals for HR Administration

Although HR administrators can gain advantages from deploying self-service portals, they are also faced with multiple disadvantages. Permitting employees to access company data through self-service portals may increase the possibility of security breaches and the associated negative outcomes, like identity theft, for affected employees. However, newer security measures, such as two-stage sign-in and account verification (using a phone, text code, etc.) may somewhat lessen this risk. Employees are concerned that even having their data in a company's HRIS can lead to misuse of such information by others in the organization and may feel their privacy is invaded when organizations fail to limit access to personal data housed in HRIS (Phillips, Isenhour, & Stone, 2008). For example, managers may learn negative information (e.g., that employees have medical disabilities) through MSS portal access that would have been unavailable in a paper record system. Even the inadvertent use or sharing of such information may preclude training or promotional opportunities for employees. Misuse of this personal information in this manner can constitute a violation of labor laws such as the **Americans with Disabilities Act (ADA)** in the United States. Privacy and security issues will be discussed in more detail later in this chapter.

In addition to security issues, HR administrators may find that unions and managers resist using the self-service portals. In particular, unions may argue that employees are "doing HR work" when they enter data and make changes online via an ESS portal. Union members who perform such transactions on their own time may request overtime pay for completing such functions or may choose to do such functions at work, thus reducing productivity. Managers may also resent having to do work that previously was handled completely by HR staff, particularly when such work involved calling the staff members rather than completing forms. For example, managers may have had relationships with HR staff that permitted the managers to bypass established procedures for requesting a new hire. Thus, using MSS portals would not only require more actual work for the managers but also enforce standardized interfaces that might lead managers to perceive a reduction in their status and power in the organization. Accordingly, HR managers should recognize and take action to ameliorate such perceptions and concerns as part of the project management planning and implementation process for an HRIS.

Shared-Service Centers and HRIS

The second structural approach to HR administration, shared-service centers (SSCs), generally appeared in response to the increasing globalization of competitive markets occasioned by the proliferation of multinational enterprises (MNEs). To compete successfully, organizations were pressured to reduce costs through the consolidation of administrative transactions while still providing excellent service. Such a challenge involved balancing the desire for control inherent in centralized administrative structures and the desire for flexibility inherent in decentralized administrative structures—a constant organizational conflict within large and expanding corporations (Lucenko, 1998; Quinn, Cooke, & Kris, 2000; von Simson, 1990). Over time, many organizations have chosen SSCs as the structural solution to that pressure.

> **Shared services** is a collaborative strategy whereby [one or more] staff functions of a firm are concentrated in a semi-autonomous organization and managed like a business unit . . . to promote greater efficiency, value generation and improved service for internal customers. (Goh, Prakash, & Yeo, 2007, p. 252)

PricewaterhouseCoopers (2016) emphasizes the increasing global importance of SSCs; some organizations have described them as "centers of excellence" (Bender, 2001). Figure 7.4 illustrates that SSCs include HR in 66% of manufacturing and 53% of service companies (Powell, 2004).

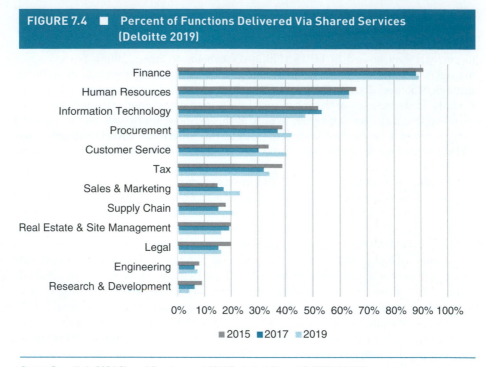

FIGURE 7.4 ■ Percent of Functions Delivered Via Shared Services (Deloitte 2019)

Source: Powell, A. 2004 Shared Services and CRM Technical Report E-0005-004RR.

Powell (2004, p. 6) identified the following common elements of SSCs:

- Centralizing or decentralizing of business processes

- Using economies of scale to reduce unit costs

- Developing customer relationship models (CRMs) to better meet the needs of customers

- Concentrating on cost reduction to enhance competitive positioning

- Deploying quality tools to ensure continuous process improvement

To be successful, a shared-service center involving HR, for example, must view itself as an independent business unit offering products (e.g., HR reports), which it must "sell" to its customers at a price (internal transaction cost) they are willing to pay. These internal customers are managers in different business units such as operations and marketing. If the HR function is unsuccessful in reducing costs, providing desirable services, and adding value, it may find itself "outsourced" by business unit managers who perceive that they can get better service and value from an external provider. To demonstrate added value to the organization, the SSC should *establish measures* that demonstrate customer satisfaction levels, productivity, cost controls, and quality. Such measures are necessary to allow internal customers to assess the value of the consolidated unit and to facilitate continuous improvement by SSC managers.

Accenture (2007) outlined several principles to embrace when considering the use of SSCs:

- Establish a "global good" vision for the SSC that includes its definition and benefits to ensure that business units "losing" functions are willing to make the commitment to transfer their work.

- Identify leaders, in all the affected groups, to sponsor the SSC vision, promote the center's value to the organization, and serve as responsible change agents.

- Support transparency regarding who (e.g., affected employees), what (e.g., which functions), when (e.g., transition plans), and where (e.g., location of the new center). This openness is essential to building the trust needed to initiate and maintain the center's effectiveness.

- Conduct initial and ongoing customer "values and requirements" meetings to build trust, establish performance and service expectations, and solve problems. Implementing jointly acceptable measures facilitates SSC success and internal customer satisfaction.

- Focus on viewing the SSC's processes in the context of the overall business functions. Examine the process behind each function from "end to end." Understanding the context of all processes in each function encourages the recognition of the interdependencies inherent in the SSC concept and bolsters the value-creating goal of SSCs.

Advantages of Shared-Service Centers for HR Administration

Advantages of SSCs for HR administration (Boglind, Hallsten, & Thilander, 2011; Robinson & Robinson, 2005; Ulrich, 1997; Walker, 2001) include (1) permitting HR administration managers to focus on delivering the timely, high-quality transactions necessary to fulfill corporate requirements, such as mandated governmental reporting, and (2) removing the artificial barriers inherent in the generalist–specialist continuum common in HR organizations, smoothing work and communication processes. This is particularly important for multinationals, which have to respond to the labor laws of multiple countries.

Combining such transactional responsibilities into a single business unit encourages the unit to focus on customer satisfaction with specific user interactions, such as responses to employee questions or requests for assistance. This frees specialists to focus on more strategic activities. SSCs also encourage the efficiency and standardization necessary to support strategic cost-control goals by consolidating individuals responsible for transactions, providing organizations with greater motivation to redesign procedures and create more effective ones. Finally, such centers facilitate development of the measures of efficiency, quality, and customer responsiveness that are necessary to demonstrate appropriate contributions to strategic goals.

Disadvantages of Shared-Service Centers for HR Managers

Although there are advantages to using SSCs, there are also some pitfalls to recognize as well. Frequently, organizations combine multiple, unrelated shared services into a combined business unit. Depending on the nature of such functions, the synergies needed to consolidate and improve processes may be less prevalent. For example, combining vehicle fleet management and HR transactions may offer few synergies. Leaders of such units may be stretched as they seek to unify and manage diverse functions. However, careful development of the mission and appropriate selection of the leaders of such units can overcome this problem by establishing a shared mindset among those involved (Walker, 2001).

In addition, creating SSCs may lead to unanticipated power shifts in organizations. For example, combining financial and HR transactions in a single center may lead to reduced emphasis on HR transactions, since business managers are especially concerned with the budget reporting associated with financial transactions. Again, establishing an effective mission and overarching goals for the center can forestall such power shifts (Cooke, 2006; Ulrich, 1997).

Finally, SSCs can lead to depersonalization. For example, line managers, accustomed to personal contact with HR professionals, may feel isolated when handling transactions through self-service portals. Similarly, they may feel abandoned when traditional communication patterns are disrupted because specialists have been consolidated in SSCs. Because such units are concerned with efficiency and cost controls, individuals working in them can become more involved with the technology with which they work and less involved with others who are engaged in the day-to-day aspects of the business (Ulrich, 1997).

Outsourcing and HRIS

The third approach to HR administration, outsourcing, is the practice of contracting with vendors to perform one or more HR services and activities. This has been described as the HR version of the make-buy decision described earlier (Greer, Youngblood, & Gray, 1999). In organizations where strategic human capital management is practiced, outsourcing is a strategic decision made by senior executives, including HRM leaders. However, when human capital management is viewed as primarily administrative, HRM leaders may not be included in outsourcing decisions (Delmotte, 2008, Seth & Sethi, 2011). Outsourcing is not new in HR administration. For example, Automatic Data Processing, Inc. (ADP) moved quickly in 1945 to offer its expertise in payroll and tax calculations to businesses facing increasingly complex employee income tax and withholding calculations (Dominguez, 2006). Nonetheless, few would have predicted the recent explosion in specialized organizations capable of providing a few or all of an organization's HR functions (Hewitt, 2005). According to the 2012 KPMG Institutes' outsourcing survey, 31% of participating global firms viewed HR as a top functional area for outsourcing. In addition, 40% of those surveyed were in the process of coordinating new global sources for outsourcing some HR functions (KPMG Institutes, 2012).

HR outsourcing (HRO) firms are hardly uniform. There are many different types of providers, reflecting the diverse needs of organizations. HRO firms provided HR services for 3.3 million employees in North America (Everest Research Institute, 2007). For example, the Everest Group (2016) has identified 11 providers who specialize in one of the fastest-growing HRO specialties: benefits administration outsourcing (BAO). These included ADP, Bswift, Businesssolver, and Willis Towers Watson, who, domestically and globally, represent 75% of the market.

Outsourcing contracts should include specific pricing agreements (e.g., flat or fixed-fee-per process or per employee served, unit prices per transaction levels, hourly and overtime rates, revenue sharing, risk-reward sharing, failure penalties), expected performance and associated measures (e.g., transaction quality standards, error rates, system availability and downtime, customer satisfaction levels, hours of operation), and terms and conditions (e.g., start and end dates, extensions permitted, termination agreements, dispute resolution procedures, audit procedures). Obviously, HR administration managers would require significant assistance from multiple groups such as the legal, operations, and information systems departments within the organization to establish and monitor the contract, ensuring that the organization is adequately protected from incompetent or unethical outsourcing providers. In addition, HR professionals need to develop skills in contract management to ensure that strategic goals associated with the outsourcing are achieved.

Reasons Organizations Pursue HR Outsourcing (HRO)

HR administration managers elect to pursue HRO for multiple reasons (Keebler, 2001). Weatherly (2005) suggests that managers may pursue discrete, multiprocess, or total-process HRO. For example, some organizations outsource only discrete or selected functions, pursuing **discrete HRO** through niche, third-party providers. This outsourcing involves having specialized external firms deal only with a particular HR function. External HR recruiting firms, for example, fall into this category. Such an approach is common in smaller organizations with limited numbers of HR professionals or in larger organizations with few, sporadic recruiting requirements. Also included in this category is the outsourcing of parts of various HR functions. For example, even organizations with large, effective recruiting staffs may elect to outsource executive or specialty recruitment functions (e.g., recruiting for multilingual positions) to external search firms that have unique expertise. Similarly, organizations may outsource only annual benefits enrollment, flexible spending accounts (FSA) administration, or payroll administration.

Generally, the outsourcing of discrete HR functions is attractive for two reasons. First, discrete HRO can achieve cost savings by eliminating the company's need to hire highly specialized HR professionals (e.g., executive recruiters) or those with the HRIS expertise necessary to perform infrequent functions (e.g., FSA administration). In addition, discrete HRO can reduce the HR administration costs associated with frequent, high-volume transactions such as payroll. In both cases, discrete HRO serves to reduce HRIS expenses and the number of HR employees while ensuring the desired strategic outcome of hiring the right executive or paying employees correctly on schedule. Although discrete tactical HRO has existed for many years, it still remains a popular HR administration approach for achieving strategic goals.

HR administration managers may also pursue **multiprocess HRO**, also known as *comprehensive* or *blended services outsourcing*. This approach involves outsourcing to niche, third-party providers all of one or more related HR functions, for example, recruitment and selection or defined and 401(k) retirement plan administration. Multiprocess outsourcing has become more popular with the increase in the number of specialized vendors providing such services and the spread of enabling Internet portal capabilities. With an HR portal and HRIS, employees can model their pension decisions independently (to determine pension amounts associated with different retirement dates, for example) and then change 401(k) investment directions by speaking to pension specialists at the third-party vendor when questions arise. This outsourcing of sets of functions reduces the number of specialized HR employees, improves service levels to employees, and reduces HRIS hardware and software upgrades and ongoing maintenance costs. Overall, such an HR administration approach can provide significant cost reductions and simultaneously maintain or enhance service levels.

Total HRO is the third type of outsourcing approach and involves having all or nearly all HR functions handled by one or more external vendors. All traditional HR administrative and functional activities would be managed through third-party vendors. For example, Johnson & Johnson Inc. contracted with Convergys to provide full HR administrative and transactional services for its global workforce for $1 billion (CBR, 2007). Under such arrangements, employees would contact the vendor for assistance or inquiries directly, without any company HR employee involvement or knowledge. Certainly, such a plan would reduce internal HR employee expenses, HRIS expenditures, and administration costs dramatically; however, such savings would be offset by costs for vendor contract administration, quality controls, and oversight. In addition, the HR *strategic functions*, such as long-term force planning and strategic business unit support, should not be outsourced, because third-party vendors frequently deal with multiple clients, one or more of whom might be competitors. It is not hard to imagine how even the most sincere vendor efforts to secure strategic HR plans might be inadvertently compromised, leading to disclosure of these plans and severe strategic disadvantages. Although this HR administration approach is not as prevalent as either discrete or multiprocess outsourcing, it is gaining in popularity. Organizations might opt for such a total HRO solution to deal with the myriad HR requirements associated with the global workforce of an MNE, to focus on HR strategic issues, or to reduce costs. That this strategy is gaining support is demonstrated in Hewitt's HRO survey (2010): 82% of surveyed companies rated their outsourcing as effective or highly effective in meeting strategic goals.

Advantages of HR Outsourcing

The advantages of HR administration outsourcing can be both financial and strategic (Keebler, 2001; Weatherly, 2005). For example, organizations seeking to increase financial profitability and enhance shareowner value might employ HRO to reduce ongoing expenses for employees and software, forestalling capital expenditures for new buildings and equipment. This decision would entail a careful "make-buy" assessment of the total costs and benefits of continuing internal operations versus contracting for them in the external market. Benefits of such an approach might include redesigned processes, improved quality, centralized or consolidated operations, access to technology, and enhanced employee satisfaction. The benefit-cost analysis (CBA) approach covered in Chapter 6 would be essential in this situation.

The strategic advantages of HRO might include the ability of the organization to better focus on its core business by transforming the HR function. By outsourcing the simpler, transaction-based function, the HR department can move from its historical focus on administrative activities to a new position as strategic business partner. Organizations recognize that, more than ever, effective talent management may be the source of sustainable strategic advantage in a knowledge-based, global economy. However, many HR professionals are mired in day-to-day transactional administrative tasks that preclude the value-added consulting, planning, and visioning activities required from them to achieve strategic goals (Fletcher, 2005; Lawler, 2005). HRO could free HR professionals to focus on strategic issues, such as talent management, while providing the firm with skilled transactional and professional services in HR functional areas such as compensation and in administrative areas such as governmental compliance and regulations. Moreover, these services would be powered by the up-to-date technology provided by the external vendor.

Disadvantages of HR Outsourcing

Although there are a number of financial and strategic reasons for considering HR administration outsourcing, there are also serious potential problems for firms that use the approach without fully understanding how to manage it to achieve desired goals. For example, firms that used HRO to achieve HR transformation and cost savings rated their success at an average of 3 on a 5-point scale, (1 equaling *benefits not at all achieved* and 5 equaling *benefits fully achieved*; EquaTerra, 2007). Thus, one big disadvantage of HRO is the likelihood that the organization will *not* achieve its strategic goals. Such a failure could have a significant, negative impact on the organization's ability to survive. Steps to minimize such a failure include realistic benefit-cost analyses, successful change management and implementation planning, unambiguous goals and measures of HRO success, rigorous vendor assessment and selection processes, and skilled vendor contract negotiation, management, and auditing (Weatherly, 2005). Indeed, one of the primary responsibilities of HR administration managers in an outsourcing environment is to ensure that contract terms are fulfilled on a daily basis and that corrective actions are immediately taken when failures occur.

Another disadvantage of HRO includes the loss of institutional expertise in the outsourced functions, making an HRO decision reversal difficult or impossible. Frequently, when outsourcing is undertaken, HR subject matter experts are reassigned or released. This restructuring can be a serious strategic error if the vendor is unable to fulfill its contractual obligations. As noted, an organization would be unwise to outsource core or strategic HR planning functions because of the possibility that competitors might learn its plans from vendors. In addition, loss of internal strategic HR expertise may be devastating to an organization over time. Unfortunately, these outsourcing organizations may lack the contract management expertise to oversee the vendor and hold it accountable for contract terms. Other potential problems include security risks in multivendor outsourcing, internal employee and manager resistance, compliance failures, and cultural clashes between the organization and its vendors.

As outsourcing arrangements continue to increase, evidence from information technology (IT) outsourcing can provide a cautionary tale for those considering HRO. For example, in a recent study, approximately one-third of organizations reported that they had canceled an IT outsourcing contract (Lacity & Willcocks, 2001). In addition, when these contracts are canceled, the functionality is often brought back in-house instead of shifted to a new outsourcing partner (Lacity & Willcocks, 2000). The effort to bring functionality back in-house, also known as **backsourcing**, can be expensive, as firms pay to reorganize twice: first when outsourcing a function and again when it is backsourced.

In summary, HRO is another approach to HR administration that offers potential for cost reduction, process improvement, and employee satisfaction. However, managers of HR administrative functions must be highly skilled at using HRO strategically to achieve organizational goals.

Offshoring and HRIS

The final approach to HR administration, offshoring, is an expansion of HR outsourcing that includes sending work outside the United States to vendors located in other countries. Technological capabilities and global competition have combined to make HRO a global business, and offshoring for MNEs is quite complex. For example, if an Australian airline has call centers in India to obtain improved cost performance, why not have its SSC for HR there as well? Based on responses from 5,231 executives in North America and Europe, Hatch (2004) reported that 19% of all companies and 95% of the *Fortune* 1000 companies considered offshore outsourcing. Moreover, there are now more than 10,000 offshore vendors in 175 countries competing for the business. Figure 7.5 shows the various reasons organizations consider offshoring.

Esen's (2004) survey of HR managers reported that organizations consider offshoring primarily for financial reasons, including lower labor costs (76%), increased profits (50%), and reduced health care costs (23%). For example, researchers found that labor costs for a software developer in India were $6 per hour as opposed to the $60 per hour earned for doing the same job in the United States (Chiamsiri, Bulusu, & Agarwal, 2005). In addition, some firms were seeking skilled employees (16%) or productivity (10%) and service improvement (7%). Only 7% considered offshoring for strategic reasons. In fact, 40% of HR managers reported that their organizations would not consider offshoring because it was inconsistent with strategic direction.

Types of HR Offshoring

When their organizations pursued offshoring, HR managers reported that manufacturing functions were most common (43%), followed by IT (29%) and computer programming (22%), customer call centers (29%), and HR functions (16%). Such organizations used

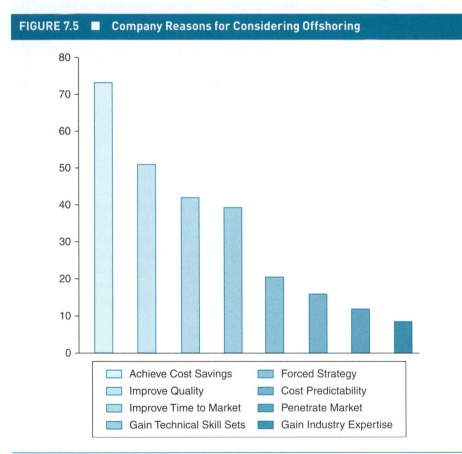

FIGURE 7.5 ■ Company Reasons for Considering Offshoring

Legend:
- Achieve Cost Savings
- Improve Quality
- Improve Time to Market
- Gain Technical Skill Sets
- Forced Strategy
- Cost Predictability
- Penetrate Market
- Gain Industry Expertise

Source: Hatch, Philip. 2004, www.ventoro.com.

both offshore ownership and offshore outsourcing (Esen, 2004). **Offshore ownership** may include opening a new subsidiary in the foreign country, entering into a joint venture with an existing firm in that country, or purchasing an existing firm. By comparison, offshore outsourcing is a traditional contractual relationship with an existing firm.

Offshore ownership is riskier than simple offshore outsourcing. In addition to appropriate strategic and financial due diligence, organizations considering offshore ownership must pay particular attention to

- ready availability of necessary employee knowledge, skills, and abilities such as language;

- information and communication systems compatibility with HRIS;

- governmental regulations and legal employment requirements such as wage laws;

- political stability of the country for facility and employee security; and

- cultural differences such as expectations about participative versus directive supervision.

Although an offshore outsourcing strategy is less risky than offshore ownership, organizations would still face more risk than they would had they outsourced domestically. HR managers should always perform due diligence in assessing the reputation and business capabilities of an outsourcing partner. However, such processes are more complex when dealing with organizations located halfway across the globe. For example, concerns about electrical power availability, which might determine whether HRIS processing can occur as scheduled, are rarely discussed with outsourcing firms in the United States but might be a significant issue in parts of Indonesia. In addition, worker availability to meet a 24/7 service center requirement is less of a problem in the United States than in countries where overtime is limited to a few hours per month, as it is in the European Union (EU). Finally, oversight and audit functions may be less onerous and expensive when U.S. companies establish offshore outsourcing agreements in nearby countries such as Canada or Mexico rather than in more distant nations such as India or China.

Summary of HR Administration Approaches

Based on the previous discussion, it is clear that HR administration managers have a number of approaches that can contribute to the goals of reducing costs, improving efficiency, and increasing service levels for internal customers. It is also clear that, without HRIS and related information technologies, HR organizations would find it difficult to respond effectively to the increasing demand for enhanced quality and quantity of information required by governments, organizations, and managers operating in a global environment. It is also important that such alternatives be pursued consistent with each organization's strategic plan to achieve sustainable competitive advantage in its industry. Multiple approaches may be appropriate based on those strategic goals. For example, HR portals may be combined with SSCs and selective outsourcing or offshoring to achieve the optimum solution for a particular firm.

In assessing whether one or more approaches is best, HR administration managers must understand the impact of their decisions on the specific administrative functions to be accomplished. Therefore, the next section describes two specific U.S. governmental reporting mandates (i.e., to the Equal Employment Opportunity Commission [EEOC] and OSHA) that are included among the many HR transactions for which HR administration is responsible. Following a discussion of the governmental mandates, their legal underpinnings, and the actual reports and records maintenance required, we explore how HR administration approaches can facilitate improved accuracy, reduced costs, and increased organizational value during the process of successfully completing such HR transactions.

LEGAL COMPLIANCE AND HR ADMINISTRATION

As noted in Chapter 1, the country and its general environment constitute a major effect on HRM and on the development and implementation of HRIS (Beaman, 2002). Whether the organization pursues a "domestic only" strategy (i.e., doing business in only one country) or an MNE approach, countries' government and labor laws are important external forces in establishing the context for business (Hersch, 1991). In particular, the labor laws provide the foundation of employee protections in the workplace. For example, in the United States, the Constitution and its amendments establish the rights of citizens in general. In addition, multiple employment laws have been passed by the U.S. Congress to complement those rights. Some of the more important of these U.S. employment laws are identified in the glossary provided at the end of the book. For a more detailed discussion of the employment laws in the United States, see Bennett-Alexander & Hartman (2018).

It is important to recognize that U.S. employment laws underpin the *general principles* used in the practice of HRM. There are a number of laws in the United States prohibiting unfair discrimination on the basis of employee sex, race, age, national origin, religion, veteran status, disability, or genetic information. There are similar laws and regulations in other industrialized nations that prohibit unfair discrimination (Briscoe & Schuler, 2004). The general principle underlying these discrimination laws and regulations is that job performance should be the primary basis for employment decisions that change the employment status of an individual. When hiring new employees, for example, a company should base its hiring decision primarily on expected job performance, which might be assessed through employment tests and interviews. Whether applicants are male or female is irrelevant in all but a few cases (e.g., restroom attendant). Similarly, decisions to award a pay raise or to promote or terminate an employee should be based on the employee's job performance without regard, for example, to the employee's sex, race, religion, or ethnicity. As noted, the general principles underlying employment laws in the United States bear significant similarities to the general principles underlying employment laws or regulations in other countries, such as those specified in the EU directives (Briscoe & Schuler, 2004; Dowling & Welch, 2005; Paskoff, 2003). Since compliance with employment laws and regulations is a critical part of HR administration, provisions for handling the employment laws of multiple countries need to be considered in the development of an HRIS for a multinational firm. For example, SAP provides specific capabilities for HRIS operations in multiple countries with differing labor and tax laws.

What complicates U.S. employment laws for HR professionals is that the 50 states frequently expand on, adopt rules and regulations that differ from, or add additional protections not covered by federal law. For example, a partial comparison of elements of the **Family and Medical Leave Act (FMLA)** with the federal and state legislation of California and Oregon demonstrates these variations. Both California and Oregon deviate from the federal FMLA statute, but they do so in different ways. The federal law specifies that its provisions apply to private employers with 50 or more employees in at least 20 weeks of the current or preceding year (U.S. Department of Labor, 2007). California law applies the provisions of the FMLA to *all* employers with 50 or more employees. In contrast, Oregon applies the provisions of the FMLA to employers with 25 or more employees in at least 20 weeks of the year. In this case, HR managers operating in both California and Oregon would be required to provide annual reports demonstrating that they have complied with both the federal and the state laws that are applicable. Since country-level and local laws can differ for all nations, administrative expenses to comply with employment laws can mushroom for firms with national and international exposure, even when an HRIS is used to support such compliance requirements. Indeed, this example reinforces the need for flexibility in HRIS software to accommodate such reporting differences.

This is, of course, just one example among many that demonstrates how governments affect HR administration. There are many laws and regulations in the United States that require organizations to report to government agencies. All these manual reports are tedious and time-consuming, and they account for a significant amount of the transactional activity of the HR department. The processing for these activities was affected significantly by the introduction of computer technology and has always been a part of any integrated HR software package. The next sections take an in-depth look at two U.S. governmental mandates associated with equal employment opportunity (EEO) and employee safety. Specifically, HR administration and related concerns associated with EEO records and reporting (EEO-1 and Component-2 reports) and OSHA record keeping and reporting will be highlighted. As you read about the reporting requirements of these laws, just imagine the tremendous amount of time it would take to complete an EEO-1 report manually for a medium-sized company of 1,000 employees; that is a considerable amount of "paper shuffling." Again, it is important to recognize that the following discussion is illustrative of HR administration, employment laws, and the use of an HRIS and, thus, could be applied to any country in the world.

HR ADMINISTRATION AND EQUAL EMPLOYMENT OPPORTUNITY

U.S. Civil Rights Act of 1964, Title VII, and the EEO-1 and Component 2 Reports

Figure 7.6 displays the broad categories of HRM administration associated with governmental mandates for meeting the requirements of **equal employment opportunity (EEO)** and affirmative action laws and guidelines. That all individuals should be considered for employment based on knowledge, skills, and abilities rather than irrelevant factors (e.g., sex, race, religion) is the *general principle* of EEO. Title VII of the Civil Rights Act of 1964 provides the requirements for such EEO. Under Section 703 of Title VII (42 U.S.C. §2000e-2), it is illegal for employers with 15 or more employees working 20 or more weeks per year

(1) to fail or refuse to hire or discharge any individual with respect to his compensation, terms, conditions, or privileges of employment because of such individual's race, color, religion, sex, or national origin, or

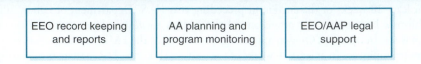

FIGURE 7.6 ■ EEO/Affirmative Action Plan (AAP) Administrative Functions

| EEO record keeping and reports | AA planning and program monitoring | EEO/AAP legal support |

Source: U.S. EEOC (2018).

(2) to limit, segregate, or classify his employees or applicants for employment in any way that would deprive or tend to deprive any individual of employment opportunities or otherwise adversely affect his status as an employee because of such individual's race, color, religion, sex, or national origin. (U.S. EEOC, 1964)

Executive Order 11246 (as amended by Executive Orders 11478 and 13672) also prohibits discrimination based on sexual orientation and gender identity for contractors working for the federal government. In addition, employers who engage in business with the federal government and have contracts valued at $50,000 or more must comply with additional requirements that include providing a written **affirmative action plan (AAP)** to the Office of Federal Contract Compliance Procedures (OFCCP). This report details how the employer is actively seeking to hire and promote individuals in protected classes. Specifically, the AAP must (1) provide a detailed comparison of the available labor force with the employer's workforce by race, color, religion, national origin, and sex; (2) specify goals and timetables for achieving workforce balance if underutilization exists; and (3) indicate the specific steps to be taken to attain the goals in order to erase underutilization. In 1967, Congress expanded protection against illegal discrimination in employment by including the age criterion (i.e., persons aged 40 or older) with the passage of the **Age Discrimination in Employment Act (ADEA)**, and in 1990, it provided protection to individuals with disabilities with its passage of the Americans with Disabilities Act (ADA). One example of the many mandated government reports is the EEO-1 report. The **Uniformed Services Employment and Reemployment Rights Act (USERRA)** of 1994 protects against discrimination based on veteran status, and in 2008, the **Genetic Information Nondisclosure Act (GINA)** banned discrimination based on genetic information.

EEO Reports

To monitor and assess equal employment opportunity practices, the Equal Employment Opportunity Commission (EEOC) was charged with gathering data, investigating alleged violations, and bringing legal charges against employers who failed to comply with Title VII requirements. Accordingly, all employers with 15 or more employees must keep records regarding their compliance with the law based on occupational category (i.e., professional, technical, managerial, craft) and sex and race/ethnicity. Although the records historically included six EEO categories (i.e., white, black, Hispanic, Asian or Pacific Islander, Native American), changes in the number and designation of categories were made based on the 2000 U.S. Census, with reporting by the revised categories beginning in 2007.

A sample of the "Employment Data" section of the EEO-1 report (Standard Form 100) with its revised categories is shown in Figure 7.7. Substantial changes in the report include expanding occupational categories from 4 to 10 and, more importantly, allowing

FIGURE 7.7 ■ EEO-1 Report

Section D – EMPLOYMENT DATA

Employment at this establishment—Report all permanent full- and part-time employees including apprentices and on-the-job trainees unless specifically excluded as set forth in the instructions. Enter the appropriate figures on all lines and in all columns. Blank spaces will be considered as zeros.

Number of Employees (Report employees in only one category)

Job Categories	Hispanic or Latino		Race/Ethnicity													
			Non-Hispanic or Latino													
			Male						Female							
	Male	Female	White	Black or African American	Native Hawaiian or Other Pacific Islander	Asian	American Indian or Alaska Native	Two or More Races	White	Black or African American	Native Hawaiian or Other Pacific Islander	Asian	American Indian or Alaska Native	Two or More Races	Total Col A–N
	A	B	C	D	E	F	G	H	I	J	K	L	M	N	O
Executive/ Senior Level Officials and Managers 1.1															
First/Mid- Level Officials and Managers 1.2															
Professionals 2															
Technicians 3															
Sales Workers 4															
Administrative Support Workers 5															
Craft Workers 6															
Operatives 7															
Laborers and Helpers 8															
Service Workers 9															
TOTAL 10															
PREVIOUS YEAR TOTAL 11															

1. Date(s) of payroll period used: _____   [Omit on the Consolidated Report.]

O.M.B. No. 3046-0007
Revised 00/2006
Approval Expires 1/2009

individuals to specify more than one race/ethnicity category. Previously, individuals were limited to a single designation. The EEO-1 report must be prepared each September 30 by

> all private employers . . . with 100 or more employees. . . . [M]ulti-establishment employers doing business at more than one establishment, must complete online: (1) a report covering the principal or headquarters office; (2) a separate report for each establishment employing 50 or more persons; and (3) a separate report . . . for each establishment employing fewer than 50 employees . . . showing the name, address and total employment for each establishment employing fewer than 50 persons . . . by sex, race, ethnicity, and each of the 10 occupational categories. (U.S. EEOC, 2018)

Revised reporting instructions include definitions of the revised designated racial/ethnic categories shown in what follows, columns for reporting individuals who specify more than one race/ethnicity, and strong encouragement to have employees "self-identify" rather than relying on the employer's visual categorization. The race and ethnic designations used by the EEOC are as follows:

- *Hispanic or Latino*—A person of Cuban, Mexican, Puerto Rican, South or Central American, or other Spanish culture or origin regardless of race.

- *White (not Hispanic or Latino)*—A person having origins in any of the original peoples of Europe, the Middle East, or North Africa.

- *Black or African American (not Hispanic or Latino)*—A person having origins in any of the black racial groups of Africa.

- *Native Hawaiian or Other Pacific Islander (not Hispanic or Latino)*—A person having origins in any of the peoples of Hawaii, Guam, Samoa, or other Pacific Islands.

- *Asian (not Hispanic or Latino)*—A person having origins in any of the original peoples of the Far East, Southeast Asia, or the Indian subcontinent, including, for example, Cambodia, China, India, Japan, Korea, Malaysia, Pakistan, the Philippine Islands, Thailand, and Vietnam.

- *American Indian or Alaska Native (not Hispanic or Latino)*—A person having origins in any of the original peoples of North and South America (including Central America) and who maintain tribal affiliation or community attachment. (U.S. EEOC, 2018, Appendix 4)

Effective for the 2019 report, the EEOC implemented additional requirements; specifically, EEO-1 now has a new section, designated Component 2, which requires that pay data be added to the report and be submitted electronically. This pay data must be reported by employers with 100 or more full-time and part-time employees using salary data from Form W-2 Box 1 compensation reported annually to employees and the IRS. This new data reporting requirement is intended to identify potential pay discrimination based on sex and race/ethnicity and represents a significant increase in data collection efforts for all affected employers (SHRM, 2016).

EEO-1 and HRIS

Recent changes to the EEOC guidelines are the most sweeping change in the history of the EEOC, as workers reclassify themselves based on the new EEO designations and organizations pore through job descriptions to classify individuals into the new work categories. For example, individuals who classify themselves as white could also classify themselves as Asian under the new plan. Even small firms without an HRIS have a large amount of work to do. HRIS changes will be significant as well. For example, HRIS and ERPs, such as SAP and PeopleSoft, have generally used a single field letter or number to represent race/ethnicity categories. Changes required by the updated EEO-1 report include the following:

- Track race separately from ethnicity (e.g., Hispanic or not Hispanic).

- Provide separate codes for Asian and Native Hawaiian or Other Pacific Islander.

- Modify limitations on reporting only one race (e.g., individual may be black and Asian).

- Ensure that queries can identify all individuals in a particular category (e.g., American Indian), even when individuals self-identify as two or more race categories.

The EEOC also now requires online reporting of the EEO-1 and, simultaneously, discourages manual reporting (U.S. EEOC, 2018). Unless a waiver is approved, data must be submitted through the *EEO-1 Online Filing System*. Using electronic reporting reduces costs associated with legislation compliance. This detailed description of EEO-1 reporting is provided to facilitate an understanding of how complex HR administration can be. The amount of paperwork required for compliance with all federal and local employment laws and regulations continues to grow and would be overwhelming without an HRIS. The EEO-1, Component 2, and I9 reports are just a few of the reports that can be compiled and electronically reported from the HRIS. The HRIS applications software helps greatly reduce this complexity. Nevertheless, no matter how sophisticated the HRIS and its reporting software, the employee and organizational data must *be entered accurately* into the system. HR professionals should familiarize themselves annually with changes in the reporting requirements through the EEOC website at https://www.eeoc.gov/employers/eeo1survey/index.cfm.

To understand the complexity of governmental reporting requirements, let us examine a second example of how these affect HRM administration. Specifically, consider the necessity of reporting data to show compliance with the Occupational Safety and Health Act (OSHA).

OSHA Record Keeping

Figure 7.8 displays the broad categories of HRM administration associated with governmental mandates for safety requirements by the Occupational Safety and Health Administration (OSHA Administration), which administers OSHA. In 1970, with work-related fatalities reaching 15,000 annually, Congress charged the U.S. Department of Labor with responsibility for establishing, monitoring, and enforcing occupational safety and health standards and practices for firms engaged in interstate commerce. OSHA primarily established, in the general duty clause of the law, that employers must provide a workplace free of known hazards likely to cause death or serious injury. The National Institute for Occupational Safety and Health (NIOSH) researches and publishes safety and health standards under the law. To ensure that all businesses with 11 or more employees

FIGURE 7.8 ■ OSHA Administrative Functions

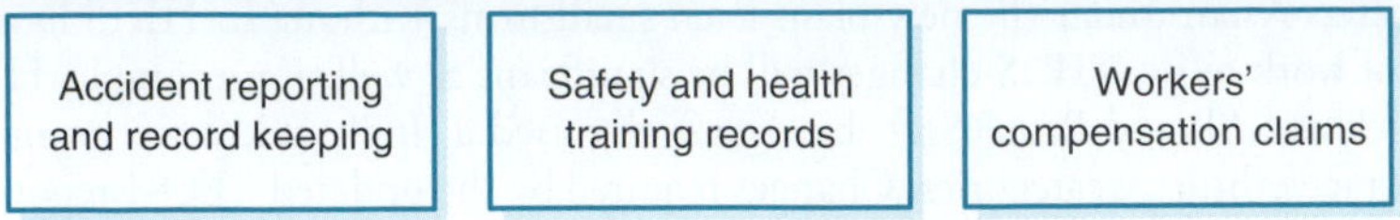

| Accident reporting and record keeping | Safety and health training records | Workers' compensation claims |

fulfill their occupational safety and health obligations, OSHA compliance officers typically arrive unannounced for an OSHA inspection. The inspector then proceeds to

- review employer records of workplace deaths, injuries, and illnesses;
- conduct on-site inspections of the work premises and note observed violations;
- conduct employee interviews to elicit any safety concerns; and
- discuss findings and violations or issue citations to the employer (Noe, Hollenbeck, Gerhart, & Wright, 2017).

Failing to correct violations or maintain required records could result in substantial fines and jail sentences for employers. For example, one of the worst U.S. mine disasters in 40 years occurred in 2010, when 29 miners died following an explosion at the Upper Big Branch-South mine in West Virginia. OSHA had issued 369 citations and orders prior to the disaster. Massey Energy Company was fined $10.8 million following the disaster investigation and agreed to an additional $210 million in remedial safety measures (U.S. Department of Labor OSHA, 2011).

OSHA Form 300 (Log of Work-Related Injuries and Illnesses) and HRIS

All covered employers are required to notify the Occupational Safety and Health Administration within 8 hours of any accident involving either a fatality or an in-patient hospitalization of three or more employees. In addition, all covered employers must complete an annual **OSHA Form 300** recording all reportable work-related injuries and illnesses. **OSHA Form 301** (Injury and Illness Incidence Report) is used to record supplementary information about reportable cases. Finally, **OSHA Form 300A** (Summary of Work-Related Injuries and Illnesses), which displays total injuries and illnesses for the year, must be posted for all employees to view. A sample of the Form 300 is shown in Figure 7.9. Regulations for OSHA administration are available at https://www.osha.gov/pls/publications/publication.AthruZ?pType=Industry&pID=152.

HR administration managers must be aware daily of any safety problems in order to meet OSHA Form 300 regulations and ensure that up-to-date records are available for OSHA inspections. Generally, details for the report must be obtained from the reporting supervisor involved in the reportable accident/illness investigation and recorded on OSHA Form 301. However, in smaller organizations, HR managers may be directly involved in accident/illness investigations. *Reportable incidents* are defined as work-related injuries and illnesses resulting in "death, days away from work, restricted work, transfer to another job, medical treatment beyond first aid, loss of consciousness, or diagnosis of a significant injury or illness" (U.S. Department of Labor, 2004). Because safety issues differ for different types

FIGURE 7.9 ■ OSHA Form 300

OSHA's Form 300 *(Rev. 01/2004)*

Log of Work-Related Injuries and Illnesses

Attention: This form contains information relating to employee health and must be used in a manner that protects the confidentiality of employees to the extent possible while the information is being used for occupational safety and health purposes.

Year 20__

U.S. Department of Labor
Occupational Safety and Health Administration

You must record information about every work-related death and about every work-related injury or illness that involves loss of consciousness, restricted work activity or job transfer, days away from work, or medical treatment beyond first aid. You must also record significant work-related injuries and illnesses that are diagnosed by a physician or licensed health care professional. You must also record work-related injuries and illnesses that meet any of the specific recording criteria listed in 29 CFR Part 1904.8 through 1904.12. Feel free to use two lines for a single case if you need to. You must complete an Injury and Illness Incident Report (OSHA Form 301) or equivalent form for each injury or illness recorded on this form. If you're not sure whether a case is recordable, call your local OSHA office for help.

Form approved OMB no. 1218-0176

Establishment name _____

City _____ State _____

Identify the person			Describe the case				Classify the case															
(A) Case no.	(B) Employee's name	(C) Job title (e.g., Welder)	(D) Date of injury or onset of illness	(E) Where the event occurred (e.g., Loading dock north end)	(F) Describe injury or illness, parts of body affected, and object/substance that directly injured or made person ill (e.g., Second degree burns on right forearm from acetylene torch)	CHECK ONLY ONE box for each case based on the most serious outcome for that case: Death (G)	Days away from work (H)	Job transfer or restriction (I)	Other recordable cases (J)	Enter the number of days the injured or ill worker was: Away from work (K)	On job transfer or restriction (L)	Check the "Injury" column or choose one type of illness: Injury (1)	Skin disorder (2)	Respiratory condition (3)	Poisoning (4)	Hearing loss (5)	All other illnesses (6)

<small>Remained at Work — Days away from work; Job transfer or restriction; Other recordable cases</small>

___	_____	___	___/___ month/day	_____	_____	☐	☐	☐	☐	___ days	___ days	☐ ☐ ☐ ☐ ☐ ☐
___	_____	___	___/___ month/day	_____	_____	☐	☐	☐	☐	___ days	___ days	☐ ☐ ☐ ☐ ☐ ☐
___	_____	___	___/___ month/day	_____	_____	☐	☐	☐	☐	___ days	___ days	☐ ☐ ☐ ☐ ☐ ☐
___	_____	___	___/___ month/day	_____	_____	☐	☐	☐	☐	___ days	___ days	☐ ☐ ☐ ☐ ☐ ☐
___	_____	___	___/___ month/day	_____	_____	☐	☐	☐	☐	___ days	___ days	☐ ☐ ☐ ☐ ☐ ☐

Source: US Department of Labor, 2004.

of businesses, the HRIS may not have a standard safety module. More likely, limited fields are added to permit tracking and facilitate federal and state reporting (Ceriello, 1991). However, including safety modules in HRIS can be beneficial. Desirable functions would include HR portal access (e.g., MSS) at remote locations so that supervisors could enter accident/illness data, make linkages to safety training and equipment records, and access interfaces with required workers' compensation claims, in addition to record keeping and report generation. Such functionality can be an important part of an overall safety program as well as a means of increasing HRM administrative efficiency (O'Connell, 1995).

Technology, HR Administration, and Mandated Governmental Reporting

Within the context of these complex legal requirements, what role can technology-enabled HR administration approaches have in increasing efficiency, quality, and cost reduction while enabling the fulfillment of mandated reporting? The answer to this question is especially important in the area of equal employment opportunities, safety, and health. Certainly, the increasing use of HRIS facilitates accurate, timely record keeping and reporting that facilitates the performance of both EEO and OSHA mandates. For example, accurate, timely completion of the EEO-1 and Component 2 reports presupposes ready access to employee records, where such information is maintained. For a smaller employer, paper records may suffice, but advances in HRIS are allowing smaller and mid-sized organizations to adopt eHRM and with it the support for EEO-1 and Component 2 reports. For larger national or international employers with multiple locations, however, paper records are inadequate. Paper record keeping would require that each location search the records of each employee, manually record the appropriate information, and forward it to a centralized location for consolidation into the company report. For organizations with centralized HRM, either operations employees or managers would be required to do the report at each remote location. However, this waste of productive time is substantially reduced by the presence of an HRIS in the following ways:

- HRIS records can be established coincident with the employee application, including optional self-reporting of EEO race/ethnicity and sex data. No separate input functions are required unless corrections are needed. Self-reported data are likely to be more accurate and are preferred for compliance reporting.

- Simple queries of the HRIS database can secure required data, categorized by employee job classification, sex, and race/ethnicity and compensation in the EEO-1 and Component 2 format if desired.

- Required information for either EEO or OSHA reporting can be secured in minutes, with minimal HR employee involvement, rather than having staff take days or weeks to manually review records, compile the information, and forward it to a centralized location for further compilation. Indeed, OSHA on-site accident reporting can be done by the local supervisor via mobile device.

- HR employees can handle the complete reporting function without interrupting productive time in operational units.

- Changes in mandated reporting requirements (e.g., an increase in the number of job classifications) can be handled mechanically by HR, without the involvement of field employees.

- Electronic reporting (i.e., computer to computer) can ensure timely receipt of reports.

- Enhanced ability to analyze data and visualize results.

If an ESS portal is available, government-mandated changes can be accomplished more easily, even when individual employees must be involved. For example, HR administration managers can communicate directly with employees, explaining the changes in EEO categories and requesting that each employee update his or her information directly via the ESS portal. In addition, the rapid expansion of mobile applications that access the ESS and MSS portals can further enhance accuracy and reporting speed. Supervisors can be notified via the MSS portal of individual employees who have not updated their information, precluding meetings with all employees to introduce and monitor this type of change. Finally, if the employee refuses to update the information, the supervisor can use the MSS portal to enter the updated data directly.

If an SSC is added to the HR portal capabilities, individual employees with questions about the reporting requirements can contact the center directly for assistance. The supervisor need not be involved, and employees will receive rapid responses, which will allow them to complete the update more quickly and accurately. Thus, an HRIS, augmented by HR portals (i.e., ESS and MSS portals) and SSCs, can substantially improve the accuracy and timeliness of mandated governmental reporting while reducing the hours wasted on routine administrative work, hours that could be spent more productively.

Similarly, HR portals, SSCs, and even outsourcing can facilitate OSHA record keeping and reporting, reducing costs and enhancing timely reporting. For example, HRIS records and MSS portals permit supervisors to complete the required record of a reportable accident electronically, filling out the 300A Form via computer terminal or mobile device immediately after an accident occurs. In addition, updates can be handled with minimal effort. With appropriate linkages, workers' compensation reporting to state agencies can be generated by the system. If an employee files a workers' compensation claim and the company disagrees, HR administration managers can access the data and provide the rationale for disallowing the claim. If an organization outsources either workers' compensation reporting or accident investigation to third-party vendors, electronic linkages can notify those groups immediately so that appropriate procedures can be instituted. Finally, HR administration managers, without involving productive employees, can generate an accurate, up-to-date Form 300 whenever one is required for inspection, posting, or safety performance analysis.

Summary of Government-Mandated Reports and Privacy Requirements

The EEO-1 and Component 2 report, along with the OSHA Form 300, are only two of the many required administrative transactions for which HR managers are responsible. In addition, privacy laws add more complexity to the administration of the HR function via an HRIS. Multinational corporations also need to be concerned with laws and reporting requirements outside the United States. For example, counterparts to OSHA include European Agency for Safety and Health at work (EU-OSHA), China's State Administration of Safety (SAWS), the Japan Industrial and Safety Health Administration and the Canadian Centre for Occupational Health and Safety. Knowing what governing bodies exist in each country and how laws, regulations, and enforcement differ is important; understanding whether HRIS capabilities support such differences is essential for successful compliance in meeting expectations for all global governing agencies,

As noted, HRIS capabilities can be enhanced by the use of one or more HR administration approaches to improve accurate and timely reporting while reducing costs and increasing productivity. These examples demonstrate how effective HR administration can help organizations comply with government mandates while supporting strategic goals. The final HR administration issue included in this chapter is how, by using a balanced-scorecard approach, an HR manager can use HRIS capabilities to measure their activities in ways that demonstrate their contribution to an organization's strategic goals. Following a brief introduction of the use of a balanced scorecard in strategic management, we will examine which HR measures that are part of an HR administration can contribute to the balanced scorecard for an organization.

HR STRATEGIC GOAL ACHIEVEMENT AND THE BALANCED SCORECARD

As should be clear from the topics covered thus far in this chapter, HR administration is crucial to effective HRM functioning, and HRIS aid in achieving effective HR administration. As discussed in Chapter 1, HR has historically been seen as performing a "paper-pusher" function in organizations and has been thought of as a cost-only operation. One of the major reasons for this situation was that the HR department could not easily or accurately generate metrics describing its value-added for its operations and programs. The paper system existed, but it was exceedingly difficult to extract HR metrics (especially the metrics described in Chapter 14). Advances in computer technology, particularly those applicable to the HR function and its HRIS programs, made the calculation of these metrics possible. Current HRIS capabilities make analyzing data and viewing results visually much easier. As a result, CBAs could also be calculated to evaluate the effectiveness of the HR department and its programs. The next step for HR was to become a part of the strategic management system in the organization.

The historic sequence and outcomes described in the previous paragraph depend on building an accurate, up-to-date database that is easy to access and manipulate. This is critical for all HR programs, and it all begins with a correctly designed HRIS that supports HR administration. The data from HR administration, particularly HR metrics (Chapter 14), are also used to support strategic goals, and one of the best examples of their use is in the balanced scorecard. Kaplan and Norton (1992, 1996, 2006), recognizing that an organization can no longer rely solely on a simple financial measure to assess its ability to achieve sustainable competitive advantage, devised the balanced scorecard to facilitate the organization's efforts to measure its success in achieving the strategic goals required to meet the needs of its stakeholder groups. A **balanced scorecard** is both a management and a measurement system that "enables organizations to clarify their vision and strategy and translate them into action, . . . [providing] feedback around both the internal business processes and external outcomes to continuously improve strategic performance and results" (Arveson, 1998).

Kaplan and Norton (1996) define the four components of the balanced scorecard as *financial, customer, internal business processes, and learning and growth*. Inclusion of these components represents an organization's commitment to balancing its strategic goals and reflects the expectations of its multiple stakeholders. An overview of all four components can be seen in Figure 7.10 along with the key question associated with each of the four.

HRM and the Balanced Scorecard

HRM is often not viewed as a strategic function in organizations, primarily because its managers fail to develop measures demonstrating its strategic business value (Lawler, 2005; Ulrich, 1997). For example, successful HR administration efforts that ensure compliance with governmental mandates (e.g., EEO and OSHA reporting) are often viewed as simple administrative transactions rather than as strategic imperatives. However, failing to hire and retain the diverse workforce documented in EEO compliance reports can result in expensive lawsuits and reduced stock prices (Hersch, 1991), as well as in diminished firm credibility (Pomerenke, 1998) and decreased long-term innovation (Florida, 2002, 2005; Page, 2007). Each of these items is directly related to the balanced scorecard categories. Specifically, lawsuits and stock price are associated with financial success, reputation is associated with the customer category, and innovation is part of the learning and growth category. Certainly, HR professionals understand the impact effective human capital management has on an organization. However, unless measures to reflect the value-added nature of HRM in leveraging human capital are developed and linked to the strategic goals reflected in a firm's balanced scorecard, it is unlikely that organizations will view such HRM-linked activities as strategic.

Figure 7.11 provides a simple example of the linkage between HR functions and an organization's balanced scorecard. The next section will highlight the development of an HR scorecard.

FIGURE 7.10 ■ Balanced Scorecard Components

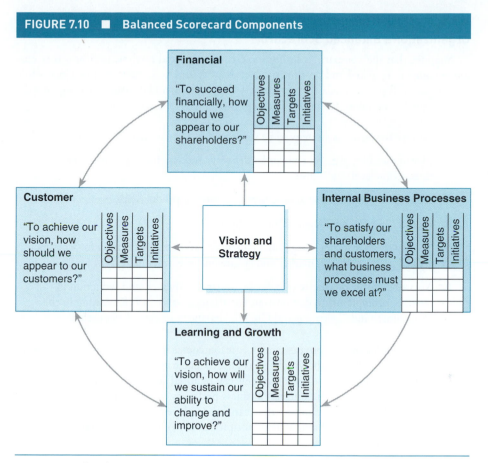

Source: Averson (1998), Balanced Scorecard Institute.

FIGURE 7.11 ■ Sample HR–Balanced Scorecard Linkages

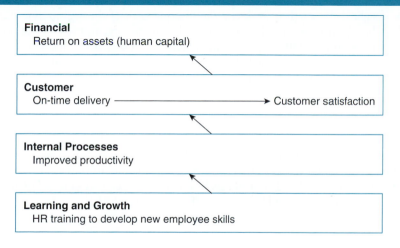

HR Scorecard, Its Measures, and Its Alignment With the Organization's Balanced Scorecard

Suppose that the company is losing some customers, and analysis indicates that customer complaints spiked and on-time product delivery and new orders declined just before these losses. HR professionals want to identify the processes and measures that support the strategic goal of customer retention. The steps they might take are as follows:

1. Specify the business strategy to be supported (e.g., customer retention).

2. Identify leading (e.g., on-time order delivery) and lagging (e.g., customer satisfaction level) indicators.

3. Identify associated internal processes (e.g., worker productivity, product quality).

4. Identify HR linkages (e.g., training, rewards).

5. Specify the HR strategy (e.g., offer enhanced productivity training for workers to reduce product time to market and ensure on-time order delivery).

6. Measure worker productivity increase, on-time deliveries, and reduction in customer complaints to demonstrate the strategic value of HR training in the "Customer" and "Learning and Growth" balanced scorecard categories.

A leading indicator is a predictor of future outcomes (e.g., on-time order delivery), whereas a lagging indicator shows what has already occurred (e.g., customer satisfaction level). Thus, to ensure the on-time order delivery required to retain customers, HR professionals must understand the internal business processes involved in this retention and identify the HR function (training) that can be employed to improve these processes (i.e., to improve productivity) and increase the probability of the desired strategic outcome (customer retention).

HR Scorecard and Balanced Scorecard Alignment

Researchers have long recognized the need to ensure goal alignment in organizations (Beatty, Huselid, & Schneider, 2003; Becker & Gerhart, 1996; Becker, Huselid, & Ulrich, 2001; Lawler, 2005). For example, Boswell (2006) reported that employees who did not have "line of sight" between their work and the strategic goals of the organization were more likely to have poor work attitudes and consider leaving the organization. In addition, Decoene and Bruggerman (2006) reported that failure to implement the business scorecard properly (i.e., by neglecting to cascade strategic goals to all levels in the organization) reduced middle managers' motivation to support strategic goals such that the organization failed to achieve its strategic financial objectives.

In recognition of the importance of alignment between the organization's balanced scorecard and HRM strategic initiatives, researchers (Becker et al., 2001) have suggested that HR professionals develop an HR scorecard as a means of establishing measures for HR that reflect this alignment. HR measures should reflect a balance of cost controls (e.g., improved productivity) and value creation (e.g., increased innovation) consistent with the business's balanced scorecard and strategic goals. Figure 7.12 identifies sample HR measures that might be included in an HR scorecard (Becker et al., 2001).

FIGURE 7.12 ■ Sample HR Scorecard Measures Linked to a Firm's Balanced Scorecard	
HR functions to support Learning and Growth category (e.g., employee development)	• Backup talent ratio—Value Creation • Competency development expense peremployee—Cost Control • No. of "special projects" for employee development—Value Creation • No. of employees with development plans—Cost Control
HR internal efficiency measures to support Financial category	• HR departmental expense/$ of sales revenue—Cost Control • HR sales training expense/$ of sales revenue—Value Creation • HR recruitment expense/R&D hires—Cost Control • No. of patents per R&D hire—Value Creation

From the previous discussion, we can see multiple opportunities for HR administration managers to utilize HRIS to align with the strategic goals covered by the balanced scorecard. For example, deploying HR portals (i.e., ESS and MSS portals) can provide simultaneous support for financial goals (e.g., cost control through reduced employee expense) and learning and growth (e.g., e-learning courses). Similarly, strategic use of outsourcing can support financial goals (e.g., cost reductions) and internal processes (e.g., improved time from vacancy request to hiring). Thus, HR administration managers can make decisions that support the strategic goals contained in the balanced scorecard, and data visualization available in HRIS can be a useful way to illustrate these balanced scorecard objectives using HR data.

Summary

Using HRIS to facilitate HR administration allows organizations to streamline processes, increase service levels, and reduce costs. This chapter discussed the relative value of HRIS in HR administration versus a traditional "paper-and-pencil" approach to HR administration. In addition, the chapter discussed the various options available in the implementation of utilizing HRIS in HR administration, including HR portals, shared services, outsourcing, and offshoring. Each of these approaches was considered in detail, and its advantages and disadvantages were outlined. The chapter also briefly discussed the flexibility that organizations have in implementing the HRIS. For example, HR portals may be combined with SSCs and selective outsourcing or offshoring to achieve the optimum solution for a particular firm.

Before developing and implementing HRIS in HR administration, the organization must have conducted a basic job analysis to determine the appropriate knowledge, skills, and abilities for each job. In addition, basic job descriptions for each job should be developed. The data from this analysis form the basis for the data that are eventually entered into the HRIS. The chapter further discussed how human resource information systems can support organizations as they conduct a job analysis. It is worth noting that newer technologies like artificial intelligence and machine learning also have promise for use in HR administration and may even be integrated into HRIS in the future.

One of the key issues in implementing HRIS in HR administration is to ensure compliance with legal requirements. This chapter discussed two specific U.S. governmental reporting mandates (i.e., EEO and OSHA reporting) as well as how an HRIS can facilitate improved accuracy, reduced costs, and increased organizational value by successfully completing such HR transactions. Even though the topic was a theme throughout the chapter, privacy, as this requirement relates to legislation and data security, was discussed in a separate section, which also presented a discussion of privacy laws and their consideration when one develops an HRIS. Finally, the chapter closed with a brief investigation of the elements important to the successful measurement of the strategic alignment of the HR balanced scorecard.

Key Terms

affirmative action plan (AAP) 172

Age Discrimination in Employment Act (ADEA) 172

Americans with Disabilities Act (ADA) 161

backsourcing 167

balanced scorecard 180

discrete HRO 165

employee self-service (ESS) 158

Employer Information Report EEO-1 (EEO-1 report) 152

equal employment opportunity (EEO) 171

Family and Medical Leave Act (FMLA) 170

Genetic Information Nondisclosure Act (GINA) 172

human resources outsourcing (HRO) 156

manager self-service (MSS) 158

multiprocess HRO 165

Occupational Safety and Health Act (OSHA) 152

offshore ownership 169

offshoring 156

OSHA Form 300 176

OSHA Form 300A 176

OSHA Form 301 176

performance appraisals 158

resource-based view 156

self-service portal 155

service-oriented architecture (SOA) 153

shared-service center (SSC) 155

shared services 161

strategic choices 157

sustainable competitive advantage 156

total HRO 166

transaction cost theory 157

Uniformed Services Employment and Reemployment Act (USERRA) 172

Discussion Questions

1. Discuss the theoretical bases for the four HR administrative approaches introduced in this chapter. Describe how such theories are useful to HR professionals in their efforts to improve transactional performance.

2. Why is service-oriented architecture enhanced by XML important to HR administration? Choose two HR administrative approaches, and discuss how each is facilitated by this architecture.

3. What are the primary advantages of HR portals and shared-services centers? Give examples of how HR professionals might use each to better achieve cost controls and service enhancement.

4. What are the primary purposes of ESS and MSS? What are the advantages and disadvantages of each?

5. Define outsourcing and offshoring. Compare and contrast the two as HR administrative tools. Give examples of the decision factors to consider when choosing one over the other.

6. Using the EEO-1 report as an example, discuss the purpose of government mandates. Give examples of penalties that organizations incur when they fail to comply with government mandates such as EEO and OSHA reporting. Explain the purposes of the EEO-1 and Component 2 reports.

7. Based on information in this chapter, recommend the most effective HR administrative approach or approaches for the owner of a small business with fewer than 50 employees and infrequent staffing needs. Would what you recommend work for a business with 5,000 employees and high turnover? Why or why not? Defend your position with information from the chapter.

8. Identify and explain the purpose of each of the four perspectives included in the balanced scorecard. Give two examples of HR measures for each of the four areas that would demonstrate the value of HR in achieving the strategic goals of organizations.

9. Return to the vignette that opened this chapter and answer the questions posed there.

Case Study: The Calleeta Corporation

Jan Samson, CEO at CalleetaCO, sat staring at the now-empty boardroom. Her board of directors had reacted negatively to Jan's growth proposals for expanding CalleetaCO globally, leaving Jan with a big problem. Shareholders, who had bought its stock as the radio frequency identification (RFID) manufacturer led the boom in new uses for its products, were restless as financial returns slowed. In addition, board members expressed concern that CalleetaCO plants in Mexico and Vietnam were becoming the targets of activists who advocated that organizations ensure that the humane working conditions common in the United States be established in American-owned offshore facilities. Finally, board members demanded that Jan move immediately to rein in the employee costs of the U.S. operation. Those costs were growing at a rate of 12% annually, compared with an industry average of 4%. HR Vice President John Nosmas defended his practice of hiring the best, paying them well, and providing them with expensive benefit programs to keep them developing the innovative products the market demanded. However, board members were adamant and demanded a plan at the next meeting, only six weeks away.

CalleetaCO, with its current 1,900 employees spread across three countries (i.e., the United States—1,000; Mexico—200; Vietnam—700), had grown rapidly over its 8-year existence. Although it started as a small entrepreneurial company, CalleetaCO was now challenging the top providers in its industry as it pursued its goal—to become the global leader in RFID products. RFID use exploded after the introduction of memory for passive radio transponders, which led to the production of RFID tags, microchip field radios embedded in products and used for electronic inventory. These tags were replacing traditional bar codes and manual scanning.

Electronic product coding associated with RFID has been embraced by retailers and consumers alike. Retailers such as Gillette, Hewlett-Packard, and Walmart benefit through more rapid restocking, less likelihood of out-of-stock items, and the electronic identification of product expiration dates. In addition, consumers can more easily return purchases. Applications seem unending. Members of Congress have introduced legislation to track sales of tobacco products using RFID technology, for example. New U.S. passports contain RFID tags. "Swipe-less" checkouts, RFID medical alert bracelets, and security identification wristbands are on the horizon. In addition, California is likely to use RFID to comply with the 2005 Real ID Act mandated by Congress (Billingsley, 2007). However, some groups are concerned that RFID proliferation could lead to the surreptitious tracking of an individual's purchases and other privacy violations, especially since individuals may be unaware that their purchases include RFID devices. In addition, hackers may be able to steal identity information by remotely scanning an individual's passport, credit card, or driver's license.

Jan's company had grown rapidly by perfecting several of these products. To keep the innovations coming, Jan and John Nosmas devised a human capital talent acquisition and retention plan to attract the most highly skilled individuals in the industry. The company had 25 HR recruiters focused solely on identifying potential employees, 17 selection specialists to test and interview them, and above-market compensation and benefits at its U.S. location to retain them: health, dental, and life insurance at no cost to the employee; six weeks of paid vacation annually; elder care; child care; on-site pet boarding; liberal performance bonuses; 401(k) matching at 10%; stock options; and onsite spa and exercise facilities. The programs had been incredibly successful in finding the right people to fuel the company's innovative products.

With the company's success had come an even larger HR department. For example, employees regularly stopped by the HR office to chat with their designated HR support representatives (there was one HR support representative for every 10 employees). The employees were thrilled with the personal service and responsiveness to inquiries on everything from health questions to veterinary referrals. Managers had access to their own HR support specialists, who handled everything from performance appraisals and salary increases to filling vacancy requests and overseeing employee discipline. When the company had formed an SSC for information technology and financial services, the HR department had balked at participating because employees were so satisfied with service levels, even though departmental costs were 20% higher than those of counterparts at competitor firms. The firm's HRIS remained under the control of HR information technology specialists in the department, and there seemed few reasons to pursue portals. However, employees who traveled to Mexico and Vietnam had begun to complain about their inability to access HR support specialists for needed information because of time differences. U.S. expatriate managers from CalleetaCO controlled employees from Mexico and Vietnam at the offshore locations. HRO firms had recently approached John about the possibility of purchasing or managing those locations, but John had not yet explored such a possibility.

Jan picked up the telephone to call John. She explained the problem and asked him to prepare a list of ideas that could help them both demonstrate how successful CalleetaCO's talent programs had been and meet the board's requirements for cost controls. Jan knew that she would need to get John to work miracles to help meet the board's demands. She didn't want to stop talent searches or above-average total compensation, but board members were unyielding. Unless

Jan could develop a successful plan to slow employee expense growth, control the activist stakeholder groups, and ultimately improve earnings, she could easily become the ex-CEO.

Case Study Questions

1. What are the key business issues facing Jan?

2. In what ways are CalleetaCO's HR operations contributing to the company's success? How do these contributions support the company's strategic goals? What changes can John make in his HR operations to meet the board's demands?

3. Describe whether each of John's proposed changes will hinder or help CalleetaCO achieve sustainable competitive advantage. Which ones would you choose if you were in John's position? Defend your choices using textbook concepts.

4. How would a balanced scorecard help Jan explain the value of her HR talent approach? Provide sample measures for each of the four categories that would support Jan in her presentation to the board.

TALENT MANAGEMENT AND HR PLANNING

Richard D. Johnson and Michael J. Kavanagh

EDITORS' NOTE

This chapter is the first of four chapters that broadly focus on the topic of talent management (TM). Talent management has become an extremely important strategic goal for organizations. At the core of talent management is the idea that to gain competitive advantage in the marketplace, an organization's talent (i.e., its people) must be managed effectively. This management of people includes attracting, selecting, training, compensating, and retaining employees. However, the underlying requirement for talent management is forecasting the need for talented employees in terms of both numbers and skills, particularly the need for employees in leadership positions. To forecast these needs, the organization must have accurate information about the knowledge, skills, and abilities necessary for effective job performance, and these are identified through job analysis. Thus, this chapter is focused on (1) managing talent, (2) forecasting future demand and supply of employees through human resource planning (HRP), (3) analyzing and defining jobs, and (4) understanding how an HRIS can assist both talent management and HRP. Chapter 9 will focus on recruiting and selecting employees with desired talent, Chapter 10 is concerned with improving talent through training and developing employees, and Chapter 11 deals with managing employees' talent through performance management and compensation practices.

CHAPTER OBJECTIVES

After completing this chapter, you should be able to

- Understand what talent management is and how it fits within human resources planning (HRP) and corporate strategy
- Discuss the talent management life cycle

- Discuss how the use of an HRIS supports talent management

- Explain the role of workforce analytics are used in a talent management program

- Discuss the steps in the development and use of an HRP

- Explain the use of HRP in forecasting supply and demand of new employees

- Explain the importance of job analysis and job descriptions

- Explain the relationship between talent management corporate strategy

INDUSTRY BRIEF

MICHELLE TENZYK, CHIEF EXECUTIVE OFFICER, EAST TENTH GROUP

Talent management will continue to be one of the biggest challenges facing leaders as we move through this decade and into the next. There are three crucial areas of talent management that must be considered: acquiring talent, keeping talent, and developing leaders from your talent.

Acquiring talent is about more than just learning how to communicate with and attract millennials and the subsequent generations; it's about adjusting to a rapidly changing, globally connected world that requires more than just the skills to do the job. You need talent that can be flexible and adaptable enough to change direction quickly, without losing their pace. As with everything else in business these days, recruitment is moving faster and must be more flexible, fluid, and responsive to the rapid changes occurring inside and outside of your organization.

According to PwC's Global CEO Survey, CEOs are worried about attracting skilled talent. More than half of global CEOs surveyed anticipate the need for adding headcount, but concerns about acquiring the talent they need is the highest it has been in a decade. To overcome talent acquisition concerns, remain competitive, and meet growth needs, most organizations will need to reevaluate their talent acquisition strategy by investing in talent acquisition, proactively seeking talent.

Retaining talent is another challenge altogether, because even when your team members aren't looking for a new job, if they are good at what they do, everyone else is looking for them. Part of the talent manager's role will be doing everything necessary to keep team members happy so that you don't lose the investment you make in acquiring and developing them. Retaining the right talent will require a flexible, open approach that is as much about clearly communicating your culture and brand. People analytics—using data to make better, smarter, and faster decisions about your human capital—will be a necessity of the future, not just for HR but for every area of your organization. Stay interviews, global mobility opportunities, rapid feedback, and leadership development opportunities will be essential for keeping strong talent.

Developing leaders should be an ongoing part of your overall talent management strategy. Changing dynamics in the workplace require business leaders to have multiple team members who are prepared for leadership positions earlier in their careers by always having multiple candidates capable of filling any key position, by hiring enough tech-savvy talent to propel the organization forward, and by always seeking nimble flexibility in team members.

Stagnating organizations will not survive, and talent management must transform by using data analytics and metrics to make better decisions, by implementing more sophisticated and modernized recruiting methods, by creating cross-functional teams, by increasing the overall adaptability of the workforce, and by creating a culture that attracts the right people. Technology will be at the center of these decisions, providing data and analysis tools to managers.

HRIS IN ACTION

Rudiger is sitting at his desk in his seventh-floor corner office in the City, gazing out over London and reflecting on life. At 43, he is at the top of his game. He has everything he could wish for—a lovely partner, a 4-year-old in a private nursery, a new executive house in the suburbs, a holiday home in southern Italy, and a remuneration package that's the envy of his peers and beyond anything his German-immigrant parents could have imagined. But it hasn't been easy. Oh no! It required hard work, long hours, geographical moves every 2 or 3 years, and sacrifices in terms of his personal life.

But now he has a problem. Rudiger has just been appointed global head of People and Talent, responsible for the future of 35,000 people worldwide, the bulk of whom are based in the United States, the United Kingdom, and Europe, and manufacturing is likely to relocate to China in the next two years, adding to his responsibilities. In his previous role, he was responsible for the United Kingdom and Northern Europe and had operational oversight for 11,000 people. An initial consideration of his responsibilities has identified a number of people issues for the next five years:

- recruiting and placing new employees in appropriate jobs as vacancies occur,

- developing the skills of current and new employees in training programs, and

- retaining unique specialists in highly skilled roles.

In addition, several other issues have been brought to his attention by the outgoing global head of People and Talent:

- some of the brightest high performers and the most experienced midlevel managers appear to be leaving the company;

- the general employee population is aging, and there will be a significant number of retirements over the next decade, which will require extensive replacements; and

- there is an aging senior directorship, most of whom are looking toward early retirement.

Although he knows he has a problem, his main concern is that he does not have enough detailed information about the employees to know the scale of the problem. He wishes he could find a general framework in which to address these problems and issues, and he wants to be able to show how the framework and programs he implements will impact the bottom line of the organization.

INTRODUCTION

I hire people brighter than me, and I get out of their way.

—*Lee Iacocca*

When looking for a new job, don't expect to get calls from "headhunters," because that title is no longer appropriate. Today, recruiters identify themselves as either a talent acquisition specialist or, more simply, talent manager. Talent management (TM) is not just a new title for the HR professional who is the manager of new hiring at a company. The field of TM brings with it a new perspective that unifies recruiting, hiring, training, promoting, and retaining talented individuals who can contribute to the overall growth and competitive advantage of a company. Historically, the management of a company's talent was primarily focused on hiring individuals who had good experience along with appropriate educational credentials—and then hoping they would fit. The concept of TM has transformed this approach. Just matching individual skills to specific job requirements is insufficient; TM requires an HRM plan that is a comprehensive program of using and developing the person's knowledge, skills, and abilities (KSAs) over time. The outcomes of a TM program are high-performing employees who can contribute to the effectiveness and profitability of the company. In this chapter, we review TM, with a specific focus on the role that an HRIS plays in support of TM, HR planning, and job analysis.

TALENT MANAGEMENT

Over the past 20 years, talent management has become critical to organization success. In general, **talent management** refers to the process of hiring, socializing, developing, and retaining employees, while at the same time attracting highly skilled individuals from the labor market. Lockwood (2006) defines TM as "the implementation of integrated strategies or systems designed to increase workplace productivity by developing improved processes for attracting, developing, retaining and utilizing people with the required skills and aptitude to meet current and future business needs" (p. 17). Take note that managers use TM for jobs at all levels in a company, from unskilled workers to CEOs. For example, if there is a labor demand (e.g., skills, quantity) for lathe machine operators due to high turnover in this job, then the general process and software used to hire new lathe machine operators would be the same as for hiring senior management. Thus, no matter if a company is looking for operators of a lathe or a CEO, the steps in the TM life cycle are the same. However, even though the steps are the same, the actual processes (e.g., recruiting, interviewing, selecting) for identifying a CEO versus lathe operators can be quite different. Thinking strategically about talent has emerged as organizations increasingly realize the importance of obtaining, developing, an optimizing talent to maximize the probability of success. For example, in a recent survey conducted by the **Society for Human Resource Management (SHRM)**, nearly half (47%) of the respondents said that in the next 10 years, identifying and optimizing talent was the top business investment challenge. This was rated higher than obtaining either financial capital (29%) or intellectual capital (12%; SHRM, 2010). In addition, organizations are investing heavily in software for TM. A recent study suggests that nearly 70% of organizations are now using some type of integrated suite to support TM (CedarCrestone, 2012). Thus, it is no longer a question of whether to focus on TM but rather how to best implement it.

The Talent Management Life Cycle

Today, organizations recognize that an important workforce issue is the lack of leadership capability. Lack of leadership in companies today is not just tied to lack of experience or training. It also comes from (1) expanding too quickly into new markets or geographies, (2) the changing needs of the employees, and (3) the ongoing retirement of the "baby boomers." Although the financial crisis of 2008 delayed retirements of baby boomers, by the end of the next decade (2029), all baby boomers (77 million) will be of retirement age and leaving the workforce. Due to this, the United States is facing a long-term talent shortage. Thus, planning for talent at all organizational levels is critical.

The first step in the **talent management life cycle** is to estimate the demand for labor, that is, the number of new leaders needed to replace the retiring baby boomers. As part of this process, the organization will need to identify high-performing and high-potential employees. Next, the organization will need to estimate the supply of leaders available in both the labor market and internal to the company. Then the *difference* between the estimated supply and demand for new and potential leaders can be calculated. The final step is to use HR programs to change the *difference* so that *supply* and *demand* are equalized (e.g., hiring new leaders when needed). Finally, any TM program must have a positive return on investment (ROI), or financial management will not support these initiatives.[1]

Identifying "High Performers"

Industry research has suggested that high-performing employees are 50% to 100% more productive than "average performers" (McKinsey and Company, 2001). However, it can be challenging to determine the attributes of a high-performing employee. One way to identify high-performing employees and high potentials (those who have the potential to develop further and wish to do so) is to look at the job performance of past individuals who have succeeded in that position and identify the attributes possessed by those individuals. The full set of specific attributes relevant to performance is likely to differ for each organization, but there are some core attributes that are relevant for all positions, such as honesty and integrity. Other attributes that are likely to be relevant for most positions are:

- *Communication skills*; high-performing individuals can communicate effectively orally and in writing and can do so over multiple media, including face to face, phone, e-mail, and social media.

- *Drive*; motivation plays a big role in determining who succeeds in any venture in life. Look at examples of people who constantly "reinvent" themselves, such as Governor Schwarzenegger—bodybuilder to Hollywood actor to California governor.

- *Ability and willingness to listen to the ideas of others*; listening is one of the most important ways of establishing good personal and business relationships.

- *Problem-solving skills*; many tasks today in business deal with solving problems, whether that involves handling a small request by a client over the phone or closing the biggest acquisition deal in a company's history.

- *Imagination*; the closest version of the word "imagination" from a business perspective is when we are asked to think "outside the box."

Organizations are developing talent pools based on criteria such as these to identify top-performing employees and develop them to meet future leadership needs. Figure 8.1 provides an example of the talent pools at Ethical Bank.[2]

Talent Diversity

In addition to identifying high-performing employees, organizations also need to consider the diversity of the talent pool. It is potentially dangerous for organizations to take the

---

FIGURE 8.1 ■ Examples of Talent Pools at Ethical Bank

- Business leaders who are likely to be future country chief executives

- A pool of midcareer hires from nonfinancial services disciplines or careers to provide a source of new talent, thinking, and perspectives

- A pool of 40 MBA recruits from key business schools globally (the plan is to double this pool)

- A talent pool for high-potential women

- An international graduate pool of over 250 graduates with high potential recruited for an international assignment as a precursor to a fast-track career under a very rigorous selection route

---

view that because they are successful now, all that is necessary in terms of a future talent pool is to clone the skills, knowledge, and competencies of current employees. Although there is always a need to retain the best current people, it is also important to recognize that the global environment is dynamic and fast moving. Therefore, a central concern within any TM initiative is what levels of talent will be included in the TM life cycle and from where they will be drawn. The most robust approach is to include the development of talent at all levels of the organization.

In addition, organizations must consider how they will address the diversity of the workforce, paying particular attention to women, people of color, people with disabilities, older workers, part-time workers, and temporary workers. In the United States, diversity will only grow in importance in the coming decades, as the country becomes more diverse. It is estimated that by 2040, no one ethnicity will constitute a majority in the U.S. (Cascio, 2016).

Diversity is valuable to organizations for multiple reasons. First, an employee base that mirrors the customer base can enhance customer service and performance. In addition, diversity can enhance innovation, problem solving, creativity, flexibility, employee engagement, business growth, and earnings (Burrell, 2016; McCuiston, Woolridge, & Pierce, 2004). However, diversity also creates challenges for organizations. It can increase conflict, and it can contribute to decreased social integration in teams (Stahl, Maznevski, Voigt, & Jonsen, 2010). Despite this tension, it is clear that diversity initiatives are here to stay, as organizations annually invest more than $8 billion in diversity training (Kirkland, 2017).

An HRIS can support diversity initiatives in several ways, including providing the data used to identify high-potential underrepresented (e.g., women, people of color, people with disabilities, etc.) talent and by assisting organizations in developing programs to mentor and train these individuals. In addition, recent advances in technology have integrated artificial intelligence (AI) into the HRIS. AI can improve the effectiveness and neutrality of talent decisions, because it does not include human biases that can affect reactions to applicants (and employees) and mislead decision makers. However, biases can still enter AI systems due to the biases that developers bring to the design of these systems. In addition, if biases are inherent in existing HR practices and data, AI may reinforce these biases because it simply focuses on patterns in the data. Amazon discovered this when developing an AI application to identify talent. Specifically, the company found that the algorithm was biased against women in the hiring process (Dastin, 2018). In addition, ethnic biases have been found in selection software (Crawford, 2016). Thus, organizations considering AI-enabled systems for TM should assess the validity and potential adverse impact of the systems.

Talent Management and Corporate Strategy

TM cannot be understood or implemented effectively without a strong understanding of an organization's strategic direction. Corporate strategy answers the question of what businesses an organization should pursue so that they can maximize their long-term profitability. An organization's TM strategy, in turn, should align with this corporate strategy to ensure that the employees have the right skills and tools to maximize the chances of the corporate strategy succeeding. For example, the 2008 economic crisis led to global layoffs, corporate bailouts, and a sense that our global economy can be affected easily by shifts in economic conditions. Corporations had to make fundamental changes not only to their business strategies but also to their TM programs. In this case, TM programs had to rapidly shift from their traditional talent strategy and instead focus on how to best manage a reduction in their workforce while also retaining the most talented and skilled employees.

A specific example of aligning talent and corporate strategies is Walmart's decision to enter China in the mid-1990s. In support of the decision to enter China, Walmart took its successful TM practices, including the Walmart Educational Institute, from the United States and implemented them in China (Trunick, 2006). In addition, the company focused on hiring highly educated and qualified managers from the local talent pool, those who knew the culture and buying habits of the local customers. Walking into a Walmart is a different experience in China than it is in the United States. In addition to fresh produce, items such as fish, turtles, clams, and eels are cleaned at the store for customers (Naughton, 2006). This example illustrates how HR must adapt and change talent programs based on future corporate needs and environmental conditions. What works today might not work tomorrow. If HR is to align itself with changing corporate and business strategy, it must be able to anticipate change and develop new HRP programs and TM practices based on forecasted future corporate strategy.

TECHNOLOGY AND TALENT MANAGEMENT

Technology can support the implementation and management of TM programs in several ways. For example, organizations can use an HRIS to track (1) the number of talented individuals hired, (2) the training of these individuals, (3) their job performance, and (4) their retention. These data can then be used to assess and illustrate the effectiveness of the individual components of a TM program as well as its overall success. An HRIS can be of great assistance in providing information on current employee skills, succession relationships, and leadership readiness (see Figure 8.2). In addition, an HRIS can assist in the implementation of these talent programs and can track adoption and participation by employees at all levels of the organization.

Given the importance of TM to organizations, it is also important that the TM software adopted by the organization supports the chosen TM strategy. As such, organizations are heavily investing in TM software solutions, and the TM software market is an important and growing segment of the overall HRIS market. According to the most recent SierraCedar survey (2019), more than 85% of all organizations indicated that they have implemented at

FIGURE 8.2 ■ Employee Skill Assessment and Succession Planning With an HRIS

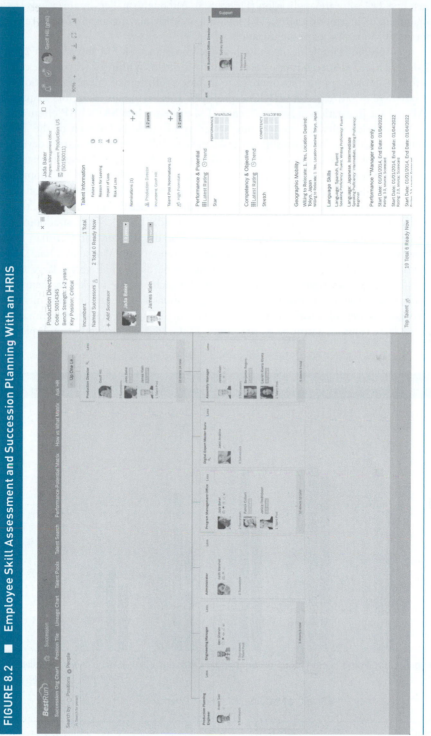

least one TM software application (Figure 8.3). Although smaller organizations lag larger organizations in adoption rates, TM software is clearly playing an important role in supporting TM for all sizes of organizations.

As a specific example of the growth in the importance of TM software, in 2001, Lars Dalgaard founded SuccessFactors as a TM software firm. Within 10 years of the company's founding, it had expanded its offerings to include a full suite of talent applications as well as system of record (e.g., core HRIS) capabilities. This led to SuccessFactors' acquisition by SAP and the integration of SuccessFactors' TM processes into SAP's ERP offerings.

Not only do software vendors offer a variety of products for each of the TM functions discussed, but they also support tasks such as skills assessment, career development, and employee life cycle management. In addition, vendors offer solutions targeted toward specific industries. Thus, a university, an airline, and a hospital could all adopt software tailored to their specific industry. Further, TM software is segmented into offerings for small, medium, or large firms based upon their different needs. For this reason, the vendor landscape is varied and diverse. According to SierraCedar (2019), the most-adopted vendors for small businesses include Ultimate Software, Workday, Paycor, and Ceridian Dayforce. However, for large businesses, the most-adopted vendors are Workday, Oracle, SuccessFactors, and Cornerstone. This illustrates how the needs of small versus large firms lead to different software products being developed for each of these market segments. Finally, as discussed throughout this book, if an organization is interested in implementing TM software, a variety of consulting firms can help with its implementation. Organizations can utilize large consulting firms (e.g., Accenture, PWC, etc.), which support multiple vendors,

FIGURE 8.3 ■ Talent Management Software Adoption Rates[3]

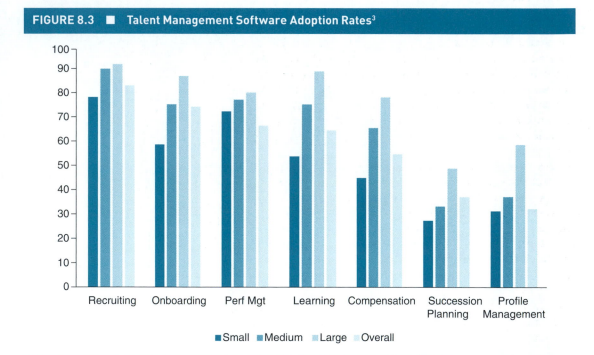

Source: SierraCedar (2019)

or can choose a specialized vendor that focuses on one specific software application (e.g., Collaborative Solutions, AspireHR).

The Future of Talent Management Software

What is the future of TM software? From the vendor's point of view, it's clear that cloud enablement is the primary direction. Most of the TM software offerings and the leading software vendors are cloud based. Many vendors are now differentiating their cloud offerings through the user experience, mobility, social tools, and/or analytics. We briefly discuss several of these trends in what follows.

Social Networking and Talent Management[4]

Although an individual's personal social network is still critical to getting hired (more than 30% of all hires come from employee referrals; Maurer, 2017), organizations are increasingly developing a social media strategy to support TM, especially for employee recruitment. **Social networking sites** (SNSs), such as Facebook, LinkedIn, Twitter, and YouTube can increase the flow of information for making social connections between candidates and the organization. In addition, SNSs can enhance corporate branding and can reach a broader audience than traditional or even web-based recruiting. As is illustrated in Figure 8.4, nearly 90% of large organizations and 70% of small organizations are using LinkedIn to support TM recruitment. Large organizations are also utilizing a breadth of SNS to support recruitment, with Facebook, Twitter, and YouTube all utilized by more than 50% of large organizations. Not surprisingly, due to more limited resources

FIGURE 8.4 ■ Adoption Rates of Social Media for Recruitment[5]

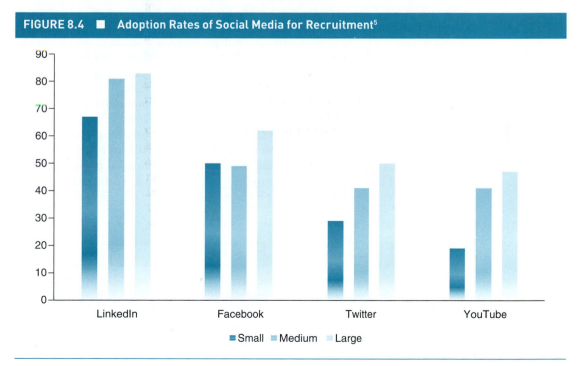

Source: SierraCedar (2019)

to dedicate to SNS, smaller organizations lag in their adoption of these tools. However, even these organizations have embraced SNS as part of talent management.

A major reason for the growth in the use of SNS tools is that prospective job candidates are increasingly using them in their job searches. For example, more than 85% of younger individuals are using social media in their job search (Economy, 2015). If recent college graduates comprise the target audience for your recruiting effort, then social networks can usually provide a direct and more efficient link to potential applicants. However, for older employees, a different social media strategy may be necessary. In addition, it is important to recognize that social media tools are always evolving, and organizations will regularly need to assess the value of using newer tools such as Instagram, Snapchat, or whatever new tool evolves. For more information on the use of social media in recruitment, selection, and training of employees, please see Chapters 9 and 16.

Workforce Analytics and Talent Management

Many organizations view workforce analytics as the future of TM. As such, organizations are heavily investing in these initiatives. The adoption rate of workforce analytics tools is expected to grow by nearly 50% in 2020 and will represent the area of greatest investment in HR for many organizations (SierraCedar, 2019). **Workforce analytics** to manage talent involves asking many questions about an individual employee or a group of employees. The major goal of analytics for TM is to model the KSAs of successful and unsuccessful employees.[6] These models can then be used for a pool of existing employees or new potential hires to determine their likelihood of success.

An employer can also utilize analytics to identify the characteristics of successful employees to see if the company is attracting the strongest individuals to the company. Employers can also use analytics to more effectively train managers on hiring tactics or to funnel resources to the most effective recruitment channels. Further, organizations can integrate internal and external data (e.g., work experiences, education, training, etc.) and analyze them to determine what helps prepare employees for success. Finally, data about performance objectives can be compared with actual business results.

However, for workforce analytics to be effective, organizations must have an integrated HRIS that allows for the sharing of data from both the HR system and other organizational systems so that strong predictive models can be designed. Ultimately, the goal of workforce analytics is to draw conclusions about employees, their skills, development needs, and performance so that HR can more effectively add value to organizational performance and make intelligent decisions regarding the company's human capital. Without data from an HRIS, insights from analytics regarding employee KSAs and performance will be limited.

HUMAN RESOURCE PLANNING

The first part of this chapter has focused on the TM process and identifying high performers and high potentials. An important part of the TM process is **human resource planning (HRP)**. HRP focuses on ensuring that the best available people are working in the proper jobs at the appropriate time, so that organizational performance is maximized. Fulfilling this goal means that an organization accurately forecasts the number of employees it will need in the future. With accurate estimates, the company can begin recruiting new employees as well as training current ones. To make these forecasts accurate, it is crucial that organizations can identify the **knowledge, skills, and abilities (KSAs)** required in the forecasted jobs. Job analysis provides this information by producing job descriptions. **Job analysis** is the process of systematically obtaining information about jobs by determining the duties, tasks, or activities of jobs, from which KSAs can be estimated.

Human Resource Planning

Human resource planning (HRP), often called workforce planning in the European Union, is derived from the manpower planning literature of the 1960s, a time when the focus was on management and control practices with short-term objectives. HRP begins with the identification of the strategic goals of the company and of how an HRP program can assist in achieving the effective use of the human capital of the company. Changes in organizational strategy and business objectives can impact the number of employees (e.g., greater or fewer) needed by the organization, their required competencies and behaviors, and the expected productivity levels for these employees. To shape the discussion of HRP, we adapt Bramham's (1994) framework (see Figure 8.5). This framework consists of four major stages that include (1) analysis and investigation, (2) forecasting, (3) planning and resourcing, and (4) implementation and control.

FIGURE 8.5 ■ HR Planning

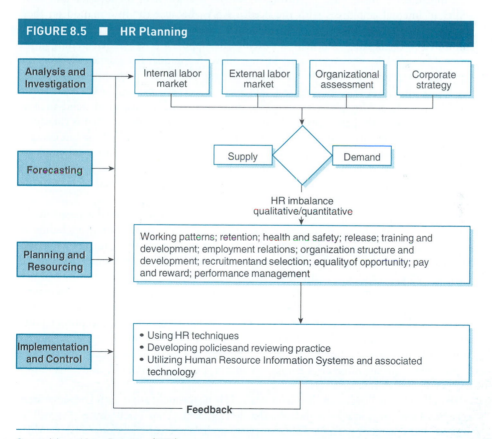

Source: Adapted from Bramham (1994).

Phase 1: Analysis and Investigation

During this phase, four key sources of information are analyzed. First is the nature of the external labor market. The **external labor market** reflects the market from which an organization derives its employees. These estimates are available from state and national labor departments, local unemployment agencies, and employee referral agencies. However, in the past two decades, the increasing use of technology in the workplace has revolutionized the geographical base of the external labor force. Thus, organizations no longer think of their labor market in terms of local or national population but increasingly in terms of a global labor market.

Despite the growth and reach of the external labor market, most jobs are still filled with internal employees (e.g., the internal labor market). The **internal labor market** reflects the availability of current employees with the requisite KSAs to fill open positions. This market is affected by and reflects the historic movement of employees within the company by job such as the number of promotions and lateral transfers of employees between jobs. The advantages of the internal labor market are that potential hires tend to be less expensive; applicants are already familiar with the culture and can start working in the position more quickly. Research also suggests that using internal labor can lead to increased training ROI and employee retention (Cappelli, 1995; Green, 1993).

Unfortunately, many large organizations are often unaware of the location and availability of internal employees with the needed KSAs, because the information on these employees is often not linked to the broader organizational information systems. An HRIS connected to the broader information systems can support a better understanding of the internal labor market in several ways. First, it allows for standardized data collection and reporting on employees that offer a snapshot of the KSAs and performance of specific employees, or classes of employees (e.g., absenteeism, revenue per employee, etc.). It also provides a good starting point for deeper examinations, such as historical trend analyses (e.g., absences over the past 5 years). As an example, consider a company that is concerned about the looming baby boomer retirements. Using data from the HRIS, it can conduct a demographic analysis that accounts for retirement projections and historical employee turnover for those in the baby boomer cohort. Ultimately, though, organizations will need to integrate and analyze data from the external and internal labor markets to identify the talent needed to meet market demands.

The third component of analysis and investigation is an organizational assessment. An organizational assessment focuses on the current state of the organization, including its philosophy, culture, values, and beliefs. One key perspective of an organizational assessment is an understanding of how the employee is viewed by the organization. For example, are they viewed as a cost or as an investment for the business? Other factors assessed may include the effectiveness of HR policies and practices and the place of the HR department in the organizational structure. An HRIS can support this analysis by providing trend analysis for the next 1, 5, or 10 years based on previous comparable periods. Exception reports, employee attitude surveys, and an employee demographic breakdown can be automated. When information regarding organizational talent is the focus, reports can be structured around the aggregate number of employees within specific talent pools, as well as knowledge and job performance levels.

Finally, as noted earlier in the chapter, any HR plan should align with corporate strategy. For many organizations, though, the development of an HRP strategy is still an organic and emergent process. This can create a challenge for traditional HRIS, which can be static and not flexible enough to meet the needs of an emergent and dynamic TM process. Organizational and HRIS processes and practices may require significant annual updating to meet HRP needs. However, research has shown that when organizations are able to link HRIS investments to organizational strategy and the environment, the ROI of these investments is higher (Aral, Bryjolfson, & Wu, 2012).

Phase 2: Forecasting

The second phase in HRP is forecasting. Forecasting is concerned with the identification of strategic options and the creation of HR scenarios about labor force demand and supply. Essentially, this means providing a calculated guess about the makeup of the employees and jobs in the organization over time. Fundamental to the success of forecasting is the assumption that the data contained in the HRIS are clean, accurate, and current. Often, this is problematic, with few HR functions being able to claim 100% accuracy and currency. Over time, though, HRIS are becoming more accurate and able to support the estimation of demand and supply of potential employees. For example, data from an HRIS can provide a breakdown of employee turnover by business unit, department, or employee cohort. More sophisticated AI-based systems may also help managers identify possible drivers of this turnover.

The goal of demand forecasting is to predict future people needs. This is done by scanning the external environment and matching this with the future organizational strategic vision, cultural style, and organizational structures. Consider, for example, a fictitious company that manufactures brake assemblies, MobiBrake. MobiBrake controls a significant share of the market and wishes to increase market share for each of the next 3 years. HR would thus need to forecast how this would increase staffing needs (e.g., forecasted demand) while also accounting for average annual turnover. To do this, HR professionals can use a number of algorithmic, statistical, or heuristic techniques using data contained in the HRIS as well as in other organizational systems (see Noe, Hollenbeck, Gerhart, & Wright, 2010, for examples).

Along with demand, estimates of supply must also be conducted. Estimating labor supply consists of identifying candidates from the internal and external labor markets and forecasting availability of potential employees from both. Data from an HRIS can also be helpful here by providing information on demographics, length of service, KSAs, leadership potential, flight risk (e.g., potential to leave the organization), and other relevant factors. Most HRIS provide these capabilities as part of standard reporting tools, and many will allow your firm to develop additional reports as needed.

Returning to MobiBrake, we would expect there to be a positive gap between our current labor demand and future needs. Therefore, we can anticipate the need to add new employees and promote some current employees to open job positions. This will require the initiation of a variety of HR programs across recruiting (external labor market) and training and development (internal labor market) geared at identifying, hiring, and promoting employees. For example, online marketing campaigns can be created to attract new applicants, and training programs can be expanded to facilitate the promotion of current employees.

Phase 3: Planning and Resourcing

Planning and Resourcing focuses on the specific development of the tactical and operational plans to support future employee needs across all functional HR areas as well as providing the resources that ensure their success. The key in this phase is to develop programs that address and eliminate the gap between current employee staffing levels and future needs. There are some choices to be made at this point regarding HRM programs. For example, decisions will need to be made about the use of technology to support recruiting and training. Additional decisions will need to be made regarding whether these programs will be implemented by internal HR staff or by an outside vendor. Further, organizations need to consider the expected benefit-cost ratio for the new programs. HR will also need to consider the type of data needed to support these new programs and their location within the HRIS. Finally, HR will need to determine what new data might be generated as the results of these programs and where these data should be stored.

Phase 4: Implementation and Control

This final phase of HRP involves the implementation of the planned HRM programs from phase 3. Regardless of the programs that are implemented, one of the most important aspects of HRP is the evaluation of these new programs to determine if they have closed the gap between supply and demand. The HRIS plays an important role in assessing the effectiveness of the HRP in closing the demand–supply gap by providing data regarding the success of the programs. In addition, data can be used for setting up future HRP programs. Particularly important is the evaluation of how useful the new HRM programs were in closing the gap. This section covered the basics of HRP programs, which can be applied to planning the utilization of human capital, whether entry level or senior management. Having established the "nuts and bolts" of HRP, we will now examine the role of job analysis.

Job Analysis

A primary goal of an effective HR department is to ensure that the organization has the best available people working in the proper jobs at the appropriate time to maximize the organization's productive capacity in pursuit of strategic goal achievement. To do this, however, the organization must know not only what each job entails but also what KSAs are necessary to perform the job successfully. Job analysis provides both types of information. As noted earlier, job analysis is the process of systematically obtaining information about jobs by determining the duties, tasks, or activities of jobs, from which KSAs can be estimated. From this analysis, job descriptions can be developed. **Job descriptions** define the working contract between the employee and the organization. Job descriptions uses include: (1) evidence for any litigation involving unfair discrimination in hiring, promoting, or terminating employees; (2) development of all the HRM programs, especially TM, in organizations, and other important HRM programs including recruitment, selection, training, and performance appraisal; (3) development of compensation structures; and (4) employee disciplinary programs and union grievances. In fact, job descriptions are often termed the "heart" of the HRM system or the "blueprints" that underlie all HR activities. Given the importance of job descriptions, it is *critically important that they be accurate and timely*. Effectively managed HR departments capture and store the results of all job analyses and job descriptions within the HRIS to facilitate future changes in jobs required by reorganizations, mergers/acquisitions, technology, and market-driven customer expectations.

Approaches and Techniques to Job Analysis

A variety of approaches to job analysis are covered in detail in other sources (Ghorpade, 1988; Morgeson, Brannick, & Levine, 2019); thus, only a general approach to conducting job analyses will be discussed in this chapter. Job analysis involves the following phases or considerations:

- Identify the types of job information needed. This information can include tasks, duties, responsibilities, the knowledge required, performance standards, job context, and the equipment used. A determination of what specific information will be used for the analysis of all jobs must be made to maintain consistency across the final job descriptions.

- Identify the sources of information about the job. The best sources are usually job incumbents and their supervisors; however, professional job analysts can be used for newly created or complex jobs. Company records and the Internet, specifically the U.S. Department of Labor's **O*Net database** (http://onetonline.org), are also good sources of information about jobs.

- Determine the appropriate methods of collecting the job data. Methods include interviews, questionnaires, observation, and focus groups. The choice of technique(s) depends on the number of jobs to be analyzed and the funding available.

- Consider using one or more of the standardized techniques for conducting job analysis to enhance the final job description—for example, functional job analysis, the **position analysis questionnaire (PAQ)**, task inventory analysis, or the critical incident method (see Ghorpade, 1988).

Regardless of the approach or technique used to analyze the jobs in an organization, the outcome must obtain accurate and timely job descriptions. Thus, a key question facing HR professionals is, how can technology assist HR in establishing and maintaining the accuracy of job descriptions?

HRIS Applications

The utilization of technology has increased the availability of information supporting reduced costs of collecting information and enhanced convenience of collecting and analyzing information. One of the earliest adopters of HRIS to support job analysis was the United States Department of Defense, which developed a mainframe-based electronic job analysis process in the 1970s (Whitman & Hyde, 1978). Today, though, organizations can take advantage of an online repository of information on more than 1,000 broad occupations, O*Net, to help guide the development of job descriptions. Consider, for example, the occupation of professor. O*Net contains generic descriptions for professors of physics, architecture, sociology, forestry, business (e.g., see http://www.onetonline.org/link/summary/25-1011.00 for the summary description of the position "business teachers, postsecondary"). To ensure that the KSAs are accurate for a specific position in a specific discipline (e.g., human resources) at a specific university, additional information and reviews of this job description would need to be conducted. The Society for Human Resource Management (SHRM) also provides many job analysis tools and templates as well. Finally, many different vendors offer these tools as stand-alone products or components of a larger product offering.

Completing job analyses and deriving job descriptions can be accomplished through online survey techniques. Job analysis questionnaires can be administered online to job incumbents and supervisors, and the resulting job descriptions can be analyzed statistically to finalize job descriptions. This online questionnaire capability can be part of an integrated HRIS software package covering multiple programs (e.g., SAP, PeopleSoft) or purchased as stand-alone software. For example, the Economic Research Institute (ERI) has an Occupational Assessor® that can assist firms in job analysis and developing job descriptions.

Maintaining accurate job descriptions can also be aided by an HRIS. Self-service portals can be used to make sure that job descriptions remain accurate and timely. For example, if work procedures or new equipment are introduced, it would be easy to request that the persons affected by the change, both employees and supervisors, access their current job descriptions via portals to make necessary updates to the job descriptions. In addition, it is a good idea to establish an annual review of all job descriptions to maintain their timeliness. If a company requires annual reviews of employee performance and these forms can be generated by the HRIS, it would be quite easy to generate a copy of the current job description to accompany each request for a job performance evaluation. The employee and his or her supervisor could then review the accuracy of the job descriptions and submit any changes necessary through portals. However, this can be perceived as time-consuming and outside of the supervisor–subordinate relationship. If organizations wish to utilize this approach, they will need to communicate the importance of accurate and timely job descriptions and the impact that out-of-date descriptions can have on the workload, performance, and compensation of each employee.

Finally, there has been some limited research on the use of technology-supported job analysis. For example, Peterson and Taylor (2004) found that the use of technology led to more accurate job descriptions and cut the time to create them by one-third. In addition, as part of the development of O*Net, experts from multiple locations provided data about job duties and utilized virtual teams to reach an agreement regarding the jobs and their descriptions. They also found that this technology-enabled approach led to more complete job descriptions and reduced completion times compared to traditional job analysis (Reiter-Palmon, Brown, Sandall, Buboltz, & Nimps, 2006).

Summary

The primary purpose of this chapter was to investigate how an HRIS and other information systems can be used to support a TM program. An organization's TM strategy should be long term, looking 5 to 10 years into the future, and should match the overall corporate strategy so that it can make a major contribution to the immediate and future strategic positions of the organization. Critical to any TM program is the identification of a diverse set of high-potential employees. The chapter further discussed how data from an HRIS can support TM in general and in the identification of high-potential employees specifically. In addition, it focused on the growing role of social networking and workforce analytics to more readily identify, attract, and retain talent. This chapter also discussed the role of HR planning, its phases, and how technology can be used to provide the data that support the HRP process. Crucial to both HRP and TM is the development of *accurate and timely* job descriptions based on job analysis. The chapter finished with a discussion of job analysis and the use of technology to streamline job analysis and improve its effectiveness.

Key Terms

acquiring talent 189
developing leaders 189
external labor market 200
human resource planning
    (HRP) 198
internal labor market 200
job analysis 199

job description 202
knowledge, skills, and abilities
    (KSAs) 199
O*Net database 203
position analysis questionnaire
    (PAQ) 203
retaining talent 189

social networking (web)sites
    (SNSs) 197
Society for Human Resource
    Management (SHRM) 191
talent management (TM) 191
talent management life cycle 192
workforce analytics 198

Discussion Questions

1. Why are job descriptions critical to the effective management of an organization? What role(s) does job analysis play in an HRP and talent management program?

2. How can an HRIS assist in establishing and maintaining accuracy and timeliness in job descriptions?

3. How does the strategic direction of the organization influence talent management and human resource planning activities?

4. Given the different needs of the HRP process discussed in this chapter, what types of data would you expect the HRIS to contain?

5. Discuss the pros and cons of using social networks in talent management.

6. How would you use workforce analytics to support talent programs such as recruiting, retention, and employee development?

7. Discuss how you would use information systems (IS) to support succession planning.

Case Study: HRIS in Action Case Continued

18 months later. . .

Once again, Rudiger is sitting at his desk in his seventh-floor office in central London reflecting on life. The move from Barcelona to England went smoothly, with the last crate arriving only two months later than the rest. He is still working hard, but the hours are slightly better since the introduction of the work–life balance policy last year, and his family has settled well into the idyllic English countryside.

As the global head of People and Talent, he still has problems, though—just different ones. The talent strategy "Our People—Our Talent—Our Future," which he presented to the board in his third month, identified the need for robust HRP information and analyses that required a new version of HRP software. It is in its early stages, but the intensive data-cleansing and updating activity has been straightforward so far. More concerning are the metrics responsible for producing the information needed to develop far-reaching HRP policies and practices for the future. The metrics are relatively easy to construct, but it is proving tricky to find the right "bundles" of predictive metrics—this is holding up progress with the analysis application package. In addition, there have been cost overruns in the implementation of the HRP software, and some senior managers are wondering if the new software should be abandoned.

At least 3 of the 12 board members will retire in the next 2 years, and they are looking to groom their successors. At least one will have to be hired from outside the organization, and the HR department is not sure what the CEO wants for this position.

In addition, employee turnover and an aggressive growth strategy mean hiring new employees as well as training transferring current employees. The work that is involved in defining competences (KSA sets) at skill levels within jobs is progressing well, with hard-won support from the unions. However, job descriptions that can be found are at least 3 to 5 years old, and some jobs have no descriptions. The new apprenticeship scheme is about to be launched, and the international graduate student package and development program has been completely revised. Overall, things are progressing OK, but there is much to be done.

Case Study Questions

1. How would you recommend that Rudiger begin to develop an HRP program? What are the steps that he needs to take?

2. How should the problem with the job descriptions be handled? Should the unions be involved?

3. What are some of the problems in the past that have led this current situation to occur?

4. Why do you think there are cost overruns? How could this have been avoided?

5. Why are there problems with implementation of the new software?

6. How will job descriptions be developed for the positions of board member and international student intern?

9

RECRUITMENT AND SELECTION IN AN INTERNET CONTEXT

Kimberly M. Lukaszewski and David N. Dickter

EDITORS' NOTE

This chapter is the second one concerned with managing an organization's talent. As noted in previous chapters, talent management is an extremely important strategic goal for organizations, both domestic and global. After the need for external hiring of new employees has been identified via HR planning (Chapter 8), the next step is to design recruitment and selection programs that will result in the successful hiring of needed talent. Successful recruiting and hiring of new talent is the first step in the talent management process (introduced in Chapter 8), which concludes with the retention of high-performance and committed employees. This chapter will cover the concepts of recruitment and selection and the use of the Internet and an HRIS to improve the operation of these HR programs. Specifically, it informs the reader on how to maximize the effectiveness of e-recruitment design and implementation. Further, with the majority of organizations utilizing technology in support of selection, the chapter informs the reader on important considerations such as equivalence and bandwidth when moving online. Finally, the chapter points out that, as with any technology implementation, there are risks associated with the use of technology in both recruitment and selection and discusses how companies can address these risks.

CHAPTER OBJECTIVES

After completing this chapter, you should be able to

- Understand the relationship between the Internet and organizational recruiting objectives
- Discuss the potential advantages and disadvantages of online recruitment in the framework of recruiting objectives

- Discuss recruitment strategies and social networking
- Discuss new technological advances in online recruitment
- Understand the relationship between e-recruitment and HRIS
- Understand how HRIS is related to selection and assessment
- Discuss technological issues that influence selection
- Understand the value of HRIS selection applications through the use of utility analysis

HRIS IN ACTION

Bank of America sought to merge its Internet-based assessment with the firm's applicant-tracking software application. In the process, the company hoped to improve the quality of the applicant pool. It was thought that adding valid selection tests would improve the quality of candidates such that those assessed by tests would be much more likely to be successful on the job than those who simply applied through the Internet. Also, by increasing applicant quality through testing, the company could reduce applicant-processing time.

Bank of America contracted with a test vendor to improve its selection system first. The vendor created competency profiles for jobs by interviewing about 50 current job incumbents and managers to ascertain that the competency profile for each job had the correct skills listed for the job. A "set of inventories was then identified to map onto the confirmed competencies and serve to identify the candidates who had the greatest potential for success in the job and would be the right candidates scheduled for final interviews" (Society for Human Resource Management [SHRM], 2004, p. 1). The next aspect of the project was to change the interface on the Web page for Bank of America so that recruiters could get the applicant information they needed to manage applications for 100 hiring sites.

Next, the promising applicants were asked to visit a Bank of America staffing facility, where they completed three tests and inventories on a computer. Once there, candidates watched a job preview video and then were again directed to a computer to key in basic contact information and complete three more tests. Candidates who were not comfortable with the software were able to access a built-in tutorial. After candidates had completed this procedure on the computer, the administrator was able to access results and conduct on-the-spot interviews with candidates who met a threshold score. In addition, this procedure allowed human contact with the candidates and maintained system security, particularly for the selection tests.

By combining online testing with its applicant-tracking system, Bank of America netted some significant results:

- Improved ability to identify successful performers. Of those who passed the test phase and were hired, 84% were rated as successful performers by their supervisors.

In fact, passing candidates were 5 times more likely to be successful on the job.

- Significant return on investment. The estimated annual return on investment from using the system in selecting for the Operations job family was more than 2,000%.

- Favorable reactions from candidates. Ninety-seven percent of respondents expressed overall satisfaction with the selection process and agreed that the

answers they were asked to provide represented their abilities.

- Valid and fair assessment of candidates. The inventories included in the system were able to distinguish between high and low performers and increase the probability of selecting the best candidates. In addition, analyses broken out by race, gender, and age showed that the inventories treated all groups fairly. (SHRM, 2004, p. 2)

INTRODUCTION

If you think it's expensive to hire a professional to do the job, wait until you hire an amateur.

—Red Adair

To remain competitive in today's global environment, organizations are searching for more efficient and effective means of acquiring and maintaining a highly qualified workforce. One popular and highly productive strategy for meeting this goal has been the use of technology, especially the Internet. Thus, the focus of this chapter is to consider the impact of the Internet and technology on the recruitment and selection processes in organizations. In the paragraphs that follow, we will discuss the effects of technology on these two key processes. In the recruitment section, we address the objectives of the recruitment process and whether online recruitment is helping to achieve these objectives. The recruitment objectives, which are based on the model of Breaugh and Starke (2000), include cost of filling a job opening, speed of filling a job opening, psychological contract fulfillment, employee satisfaction, retention rates, quality of applicants, quantity of applicants, and diversity of applicants. We also discuss the impact of the attributes of the organizational website on applications and the use of social networking. In addition, the relationship between e-recruitment and HRIS is explained. In the selection section, we address the importance of assessment and its role in HRIS. Technology issues surrounding selection, such as validity, computerized assessment, security, and proctoring, are also discussed. We then present the ways in which the HRIS has been integrated with the function of selection and assessment to address the issues mentioned previously. Finally, we demonstrate the value of selection with HRIS selection applications through the use of utility analysis.

RECRUITMENT AND TECHNOLOGY

The goal of the **recruitment** function is to identify, attract, and hire the most qualified people (Cascio, 2019). Recruitment has become more challenging due to the fierce competition for talent in the labor market and the number of jobs available (Jobvite, 2014). For example, there are 5.8 million unemployed persons versus 7.1 million open jobs in the U.S. (BLS, 2019a, 2019b). As a result, companies are increasingly being required to expand their search for applicants beyond local and domestic borders in order to find enough qualified talent. Organizations have begun using the different technologies as a means of attracting job applicants. These technologies include: Internet (e.g., company websites, job boards), social media (e.g., LinkedIn, Facebook), mobile recruitment, and artificial intelligence. In the United States, more than 95% of large companies use the Internet in some fashion to recruit applicants for job openings (Maurer & Cook, 2011). For example, almost 85% of companies use social media, with another 9% planning to adopt it in the near future (SHRM, 2017). There has been greater reliance on mobile recruitment, since almost 90% of job seekers find the use of their mobile device critical in the hiring process (Verliden, 2019). Artificial intelligence is also gaining popularity in human resources, especially recruitment and selection. More than 40% of global organizations have incorporated this technology in their HR functions (PWC, 2017).

With more than 54% of job seekers looking for online for jobs (Smith, 2015), it is no surprise that many organizations, both large and small, are turning to online recruitment technologies as part of their recruitment strategies. Online recruitment is the use of technologies, such as websites and social media, to find and attract potential job applicants, to keep them interested in the organization during the selection processes, and to influence their job choice decisions (Chapman & Gödöllei, 2017). Besides utilizing the Web as a way of attracting candidates, they are also using Web-based tools (e.g., applicant tracking systems) to support the recruiting process (Figure 9.1).

Although there are certainly a number of benefits associated with using online recruitment, there are also several issues that need to be considered before organizations adopt this strategy. For instance, is online recruitment a win-win situation for both job applicants and organizations? A good way to answer this question is to step back and examine the degree to which online recruitment (a) enables organizations to meet their recruiting objectives and (b) provides applicants with the means of obtaining jobs. We discuss these issues in the following sections.

The Impact of Online Recruitment on Recruitment Objectives

Research by Breaugh and Starke (2000) has identified a number of objectives for the recruitment process, including (a) cost, (b) speed of filling job vacancies, (c) psychological contract fulfillment, (d) satisfaction and retention rates, (e) quality and quantity of applicants, and (f) diversity of applicants. To what extent does online recruitment help organizations meet each of these objectives?

Recruitment Objective: Cost of Filling the Job Opening

One important recruitment objective that organizations constantly strive for is to minimize the cost of filling job openings (Breaugh & Starke, 2000). The average cost of recruiting and hiring someone is more than $4,100, and the average time it takes to fill a given position is 42 days (SHRM, 2016). This has prompted many organizations to

FIGURE 9.1 ■ Screen Shot of Current Applicants Form. (Applicant records shown are fictitious examples.)

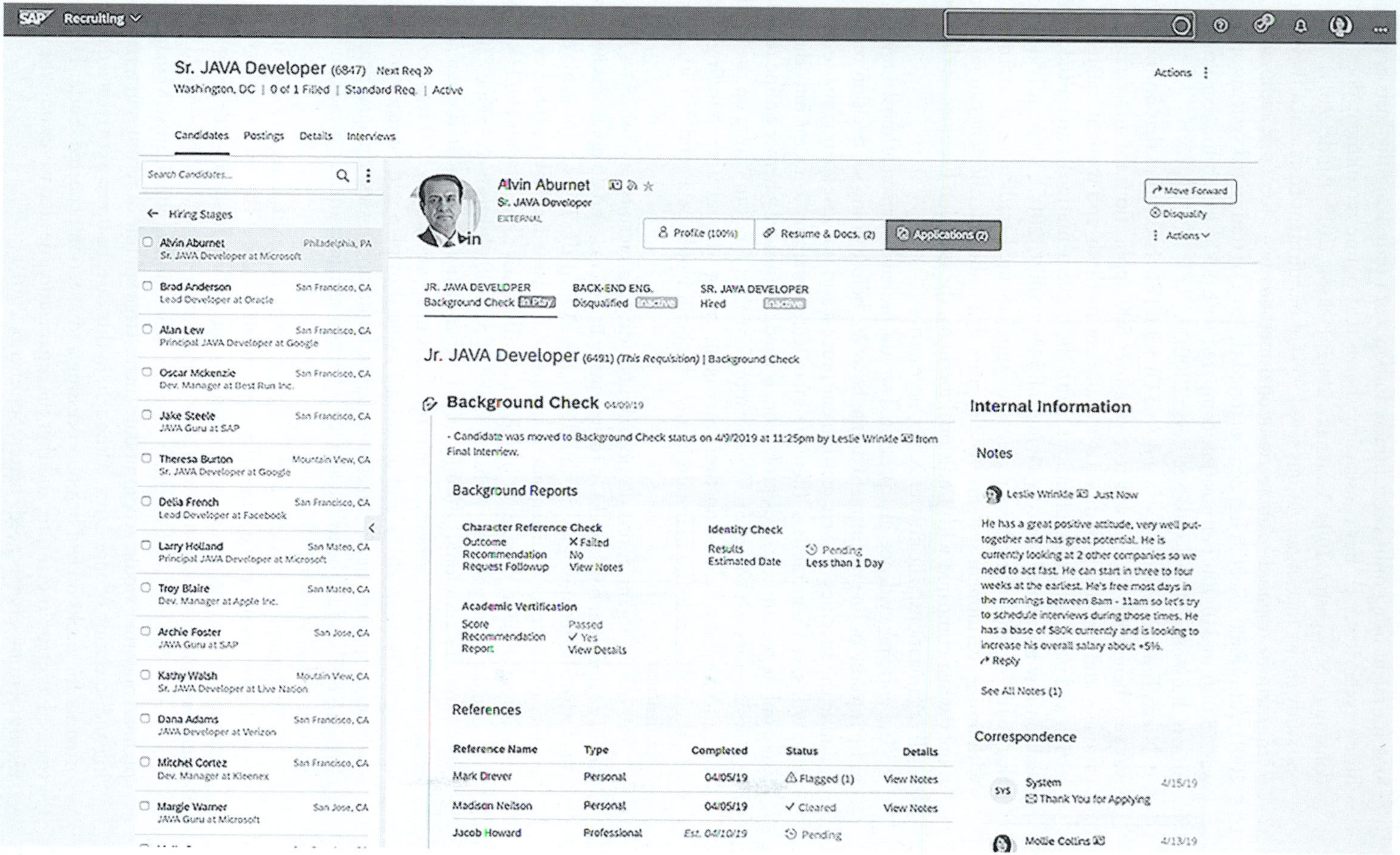

Source: © SuccessFactors, Inc. All Rights Reserved

look for talent using online recruitment in hopes of minimizing the costs and time of the hiring cycle. Research has consistently shown that online recruitment does reduce costs (Chapman & Webster, 2003; Galanaki, 2002; Jackson, 2019; Pande, 2011). For example, one study shows that organizations saved 95% of recruitment costs when they used online recruitment as opposed to more traditional methods (e.g., job fairs, radio ads; Cappelli, 2001). Additional research has demonstrated the cost of traditional systems of recruitment was $8,000 to $10,000 per position compared with $900 for online recruitment (Cober, Brown, Blumental, Doverspike, & Levy, 2000).

Nike's Europe, Middle East, and Asia Division (EMEA) found that online recruitment was very beneficial. EMEA was receiving over 800 applications for an average of 120 job vacancies and was using traditional recruitment methods and manual means for the collection and processing of applications. With the implementation of an online solution, the division saw an immediate cost savings of 54% (Pollitt, 2005). Thus, it is not surprising that many organizations have replaced or supplemented traditional recruitment systems with online recruitment systems. As it appears that online recruitment can save companies money when compared with traditional methods, the question becomes, is this applicable to all organizations? The answer is, not necessarily.

The enticing evidence just presented would probably persuade most organizations to jump into the online recruitment arena; however, before doing so, decision makers should examine the specifics of their recruitment process and not just assume that online recruitment will save them money. There are many considerations to factor into the decision of using online recruitment. HR professionals need to consider whether online recruitment is appropriate for their company. Organizations are often quick to "jump on the bandwagon" with a technology their competitors may being using without understanding its capabilities, the skills needed to maintain it, and whether it would be a good fit with their specific organization.

Too often, organizations do not map out existing recruitment processes fully, do not identify important bottlenecks in the recruitment process, and do not assess how these may align with the technology's capabilities or the ROI of the investment. This can be problematic, as unintended consequences may result. Infusing technology into any HR process, such as recruitment, may result in greater administrative burdens for the HR department or managers (Chapman & Webster, 2003; IES, 2019; Johnson & Stone, 2019; Russell, 2007), and this additional administrative burden should be considered when adopting. For example, online recruitment, on average, leads to approximately 250 resumes for each job opening (Glassdoor, 2015), and organizations need to plan and be ready to process large amounts of applications to screen out those who do not possess the qualifications needed. This can easily add time to the average 2 hours a recruiter already spends on their administrative tasks (Maister, 2017).

As an example, consider Sutter Health, a nonprofit health care network. Sutter decided to post jobs online to facilitate the recruitment process. The use of online recruitment generated an enormous number of resumes—more than 300,000—for fewer than 10,000 open positions. In most situations, this is something an organization would desire; however, Sutter Health failed to think past the generation of applicants. Managers had not planned how they would accommodate such a large volume of resumes in terms of processing and screening of applicants. Although, in this case, resumes were received quickly, they often sat for weeks on end before processing and selection occurred. Sutter Health quickly realized its error in planning and that the organization needed to revamp the use of online recruitment to serve its needs better (Seminerio, 2001).

One way to reduce this burden is to use an **applicant tracking system (ATS)**. More than 75% of recruiters use such a system, with almost 95% citing the improvements to their recruiting and hiring processes (Deutsch, 2019). A second way to reduce administrative burdens is to incorporate screening capabilities into your process that will automate the screening of individuals before an application is completed and submitted for consideration. For example, this screening may include a series of questions related to organizational culture, job qualifications, personality traits, or basic skills (e.g., math). Third, automated emails from pre-loaded templates can facilitate communication with applicants, reducing the number of emails and phone calls required by recruiters.

Organizations also need to track the effectiveness of online recruitment through common recruitment metrics (such as yield ratios, placements made, quality of new hires, job performance of new hires, cost per hire, turnover rates). Many organizations find it useful to monitor the numbers of hits your website receives on its career pages. However, the number of hits on a website is only one small component in measuring effectiveness (Cober et al., 2000). Further, monitoring conversion rates (those who view the openings and those who actually complete the application) can also help assess the effectiveness of online recruitment.

Research has found that more than 80% of applicants would use or were actively using online sources to find information about open positions, but only 41% found their present positions through online means (Starr, 2019; Stevens, 2007). This could be explained by the complexity and length of organizations' online applications. Research found 60% of job seekers quit in the middle of filling out an online job application if it is too long or too complex (Zielinski, 2016). Applicant abandonment can lead to longer searches, which may, counterintuitively, increase recruitment costs. Therefore, organizations should monitor the conversion rate for applications and review their online applications to make sure they are user friendly and can be completed in a timely fashion.

Echoing these concerns, a study of large organizations (5,000 employees or more) in the United Kingdom, which show that only about 40% of the organizations considered online recruitment to be a more effective means than any other traditional method of recruitment (Reed Company, 2003). Together, these results imply that organizations need to track the outcomes and calculate common metrics (e.g., successful placements) of their online recruitment process, monitor and evaluate its effectiveness, and compare these outcomes with those achieved by other recruiting methods. Further, current recruitment processes need to be examined to see where technology would align or where potential improvements can be made by its use. As a result, organizations need to consider the overall costs associated with the entire recruitment process before deciding upon investing in and implementing such systems.

Recruitment Objective: Speed of Filling Job Vacancies

Another way to assess the effectiveness of recruitment is the speed of filling the job vacancy (Breaugh & Starke, 2000). Online recruitment is about 70% faster than traditional hiring methods and provides the opportunity to speed up the hiring cycle at every stage from posting to receiving resumes/applications to onboarding (Kaur, 2015). Online recruitment can also increase the efficiency of the process by allowing organizations to spend less time gathering and sorting data from applicants (Chapman & Webster, 2003; Cober, Brown, Levy, Keeping, & Cober, 2003; Lee, 2005; Sylva & Mol, 2009). Based on data from 50 Fortune 500 companies, research showed that the use of online recruitment reduced their average hiring cycle time of 43 days by 6 days and allowed them to cut 4 days off the application process (Recruitsoft/iLogos, cited in Cappelli, 2001). Further, more than 70% of recruiters found the use of web-based recruitment reduced their hiring cycle for nonmanagement positions, and 67% of recruiters found similar results for management positions (SHRM, 2017).

It is evident from this brief review that online recruiting can decrease the cycle time and enhance the speed with which vacancies are filled, but this leads to other questions that need to be answered. Does this speediness enable organizations to hire the most qualified employees? Do these hires remain with the organizations? What is the diversity of these new hires? These questions and others need to be examined further to determine whether certain disadvantages of online recruiting may offset the benefits of the shortened hiring cycle.

Recruitment Objective: Psychological Contract Fulfillment, Employee Satisfaction, and Retention Rates

Psychological contract fulfilment, employee satisfaction, and retention rates are three other important goals of the recruitment process. These three goals have a close relationship. The psychological contract refers to the employees' beliefs about the reciprocal obligations and promises between them and their organizations (Morrison & Robinson, 1997). Not surprisingly, when employees believe that their psychological contracts with the organization have been breached, they are more dissatisfied and more likely to leave the organization (Rousseau, 1990). Thus, it is important to explore the extent to which online recruitment can help ensure that employees' psychological contracts are fulfilled.

The information gathered and disseminated during the recruitment process shapes the expectations that lead to psychological contract fulfilment, which directly affects employee satisfaction and retention rates (Breaugh & Starke, 2000). Numerous types of expectations shape the psychological contract. These expectations include the work role (skills use, job performance), social relations (co-worker and customer interactions), economic rewards (raises, monetary incentives), and company culture (Baker, 1985). So let's look at one factor, such as corporate culture, to provide an example. Chen, Lin, and Chen (2012) found that online applicants' perceptions of organizational culture positively influence the perception of their fit with the organization and the choice of organization to work. In addition, Braddy, Meade, Michael, and Fleenor (2009) found websites that incorporated culture-specific, or relevant, testimonials would more strongly convey culture perceptions to viewers than would websites containing null testimonials and policies.

A mismatch between the culture of the organization and the expectations of the culture from the new hire can result in turnover, which cost an organization between 50% and 60% of that person's annual salary (Bouton, 2015). For example, research found that departments whose work environments lined up with the company's actual cultural goals had 30% less turnover than those that did not (Monster, 2019). Therefore, online recruitment can impact the psychological contract and may aid in employee retention. It is critical during the recruitment phase that both the potential employee and the employer communicate what these expectations are and recognize whether this employment relationship will be able to meet the expectations of both parties (Baker, 1985). An employer could demonstrate these expectations on the company website in various forms (e.g., employee testimonials, informational sections) and using their social media. This could provide the applicant the opportunity to self-select out of or into the process based on a perceived mismatch.

Information that is provided by the applicant and by the recruiting company is a crucial part of the recruitment process. Often, the recruitment process is rushed by the recruiters, who want to complete the task of filling job openings. When a process is rushed, job seekers may find incomplete or vague information regarding job openings and company expectations. Research shows that although 60% of job seekers had expectations of receiving a timely reply from the organization, the reality was only 20% had this expectation met (Jibe, 2014). In addition, while 40% of job seekers felt they would be valued applicants by organizations, the reality was only 15% had this expectation met (Jibe, 2014). Therefore, organizations may want to ensure they communicate with applicants in a timely and meaningful manner so potential violations of psychological contracts are avoided.

Furthermore, when job seekers receive sugar-coated information from recruiters that exaggerates the opportunities and provides unrealistic expectations about the company, the expectations of employees are incongruent with those of the organization. Inaccurate, overly optimistic, or vague information is something organizations need to minimize or avoid. The use of such information can often lead to unrealistic expectations about the psychological contract between the organization and the individual. This circumstance is problematic for organizations because the new hires may begin to see the inconsistencies between their actual experiences and their expectations, which were formed throughout the recruitment process, and feel that their psychological contracts have been breached by their employer. Violations of the psychological contract can often result in negative attitudes and behaviors and higher levels of employee dissatisfaction and, eventually, will lead to greater turnover (Morrison & Robinson, 1997). Therefore, organizations really need to monitor and distribute accurate and balanced information to potential job seekers to avoid such problems in the workplace. Utilizing their organization's website and social media, such information can be available and easily updated.

Given that numerous companies have their own websites, which contain a careers section and endless space to provide information, more comprehensive and realistic information can be offered to job seekers. In addition, since the information is posted in real time, changes in content can be made at a moment's notice so that information is up to date and accurate. In fact, research has shown that the company career site is considered the most valuable resource by job seekers when researching a company (Zappe, 2016). Other important online resources include platforms like Glassdoor, where job seekers learn about organizations from current and former employees (Westfall, 2017). On Glassdoor, reviews focus on culture/values, work/life balance, senior management, compensation and benefits, and career opportunities.

Therefore, it is no surprise that career sites and review platforms help candidates form their expectations about the job and the company. Allen, Mahto, and Otondo (2007) found the amount of company information provided on their website is positively related to job seekers' attraction to the organization. They also found the amount of job and company information provided on the company website is positively related to attitude toward the website. Thus, employers can use websites to help provide realistic expectations about their companies and form psychological contracts. Companies need to make sure that the message being conveyed on their websites is producing the psychological contract that can be fulfilled for both the employees and the employer. Further, organizations should be aware of the reviews being placed on such platforms like Glassdoor. Once again, because the fulfilment of the psychological contract affects satisfaction and turnover levels, it is worthwhile for companies to convey realistic information about what new hires should expect and what will be expected of them—these expectations form the basis of the psychological contract. The use of a realistic recruitment message and the employment brand message should be the focus.

Realistic Recruitment Message. A realistic recruitment message is one that describes the organization and the job as they truly are without sugar-coating (Heneman, Judge, & Kammeyer-Mueller, 2019). One important tool many organizations use is the **realistic job preview**. A realistic job preview shows applicants the positive and negative attributes of a job they are applying for to see if this job is truly what they desire or thought it was (Wanous, 1992). Realistic job previews are often communicated through video clips that allow candidates to view what it is like to work for the organization. For example, Salesforce offers a variety of video testimonials from different employees that represent various positions (https://www.salesforce.com/company/careers/). Providing the characteristics of the jobs can provide insight into whether there is a potential fit for the job seeker. In addition, Netflix offers WeAreNetflix podcasts in which Netflix employees talk about work and life at Netflix, interviewing at Netflix, and new hire experiences (https://jobs.netflix.com/wearenetflix).

In addition to realistic job previews, organizations are also providing a **realistic culture preview** (Cober et al., 2003; McCourt-Mooney, 2000). A realistic culture preview allows an organization to expand beyond the traditional job information and provide information about the company philosophy, value systems, history, diversity, salary structure, and benefits. This information could be vital for constructing realistic expectations in forming the psychological contract. A realistic culture preview is also helpful, because applicants often seek out jobs and organizations that best fit their own personal values and beliefs (Dineen, Ash, & Noe, 2002, Harrison & Stone, 2018). Providing information about corporate culture could help develop a better relationship between the organization and the applicant and could lead to the building of trust between the applicant and the organization, which is key in the psychological contract. In addition, if the company fits the applicants' values and beliefs, they may experience higher satisfaction and stay with the company longer.

Since research has shown that applicants feel that they have a better chance of collecting realistic information from websites than from traditional sources (PSI, 2016; Rozelle & Landis, 2002), online recruitment is a critical recruitment tool. Information found in the career sections can offer a very unique insight into the jobs offered, culture, values, and benefits. The availability of such information (e.g., advancement opportunities, salary, organizational culture) can have a positive impact on applicants' attraction to an organization (Cober et al., 2003; Mohamed, Orife, & Wibowo, 2002). Research shows that the use of videos with job postings on career pages gets 36% more applicants (Reiners, 2018). Table 9.1 provides five examples of how companies are utilizing their websites to create realistic cultural previews.

Overall, the use of realistic recruitment messages in online recruitment should enable organizations to increase the degree to which employees perceive that their psychological contracts are fulfilled and should also enhance satisfaction and retention levels. Realistic recruitment messages should not only help organizations attract applicants who possess the skills and values that are aligned with those of the company but also communicate what employers are looking for in candidates applying for job openings. This communication could potentially help applicants construct realistic expectations, which could lead to a well-developed psychological contract that could be fulfilled in the future on the job if candidates are selected for positions. The fulfillment of the psychological contract could lead to

TABLE 9.1 ■ Examples of Companies Using Their Website for Realistic Cultural Previews	
Company	**URL**
Accenture • Provides detailed information about their core values, focus on teamwork, investing in training and development, providing a supportive work environment, and sharing their skills in the community. This company definitely provided information beyond the basic job and company information and would help to gauge if one should apply to such a place.	www.careers.accenture.com/us-en/working/overview/pages/index.aspx
HubSpot • Offers 128 online slideshows that offer insights into their company culture. The section discusses benefits, perks, allows you to see and meet different employees, opportunities for career growth and diversity and inclusion.	https://www.hubspot.com/jobs
Payscale • Provides information about pay, benefits, company perks, available jobs, and their distinct culture in a very colorful layout. Employee photos are displayed and, when clicked upon, a chart appears that breaks down their personality into fun categories (e.g., dog mom, baker, gamer, volunteer).	https://www.payscale.com/about/jobs
Spotify • HR Blog on their careers site covers such topics as employee engagement, incentives, and mental health at work.	https://hrblog.spotify.com/

a long and productive relationship for both the employee and the employer, so satisfaction and retention rates could be increased.

Employment Brand Messages. A company's **employment brand** can be a powerful tool to attract applicants to its website. A company's employment brand is often based on the organization's well-known values or distinctive image and culture (think Southwest Airlines or Apple). A company often sets itself apart from competitors by means of its employment brand (Kim, Jeon, Jung, Lu, & Jones, 2011; Stone, Stone-Romero, & Lukaszewski, 2003; Ulrich, 2001) or uses the brand to help create a particular image in hopes of attracting job applicants (Galanaki, 2002; Love & Singh, 2011; Sokro, 2012). Branding is particularly important in recruiting. Three out of four job seekers consider the brand of a prospective employer before even applying for a job (CareerArc, 2015). In addition, when an organization actively manages its employer brand, 94% of candidates are likely to apply for a job, and the quality of applicants increases by 50% (LinkedIn, 2014). Further, companies with a stronger employer brand see a 43% decrease in the cost per candidate (McDonagh, 2018). Conversely, if the online presence of the employer brand is poor, more than 90% of job seekers find this damaging to the firm (LinkedIn, 2014). Therefore, it is not surprising that more than 70% of recruiting leaders worldwide at small to medium organizations believe that employer brand has a significant impact on hiring and plan to extend their employer brand online (LinkedIn, 2014).

A great example of using the website to build an employment brand is Marriott International. According to its website, its core values are: *putting people first, pursuing excellence, embracing change, acting with integrity, and serving the world* (https://www.marriott.com/marriott/aboutmarriott.mi). In support of this, the career section emphasizes career opportunities, diversity and inclusion, veterans initiatives, the TakeCare relief fund (emergency funding for employees), and Heart of the House (stories from employees). The career opportunities section begins with the tagline "Here's the journey. . . ." and focuses on helping job seekers understand how they can: (1) make your own way, (2) explore endless possibilities (30 hotel brands in more than 131 countries), (3) explore new opportunities (various career paths in the restaurant/bar, hotels, or corporate), (4) access travel perks, never settling, and wandering the world. Their brand is further enhanced through Twitter, Instagram, LinkedIn, and Facebook, allowing them to cast a very wide net to lure potential applicants.

In addition, the current brand or reputation of an organization's product and services can also attract applicants to its career opportunities. This can be quite helpful in attracting applicants who are familiar with the company's products but possibly never thought about working for the company. Employment brand has been shown to be an important determinant of applicants' attraction to organizations and of subsequent satisfaction and retention rates (DelVecchio, Jarvis, Klink, & Dineen, 2007; Saini, Rai, & Chaudhary, 2014). When a person believes in and identifies with a particular company, he or she may find fulfillment and satisfaction and stay there if extended a job opportunity (Sokro, 2012). Therefore, the use of online recruitment coupled with the presence and strength of an online organization's employment brand strategy could be quite effective in attracting the right candidates for open positions. However, it appears many companies do not utilize this approach, with only 57% of organizations having an employment brand strategy (CareerArc, 2015).

Recruitment Objective: Quantity, Quality, and Diversity of Applicants

The quantity, quality, and diversity of applicants are three other important recruitment objectives (Breaugh & Starke, 2000), each of which can be affected by online recruitment methods. Each topic will be discussed in greater detail.

Quantity of Applicants. Online recruitment is extremely convenient for organizations and applicants and available 24 hours per day and 7 days a week. It also allows job seekers to fill out an online application or upload a resume for various positions in a matter of seconds. Further, it allows them to view and find various job openings through company websites, job boards, and social media. Although this convenience can be very beneficial, it may encourage applicants to apply for jobs without assessing their own qualifications for each job, which can result in a large number of applicants for every job opening (Sullivan, 2013).

To offset this volume, organizations need to put into place methods to screen out applicants who are not qualified. Most companies, including almost 100% of Fortune 500 organizations, use applicant tracking systems (ATS; Shields, 2018) that allow for keyword searches (i.e., of specific degrees or skills) to scale down the large volume of applications. The use of such systems can allow for searching resumes based on keywords form the job description or job specifications.

Although this seems like a great way to handle large volumes of applicants, caution is needed when using keyword searches. Applicants may tailor the content of their resumes to the words in the job descriptions to enhance their chances of passing through ATS (MacMillan, 2007; Mohamed et al., 2002; Shields, 2018). Several online lists provide examples of keywords for applicants to incorporate into their resume (Shields, 2018). This may result in unqualified or marginal individuals advancing into your selection process. This makes initial screening more difficult than before and can translate into more time, efforts, and costs to identify and eliminate unqualified or marginal applicants. Therefore, HR professionals must ensure that keywords are strictly job related and not picking up on dimensions (e.g., gender, age, religion) covered by equal employment laws (e.g., Civil Rights Acts, ADEA; Mohamed et al., 2002).

Quality and Diversity of Applicants. Two other important goals of the recruitment process are to generate highly qualified applicants with diverse backgrounds. The quality and **diversity of the applicant pool** are affected by the characteristics of those who take advantage of online recruitment. Some research indicates that online recruitment systems place artificial limits on the applicant pool. There are ethnic differences in the use of online recruiting (Smith, 2015). Some potential contributing factors to these figures may include lack of access to computers, lack of computer skills, and poverty (Kuhn & Skuterud, 2000). More specifically, when compared to whites, African American and Hispanic adults are less likely to own a traditional computer or even have high-speed internet at home (Perrin & Turner, 2019). Ownership of a computer and having Internet connection in homes is greater among whites (80%) than blacks and Hispanics (60%; Perrin & Turner, 2019). Further, researchers have argued that cultural differences in relationship orientation may affect Hispanics' use of online recruiting systems (Harrison & Stone, 2015; Stone, Lukaszewski, & Isenhour, 2005). However, the research findings on ethnicity and online recruitment usage have been somewhat contradictory. For example, one study found that African Americans often react quite favorably to online recruiting and use it to self-select themselves out of the application process for a poor-fit job or organization (McManus & Ferguson, 2003).

There is also contradictory evidence about gender and online recruitment. Employed men are more likely to search for jobs on the Internet than employed women (Kuhn & Skuterud, 2000, Weghoeft, 2018). The reason for this may be that females generally lower computer self-efficacy than males (Jackson, Ervin, Gardner, & Schmitt, 2001). However, other research did not find any gender differences in the rates at which men and women use online recruitment systems (Perrin & Turner, 2019).

Research has also shown there are age differences in online recruitment. The Pew Research Center (2015) found that younger individuals were more likely to search for jobs online than older individuals (80% for 18–29 down to 32% for those 50–64). Older individuals (55 or above) tend to have lower computer self-efficacy (Reed, Doty, & May, 2005) than younger adults, which may inhibit older applicants' ability and perceived ability to use online recruiting.

Lastly, the use of online job searches increases with education, income, and proximity to more urban/suburban locations (Perrin & Turner, 2019). Further, approximately16% of

U.S. adults (from ages 16–65) are not digitally literate (Mamedova, Pawlowski, & Hudson, 2018). Given the differences in online recruitment usage by various demographics, it is clear that the use of online recruitment may limit the extent to which an organization attracts a diverse applicant pool. Therefore, organizations should be mindful, especially for positions being recruited online that do not require computer skills, that other recruiting methods need to be deployed to meet the goals of attracting high-quality and diverse applicants.

If companies fail to consider the impact of their recruitment approach, the risk of adverse impact may increase. **Adverse impact** occurs when unintentional discrimination towards protected groups occurs in your hiring process. This could lead into legal issues for organizations. For example, one study found that of more than 25,000 applicants for restaurant and retail job positions, more than 40% of phone applicants were people of color, but only 20% of Internet applicants were people of color (Adverse, 2008). Thus, for some positions, the use of online recruitment may negatively affect the diversity of the applicant pool.

Not only may an online recruitment method exclude protected groups, but it may cause the organization to miss out on high-quality talent. If your organization finds the use of online recruitment is an appropriate approach, then another consideration is the design of your recruitment portal. Research found 60% of job seekers quit in the middle of filling out online job applications if it is too long or too complex (Zielinski, 2016). However, when the application takes less than 5 minutes, the conversion rate can go up by 365% (Zielinski, 2016). Therefore, the effectiveness of online recruitment may be hindered by the actual design of the online application. Unfortunately, despite this finding, about 50% of employers feel a lengthy application process is a great way to weed out applicants (Zielinski, 2016). High-quality talent could be lost, and applicant word of mouth will be poor. For these reasons, it is important that organizations evaluate their current online application process and track the time to complete and the conversion rates they are experiencing.

Another source of quality in your applicant pool is the type of job seekers you desire to apply for your openings. One particular group that organizations desire is passive job seekers, and online recruitment may help organizations connect with such job seekers. The **passive job seeker** is a currently employed individual who is not actively seeking employment but could be enticed if a particular opportunity came their way. They are usually very happy with the job and organization where they are currently employed. They also tend to be highly skilled, with a wealth of experience. Currently, passive job seekers make up 70% of the labor market. Social platforms, such as LinkedIn, can provide access to such a group to source for your job openings. Further, organizations can have a presence on LinkedIn to attract such candidates to apply online. However, attractive as this may be to organizations, the demographics of the users of such a platform should be considered (see Chapter 16 for more information on the different use rates for social media platforms), and a determination made in regard to recruiting through these sources may affect the quality and diversity of the applicant, pool.

In summary, if an organization relies only on online recruitment, there is a risk that the overall composition of the workforce will contain less diversity, and quality may suffer (Stone et al., 2005). Therefore, online recruiting may facilitate workforce homogeneity and, as a result, hinder innovative and creative decision making (Schneider, Goldstein, & Smith, 1995). Organizations must be aware of the potential biases created by their recruiting practices and align their recruiting strategies with their overall business strategies to create competitive advantage (Becker & Gerhart, 1996; Wright & Snell, 1998). For example, if an organization wants to hire an individual for an HRIS-related job, the organization may find online recruiting to be a cost-efficient and effective source of recruitment, because members of the applicant pool are technologically proficient and would most likely use the Internet in their job searches. Conversely, if the organization is looking for a person in a nontechnical position (e.g., staff writer, creative consultant), then the use of traditional recruitment sources (e.g., newspaper ads, job fairs) may be more effective and legally defensible than the use of online recruitment alone. For this reason, we recommend that organizations consider using online recruitment in conjunction with other recruitment sources to ensure that their recruitment processes are fair.

Attributes of the Recruiting Website

Another factor that may affect the acceptance and effectiveness of online recruiting is the design of the website. In general, the best website design is user friendly in that users can easily navigate and browse through multiple Web pages to find information. The extent to which the website is usable or not has been referred to as "website usability" in the empirical literature (Cober et al., 2003; Karat, 1997; Nielsen, 2000). The construct of website usability has been conceptualized as encompassing a number of dimensions, including navigability, content information, and aesthetic features. Each dimension and its use in recruitment is further discussed in this section.

First, **navigability** can be defined as the overall ease with which a user can browse through multiple Web pages to locate topics of interest. Hosting a website that displays current information and includes active hyperlinks to retrieve information is essential in maintaining user interest within the site. To achieve this goal, organizations should follow the "three-click" rule for users to locate information of interest. For instance, users who wish to browse job opportunities on the organization's website should be able to reach the desired Web page by the third hyperlink from the home Web page. Accordingly, research has shown that applicants have more favorable impressions of an organization when its website is easy to navigate as opposed to being difficult to navigate (Braddy, Meade, & Kroustalis, 2008). Such favorable impressions are important to elicit within applicants, because they may lead to greater organizational attraction (e.g., Allen et al., 2007; Lyons & Marler, 2011).

Next, **content information** refers to the degree to which the website hosts relevant information that the user deems valuable and informative in nature. Providing information that the user desires is another mechanism by which organizations can sustain user interest and satisfaction with the website. The **media richness** theory (Daft & Lengel, 1986) has been frequently applied to explain why hosting relevant content information is beneficial to applicants. Specifically, this theory contends that communication effectiveness is a function of the degree to which media sources reduce user uncertainty and equivocality (Daft & Lengel, 1986). Rich media sources (a website) contain enough relevant and accessible information to reduce user uncertainty and subsequent anxiety toward the target source (an organization). Conversely, when a source has a low degree of richness, inadequate information fails to reduce users' uncertainty about the organization, which may then lead to ambivalence and anxiety toward the target source. The result of this process may stimulate positive or negative attitudes toward the organization, such as more favorable impressions of an organization's image (Cable & Yu, 2006). Thus, an organization would be advised to host a website that includes information about the organization and its products, available job opportunities, developmental opportunities, compensation, and culture (Barber & Roehling, 1993; Cable, Aiman-Smith, Mulvey, & Edwards, 2000; Cable & Graham, 2000; Judge & Cable, 1997). For example, Walker, Field, Giles, Armenakis, and Bernerth (2009) found when organizations posted employee testimonials on their employment Web pages, their sites generated greater organizational attraction than other websites that did not have such testimonials. Consequently, hosting information that applicants value will most likely facilitate person–job (P-J) and person–organization (P-O) "fit"-related decisions.

Specifically, when applicants perceive similarity between their qualifications and what is required by the job (P-J) and between their personality and the organization's values (P-O), it is more likely that they will pursue employment with the organization (e.g., Kristof-Brown, Zimmerman, & Johnson, 2005). Indeed, perceived fit has been found to be one of the strongest predictors of organizational attraction (Uggerslev, Fassina, & Kraichy, 2012). Overall, these applicant-evaluative processes cannot be formed if the organization does not include useful information on its website. For example, many organizations (e.g., Texas Instruments) provide a list of cultural values on their employment Web pages. It is important to note, however, that the more customizable information an organization provides on its Web page, the more likely an applicant will engage in appropriate **self-selection** behavior (to apply or not apply for a job within the organization). In other words, if the website provides direct feedback to applicants regarding their P-O or P-J fit, the online recruiting effort will likely attract a more qualified applicant pool (Dineen et al., 2002; Dineen, Ling, Ash, & DelVecchio, 2007; Dineen & Noe, 2009). Therefore, in order to avoid the "dark side" of Web recruitment, an organization must first determine and maximize the information that is most likely going to influence fit perceptions and then engage the user to seek and understand this information. For example, professional sports teams that advertise job openings on a third-party website, www.teamworkonline.com, frequently have potential applicants respond to a few P-J fit-related questions before they are allowed to apply for the job in question.

Finally, companies should consider how the **aesthetic features** of their websites engage user interest and attention. These features encompass the overall stylistic or innovative aspects of a website, such as contrasting colors, pictures, animation, and playfulness, which keep the user engaged while he or she navigates through multiple Web pages (Cober, Brown, Keeping, & Levy, 2004). When a user is engaged, it is more likely that he or she will maintain interest in the organization and browse for more information about the organization (Cober et al., 2003). Ultimately, an applicant may perceive these innovative features of a website as "signals" about broader organizational attributes, such as the organization's culture and image (Lyons & Marler, 2011). For example, if a website has attractive stylistic features (e.g., Goldman Sachs's website, www.gs.com), it may stimulate more favorable perceptions of organizational image, which has been found to be positively related to organizational attraction (Lyons & Marler, 2011). These results are especially important for entrepreneurial or smaller firms that wish to attract qualified applicants to their organizations. That is, when an organization invests in the latest Web design, a user or applicant will be more likely to perceive that organization as reputable. Similarly, an information technology (IT) firm would be wise to invest in the latest Web design software to generate applicant or even customer perceptions that the organization values innovation and creativity. This investment is especially prudent from the perspective that this firm's potential applicants will most likely be attracted to an organization that values innovation and creativity.

Integrating these attributes, a website's **usability** has been found to affect applicant perceptions and attitudes toward the organization. A recent meta-analytic study by Uggerslev et al. (2012) found a corrected correlation coefficient of .41 between website usability and organizational attraction—in other words, the more usable the website was perceived to be, the more likely the applicant was attracted to the organization. A study by Allen et al. (2007)

found that website **attributes** were positively related to applicants' intentions to pursue employment, which is the immediate precursor to the actual behavior of applying for a job within an organization. Toward this end, in a sample of U.S. state government recruitment websites, Selden and Orenstein (2011) determined that website usability was positively related to applicant pool quantity (i.e., total number of applicants). All these studies converge on the finding that website usability perceptions influence applicant attitudes toward an organization. As a result, organizations should be attuned to how their websites influence applicant perceptions and be prepared to update their Web design to embody high navigability, content fidelity, and engaging aesthetic features. HR and IT employees should monitor the usability of their firm's website by surveying applicant perceptions of and reactions to the Web recruiting process, especially in situations in which the Web recruiting function entails gathering applicant data and preliminary online ability testing.

The decision to host job openings on organizational websites and to have the capability of screening job applicants for positions should be based on the firm's resources and strategy. With this statement in mind, we can see that the purpose of an organization's recruitment website can be classified either as recruiting and screening oriented or as just recruitment oriented (Williamson, Lepak, & King, 2003). A **recruiting- and screening-oriented website** has the capability to list job openings and accept applications through a secure server. Conversely, a website that focuses only on recruiting just hosts a list of job openings, with the option of submitting an application via mail, e-mail, or fax to an organizational representative. Williamson et al. (2003) articulated that both recruitment orientations can be effective in attracting applicants; however, it could be contended that applicants may prefer submitting personal information through websites that they perceive to be secure and trustworthy (Stone et al., 2003). Therefore, if an organization does not have the financial resources to invest in building a secure server to accept applications, an alternative would be to still offer information about the organization and its culture on the website's employment Web page and then have a hyperlink that connects interested applicants to jobs that are hosted by a third-party vendor, such as Monster.com. A more logical alternative would be to host an organization's job opportunities on a third-party vendor's website (e.g., Monster.com, Careerbuilder.com) and include a hyperlink on each announcement that connects the applicant to the organization's home Web page. These alternatives would allow the organization to achieve the benefits associated with Web recruiting and provide the applicant an opportunity to learn more about the organization by browsing the firm's home Web page. Also, from the applicant's perspective, these options would reduce any anxiety or adverse perceptions about lack of privacy or about Web security concerning those organizations that the applicant does not know well or does not entirely trust.

Recruitment Strategies and Social Networking

Organizations have always used social relationships and networking, including employee referrals, to attract talent. Increasingly, social networking sites such as Facebook, Twitter, and LinkedIn are gaining in use and popularity, and they now provide a unique method of allowing recruitment professionals to source, contact, and screen both active and passive job candidates. For example, domestically in the United States, the United Parcel Service (UPS) uses Facebook, Twitter, and LinkedIn to post job openings and host relevant information about the company and its culture (Zielinski, 2012). Internationally, the Hard Rock Café solely used Facebook as a recruiting source to hire 120 employees for a new restaurant in Florence, Italy (Colao, 2012). Although there are benefits to using social networking websites (SNWs) for recruitment and selection purposes, there are also concerns regarding its proliferation, targeted applicant pool, use in selection, saliency of more negative profile information than positive, and merit as a worthwhile recruiting source. For a further discussion about the role of social recruitment, please refer to Chapter 16.

Advancing Online Recruitment With New Technologies

The last 5 years have brought with them dramatic change. Although Chapter 17 discusses the future of HR technology, we briefly want to discuss several trends affecting employee recruitment. First, mobile recruitment is becoming a necessity. Mobile technology now connects with an ATS, allowing recruiters to receive and view candidates, view calendars, and make notes about candidates, all from their smartphones (McHugh, 2019). In addition, almost 90% of job seekers believe mobile devices are critical in their job searches, 70% actively use mobile devices to search for jobs (Rossheim, 2019), and approximately 50% have used their smartphones to apply for jobs (Smith, 2015). Among Millennial job seekers, 37% expect to be able to view career sections and 27% expect to be able to apply for jobs using their mobile devices (Jobvite, 2016). Therefore, it is imperative that organizations make sure their applications, job postings, and career sections are designed and formatted for all common mobile devices and understand how interface design principles are applied to mobile design.

Mobile technology is convenient and provides 24/7 access for job seekers. Further, when paired with the ATS, the organization can send automated text messages to job candidates about scheduling and other updates, which allow for more personalized connections with job seekers. However, only about 8% of recruiters actively use texting in their process (Deloitte, 2017). If organizations utilize texting, they need to make sure there are rules (e.g., sending appropriate and professional messages) in place to guide recruiters. Mobile technology may also help organizations bridge the digital divide. The digital divide reflects the gap between individuals who have access to computers and ability to use them and those who do not (Hoffman & Novak, 1998). As noted, people of color are less likely to have computing access. However, African-American and Hispanic smartphone usage is very similar to that of whites. In addition, for African-Americans and Hispanics, their smartphone is often their main access to the Internet (Perrin & Turner, 2019). Thus, mobile recruitment can help the organization cast a wider net for job openings and to tap a broader pool of skills and knowledge.

Another exciting technology being used in online recruitment is artificial intelligence (AI). AI is an umbrella term that includes areas such as machine learning and cognitive computing. AI deals with the simulation of intelligent behavior in computers. Success has been found with AI in visual perception, natural language processing, speech recognition, speech-to-text conversion, language translation, tone analysis, and other areas (Guenole & Feinzig, 2018). AI is used in 40% of international companies in their HR functions (PWC, 2017).

AI is supporting HR in multiple ways. First, it is used to automate the screening process of resumes (Ideal, 2019a). Since organizations often receive 75% to 88% of resumes from unqualified applicants (Ideal, 2019a), the time to screen candidates for a single position and identify those who move forward averages approximately 23 hours (Ideal, 2019a). Second, the technology can standardize the ability to match the candidate to the knowledge, skills, abilities, and other characteristics (KSAOs). This has led to a 35% decrease in turnover, 20% performance increase, and 4% increase in revenue per employee (Ideal, 2019a). Ultimately, automating these processes with AI can lead to greater savings of time and costs.

A third way is through the use of chatbots. A **chatbot** is a computer program that simulates conversation with humans, mainly over the Internet. Common examples of chatbots would be Alexa or Siri. Chatbots can reduce the burden recruiters face with sustaining regular communications with each job applicant. This is important because, on average, 40% of candidates never hear back from organizations after submitting an application (Ideal, 2019b). Chatbots can be deployed through email, social media, the ATS, and SMS. Organizations are using chatbots to gather information about applicants, to provide automated FAQ answers, to ask screening questions, and to schedule interviews (Ideal, 2019b). Information collected can then be integrated into ATS or given to a recruiter for follow-up. For example, the U.S. Army uses the SGT STAR chatbot. To date, it has answered 11 million questions, the equivalent volume of 55 recruiters (Ideal, 2019b). Research also found that almost 60% of candidates would be comfortable interacting with AI and chatbots in the recruitment process (Fisher, 2017). However, there are some challenges in the use of chatbots. The lack of standardization in how people text (acronyms, emojis) and lack of human-like responses by chatbots can limit their effectiveness. Although chatbots are increasing in popularity and job candidates are responding positively, more research is needed to determine how to best deploy them in recruitment to improve hiring outcomes.

The Relationship of e-Recruiting and HRIS

The applicant's information acquired through the company's online recruitment can be funneled into the company's HRIS. This information may come from computers or mobile phones. The use of the HRIS in the recruitment process can make the process more efficient and effective by having information readily available and usable at a moment's notice. Many of the suggestions made in the earlier sections are illustrated here. One important function the HRIS provides is applicant tracking. Applicant tracking allows for the generation of applicants' profiles, which are compiled through application blanks and/or resumes. These profiles can aid the hiring managers in their employment decisions. Recruiters or the hiring managers can perform key word searches to find qualified applicants for available jobs. Applicant tracking also allows recruiters, hiring managers, and sometimes the applicant themselves to see where they are in the recruitment process. The HRIS can provide information about the yield ratios for each recruiting source, cost effectiveness of the recruitment process as a whole or by recruitment source, and to support EEO/AA analyses. Applicant data can be also stored and searched for future vacancies. Lastly, when applicants become new hires, the HRIS provides the data to populate the core HR system and other HR purposes, such as payroll and benefits.

ONLINE RECRUITMENT GUIDELINES

Stone et al. (2005) offer the following research-based guidelines on the effective design and use of online recruitment strategies:

- Online recruiting is more suitable for well-known firms with excellent employer branding.

- It should be used as one of many sources of recruitment.

- Organizations should be aware of the limitations of this method, such as its limited ability to attract older individuals and minority candidates.

- The websites should be easy to use and navigate and designed to attract, not screen, candidates.

- Online screening systems should be based on job analyses.

- E-recruiting systems should provide realistic previews of jobs and of the firm.

- Effectiveness should be regularly reviewed and continuously improved based on feedback from job applicants.

- Online recruiting should be culturally sensitive and suit people from diverse backgrounds, including those with low education levels and low computer self-efficacy.

- Online recruiting must incorporate privacy protection policies, including those limiting the collection of information to only employment-specific data and those restricting access to and distribution of such data.

In summary, organizations should consider the extent to which online recruitment enables them to meet their recruitment objectives. Our previous discussion provides evidence that online recruitment can help organizations reduce the costs of recruiting, decrease the cycle time of filling job vacancies, and generate large quantities of applicants. However, organizations must remember that these are not the only recruitment objectives and must focus on finding the impact of online recruitment on the other recruitment objectives (quality and diversity of applicants, psychological contract fulfillment, employee satisfaction, retention rates). In addition, the attributes of the website can affect the acceptance and effectiveness of online recruiting. The best website design is user friendly in that users can easily navigate and browse through multiple Web pages to find information that is valuable and conveys whether the applicants fit not only the job requirements but also the organization's value system. Last, the aesthetic features of a website, combined with the content presented, may shape the attributions of job seekers toward the organization in a positive manner. However, the attraction of applicants to job openings is only the beginning—organizations now have to focus on assessing the applicants who constitute their applicant pools. Therefore, we now need to switch our focus to a discussion of selection.

SELECTION AND TECHNOLOGY

This section focuses on tests and assessments of individual employees and candidates, which underlie the evaluation processes that enable organizations to manage their talent. These tools are used for selecting employees, as well as placement, training and development, promotions, and evaluations. Tests and assessments are important for HRIS because they provide data that are used for making organizational decisions. To explore the data-based decision-making process in further detail, we focus our discussion on the use of tests and assessments to make a critical decision—whether to hire a particular candidate.

What Are Selection Tests and Assessments, and Why Are They Used?

Most organizations that seek HRIS expertise on selection will likely consider the term *test* to refer to traditional multiple-choice examinations that can be used to measure ability, personality, or knowledge, as well as skills tests, such as typing tests. Organizations seeking assessments may be referring to these same tests, or, alternatively, they may be thinking of different types of **selection procedures** and tools, such as reference checks or work samples. Whatever the label, tests and assessments are job-related decision-making tools that provide information about candidates, information that organizations can use in selection. Figure 9.2 contains examples of the major tests and assessment instruments. For this section of the chapter, we use the terms *test, assessment, selection tool,* and *selection procedure* interchangeably to refer to any tool designed to measure attributes of individuals for the purpose of selecting employees.

Here is a more comprehensive list of assessments, as provided by the Society for Industrial and Organizational Psychology (SIOP):

> Depending on one's focus, selection procedures or predictors can be described in terms of what they measure (content/constructs) or how they measure what they are designed to measure (methods) . . . Examples of these selection procedures methods include, but are not limited to, paper-and-pencil tests, computer-administered tests, performance tests, work samples, inventories (e.g., measures of personality and interests), individual assessments, interviews, assessment centers, situational judgment tests, biographical data forms or scored application blanks, background investigations, education, experience, physical requirements (e.g., height, weight), physical ability tests, and appraisals of job performance. In addition, unproctored internet-based tests, "big data" and machine learning methods (e.g., harvesting information about candidates from social media sites, resumes, or other sources of text or information), gamification, and computer-based simulations of varying levels of technological sophistication are examples of contemporary testing and assessment approaches. (SIOP, 2018, p. 4)

FIGURE 9.2 ■ Specific Examples of Tests and Assessments

Knowledge test: A multiple-choice training posttest of knowledge of the tools, machines, and equipment used in a factory and designed to measure how well the new hire has learned essential job information taught in classroom training.

Skill test: A practical exercise or simulation that tests the candidate's effectiveness in using Microsoft Word software.

Ability test: The Watson-Glaser Critical Thinking Appraisal, a multiple-choice reasoning test, in which the examinee reads a short or medium-length passage and draws logical conclusions about the statements, choosing the answer that makes the best logical sense. Many other ability tests are similar in appearance and format to educational tests that are familiar to students (e.g., the Scholastic Aptitude Test [SAT], the Miller Analogies Test [MAT], and the Graduate Record Examination [GRE]).

Personal attributes test: A multiple-choice personality assessment in which the examinee reads statements such as "I enjoy making presentations in front of large groups of people" and indicates the extent to which she or he agrees or disagrees with these statements. Results are scored on several scales or dimensions.

Work simulation: An in-basket exercise in which the examinee must examine the variety of types of information (correspondence, reports, and other information) and also interact with simulated coworkers, employees, or other business associates (whether computer simulated or role-played by actors over the telephone or in person). The examinee is evaluated on a variety of dimensions, from accuracy and the quality of decisions to work-related competencies, interpersonal skills, and other personal attributes.

Why Is Understanding Assessment Important for HRIS?

When used for employee selection, assessments have value because they assist organizations in identifying those individuals who are more likely to succeed on the job and prevent the hiring of those who are less likely to succeed. HR managers need to understand the purpose and use of assessments for a variety of reasons, including the following:

- All organizations use assessments.
    - Organizational leaders know that employees' abilities, skills, and personal attributes are critical for success.
    - The range of assessments and methods of administering them with technology is already broad (SIOP, 2018) and will only grow.
- The value of selection is quantifiable.
    - *Some selection systems work better than others.* Effective assessments must be valid, provide information that is clearly related to their intended use, and the information must be related to the job's requirements.
    - Unfortunately, some commercially available assessments are poorly designed and researched, and their creators may make unjustifiable claims about their effectiveness.
- Employee selection is regulated by antidiscrimination laws.
    - These laws prohibit employment practices that unfairly discriminate against people in various protected groups, such as racial/ethnic minorities, women, and older candidates. HRIS experts must be aware of these **antidiscrimination laws**.

In order to be fair and legal, selection decisions that differentially affect protected group members must provide equal treatment and be equally predictive of success for people of color and other protected groups.

Although this chapter will address a variety of important concepts about selection and assessment for personnel decision making, a full discussion is beyond the chapter's scope. Interested readers are encouraged to consult additional sources, including the SIOP document. We also recommend classic texts by Guion (1998) and Farr and Tippins (2017), two of the essential references on the topic. In addition, The U.S. Department of Labor (1999) offers a less technical summary white paper that remains relevant, and the SIOP website (www.siop.org) provides links to many useful websites and papers.

Technology Issues in Selection

The most common use of technology for selection systems is the use of software or Internet-based services (digital services) to administer and score tests. HRIS experts need to be aware of several general concerns about the digital administration of selection procedures. First, does mode of administration of an assessment—in particular, the devices used, such as paper and pencil, computer, tablet, or smartphone—affect the measurement properties of the test? Second, as computing capabilities increase, it is possible to make assessments that more closely simulate the job, that is, ones that closely approximate the work that would be done once the candidate is hired. What are the benefits and risks of high-fidelity work simulations? Third, how does online testing affect the validity of selection systems? Does the technology that allows candidates to take tests anywhere, and organizations' increasing interest in using that technology, compromise the test security that is present in traditional settings with proctored (supervised) examinations?

Equivalence Between Modes of Assessment

Most of the first **computerized assessments** were meant to look like their paper-and-pencil, low-tech counterparts, except that they were delivered on a computer and required candidates to answer questions (generally multiple choice) via a keyboard or a mouse or to take a computerized skill test (e.g., a typing test). The primary concern, then, was that the mode of administration (paper or computer) might affect the measurement properties of the test, such that a score taken on paper might not be equivalent to a score taken on a computer. Today, the availability of different computing devices (laptops, tablets, smartphones, watches, etc.) amplifies concerns about equivalence for certain types of assessments and requires the HRIS expert to know when caution is warranted about interpreting test scores from different devices. For some types of assessments, most researchers have little concern that the mode of administration will result in a different measure. For example, for **personality tests** and career interest inventories, for which job candidates answer questions at their own pace about their beliefs and characteristics or their interests in different types of work, the presentation format of the questions is expected to matter little (for example, see Tippins, 2015). On the other hand, there is clear evidence that the mode of administration matters for certain types of **ability tests,** particularly **speeded tests,** which are time pressured, such that candidates may not finish all the items in the allotted time (e.g., see Mead & Drasgow, 1993; Potosky & Bobko, 2004). For such tests, the physical or virtual materials and test administration methods affect the time (in seconds) it takes to complete a test item and, thus, the results. For instance, think of a paper test form that requires a candidate to match questions printed in booklets to an answer sheet; now imagine a computer screen on which the examinee sees one item at a time and uses a mouse to click on the answers. Alternatively, one candidate may take a test on a large screen that displays the entire question at once, whereas another might take the test on a small tablet and may need to use time to scroll down in order to see the whole question. Total scores, average scores, and performance on individual test items may be affected. The more speeded a test is, the more likely it is that there will be differences between the modes of administration.

In contrast, **power tests**, tests in which there is no designated time limit to create time pressure or in which the time limit is set such that most candidates will complete the test without working hastily, typically do not show differences between testing modes. Where a difference in scores is expected, an industrial/organizational psychologist or other expert in tests and measurements can conduct a study of the equivalence between the two. The study entails administering both types of tests, ideally to the same individuals, with the order of administration counterbalanced across participants, and examining and comparing the overall results and the statistical results for each item. Then, when necessary, a formula equating the two can be developed to adjust for differences. The result is a method of ensuring that, irrespective of whether the candidate takes the test with one device or another, he or she will have the same opportunity to perform well.

Bandwidth Versus Fidelity: How Closely Should We Simulate the Job?

Technology has enabled organizations to create work sample simulations that represent the job with high fidelity. Company leaders may want this because they believe that no assessment could be nearly as good as a simulation that closely matches the work that will be performed on the job. However, as Figure 9.3 illustrates, an analysis of decades of assessment research has found that general cognitive ability tests can, on average, predict success virtually as well as simulations, and, when combined with other types of assessments, they can exceed the predictive ability of simulations. The bar chart in Figure 9.3 displays statistical correlations between assessment scores and job performance data. Schmidt and Hunter (1998) provided these data in a comprehensive meta-analysis, research that quantitatively summarizes the data from many studies on a particular topic—in this case, the personnel selection research literature. The research is most supportive of **work simulations**, ability tests, structured interviews, and personality testing. Higher scores on these types of assessments are predictive of higher job performance. For comparison, less valid assessments are also shown, such as education and training ratings and graphology (handwriting analysis), which has been shown to have little or no validity.

Work simulations give candidates a sense of what it would be like to perform some aspect of the job, such as answering customer service calls and entering client information or writing emails to managers and co-workers. As computing power increases, so does the capacity for more and more realistic and complex simulations, as do the amount and varieties of data

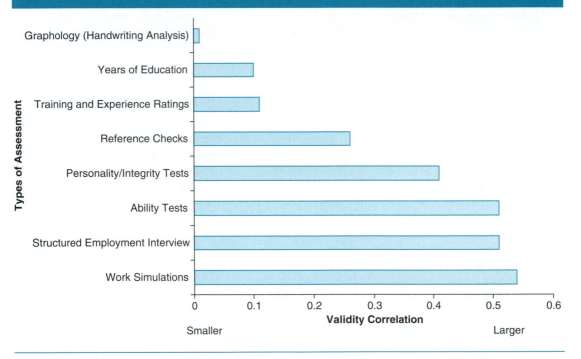

FIGURE 9.3 ■ Correlations Between Assessment Scores and Job Performance

Source: Schmidt and Hunter (1998).

that can be collected about the candidate's behaviors during the simulation. Candidates may now operate avatars to move through a game-like virtual environment that records not only their answers to questions or puzzles but also tracks all they items of information they viewed and for how long (see Fetzer & Tuzinski, 2013). This assessment frontier opens new avenues for the HRIS expert to explore the best methods of coding, scoring, storing, and applying the collected data.

It is also important to be aware of the trade-off between **fidelity** and **bandwidth**, the range of settings to which the simulation might apply. For example, suppose that a management simulation is designed to closely represent a particular line of business in the actual organization chart and reporting structure, as well as the unique subject matter that is addressed in the management job from day to day. If the company then wants to use the simulation for a different business unit or job, the details that made the simulation highly appropriate in the first setting may interfere with its use in the other setting. The same problem applies to jobs and settings that change over time, as most do. Therefore, although as the HRIS expert you may be adept at creating an assessment that looks just like the job, such a tool might have a narrow range of uses. Also, simulations generally require that the job candidate already knows how to do the job, at least at some basic level, or that the job is simple enough that the candidate can learn the job tasks quickly to perform the simulation. In general, HRIS managers should keep in mind that, depending on the effort and expense one is willing to expend on assessment development and installation, lower-fidelity simulations or combinations of other types of assessments might be preferable to a simulation that is highly job specific and costly.

Validity and Security Issues Created by Unproctored Online Testing

Numerous consulting companies offer **online tests**. While these tests may be conducted in an office by a proctor who checks identification and monitors the test session, frequently they are delivered in **unproctored testing** (unsupervised) situations. Such testing can be attractive to organizations because of its anywhere-anytime convenience for both the candidate and the hiring organization.

However, this convenience may come at a cost. A panel of industrial/organizational psychologists convened at the annual SIOP conference in 2006 and published a well-known article that summarizes the issues. These individuals were employed by a range of different types of organizations: a university, several test-publishing firms, the U.S. government, and a publicly held company in the finance industry (Tippins et al., 2006). The issues they identified include candidate identity, test security and cheating, and fair access to testing for people of color. These issues still hold up well today (e.g., Farr & Tippins, 2017; Tippins, 2015).

Establishing candidate identity is a straightforward problem, currently without a straightforward solution. There is currently no failsafe method. In contrast to in-office testing requiring identification, when testing is unproctored, someone could be taking the test in the candidate's place. A live video feed or a biometric method of verifying the candidate's identity would provide more assurance, and there are now companies that offer such services. Alternatively, the organization might choose to retest all the candidates who qualify, using a proctored setting. A related issue is **test security**. One facet of this is keeping the test content under lock and key for future use. The HRIS manager must take precautions to prevent the test content from being copied and compromised, whether locally or via Internet hacking. Certainly, a related concern is protecting the privacy and security of the candidate scores and other personal information (see Zafar & Stone, 2018, for a useful overview on this topic). Another facet is preventing cheating. In addition to having someone else take the test or assist the candidate, the candidate might use resources that are not permitted (e.g., Internet search engines, offline dictionaries, calculators). Cheating is of particular concern when the tests have right answers (e.g., ability tests) or require skills that the candidate can have others perform (e.g., typing tests). Common sense tells us that the higher the stakes in a testing situation, the higher the likelihood of cheating.

HRIS experts also must be aware of a third issue: equal and fair access. In particular, tests must be fair to legally protected groups, yet unproctored testing and, indeed, Internet recruitment and candidate processing in general run the risk of having a chilling effect on people of color, who, because of the so-called digital divide, might have greater difficulty accessing the Internet to apply for jobs. People of color also might be disadvantaged by having to rely on small-screen devices such as smartphones to take ability tests if this is their only portal to the Internet. Organizations must provide for multiple ways to gain entry.

These problems do not have easy solutions for organizations that wish to rely on unproctored Internet testing. Tippins et al. (2006) discussed the pros and cons of unproctored Internet testing but did not come to a consensus about the ethics of administering unproctored tests and keeping the process fair. A practice commonly suggested by test providers is to follow up unproctored testing with proctored testing of applicants who "pass" the unproctored test and who satisfy other job qualification requirements (Tippins, 2009). This approach has been officially recommended by the International Testing Commission's (2006) guidelines on computer- and internet-based testing. However, there are technical problems with evaluating and acting on score differences, and retesting diminishes the convenience and cost savings that were the original reasons for unproctored testing (Tippins et al., 2006). A review article by Stone, Lukaszewski, Stone-Romero, and Johnson (2013) provides interested readers with further information on the use and acceptance of various types of assessment technologies and systems for selecting candidates into organizations.

Applying HRIS to Selection and Assessment

Selection systems are information management systems for organizational decision making and administration. Therefore, human resource information systems play an important part in their development and use. Where once these systems operated using local software and storage, the availability of **cloud computing** for remote storage, and licensed, remotely hosted **software as a service** now means that HRIS managers will frequently be partnering with or working for consulting firms offering assessment services. One uniquely HRIS-centered role is database design. Selection systems require the careful design of databases to store and keep track of selection data, both before and after individuals are hired, and the ability to link information in interrelated systems, such as candidate test data and demographics, employment data for those who are hired, and job movement and position histories within the company. Increasingly, HRIS experts will be called on to assist in integrating the organization's various HR systems. At a minimum, integration involves linking data in two or more systems, such as the candidate and employee identification data, so that one may conduct database queries and follow individuals as their information passes through the different systems. Integration often also involves linking transactional operations in a system such that, after the first system has conducted a transaction that requires follow-up in the next system, the first system contacts the next system to launch the required transaction. For instance, once a candidate has completed an online application, he or she may be automatically sent to another Web-based application to complete an assessment. The HRIS manager must have a conceptual understanding of what it means to link a test delivery system with other systems, such as applicant-tracking systems. Another general HRIS role in selection systems is the development of scoring and decision rules and of the administrative functions of the system. Whether the output of the completed assessment is simple to interpret (e.g., pass/fail) or complicated (e.g., multiple sources of information, levels of performance, and data from various screening events that could follow), the HRIS expert who participates in the creation of scoring or decision rules must be sure that they are easy for the HR department and others to understand and apply consistently throughout the organization. Another key HRIS role is helping to design and apply the administrative functions of the system, the features permitting access to assessments results and the right to distribute candidate information. Following are some more specific considerations for designing a computerized or Web-based selection system (Kehoe, Dickter, Russell, & Sacco, 2005):

- *Test access and security:* The HR department must decide how candidates will gain access to the test (By permission? Will there be prescreening? Is testing open to anyone?) and how the test content will be kept secure.

- *Test inventory and administrative privileges:* The HRIS expert must consider how the computerized tests will be purchased and inventoried (if accessed from a vendor) and the administrative privileges that determine

  1. Who should be assigned the right to work with particular types of test data,

  2. Whether there will be multiple levels of access, and

  3. Whether individuals will be able to delegate record-viewing rights to others.

- *Options for scoring:* Will there be multiple ways to score an assessment, with a variety of possible scoring rules? How might examinees' scores be compared with those of reference groups to make these scores more meaningful?

- *Accessing results:* In what data format and by what methods will test results be stored, transmitted, and interpreted?

- *Applying test policies:* What organizational requirements will affect the testing methods (e.g., systems that allow accommodations for disabilities) and the data that are kept and used (e.g., mandatory waiting periods before retests)?

A new area for HRIS is **big data**—large-volume datasets with a variety of information that may be collected rapidly. For example, information posted on social media is not only high volume but also contains text, internet links and photos, all of which are updated frequently. Data scientists have begun mining these data to learn about the people who post to social media sites, including their personalities and attitudes toward work. Guzzo and colleagues (2015) provide numerous examples as well as cautionary advice regarding the analysis of big data. Of particular concern are the ethics of using such data, for example, when the individuals posting online did not give consent for their data to be used in research or to make application decisions, or where it might be possible to connect datasets in such a way that identifies people who posted information privately. Another concern is that such data might be incorrect. It may be difficult to amend one's own inaccurate data online, or as a researcher, to verify the quality of the information gathered there. Big data is a rapidly growing field that will be of interest to many who pursue a profession in HRIS.

Another advancement in HRIS and selection technology is the use of machine learning and artificial intelligence. Technology such as IBM's Watson platform is available to assess a candidate's fit within an organization's culture using data analysis algorithms known as machine learning, transforming previously labor-intensive work into automated processes (Dickter, Jockin, & Delany, 2017) and permitting new analyses such as the processing of human speech (Landers, Fink, & Collmus, 2017). Given the troves of data that may be available on the Internet about applicants, such as in social networking sites and video content posted online, using automation to make sense of it seems practical. However, there are ethical concerns with using personal data that were not provided in the context of applying for a job (Lukaszewski & Johnson, 2017).

Demonstrating the HRM's Value With HRIS Selection Applications

As mentioned earlier, the HRIS manager plays a key role in proving the value of a selection system, through knowledge of how to obtain and use the right data on individual and organizational outcomes and to demonstrate a return on investment in the system. This expertise is also critical for defending the selection system, which is generally a high-stakes event: The use of the selection information determines individual careers and the company's ultimate success.

Demonstrating the value of selection requires that we know how well the employees who were assessed eventually perform on the job. For instance, if we measure their productivity (e.g., more products assembled or repaired, customers served, or products sold), we may find that people who score higher on the tests also are more productive. As another example, suppose the assessed individuals are supervisors. Among this group, we may find that the higher the supervisors' assessment scores, the better they supervise their subordinates, who have higher skill levels (perhaps as measured with a **knowledge test**) and lower turnover than the subordinates of people whose assessment results were not as high. Testing experts refer to this value or return on investment as utility: the extent to which a selection system results in the selection of better candidates than would have been possible if the system had not been used (Blum & Naylor, 1968). The quality of the candidates may be defined in terms of one or more of the following (Cascio & Aguinis, 2011):

1. The proportion of candidates who are successful on the job

2. The average numeric value of an outcome of interest (such as number of products sold or customers served)

3. The dollar amount of benefit resulting to the organization (such as the annual increase in revenue)

If a selection system produces a higher proportion of successful candidates (e.g., a 10% increase in the number of new financial advisers who, once hired, can pass a government-mandated licensure exam), then that system has clear value to the company. The same can be said of a selection system that results in an increase in some **performance criterion** (e.g., cable service technicians who are able to complete an average of 20% more installations per day as a result of testing). And the same can be said for a benefit that can be measured in dollars (e.g., for every 10 points higher a salesperson scored on a sales skill assessment, annual sales increased by $1,000).

There are many approaches to estimating utility. Apart from an anecdotal approach (Does it seem like more people are successful on the job now?), perhaps one of the simplest approaches is to conduct pre- and post-comparisons of measurable performance to see if use of the selection system coincides with a change in performance. As a more precise alternative, industrial/organizational psychologists frequently use a **utility formula** that takes several factors into account: the **selection ratio**; the **validity coefficient**, expressed as the correlation between assessment scores and criteria (outcomes); and information about the dollar value of performance. The utility formula and related concepts are described here in some detail.

The selection ratio is the number of candidates who, based on the assessment, are chosen for the job, divided by the number of candidates who are assessed. The validity coefficient is a statistical correlation that indicates the correspondence between test scores and job performance or some other important work outcomes. When validity is high, there is a close correspondence between assessment performance and work results. In general, a high-validity, low-selection-ratio system produces the greatest benefit of selection but also incurs the highest cost of selection, all else being the same. When the selection ratio is low, the bar is set high on the assessment, and more rarified, higher-performing candidates will be chosen. (This generalization works as long as the selection ratio is not so high or so low that nearly everyone is hired or no one is hired, respectively; in those cases, the assessment has little value as a decision-making tool.) Information about the process used to estimate the dollar value of job performance follows. The value can be obtained from job experts at the organization. Alternatively, published research may be used to estimate this value, and, in many cases, the published value is used for utility estimates.

The result of the utility calculation is the dollar value of the selection system per individual or group of individuals hired. (Note that here utility refers to the dollar benefit of selection, without consideration of the cost. Certainly, it is important to compare this benefit with its corresponding cost to make good business decisions about selection systems.) The formula for utility is $\Delta U = r_{xy} \times SD_y \times N \times \phi/\rho$, and the elements of the calculation are as follows:

1. ΔU is the utility or annual change in the dollar value of productivity. Items 2 through 5 will be multiplied to calculate this number.

2. r_{xy} is the validity coefficient of the assessment, quantified as a correlation that falls between −1 and +1 and notated as a correlation between x (the assessment score) and y (the performance criterion score). Positive values indicate that the assessment (also called the predictor) and the criterion (work outcome) increase together; for instance, looking at the range of candidate data, as ability test scores increase, so might evaluations of ability to learn on the job. Negative values indicate that as one increases, the other decreases. For instance, as scores on an assessment of conscientiousness and work ethic increase, the frequency of absence and tardiness might decrease.

3. SD_y is the standard deviation (SD) of performance (y). This is the difference, in dollar terms, between an average performer and a performer whose superior performance puts them 1 SD above the population mean. Using data from across the spectrum of jobs in the U.S. economy, the value of SD_y has been estimated to be approximately 40% of salary (Hunter & Schmidt, 1982). Thus, as salary and likely responsibility increases, SD_y increases.

4. N is the number of employees hired.

5. ϕ/ρ refers to the test score of applicants who are selected by the organization and is expressed in a statistically standardized form (the standard deviation units in this

value and the standard deviation of performance in Item 3 cancel out, leaving a dollar value for the utility estimate).

For example, suppose an employer tests 2,500 clerical job candidates on an assessment with a validity of 0.43 and hires the top 1,000 scorers at an annual salary of $20,000. Therefore, r_{xy} = 0.43. The standard deviation of job performance (SD_y or 40% of salary) is estimated to be $8,000. One thousand employees are hired ($N = 1,000$). The selection ratio is 40% (4 out of 10 qualify); for this ratio, ϕ/ρ can be determined from statistical tables of the normal curve; this value is 0.64. Therefore, ΔU = (0.43) × (8000) (1000) × (0.64) = $2,201,600, meaning that the average increase in utility per person hired is $2,202 per year. If all 1,000 employees were to stay 3 years, we would estimate the utility over that period at approximately $6.6 million. Supposing that the testing program expenses were $300,000 per year, the return on investment for a 3-year period would still be about $5.7 million. This example serves to illustrate a method of estimating utility and also shows that, when many people are hired, the total value of the assessment quickly yields high numbers. Although organizational stakeholders occasionally are skeptical because of the extremely high utility values that are possible, the principles behind the numbers are sound.

After reading this section, you should reasonably conclude that there are a variety of technical concepts related to selection and assessment with which HRIS experts should familiarize themselves. Our intent has been to provide an overview of these topics and of the trends that are currently taking place in organizations, in the testing industry, and in research programs. By becoming familiar with this work, the HRIS student will gain awareness of the major issues he or she is likely to face when implementing database-based decision-making systems.

Summary

In summary, this chapter explained the intersection between the use of technology in the recruitment and selection process and the use of HRIS in organizations. This highlighted the need for HRIS experts to understand how to use the Internet for recruitment as well as selection-related data in order to provide strategic information to the company and demonstrate the return on the company's investment in assessments. In addition, technology issues surrounding the selection process were addressed. Measurement properties of paper-and-pencil assessments and their computer versions were discussed. The mode of assessments that do not include measurements of ability is of little concern for researchers, since giving these tests on paper will not result in a different measure from that obtained with a computerized test. However, there is clear evidence that the mode of administration (paper vs. computer) matters for ability tests that are speeded. The more speeded a test is, the more likely that there will be differences between the paper and computer test results.

A second issue focused on in this chapter is the trade-off between fidelity and bandwidth. Technology has enabled organizations to create work sample simulations that represent the job with high fidelity. However, if the company then wants to use the simulation for a different business unit or job, the details that made the simulation highly appropriate in the first setting may interfere with its use in the other setting. In general, HRIS managers should keep in mind that, depending on the effort and expense one is willing to expend on assessment development and installation, lower-fidelity simulations or combinations of other types of assessments might be preferable. One of the final issues dealt with was unproctored testing, which can be convenient to both the applicant and the organization. Unfortunately, this means of delivering assessment gives way to a floodgate of concerns such as how to verify candidate identity, provide test security and eliminate cheating, and ensure fair access to testing for people of color. The chapter further examined the role that HRIS experts have to play in solving these problems through the use of technology and the decision to develop and use an HRIS.

Key Terms

ability test 229

adverse impact 220

aesthetic features (of a website) 222

antidiscrimination laws 228

applicant tracking system (ATS) 213

attributes (of a website) 223

bandwidth 231

big data 233

chatbot 225

cloud computing 232

computerized assessments 229

content information 221

diversity of the applicant pool 219

employment brand 217

fidelity 231

knowledge test 234

media richness 221

navigability (of a website) 221

online test 231

passive job seeker 220

performance criterion 234

personality test 229

power test 229

psychological contract 214

realistic culture preview 216

realistic job preview 216

recruiting- and screening-oriented website 223

recruitment 210

selection procedures 227

selection ratio 235

self-selection 222

software as a service 232

speeded test 229

test security 231

unproctored testing 231

usability (of a website) 222

utility formula 235

validity coefficient 235

work simulations 230

Discussion Questions

1. What recruiting objectives are being met through the use of online recruitment?

2. What are some of the advantages and disadvantages of using online recruitment?

3. Should organizations rely solely on recruiting through the Internet? Why or why not?

4. What are some of the technological issues that arise through the use of technology in the function of selection?

5. Describe how the use of technology in the selection process is adding value to organizations.

Case Study: Recruitment and Selection in a Global Organization

The case from Chapter 8 will be used here, since recruitment and selection are the next step in the operationalization of a talent management strategy. The background for this chapter case is the case material from Chapter 8; at the end of this background material, more details relevant to the recruitment and selection of new employees will be presented.

Rudiger is sitting at his desk in his seventh-floor corner office in the City, gazing out over London and reflecting on life. At 43, he is at the top of his game. He has everything he could wish for—a lovely partner, a 4-year-old in a private nursery, a new executive house in the suburbs, a holiday home in southern Italy, and a remuneration package that's the envy of his peers and beyond anything his German immigrant parents could have imagined. But it hasn't been easy, oh no! Hard work, long hours, geographical moves every 2 or 3 years, and sacrifices in terms of his personal life.

But now he has a problem. Rudiger has just been appointed global head of People and Talent, responsible for the future of 35,000 people worldwide, the bulk of whom are based in the United States, the United Kingdom, and Europe, and manufacturing is likely to relocate to China in the next 2 years, adding to his responsibilities. In his previous role, he was responsible for the United Kingdom and Northern Europe and had operational oversight for 11,000 people. An initial consideration of his responsibilities has identified a number of people issues for the next 5 years: the company needs to recruit and retain particular specialist and skilled personnel; some of the brightest and most experienced midlevel managers are leaving; an aging senior directorship is looking toward early retirement. But the main difficulty is that, although he knows he has a problem, he doesn't have enough detailed information to know the scale of the problem.

18 months later . . .

Once again, Rudiger is sitting at his desk in his seventh-floor office in central London, reflecting on life. The move from Barcelona to England went smoothly, with the last crate arriving only two months later than the rest. He is still working hard, but the hours are slightly better since the introduction of the work-life balance policy last year, and his family has settled well into the idyllic English countryside.

As the global head of People and Talent, he still has problems though—just different ones. The talent strategy "Our People—Our Talent—Our Future," which he presented to the board in his third month, identified the need for robust HRP information and analyses that required a new version of HRP software. It is in its early stages, but the intensive data-cleansing and updating activity has been straightforward so far. More concerning are the metrics responsible for producing the information needed to develop far-reaching HRP policies and practices for the future. The metrics are relatively easy to construct, but it is proving tricky to find the right "bundles" of predictive metrics—this is holding up progress with the analysis application package. In addition, there have been cost overruns in the implementation of the HRP software, and some senior managers are wondering if the new software should be abandoned.

At least 3 of the 12 board members will retire in the next 2 years, and they are looking to groom their successors. At least one will have to be hired from outside the organization, and the HR department is not sure what the CEO wants for this position. In addition, employee turnover and an aggressive growth strategy mean hiring new employees as well as training transferring current employees. The work that is involved in defining competences (KSA sets) at skill levels within jobs is progressing well, with hard-won support from the unions. However, job descriptions that can be found are at least 3 to 5 years old, and some jobs have no descriptions. The new apprenticeship scheme is about to be launched, and the international graduate student package and development program has been completely revised. Overall, things are progressing reasonably well, but there is much to be done.

Case Supplemental Material

On the basis of your analyses and answers completed for Chapter 8, assume that Rudiger has completed an acceptable HRP program, and his staff members have completed current and accurate job descriptions for all positions in the talent management project. These job descriptions all contain the specific duties, tasks, and responsibilities as well as the KSA sets needed for each job.

Rudiger's next task is to recruit and select individuals for jobs. He wants to use the new HRIS software applications that the company has purchased and implemented for recruiting and selecting new employees. Fortunately, he can get assistance on this task from the IT department, which has built

and maintains the company's website. In addition, he has several staff members with doctorates in industrial/organizational psychology who can work with the IT professionals to develop recruitment and selection materials. However, Rudiger must provide the guidelines for the selection and recruitment of individuals who can fit into the talent management project.

Case Study Questions

1. What guidelines would you establish as part of Rudiger's plan that emphasized the use of the Internet via the company's website to communicate the recruiting objectives of the talent management project?

    a. What are the potential advantages and disadvantages of online recruitment to communicate recruiting objectives?

2. What guidelines would you establish for the use of an HRIS for the selection and assessment of potential employees?

    a. What selection and assessment tools could be used on the Internet, and which ones would need to be done on a face-to-face basis?

    b. What are the technological problems that affect selection via the Internet and the solutions that have been suggested?

    c. What guidelines would you develop to make sure that a utility analysis was done for all HRIS selection applications?

10

TRAINING AND DEVELOPMENT

Ralf Burbach and Steven D. Charlier

EDITORS' NOTE

Training and development (T&D) is central to the success of any organization and an important aspect of an organization's talent management program. Organizations use training not only to improve employee skill and knowledge but also to develop employees for future positions. In addition, training plays an important role in the motivation of employees. It shows that the organization is concerned about the development of its employees and would like to retain them. However, training generally captures the largest portion of the HR departmental budget. Due to these heavy costs, the application of an HRIS to save money is very important. In this chapter, you will learn more about the effective design of training and development and how technology is transforming T&D. Specifically, you will learn how training can be made to be cost-effective through an HRIS that serves both as a more efficient transaction processor and as an aid to managerial decision making.

CHAPTER OBJECTIVES

After completing this chapter, you should be able to

- Discuss how training can be used as a source of competitive advantage
- Differentiate between training and development (T&D)
- Understand how training and development affect both learning and motivation
- Explain the steps in a systems model of training
- Understand the essential features of the culture of a learning organization
- Explain the factors that influence transfer of training

- Understand both the costs and the benefits metrics associated with training
- Discuss the critical importance of the evaluation of training
- Understand MIS, HRMS, and DSS (see Chapter 1) training applications
- Explain the advantages and disadvantages of Web-based learning
- Develop a practical application, using EXCEL, in the evaluation of training

INDUSTRY BRIEF

RICHARD GEGENWARTH, STRATEGIC CHANGE MANAGEMENT LEADER, GUARDIAN LIFE

Learning and development (L&D) plays a key role in shaping the workforce of the future. This is a time of great opportunity for L&D, with a more dynamic means of delivering content and a convergence with core ERP systems and data analytics that provide L&D with ability to demonstrate the financial value of learning investments. It is also a time of challenge, because L&D professionals must integrate new technologies and deliver on the expectations of a new generation of employees and stakeholders, all while balancing investments in HR systems, existing knowledge assets, and leading practices for adult learning.

Healthcare providers are a great case for the evolving role of L&D. These complex organizations bring together medical research, teaching, and treatment teams, with many deep specialists involved in addition to sophisticated operational, administrative and functional teams. Providers are moving to new delivery models that can elevate care outcomes, improve patient experiences, and achieve efficiency and safety goals. Learning teams play a central role in successfully building new skills and measuring outcomes.

One of the common challenges for learning teams is the development of management and leadership skills for physicians. Surgeons, for example, rise to the top of their field based largely on their skills in the operating arena but are often then tasked with managing teams, surgery centers,

and facilities, for which they are less prepared to lead. Leading hospitals are making investments in leadership programs to address this situation and are using integrated HR and operational data to inform the selection of participants and to measure the effectiveness of these programs. A mixed approach is used that takes physicians out of the clinical setting for an intensive opening experience and then provides them with on-demand videos, virtual learning, and coaching to practice over an extended period on the job at a time that is convenient for the physician.

In addition, training the broader workforce on the mandated electronic health record systems, new codes for classification of diseases, and related health problems, and reporting of various hospital and physician quality and outcome measures is critical for these organizations. Professionals in these environments need training and development experiences to work within their highly variable and demanding schedules, and hospitals need to be able to monitor course completion, understand the efficacy of training, and how training impacts team performance and patient outcomes.

Increased sophistication in the capture, aggregation, analytics, and reporting of operational data places L&D organizations in a position to measure higher-level returns on training investments in a much more rigorous manner

(Continued)

(Continued)

than was previously possible. In conjunction with operational outcomes (e.g., patient health outcomes, efficiency, lapses in clinical standards), learning systems allow organizations to more efficiently address concerns and update employee skills. Finally, organizational adoption of cloud-based systems are acting as a catalyst to upgrade L&D capabilities and services. HR technologies offer new ways of providing content and access for learners at their point of need, so employees can enjoy both richer and more targeted learning experiences.

HRIS IN ACTION

Midwestern Mighty Markets (Triple M)[1] is one of the largest supermarket chains in five states, with 275 store locations. The corporate director of training, June Grady, was hired externally and has been on the job for 2 months. She has inherited the job with little information about what had been happening in the past relative to training and the use of any computer-based technology to manage the training activities and programs. She has begun a careful examination of the training activities, particularly supervisory training, since that is where the next higher-level managers will be identified. The annual budget for training has been $2.2 million, of which $1.1 million is devoted to supervisory training.

Supervisory training is 1 week in length and occurs on a monthly basis in each state at a central location. It is focused on training assistant department managers (e.g., produce, meat, and grocery) in the supervisory skills needed to be a department manager. Based on department managers' recommendations, assistant managers are sent to training at a central location in their state. However, all assistant managers across the states have the same training content and training activities. At the conclusion of the training, all trainees complete an evaluation of the training program based on their experiences.

The company has an HRIS software application developed by PeopleSoft and implemented 3 years ago. It is used for the management of all the training in the company. A number of reports can be generated from the software, including attendance by states, stores, and departments within the stores. This information is useful for June, so she can make sure that training is occurring evenly across departments, stores, and states. Other reports are also available that can be sent to department and store managers as well as to the regional managers of Triple M.

June has been examining all these reports available from the HRIS software to determine if anything is missing. During her examination, she notices that no one has been accessing the reports summarizing the trainees' evaluations of the training programs. On further examination, she finds that some store managers receive these summary reports but rarely use them. Also, she discovers that there is an additional report that has been designed to be generated by the software. This report is based on evaluation data that are to be collected from department managers 3 months after the trainees have returned to their jobs. This report appears quite important, since it asks the department managers to rate the trainees' job performance after they have completed training to determine any effects of the training.

June sees a serious problem with this lack of training-evaluation data collection and assessment; the trainees' posttraining evaluations are not being analyzed by the available software, and, more important, the department managers' ratings of trainee job performance are not being completed. Therefore, even though the company owns sophisticated (and costly) software, it is not being used to evaluate the supervisory training programs. More seriously, June has no idea if the $1.1 million being spent on supervisory training has had any effect on the job performance of the trainees.

INTRODUCTION

The only thing worse than training your employees and having them leave is not training them and having them stay.

—Henry Ford

The nature of work and the structure of organizations are rapidly changing. Internationalization, globalization, technological advances, and changing customer expectations of service and quality standards require firms to improve and transform themselves perpetually to remain competitive. Emerging concepts such as the global marketplace, knowledge economy, knowledge workers, information age, and digital revolution underscore that an organization's ability to survive in a constantly changing business environment is founded on its capacity to generate new knowledge, to share knowledge, and to innovate continuously (Alavi & Leidner, 2001; Gold & Malhotra, 2001; Nonaka & Takeuchi, 1995; Porter, 1990; Senge, 1990). In the new global economy, knowledge is now the new lever for success, since knowledge potentially adds more value than the traditional factors of production—capital, raw material, and labor (Harrison, 2009). In a knowledge economy, sustainable economic growth is thus based on investments in intangible assets, that is, knowledge-based capital (KBC) which comprises information resources, innovation, and organizational competencies (OECD, 2013).

Knowledge is created by a firm's knowledge assets, that is, its **human capital**[2] (see OECD, 2001, p. 18), which has long been recognized as one of the key sources of competitive advantage (Barney & Wright, 1998; Grant, 1996; Hatch & Dyer, 2004; Prahalad & Hamel, 1990; Wright, Dunford, & Snell, 2001). Hence, the **learning, training, and development (LT&D)** of employees is now center stage in today's organizations to ensure long-term competitiveness, excellence, quality, flexibility, and adaptability. Changing work practices and new services and products necessitate new knowledge, competences, and skills. It may also be argued that today's organizations ought to learn faster and more effectively than their rivals in order to remain competitive. However, a range of other reasons exists as to why organizations train and develop their workforces—for instance, to enable employees to cope with daily workloads. T&D activities can also alleviate possible future skill shortages and play a fundamental role in talent management. High-commitment organizations train and develop their employees to foster employee motivation and satisfaction (Pfeffer, 1996, 1998). In a time when job security is diminishing and employability is of increasing value, employees place much greater emphasis on career prospects and career development in their choice of employer. This point is of particular relevance for specialist knowledge workers who are in short supply in a tight labor market. The strategic importance of individual and organizational learning and development is mirrored in the continued interest in the concepts of the **learning organization** and **organizational learning**. These terms are often used interchangeably. However, the learning organization is the ultimate state of organizational learning at which the organization is able to facilitate the learning of all its members and can continuously transform itself (Argyris & Schon, 1978; Pedler, Burgoyne, & Boydell, 1991). "It is the potential of organizational learning to enable organizations to reinvent themselves in order to compete in the changing and increasingly uncertain and competitive environment that is making it such an attractive proposition for many managers" (Burnes, 2004, p. 129).

Yet it has been argued that few firms, if any, have actually achieved this aim. Nonetheless, the notion of the learning organization illustrates that organizational learning is inextricably linked to individual LT&D. It is also closely linked to the notion of lifelong learning and continuous professional development. Employees at all levels of the organization will have to demonstrate their commitment to these, especially when they seek a new employer, pay increases, or promotions. T&D activities are thus closely allied with **performance management** and talent management. Most large organizations use human resource information systems (HRIS) to collect, store, and analyze T&D information. This information is generally contained in specialist talent management modules, T&D modules, and learning management systems to reflect the strategic importance of LT&D in the organization. This chapter examines the strategic implications of T&D before it covers the **systems model of training and development**. The section on the systems model will look in detail at its four stages—identifying T&D needs, designing T&D solutions, implementing T&D, and evaluating T&D—along with a brief discussion of identified success factors specific to technology-based learning. Then training metrics and benefit analysis will be discussed. The next section investigates some HRIS applications in training and some implementation issues. The chapter concludes with a summary of the key issues.

TRAINING AND DEVELOPMENT: STRATEGIC IMPLICATIONS AND LEARNING ORGANIZATIONS

The introduction to this chapter has already alluded to a number of key terms associated with T&D. Some of the terms, such as *learning, training, development,* and *education,* are frequently used in combination and sometimes even, incorrectly, as substitutes. To comprehend the processes involved in LT&D, we must differentiate these key concepts. *Education* is aimed at developing, usually as part of a formal program of study, general knowledge, understanding, and moral values. *Training* refers to the planned acquisition of the knowledge, skills, and abilities (KSAs) to carry out a specific task or job in a vocational setting. The purpose of training interventions is to attain a positive change in performance. *Development* is a continuous process of systematic advancement, of "becoming increasingly more complex, more elaborate and differentiated, by virtue of learning and maturation" (Collin, 2007, p. 266). Development in an organizational context ensures that employees possess the KSAs required to fulfill future roles in the organization. Hence, development may be conceived as a lever for career development, succession planning, performance management, and talent management (Gunnigle, Heraty, & Morley, 2017). Training focuses on immediate job performance, whereas development centers on long-term, continuous changes of an individual's potential. Learning is defined as the process of assimilating new knowledge and skills in consequence of experience or practice that will bring about relatively permanent changes in behavior. However, the manner in which adults learn and are motivated to learn differs fundamentally from the ways in which children and adolescents learn. Andragogy, or the study of adult learning, purports that adults learn best when

1. They know the reasons for learning a new concept or skill

2. They are actively involved in creating or setting the learning activity

3. They can connect new learning to the knowledge and experience they have developed over time

4. Learning is problem centered

5. They believe a learning activity is immediately relevant to their job

6. They are internally rather than externally motivated to learn; in other words, they learn when they can see a benefit (Knowles, Holton, & Swanson, 2005)

Learning at an individual or organizational level is ineluctably linked to the creation and management of knowledge. Learning is the basis for any T&D activity. The outcomes of learning include skills, competencies, know-how or tacit knowledge, and higher-level cognitive and other skills (Collin, 2007). Skills are directly related to performance and the ability to carry out a task. It has been argued that new organizational realities require higher levels of cognitive skills. Bloom's taxonomy of learning, for example, identifies six increasingly higher levels of thinking—knowledge, comprehension, application, analysis, synthesis, and evaluation (Bloom, Engelhart, Furst, Hill, & Krathwohl, 1956). Competencies consist of KSAs and the underlying characteristics of a person that allow the jobholder to perform a task effectively. The knowledge of employees is a tacit commodity, an intangible asset. It is associated with an understanding of and a constructive application of information (Grant, 1996). In a knowledge-based economy, organizations must become knowledge productive, and employees, knowledge workers and knowledge assets. Knowledge-intensive organizations are those that heavily depend on knowledge creation and knowledge sharing, such as firms with a significant research and development focus or consultancy firms. **Knowledge management (KM)** essentially consists of five separate activities, which are the acquisition, documentation, transfer, creation, and application of knowledge (Yahya & Goh, 2002). Whereas knowledge is generated by individuals, organizational knowledge and learning are the result of the combined learning of everybody in the organization and the acquisition of knowledgeable individuals (Grant, 1996).

Hence, if a firm's organizational culture rewards learning, it facilitates KM and the transformation of the firm into a knowledge organization (Mayo, 1998; Soliman & Spooner, 2000). The sharing, codifying, storing, and replicating of knowledge within the organization is greatly facilitated by **information and communication technology (ICT)**.

Consequently, KM focuses on the interaction of human beings and ICT and the subsequent creation of knowledge and, in addition, on the alignment of technology with people systems within a firm. The HR department plays a vital role in determining where, among employees, tacit knowledge exists, what type of knowledge is present, and whether and to what degree this knowledge is conducive to attaining present and future organizational goals (Soliman & Spooner, 2000). Should the HR function detect a gap between existing knowledge and the knowledge necessary to pursue strategic objectives, it can initiate procedures to remedy this shortfall through recruitment, socialization, and T&D initiatives. It is evident that the concepts of KM and organizational learning are closely related. Organizational learning is by no means a new concept. Argyris and Schon (1978) suggested a three-level model of organizational learning, consisting of single-loop, double-loop, and triple-loop learning. Single-loop learning is adaptive and focuses on the detection of deviations in performance from established organizational norms, practices, policies, and procedures. Double-loop learning questions the suitability of norms, practices, policies, and procedures that define performance standards. Triple-loop learning challenges the rationale of the organization with the aim of completely transforming it (Burnes, 2004). One of the most influential proponents of the learning organization is Peter Senge. In his book *The Fifth Discipline*, he puts forward five interrelated disciplines that an organization should cultivate among its employees to engender learning and success (Senge, 1990):

1. *Personal mastery:* individual growth and learning

2. *Mental models:* deep-rooted assumptions that affect the way in which employees perceive people, situations, and organizations

3. *Shared visions:* a shared view of the organization's future

4. *Team learning:* a shift from individual learning to collective learning

5. *Systems thinking:* or the "Fifth Discipline," which connects the previous disciplines (Burnes, 2004)

Other writers promote generic organizational characteristics that stimulate organizational learning. Cummings and Worley (2009), for instance, advocate a flat teamwork-based organizational structure to facilitate networking; the use of information systems to collect, process, and share information; human resource practices such as appraisals and rewards that reinforce learning; effective leadership that is supportive of organizational learning; and an organizational culture that encourages openness, creativity, and experimentation among members of the firm. A learning culture is one of the key levers for organizational learning, training, and development. Transfer of training is far more likely to occur in an environment in which the basic assumptions, shared values, norms, and artifacts of an organization espouse successful LT&D and in which employees are encouraged to create, process, and share information and knowledge (Cummings & Worley, 2009). A T&D intervention can only be considered successful if transfer of training has occurred and a permanent change in behavior has taken place.

HRIS training and development applications play a fundamental role in fostering organizational learning. These applications provide organizations with a mechanism to assess, measure, facilitate, manage, and record systematically the LT&D of each employee and thus the entire organization. In that way, HRIS LT&D applications also support HRIS talent management and performance management applications. For instance, LT&D applications may be utilized to manage the training and development of high potential employees. In addition, employees' training records could feed into their performance evaluations.

Systems Model of Training and Development

The approaches to T&D adopted by organizations are quite possibly as diverse as the organizations that employ them. The literature is teeming with different, sometimes competing models that mirror the approaches to T&D found in practice. One of the most frequently cited models is the systems (or systematic) approach. This formal or planned approach to workforce T&D consists of four interrelated and connected steps, which are illustrated in Figure 10.1. The steps are arranged as a cycle to highlight the cyclical and continuous nature of the process; the systems model, then, is conceptualized as an ongoing activity, in much the same way as is employee development. Thus, the model is applicable to both training and development. Its simplicity and clear structure make it ideally suited in the context of HRIS applications in this area. In addition, the model provides a rational foundation for the allocation of resources throughout the T&D process. However, the systematic model has also received some criticism *because* of its simplicity, because of the fact that it is a closed system, and because it does not take account of individual differences among the learners. Notwithstanding these criticisms, the model continues to find broad application, for instance, in the development of national training standards and, indeed, in many IT-based T&D applications that are designed based on the four steps (Stewart, 1999).

Step One: Identifying T&D Needs

The first step of the systems model is concerned with the identification of the learning and development needs of organizational members. The **training needs analysis (TNA)**

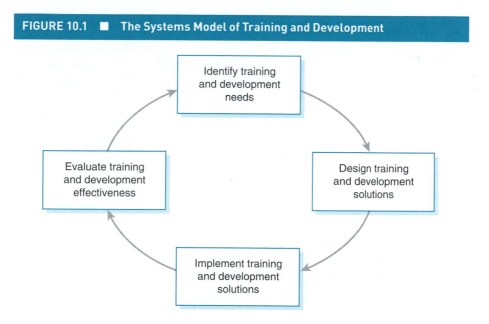

FIGURE 10.1 ■ The Systems Model of Training and Development

is the key activity of the systematic approach and essentially serves to identify any discrepancies, the T&D "gap," between existing KSAs and those required in the present and in the future. Thus, it ensures the integration of employee T&D activities with the business needs of the firm. Hence, the TNA must assess the validity of initiatives, it ought to assist in prioritizing T&D objectives and initiatives, and it has to be able to determine the actual training needs. Training needs may arise at three distinct levels (Boydell, 1983):

- At an organizational level (current and future employee T&D requirements that an organization has to fulfill in order to attain its strategic long-term objectives)

- At a job level (relevant KSAs that are part of specific jobs)

- At a personal level (the competences required)

Because of the crucial importance and comprehensive nature of the TNA, many organizations employ an HRIS to collect, store, and analyze training needs data, thus ensuring that the resulting information is both timely and accurate. Data sources range from business objectives and statistics at the organizational level to job descriptions and output levels at the job level and staff appraisals biographical data, and individual training records at the personal level. Most HRIS can be configured to gather data from these and other sources. However, a host of specialist T&D software (discussed further on in this chapter) exists that will aid a firm in accomplishing its T&D activities. In the event, however, that the TNA highlights a considerable gap between existing and desired KSAs, an organization may decide on external recruitment to hire individuals who already possess the required competencies. In that case, it will be of vital importance that the organization has access to skilled personnel and demographic data, which might provide some indication regarding the skill levels of the wider population and the environment in which the firm operates.

Step Two: Developing T&D Initiatives

The second stage of the cycle focuses on the development of T&D initiatives, objectives, and methods that should be capable of meeting the three levels of needs identified during the first phase, the TNA. Organizations have a wide array of T&D methods at their disposal, and advances in and access to ICT and mobile technologies will further increase the number of methods and ways of content delivery available. Faced with an apparent overabundance of methods, how should organizations choose the ones most appropriate for their needs? A number of criteria will guide the decision-making process.

The effectiveness of individual learning plans and events ultimately hinges on the design of these T&D interventions. A learning activity can be considered successful if it leads to transfer of learning as well as a noticeable and permanent change in behavior in the trainees. The aim of the HRIS in this context is to compare employee training data with subsequent performance data. Successful learning events must achieve a "best fit" between

- the content of what is to be learned,

- the media through which content is delivered, and

- the method used to facilitate learning (see Figure 10.2).

FIGURE 10.2 ■ Best-Fit Learning Event Model

With regard to individual learning, it is important to note that every individual has his or her preferred learning style and that these learning styles must be taken into consideration when one designs a training event to encourage learning transfer (explained in what follows). Based on Kolb's (1984) learning cycle, which involves a concrete experience, reflective observation, abstract conceptualization, and active experimentation, Honey and Mumford (1992) developed four preferred learning styles—activist, reflector, theorist, and pragmatist. Additionally, the VARK framework (Fleming, 2001; Fleming & Mills, 1992) has been proposed as an alternative view of learning styles, proposing four different preferences for learning activities—visual, aural, read/write, and kinesthetic.

In today's highly regulated working environments, it is also essential to attain internal and external consistency. Internal consistency is achieved if learning interventions are mutually supportive of one another and of the business objectives. External consistency is attained if T&D activities are aligned with external regulations (e.g., health and safety legislation), best practices in the industry, and the stipulations and standards of external training award bodies. The conditions for a successful learning event are illustrated in the **best-fit learning event model** in Figure 10.2.

T&D methods essentially fall into two broad categories—on the job and off the job, albeit the emergence of e-learning has somewhat diluted this distinction, as it can be either (Welsh, Wamberg, Brown, & Simmering, 2003). **On-the-job training** usually involves peer observation and can be informal, structured, or unstructured, although successful learning outcomes are more likely to occur in a structured rather than an unstructured environment. Compared with **off-the-job training**, on-the-job training is relatively inexpensive. While off-the-job methods may provide greater exposure to expert knowledge, they may also be more time-consuming and may not encourage knowledge transfer. Table 10.1 lists a number of examples of T&D methods in each category.

TABLE 10.1 ■ Training Methods	
On-the-Job Training Methods	**Off-the-Job Training Methods**
Observation	Simulation
Mentoring	Role play
Coaching	Case study
Job rotation	Business games
Apprenticeship	External course or workshop
Self-directed learning	Behavior modeling
	Placement
	Open, distance, or blended learning

E-learning

We pause in our coverage of the systems model at this point to discuss **e-learning**, an umbrella term that broadly refers to any learning activity that is facilitated using electronic means. Recent reports by the Chartered Institute of Personnel and Development (CIPD, 2015; Insala, 2014) and Association for Talent Development (2015) indicate that the number of people accessing the Internet using a mobile device surpasses the number of people doing so using ordinary desktop computers. Mobile learning, virtual classrooms, and social media are rapidly replacing traditional forms of learning and early forms of e-learning, such as computer-based training. Yet confidence levels in the ability of organizations to effectively harness technology for T&D needs are lagging (CIPD, 2015), and overall effectiveness of e-learning is a concern for many organizations (CIPD, 2015; Insala, 2014). Nevertheless, e-learning has the potential to capitalize on a variety of different technologies that have emerged as a result of rapid developments in information technology and the World Wide Web. The technologies can be commonly categorized as **Web 1.0, Web 2.0, and Web 3.0**. These are explained in Table 10.2.

Other technologies used in e-learning encompass computer-aided assessments, animations, simulations, games, and electronic performance support systems (EPSSs). EPSSs are not learning technologies per se. However, they provide an electronic support infrastructure that allows employees to carry out their work. An EPSS would typically include assistants (e.g., Microsoft Office Assistant), wizards, knowledge bases, help, and advice functions. A number of Web 1.0 e-learning methods to address different training needs are identified in Table 10.3.

The e-learning methods explained in Table 10.3 are arranged according to the extent to which they use the Internet, the degree to which they facilitate interaction between peer learners and instructors, and the degree to which computers are networked or not networked. They are arranged in increasingly complex order; **mobile learning** shows the highest level of interaction and networking. However, this does not imply that methods that rely on greater student interaction or that allow greater access to external resources are necessarily the best options for all situations—the choice of e-learning method will depend on the best fit with the training needs that ought to be addressed (see Figure 10.2).

TABLE 10.2 ■ Web Technologies

Technology	Explanation
Web 1.0	The first-generation Web, including CD-ROMs, interactive videos, DVDs, video streaming, Web pages, and software programs
Web 2.0	Web-based file sharing and user-generated interaction using discussion forums, e-mails, blogs, wikis, and/or social media websites such as Yammer, MySpace, YouTube, Twitter, Facebook, Renren, LinkedIn, etc.
Web 3.0	The "intelligent Web" based on a number of developments such as the semantic Web, open access, augmented reality, and intelligent applications (e.g., speech recognition). Web 3.0 focuses on the use of software as a service, cloud computing, multiple technologies, and mobile devices. This is often associated with mobile learning.

TABLE 10.3 ■ Web 1.0-Based E-learning Methods

E-learning Methods	Explanation
Computer-based training (CBT) or technology-based training, computer-managed instruction (CMI), computer-aided (assisted) instruction (CAI), computer-based learning (CBL)	Interactive training experience using a stand-alone computer, when no collaboration and access to external resources is necessary; media used include CD-ROMs, DVDs, interactive video
Multimedia-based training (MBT)	Training experience that combines text, colors, graphics, audio, and video to engage the learner; MBT can range from a simple graphical presentation of text to a complex flight simulation
Distance learning (or education)	Learner and tutor are in different locations; the approach uses both synchronous and asynchronous communication; the course provider usually provides online support and supplies students with a course pack, including printed and audiovisual materials; courses follow a predetermined curriculum and schedule
Open learning (or education)	Learner has complete control over how, what, when, where, and at what pace learning occurs; any type and combination of media may be used
Open distance learning (ODL)	Umbrella term that covers both open and distance learning
Virtual learning environment (VLE) or virtual classroom	Online environment in which learning takes place
Web-based training (WBT) or online learning (or education), **Internet-based training (IBT)**	Any training and learning that takes place online, that is, via the World Wide Web
Mobile learning	Any T&D offering that involves mobile technologies; mobile technologies include notebooks, tablets, smartphones, MP3 players

However, rapid developments in ICT also imply that many methods and approaches have a relatively short shelf life; that is, they quickly become obsolete (e.g., computer-based training). In addition, the distinction between some of these e-learning methods has become blurred, and the terminology can be confusing, as terms are often used interchangeably. Increasingly, the media employed in e-learning are interactive; that is, the learner interacts with the media. Using Web 2.0 and Web 3.0 technologies, the e-learning content is generated by the users themselves, and learning occurs "socially"; that is, the learner interacts with other learners and media to create their own learning environment.

Thus, online learning relies on digital collaboration. The term *digital collaboration* denotes networking and communication via the Internet using a variety of mobile devices. Although digital collaboration is of vital importance in the effectiveness of virtual teams in the business world, online collaboration between learners also tends to increase learning and learning transfer. Intranet-based **collaborative technologies**, such as groupware (electronic meeting software), provide a company forum for tracking, sharing, and organizing information. Collaboration software generally combines e-mail, document management, Web conferencing, and/or calendar management tools that allow users to collaborate on projects and documents simultaneously. Numerous options exist in the current market, including Slack, Basecamp, Trello, and JIRA among many others. Internet-based collaborative Web 2.0 technology, or social networking technology (e.g., blogs, wikis, or podcasts), play an increasingly important role in informal peer-to-peer learning, which is much faster, more flexible, and more responsive than formal modes of training (Frauenheim, 2007). Collaboration and communication in this context may be synchronous or asynchronous. **Synchronous communication** refers to "real-time" or live communication using tools such as messenger services or videoconferencing. Smartphones have become the device of choice for this type of communication, and various apps are available for the various mobile platforms such as iOS and Android. Web 2.0 and Web 3.0 technologies thus create virtual classrooms that can be accessed anytime, anyplace and which have the potential to be far more interactive than traditional classrooms could be.

However, not all collaboration can occur in real time, especially if learners are geographically dispersed across different time zones. While **asynchronous communication** still makes use of the Internet, communication is delayed, and learners access the learning spaces at their own convenience. Table 10.4 provides some examples of synchronous and asynchronous methods of e-learning.

Although it is important to make a distinction between different forms of collaboration, most e-learning combines various types of communication, collaboration, e-learning methods, and, in some cases, more traditional approaches to maximize learning transfer. Testing and assessment of e-learning may rely on traditional paper-based methods, the electronic submission of files, or interactive assignments (including online discussions). The combination of e-learning methods with traditional face-to-face methods is referred to as **blended learning**. This hybrid approach promises to combine the advantages of both traditional and e-learning approaches to training. For instance, one of the key issues in workplace training is the ability to apply new skills to the actual job. However, most online training does not provide for the application of new knowledge and skills, which is one of the key elements of Kolb's learning cycle. Blended learning, thus, allows the learner to apply new skills in a real-life situation, either in a classroom or on the job. Nevertheless, recent research suggests that students' individual differences may play a key role as to whether a blended learning system will be effective. Individuals with higher self-efficacy and a more internal locus of control may be better equipped to persist in the face of challenges presented by a

TABLE 10.4 ■ E-learning Communication Typology	
Synchronous	• Virtual learning environments (VLEs) • Instant messaging/texting services • Audio- and videoconferencing • Digital chat rooms • Shared whiteboard applications • Application sharing
Asynchronous	• E-mail • Discussion forums or blogs • Threaded discussions • Self-paced learning

blended learning environment (Beaudoin, 2013; Sitzmann & Ely, 2011). Harvard, Taylor, and Eggleston Schwartz (2018, p. 27) argue that a focus on blended experiences based on a "multimodal approach to learning" facilitated by technological advancements will be far more effective in increasing knowledge retention and changing behavior than traditional blended learning approaches.

The development of e-learning programs and resources requires significant investments of time and money. However, the volatile nature of the global marketplace and the rapidly changing information needs of firms necessitate a different approach to e-learning. While standard e-learning solutions can take months to develop, **rapid e-learning (REL)** or just-in-time learning solutions may be developed in weeks, days, or even hours, depending on the complexity of materials to be created. Essentially, REL allows companies to produce a large amount of content, using limited resources, in a short time interval, and deliver this content in real time to a large number of people. In 2014, almost 50% of U.S. organizations utilized an REL tool in their T&D activities (Training, 2014).

Although e-learning methods diverge on a number of levels, for instance, the level of interaction between learners, e-learning, in general, offers a range of advantages and disadvantages to the learner and to the organization. These are shown in Table 10.5. The key advantage of e-learning is flexibility; that is, it affords learners the choice of what, when, where, and how much is learned. The key disadvantages center on the lack of human contact and technological issues.

Despite the increasing global popularity of e-learning initiatives, they suffer from several shortcomings. Nunes, McPherson, Annasingh, Bashir, and Patterson (2009) identify several of these:

- Some of the most advertised advantages of e-learning, such as reductions in the travel and accommodation costs associated with face-to-face training, are not well accepted by learners. Often, trainees have to undergo e-learning in addition to their normal workloads while in the office and subject to their usual daily work pressures.

TABLE 10.5 ■ Advantages and Disadvantages of E-learning	
Advantages	**Disadvantages**
Cost advantages compared with traditional methods	Basic computer skills necessary
Improves computer skills	Use of computers might cause apprehension
Self-paced	Not suitable for certain content
High degree of learner control	Privacy concerns if based online
Choice of learning environment	Requires self-motivation to learn
Interactive	Learners may feel isolated from instructors and peers
Easy tracking of learner progress and engagement	Lack of human contact in general
Real-time feedback	Technical difficulties impede access
Consistent delivery method	
Variety of formats and methods available	
Consistent content	
Unlimited access in terms of time and locale	
Better support, help functions, knowledge base than other methods	
Appeals to several senses simultaneously	
Increased benefits through the combination with traditional training methods	
Can be both synchronous and asynchronous	
Accommodates different learning styles	

- Another source of dissatisfaction with e-learning is its lack of human touch: the lack of interaction with knowledgeable trainers and the lack of socialization with fellow learners.

- Generic multimedia simulations without an organizational and work-specific focus tend to alienate learners.

- Organizations still tend to rely on the conservative "drill-and-practice" model and "force-fed instruction" and, in the process, ignore the social, informal, and collaborative aspects of learning.

- There is also less emphasis on learner-centered approaches that take advantage of social negotiation, on-the-job learning, on-demand learning, and peer support. New learning models are moving in the direction of "casual, instant, and informal" learning facilitated by Web 2.0 technologies, such as blogs, Webcasts, online conferencing, and mobile learning using mobile devices.

- There is little research that links e-learning to employee creativity, innovation, and adaptability—all of which are essential to any workforce in the 21st-century knowledge economy.

- Often, learners are pushed into e-learning without being properly equipped with the basic skills required for being successful in a networked learning environment.

- Finally, e-learning is currently serving the needs of mainly large organizations and has yet to address the learning needs of small and medium-sized enterprises.

Salas, DeRouin, and Littrell (2005) offer several research-based guidelines for designing e-learning packages. Even though these guidelines pertain to **distance learning**, they are relevant and useful for other e-learning methods as well:

- Only provide e-learning when you are sure it meets the organization's specific learning and development needs.

- Train learners on computer basics before offering computer-based training.

- Take into consideration human cognitive processes when designing e-learning programs.

- Enhance the learning experience by including multimedia and learning games in the presentation of learning topics.

- Keep learners "engaged" by offering blended learning and allowing interaction among trainees and between trainees and facilitators.

- Offer trainees control over certain aspects of instruction, and guide them through the learning process by using tools, such as cognitive maps.

We discuss the primary factors that influence the success of e-learning initiatives (in regard to learner outcomes like satisfaction, learning performance, and learning transfer to the job) in a later section but now return to the discussion of the systems model and implementation.

Step Three: Implementing T&D

The third stage of the systems model of T&D involves the implementation of training. Although this stage is depicted as a separate phase of the training process, it is closely linked with the preceding stage, the design stage. Indeed, many book chapters on T&D consider both stages in unison. The reason for this is that the design of a training solution ultimately determines its implementation, as any issues and factors that could arise during the implementation phase should be anticipated at the design stage (Stewart, 1999). For instance, if an organization wanted to roll out e-learning to its entire workforce via the company intranet, the firm would have to ensure that every employee had access to the intranet. To ensure that the implementation phase runs smoothly, organizations ought to formulate an implementation plan that should specify

- the resources required,
- how the training should be carried out,
- who should facilitate the training, and
- the period within which the training should occur.

The requisite resources vary with the training method chosen. While traditional face-to-face training necessitates physical training rooms and equipment, e-learning requires initial investments in ICT. Available resources are normally set out in pre-determined annual training budgets. The training design will provide answers to the questions of how, by whom, and when training should be implemented. The implementation of a T&D initiative can only be considered successful if transfer of learning has occurred.

Training Transfer

Positive and long-lasting changes in employee behavior and, ultimately, increased shareholder value can only be attained if training (or learning) transfer occurs. **Training transfer** is the continuous application of the KSA acquired during the training exercise. Various classifications of transfer of training exist depending on the context:

- Near versus far (how close the training task is to the actual job task)
- Specific versus general (transfer of skills versus transfer of principles)
- Positive versus negative (linked to the perception of the training experience)
- Lateral versus vertical (Hayashi, Chen, & Terase, 2005)

Lateral transfer is about the application of training to similar tasks at the same level of complexity, while vertical transfer implies analysis and synthesis, that is, the ability to apply training to more complex tasks (Gagné, 1985). Training transfer depends on a number of variables, which can be summarized under five headings (Baldwin & Ford, 1988):

1. Trainee characteristics (the trainee's predisposition to training)
2. Training design (the organization of the learning environment)
3. Work environment (the immediate factors at work that affect transfer)
4. Learning and retention
5. Generalization and maintenance (ensuring that the trainee is given the opportunity to continuously use the acquired KSA)

Learning and retention are most likely to occur when the trainee possesses the necessary characteristics (e.g., high cognitive ability, high conscientiousness, and voluntary participation), the training design and workplace environment foster learning transfer (e.g., supervisor support), and the trainee is given ample opportunity to apply the training (Blume, Ford, Baldwin, & Huang; 2010). In addition, it has been demonstrated that transfer of training is *critically* dependent on the organizational climate that supports the training transfer (Lance, Kavanagh, & Brink, 2002; Rouiller & Goldstein, 1993; Tracey, Tannenbaum, & Kavanagh, 1995; Velada, Caetano, Michel, Lyons, & Kavanagh, 2007).

Step Four: Evaluating T&D

To assess whether a particular training initiative, method, or solution has met the training needs and objectives of the firm and whether transfer of learning has taken place, organizations must evaluate their T&D efforts. Training evaluation is not an isolated activity. It is part of the T&D cycle and must be considered alongside and aligned with **needs analysis**, design, and implementation to provide a holistic picture of the entire T&D process. Similar to the T&D cycle, the evaluation process should be viewed as cyclical. The steps in the evaluation process are illustrated in Figure 10.3.

FIGURE 10.3　■　The Evaluation Process

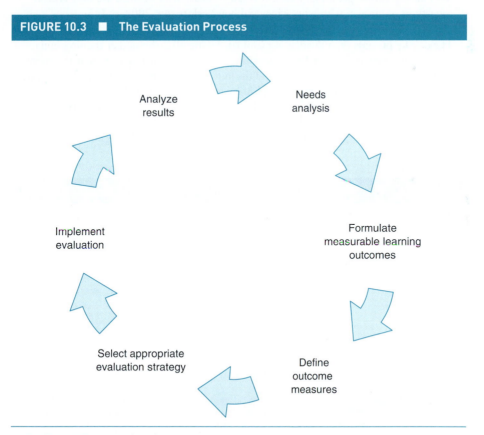

Source: Developed from Noe (2002).

The evaluation process commences with the needs analysis. Training needs must then be translated into measurable learning outcomes. Appropriate metrics must be identified against which outcomes can be measured. The next step involves the selection of an appropriate evaluation strategy. Not all training can be assessed in the same manner because of the diversity in training methods. Once an evaluation has been carried out, the results must be analyzed and fed back into the training process. This final step is omitted in many evaluation models, even though it is crucially important to use evaluation data to make decisions about future training initiatives. An HRIS can be invaluable in supporting this process, as it contains a vast amount of data related to training and performance that can form the basis of any T&D decision.

However, many organizations pay lip service to evaluation without having a clear concept of what evaluation means and what purpose it serves.

People often confuse the process of monitoring, validation and evaluation. The purpose of monitoring is to take the temperature of a learning event from time to time, picking up any problems or emerging needs. Validation measures the achievement of learning objectives set for a learning initiative or process. Evaluation looks at the total value of that event or process, thereby placing it into its organizational context and aiding future planning. Faced with an evaluation task, there are four crucial questions to answer: why, who, when and how? (Harrison, 2009, p. 143)

Hence, the purpose of evaluation is manifold. Figure 10.2 shows that training initiatives must attain internal and external consistency to be effective and to ensure that the training needs and objectives of the organization and the individual have been addressed. The purposes of evaluation discussed in the literature are plentiful (see, for example, Gibb, 2002; Griffin, 2014; Hayden, 2018). The primary purposes of evaluation could be summarized as in Table 10.6.

So what should be evaluated? As a rule, criteria for evaluation should be based on the training objectives (see Figure 10.3). In addition, the criteria ought to be relevant;

TABLE 10.6 ■ Purposes of Evaluation	
Summative	Quantitative in nature; establishes whether T&D program was effective, was efficient, has added value, and has met its objectives
Formative	Qualitative in nature; assesses how training, learning, and development can be improved, that is, how they could be made more efficient and effective
Learning	Quantitative and qualitative assessment of learner's posttraining performance to evaluate whether learning transfer has occurred
Power and Politics	Subjective in nature; is used to serve the interests of specific stakeholders within the organization

Source: Based on Easterby-Smith (1986).

that is, they should not be contaminated (biased) or deficient. However, criteria should also be reliable, practical, and discriminative. Training outcomes fall into a number of distinct categories. The number of training evaluation models in the literature seems almost infinite. Kirkpatrick and Kayser Kirkpatrick's (2016) New World Kirkpatrick Model, which is based on Kirkpatrick's (1960, 1994) training evaluation model, consists of four levels of learning outcomes: reaction, learning, behavior, and results. Building on these four levels, Phillips (2012) added a fifth—the assessment of return on investment of training. However, Saks and Burke (2012) found that with respect to the Kirkpatrick (1960, 1994) framework, only behavior- and results-related evaluations of training were correlated with higher levels of learning transfer. Warr, Bird, and Rackham's (1970) CIRO framework also has four levels: context, inputs, reactions, and outcomes (immediate, intermediate, and ultimate). Easterby-Smith (1986) suggests a CAPIO framework comprising context, administration, process, inputs, and outputs. In yet another model, Brinkerhoff (2009) focuses on what he refers to as the "Success Case Study Method," which surveys both the most successful and least successful training participants to ascertain the enablers and barriers to training success. Finally, individual outcomes of training programs have been identified as falling within **Bloom's taxonomy** of learning domains (cognitive, psychomotor, and affective), which is one of the most widely used models to describe learning outcomes (Bloom et al., 1956; Bloom, Masia, & Krathwohl, 1964). A comparison of these and other frameworks reveals a significant overlap between these evaluation models, as well as between a number of the key learning outcomes contained within them.

The key objective of any evaluation process will be to assess the broad range of individual and organizational outcomes as well as return on investment (ROI). Hence, one of the key considerations will be whether a T&D program has had any measurable impact on the firm's bottom line, so as to justify training expenditure and training budgets. The following section will consider some of the complexities involved in establishing the costs and the actual benefits of T&D initiatives.

Success Factors in E-learning

In their recent review of the e-learning literature, Johnson and Brown (2017) propose a model of learning effectiveness that encompasses several factors pertinent to the focal training outcomes of learner satisfaction, actual learning, and transfer of learning to job performance. These factors include the organizational context, technology, learning design, and the characteristics of the instructor and trainees. We briefly discuss each of these factors as follows but encourage readers to review the Johnson and Brown (2017) article for a fuller discussion of these topics.

In regard to organizational context, two areas that have been highlighted in recent research involve the level of **organizational support** for learning activities and the **learning climate** within the organization. Organizational support refers to the resources (e.g., tools, time allocation, and financial support) available to employees to pursue e-learning activities, while learning climate relates to individual perceptions of the overall environment related to e-learning. In short, research has shown that when organizations provide requisite resources and create a positive learning climate, motivation (Colquitt, LePine, & Noe, 2000; Hurtz & Williams, 2009; Noe & Schmitt, 1986), satisfaction (Sawang, Newton, & Jamieson, 2013), and learning transfer (Kodwani, 2017; Park, Sim, & Roh, 2010) are higher.

Technology is obviously an integral part of any e-learning activity and comprises an array of hardware, software, and networking considerations. Broadly speaking, we can view technology in terms of its **reliability**, its **perceived usefulness** and **ease of use**, and **media richness** to determine the impact of technology on e-learning outcomes. Research has consistently shown that technology reliability positively influences learner outcomes (Islam, 2011; Johnson, Gueutal, & Falbe, 2009; Kim, Trimi, Park, & Rhee, 2012; Liaw, 2008), while the results are less clear in regard to the other technology characteristics. That is, for e-learning to be successful, trainees need to believe that the course materials will be available, accessible, and reliable at speeds commensurate with the media (e.g., audio, video, text) that they are utilizing. In turn, it suggests that although it is important that the software be easily used and provide useful content, these alone may not drive learner outcomes unless coupled well with organizational context and course design factors.

Design factors include **training complexity** (the level of information load, diversity, change, and interconnectedness required of learning tasks; Sweller, 1988), **learner control** (the level of control trainees have over pace, content, and structure of the training itself; Fisher, Wasserman, & Orvis, 2010), and **training guidance** (advice on how best to navigate and use e-learning tools; Johnson & Brown, 2017). The majority of research in traditional environments suggest that training complexity is negatively related to learner outcomes (Argote, Insko, Yovetich, & Romero, 1995; Fisher & Ford, 1998; Warr, Allan, & Birdi, 1999), and this negative relationship is perhaps even stronger in e-learning environments (Granger & Levine, 2013; Hornik, Saunders, Li, Moskal, & Dzuiban, 2008; Salas, DeRouin, & Littrell, 2005; Welsh, Wanberg, Brown, & Simmering, 2003; Yanson & Johnson, 2016), particularly when it comes to skill development.

Although learner control has been shown to have positive effects on learner satisfaction (Fisher et al., 2010; Karim & Behren, 2014; Orvis, Fisher, & Wasserman, 2009), the empirical findings on its effects on learning and transfer are mixed (DeRouin, Fritzsche, & Salas, 2004; Granger & Levine, 2010; Orvis, Brusso, Fisher, & Wasserman, 2011). However, proper training guidance, in the form of adaptive guidance or technological scaffolding (temporary support structures that help learners focus on important content and suggestions for improvement; Bell & Kozlowski, 2002; Janson, Söllner, & Leirmeister, in press) and self-regulated learning strategies (Santhanam, Sasidharan, & Webster, 2008; Sitzmann, Bell, Kraiger, & Kanar, 2009), can improve trainee outcomes.

Finally, characteristics of instructors and trainees play crucial roles in the effectiveness of courses in both traditional and e-learning training environments. Instructors that have confidence/self-efficacy in their ability to utilize e-learning (Chien, 2012; Ferdousi & Levy, 2010; Webster & Hackley, 1997) and have positive attitudes toward e-learning (Liaw, Huang, & Chen, 2007) can improve student outcomes. In terms of instructor behaviors, the level of instructor engagement and interaction with learners also demonstrates consistently positive results in regard to student outcomes (Arbaugh, 2001, 2014; Marks, Sibley, & Arbaugh, 2005; Sitzmann et al., 2008; Yang & Durrington, 2010). Student characteristics have also been the focus of research in the e-learning environment, including demographic variables, personality traits, attitudes, and experience. Yet the results for many of these characteristics have been inconsistent across studies. Table 10.7 provides an overview of the research findings to date.

TABLE 10.7 ■ Effects of Trainee Characteristics on Learner Outcomes		
Characteristic	**Traditional Learning**	**E-learning**
Age	Negatively related to training motivation and performance; positively related to transfer (Colquitt et al., 2000).	Unclear—empirical results have shown positive relationship to motivation and satisfaction (Hashim, Ahmad, & Abdullah, 2010; Kim & Frick, 2011), mixed results (Bausch, Michel, & Sonntag, 2014), and no relationship (Brown, 2001; Chu, 2010).
Locus of control	Internal locus of control (LOC) → higher learner motivation and outcomes (Colquitt et al., 2000).	Unclear—Yukselturk, Ozekes, & Turel (2014) found lower dropout rate and higher satisfaction among internal LOC individuals; Johnson et al. (2009) found no relationship between LOC and training outcomes.
Conscientiousness	Positively related to training outcomes (Colquitt et al., 2000).	Unclear—may be more relevant to longer-duration e-learning events (Kleitman & Costa, 2014) vs. short duration (Orvis et al., 2011).
Computer self-efficacy	Not applicable.	Positively related to satisfaction (Eom, 2011; Johnson, Hornik, & Salas, 2008; Liaw, 2008). Mixed (but generally positive) relationship with performance (Galy, Downey, & Johnson, 2011; Johnson et al., 2009; Sun, Tsai, Finger, Chen, & Yeh, 2008).
Computer anxiety	Not applicable.	Research has primarily focused on decisions to use e-learning; negative relationship with satisfaction (Saadé & Kira, 2009) and performance (Fuller, Vician, & Brown, 2006), but minimal studies to date.
Motivation to learn	Positively related to training outcomes (Colquitt et al., 2000).	Limited but generally positive in regard to learner outcomes (Brown, 2005; Garavan, Carbery, O'Malley, & O'Donnell, 2010; Kim & Frick, 2011).
Learning goal orientation	Mastery orientation → small positive relationship with training performance; no significant relationship for performance orientation (Cellar, Stuhlmacher, et al., 2011)	Unclear—mixed results for mastery vs. performance orientation in regard to performance (Bell & Kozlowski, 2002; Brown, 2001; Kickul & Kickul, 2006) and off-task behavior (Brown, 2001; Orvis et al, 2011).
Previous e-learning experience	Not applicable.	Generally positive relationship with satisfaction and performance (Arbaugh, 2002, 2004, 2014; Salyers, Carter, Myers, & Barrett, 2014; Yanson & Johnson, 2016); negative relationship with dropout rate (Dodd, Kirby, Seifert, & Sharpe, 2009).

TRAINING METRICS AND BENEFIT-COST ANALYSIS

The costs involved in training can be established relatively easily, yet they can be substantial and involve both direct costs and indirect costs (Noe, 2002). A considerable direct cost is the loss of production sustained through the absence of trainees from work for the duration of the training. E-learning significantly reduces this element of direct costs, as trainees generally do not have to leave their place of work to participate in online training (provided they have access to a computer). Online courses may also be taken outside of work. In many cases, employees can avail themselves of online training through an intranet, which can be accessed from work and from home, thus allowing for greater flexibility at a reduced cost.

Conversely, the actual benefits to the firm may be much more difficult to ascertain, as many of the benefits take a long time to materialize or can often be of an intangible nature. Moreover, it may prove almost impossible to isolate completely from other organizational variables the effects of training on performance. Ascertaining these effects is of great significance, though. In fact, this preoccupation with the quantification of the business benefits of training has frequently been described as the search for the Holy Grail, and those organizations that evaluate training employ a number of different models and approaches to pursue this quest, including the balanced scorecard (Kaplan & Norton, 1992, 1993) and ROI (Phillips, 1996b). Russ-Eft and Preskill (2005) highlight three critical factors in HR development evaluation that complicate the assessment of training outcomes:

1. Evaluation occurs within a complex, dynamic, and variable environment.

2. Evaluation is essentially a political activity.

3. Evaluation ought to be purposeful, planned, and systematic.

Notwithstanding these factors, Phillips (1996a) advocates that any available posttraining data should be analyzed and converted into monetary values to establish ROI. Phillips's (1996c, 2005, 2012) ROI methodology (or ROI process) produces six types of data, which are based on **Kirkpatrick's** (1960, 1994) **evaluation taxonomy**:

1. Reaction, satisfaction, and planned action

2. Learning and application

3. Implementation

4. Business impact (see Table 10.7)

5. ROI

6. Intangibles

The ROI method advocates five useful steps for converting hard (tangible) data and soft (intangible) data into monetary values:

1. Focus on a single unit of improvement in output, quality, or time.

2. Determine a value for each data unit.

3. Calculate the change in output performance directly attributable to training.

4. Obtain the annual amount of the monetary value of the change in performance.

5. Determine the annual value (the annual performance change times the unit value).

Having identified relevant data sources and applying these best practices, firms can use a number of approaches to quantify the relationship between training costs and benefits. These approaches are shown in Table 10.8. Organizations may use one or more of these ratios to determine the costs and benefits of planned and existing learning technology projects.

It is possible to enter basic values into a spreadsheet application to calculate the ratios listed in Table 10.7. However, the variety of possible outcomes from training, the variety of factors that affect these outcomes, and the variety of data to be collected to produce any meaningful results appear to make the evaluation process a rather tedious task that would be next to impossible to complete efficiently and effectively without the help of a computerized system. Most commercial HRIS can be customized to record, analyze, and report on the training metrics that have been identified by a firm. For instance, the system could be configured to collect information on the monetary benefits of T&D projects, such as increased production output or a reduced number of complaints, and compare this information with data collected on the costs of T&D projects. In addition, the satisfaction with or the success of particular training interventions could be assessed. T&D data will usually be stored in the T&D module of the HRIS. The human capital management (HRM) modules included in the HRIS of the largest ERP systems (for example, SAP or Oracle) incorporate functionalities for creating employee development plans, competency management tools, and online learning environments, as well as numerous training metrics. In addition, many dedicated T&D systems are commercially available. The following section will discuss the data elements and various HRIS applications used in the training function.

TABLE 10.8 ■ Benefit-Cost Approaches	
Approach	**Explanation**
Benefit-cost ratio (BCR)	Monetary benefits of T&D projects Costs of T&D projects
Payback period	Costs of T&D projects Annual savings
Return on investment (ROI)	Monetary benefits of T&D projects Costs of T&D projects

Source: Sadler-Smith (2009).

HRIS APPLICATIONS IN TRAINING

Traditionally, training software applications have been employed to record information associated purely with training administration purposes (Noe, 2017). Today, firms place much greater demands on training applications in terms of compatibility with existing systems, analytical functionality, and accessibility to meet business needs. The primary demand on any system, however, must be that it furnishes usable information to key decision makers to achieve both administrative and strategic advantages (Kovach, Hughes, Fagan, & Maggitti, 2002).

Hence, useful HRIS information should possess three key characteristics:

1. It must be presented in a user-friendly manner and must be easy to use.

2. It must be meaningful and appropriate (Keebler & Rhodes, 2002).

3. It must be used effectively in the decision-making process to support an organization's overall business strategy (Kovach & Cathcart, 1999).

According to the Society for Human Resource Management (2011), HRIS training and development applications need to:

- Be easy to use

- Be customizable

- Be integrated with other HR systems and functions

- Offer a fully digital experience

- Provide mobile access to all users

- Be integrated with social media platforms

- Be available as software as a service

Elementary HRIS training databases are easily set up using commercial or open-source desktop software (see Figures 10.4 and 10.5). These databases may then be used to collect, store, and analyze training-related HR information. The amount of data that can be stored, the manner in which it is collected, and the level of analysis possible will depend on the application used. Table 10.9 shows the basic data elements an electronic T&D database should contain. The first column, "Data Element," shows the main categories of data elements, while "Subcategory 1" and "Subcategory 2" provide examples of the type of information these data elements could include.

Using these essential data elements, we could create a spreadsheet (see Figure 10.4). This basic database contains relevant training information and possesses limited search and reporting capabilities. Should a firm decide to upgrade to commercial training software, data stored in a spreadsheet can be imported into most training applications.

Clearly, both the amount of information that can be collected and stored using a spreadsheet and the level of analysis that this application permits are limited. Therefore, many organizations create bespoke databases, which offer greater possibilities regarding the collection and presentation of training data. These database applications allow users to run queries using customizable search criteria; they provide greater reporting options; and information on different screens can be linked to avoid multiple entry of data. An example of such a database, one that includes the data elements and subcategories of Table 10.9, is shown in Figure 10.5. As more functionality is desired, organizations can also use a more sophisticated learning management system (LMS) to collect and manage training data (see Figure 10.6).

FIGURE 10.4 ■ Example of an HRIS T&D Database in Spreadsheet Format

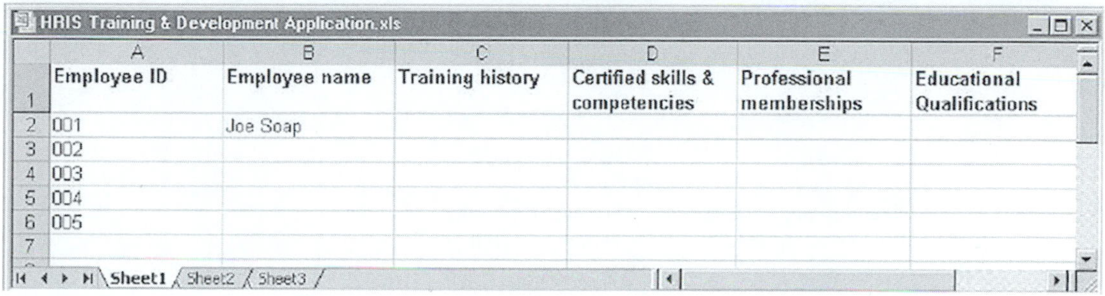

FIGURE 10.5 ■ Example of a Database

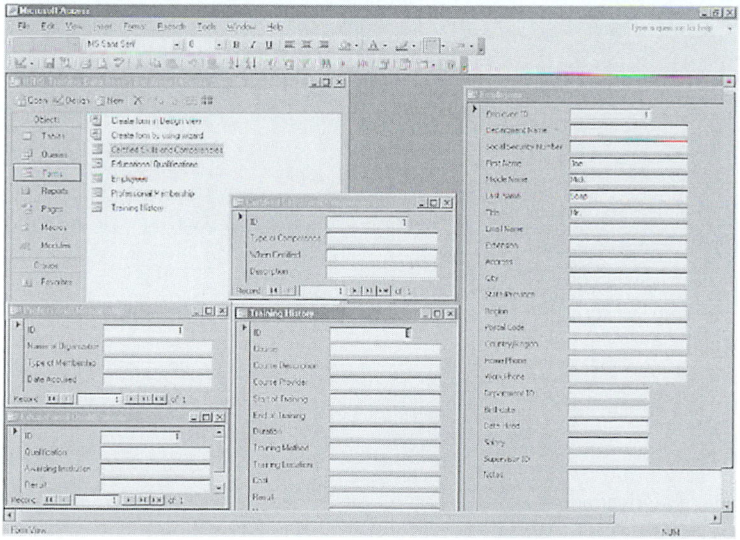

TABLE 10.9 ■ Basic Data Elements for an HRIS Training Database

Data Element	Subcategory 1	Subcategory 2
Employee information	Employee ID	
	Employee name	Title
		First name
		Middle name
		Second name
	Social Security number	
	Department	
	Position	
	Reporting to	
Training history (training course completed)	Date of training (start and end)	
	Training methods	(see above)
	Course (including description)	List of common courses
	Course provider	List of common providers
	Training location	In-house
		Out-of-house
	Result	
	Duration	
	Cost	
	Notes on performance	
Certified skills and competencies		
Professional memberships		List of professional organizations
Educational qualifications		

FIGURE 10.6 ■ Training Module With OrangeHRM (an open-source HRIS)

As firms grow in size, their need to manage training activities and training data more effectively and efficiently increases accordingly. A host of commercial systems service the broad spectrum of T&D, ranging from stand-alone training administration software to fully integrated expert systems. T&D software is available in many guises. The most common applications are discussed here.

HRIS/Learning Applications: Learning Management Systems

The vast majority of large organizations rely on fully integrated enterprise-wide systems, called enterprise resource planning (ERP) systems, to satisfy their information needs. An ERP system amalgamates the management information systems (MIS) capabilities from all functional areas in a business, for example, finance, production, marketing, and HRM, into a single integrated system. The ERP component that supports the HR function is commonly referred to as an HRIS. These data repositories for HR-related data typically comprise a number of modules, which in turn can support every area of HR, including T&D. Traditionally, firms used HRIS T&D applications and modules for administrative purposes only. The capabilities of today's HRIS T&D applications—complete learning technology solutions that are usually referred to as **learning management systems (LMS)**—range from training administration to training and talent management. The key users of LMS are training administrators and learners. The uses and capabilities of an LMS are shown in the LMS classification presented in Table 10.10.

The use of administrative systems is restricted to transaction processing, including the calculation of training costs. Training management systems can facilitate the entire

TABLE 10.10 ■ Learning Management System Characteristics, Uses, and Capabilities	
Characteristics	**Uses and Capabilities**
Administration	Basic employee and T&D records
	Calculation of training costs
	Management of administrative permissions
	Establishment of learning plans
	Administration and reporting (including tracking of training progress)
	Training course and catalogue management
Training management (including learning content management)	Creation of training courses and initiatives
	Scheduling and access to training courses
	Assignment of training based on skills and certification requirements
	Authoring of training courses and initiatives
	Online access to courses
	Training evaluation
	Tracking of training attendance and results
	ROI measurement
Talent Management	Employee onboarding (induction)
	KSA assessment
	Attract, recruit, manage, and retain talent
	Performance reviews and appraisals
	Succession planning
	Career planning
	Management development

Technology-Enabled Features	Social (media) learning
	Artificial intelligence
	Augmented reality/virtual reality
	Application programming interfaces (third-party integration)
	Gamification
	Microlearning
Types of Training Examples	Compliance
	Certification
	Sales and marketing
	Customer service
	Machine maintenance

T&D process (see the systems model of T&D described previously) from TNA to training evaluation. A **learning content management system (LCMS)**, as the name implies, can be used to store and develop T&D content, such as multimedia files, templates for training courses, or assignments. It may also be employed to track training attendance and completion records or for quality assurance purposes. LCMS is frequently used in combination with REL. A **talent management system (TMS)**, sometimes referred to as a human capital management system, is an integrated software suite that can comprise a range of applications, such as applicant tracking, succession and career planning, performance management, compensation and benefits management, and learning management. Talent management systems allow employees to create personal electronic *talent profiles*, which can be updated and usually reflect their KSAs and goals. Organizations can use these data to generate information on the talent profile of the organization and to develop macro- and microlevel employee development plans. The LMS market is large and diverse (see Table 10.11 for a small sample list of these vendors). LMSs may be open- or closed source, enterprise solutions, cloud-based or installed, industry and/or education focused. The choice of system will be determined principally by an organization's LT&D needs, LT&D budget, and ICT capabilities. The reporting, analytical, and strategic potential of these systems will diverge accordingly.

LMS also provide a number of metrics and reports that firms can use when assessing the effectiveness of their training initiatives (Pappas, 2016; Powell, 2019). Table 10.12 contains a sample of such reports.

The degree to which learning management systems can assist strategic decision making can be assessed using Beckers and Bsat's (2002) decision support system (DSS) classification. Their model consists of five levels:

1. Management information systems (MIS)

2. Decision support systems (DSS)

3. Group decision support systems (GDSS)

4. Expert systems (ES)

5. Artificial intelligence (AI)

TABLE 10.11 ■ Leading Cloud–Based Learning Management System Vendors		
Vendor	**Website**	**Twitter**
360Learning Engagement Platform	https://en.360learning.com	@360Learning
Absorb LMS	https://www.absorblms.com	@AbsorbLMS
Adobe Captivate Prime	https://www.adobe.com/products/captivateprime.html	@Adobe
Agylia	https://www.agylia.com	@AgyliaGroup
Aptara, Inc.	https://www.aptaracorp.com	@Aptara
Asentia LMS	https://www.asentialms.com	@asentialms
BizLibrary	https://www.bizlibrary.com	@BizLibrary
Blackboard	http://www.blackboard.com/	@Blackboard
Brainier	https://www.brainier.com	@brainiersol
Bridge LMS	https://www.alturalearning.com/bridge-lms/	@AlturaLearning
Brightspace	http://www.brightspace.com/	@_Brightspace_
Canvas LMS*	https://www.instructure.com/canvas/	@Instructure
Chamilo*	https://chamilo.org/en/	@chamilo_news
Coassemble	https://coassemble.com	@coassemble
CoreAchieve	https://www.coreachieve.com	n/a
Cornerstone	http://www.cornerstoneondemand.com/	@CornerstoneInc
CrossKnowledge	https://www.crossknowledge.com	@CrossKnowledge
Docebo	https://www.docebo.com	@docebo
DuPont Sustainable Solutions	https://www.consultdss.com	@ConsultDSS
Edmodo	https://new.edmodo.com/	@edmodo
EduMe	https://www.edume.com	@EduMeSocial
eFront	https://www.efrontlearning.com	@eFrontLearning
Fuse Universal	https://www.fuseuniversal.com	@Fuseuniversal
G-Cube	https://www.gc-solutions.net	@GCubeSolutions
GP Strategies	https://www.gpstrategies.com	@gpcorp

Growth Engineering	https://www.growthengineering.co.uk	@growthengineer
Gyrus Systems	https://www.gyrus.com	@gyrussystems
iSpring Learn	https://www.ispringsolutions.com	@iSpringPro
LearnUpon LMS	https://www.learnupon.com	@LearnUpon
Looop	https://www.looop.co	@LooopCo
Mindflash LMS	https://www.mindflash.com	@mindflash
Moodle*	http://moodle.org/	@moodle
NetDimensions	http://www.netdimensions.com/	@NetDimensions
Open edX*	https://open.edx.org	@OpenEdX
ProProfs LMS	https://www.proprofs.com/training/lms-software/	@ProProfs
SAP Litmos	www.litmos.com	@Litmos
Schoology	https://www.schoology.com	@Schoology
Skillcast LMS	https://www.skillcast.com/compliance-learning-management-system	@iSkillcast
SkillSoft	http://www.skillsoft.com/	@Skillsoft
SkyPrep	https://skyprep.com	@SkyPrep
TalentCards	https://www.talentcards.io	@TalentCardsApp
TalentLMS	https://www.talentlms.com/	@TalentLMS
Teachlr Organizations	https://organizations.teachlr.com	@TeachlrOrg
Top Hat	https://tophat.com	@TopHat
Totara Learn*	https://www.totaralearning.com	@totaralearning
uCertify LEARN	https://www.ucertify.com/#	@uCertify
Wisetail	https://www.wisetail.com	@Wisetail
WorkWize	https://www.workwize.com	@EssentialSkillz
Valamis	https://www.valamis.com	@Valamis

*Open Source

Note: Table is based on the following rankings: eLearning Industry—The 20 Best Learning Management Systems (2019 Update); FinancesOnline—20 Best LMS Software Solutions of 2019; Training Industry—2018 Top Learning Portal/LMS Companies; SIIA—Accelerating Innovation in Technology, Data & Media—SIIA CODiE Awards—2019 Finalists—Best Corporate/Workforce Learning Management Solution

TABLE 10.12   ■   Training Metrics and Reports Available Through LMS

Course progression and completions	Course subscription dates
Last access by user	Learner proficiency and competency
Total time spent on courses and learning plans	Active courses
Most-viewed courses	Course (and trainer) evaluations and ratings
Test/assessment scores (highs and lows)	E-commerce transaction data
Learning plan reports	User activity reports
Audit trail reports	Gamification reports (e.g., badges and contests)
Certification reports	External training activity reports
Return on investment	

Each consecutive category offers the users more extensive reporting and analytical capabilities that can support strategic T&D decision making. MIS can be used to support T&D decision making at the operational, functional level of the organization. DSS and GDSS are designed to facilitate senior management decision making in the long term and relate to the overall mission and objectives of an organization. They are based on "what if" scenarios. Expert systems consist of a knowledge base, a decision-making function, and an interface. They replicate the decision-making capabilities of human experts. An example of a system that uses AI is an intelligent tutoring system (ITS). An ITS can be employed to tutor, coach, or empower employees. The advantages of these systems are that instruction can be aligned with learner needs, the system can respond to learner actions, and learner progress can be modeled (Noe, 2017). ES and AI aid strategic T&D decision making at the board level of the organization. However, capital investments in sophisticated HRIS T&D applications alone will not necessarily improve LT&D in the organization, nor will they lead to knowledge creation or organizational learning. Any HRIS project requires careful planning and ample resources (time, money, and expertise). Bonadio (2009) puts forward five key issues that could enhance the effectiveness of an LMS:

1. Employee development should be linked to learning delivery.

2. Learning activities ought to be aligned with business objectives.

3. Regulatory compliance must be maintained.

4. Learning effectiveness must be measured throughout the organization.

5. An integrated approach to employee onboarding (employee orientation) should be established.

Nevertheless, LMS are somewhat limited, as they typically only track formal learning as opposed to experiential learning or learning acquired from mentoring programs (Torrance, 2016). However, a relatively new application specification called **Experience Application Programming Interface**, or **xAPI**, or sometimes also referred to as Tin Can API, allows the sharing of a variety of synchronous and asynchronous learning experiences between different LMSs independent of the context within which the learning took place. Today's learning contexts range from collaborative learning, social media learning, experiential learning, mobile learning, simulations, gamification, to real-life scenarios. xAPI allows the recording of learning experiences as simple statements—who learned, what learning activity was used, what was learned—which are then stored in a learning record store. This data can be shared easily across platforms and also analyzed using learning analytics software, which typically form part of an LMS to evaluate the effectiveness of a variety of training interventions and contexts.

As user demands and system capabilities evolve over time, a natural evolution of the LMS is to learning experience platforms (LXP). As their name implies, the focus of these platforms is to provide better user experiences and flexibility than traditional LMS by incorporating the newest developments in artificial intelligence, gamification, AR/VR, and social and microlearning (Bersin, 2018). Many of the LMSs listed in Table 10.10 also offer LXPs. These developments are echoed by the latest Sierra-Cedar 2019–2020 HR Systems Survey White Paper, which states that organizations are moving away from a single LMS setup to a software architecture consisting of multiple learning applications, which may or may not be integrated into existing HRIS or TMS (Sierra-Cedar, 2019).

The white paper also highlights that talent-driven firms are more likely to employ a broader range of learning tools than those that are not. These learning tools can include:

- Content creation

- Content libraries

- MOOCs (massive open online courses).

- **Adaptive learning platforms** (using AI to adapt learning in real time to user needs)

- Learning adoption/engagement platforms

- Microlearning platforms

- Learning Record Stores (based on experience API (xAPI) specification, which enables the capture of a variety of learner experiences across different devices, LMS, organizations; Torrance, 2016)

HRIS T&D Applications: Implementation Issues

Many HRIS T&D projects fail to meet the expectations of key decision makers. The reasons for these failures are manifold. Some firms introduce a new TMS only because competitors have done so, yet these companies may not have the necessary expertise to operate the system. Frequently, decision makers have false expectations of ROI or apply training metrics that merely focus on cost savings and fail to take note of intangible gains derived from T&D (see the section "Training Metrics and Benefit-Cost Analysis"). In other cases, the HRIS T&D application strategy is not aligned with training needs and the overall T&D, HR, and business strategies. Few organizations involve employees during the implementation stage of the HRIS, which can lead to underutilization and dissatisfaction with the system (Burbach & Dundon, 2005). According to the 2019 Deloitte Human Capital Trends report, some of the latest trends in TMS focus around improving the digital experience of their workers by integrating AI, cognitive interfaces, robotics and other technologies. However, the report also highlights that in reality the notion of digital HR is still only aspirational.

For a variety of reasons (see "Disadvantages" in Table 10.4), many employees never actually complete the e-learning programs in which they are enrolled. Sometimes, disenchantment is simply the result of poor planning and the consequent incompatibility of various disjointed HR systems, albeit an increasing number of organizations purchase one or more items of their training management system from a single vendor to prevent these problems (Frauenheim, 2006). A number of authors have suggested success factors for the introduction of HRIS T&D applications (Gascó, Llopis, & González, 2004; Noe, 2002; Sadler-Smith, 2009; Troshani, Jerram, & Rao Hill, 2011) and for increasing e-learning usage and completion rates (Brown & Charlier, 2013; Frankola, 2001):

- Align e-learning strategy with T&D strategy, HR strategy, and overall business strategy.

- Create a corporate learning culture that fosters e-learning and the use of HRIS T&D applications.

- Assess HRIS T&D projects based on their suitability to meet the T&D strategy of the organization rather than the technical sophistication and elegant features of the system.

- Carefully plan HRIS T&D projects to guarantee compatibility with legacy systems, affordability in terms of budget allocations, and the existence of expertise to use the system.

- Ensure senior management support for HRIS T&D projects.

- Involve line managers and employees in HRIS T&D projects to ensure greater buy-in.

- Match HRIS T&D applications and e-learning initiatives with their ability to meet training needs to encourage learning transfer.

- Establish a suitable evaluation strategy to assess the extent to which training technology meets training needs, and evaluate this fit regularly.

- Identify suitable T&D metrics that take account of all direct and indirect training outcomes.

- Promote the benefits and create a sense of urgency toward the use of HRIS T&D applications and e-learning.

- Make managers accountable for the uptake of e-learning and for HRIS T&D utilization.

- Create an organizational climate in which use and knowledge transfer of e-learning by employees is supported.

- Reward employees for their use of e-learning.

- Ensure that e-learning and T&D systems are user friendly and provide quality information.

- Develop a data security policy for the T&D system and applications.
- Do not focus on only financial gains from HRIS T&D projects.
- Train managers and employees in the use of T&D technologies.

Summary

This chapter highlighted the strategic importance of LT&D in an increasingly knowledge-intensive global economy. The discussion showed that it is important to distinguish between learning, training, and development to understand the processes that lead to the acquisition of knowledge, skills, and abilities (KSAs). Other key concepts, such as knowledge management (KM) and the learning organization, were also explained. Knowledge creation, innovation, and organizational learning are inextricably linked to an organization's capacity to remain competitive. This chapter identified and explained various e-learning methods, their role in knowledge acquisition, and their advantages and disadvantages, as well as the factors that influence e-learning outcomes. Nonetheless, traditional face-to-face methods still carry considerable credence, which is reflected in the increasing use of blended learning, an approach that combines both traditional and online methods of learning. Notwithstanding the effect of face-to-face learning, emerging Web 2.0 and Web 3.0 technologies, such as social media and mobile learning, furnish organizations with a multitude of exciting new ways in which LT&D can be delivered and measured. The key differences to early e-learning options are that the learners actively participate in creating the learning materials and that learning increasingly occurs in an informal virtual and social setting among peers rather than in the training rooms of a corporation. A careful analysis of training needs, various LT&D methods, and individual learning styles is necessary to ensure that transfer of learning occurs and that, ultimately, the strategic objectives of the organization can be attained. HRIS T&D applications are vitally important tools in pursuing a systematic approach to LT&D, which necessitates identifying training needs, designing LT&D solutions and methods, implementing these initiatives, and evaluating the effectiveness of training (including completing an assessment of ROI on training). As many LT&D outcomes are of an intangible nature or take a long time to materialize (note the definition of development in this context), it is inherently intricate to determine appropriate training metrics that may be employed to perform any meaningful CBA. The key is to analyze any available data. Notwithstanding these difficulties, a number of approaches to ascertain ROI using HRIS T&D applications were offered. This chapter also expounded on how an elementary T&D system can be created using a spreadsheet or database desktop application. A variety of HRIS T&D applications exist. Learning management systems may be embedded in an HRIS or ERP. These learning management systems vary considerably in their capacity to manage the training process, generate reports, or assist in strategic decision making. Talent management suites integrate a range of applications, including succession planning and learning management. Learning management systems with DSS and ES capabilities offer the greatest strategic value. However, the choice of system is contingent on the T&D needs of an organization, its budget, and its ICT capabilities. This chapter concluded with a discussion of the implementation of HRIS T&D applications.

Key Terms

adaptive learning platforms 273

asynchronous communication 252

best-fit learning event model 249

blended learning 252

Bloom's taxonomy 259

collaborative technologies 252

distance learning 255

ease of use 260

e-learning 250

Experience Application Programming Interface (xAPI) 272

human capital 243

information and communication technology (ICT) 245

Internet-based training (IBT) 251

Kirkpatrick's evaluation taxonomy 262

knowledge management (KM) 245

learner control 260

learning climate 259

learning content management system (LCMS) 269

learning management system (LMS) 268

learning organization 244

learning, training, and development (LT&D) 243

media richness 260

mobile learning 250

needs analysis 257

off-the-job training 249

on-the-job training 249

organizational learning 244

organizational support 259

perceived usefulness 260

performance management 244

rapid e-learning (REL) 253

reliability 260

synchronous communication 252

systems model of training and development 244

talent management system (TMS) 269

training complexity 260

training guidance 260

training needs analysis (TNA) 247

training transfer 256

Web 1.0, Web 2.0, and Web 3.0 250

Web-based training (WBT) 251

Discussion Questions

1. What is the systems model of T&D? Discuss how HRIS T&D applications can assist in carrying out the steps in the systems model.

2. Explain synchronous and asynchronous communication in relation to e-learning.

3. What are the advantages and disadvantages of e-learning?

4. How can HRIS T&D applications help firms foster organizational learning?

5. Explain how organizations should choose appropriate T&D methods.

6. What is transfer of training? What role does transfer of learning play in e-learning?

7. Explain the issues involved in establishing ROI for T&D initiatives. What role do HRIS T&D applications play in establishing ROI?

8. Outline how standard desktop applications such as a spreadsheet or database can be used to set up a basic T&D system.

9. Discuss the different types of HRIS T&D applications and their reporting and decision-support capabilities.

10. What issues might arise during and as a result of the implementation of HRIS T&D applications?

Case Study: Training and Development at Meddevco

Meddevco (name changed) is a large multinational corporation that operates in the medical devices sector. The firm employs around 33,000 people in five divisions and has operations in 120 countries. A total of 66% of the multinational's revenue is generated from products that are less than 2 years old, and 80% of employees are working on products that are less than 2 years old. These figures illustrate the highly competitive and fast-paced nature of the medical devices sector. This sector is also characterized by high levels of regulatory control and a need to comply with industry norms. Meddevco is headquartered in the United States and Switzerland. The information needs of a firm of this size are substantial, and it would be next to impossible to collect, store, and analyze HR-related information without the use of a fully integrated global HRIS. Moreover, the diversity of the workforce, the multiplicity of skills required in the different divisions and to support the various product lines, and the pressure of compliance necessitate a perfectly orchestrated T&D effort. Needless to say, HRIS T&D applications play a major role in managing the T&D function. Meddevco uses an HRIS by PeopleSoft (now Oracle) to manage the majority of its global HR processes, including e-recruitment and performance appraisals. With regard to data entry into the system, the corporation operates a strict "no customization unless legally required" policy to ensure data compatibility across the system. In the United States, most HR services are centralized in an HR shared services center. The corporation has a dedicated HRIS center in Europe, and negotiations are ongoing to implement a European HR shared services model. The company uses a number of different payroll systems in Europe for compliance reasons. All employees in the corporation have access to a company intranet called My Meddevco, which also includes a learning portal that provides access to online training programs, which employees can use at work and at home. The intranet also includes a knowledge base and detailed company information, including a full listing of all employees and their job titles and locations. Employee transfers and promotions are also listed.

A number of years ago, the corporation made the decision not to use the training module included in PeopleSoft and opted for a training management system called SABA to coordinate and manage training initiatives; for example, the recent rollout and training for the use of SAP (an ERP system) for production facilities was managed through SABA. In addition, Meddevco has recently commenced using the talent management module included in PeopleSoft to identify and track high-performing employees for promotion. Every employee is required to complete an online talent profile, which is similar to an online CV and which can be updated by the employee. The combination of systems and applications and the careful analysis of HR information contained therein allow the organization to develop and implement a global T&D strategy. However, the firm also faces some challenges arising from the use of these systems. As the organization largely grew through acquisition, a number of legacy systems still coexist with the global HRIS at some of its subsidiaries. Data compatibility issues also derive from the use of SABA, which is not part of PeopleSoft. In addition, the firm is also using SAP, and it is questionable whether Oracle (the owner of PeopleSoft) will support data exchanges with a system supplied by its chief competitor. Furthermore, because Meddevco did not involve the workforce in the implementation process of the TMS, employees are reluctant to complete their talent profiles. Moreover, the need to customize the HRIS locally to comply with the national legislation affecting Meddevco subsidiaries further complicates the collection and transfer of data within the global HRIS.

The example of Meddevco illustrates how large organizations employ HRIS to manage their workforces and how they leverage HR development through the use of HRIS T&D applications, learning portals, and specialized learning management systems. However, it is also apparent that careful planning is essential to avoid compatibility issues and to ensure a consistent global flow of HR- and T&D-related information.

Case Study Questions

1. What should Meddevco have done to avoid some of its problems?

2. How could Meddevco now solve the problems created by not involving employees during the implementation of the HRIS?

3. What else should Meddevco do now to improve the operation of its system?

11

REWARDING EMPLOYEES AND HRIS

Charles H. Fay and Hadi El-Farr

EDITORS' NOTE

This chapter is the fourth one involving an organization's talent management program and the support an HRIS can provide through its data collection and analysis capabilities. It completes our look at the cycle of activities involved in talent management—planning and forecasting the need for talent (Chapter 8), recruitment and selection of talent (Chapter 9), and training for talent management (Chapter 10). As noted previously, the purpose of talent management is to achieve the organization's strategic goal of remaining competitive in its market. This chapter describes the role of performance management as part of the talent management process and how in concert they maintain market competitiveness for the organization. The authors focus on the management of employee performance in a systematic manner. This includes the formal performance management system as well as the reward system that supports the evaluation. The reward system of the organization involves the design, decision making, and administration of both compensation and benefits practices. Throughout the chapter, the authors discuss the role of technology in supporting the data needs for organizations as they implement performance management, compensation, and benefits systems.

CHAPTER OBJECTIVES

After completing this chapter, you should be able to

- Understand the performance management (PM) cycle and the role of the HRIS in PM design, decision making, and administration

- Understand typical compensation practices and the role of the HRIS in compensation design, decision making, and administration

- Understand typical benefits practices and the role of the HRIS in benefits design, decision making, and administration

- Understand payroll systems and the role of the HRIS in payroll administration

- Be able to discuss the meaning of work to employees in terms of their identities and self-esteem

- Discuss a motivation theory that helps to understand why work is so important to employees and how the HR programs in talent and performance management affect employee motivation.

INDUSTRY BRIEF
MATTHEW COTUGNO, LEADER, TOTAL REWARDS, MVP HEALTH CARE

Developing a New Compensation Structure at MVP Healthcare

In order to flourish, organizations must be willing to adapt to a constantly changing environment, as well as taking calculated risks to adapt to a changing business landscape. With these thoughts in mind, MVP Health Care's Total Rewards team began a multiyear journey to dramatically redesign both its salary structure and approach to deriving employee titles all at once. It was a monumental undertaking that involved many steps.

Before getting started on any business initiative, you need two critical drivers of change—a clear purpose/direction and buy-in from Executive leadership. MVP's path to creating a new salary structure started with an organizational need. The existing salary structure was not functioning the way a structure should, and, at the minimum, it needed a redesign. Since this was something we all agreed upon, the next question was how much do we want to change our approach.

In order to make the best decision for the organization and get the needed executive buy-in, MVP chose to bring in external consultants to collaborate on the design and execution of the new structure. Their expertise, combined with the Total Rewards team knowledge, allowed for meaningful discussions on long term strategy,

employee impact, delivery, and of course, the structure itself. After six months of effort with a team that included the Total Rewards team, external consultants, and two top executives of the organization, MVP was ready to begin socializing the new approach to other top leaders in the organization.

As mentioned earlier, executive buy-in on any major initiative is paramount to its success. Therefore, the team took the needed time to conduct one-on-one meetings with a handful of the top leaders at MVP to make sure they understood and could support this new direction. Although these meetings resulted in mixed reaction, we were able to absorb that feedback and make minor adjustments to create an enhanced structure that made more sense for the organization. At the conclusion of these executive meetings, the subteam felt confident about starting to build a communication plan to roll out this new structure to the rest of the organization.

Despite taking all the right steps to design a viable new salary structure, we knew an effective communication plan would be crucial. Our plan was to leverage MVP's brand promise of making it personal. We did this by establishing a plan that involved rollout meetings with every department in the organization. For a company of 1,700 employees across multiple locations in New York State, we knew this would be quite the undertaking. However, we were resolute in our mission to deliver what we promised from the start.

A salary structure can be complex even for HR professionals. Therefore, we built a presentation that met key objectives. From the beginning, we knew that the presentation needed to be concise to make sure we did not lose our audience with the content. Moreover, we made sure to establish the how and why from the very start to make sure employees understood our purpose. Lastly, we clearly articulated the next steps while sharing the reality of the effort and time required to fully execute this new structure across the organization.

The 12-month communication/rollout period was quite extensive. In addition to numerous presentations to each department, we also needed to collaborate with each department's leadership team to assess the impact of the new structure to their group. During this same time, we also needed to work with our HR systems team to ensure that this new structure could be seamlessly built into our HCM platform.

Integrating a unique and customized salary/titling structure into an HR system was both complex and labor intensive. First, we needed to collaborate on how our existing system (Infor) could accommodate the new approach. After considerable internal discussion, we agreed that building custom fields would best suit our needs. Second, we needed to devise a plan on how add all this new data into our system in a timely fashion. The approach we took was to create upload files that would be entered in an iterative fashion. Third and last, we needed to build the HR process flows (in Infor) that would allow for HR representatives to quickly and easily make changes to an employee's placement in the structure. Ultimately, we were forced to use a more custom approach, because the delivered HRIS functionality did not meet our business requirements.

Although there were some lessons along the way, the roughly one year dedicated to the preparation and planning resulted in what we deemed a fully successful rollout.

HRIS IN ACTION

As Mark walked into his work area, he was fuming. "Those idiots in HR and payroll are really the gang that couldn't shoot straight," he announced to everyone in the vicinity.

"What did they do now?" asked Marsha. "Don't tell me they got it wrong again!"

"They sure did," said Mark. "After I complained last month, you'd think they would at least check to make sure they corrected their mistake. If I treated a customer this way, I'd get fired!"

Mark's paycheck is wrong once again, and the story is a complicated one. It started with the performance review Mark had received from his boss the previous month. The review was good, and Mark had earned an "Exceeds standards" summary rating. Somehow, when an HR data-entry clerk entered the approved rating into the system, an error was made, and "Does not meet standards" went into the compensation review system. The error snowballed, and Mark received no merit increase or

(Continued)

(Continued)

bonus for the year. In fact, because of increased deductions for health coverage, his check was actually smaller than the one he had received 2 weeks earlier. Apart from the financial costs, Mark was psychologically shattered, because his boss had discussed in their performance review meeting how good his performance was.

After his boss intervened, HR and payroll corrected the error and noted that Mark would receive the expected increase and a one-time adjustment for back pay. On the strength of that, Mark made additional financial commitments. When the latest check was direct deposited into Mark's bank account, the mistake had not been corrected, and a check Mark had written was returned for insufficient funds. Payroll's excuse? HR had not received the approved changes at least 1 week prior to check issuance—payroll's deadline for changes.

How can errors like this be avoided? They are not uncommon. A large state university in the Northeast makes salary adjustments to faculty who receive performance increases in two stages: The adjustment becomes part of the biweekly paycheck in late spring, and the adjustment for January 1 through late spring is paid out as a lump sum in summer. Last summer, the back-pay adjustment was considerably higher than it should have been because of a data-entry error in the adjustment formula. No one caught the error until this year, when the university had to notify all faculty members that the back-pay adjustment for this year would be reduced by the excess adjustment received the previous year.

PM, compensation, benefits, and payroll are sensitive areas for most employees. The typical employee tends to "keep score" on his or her relationship with an employer through these systems. It is critical that information technology (IT) systems in these areas be flawlessly executed from the employee's perspective because getting the wrong (or no) paycheck sends a very bad message to the employee. Given the amounts of money involved, it is critical that IT systems in these areas be flawlessly executed from the employer's perspective as well.

In this chapter, we will provide an overview of PM, compensation, benefits, and payroll, so that you have an idea of the complexity that must be captured if the HRIS is to work well.

INTRODUCTION

Appreciate everything your associates do for the business. Nothing else can quite substitute for a few well-chosen, well-timed, sincere words of praise. They're absolutely free and worth a fortune.

—Sam Walton

Performance, rewards, and payroll systems focus on the basic exchange of inputs and outcomes between employees and employers. Employees provide performance, and, in exchange, employers provide rewards, which are distributed via payroll systems. These systems also serve as good examples of several IT issues in human resources management (HRM). **Performance management (PM)** systems are usually entirely internal to the organization, but data must be linked to several other systems, including rewards, staffing, training and development, and career development. PM systems are used as working tools by managers to motivate employees to perform well in their jobs and must, therefore, be inherently self-explanatory. Often, data are specific to the individual, although various summary measures must be comparable across subsets of employees or all employees. Since job performance is a function of individuals' knowledge, skills, and abilities (KSAs) and their motivation to work, a good starting point to understand how a PM program works is to examine the meaning of work.

The Meaning of Work

For most of us, work takes up a large part of our time and effort and is our major source of income. It shapes our identity, is critically important in how we perceive ourselves, and affects our self-esteem and self-worth. Each is an important part of the meaning of work and strongly affects our motivation to work and perform effectively. The employee–employer exchange is the basis of a work motivation theory called **Equity Theory** (Adams, 1963, 1965). Basing our discussion of PM in motivation theory is necessary, since the primary purpose of a PM program is to both help align employee performance with organizational outcomes and to motivate employees to perform well. Due to the importance of effective employee performance, we will cover the major tenets of Equity Theory.

How does the theory apply to work and management? All employees seek a fair balance between what they put into their jobs and what they get out of it. But how do we decide what is a *fair balance*? The answer lies in Equity Theory. Importantly, we arrive at our measure of fairness, or equity, by comparing our balance of effort and reward, that is, the ratio of input and outcome, with the balance enjoyed by other employees whom we deem to be relevant reference points. None of us like to feel that we are placing more effort into our work and receiving fewer rewards (e.g., salary, bonuses, benefits, etc.) than those around us. Equity Theory can therefore help explain why people can be happy and motivated by their situation one day and yet, with no change to their terms and working conditions, can be made very unhappy and demotivated, if they learn for example, that a colleague (or worse an entire group) is enjoying a better reward-to-effort ratio. Use of this theory can help us understand why people select one job over another or seek a raise because one's coworker has gotten a raise. Thus, the effectiveness of the PM system in motivating employees' performance has its basis in Equity Theory.

In contrast to performance management systems, which are entirely internal to an organization, reward systems have both internal and external ties to multiple other information systems. Both pay and benefits must be linked (or linkable) to external survey data, legal requirement data, and internal systems such as budgeting and planning systems. Usage of parts of reward systems must be restricted to HR professionals, although other parts must be widely available to employees for self-queries. Most organizations consider rewards data to be highly confidential, so system security is critical. Reward systems data focus on the individual, small-group, unit, and organization levels for different purposes, and the same variable (e.g., value of a specific benefit, seniority, option value) may have to be defined, calculated, stored, and reported in multiple ways depending on the need.

In the case of payroll systems, flawless data integrity and even more flawless execution are critical. Anyone who has received an inaccurate paycheck will understand the frustration and anger that occur; a payroll system that is not flawless is an administrator's nightmare. Payroll systems must be linked to external data (e.g., federal and state requirements for minimum wage) and internal data (e.g., general ledger, benefit choices) and must be capable of incorporating constant change. The payroll system is generally used only by payroll specialists, but every employee "audits" his or her own results. One final aspect of payroll is that some summaries of payroll data are not likely to match summaries of the same variables used in compensation or other HR systems. Even in a question as seemingly simple as number of employees, there will be discrepancies in these data summaries. For example, the compensation system is likely to contain only currently active employees; benefits might also include employees on leave, retired employees, and those former employees who have elected continuation of benefits under the **Consolidated Omnibus Budget Reduction Act (COBRA)** of 1986; and payroll files will contain everyone for whom a check is cut.

Although the interrelationships between performance management, rewards, benefits, and payroll are clear, and it is obvious that the HRIS applications for these four functions need to interface seamlessly, it would be a mistake to assume that these four functions can be considered independently of other HR applications or, indeed, of any of the information systems operated by the organization. The HRIS must allow for all aspects of the employment relationship (including relationships with prospective and past employees that affect equity perceptions) to be considered, analyzed, and acted on. Neither managers nor employees see the relationship between the organization and the employee through a single lens. In turbulent times, it is difficult to predict how information may need to be used. The potential must be there for any data sets currently collected by the organization to be retrieved and analyzed based on the requirements of the problems faced, not on the bin in which the data currently reside.

This chapter focuses on the data inputs, the typical reports that are generated, data outflows to other systems, and the ways that the IT system can provide decision support to organizations and managers in the areas of PM, rewards, and payroll. Before that discussion can be meaningful, however, a brief overview of each of the areas is necessary. Although most employees have a good "feel" for performance management (after all, their performance has been graded throughout their school years), few people not working in the field understand the intricacies of compensation or benefits, and may assume payroll is just a bookkeeping task.

There are many talent management solutions available in the market (performance management, succession planning, recruitment, learning and development, compensation, etc.), but it can be challenging to integrate them into a single talent management suite; a one-stop-shopping platform (Accenture, 2014; Keys, 2015). A single solution enables organizations to align their HR processes, take comprehensive, insightful, and prescriptive HR decisions, and leverage data generated under each HR activity to assist decisions in other activities (Accenture, 2014; Rogers, 2018).

PERFORMANCE MANAGEMENT

Overview

Performance management was briefly introduced in Chapter 8 as a critical part of talent management. This chapter examines performance management in more detail and relates it more closely to the other human resource functions that make up talent management.

Until recently, most discussion in organizations focused on the performance appraisal process. The emphasis was on getting the "best" appraisal format and training managers to "rate" employees using the format. Most research, whether by scholars or professionals, was on rating formats, rater error, and the training of raters. The assumption was that, if the correct format could be developed and managers were trained to use it, the resulting ratings would be accurate.

During the 1980s, professionals and some scholars became interested in a different goal: improving performance (Banks & May, 1999; Bernardin, Hagan, Kane, & Villanova, 1998). This interest led to a reconsideration of the whole performance process, and attention shifted to PM. The PM process consists of three parts: performance planning, **performance observation**, and providing **positive feedback** and/or **corrective feedback**. In support of this process, periodic performance summaries are developed to serve as a basis for performance planning for the next period while providing data for a variety of HR decisions, including rewards, staffing, training, and other decisions affecting the employee's relationship with the organization. This description of the process of performance management is based on the motivational theory of goal setting (Locke & Latham, 1984, 1990a, 1990b).

The fundamental tenet of **goal-setting theory** is that goals and intentions are responsible for human behavior. After years of research on this theory, the evidence for this tenet was strong (Locke, Shaw, Saari, & Latham, 1981). On the basis of this extensive research, several other tenets of the theory were verified. First, it was found that if goals determine human behavior, higher or more difficult goals result in higher levels of performance than those resulting from easy goals. Second, it was found that specific goals (such as reducing employee absences by 25%) result in higher levels of effort than vague goals such as "Why don't we reduce absenteeism." Third, it was found that incentives such as money, feedback, and competition will have no effect on behavior unless they lead to the setting and acceptance of specific, hard goals.

PM is now considered within the framework of "talent management," which encompasses all areas of HR that have to do with onboarding, developing, evaluating, and managing the workforce through all the normal cycles (see Chapter 10 for more complete coverage of talent management and HRIS). PM is just one of the areas connected to others such as

- recruiting (external),
- staffing (internal),
- career management,
- 360° assessment,
- development management/training,
- retention management, and
- workforce planning.

The model of contemporary talent management is shown in Figure 11.1.

Note that many organizations today, although having installed expensive and expansive enterprise resource planning (ERP) systems to provide a single platform for all these integrated applications, found that it was necessary to add specialized talent management solutions from third-party vendors to achieve the necessary functionality.

The link from the resulting performance and compensation processes to the core payroll systems, however, still remains as an integral link between the ERP systems and the specialized talent management solutions. This link would also be consistent with the findings

FIGURE 11.1 ■ Model of Contemporary Talent Management

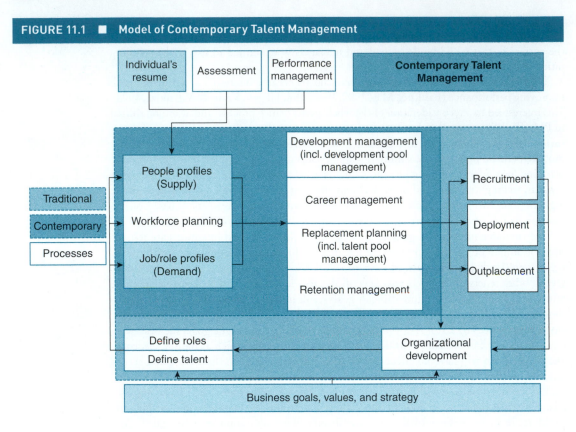

from goal-setting theory. In the example given in the opening vignette, if there were an integrated talent management system linking the performance module and compensation, there would be no need for anyone to enter the performance rating into the compensation system, since the performance rating would have already been there as a result of the approved employee review.

Performance Planning

Performance planning, like most management processes, must be constructed in such a way that any manager can do it, regardless of management style or skills. Better managers involve the employee collaboratively in all phases of the PM process, but the system is designed so that even directive managers can follow the process. This discussion assumes that the manager is more directive than collaborative.

The manager must first define what performance means in the case of a specific **direct report** (i.e., the employee whose job performance is being evaluated). At the broadest level, this definition of performance would encompass any employee who fills the job position. Remember that the job position is described in terms of duties and tasks outlined in the job description. Another way to conceive the definition of performance is that it is the performance expected of a new employee in the position if the direct report were terminated.

Ideally, this definition is developed by a cascade of goals, fitting the research findings on goal-setting theory, beginning with the organizational strategy and operating plan, with the immediate source being what the manager is expected to accomplish during the period and ending with the direct report's expected part of that accomplishment (Evans, 2001). The manager must then move from the general to the specific, usually expressed in terms of desired outcomes. This constitutes the performance dimensions for the direct report and is consistent with the findings from goal-setting theory.

When outcomes are difficult to observe or measure, behaviors that are expected to lead to desired outcomes are added. For each performance dimension, the manager must develop specific outcomes and behaviors that will be used to measure the direct report's performance. For a performance dimension of budget management, an outcome might be "Actual expenses are within 2% of budget for each budget category." A behavior on the same dimension might be "Checks expenditures against budget." After the measures are determined, the manager must set appropriate standards for each measure. The standard for "Checks expenditures against budget" might be "Checks expenditures against budget weekly." After defining standard performance, "Exceeds standards" and "Fails to meet standards" would be defined. The "Exceeds standards" level for "Checks expenditures against budget" might be "Checks expenditures against budget weekly; where discrepancies exceed 2%, checks those categories daily until discrepancies disappear." The "Fails to meet standards" level might be "Misses weekly check of expenditures against budget; allows discrepancies to continue without any follow-up." It should be noted that performance dimensions, measures, and standards are unique to each position, although attempts should be made to develop common standards for employees with identical job titles.

When performance dimensions, measures, and standards have been developed, the manager must communicate them to the direct report. The manager must make certain that the direct report understands measures and standards. The manager then gets the direct report to set goals for performance for the coming year. Note that goals and standards are not the same thing. The standard is what is expected of a fully job-knowledgeable employee who exerts normal effort. One purpose of PM is to get employees to set stretch goals, to be better than the standard. At the end of the goal-setting discussion, the direct report has agreed on some performance level as a goal. The set of performance measures, with standards and goals, becomes the **performance contract** for a defined performance period, typically a year. Most effective performance management systems encourage more frequent performance conversations and reviews rather than waiting for an annual review.

Automation of HR and organizational processes through artificial intelligence (AI) and robotics is increasing and has a direct impact on the workforce. Currently, around 50% of global work activities can be automated, and, by 2030, up to 32% of the U.S. labor force may be displaced by automation (Manyika et al., 2017). Some job tasks might be eliminated due to labor substitution, although new jobs might emerge as organizations adopt AI-enabled workforce automation solutions (Wisskirchen et al., 2017). As a result, jobs will need to be redesigned to incorporate these changes, and KSAs needed for specific jobs will have to be altered. Some tasks might be dropped as obsolete, others might emerge as more important, and still others will be newly added to the job occupant's required competencies. The higher the possibility for a skill to be automated, the less vital it is for organizations. Therefore, PM should focus on giving more weight to skills that are less likely to be substituted, which in return results in higher rewards and retention rates for employees who possess them. Moreover, automation and can help in job redesign, internal and external recruitment requirements, training and development plans, and resource allocation. Those solutions, combined with labor adjustments, aim to increase employee productivity and organizations' profitability.

Due to technological advancements, changing workplace and employment conditions, and preferences of younger generations, organizations are more reliant than ever on remote employees, individual contractors, and **outsourcing** service providers. In 2016, the gig economy composed 34% of the U.S. labor force and was expected to grow to 43% by 2020 (Gillespie, 2017). Approximately 30 million American workers earn their primary income from gig work, and an additional 15 million supplement their traditional income through freelancing (Metlife, 2019). Nontraditional employees and contractors are as important as traditional employees to success in many organizations. Thus, retaining high-performing remote and contingent workers is vital. For this reason, PM records should include not only traditional employees but also all contingent workers, and appropriate rewards should be offered to ensure goal achievement and repeated employment agreements for contingent workers.

Formats

Most organizations define the performance instrument differently depending on the type or level of the employee. For example, a nonmanagement or clerical position may have a relatively standard set of criteria that requires little or no change year after year. On the other hand, management employees tend to use a format that combines both goals and objectives with a competency evaluation. A well-designed performance application can automatically map the correct "format" based on the employee who has logged into the performance website.

For the management "format," the performance evaluation can reflect a weighting of a goal portion and the competency portion (e.g., 60% of the overall rating will be based on the goals results, although 40% will reflect the competency ratings). Also, within each of these sections, a specific performance level for each goal or competency might be rated. Therefore, the overall result could reflect a weighted calculation of each goal, competency, and section. Web-based performance systems can easily perform these calculations for the user. Even if the organization prefers that the employee and/or the manager actually determine the overall rating, the system can provide "advice" as to the reasonableness of the entered rating versus the underlying ratings.

Performance Period

During the performance period, the manager uses the performance contract as a benchmark for observing the direct report. When performance above standard is observed, the standard becomes the basis of positive feedback. When performance is below standard or below the goal set by the direct report, corrective feedback is used, again relying on the standard and on the goal set as the benchmarks for the performance observed. When discussion about performance is couched in terms of known measures, standards, and performance goals, feedback can be much more objective, and it is less likely to be seen as criticism of character. The direct report is not bad per se, but is simply not performing at the agreed-upon level on one or more measures. Stone, Deadrick, Lukaszewski, and Johnson (2015) note that employees will react differently to feedback from an electronic system than from a supervisor. This suggests that some combination of automated feedback and supervisory feedback is optimal in any performance management system.

AI-enabled PM solutions can contribute to a better employee performance management experience, because the system can provide immediate performance feedback for both individuals and teams. Moreover, performance scores can be reported in real time, motivating employees to take corrective actions to meet targets immediately rather than waiting for periodic performance reports. For example, chatbots have become a widely utilized tool to address employee inquiries on salary, incentives, benefits, and performance results. Employees can communicate with a chatbot to get fairly accurate performance assessment based on up-to-date data. This in turn can help build realistic appraisal expectations and can help employees and teams develop goals to improve future performance.

Periodic Performance Summary

At some point, a summary of performance during the period is provided to the direct report. In most organizations, this is an annual event, but some organizations have quarterly or semiannual performance summaries. At this point, the manager provides a summary of how the direct report has done on each performance measure and whether standards and goals have been met. In performance systems that offer both the employee and the manager Web-based input capabilities, periodic review of the employee's progress toward achieving goals is much easier. Once the employee self-assesses her or his own performance, the manager can also review each goal while viewing the employee's comments (see Figure 11.2 for an example).

Consequences of achieving various performance levels are communicated, and planning for the next period's performance begins. If PM has been done correctly, the summary appraisal should have no surprises for the direct report. As shown in Figure 11.1, development is a critical component. One of the more important outputs of the performance process is an **individual development plan (IDP)** that is used to document any steps necessary to improve employee performance. Each employee should have an IDP.

The process described applies to PM at the individual level. Yet most employees today work as an integrated part of one or more teams. The PM process does not change significantly for a team. It is usually easier to get outcome performance measures for a team than for an individual, and it is more difficult to get individual performance measures for a team member (Bing, 2004). Some organizations have elected to use team output as the primary outcome measure of performance for all team members and then develop a "team citizenship measure" for each team member.

Typical Data Inputs

Data inputs for PM systems include organizational-, job-, and individual-level data. Organizational-level data consist of links to organizational and unit goals and strategies and business plans. Performance plans should be able to tie back to unit and organizational plans; ideally, it should be possible to consolidate individual performance plans to the unit level and consolidate unit plans to the organizational level.

Job-level data is a significant part of the PM system. Key tasks, responsibilities, and outcomes should flow from job data sets to individual performance plans. Performance exists only within the context of the job.

Because performance begins at the individual level, most of the data in the PM system are individual-level data. Data include all the performance criteria developed by the manager for the individual, the particular measures that will be used to rate the individual's performance on each criterion, and the performance standards for each measure. If rating information is to be provided by more than the manager, the names of other raters and the criteria for which they will provide rating information need to be in the system as well. Usually, the entire performance contract will be a part of the system. Most systems will

FIGURE 11.2 ■ Performance Planning and Rating Module Screen

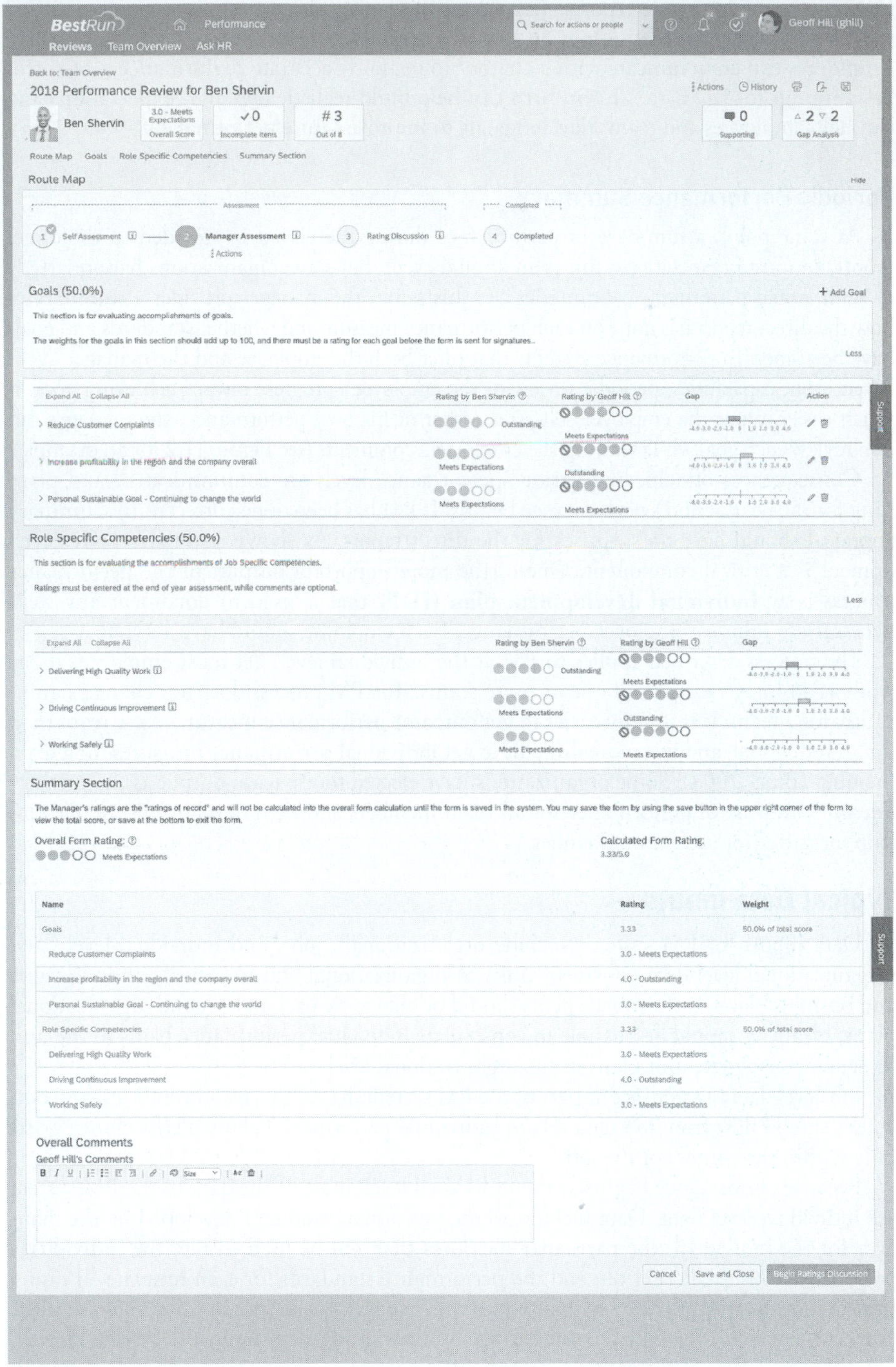

Source:

include space for the supervisor (and other raters) to enter observed performance and performance incidents. Contemporary systems allow both employees and managers to enter comments and observations at any time during the review period and provide the option of having all those comments swept into the final review, presenting them in a concatenated area for editing by users. There should also be space for documentation of positive and corrective feedback. While creating an IDP, many systems can recommend and provide a library of development activities that can be used to correct specific problems.

Performance management systems must interface with staffing and training applications. As an example, if certain jobs are hard to staff, the PM system will want to add the competencies required for that job so that more internal candidates can be surfaced. Similarly, training applications need to be coordinated with the PM system so that evaluation of training (and development) programs will be possible.

Typical Reports

The most important standardized reports produced by the HRIS are the performance contract and the annual summary appraisal for each employee. Other reports include aggregate performance data by unit and reports comparing aggregated unit performance with unit output (Cohen & Hall, 2005, p. 64). The HRIS needs to have the capability of archiving data so long-term performance trends for individuals and groups can be tracked. If competency assessments are used as a part of the review, the HR department can monitor systemic developmental requirements based on the aggregated competency results (e.g., those for business unit, location, or level).

Data Outflows

Performance data are used in many HRM decisions and will flow automatically into some processes or be available for others as needed. One automatic flow will be into compensation. Organizations with merit pay need performance distributions to construct a merit matrix. (Note that many performance applications are capable of having compensation functionality built in.) The performance measure used is the summary performance level for each employee. Performance data on various performance dimensions are used in decisions relating to promotion, layoffs, assignment to training programs, and developmental assignments. Performance data are also central to HR planning. Other applications that make use of performance data are training and development (so that training needs can be analyzed based on current weaknesses in employee performance) and staffing, where aggregated strengths and weaknesses of currently needed skills and competencies can trigger recruitment and staffing goals. Performance processes utilizing competency assessment can also be used by manpower planning applications to assist in forecasting future deficiencies based on required skill profiles. In addition, enabling employees to access and visualize automatically generated data (either as statistics or as charts or graphics) is vital to accommodate various employees' needs and preferences. For example, the accommodation for different generational preferences (Generation X, Y, and Z) could be provided by allowing employees to access HR systems on their PCs or via apps on mobile devices (König, 2015).

Decision Support

The basic decision support system in the area of PM is the entire system. Having performance criteria, performance measures, performance standards, goal-setting results, and recent performance documentation in a single place allows managers to keep track of how each direct report is doing and what interventions need to be made to improve performance (Evans, 2001). This self-service feature for managers makes the performance management module a management tool for daily use. All performance management documentation activities required of the manager can be dealt with through the system. Performance planning, documented observation of performance, feedback documentation, and the formal appraisal can all be developed on the system itself and stored there for future reference by managers. Similarly, the system can provide self-service for employees by allowing them to view the same data and use those data as a basis for deciding on areas in which improvement is needed. For example, were performance "specific" goals set at a high enough level to motivate employees to perform at higher levels on their jobs? Appropriate interfaces between the performance management module and training and development modules can lead either the manager or the direct report to training programs or other developmental activities based on the specific performance problems noted. Indeed, PM software can be categorized as either preformatted appraisal systems—systems that allow the development of customized appraisals—or systems that diagnose performance problems (Forrer & Leibowitz, 1991, pp. 104–106). Research suggests that as many as 93% of large organizations use electronic performance management systems of one type or another (CedarCrestone, 2014).

Flowers, Tudor, and Trumble (1997) note that such systems should allow managers to update information, serve as a support in conducting the appraisal interview, allow the creation of effective appraisal forms, and support all legal mandates relevant to performance appraisals. In some systems, a copy of the current job description for the position is available to the manager so that it can be reviewed for accuracy on an annual basis. A system supporting multisource feedback appraisals such as **360° appraisals** is described by Meyer (1998).

Drawing from performance data of successful (and unsuccessful) employees, we can identify the best profiles for candidates in the recruitment process (Rogers, 2018). Organizations can utilize machine learning to better identify which performance measures are effective in predicting better work results. They can also use these tools to predict which performance measures are becoming more important, less important, or even obsolete. We can also identify potential new measures for each job. Accordingly, we can be proactive in planning our future talent through selection methods that are good predictors of employee performance and training programs that address current and future skills needs (Rogers, 2018).

Group performance can also be tracked and the data used for performance improvement; because most employees work as part of teams, there has been increased interest in measuring and managing team performance (e.g., Jones & Schilling, 2000). Stegner and Kofahl (2004) provide a case study of a process for group performance improvement that could not exist without heavy input from the HRIS. In some cases, systems tie closely with marketing and management information systems; Charles, Kurlander, and Savage (2000) describe a sales performance tracking system that keeps home office and sales personnel aware of results against quotas and suggests where efforts need to be made to enhance sales performance.

Finally, automated PM systems allow managers and HR managers to track the administrative aspects of PM: Have all managers completed performance contracts with their direct reports? Are summary appraisals done on time? Do ratings by a manager and the performance of the manager's unit jibe? These are questions that can be answered by the system. Additionally, performance ratings can be checked for possible bias against protected groups. This checking can include not only the ratings themselves but also their use in HR decisions. Under the *Uniform Guidelines on Employee Selection Procedures* (U.S. Department of Labor & U.S. Department of Justice, 1978), performance appraisals are considered "tests" when used for HR decisions, such as promotions, and are subject to the same validity and reliability requirements as other tests when they are found to have an adverse impact on protected groups.

FIGURE 11.3 ■ Example of Relating Performance to Compensation

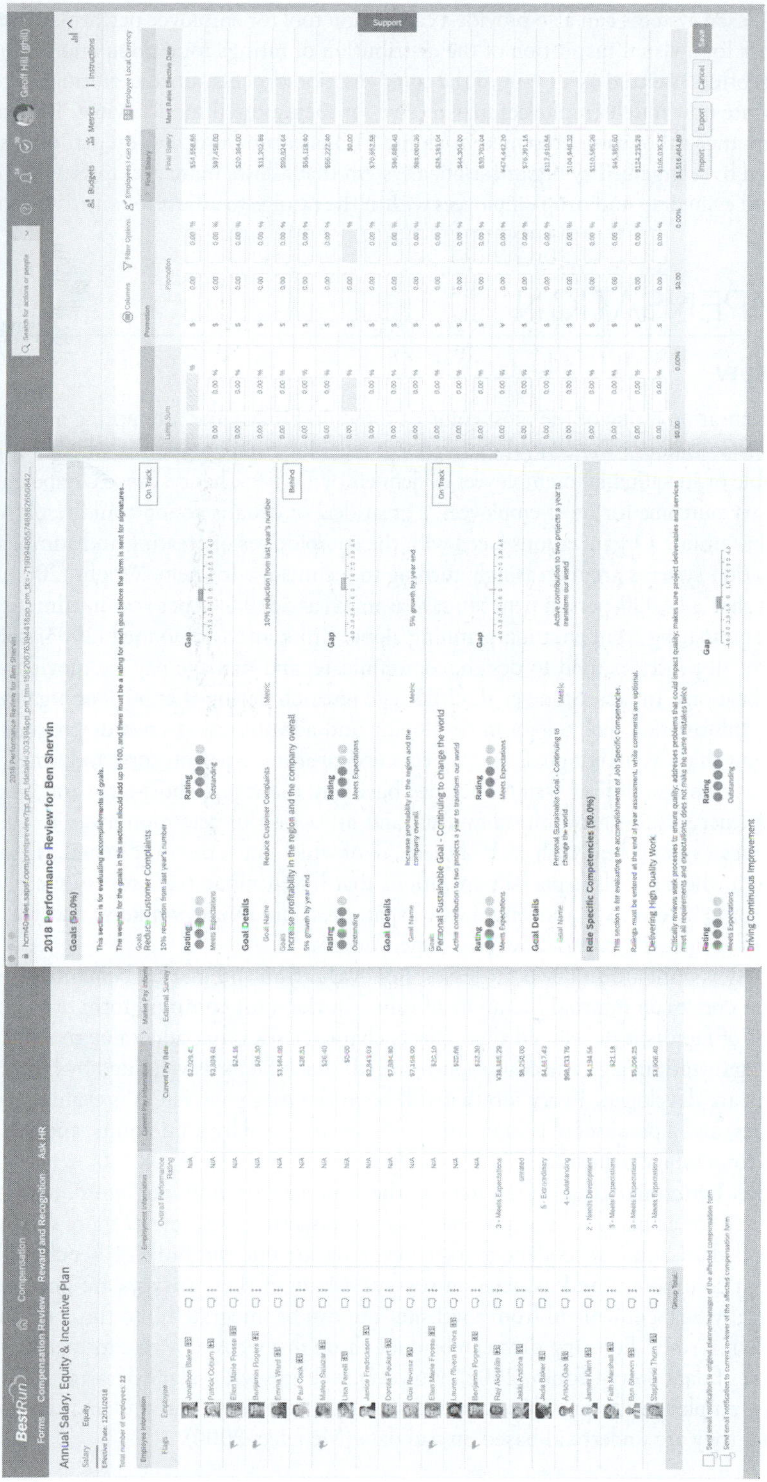

Web-based systems can also provide a calibration tool for employee performance ratings that allows for a visual inspection of the distribution of ratings for a population. This calibration is often essential as a tie-in to the compensation process, since performance ratings often dictate how much employees may receive for their annual merit review. The example of performance calibration presented in Figure 11.3 is part of a succession planning system being used by a large utility organization, a system that allows managers to view the distribution and even drag and drop employees within the ratings to adjust for any discrepancies.

COMPENSATION

Overview

Compensation is one of the most complex topics in HRM, and attempting to present an overview is ambitious. The central motivational issue for compensation is whether it is seen as equitable or inequitable to employees as defined by Equity Theory. Since compensation is the primary outcome for most employees, a great deal of dissatisfaction could result when it is viewed as unfair. Organizations faced with the complexities of creating and administering compensation systems are increasingly turning to technology for help. Wright (2003, p. 55) estimates that a 12,000-person firm can save as much as $850,000 per year in administrative costs by automating compensation planning alone. Brink and McDonnell (2003) point out that nearly all processes used to design, communicate, and manage pay are moving toward Web applications. In fact, Stone et al. (2015) cite research noting that 50% of organizations are using information technology in developing and administering rewards programs, and they suggest that two major goals are the reduction of administration costs and time.

The basic compensation system includes **base pay**, merit pay, short-term and long-term incentives, perquisites, recognition awards, and attraction or retention awards. There are many processes associated with each of these, all of which must be coordinated. If that were not enough, there are also special populations that have unique pay processes: executives, sales personnel, scientists and engineers, expatriates, unionized workers, and the whole panoply of temporary, contract, or part-time workers.

Base pay is built around two processes: **job evaluation** and market benchmarking. Job evaluation creates an internal hierarchy of value. In the most common form of job evaluation, a set of factors is developed that reflects characteristics that add value to work in the specific organization (e.g., the education required). Each factor is weighted by importance, and scales are developed. Every job that will be in the base pay system is evaluated on the set of scales, and a point score is calculated. Jobs are arranged by total points, and this forms the basis for a salary structure.

Market benchmarking is used to price the structure (or individual jobs). Market data are collected for as many jobs as possible. In most organizations, one or more surveys may be developed in-house to collect market benchmarks; but the bulk of benchmark data come from commercial and association surveys. Many of these surveys are now available electronically (via a download from a website) and can be integrated into the compensation information system. Entering data can be done through a website with a format that maximizes ease of data entry (Tobin, 2002). However, websites with salary data are not without problems; employees frequently access websites that may have unrepresentative data and argue that they are underpaid based on bad data (Menefee, 2000).

An employee is placed in the salary grade appropriate for her or his job. Each grade has a midpoint that serves as a proxy for all the jobs in that grade, and a range is built around that midpoint. (This range defines the minimum and maximum salary for jobs in that grade, usually ±20% from the midpoint.) Exact placement in the range is usually a function of performance and individual characteristics (quality of degree, job seniority, and experience).

Because of economic difficulties arising from the recession of 2008–2010, some organizations (especially public-sector organizations) could not afford to keep up with the market or provide cost-of-living increases, and they found themselves dramatically behind salaries paid in other industries. This was especially true for IT jobs, and many organizations are still trying desperately to catch up to market levels. Current difficulties associated with COVID-19 may exacerbate this problem and extend it to other organizations. To stay current, organizations adjust salaries each year based on market movements. If the market were to increase by 3%, for example, the midpoints would increase by 3% as well. However, not all employees receive a 3% increase if the organization uses a merit pay system. In a merit pay system, the size of the increase is a function of performance level and of where an employee is in the range: the higher the performance, the larger the increase and, generally, the lower the place in the range, the higher the increase. A merit matrix, developed to provide guidelines based on performance and place in the range, ensures that the total amount spent by the organization is no more than the specified percentage of payroll.

There are many forms of short-term **incentive pay**. Unlike merit pay, short-term incentive pay is rarely added to base pay and must be re-earned every year. Typical short-term incentive programs include bonuses, gain sharing, goal sharing, small-group incentives, and profit sharing. Short-term incentive programs usually have specific measures, set up prior to the beginning of the program, that will drive payout (profit sharing as an incentive is not typically covered by these measures). Gain sharing, for example, bases payouts on reductions in production costs due to more efficient use of labor. Specific preplanned formulas based on past production costs drive payouts. Bonus systems can be driven by preplanned criteria related to manufacturing, customer service, safety, or anything else that the company wishes to motivate employees to achieve. Profit sharing is usually retrospective, however; the board decides after the books have closed for the fiscal year that some percentage of profits will be shared with employees. In all cases, the measures driving short-term incentive payouts must be collected, either through existing measurement systems or through special systems designed for the purpose.

Long-term incentives are primarily based on organization stock, options to buy organization stock, or phantom (make-believe) stock. The goal of long-term incentives is twofold: to align the interests of employees with those of shareholders and to motivate aligned performance over periods of more than 1 year.

Perquisites are rewards that are a function of organizational status. Executive dining rooms, first-class or corporate jet air travel, and club memberships are examples. Perquisites frequently have tax consequences to the employee receiving them and, thus, must be included as part of the pay system. In the past several years, some organizations have transformed perquisites into incentive rewards based on performance; go to any Disney property, and you will see parking spaces near the employee entrance that are reserved for high performers.

Recognition awards are low-cost or no-cost awards that are retrospective: When an employee does something of note, he or she receives an award that may have little financial value but is psychologically rewarding. The use of websites in recognition programs, so that every employee can go online and find where he or she stands in comparison with other eligible employees, can greatly enhance the motivational impact of such programs (Perlmutter, 2002). **Attraction** or **retention awards** are one-time awards that are used to attract prospective employees to the organization or persuade them to remain with the organization. These awards may take the form of cash, stock options, benefits, or adjustments to benefits rules. The goal is to incur a one-time cost that does not drive up base pay.

Although the types of compensation already described are made up of multiple programs, it is critical that all compensation programs be integrated so employees receive a single message about what adds value in the organization and the type of behavior and culture that is desired.

Compensation programs must also meet federal and state statutory and regulatory requirements. The **Fair Labor Standards Act (FLSA)** differentiates **exempt workers** and **nonexempt workers**; the organization must pay nonexempt workers at least the minimum wage, must pay for time worked in excess of 40 hours a week at an overtime rate of 1.5 times the normal pay, and must provide records to the federal government on hours worked and regular and overtime pay for all nonexempt workers. Different states and municipalities may have higher minimum wages than the Federal level, and a company doing business nationally must keep track of changing rates across the country to make sure they are compliant; the HRIS must be capable of tracking changing worker locations and state and local minimum wages and adjusting payroll accordingly. The **Office of Federal Contract Compliance Programs (OFCCP)** requires annual evidence of no unfair bias with respect to race and gender for similarly situated employee groups (SSEGs) and requires multiple linear regression analyses as evidence.

Typical Data Inputs

Compensation data inputs include internal, external, and generated data. Internal data include information about jobs (descriptions, specifications), people (performance, salary history), and organizational units (salary budget, job evaluation system). External data would include market survey data and information on rewards practices. Internal and external data would be combined and used to generate job evaluation results, salary structures, merit matrices, and a variety of reward guidelines. Incentive programs will require input data on whatever behavior or outcome is being encouraged; such data might include customer survey results, accident data, time-to-market data, or product quality data. Data from the staffing function can highlight problem areas, for example, jobs for which compensation may be too low.

Compensation for a special employee group usually requires data specific to that group. Executive compensation is likely to require organizationwide sales, productivity, profit, share price, market share, and other financial, market, and production data indicative of organizational success. Sales compensation systems may require data on quotas, sales, bonus or commission rates, and competitive market data. Gain-sharing programs require historical averaged data on labor costs as a proportion of value of production. Bargaining unit employee pay systems require data on contract specifics. For nonexempt employees, hourly rates and hours worked per week are required.

In short, there are very few data within the organization that might not be required by some part of the compensation system. As an example, a company that market-prices jobs will collect as much market data on wages as possible. Even so, it is unlikely that market data can be found for all jobs. The "market rate" for these jobs must be estimated.

It is common to use multiple linear regressions for this purpose. As much information about all jobs is collected as possible, using either job specification data or aggregate information from job incumbents. Some specific information that might be collected from the HRIS includes the average education level of job incumbents in each job, the average amount of training incumbents in each job have had, the average number of direct reports each incumbent in a job has, and so forth. Although logic guides the choice of which independent variables to use in the regression equation to predict market rates, the goal is to get the best prediction, so whatever variables end up providing the best prediction are the ones that will be used. Similarly, incentive programs may make use of any financial, market, or production data to determine whether bonuses should be paid and, if so, how much and to whom.

Typical Reports

There are several standard reports in the compensation arena; however, because of the sensitive nature of compensation information, they are not widely circulated. The most common reports include budget reports to managers showing how their actual compensation costs compare with the projected costs. Most organizations provide each employee with an "Annual Compensation Report" showing the total amount of money spent by the organization on the employee, including money spent on wage or salary, incentive pay, and the cost of benefits paid for by the organization. Similar reports, such as incentive reports that tell people how they are doing with respect to earning a specific incentive award, become much more effective when a website is used for communication (Stiffler, 2001).

Companies participating in wage surveys produce reports for use by surveying organizations. In some cases, a compensation analyst draws the data from the HRIS and enters them into the survey, but, in other cases, an automated application gathers data from the HRIS and enters them into the survey program.

A new report on the analysis of possible "systemic compensation bias" among "similarly situated employee groups" is now required by the U.S. OFCCP. This report will be due annually, along with the organization's EEO-1 Report.

Data Outflows

The primary data outflow from compensation modules is to payroll. Compensation analysts draw on the data for additional analyses, however. Managers preparing budgets draw on compensation data as they project costs over the next budget period. Benefits analysts draw on compensation data as they analyze probable future costs of wage-based benefits (pensions are usually a function of salary level, while health benefits are largely independent of salary level).

Data are sent to federal, state, and local agencies, including taxing agencies, labor departments, and other units tracking wage data. Many organizations also provide data to firms conducting reward surveys.

Decision Support

The major rewards decision that must be made about every employee is how much to pay that individual to be seen as fair by the employee. Decision support systems in compensation are all aimed at that decision. Because of the complexity of compensation, though, a series of decisions must be made before a final compensation decision is made. Thus, there are decision support systems dealing with job evaluation, the use of market data, market pricing, building a salary structure, developing a merit matrix, and running incentive programs. Although much of this activity is carried out by compensation and other HR managers, other managers can do much of the work themselves if the system is set up correctly as a self-serve system. The most common areas that managers would handle themselves include salary budget planning, merit, promotional and other increases, and most incentive programs. Using Web-based compensation modules, managers can perform salary-planning functions much more easily than was possible with paper-based processes. Data such as current salary, compa-ratio, and salary ranges can be viewed for all their employees at once; for international organizations, such systems can handle multicurrency requirements; and these systems can ensure that the total of the projected salary increases recommended by each manager does not exceed budgeting guidelines. Figure 11.4 depicts the work area of a Web-based application that enables managers to do compensation planning for their employees.

Koski (2003) describes a project that automated a worldwide employee bonus system; executives and managers got a self-service system, and compensation executives could keep track (in real time) of award amounts and payouts. Supported by computer and Web-based products, these processes generally offer advantages to the organizations using those (Zingheim & Schuster, 2005). Indeed, Zingheim and Schuster (2004) argue that Web management of pay and rewards is one of two great innovations in the rewards field.

Employees do not make many compensation decisions themselves, so self-service functions are largely restricted to providing information. Most companies now make salary structures available on the company intranet, and job postings typically provide either structure information or the salary grade of a job, so employees can look up what the range of pay for any job would be. The merit matrix, average salary increases, average bonuses of various kinds, and other reward information are all posted by some companies. Most public-sector salaries are publicly available under state and local "freedom of information" acts, and, in these cases, salaries (and total earnings) of specific employees are available; private organizations almost never post such information.

There can be difficulties with Web management of pay. Van De Voort and McDonnell (2003) point out that working "live" can create problems when numbers change during the process. As an example, if a manager is calculating merit pay and is working off a specific budget number, changes to that number by a senior manager can create confusion and bad decisions. The use of a frozen or static database ensures that everyone is working with the same data, formulae, and figures.

Other decision support systems deal with sales compensation. Cocks and Gould (2001) note that compensation software is critical in defining commission levels, designing compensation plans, and managing compensation, since all three areas require on-the-fly complex calculations on a repeated basis. Weeks (2000) notes that virtual sales teams in widely separated areas can be much more effective in maintaining customer satisfaction; only the Web allows the coordination between team members required to pull off this strategy, and it also allows sales compensation experts to audit and fine-tune the sales compensation system to maintain high motivation levels.

FIGURE 11.4 ■ Screen of Salary Review Module for Department Manager

Salary Review - USA

Budget Figures

Total Budget for United States: 1467
Budget Used: 13500.7
Budget Remaining: 1173.29

USA Merit Increase Matrix

The following table is used to determine the merit increase percentage based on the employee's Consolidated Rating and RSP scores:

Rating	RSP 70 - 100 (From)	RSP 70 - 100 (To)	RSP >100 - 130 (From)	RSP >100 - 130(To)
10 - 24.9 Points	0	0	0	0
25 - 34.9 Points	0	0	0	0
35 - 44.9 Points	3	5	0	3
45 - 54.9 Points	5.5	7.5	3.5	5.5
55 - 70 Points	8	10	6	8

Employee Merit Increase

The local currency is: US Dolloar: The Euro exchange rate is: 0.830220

Employee	Rating	Consolidated Rating	Range %	Current Salary Local	Current Salary	Merit Range From	Merit Range To	Merit Increase %	Merit Increase Amount	Salary with Merit	Adjustment Increase %	Adjustment Increase Amount	Salary with Adjustment	New RSP
Blasi, Charles	60	20	90.00	27,000.00	22,416.00	0.00	0.00	3.00	672.48	23,088.48	0.00	0.00	23,088.48	90.00
Flint, Fred	38	38	108.00	35,000.00	29,058.00	0.00	3.00	4.00	1,162.32	30,220.32	0.00	0.00	30,220.32	111.00
Rossi, David	43	43	101.00	35,500.00	30,303.00	0.00	3.00	5.00	1,515.15	31,818.15	0.00	0.00	31,818.15	114.00
Bowen, Chris	45	50	79.00	36,000.00	29,888.00	5.50	7.50	5.50	1,643.84	31,531.84	2.00	630.64	32,162.48	89.00
Steinberg, Maureen	56	56	85.00	45,000.00	37,360.00	8.00	10.00	8.00	2,988.80	40,348.80	0.00	0.00	40,348.80	92.00
Innocenti, Cynthia	59	70	90.00	73,000.00	60,606.00	8.00	10.00	8.00	4,848.48	65,454.48	0.00	0.00	65,454.48	98.00
				252,500.00	209,631.00				12,831.07	222,462.07		630.64	223,092.71	

When integrated with payroll, AI-enabled PM systems can help organizations better understand which incentives are working best to modify employee performance. Through machine learning, organizations can optimize incentives at the organizational, team, and personal levels. Moreover, incentives' impact might vary based on teams, locations, and individual employees. Thus PM data could enable organizations to customize incentive plans and better predict the cost of each, resulting in higher performance, more accurate budget forecasting, and, potentially, lower labor costs. Due to automation and the changing nature of the workforce, it is projected that future compensation packages will be more based on performance-related pay than fixed pay (Gayeski, 2015; Wisskirchen et al., 2017). Compensation based on hours spent at the workplace is becoming less practical and desirable due to flexible work arrangements and work preferences for generations Y and Z (Gayeski, 2015; Manyika et al., 2017). Therefore, AI-enabled PM systems will be essential for organizations in the future.

A whole set of applications relate to executive pay. Since the Enron scandal and the subsequent passage of the **Sarbanes-Oxley Act (SOX)**, compliance reports, including those dealing with executive pay, are required. SOX compliance is greatly supported by data from the HRIS ("How HRIS Can Help with SOX Compliance," 2005; Sherman, 2005). Additional regulations covering executive pay have come about as a result of the **Troubled Asset Relief Program (TARP)** of 2009 and the financial bailout of troubled financial services firms and automakers. More financial regulations restricting executive pay in financial firms were enacted in the **Dodd-Frank Wall Street Reform and Consumer Protection Act of 2010**, and regulators continue to press for new controls. The HRIS must be flexible enough to add any new fields required by these regulations and capable of running the audits required.

BENEFITS

Overview

A full discussion of benefits programs is beyond the scope of this chapter. There are five broad types of benefits programs in most U.S. organizations. Because some company-provided benefits in this country are government provided in other countries, a different typology would be required for organizations abroad. As might be expected by Equity Theory, benefits are becoming important outcomes from the organization and could affect employee turnover.

The first set of benefits programs common in U.S. companies includes **pension plans** (both defined benefit and defined contribution), individual savings plans (such as Keoghs, **simplified employee pensions [SEPs]**, and **individual retirement accounts [IRAs]**) and Social Security. Although few Americans think of Social Security as a benefit, the organization must fund contributions to Social Security just as an employee does. The goal of all these benefits programs is to ensure that the employee will have continuing income after retirement. The second set of benefits programs includes workers' compensation, unemployment insurance, long- and short-term disability insurance, and life insurance. The goal of these programs is to ensure that employees who cannot work (through no fault of their own) have some income until they can work again and to provide income protection to employees' families.

The third set of benefits programs includes medical and other health benefits, such as hospitalization and medical care insurance; surgical and major medical care insurance; long-term care; dental, vision, and hearing care insurance; and prescription drug coverage insurance. These benefits are designed to make sure that employees and their families are not bankrupted by illness or accident and can obtain preventative and curative care. The fourth area of benefits is paid time off and includes vacation, holidays, personal days, special-purpose days (because of jury duty, bereavement, or military service, for example), and family leave. The purpose of paid time off is to allow employees to recharge their batteries, spend time with their families for celebrations, and participate in other significant life events.

The fifth and final category of benefits includes miscellaneous benefits such as dependent care, flexible working benefits (telecommuting, job sharing, and compressed workweek), employee assistance programs, professional memberships, tuition reimbursement, holiday parties and gifts, subsidized cafeterias and gyms, legal advice benefits, and employee discounts. These benefits round out the benefits package and are typical of organizations found in the "best companies to work for" lists.

Benefits programs differ from compensation in two major ways. First, in the majority of organizations, employees pay part (or all) of the costs for most benefits. (Even when benefit costs are borne entirely by employees, group purchasing reduces the cost that the employee would pay for an equivalent self-purchased benefit.) Second, most organizations offer some flexibility in their benefits programs. All employees receive a core benefits package but then choose additional coverage or additional benefits, or both, up to the level of the total benefits package. These **flexible benefit plans** also allow the employee to purchase additional coverage or benefits, or both, at cost.) These two characteristics of benefits programs make them relatively complex to administer; each employee in the organization may have a slightly different benefits package with a unique salary deduction profile. Things even get complicated with paid time off. Not only may different employee groups (e.g., bargaining units, executives) have different configurations for paid time off, but these configurations may also differ within groups based on seniority. In addition, many organizations have what is called a paid-time-off bank, through which employees can trade paid time off for cash or other benefits, can buy additional paid time off, or can donate paid time off to other employees (e.g., in cases of long-term illness). All this makes benefits programs extremely complex and difficult to administer.

Another major difference between benefits and compensation programs, one that strongly affects HRIS configuration, is the growing trend to outsource benefits programs and administration. Few parts of the typical compensation program are outsourced. The most common is the outsourcing of wage benchmarking. Although consultants are frequently used in compensation, they tend to work offline. In benefits, however, program design, benefit delivery, and program administration (including employee communications) are increasingly outsourced. As a result, the HRIS must interface not only with other internal systems, such as rewards and payroll, but also with the IT systems of other organizations. The necessity of establishing these interorganizational linkages introduces problems such as how to define fields, which fields can be included, what protocols for interaction to establish, and how to maintain security.

Legal requirements for benefits programs are also more stringent than those for compensation programs. Most benefits programs are influenced by the

Employee Retirement Income Security Act (ERISA), which grants benefits a tax-favored status. However, to qualify for favorable tax treatment, the benefit must meet stringent requirements. These include reporting to recipients of benefits and to the federal government, demonstrating that requirements for qualified status are met. In addition, many organizations offer nonqualified benefits to some employee groups, particularly to executives.

Aside from legal requirements, most organizations (and their employees) are concerned about the safety and security of personal data stored in the HRIS (Zafar, 2013). Data required for benefits include many characteristics of employees that they wish to keep private (e.g., addiction treatment, psychiatric care, adoption records, and health information). Because benefits information is shared with organizations outside the employer (e.g., insurers, medical providers), data security can be breached, not only in the employing organization but also in other organizations. More information on how organizations can protect their employees' privacy and secure data is provided in Chapter 15.

Typical Data Inputs

There are HRIS benefits modules with different purposes, and each requires a different type of data input. One set of functions focuses on the organization's relationship with current and prospective benefits vendors (of health insurance, for example). Inputs, in this case, will include aggregate data about the people to be covered, data outlining the relevant demographics for the covered groups, and data specifying the program coverage desired and cost limitations.

A second set of functions focuses on the internal management of benefits programs and will be used to track usage, employee choices (in the case of flexible benefit plans), and costs. Experience, usage, and costs will be fed into this program.

A third (and the most common) set of programs focuses on employee input about enrollment and other coverage choices, changes in coverage desired, and changes in employee status (e.g., addition of a dependent, change in marital status) that may affect coverage and employee costs. These programs may also allow employees to file claims with the organization. In these programs, many of which are Web based, employees feed in personal data, coverage choices, and other data relevant to their use of the benefit.

The fourth set of data placed in the system consists of the myriad federal, state, and local laws and regulations governing benefits practice. These laws and regulations provide decision support system "rules" for managers using the system.

Typical Reports

Dozens of reports are required by federal and state government units, including the IRS, units of the U.S. Department of Labor, other federal agencies, and similar units at the state level. The most common report is the annual benefits report to employees required for tax-qualified plans under ERISA. This regulation requires organizations to report to employees annually about certain benefit facts, such as vested pension levels. Most organizations have gone beyond the ERISA requirements and provide a report to each employee showing the total value of all compensation and benefits received by the employee during the year. This annual compensation report is the "rewards scorecard" for the employee. Ceccon (2004) estimates that putting this annual report online rather than distributing printed copies can save a company with 30,000 employees $678,000 in actual costs over five years and that productivity savings from reducing the amount of time employees use to find benefit account balances, pay information, and other rewards information on multiple sites or via phone calls to the HR department can save $625,000 per year. HR productivity increases net an annual savings of $30,000, and increased employee retention would reduce costs by $150,000 per year. With a 5-year savings of $678,000 and an annual productivity savings totaling $805,000, Web reporting is clearly advantageous.

With Web-based access to benefits and other employee information, staff can view summary reports at any time, which, in many cases, eliminates the need for a company to produce expensive paper versions. With a Web-based system, an employee can, at his or her convenience, view his or her current benefits, salary, and other information directly (as shown in Figure 11.5) and decide to print a paper copy if one is needed. For an international company that distributes benefits or pay in multiple currencies, the system could normalize that data into a single currency.

Data Outflows

Data generated by benefits programs have to be transferred to payroll and accounting internally. Data are sent externally to benefits providers, outsourced benefits administrators, and a variety of federal, state, and local agencies. Aggregate data are provided to benefits survey firms.

The real-time transfer of data can result in large cost savings. Moynihan (2000) notes that AT&T saved $15 million when it switched to providing updated enrollment information to all its various health plans. Previously, tardy data transfer resulted in health plans denying coverage to employees who were in fact eligible and in claims being paid out to people who no longer worked for AT&T.

Decision Support

Decision support tools overlap to some extent with reports in the benefits arena because, frequently, these reports trigger the need to make changes to comply with federal, state, or local requirements. As an example, McCormack (2004) notes that the Family and Medical Leave Act (FMLA) has complicated the administration of employee leave. Many states have more stringent leave requirements than FMLA or the 40 other federal leave laws. A system that tracks these laws and can tell the HR manager exactly what the leave requirements are in a specific locality ensures compliance and minimizes the risk of lawsuits and fines.

Similarly, tax-qualified benefit plans are subject to federal bias regulations. In this case, "bias" refers to income level rather than protected group status. Federal policy is that tax laws should not underwrite benefits that are available only to highly paid employees. If an organization is to have a qualified 401(k) retirement plan, for example, the plan must be available to both low- and high-paid employees, and, in addition, it must be used by both. Tracking enrollments against those eligible for participation can trigger efforts to get more low-paid employees to participate in the plan.

FIGURE 11.5 ■ Compensation and Benefits Planning Screen

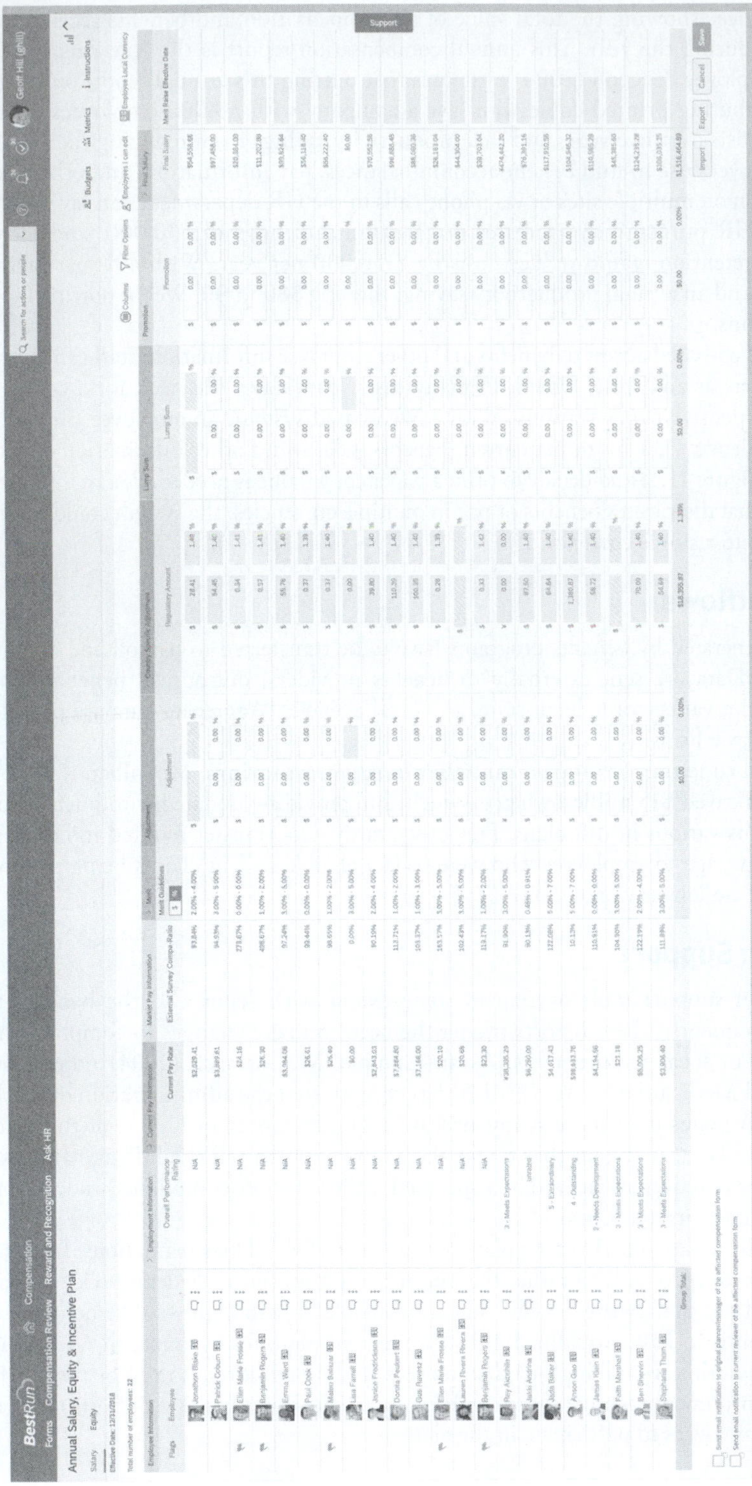

Source: © SAP. All Rights Reserved.

When organizations offer flexible benefit plans, it is common to track the choices made by employees to guide plan development. A few organizations have looked at benefits choices made by high performers to see if they differ from the choices made by low performers. Others look at the choices made by protected groups. Recruitment literature can then be tailored to specific groups to ensure a better yield of desirable applicants.

Web-based services also offer decision support to employees deciding what levels of coverage to sign up for (Dawson, 1997). Employees can readily compare the cost of various levels of benefits service and more readily understand the cost-benefit trade-off that they are going to make. Similarly, transferring the enrollment process to the employees themselves can save the organization money (Teer, 1997). However, such savings are not likely to occur unless the system is easy to use for all employees, not just the technologically savvy (Ashley, 2006).

Self-service systems for managerial use in the benefits area are not frequent, as few managers have a role in benefits decisions concerning their direct reports. However, self-service systems for employees are increasingly relied on by employers to lessen the burden of benefits transactional administration (Stone et al., 2015). Employees typically make and change selections in flexible benefits plans through the company intranet. They can change beneficiaries or dependents as births, deaths, and divorces occur. They can increase tax-deferred or pretax contributions to various benefits categories such as 401(k) plans, health spending accounts, and similar programs. They may buy or sell vacation days from the paid-time-off (PTO) bank. They may transfer PTO days into their 401(k). (Timing and contribution limits and other rules must be observed, but these can be built into the application.) Employees can also find out the status of various benefits through self-service approaches. At least one organization allows employees to do "what if" scenarios with respect to retirement: for example, "If I retired tomorrow, what would my pension be?"

The outsourcing of benefits creates additional issues for the HRIS. Some major corporations have outsourced all benefits. An extensive interface must be built connecting the organization's HRIS with the outsource firm's system. The benefits advisers at the outsource firm must have current, accurate data on the benefits status of every organizational employee to be able to answer questions and provide advice. Outside access raises security issues to a greater level of concern; benefits data (including hospital and other medical billing and psychiatric care and employee assistance program billing) are the most sensitive employee data held by the organization, and privacy standards (including Health Insurance Portability and Accountability Act [HIPAA] requirements) must be met.

A whole range of decisions concerning benefits is made outside the HR department. Benefits costs are the most rapidly increasing part of labor costs, particularly costs for health care benefits and defined benefit pension plans. Consequently, senior executives (especially the CFO) are interested in the aggregate costs of the various benefits packages offered by the organization. However, determining these costs is complicated. For many benefits, such as workers' compensation, cost is a function of experience; for others, such as insurance, cost depends on usage; and for others, such as health insurance and pensions, employee demographics are particularly significant. Therefore, the organization needs to be able to price current benefits packages and project costs based on expected demographic changes. It also needs to be able to run "what if" scenarios based on alternate benefit packages: What would we save over the next five years if we switched from a defined benefit pension to a cash balance plan? How would that compare to switching to a 401(k) with match?

PAYROLL

Overview

Payroll is the transactional process through which compensation is transferred to employees and federal, state, and local income and payroll taxes are withheld from employees' checks. It is also through payroll that any benefits costs borne by employees are withheld. Although some employees receive actual checks for net pay, it is more common, especially among large organizations, for **direct deposits** to be made to employees' bank accounts. Companies that outsource need to make sure that the compensation and benefits modules of the HRIS interface flawlessly with the provider's payroll input. Even when companies do payroll in-house, the payroll module is usually part of the accounting system rather than the HRIS, so it is critical that the interface between the HRIS and the payroll software work flawlessly (Walker, 1987).

In the majority of organizations, payroll is a function administered by finance or accounting rather than the HR department. HR departments feed compensation data and benefits coverage (and employees' coverage choices) to payroll, which makes sure that all appropriate federal, state, and local income and payroll taxes are withheld at the correct rate and that any deductions for benefits are also withheld at the correct rate. Payroll usually has the responsibility for keeping track of income and payroll tax rates and applicable salary levels. Payroll results are fed back into the general accounting system by payroll. Because labor costs are the largest variable cost for most organizations, it is critical for the organizations' financial well-being that payroll records be accurate and timely. Because the paycheck is a signal of the employment relationship and because many employees rely on their paychecks to meet bills that are due, it is critical that the payroll system deliver accurate and timely paychecks or bank transfers. Little will anger or demoralize an employee more than a missing or inaccurate paycheck or transfer. In short, payroll is a transactional task that must be flawless.

Currently, AI-enabled payroll solutions ensure legal compliance and minimal errors in routine payments; thus, human involvement focuses on irregular transactions and errors. Moreover, technologically advanced payroll systems allow the automation and streamlining of payroll processes, comprehensive employee self-service, and addressing employee inquiries with no human interaction (Robert Half, 2018). Current solutions are enabled to generate advanced descriptive and diagnostic analytics based on big data and provide future predictions and prescriptive solutions (Thompson, 2018).

Payroll is the most heavily outsourced HRM function. Great economies of scale can be achieved by a payroll processor with respect to keeping up with the intricate requirements of income and payroll tax deductibles or maintaining (and upgrading) software that ensures that payroll is accurate and completed in a timely manner. However, outsourcing companies do not work in a vacuum, and compensation and benefits functions must deliver data to the outsourcer, and the accounting and finance functions must receive data back from the outsourcer. Also, some companies argue that integrating the HR and payroll functions makes sense and saves data entry and labor costs while providing greater accuracy and timeliness (Gale, 2002).

Typical Data Inputs

Data entered into the payroll system from inside the organization include compensation data, benefits data, and other payroll addition data (e.g., special awards) and deductions data (e.g., union dues, wage garnishments for child support, credit union repayment installments). Time and attendance data are usually handled in a special module, and data from this module are also fed into payroll (Robb, 2004). Data external to the organization include federal, state, and local income and payroll tax rules that allow the organization to withhold appropriate amounts from each employee's paycheck. There may be payments made to individuals who are not active employees. Although these are usually taken care of in a separate COBRA module, there may even be payments from ex-employees for the continuation of benefits. The most frequent data input are changed data. Every time a new employee goes on the payroll, an employee changes status, an employee makes benefits elections changes, governments change tax or withholding rates, or the organization makes changes such as pay increases, data reflecting the changes have to go into the payroll system. Many of these elections can be performed by employees themselves using the self-service capability of a Web-based payroll system. Through a direct entry screen (shown in Figure 11.6), the employee can enter or update any data that he or she controls, such as the number of exemptions or extra withholding, without the need for HR intervention. For an international company, the system could automatically present any financial data in whatever currency the employee requested.

In addition to internal and external data, the system generates data that it stores and uses over time. For example, in 2020, FICA (**Federal Insurance Contributions Act**, i.e., Social Security) taxes were withheld on the first $137,700 of income, and the maximum tax withheld for any employee was $8,537.40. Payroll must keep a running total of FICA paid to date so that it does not deduct too much from the employee's paycheck.

Typical Reports

There are a number of standard payroll reports. These show—for the organization as a whole (or for subunits)—the actual amount paid to employees for a period (and cumulatively) and the amounts deducted for various purposes. Reports go to federal, state, and local agencies, including taxing authorities, and to benefits providers. Employees receive reports with their paychecks or notices of deposit; the report shows gross pay and all deductions. Usually year-to-date accumulations are also provided.

Data Outflows

Payroll data go to accounting; federal, state, and local agencies; benefits outsourcing firms; and individual benefit program providers. These payroll data are the input for a variety of processes in those units, so it is critical that systems interface flawlessly. Interface

FIGURE 11.6   ■   Screen Used for Entering Data for a Paycheck

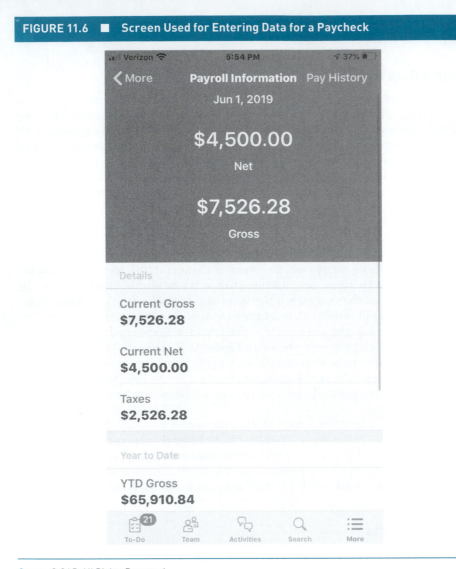

becomes even more complicated as external systems communicate not only with payroll but also with compensation, benefits, and other HR systems.

Decision Support

Payroll data are not usually used by HR departments or line managers for decision-making purposes. They are used extensively for audit purposes. Employees, on the other hand, like to know from time to time how much money they have earned in a given year, how much income and payroll taxes have been paid, and the level of pretax and deferred tax contributions made for various benefits. This information can be made available through a self-service system. Similarly, a self-service system can allow employees to increase with-holding or make other (limited) changes in their pay.

Summary

The overall goal of this chapter was to provide the reader with a broad understanding of the role and focus of HRIS in supporting performance management, compensation, benefits, and payroll processes. The combined PM, compensation, benefits, and payroll systems constitute some of the most important parts of the HRIS. Money may not be at the forefront of how people talk about the organization and their linkages to it, but if performance ratings result in lower than expected salary increases, bonuses are miscalculated, benefits elections are not implemented, or a paycheck is wrong or (worse still) not delivered, employees become vocal. Because pay and benefits constitute the largest variable cost to any organization and the largest overall cost for many organizations, it is critical that managers plan, track, and audit outlays on a real-time basis. A significant proportion of the data and reports owed to federal, state, and local agencies come from the compensation, benefits, and payroll modules. The consequences of inaccurate, misleading, or missing data and reports include embarrassment, fines, and even jail time. And these are the risks associated with poor data from just the transactional part of these modules. The additional fallout would be the negative effects on the motivation of the employees to work at higher levels and/or to leave the company for a company that does not have these problems. Thus, one of the major purposes of an HRIS is to help organizations administer their performance management, compensation, benefits, and payroll systems.

The role of motivation in work performance was covered, with a specific discussion of Equity Theory. It is easy to see that employees who perceive their job situation in terms of the ratio of their inputs to the company's outputs as inequitable will not be highly motivated to perform adequately on their jobs. A key part of strategic HR is aligning employee behaviors with the strategic intent of the organization. As seen in the discussion of goal-setting theory, the process of the PM system needs to follow the research findings on goal setting. It is important to hire the best people and provide them with the training and development needed. Without PM, the success of hiring strategies is unknown, and, similarly, the need for training and development interventions is unknown. PM systems support the translation of corporate strategy into individual performance plans. Compensation and benefits systems can be used to hire the right people, retain the high performers, and motivate all employees to perform at a higher level. Compensation can also be used to motivate poor performers out of the organization. As systems technology has progressed, managers have become better able to enhance the performance of their direct reports and to tailor compensation and benefits programs to attract, retain, and motivate the best. Thus, the importance of understanding the central role of an HRIS in assisting managers in making key decisions regarding performance, compensation, benefits, and payroll cannot be underestimated.

Key Terms

360° appraisals 292

attraction awards 296

base pay 294

Consolidated Omnibus
   Budget Reduction Act
   (COBRA) 284

corrective feedback 285

direct deposits 306

direct report 286

Dodd-Frank Wall Street
   Reform and Consumer
   Protection Act of 2010 300

Employee Retirement Income
   Security Act (ERISA) 302

Equity Theory 283

exempt workers 296

Fair Labor Standards Act
   (FLSA) 296

Federal Insurance
   Contributions Act
   (FICA) 307

flexible benefit plans 301

goal-setting theory 285

incentive pay 295

individual development plan
   (IDP) 289

individual retirement account
   (IRA) 300

job evaluation 294

market benchmarking 294

nonexempt workers 296

Office of Federal Contract
   Compliance Programs
   (OFCCP) 296

outsourcing 288

pension plans 300

performance
   contract 287

performance management
   (PM) 282

performance
   observation 285

performance
   planning 286

perquisites 295

positive feedback 285

recognition awards 295

retention awards 296

Sarbanes-Oxley Act
   (SOX) 300

simplified employee pensions
   (SEPs) 300

Troubled Asset Relief Program
   (TARP) 300

Discussion Questions

1. Discuss how a manager might make sure that the performance plan for each of her direct reports was driven by organizational strategy and the business plan. How can information systems support this goal?

2. Merit increases require a single "performance" number, while most incentive plans have multiple and varying performance measures. How can the PM system meet both needs?

3. Compensation strategy includes how competitive the organization wants to be, the number of different compensation systems the organization wants to have, the mix of various reward and benefit components, and the basis of increases.

Discuss the data inflows required if an organization wanted to automate its compensation design and administration processes.

4. Both PM and benefits information systems make provisions for employee access and input. What access would you provide in each of these systems, and what leeway would you provide employees in reading, entering, and changing data?

5. A lot of compensation information is available to employees today on the Web (e.g., www .salary.com). How can an organization assure employees that they are fairly compensated (assume they are) when public data suggest otherwise?

6. Flexible benefit plans are common today. Discuss ways in which employers can ensure that employees make good choices about the benefits and benefit levels that they choose within the benefits information system itself.

7. Payroll and benefits are commonly outsourced. Discuss which parts of PM, compensation, benefits, and payroll you would consider outsourcing, justifying your views.

Case Study: Grandview Global Financial Services, Inc.

Grandview Global Financial Services is an international corporation providing multiple financial services. Although it is one of the smaller players in the field, the firm has about 20,000 employees worldwide. Corporate strategy has focused on serving a niche market comprising high-net-worth individuals, providing them with all the wealth management services they require. These services include investments, insurance, banking, real estate, financial planning, and related services.

The linchpin making all these services work well is the quality of the employees—the degree to which they are motivated to provide "over-the-top" attention to clients' needs. Clients have come to expect this level of service regardless of where they might happen to be and regardless of the time. Because of clients' high expectations, every employee is expected to provide flawless service.

As it has expanded globally, Grandview has hired employees from all the countries in which it does business. Although all employees are expected to speak English, business is conducted in nine different languages in 45 locations. Grandview has invested heavily in developing a uniform corporate culture but has not succeeded in doing so in all locations.

One difficulty has been the PM and reward systems. Each geographic area developed its own PM tools, which reflect the national culture and the past experiences of local employees. There are a variety of systems using different performance criteria. Most of the PM materials are in Microsoft Word. Some of the systems seem to work all right, although others do not. None of the systems are coordinated, except to the extent that those final performance ratings are sent to the Grandview corporate HR department. There has been enormous pushback and noncompliance with PM policies from the employees because of the difficulty of the paper performance process as well as the nine different languages being used worldwide.

Rewards systems are similarly localized. Base pay, incentive systems, and benefits have grown up in each geographic location in accord with local market practices, laws, and customs. The complexity and number of Excel spreadsheets needed to manage the financial targets and the resulting compensation plans for that many employees have created perceived and actual inequities. It is difficult to transfer employees across geographic areas because of the different systems in place, and awareness that employees in different locations have very different terms and conditions has created morale problems.

Corporate HR has PM and rewards modules in its HRIS covering U.S. employees, but this takes care of only about 60% of Grandview's employee population. An executive rewards module does cover about 2,000 senior executives worldwide, but all foreign data are sent from different locations and entered into the module at headquarters. Part of the historic reason for this process involves the legal requirements concerning privacy of information in the EU and some other locales; it is easier to get executives to grant permission for the transmission of specific data when those data are used to calculate stock option awards and other executive incentive payments granted by the corporation.

Corporate HR would like to move away from local systems and institute a corporatewide system that relies neither on Word documents for performance reviews nor on Excel spreadsheets for the resulting compensation plans that result from the overall performance ratings. It was thought that common systems for PM and rewards would support a more unified culture and help translate Grandview's corporate strategy into individual performance plans worldwide.

The ideal system would be a Web-based, multilingual, integrated PM and compensation system. The PM system would be accessible by managers and their direct reports and would be tied to corporate strategy and the current business plan. Managers and their direct reports could access the system at any time to see performance criteria, measures, and standards and to look at current progress against standards. The rewards and benefits modules, although based on local law and customs, would be standardized with respect to process, fostering a more uniform rewards culture. It is critical to HR managers that the technology selected is flexible enough so that yearly changes to the application could be made efficiently and legal requirements in different locations could be accommodated, as well as changes in those requirements.

Because the performance goals are based on financial targets, and employees' merit and incentive payments are directly related to employee performance as well as Grandview's overall results, all necessary functionality for the compensation process should be built into the performance system. At year end, results should be able to be imported directly from corporate financial systems and used to generate performance reviews and compensation plans for the employees. The resultant pay increases and bonus payments would be fed directly into the payroll system already in use by Grandview in the United States and abroad. The system administrators should be able to ensure worldwide compliance with the performance process directly from the system through a variety of reports.

Case Study Questions

1. What is the role of PM in establishing and maintaining corporate culture?

2. What is the role of compensation and benefits in establishing and maintaining corporate culture?

3. Since laws, labor markets, and customs relevant to PM, compensation, and benefits differ from country to country, does it make sense to try to maintain a common global process for managing each of these areas?

4. Given all the cross-country differences, why would a global organization want to have a common HRIS?

5. How should Grandview go about implementing a global PM system?

6. How should Grandview go about implementing a global rewards system?

7. How should Grandview go about implementing a global benefits system?

8. How should Grandview go about implementing a global HRIS to manage these functions?

STRATEGIC CONSIDERATIONS IN HRIS

Huub Ruël and Tanya Bondarouk

EDITORS' NOTE

The purpose of this chapter is to provide an overview of the internal and external considerations that occur as part of the implementation of an HRIS and a move toward an eHRM approach to delivering HR functionality. The decision to invest in HR technology is not made in a vacuum but instead occurs in conjunction with the organization's overall strategy and its HR strategy. For optimal results, these must be in alignment. In this chapter, the authors present two models of the eHRM environment. In each model, they discuss key strategic considerations such as economic environment in which the purchase is considered, the local legal and regulatory environment, the needs of employees, HRIS vendors, the design of the HRIS adopted, and more can affect the success of the implementation and use of an HRIS. The chapter further discusses how eHRM can be adapted to support different HRM strategies up to and including outsourcing parts (or all) of the HRM function. In addition, it briefly discusses the changing role and skill sets needed for HR professionals as they navigate eHRM. Finally, the chapter looks ahead toward new challenges and opportunities for eHRM. After reading this chapter, you should better understand the strategic considerations associated with the implementation and use of eHRM.

CHAPTER OBJECTIVES

After completing this chapter, you should be able to

- Explain how each aspect of the eHRM domain (e.g., implementation, content, design, effects, and target groups) shapes how it is implemented and used by the organization
- Discuss why it is important to link HRM strategy to eHRM strategy

- Explain why eHRM must consider both technical and social aspects during its design, implementation, and use

- Discuss how the use of eHRM will change the nature of HR jobs and what the jobs in HR may look like in the future because of eHRM

HRIS IN ACTION

HR Technology at Unilever

Unilever, a large Dutch-British multinational (known for brands such as Becel, Axe, Rexona), applies automated facial recognition in its recruitment process. It uses an online video-based interview platform called HireVue. Applicants are asked to answer a set of questions that will be captured on video through this platform first. The platform has built-in emotion-recognition technology that can recognize whether the displayed emotions are "real" and the extent to which the applicant is enthusiastic, bored, or honest. Unilever claims that HireVue has saved the application process 50,000 hours in 18 months' time. With technology, recruit-ers only have to talk to the best applicants. The company says that technology also produces a less subjective and fairer recruitment process. Applicants are more strongly assessed by the technology on their personal characteristics but then objectified by the technology rather than e.g., rejected because they followed the "wrong" training. The question remains, of course, whether the assessments of the emotion-recognition technology are indeed correct, because the algorithms are trained on the basis of human assessments and interpretations of emotions. Also, there is a question of whether privacy legislation allows emotion-recognition data to be stored and retained.

INTRODUCTION

We live in an age in which technological developments succeed each other at a rapid pace, or at least that's how we experience it. But is it indeed getting faster, or is it also the way we live? If modern technology were to suddenly break down, our morning would be full of smaller and bigger annoyances: no electronic payments, no coffee available, no Google Home responding, no direct news or social media updates, and it might not even be possible for most people to start work, because we could not use our laptops, desktops, and other electronic and digital devices. If all digital networks were to fail, panic would break out. Just like us, human resources (HR), top management, line management, and employees would not be able to start the day normally without electronic and digital resources. Even though HR management is a field by and for people, technology has become an important foundation for its practice. Whether it concerns an old-fashioned process such as employee record keeping or decisions about launching a new employer branding campaign, technology is required.

Although many in the C-suite (approximately 27% in a recent study) do not view employee issues as their concern, they do believe that the data to make effective "people" decisions is an enabler of greater productivity (EIU, 2019). Technology has become a key facilitator of these people decisions and has impacted HRM strategy, services, and practices. For investments in technology to be most successful, though, HR must align its investments in HRIS with both its HR strategy and its **organizational strategy** while balancing employee and organizational needs and knowing that the C-suite may not be actively engaged in shaping that strategy. This chapter touches on how organizations can accomplish these goals.

HRM AND TECHNOLOGY

Before discussing the strategic role that a **human resource information system (HRIS)** can play in organizations, it is important to indicate that we focus our discussion on information and communication technology rather than all types of HR systems (e.g., processes). Although technology has not always had such a central role in HR, the last two decades have seen a dramatic increase of the centrality of technology to accomplishing HR tasks, including recruitment and selection (see the Unilever case), in onboarding and socialization processes, talent training and development, and evaluation and performance management at strategic, tactical, and operational levels. But it is important for us to more clearly define what is meant by the use of technology in HR. Chapter 1 briefly contrasted HRIS with eHRM, and we go into a bit more detail in this chapter. Recall that an HRIS was defined as a system used to acquire, store, manipulate, analyze, retrieve, and distribute information regarding an organization's human resources to support HRM and managerial decisions (Chapter 1). This is similar to Haines and Petit's (1997) definition of an HRIS as a system used to collect, store, edit, analyze, query, and disseminate necessary information about the human resources of an organization.

However, in the late 1990s, researchers realized that the definition was a bit limiting, because it focused on the data and technology regarding employees rather than the richness of technology-enabled HR processes. For this reason, a proliferation of definitions and terms came into fashion. These included terms such as electronic human resource management (eHRM), virtual HR, Web-based HRM, and Intranet-based HRM. For example, virtual HR referred to a network-based structure that relies on partnerships and collaborations that run through information technology to help recruit, develop, and operate an intellectual capital organization (Lepak & Snell, 1998). Put more simply, virtual HR is primarily a digital network that connects parties to recruit staff, develop them, and make them productive.

It is instructive to see that in the early years, the range and impact of technology for human resources was not yet fully recognized. Most simply looked for opportunities to automate existing processes rather than understanding how an HRIS could provide greater opportunities for sharing information within organizations and across organizational boundaries. With the emergence of the internet, HRM was also able to improve its service to employees and managers by infusing their processes with technology. Thus, scholars developed a new term to reflect the increasing infusion of technology into HR processes and the improved communication capabilities of these systems, **electronic human resource management (eHRM)**.

eHRM has been defined in many ways. Lengnick-Hall and Moritz (2003) defined eHRM as conducting HRM operations via the internet or intranet. Voermans and Van Veldhoven (2007) defined it as using internet technology for the administrative support of the HR function. Ruël, Bondarouk, and Looise (2004) defined eHRM as implementing HRM strategies, policies, and practices in organizations with the conscious and direct support and full use of web technology-based channels. Finally, Strohmeier (2007) defined eHRM as the planning, implementation, and application of information technology for both networking and supporting at least two individuals or a collective in the joint implementation of HR activities. This is similar to the definition provided in Chapter 1 of eHRM as the "implementation and delivery of HR functionality enabled by a HRIS that connects employees, applicants, mangers, and the decisions they make" (Johnson, Lukaszewski, & Stone, 2016a, p. 536). The key takeaway from these definitions is that eHRM is an umbrella term for all possible integration mechanisms between **strategic HRM**, plans, practices, and information technology and its implementation in organizations to create value for organizational activities aimed at employees and managers (Bondarouk & Ruël, 2009).

The eHRM Domain

The definition of eHRM with which we ended the previous section deserves further exploration. Specifically, there are multiple factors and defining characteristics of eHRM that must be considered (Figure 12.1). These are eHRM implementation, eHRM content, eHRM design, eHRM effects, and eHRM target groups. Figure 12.1 visualizes these characteristics and makes it clear how extensive eHRM is as a phenomenon. We are talking about much more than just the use of technology in HRM. eHRM is about the integration of HRM and technology that is continuously evolving, with a wide scope and multiple components. We briefly outline each in the following sections.

FIGURE 12.1 ■ The eHRM Field (adapted from Bondarouk, 2014)

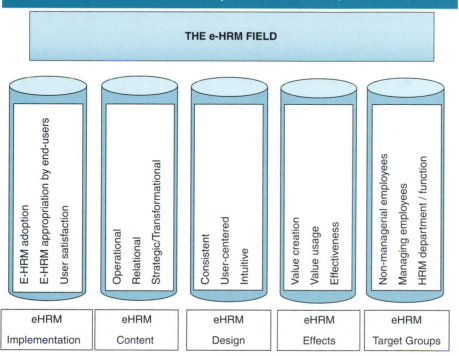

THE e-HRM FIELD

eHRM Implementation	eHRM Content	eHRM Design	eHRM Effects	eHRM Target Groups
E-HRM adoption; E-HRM appropriation by end-users; User satisfaction	Operational; Relational; Strategic/Transformational	Consistent; User-centered; Intuitive	Value creation; Value usage; Effectiveness	Non-managerial employees; Managing employees; HRM department / function

eHRM Implementation

First, when moving to eHRM, organizations must consider how to best implement an HRIS that will support the transformation of HR processes to eHRM processes. This involves the development of an **eHRM strategy** and making decisions regarding which HRIS to adopt, what functionality to deploy, and how these applications will be used by employees and managers. This part is very important, because technology will only have an impact if it is actually used. Our systems, processes, and devices only work because people, organizations, and societies use them. A lot of technological applications that are being developed will not succeed because they are not accepted and put into use by people. Many of the possible applications that people have at their disposal in work or at home are often unused and will therefore not have any impact.

eHRM Content

Second, it is important to understand both the context and content of eHRM. eHRM can transform any type of HRM practice that is technology supported. This includes e-recruitment, e-selection, e-training and development, e-performance management, e-personal data management, e-employer branding, e-compensation, and so on. In addition, an organization will need to consider at what level the organization is using eHRM. Data and process needs will be unique at the operational, tactical, and strategic levels (Dulebohn & Johnson, 2013).

eHRM Design

Third, organizations must also consider the ability of eHRM to facilitate all types of HRM practices, whether they are web, mobile, cloud-based, or part of a larger enterprise resource planning (ERP) system. In addition, organizations must be aware that technology continues to evolve and that the future will be dominated by artificial Intelligence (AI), robotics, blockchain and more (see Chapter 17). It is important to emphasize that information technology can play a facilitating role but never a leading role. Design considerations made by vendors can affect the use of the HRIS by different organizational stakeholders (Davis, Bagozzi, & Warshaw, 1989) and how they are used to manage employees and make decisions about them (Johnson, Lukaszewski, & Stone, 2016b).

In addition, without human intervention or an aim conceived by people, information technology cannot effectively support HRM. It is often said that information technology influences society, organizations, and people, but without human action and without people, organizations, and society using technologies, they have no influence. In short, technology will only have an impact when it is used. Technology therefore has both a technical dimension and a social dimension (see also Orlikowski, 2010).

e-HRM Effects

Fourth, eHRM must create value for employees and managers in organizations and across organizational boundaries. Value creation is a broad concept, and every organization must determine how to define it for their specific situation. Most often, value creation occurs through efficiency savings by focusing on how much can be saved by introducing new eHRM applications (see Chapter 6). Given the complexity of eHRM, though, it can be difficult to express the eHRM outcomes financially beyond efficiency and cost savings. Recall that eHRM has both a technical and a social side, and new eHRM applications can only deliver something if they match the wishes and working methods of the organization and its employees.

Beyond efficiency gains, eHRM can also improve the quality of service delivery of HRM and the positive experiences that it creates for key stakeholders (e.g., employees, managers, applicants, etc.). For example, eHRM applications can shorten time to hire (the time between the creation of a vacancy and filling the position), preferably with a higher likelihood that the person is the most qualified and best-fitting individual for the firm. In addition, eHRM can help the recruitment, selection, and onboarding process run more smoothly and efficiently. Research has found that efficiency benefits can play out across many different HR functions, including recruitment (Cober, Brown, Blumental, Doverspike, & Levy, 2000), employee selection (Alkhadher, Anderson, & Clarke, 1994), training and development (Welsh, Wanberg, Brown, & Simmering, 2003), and self-service (Gueutal & Falbe, 2005).

e-HRM Target Groups

Finally, the various target groups (e.g., stakeholders) of eHRM such as managers, employees, and applicants must be considered. Although systems developed in the 1980s and 1990s focused on the HRM department, the emergence of internet dramatically changed who is impacted by the HRIS and eHRM practices. Data from the HRIS can now be put into the hands of employees and managers, allowing them to own and manage data rather than having to wait for HR. These self-service applications have been adopted by most organizations and can dramatically lower the costs of many HR transactions (Gueutal & Falbe, 2005). However, when considering the target groups, organizations must acknowledge and account for the differing, and sometimes conflicting interests of the different groups.

Not all employees will have the technological and business expertise to use the HRIS and move to eHRM. An investigation of 10 UK organizations showed that although they are achieving process efficiency and realizing effectiveness benefits with eHRM, the extent of value gained depends on the quality of the design and implementation of eHRM, including involvement from the organization and training of HR staff (Parry & Tyson, 2011). Thus, training will be needed as a part of any eHRM innovation.

eHRM: FROM STRATEGY TO RESULTS

For optimal value creation to occur, organizations must account for both the technical aspects of eHRM and the social aspects of the implementation. As illustrated in Figure 12.2,[1] this can include a broad set of internal and external stakeholders, including the software vendors, the various government agencies that regulate employee treatment, and more. In this section, we pivot from the discussion of the eHRM domain to present a model that focuses on the environmental factors that enable and constrain organizations as they seek to create value through their eHRM strategy. This model consists of five components: eHRM context (expanded from the last section), eHRM strategy, eHRM goals, eHRM types, and eHRM outcomes (Figure 12.2). We will discuss each in turn.

FIGURE 12.2 ■ The eHRM Model (adapted from Ruël et al., 2004)

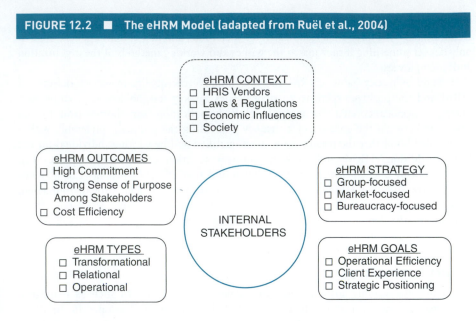

eHRM Context

The development of an eHRM strategy is influenced by several factors outside of the organization's control. These include HRIS vendors, local laws and regulations (political, legal), economic influences (market forces and the government), and societal influences (Shapiro et al., 2007; see also Figure 1.3). Organizations pursuing eHRM innovations must prepare an analysis to anticipate or to react adequately to these external influences.

HRIS Vendors

HRIS vendors are the developers of the software used to support HR processes. These vendors can provide either core HR systems (e.g., Oracle, SAP, Workday, Ultimate Software, etc.) or can provide niche systems for specific HR processes such as payroll and benefits (e.g., Zenefits, Paycor, TrakStar, etc.). HRIS vendors develop applications with the goal of motivating the maximum number of organizations to choose their software. Each of these providers tries to be distinctive and better than the competition. This drives technological development. However, a technologically driven eHRM approach does not guarantee an effective implementation. Simply being on the cutting edge does not ensure success. For many organizations, the technology supporting HR is so advanced and there are so many choices in the market that it is difficult for organizations to determine what system is best for them and which functionality should be implemented in their own organization.

The results of research focusing on the effects of investing in HRIS on HR and organizational performance have been mixed. Some studies have found that eHRM results in cost savings, greater efficiency, better HRM services, and more employee engagement (CedarCrestone, 2015). This suggests that the vendors are offering excellent products and services to support HR processes.

However, other studies have argued that eHRM can increase stress, increase administrative burdens, and disappoint users with the available functionality (Johnson & Stone, 2019). This contradiction can be explained to a significant extent by contextual influences. One of those

TECHNOLOGY KNOWLEDGE OF HR PROFESSIONALS IS LIMITED

A recent survey of 190 HR professionals con-ducted by AFAS (an HR technology provider) in collaboration with Tilburg University found that only 25% of HR professionals believe that they have the necessary knowledge and skills to effec-tively use modern HR technology. One-third were very dissatisfied with their own knowledge of HR technology and how to best utilize it.

influences derives from eHRM developers and technology providers. eHRM is not a static phe-nomenon, nor is it a standardized system or set of applications. New systems and applications continue to appear on the market, and any new customization or application can influence the effects of eHRM in organizations. And unfortunately, HR professionals often do not feel pre-pared to meet the challenges of deploying new technology and embracing eHRM.

Laws and Regulations

Just as traditional HR processes had to comply with local and national laws and regu-lations, so also will eHRM processes. This can be challenging for global firms, which must consider the regulations of many different countries. For example, in the Netherlands, there are extensive legislation and regulations in the field of labor law and privacy, and HRIS data storage and protection capabilities must comply with these laws. Data that are typically covered by these laws include access to electronic personnel records, storing electronically processed data, and monitoring electronic communications traffic. There may also be frameworks at the sector level or organizational level with which eHRM applications must comply. However, in the United States, there are different, and often less stringent, laws regulating data storage and protection (see Chapter 15).

In larger European organizations, there are also works councils (private sector) or par-ticipation councils (public sector) that have a voice in personnel decisions and that should be involved in an eHRM implementation. The resulting agreements with these councils form a framework that affects what eHRM innovations are going to look like. When these councils are not involved or when they resist, the implementation of eHRM processes will not be as successful. For example, the works council of one large airline was very critical of eHRM, and for this reason, relatively little use was actually made of the HRIS and eHRM capabilities. In other words, this organization remained far behind what the market had to offer technologically.

Economic Influences

Companies experience turnover based upon the degree to which the economy grows, stands still, or shrinks. These economic factors can also affect the investments in human resources and in HRIS. In other words, eHRM innovations generally are reduced during an economic downturn. However, companies may choose to invest during economically difficult times, because using eHRM can save costs and can enable more smoothly func-tioning HRM processes and quicker attraction of high-quality new staff once the economy grows again. Public-sector employers (e.g., government) can also be impacted by economic conditions. The government receives fewer taxes and needs to cut back as soon as the econ-omy shrinks or stands still, and eHRM innovations are often attractive items to cut back.

In addition, the dynamics of government involvement in the economy can also affect how organizations invest in eHRM. For example, compared to the United States, the Dutch economy is characterized by a relatively present and coordinating role of the government. Public policy in the field of reintegration of sick employees, working time, parental leave, diversity, and lifelong learning each influence the choices organizations make regarding what eHRM applications and which functionality to implement. In addition, any new piece of government legislation can require an updated or new eHRM application. As such, HRIS vendors will quickly jump in and approach organizations actively to use their applications.

Society

Finally, organizations do not operate in a vacuum but are part of a society. Society is made up of people, citizens who have developed implicit and explicit rules, manners, and behavioral patterns (e.g., culture). These rules, manners, and behavioral patterns reflect what is and what is not permissible at home and at work, what is considered nice and what is not, how to set up cities, build homes, and what the landscape should look like. For example, in the Netherlands, a change process requires a very participative approach to be successful, but in many societies, a much more direct and top-down approach is desirable. Citizens of such societies expect managers to give clear directions and to assert their authority.

These societal and cultural contexts in which eHRM occurs cannot be ignored. eHRM is not only influenced by the organizational context, but it must also "co-evolve" with external stakeholders such as market parties, government, and society (Marler & Parry, 2016). The implementation of new eHRM applications must adhere to country and societal rules, norms, and behavioral patterns. For example, in many countries, payroll data is considered private and may be accessible to the employee but not to management. In addition, in some emerging economies, expatriate employees (an employee not native to the local country) may not officially be appointed as managers. Therefore, they are often hired as external consultants whose roles are essentially that of managers. The capabilities of the HRIS and eHRM processes must therefore be adapted to the local rules. In short, the effects of eHRM are linked to and develop in continuous interaction with the environment in which the organization operates. For multinational organizations, this means that the intended and realized results of eHRM innovations differ by country or region (Bondarouk et al., 2016).

eHRM Strategy

eHRM innovation requires guidance, especially an eHRM strategy. Without a clear strategy, it is almost certain that HRIS applications will not function adequately in conjunction with each other, overlap will be created between applications, and users will not be clear about what the organization expects. This leads to suboptimal results and can even move the organization away from eHRM. Just as HR strategy must be linked to an organizational strategy, so also should an eHRM strategy link to the overall HRM strategy and practices (Ruël et al., 2004). Although HRM strategies and practices differ from organization to organization, there are three main architypes (Beer et al., 1984). These are "bureaucratic," market, and team-focused (e.g., "clan"). Organizations that want to implement eHRM innovations do not start from scratch with eHRM; they have already made implicit or explicit strategic HRM policy choices in employee participation, staff through-flow, remuneration, and organization of labor based upon the HR strategies chosen (Beer et al., 1984). In addition, there can also be several HR strategies existing within an organization. For example, in a hospital, there can be an HRM strategy for the non-medical staff and one for the medical staff.

The "Bureaucratic" Approach to HRM

The **"bureaucratic" HRM strategy** is particularly evident in organizations that operate in stable environments in both technological and socioeconomic terms (e.g., larger, established companies and government organizations). Although "bureaucratic" often has a negative connotation, we use it to describe an organizational form based on elaborate rules with a clear hierarchy. This has the benefit of clarifying where the responsibilities and controls lie, but it can be negative when maneuverability and responsiveness are desired, as rules and hierarchy quickly get in the way.

The Market Approach to HRM

A **market-oriented HRM strategy** is mainly found in organizations that need to react quickly to market and environmental developments. In such an organization, employee participation is not strongly formalized and depends on the space and openness of the leadership; personnel flow depends on individual aspirations and attempts to "advance" rather than a formalized development trajectory; remuneration of staff has a basic framework, but depending on the situation on the labor market, the leadership may decide to pay new staff more than people in similar positions; the furnishing of labor and the organization often have a more flexible, flatter form. In newer companies, ones that are highly seasonal, technology companies, and start-ups that have survived the beginner phase, HRM is characterized as market oriented.

The Group-Focused Approach to HRM

A **group-focused HRM strategy** suits organizations for which high quality and innovation are important. Staff in these organizations consist of highly skilled professionals with specialized skills. Companies consisting of technical specialists, accountancy firms, and medical specialists are examples of organizations with a group-oriented HRM strategy. Employee participation is critical, as staff members' best insights are needed to deliver quality and remain innovative; there is a strong connection with the company's specialization and with peers, staff flow reflects loyalty to the organization, rewards are based on benchmarks with peers and dependent on seniority (e.g., joining as "partner"), and the establishment of labor and organization is often motivated by specialization of the organization.

Linking eHRM & HRM Strategy

The organization's HRM strategy and policy choices are the starting point for the eHRM strategy. In an organization with a "bureaucratic" HRM strategy, an eHRM strategy will primarily have to align with and conform to the existing rules and hierarchy, communicate these rules better, and apply them more effectively and efficiently. In an organization with a market-oriented HRM strategy, an eHRM strategy may focus on facilitating the organization's agility. eHRM applications will be highly employee self-service focused, strongly focused on strategic management information (HR analytics, personnel file analyses), productivity-enhancing work, and communication and interactivity between management and employees. Much more authority is placed in the hands of managers in market-oriented strategies compared to those with a bureaucratic strategy.

With a group-oriented HRM strategy, an eHRM strategy will focus on supporting the functionality of the specialist as much as possible. There will be a specific focus and connection to the wishes and needs of specialists and professionals so that they can exercise their profession optimally, deliver high quality, and continue to improve themselves. Although the choices described here reflect choices that organizations will make when linking eHRM and HRM strategies, the reality is a lot more complex than described here. That is, technology, organizational strategy, and employee desires can all mutually influence the successful link between eHRM and HRM strategy (Marler & Parry, 2016). In addition, research from CedarCrestone (2014) found that the organizations that found the most success from eHRM implementations were also those that had the strongest HRM practices.

eHRM Goals

As organizations determine their eHRM strategy, they will also focus on the specific goals that an organization wants to achieve with eHRM. Here, too, the influence of eHRM vendors is clearly visible. Vendors make certain assumptions about HR processes and design their products with certain capabilities. These processes may differ from how an organization currently operates. In addition, vendor salespeople can promise unrealistic and too-optimistic outcomes. The risk is that without knowledge of both your firm's HR processes and the capabilities and limitations of an HRIS under consideration, organizations may not be able to make the right choices for eHRM innovation. Therefore, an organization must articulate its goals for moving forward with eHRM *before* seeking recommendations from vendors.

Typically, organizations focus on three main goals with eHRM. These include providing cost savings and improving the efficiency of HRM processes, improving the strategic orientation of human resources (e.g., HRM as strategic business partner), and improving the quality of service to HRM clients (Bondarouk & Furtmueller, 2012). eHRM innovations oriented toward achieving cost savings and improving HRM processes focus on replacing paper forms with electronic processes. Examples of this include employee and management self-service applications. However, realizing cost savings can be difficult to achieve. The costs of adoption can often end up higher than estimated, and the proposed savings are often unrealistic (Bondarouk & Ruël, 2005; 2013).

eHRM innovations aimed at improving the strategic role of HR mainly focus on using data from the HRIS to improve HR data analyses and decision making and providing more robust analytics capabilities. Finally, improving the quality of HRM services means investing in eHRM applications that are very well aligned with the needs of clients. The applications must be intuitive to use, and users must have a quality experience. In fact, research found that a good design of eHRM applications is the most important factor needed to start using those applications (Bondarouk & Ruël, 2005).

Each of these three eHRM goals can be pursued jointly in eHRM innovation projects, but research shows that organizational goals surrounding all of them are often not realized. An important explanation for this lies in the "mismatch" between the technical design of applications and the perceived usability and experienced user convenience between the technical system and the social system. Organizations often forget that by transferring HRM tasks to employees and managers through self-service, the demand for HRM services does not decline. The effort is simply transferred. This means that employees will have to do additional work and that managers' HRM-oriented tasks expand; unfortunately, many managers lack the HR knowledge to complete those tasks and will likely require training to remain compliant with local laws and HR procedures.

Does this mean that eHRM innovations are pointless? Hardly. However, it does mean that because eHRM innovations are often not familiar to organizations, they need clear strategies and realistic objectives. To achieve this, an eHRM innovation project should be considered an organizational change process and not simply an IT project. One reason for this is that employees often implicitly assume that many things can easily be arranged or selected via a mobile device. After all, in everyday life, the smartphone or other smart devices support communication, shopping, and financial matters. But when forced to use the new HRIS and employee eHRM, they realize how complex these systems are. Preparing and training employees in advance can reduce resistance and underutilization of the system once in place.

eHRM Types

Once the organization has formed an eHRM strategy and has articulated the goals for eHRM investments, they can then determine what level of organizational functioning their system will support. Ruël et al. (2004) distinguish three types of eHRM: operational eHRM, relational eHRM, and transformational eHRM. Let's examine these three types.

- **Operational eHRM** concerns the use of eHRM to facilitate employees' daily tasks by making information easily available and their development through competency development, performance management, and reward. This form of eHRM supports the transactional HR activities discussed in Chapter 1.

- **Relational eHRM** concerns the implementation and use of eHRM to support HRM service processes. Think of efficiently organized processes for recruitment, selection, and introduction (onboarding), for employee development, HR communication, and participation, for performance management and assessment and reward. Relational eHRM connects middle management and employees and helps support the traditional HR activities discussed in Chapter 1.

- **Transformational eHRM** concerns the implementation and use of eHRM to facilitate strategic decision making and strategic change processes. For example, transformational eHRM would focus on strategic personnel planning and corporate branding with the aim of attracting the desired talent. Transformational eHRM supports the transformational HR activities identified in Chapter 1. Strategic HR analytics applications are suitable for this purpose, but they require more advanced levels of personnel data such as competency development, performance, and ambitions. Without this kind of good-quality data, it is difficult to make analyses for the future. Transformational eHRM is the most ambitious type of eHRM, because it demands effective eHRM innovations at both the tactical and operational levels.

The three eHRM types described here are suitable for use by professionals and consultants as a means of looking at how eHRM is implemented in organizations. In practice, organizations will use eHRM applications that have characteristics of all three types. And not all the parts will be equally well integrated and widely used. There are many anecdotes about managers who need to approve employee leave requests in an eHRM application, but in daily practice, they "outsource" this task to their assistants. They often do not have the formal power to do so, and it can also prevent them from actually being able to access data that should remain confidential. The eHRM types can also help organizations understand how to align their eHRM strategy and objectives with eHRM types to ensure that the strategy, objectives, and types form a coherent whole. This is quite difficult for organizational practice to realize and a source of failures or disappointing results in eHRM innovations.

eHRM Outcomes

eHRM should deliver results and create value for organizations and support key HR policies and goals. Otherwise, organizations will not invest in them. Beer et al. (1984) identified a number of these goals:

1. Profound commitment of all employees (high commitment),

2. Competent human resources (high competence),

3. Cost-effective human resources (cost effectiveness),

4. Better relations between different internal stakeholders, between management and employees, and a good balance in the rewards for various staff groupings (higher congruence).

Each of these goals can support organizational performance. For example, highly engaged and committed employees are motivated to support the organization's goals. As experts in the people aspects of the firm, HRM can act as a change agent as an organization evolves its "human capital" in a competitive marketplace (Ulrich, 1996). Competent human resources refer to the capacity of employees to continue to develop and to ensure that their knowledge and skills are and remain up to date. For HRM, this means that it must be able to fulfil the role of employee champion by stimulating and facilitating the development orientation of employees.

Cost-effective human resources refer to the pursuit of a reward system that promotes maximum productivity for optimal wage costs while considering organizational needs, employee needs, and local labor market conditions. In this case, it is important for HRM to be able to fulfil the role of "administrative expert." Finally, better relationships between different organizational groups contribute to organizational performance. It also means that there is a good dialogue between the management and staff, which makes it possible to constantly discuss changes that are needed to remain successful in a collaborative manner.

eHRM can facilitate each of these goals in several different ways. However, as introduced in Chapter 1, a major role that an HRIS can play is by providing the data that organizations need to make people decisions. Technology-enabled eHRM processes in turn can streamline decision-making and support communication between employees as they perform key tasks. eHRM can promote transparency about reward structures, improve industrial relations in organizations, facilitate communication and interaction between employees, and help them self-evaluate and develop support.

eHRM AND THE HRM FUNCTION

In the previous section, we discussed the five components that form the core of successful eHRM innovations in organizations: the context of eHRM, eHRM strategy and policy choices, eHRM goals, eHRM types, and finally eHRM outcomes. eHRM innovations cannot be consigned to just pieces of technology; they require an integrated approach in which the "social system," the organization, and the "technical system" (e.g., the HRIS) inform the design and content of eHRM. As such, eHRM is not static but dynamic, evolving as the social and technical environments change, as organizations better understand eHRM, and as the organization's strategy evolves.

Technology is not neutral but is designed by people and only "comes to life" during use. And it must remain that way. If technology is no longer understood by people or is not under their control, undesirable situations can arise. This may sound like science fiction and futuristic, but with the rapid developments in, for example, artificial intelligence (AI), there are risks of technological developments getting out of hand. That is why in the eHRM model (Figure 12.1), the central focus is on the stakeholders (e.g., employees and management). That is, people must be at the core of eHRM. They must give direction and substance to eHRM innovations. HRM and technology are inextricably linked. HRM naturally revolves around people and helping them move forward in their roles, ways of working together, well-being, development, and performance in organizations, but technological applications are needed to make this possible now and in the future. But what does eHRM mean for the design, organization, and role of the HRM department?

Shifting Roles of HRM Professionals

The eHRM developments of recent decades have not left HRM unaffected. The types of eHRM shown in the eHRM model mean that HRM must also innovate. The transactional importance of HRM has not diminished; instead, most basic HR tasks have been automated through self-service applications. An important consequence of this is an evolution of the role of HRM to that of strategic business partner. It also means that instead of spending time conducting basic transactions, HR staff should begin focusing on transformational activities that link HR strategy to an organization's strategy. Thus, HRM needs professionals who can think strategically and have a vision of what HRM information and analyses are needed.

The role of the HRM professional has also been changed by eHRM and will continue to change as eHRM evolves (Gueutal, Marler, & Falbe, 2007). Much has been said in recent years about the lack of information technology interest and skills among HRM professionals. However, the HRM professional of today and tomorrow must constantly keep an eye on what eHRM innovations are available on the market and how they can contribute to improving the performance of the HRM department. eHRM developments also influence the level and roles of HRM professionals. Greater levels of education are required to function as an HRM professional, and there is also a greater variety of roles: generalist, specialist, consultant, technology-oriented specialist, and business partner. eHRM has also contributed to strengthening a focus on the role of the HRM department as a service provider to employees and management. Through good use and support of eHRM, the quality of the service can be improved, and HRM professionals can function much more as internal consultants.

eHRM and Outsourcing HRM

eHRM developments have also supported speculation about the usefulness of an internal HRM department. Today, it is possible to outsource all HR services to an external party and deliver them online. However, eHRM has not led to the systematic disappearance of the HR department that was predicted. Instead, organizations have strategically outsourced specific HR functions such as payroll benefits administration, and some HR administrative tasks (e.g., background checks, some training, etc.). Placing personnel data entirely outside the organization still encounters many objections, not least of which is security. In addition, eHRM has emphasized and strengthened the demand for the value-added service of personal interaction. And the oft-quoted statement that HRM must be in line (i.e., that the line manager is actually the daily HR manager) emphasizes that the support for this responsibility can only be partly delivered from outside the organization. The "real" HR work has remained a person-to-person affair.

It can be concluded that eHRM has contributed to making the HRM field much broader. With the possibility of deploying increasingly sophisticated technology, a new palette of HR activities has emerged. For example, employer branding, establishing an organization as a strong brand as an employer, has increased in importance over the past decade (see also Chapter 9, Recruitment and Selection).

THE FUTURE OF eHRM

eHRM innovations have made it possible to collect and analyze much more HRM data than was previously possible. The nature of the data that can be collected has also greatly increased and continues to expand. For example, organizations are using smart devices to assess employee stress, which can then be used to help the organization take precautionary measures in the event of high stress to prevent failure due to illness. When organizations decide to place monitoring of employee actions in the hands of their employees, it gives employees room to decide when and how to analyze themselves and to whom to send which data. It could bring about an actual learning organization. Employees could use this data to learn and work on the continuous improvement of their performance. However, it also raises ethical and privacy-related questions. Is it desirable to continuously monitor? What are the implications for employee privacy? Does the organization have the authority to monitor employee activities outside the workplace if the company provides the mobile device to the employee?2 Finally, questions arise with respect to who has access to the data and where and how it is stored.

In addition, developed economies are increasingly becoming smart economies, ones in which production technology, digitization, and networks combine to create new opportunities for companies and society. The connection of user applications to the internet and all kinds of online networks also creates new opportunities for HRM that can serve organizations and employees. However, people dictate the direction and content of those possibilities, not the technology. And for eHRM, the HRM strategy and policy choices must indicate the direction and content for eHRM applications, even in the smart era. Our argument is that these decisions must be "people centric."

Organizations are also starting to invest in artificial intelligence (AI)-enabled eHRM, which strives to "learn," or to improve its own performance over time with the help of continuous collection of data. Chatbots, or robots with which people can "chat", talk, and ask questions, improve their performance based on conversations that people have with them. AI offers new opportunities for organizations and HRM; it can replace human actions, and it has the potential to better facilitate HRM. Replacing human actions mainly involves AI-driven robotics and "service automation." For example, customer questions can be handled through an AI-driven application that learns and improves itself based on those questions.

AI-enabled eHRM processes are heavily utilized in some sectors, such as the high-tech sector. However, AI-enabled eHRM is also moving to nontechnology organizations such as catering or cleaning companies that work with many people on flexible contracts and work on location. For larger government organizations, eHRM innovation and the use of these applications may also be slower. It is likely that the institutional context or even country will make a difference in the speed of adoption of AI-enabled eHRM. To maintain control over these new technological developments, it is important for organizations to develop a strategy for how to deploy AI. Whatever decisions are made regarding future technology innovations, we return to our core principle . . . that is technology should not be in control, people should be guide and control how these innovations are deployed.

Summary

This chapter describes the relationship between HRM and technological developments that support HRM. That relationship is brought together in the term eHRM. Technological developments have influenced HRM and have encouraged innovation and change. In addition, they have enabled new ways of organizing HRM and delivering HR functionality. eHRM can support the strategic goals of HR in several ways (Bondarouk & Furtmueller, 2012; Ruël & Bondarouk, 2014; Stone et al., 2015; Strohmeier, 2007):

- Automation of routine HRM work and digital archiving of employee records

- Reduced transaction costs for talent management

- Facilitates managerial decision-making about their people

- Facilitates working with HR metrics and HR analytics. Data processing and analysis provide insights for strategic decision-making.

- Improved HR and organizational "branding" and improving the image of organizations as an attractive employer

- Reduces the administrative burden of conducting HRM transactions and providing opportunities for improved strategic focus

- The transformation of HR professionals from administrative paper handlers to strategic partners

It is clear from these findings that eHRM has already had an impact on and provided opportunities for HRM. However, it is important to remember that eHRM cannot be implemented effectively without an understanding of how it supports an organization's overall HR and corporate strategies. In addition, organizations must consider the technical aspects of eHRM (e.g., the HRIS), the social aspects of eHRM (e.g., the employees, managers, and their relationships), and the goals of HR and the organization to most effectively deploy and manage any eHRM initiative.

Key Terms

bureaucratic HRM strategy 323

electronic human resource management (eHRM) 316

eHRM strategy 318

group-focused HRM strategy 323

human resource information system (HRIS) 316

HRIS vendors 320

market-oriented HRM strategy 323

operational eHRM 325

organizational strategy 316

relational eHRM 325

strategic HRM 317

transformational eHRM 325

Discussion Questions

1. Identify and define the five components of the eHRM domain.

2. Why is it important to consider the target groups when implementing an HRIS? How might each group's needs and motivations impact the use of an HRIS and the effectiveness of eHRM?

3. How do each of the four aspects of the eHRM context affect how an organization might choose to implement eHRM?

4. How would the use of eHRM look different in a bureaucratic HRM strategy compared to a market-based approach?

5. Why is it so important that an organization's eHRM strategy is linked to its HRM and organizational strategies?

ADVANCED HRIS APPLICATIONS AND FUTURE DIRECTIONS

PART IV

13

HRIS AND INTERNATIONAL HRM

Michael J. Kavanagh and Miguel R. Olivas-Luján

EDITORS' NOTE

Today, most organizations of any scope have some form of international presence. For organizations, "going global" is a necessary part of competing, but it can bring with it some of the most important issues for HRM. Frequent conflicts can arise when there is a difference between the culture of the country and the culture of both the organization's and HR's environments. The cultural differences between countries will influence HR programs and practices. In this chapter, some of the significant differences between domestic HRM and international human resource management (IHRM) in multinational enterprises (MNEs) are covered. In addition, the authors discuss some of the key HRM issues involved in an international organization. Further, global operations pose a number of additional complexities and challenges for data collection, management, and use, as well as for the design, development, implementation, and use of an HRIS. These challenges are discussed by the authors throughout the chapter.

CHAPTER OBJECTIVES

After completing this chapter, you should be able to

- Understand the differences between domestic HRM and international HRM
- Identify the types of organizational forms used by firms competing internationally
- Understand the different types of employees who work in MNEs
- Discuss the staffing process for individuals working in MNEs
- Understand the problems that handling expatriates poses for the IHRM department

- Describe the training needs of and programs for international assignees
- Reconcile the difficulties of home-country and host-country performance appraisals
- Identify the characteristics of a competitive international compensation plan
- Understand the modifications necessary for using HRIS applications in an IHRM

INDUSTRY BRIEF

ROY J. WOOD, JR., EXECUTIVE VICE PRESIDENT OF PROFESSIONAL SERVICES, INSURITY

Increase revenue! Increase profits! Increase market share! Innovate! Attract the best talent!

There is tremendous pressure on domestic (e.g., U.S.) companies to "do more with less" and to do it "the right way." With increasing labor shortages in most key sectors and decreased patience by Wall Street and private equity financiers in how quickly a company should grow and expand, today's strategic decisions must look outside our borders for creative answers to key business questions such as "How do I lower cost while producing more?"; "How can I be more profitable through innovation while not being able to spend more on R&D?"; and "How do I service my customers around the clock?" Expectations are sky high. Corporate management needs to excel in all areas now! Companies are thus forced to look to options outside the U.S. borders to increase the ability to scale with cheaper resources while striving to expand market share while innovating to levels they never have before.

This expansion has come in two forms. First, domestic companies are opening offices in offshore locations to reap the benefits of the economics those countries have to offer. In addition, around the world, innovative companies are sprouting up that are focused solely on partnering with first-world-country companies to meet today's demand through well trained and flexible workforce options. The desperate search for cheaper trained

labor, more flexible employees, and, in some cases, less involvement from labor unions, have produced promising results as U.S. companies have become more competitive, but they have also become more reliant on their international strategies. This has greatly changed the role of human resources management at these companies as HR becomes more strategic in helping companies reach their top and bottom lines through policies and strategies that stretch around the globe.

This opportunity to solve a host of current manager problems by working with a global workforce of course comes with a host of acute issues for human resources. First and foremost, it is a challenge to manage the culture of a workforce that is both multicultural and working on teams that span thousands of miles and multiple time zones. Whether working with internal employees or a business partner overseas, there is frequently resentment as jobs and focus leave the U.S. and move toward the lower-cost locations. There are also the challenges of higher employee attrition rates that are prominent in many of the offshore option sites, as well as the process of attracting and recruiting top talent, retaining that talent, and compensating in line with local market demands. Managing this workforce is a new dynamic for U.S. companies as they learn to deal with issues such as what motivates employees from other cultures, how

(Continued)

(Continued)

to accommodate for their differences in working habits, and how to hold international employees accountable for results.

Companies looking to solve their core business issues with strategic international plans can solve these issues only if they *actively confront and have a strategy for how to solve the issues* that come with the strategy. This typically falls on the human resources team. They will be responsible for developing programs and a culture that is attractive to both the domestic employees as well the additional labor markets with which they choose to align. This results in the HR role being very different than it was even a decade ago as the specialists needed for HR to succeed expand exponentially. For instance, having someone with deep knowledge of the local labor laws where business is being done is now critical. An acute knowledge of localized benefit plans, compensation expectations, local holiday schedules, satellite vacation expectations, etc. all become an important focus of the human resources function and a critical aspect to the overall success of the strategy.

In addition, in looking to expand to global markets for revenue opportunities, as well as to enhance their current workforce, domestic companies need to consider localized data privacy laws, technologies that cross over country borders, and the battle for data ownership. As strategic workforce planning becomes key to strategic decisions to move overseas, more and more pressure is placed on Human Resources to provide critical data points so that the right decisions can be made, so that business objectives are in line with the realities of the landscape within which they operate.

It can be said that the move to solve core business issues with an international strategy has put the human resources function at the head of the table in the board room as a critical and active part of strategic decision making. As we move forward, more deeply into the global work world, it becomes increasingly important to continuously reevaluate and change. Offshore companies that support the growth of U.S. companies are also being courted by other first-world countries (United Kingdom, France, Germany, Canada, etc.), creating competition and conflicts. Sometimes these off-shore companies become too expensive over time, resulting in a strategy to move to even lower-cost countries and options. As we move deeper into the 2020s and beyond, it will be those domestic companies that operate with a well-defined complementary global strategy that will win. *This will take a strategic, well-informed, and high-performing human resource function to do accomplish.* The stakes are high. Those that resist expanding internationally will cease to be able to compete. Those that embrace the challenges and grow their human resource competency to do so will excel.

HRIS IN ACTION

Skylor Electronics,[1] an MNE with headquarters in Seattle, Washington, learned that the European Union (EU) and the U.S. Department of Commerce had just published a Privacy Shield Framework (PSF) to enable data transfers between subsidiaries under EU information protection laws. The vice president for HR, Rosa Martins, became concerned about the costs of internalizing its implementation. An alternative was to hire a vendor, which might offer some advantages, but at a price.

Rosa was looking for the best answer to this problem; she called a meeting with Director of Overseas Operations Elaine Peterson and Director of Career Development Bill Seamon. Bill was quite happy about the new developments, as the previous arrangement, the U.S.–EU Safe Harbor Framework, had shown a number of shortcomings. Elaine did not understand why there was a problem, since she, along with Director of Domestic Operations Dawn Fisher, had successfully managed the automation of HRIS for Skylor in a couple of countries. However, none of them had experience navigating the complexity that compliance with the new PSF regulations would surely entail.

Rosa indicated that she had spoken directly to a few fellow VPs of HR at a local SHRM meeting, and some of them were very uncomfortable with many of the nuances of the new PSF. Rosa directed Bill and Dawn to investigate this problem and to provide a report in 2 weeks. Elaine indicated that she would provide a member of her staff to help with this investigation.

Two weeks later, Bill and Dawn presented their report to Rosa and Elaine. The gist of the report was that they could not make a strong case for one of the two scenarios (hiring an external consultant or joining the PSF without external help). There were pros and cons for each scenario, but their analysis did not seem to identify that one was clearly more advantageous than the other for a company with annual revenues of about $600 million, like Skylor. Bill and Dawn suggested that rather than a cost consideration, this would be a managerial preference. When Rosa mentioned that other companies in the area were seriously considering hiring a vendor, Bill and Dawn showed their benefit-cost analysis (BCA), as described in Chapter 7, in which the benefits, in costs saved, by hiring a vendor minimally exceeded the apparent costs of current employees performing these additional tasks.

INTRODUCTION

Globalization has changed us into a company that searches the world, not just to sell or to source, but to find intellectual capital—the world's best talents and greatest ideas.

—Jack Welch

As noted in Chapter 1, the **globalization of business** is one of the major changes in the world of work. Data from the World Trade Organization (2015) show that merchandise exports around the world have almost quadrupled, from $5,168 billion in 1995 to $19,002 billion in 2014. With respect to commercial services, growth has also gone from $1,179 billion in 1995 to $4,872 billion in 2014. Even though the great recession of 2008 slowed down world trade, the past 20 years show that companies that remain domestic in their geographic scope have a lot to lose. In simple terms, the world's GDP (gross domestic product) is estimated to have reached US$74.152 trillion in 2015; even though the United States, the largest national economy, exceeded US$18.036 trillion in the same year, more than 75% of the world's economic activity takes place elsewhere (World Bank, 2016).

Further illustrating the growing importance for HRM, the strategic implications of globalization for chief human resources officers (CHROs) is the topic of recent reports from the Conference Board (Ark, Ozyildirim, & Levanon, 2015). These reports, which deal with HR's role in mergers, acquisitions, and divestitures, with labor market trends, and with the pressures felt for HR transformation (among other themes), offer evidence that globalization is strongly affecting the HRM field.

Perhaps one of the major changes in the world's business economy has been the formation of regional free-trade zones. The passage of the **North American Free Trade Agreement (NAFTA)** in 1994 established the world's largest free market, increasing trade between the United States, Mexico, and Canada, even if the election of its outspoken critic, Donald Trump, as the 45th president of the United States, suggests that changes are imminent. Subsequently, the European Union (EU) was formed and now includes more than 25 member countries engaged in free trade; this membership has kept growing, despite the UK's "Brexit" vote in mid-2016. Other trade agreements, such as the Association of Southeast Asian Nations (ASEAN), the East Asia Economic Caucus (EAEC), the Asia-Pacific Economic Cooperation (APEC), and the South Asian Association for Regional Cooperation (SAARC), have improved trading relationships in Asia. One can easily foresee that there might be an African and perhaps a Middle Eastern free-trade zone in the future. Even the United States' pulling out of the "Trans-Pacific Partnership" or "Trans Pacific Partnership Agreement" will likely bring about another country coalition that will be ratified in the near future.

A variety of factors have led to the increased globalization of business and the increased importance of the IHRM function in organizations. These factors include: (1) a dramatic increase in global competition; (2) deregulation in the United States, Germany, and other industrialized countries, which has liberalized the domestic business environment and encouraged transnational investments; (3) an increase in international mergers and acquisitions; and (4) an increased awareness of the existence of talented human capital throughout the world. IHRM requires managing human resources worldwide, or, at a minimum, in more than one country.

One of the major factors related to a firm's choosing to have an international presence is the availability and cost-effectiveness of information and communications technology. Information and communication technologies have had a major influence on the acquisition and use of physical and financial resources, as well as greatly enhancing the marketing capabilities of MNEs. However, a most important impact of computer technology has been in HRM. Improved communications, worldwide recruiting and selecting, and better talent and performance management programs tied to career planning are only a few of the HR programs in MNEs that have been improved by the use of computer technology. Still, the increased use and integration of data within the organization faces several challenges and pressures, because the laws with which these systems must comply often differ from country to country. In this chapter, we examine the characteristics of MNEs and the management of people within these enterprises. In addition, we cover the various ways in which computer technology and a well-developed HRIS affect the field of International HRM.[2]

Types of International Business Operations

In today's global economy, organizations tend to compete based on different levels of participation in international markets (Noe, Hollenbeck, Gerhart, & Wright, 2017). International business operations differ primarily by their level of global participation on a continuum from an international corporation to a global corporation. Although many organizations have only limited global scope, a growing number, such as Dell and icrosoft, have a large number of personnel and facilities throughout the world (Snell et al., 2016). The following section provides a brief description of the four types as identified by Beaman (2011) and are based on the types of international business operations described by their level of global participation (Bartlett & Ghoshal, 1998).

International Corporation

An **international corporation** uses its existing core competencies to expand operations into foreign markets (Snell et al., 2016). These organizations' approach is centralized and focused on learning and sharing. This type of organization competes in the global marketplace by exporting existing products and eventually opening facilities in other countries. While their corporate headquarters typically reside in the parent country, international corporations have foreign operations in one or more host countries. Companies operating as international corporations include Honda, General Electric, and Procter & Gamble (see Snell et al., 2016).

This type of international business operation presents various unique challenges for the HRM function of the organization. Two issues particularly relevant to international corporations are the host country's legal system and the host country's national culture. Legal issues might arise because of a country's minimum wage, for example. In some countries, the minimum wage is relatively high, driving up labor costs (Noe et al., 2017). Examples of cultural differences affecting international corporations are communication styles or the meaning and importance of work in the host country; such differences often impact work outcomes such as organizational commitment, job satisfaction, and intention to stay.

Multinational Corporation

A **multinational corporation** is a more complex business operation than an organization that is simply international. In an attempt to capitalize on lower production and distribution costs, multinational corporations' HR role is highly decentralized, is locally responsive, and operates fully autonomous units in multiple countries (Noe et al., 2017; Snell et al., 2016). An example of a multinational corporation is General Motors (GM). While GM's headquarters and some of its operations are located in the United States, many of its manufacturing facilities have been relocated to places such as Mexico and China with the goals of reducing production costs and accessing local markets. Locating facilities to China has allowed GM to sell to the Asian markets with reduced distribution costs. The HRM issues experienced by multinational corporations are similar to those encountered by international corporations, but exacerbated by the fact that there are more countries—and country differences—to take into consideration.

One approach taken by multinational corporations has been to hire local managers or third-country nationals to help with staffing and management issues (Noe et al., 2017). However, according to Noe and colleagues (2017), although hiring local or third-country nationals has its disadvantages, such issues can often be overcome by requiring greater cross-training in cultural and managerial skills.

Global Corporation

Global corporations are similar to international corporations in that their HR functions are highly centralized and focused on efficiency; however, the **global corporation** also integrates its worldwide operations through a centralized home office (Snell et al.,

2016). Multinational corporations produce and distribute identical products and services worldwide. Global corporations, on the other hand, emphasize flexibility and mass customization to meet the needs of differing customer groups worldwide (Noe et al., 2017). Ford represents an example of a global corporation. Ford offers two different lines of automobiles, one to its American consumers and the other to its European consumers. For example, it meets the need of European consumers for smaller, more fuel-efficient cars by offering the Ka—a car similar to Daimler's smart car.

Because of this integrative international focus, global corporations must manage their human resources through a multicountry HRM system. This type of system is characterized by three essential attributes: (1) HR decisions are made from a global rather than a national perspective, (2) the company's management is composed of people from all over the world, and (3) decision-making and planning processes include people from a variety of cultures and backgrounds (Noe et al., 2017).

Transnational Corporation

A **transnational corporation** uses an HR approach that is locally responsible to its country location and is focused on being highly efficient plus emphasizing learning and sharing. The type of international business operation will inevitably influence the way in which the organization manages its human resources. It is feasible to conceptualize organizations on a continuum based on their level of global participation, from the domestic corporation representing the lowest level of global participation to the global corporation representing the highest level of global participation. With this in mind, we provide in the following sections of this chapter a discussion of issues surrounding the management of human resources internationally. Although these distinctions among MNEs are important, the actual structure of the MNE determines its effectiveness. There is no "best structure" that fits the distribution and marketing needs of all MNEs. Perhaps having a flexible approach to structure is the best way to manage an MNE. For example, an HR approach that is locally responsive to its country location is highly efficient and focuses on learning and sharing.

Going Global

For domestic and international firms, becoming a global corporation is a desirable and important step due to potential sales in international markets, in addition to the ability to improve products and services through the lessons learned in different markets. Since going global requires a significant investment, most companies that go global are fairly large and have products or services that would appeal to an international market. However, there are specialty companies for which the international market is also desirable due to country-by-country market niches. Briefly, going global requires considerable planning and learning how global companies and domestic competitors operate. The first step in going global for most companies is to establish a sales office in the countries being considered as potential subsidiary locations. This enables the company to gain important knowledge of the local culture, its regulations, competition, and living conditions. When it is possible, companies also will calculate an initial benefit-cost analysis to determine if the potential ROI indicates they should continue to explore the establishment of a subsidiary in the country.

A number of important HR issues will also need to be addressed when companies make the switch to global expansion. Roberts (2000) raised four issues that companies should consider before deciding to go global: (1) understanding the power of the people, (2) technical issues, (3) cultural clashes, and (4) privacy law hurdles. An example of understanding the power of the people cited by Roberts was that of an electrical component manufacturer in Tennessee that needed 83 faxes just to get a worldwide head count. The company had more than 26,000 employees at 163 sites in 24 countries, so getting an accurate head count was difficult but quite important. Often, companies feel that globalization will surely be able to solve this problem. Related to the power of the people was that a company needs more than monetary resources to go global. It also needs the willing participation of all parties involved. This process of globalization was a major organizational step, and it needed to be implemented carefully (see Chapter 9).

The second problem, according to Roberts, that most people assume to be solved easily involves the technical issues and changes needed to globalize. Decisions will have to be made about in which technologies to invest, how to integrate them, and how data are shared between countries and divisions. In addition, issues such as employee readiness for new technology, privacy laws, and the types of devices (e.g., mobile, laptop, desktop, etc.) that will be utilized will need to be addressed. Mason (2009) argues that technology can help to standardize and streamline HR practices globally. We discuss more about this later in the chapter when we discuss the role of HRIS in these firms.

Culture, the third of Roberts' issues, is also highly important; some even argue it to be the most important for any company going global. Many attempts to go global have failed because the employees from the home country location have difficulties with the cultural diversity in other countries. Working styles in countries may be entirely different, with strict levels of hierarchy and formalities expected in some countries, while others may not have this structure.

The fourth issue deals with the varying, country-by-country, privacy laws. For example, the privacy laws in the United States are more liberal than the ones in the **European Union (EU)**. In addition, most countries, including those in the EU, have data privacy laws specific to their own country. Batyski (2008) notes that this will require HR staff, and even managers who handle employee data, to be well trained in the privacy laws for each country in which the company operates. Notwithstanding the emerging Privacy Shield Framework (PSF) recently negotiated between the U.S. and the EU (see HRIS in Action section), differing privacy laws can also impact HR reporting requirements. HR must be aware of country-specific requirements surrounding the tracking of employee data, and the HRIS utilized must be able to account for these differences. For example, in some countries, the tracking of union membership is allowed, but in others, it is not. These differing regulations and reporting requirements make it very difficult to implement an HRIS that spans multiple countries and accounts for the country-specific nuances in data collection and reporting. Thus, many firms are likely to implement multiple HR systems throughout the world to remain compliant with these differences.

In the *2011–2012 Going Global Report: HCM Trends in Globalization*, Beaman (2011) describes the decision of "going global" as quite difficult and time consuming. Jeitosa Group International, in collaboration with the **International Association for Human Resource Information Management (IHRIM)**, completed a survey of 130 multinational organizations from diverse industry sectors that focused on the factors that lead a corporation to "go global." The survey was designed to answer these questions:

1. How does an organization decide when it should go global?

2. How does it determine whether its HR department and HRIS are ready?

3. Are its business and HR functions capable of supporting a move to a global level for the organization?

Figure 13.1 lists a number of challenges that organizations face when going global. Interestingly, the top four challenges identified in this survey—time zone differences (39%), lack of resources (36%), cultural differences (33%), and international compliance (33%)—are the same challenges facing global organizations for years (Adler, 2002; Briscoe & Schuler, 2004; Dowling, Festing, & Engle, 2013). This survey also queried respondents about the key competencies for successful global work. As seen in Figure 13.2, the top five are a global mindset (67%), cultural intelligence (64%), strategic thinking (64%), adaptability to change (47%), and accommodation/flexibility (38%). The next five key competencies are all focused on management: leadership skills, decision-making ability, analytic thinking, interpersonal skills, and business acumen. As a set, these 10 competences indicate that professionals and managers working in global companies need to develop these competencies through training and experience in order for the global company to be successful. We agree with Beaman (2011):

> Going global with HR and HR technology is challenging, but can be rewarding too. While the industry is making progress, there is more work to do. (p. 28)

The difficulties involved in managing the workforce of any MNE, including a global one, are covered in the remainder of this chapter.

Differences in HRM in MNEs

Even though a number of different types of international business operations were described in the previous section, for convenience, these types will all be referred to as **multinational enterprises (MNEs)**. As one might expect, there are significant differences in HRM programs and practices between a domestic enterprise and an MNE. Because the

FIGURE 13.1 ■ Top Challenges in Working Globally

Source: Beaman (2011, p. 5). Reprinted with permission. Group International & IHRIM, New York, NY. Figure 4.

FIGURE 13.2 ■ Key Competencies for Successful Global Work

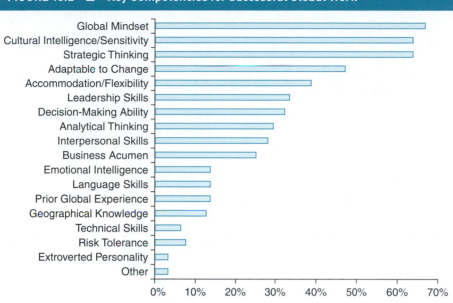

Source: Beaman (2011, p. 13). Reprinted with permission.

domestic organization only operates in one labor market, managing its human resources is much easier than is the case for MNEs. MNEs operate in multiple countries and must have information on the labor markets in all the countries in which they do business.

In addition, a MNE includes three types of employees, as opposed to one type in a domestic firm. These MNE employees include **parent-country nationals (PCNs)**, **host-country nationals (HCNs)**, and **third-country nationals (TCNs)**. PCNs are from the country in which the corporate headquarters of the MNE is located, while HCNs are from the countries where subsidiaries are located. TCNs are employees from countries other than the parent or host countries. In spite of these differences in the types of employees hired by a domestic enterprise and an MNE, the major programs of HRM, for example, talent management and compensation, exist in both domestic and international organizations. However, the fact that an MNE competes in multiple countries versus the single-country orientation of a domestic company contributes to the complexity of IHRM. Dowling et al. (2013) identify six key factors that contribute to the complexity of international HR management:

- More HR activities: An HR department in an international firm must be concerned with activities that would not be part of an HR department in a domestic firm, for example, relations with host governments; differences in labor laws and guidelines in the host country; and administrative details of the employees, such as international taxation, international relocation, orientation, and language training.

- The need for a broader perspective: The HR department and managers in MNEs need a broader worldview in dealing with PCNs, HCNs, and TCNs, and recognition of both the cultural differences among employees and the differences in work ethic, practices, and expectations in the employees' home countries.

- More involvement in employees' personal lives: The IHRM department is more involved in the lives of employees in the areas of taxation, education, and even banking services. It also has to address the issue of visas and housing arrangements for PCNs (expatriates) and TCNs.

- Changes in emphasis of HR programs, such as compensation, managerial style, and tolerance of employee diversity, as the workforce mix of expatriates and locals varies. The immense pool of talent available to MNEs means a varying mix of PCNs, HCNs, and TCNs in the workforce. Consequently, a number of different languages will often be spoken. This situation would dictate language training to support a common language for employees and to improve communication in the working environment.

- Risk exposure: The IHRM department must be aware of the risks to its employees and keep them apprised of any significant problems (e.g., terrorist threats, impending war, crime in specific locations, and environmental disasters). It must be prepared for any necessary evacuation of employees.

- Broader external influences: Many factors can affect the operation and activities of IHRM in multiple countries, such as government regulations and relations, the labor market, societal concerns, and the level of technology.

Key HR Management Issues in MNEs

Managing in the global business environment creates unique complexities for managers—especially expatriate managers. In the past, organizations have relied on expatriates as a major source of staffing for their overseas operations (Schuler & Tarique, 2007). Today though, organizations are increasingly shifting from an expatriate-focused workforce to a global workforce. Beaman (2008) argues that "it is only by first 'thinking locally' to truly understand the needs of our local business communities, and then 'acting globally' to seamlessly knit together diverse business functions and (HR) systems into a holistic, global approach that we can build an effective, efficient and competitive organization" (p. 6). In other words, building a global workforce will require a mix of local and expatriate employees working together. Some of the most important cultural factors include diversity, education, politics and law, and economics (see Snell et al., 2016).

Global Diversity and Inclusion

In many locations, the drives for increased diversity and inclusion have their basis in equal employment legislation. But beyond the legal requirements, there are additional reasons for supporting a diverse workforce. These include (1) the moral issue of discrimination in hiring and promotion on the basis of gender and race and (2) the business case that increasing diversity and inclusion will improve the financial position of the MNE. The business case simply states that if the consumer population is diverse, it behooves an MNE to have a diverse workforce.

Organizations are increasingly recognizing the importance of having a global approach to the hiring and management of employees in order to remain competitive in the global marketplace. This search for new employees must take account of cultural differences in multiple countries by recognizing the importance of developing greater cross-cultural competence in their employees. "Driven by a need to compensate for talent shortages—and compete in an increasingly diverse marketplace—companies are extending their recruiting and promotion efforts to groups that traditionally were under-represented or not present at all" (SHRM, 2009, p. 5).

Having this type of a workforce means that the educational level, skills, background, and cultural values of the workforce will be highly varied. It is important for managers to understand and deal with the human capital needs of a highly diverse workforce made up of individuals (1) coming from different cultural backgrounds, (2) possibly speaking different languages, and (3) having different educational experiences. These education differences require that managers provide a supportive work environment for their employees. One important aspect of support is training on (1) cultural differences, (2) verbal and nonverbal communication, and (3) specific skill sets particular to the employee's job. In order to survive, organizations must manage differences so that employees from all backgrounds can be heard, be understood, and be able to work together productively.

Political and Legal Systems

The political and legal systems within the host country will affect the type of HR practices that can be used (Noe et al., 2017). The laws and regulations of the host country are determined in part by the societal norms of that country. For example, the United States has created laws governing issues such as equal employment opportunities and fair pay standards (Noe et al., 2017); however, these laws are specific to the United States, and similar laws may or may not necessarily exist in other countries. In addition, free speech is a **cultural norm** in the United States and is protected by law. It is acceptable for organizations and individuals to speak out against the government if they do not like certain government regulations or taxes or if they think they are being unfairly treated. However, in other parts of the world, it may be highly inappropriate, and occasionally even dangerous, for organizations to speak out against the government. On the other hand, U.S. companies may impose a certain degree of censorship on employees, as long as a business necessity exists. In other countries, employees might be protected by law or by highly regulated severance practices.

Economic System

The economic system of the host country is one determinant of the way in which HR programs and practices are used. This economic system affects human capital primarily through its compensation system (Noe et al., 2017). Countries such as Germany, Switzerland, and Japan have strong educational systems and provide employees with high wages. In comparison, third-world countries such as the Philippines, Afghanistan, and Haiti have poorer educational systems and provide substantially lower compensation to their workforces. A study by the U.S. Department of Labor (2012) indicates that the average compensation for employees in the manufacturing sector in the Philippines was $2.01 per hour, compared to $35.53 per hour for manufacturing employees in the United States. If the workforce of an MNE in the Philippines were composed of employees from both the Philippines and the United States, an equity issue might arise and must be managed effectively.

HR PROGRAMS IN GLOBAL ORGANIZATIONS

International Staffing

The complexities inherent in managing a global organization make staffing an especially important part of the IHRM system. When staffing for managerial and nonmanagerial positions, the MNE needs to determine if personnel will be selected from the home-country, host-country, or third-country talent pool.

As described by Snell et al. (2016), each of these employee groups provides a different advantage for the MNE. A common issue for all of these employee groups, however, is the underutilization of and lower pay for female employees (Adlung, 2010). Adlung found that in a number of European countries, females received approximately 25% less salary than their male counterparts. This point suggests that MNEs should emphasize hiring female employees and paying them fairly. Adlung suggests that companies could utilize an integrated talent management system such as PeopleSoft, TalentSoft, or SuccessFactors to leverage this untapped talent pool and reduce the salary gap between male and female employees.

Selecting Global Managers: Managing Expatriates

One of the most difficult but important responsibilities of the IHRM function is the selection of managers from the parent country for assignments in host countries. Most of the literature on this topic is focused on the selection of expatriates, whether they are PCNs, HCNs, or TCNs. The reason expatriates can be from any of these three categories is that, at the managerial level in an MNE, these individuals will move from country to country. Thus, the term **expatriate** will be used to designate global managers, regardless of the home country. To understand the difficulty in selecting expatriates, we will discuss in this section (1) the **cultural environment of countries**, (2) expatriate failure and its causes, and (3) selection criteria and procedures for expatriates.

The Cultural Environment of Countries

One of the most important aspects of an expatriate's job that will significantly affect performance is his or her interaction with the local government and people of a country. Because of this interaction, most expatriates will experience **culture shock** as they move from country to country within an MNE. Culture shock can be mild, for example, for a German manager who relocates to a subsidiary plant in France, or quite severe, for example, for an Australian manager who moves to a subsidiary in Egypt. Thus, one of the most important tasks of the IHRM department is to gather information about the culture of countries where the MNE does business to try to estimate the cultural differences between the home countries of employees and the countries where they may be assigned. An HRIS can be very useful in that it can serve as a repository of this information, and, thus, cultural profiles of countries can be quickly generated.

Further emphasizing the importance of a country's culture, Briscoe and Schuler (2004) state,

> Knowledge about and competency in working with country and company cultures is the most important issue impacting the success of international business activity. And possibly the area of business that is most impacted by cultural differences is the human resource function. (p. 114)

Culture, as defined by Hofstede (1991), "is the collective programming of the mind which distinguishes the members of one group or category of people from another" (p. 6). Hofstede's research was the first systematic study of the dimensions of **national culture**, and he identified five dimensions on which the cultures of countries differ. In addition to Hofstede's work, other studies have examined differences in national culture (GLOBE Research Team, 2002; Trompenaars, 1992). Trompenaars, like Hofstede, found five distinct cultural factors that differentiated country cultures, while the Global Leadership and Organizational Behavior Effectiveness (GLOBE) research project categorized countries on nine cultural dimensions. Regardless of which study we examine, all of the authors cited in this chapter agree that the cultural environment of a country has a strong effect on the management of employees and should be considered when selecting expatriates or implementing people management practices.

To define the culture of a country, Snell et al. (2016) list the following elements that will differentiate countries in terms of their cultural environment for international business: (1) education/human capital, (2) values/ideologies, (3) social structure, (4) religious beliefs, and (5) communication. Information gathered in these five categories could be used to create profiles of the cultural environment of countries in which the MNE does business. It is most important to emphasize that this information could be stored electronically in the HRIS and maintained by the IHRM department. Major HRIS suites such as Oracle's and SAP's have this capability, or it can be customized by the MNE.

A final note on country culture: It will have an *effect on all the activities and programs* of the IHRM function, including selection, training, compensation, and performance management.

Expatriate Failure and Causes

Expatriate failure is defined as the return of an expatriate to the home country before the period of the assignment has been completed. Thus, expatriate failure represents an error in a selection or follow-up decision. There is such an emphasis on expatriate failure because of its costs to the MNE. These costs are both direct and indirect. Direct costs include the actual money spent on selecting and training, relocation costs for the expatriate (and family), and salary. These costs can be quite substantial. However, indirect costs can frequently be higher than direct costs. Indirect costs are harder to quantify, but they could include loss of market share in the country, negative reactions from the host country's government, and possible negative effects on local employee morale. For example, expatriate failure could lead a local host government to insist that, in the future, only an HCN fill the position. Finally, there will be the indirect costs experienced by the returning expatriate in terms of personal failure, loss of respect by peers, and possibly negative influences on future promotions.

What are the causes of expatriate failure? Although there has been considerable research on this topic, the answer is not completely clear. It is safe to say that one cannot generalize from the research results to every expatriate situation; however, the results do provide a guide to the information that should be collected during the selection of expatriates. In general, one could state that the major factor affecting expatriate failure is the *inability to adjust to the new situation and culture* by the expatriate and her or his family.

In terms of specific reasons for expatriate failure, Dowling et al. (2013) cite the global surveys of the Organizational Research Counselors (ORC; 2002) and the GMAC Global Relocation Services and Windham International (2002). The problems reported by expatriates and companies in these surveys were

- spouse/partner dissatisfaction,

- inability to adapt,

- difficulties with family adjustment in the new location,

- difficulties associated with different management styles,

- culture and language difficulties, and

- issues associated with the accompanying partner's career development.

Similarly, Briscoe and Schuler (2004) indicate that "a number of surveys and studies have found that the most important factors in the early return of expatriates . . . lie in the inability of their families (and/or themselves) to adjust to the foreign environment" (p. 242). The clear implication of these findings is that the expatriate's family or partner must be considered in the selection decision process.

Selection Criteria and Procedures for Expatriates

In selecting expatriates, IHRM professionals should remember that the selection process is an exchange between the organization and the employee. Furthermore, the prospective expatriate's family must be involved in the exchange. In terms of the utility of selection, that is its cost-effectiveness (covered in Chapter 12), making a mistake is extremely costly. IHRM professionals must be cognizant of the causes of expatriate failure when developing the selection procedures, for example, tests or interviews, and also have an understanding of the cross-cultural issues in the evaluation and recommendation of employees for an expatriate assignment.

The factors involved in the selection of expatriates can be divided into two general categories—individual and situational (Dowling et al., 2013). In the individual category are technical ability, **cross-cultural suitability**, and family requirements. Technical ability is quite clear and would include both managerial and technical skills. The person selected must be technically proficient in his or her field (e.g., electrical engineering) and also must have a good performance record as a manager. Technical ability is very important to the selection process, as indicated by the results of the ORC worldwide survey (2002), in that 72% of responding firms used it as the first screening criterion in their selection procedure. In selection terms, technical ability would be the *absolute minimum* requirement for the first screening of prospective employees for the assignment. Note that technical incompetence or poor performance is not mentioned as a cause of expatriate failure; however, job-related factors could possibly cause premature departure—for example, the nature of the job not being as described or the expatriate being unable to transfer technical or managerial skills to the new assignment.

The second individual factor, cross-cultural suitability, has several aspects. It could include language ability, cultural empathy, adaptability, and a positive attitude toward the assignment in the specific country being considered. Although technical ability is very important for success in the assignment, cross-cultural suitability is equally important, since a number of the causes of expatriate failure are directly related to this factor.

The third individual factor, family requirements, has a great deal to do with the success of the expatriate's assignment. In all the research and surveys on causes for expatriate failure, the poor adjustment of the accompanying spouse or partner and children has been well documented as one of the major causes of expatriate failure. Although it is appropriate to use standard testing and interview techniques to assess the technical ability and cross-cultural suitability of potential expatriates, evaluation of these factors means the involvement of the family. Interviewing the candidate's spouse or partner and children regarding the assignment is frequently done. In addition, most MNEs have learned to build in a preassignment visit for the expatriate candidate and his or her family as part of the selection process. This involvement of the entire family in the selection process has become a common practice for MNEs. In fact, if there are two possible locations for the assignment, companies may encourage a preassignment visit to both countries.

With regard to the general factors that affect the assignment situation, Dowling et al. (2013) list country and cultural requirements, language, and MNE requirements. Country and cultural requirements could include work permits and visas. Generally, the work permit is given to the expatriate, and the accompanying spouse or partner may not be permitted to work. As for the children, there may not be schools that would be acceptable, particularly if the children do not speak the language of the host country. In some expatriate assignments, the children either receive language training or there is a school in which their native language is spoken. The opportunity for the spouse or partner and the children to learn another language is sometimes seen as a benefit of the international assignment.

Of course, this relates to the second factor of language. Difficulties in language are a major barrier to cross-cultural communication; thus, this is a very important factor for the expatriate and the family. Fortunately, many companies offer language training to the entire family prior to departure for the assignment. In addition, the increasing availability of technologically mediated language training (including smartphone apps, Web-based courses, etc.) as well as translation services, may reduce the magnitude of language difficulties. The final factor, MNE requirements, could involve getting permission from the host country for the selection of any expatriate. This is common in joint international ventures. Other factors could be the duration and type of assignment. When the duration of the assignment is for only 2 to 3 months or the assignment is in a "high-risk" country, the family members usually would not accompany the expatriate.

Selection of expatriates is a critical function of IHRM, particularly in MNEs where expatriate assignments are used to "groom" managers for higher levels of management. Many of the factors to consider in selecting expatriates and the factors causing expatriate failure are handled by training. However, the software applications available can greatly reduce the time required to make this process work. The next section focuses on training in the MNE, primarily the training of expatriates.

Training and Development of Expatriates

As was done in the previous section, all managers in an MNE will be considered as expatriates, since their career assignments and development typically mean that they will move from country to country. Training and development activities and programs in MNEs also include nonmanagerial employees of all types—PCNs, HCNs, and TCNs. Because traditional training and development were covered in detail in Chapter 11, most kinds of typical organizational training (e.g., orientation or technical training) will not be discussed. However, the use of an HRIS and its applications will still be discussed. In fact, the training applications that are integrated into the HRIS are increasingly useful for training expatriates. Not only will the expatriates' personal, work experience, and skills information stored on the HRIS be easily accessible, but also the results of the training in terms of expatriate success or failure can be recorded. This information should be useful for future expatriate selection.

The corporate IHRM department has responsibility for all training; however, this responsibility is usually decentralized by delegating it to the MNE's subsidiaries. There may be training programs developed at the headquarters of the MNE, but it is unusual for these IHRM professionals at headquarters to deliver programs to the subsidiaries when it can be done more economically by the local IHRM professionals. Most of this local training for nonmanagerial employees will vary by different geographic locations of the MNE. Therefore, some cross-cultural training for nonmanagerial employees who are not HCNs will be necessary, for example, language training.

This section will cover expatriate training in detail and will be divided into the following subsections: (1) the purpose of expatriate training, (2) **predeparture training** and the repatriation of expatriates, and (3) **transfer of training**.

Purpose of Expatriate Training

The dual purpose of any training program is to inform and motivate employees. Even training that is focused on learning a manual skill, for example, keyboarding, has both knowledge and motivational aspects. Clearly, the employee is learning a new skill, but with the proper training method, the employee can be encouraged to be more productive; and with the improved skill, the employee may be happier in the job. In addition to these two purposes of training, the first specific purpose of expatriate training is to supplement the selection process and assist the expatriate and her or his family in adjusting to the new situation. It must be emphasized that selection of expatriates is never perfect. Why else would there be expatriate failure? Thus, the training program content for expatriates should incorporate adjustment training and discuss the causes of expatriate failure.

The second specific purpose of expatriate training is economic. Recall that the expatriate brings both technical and managerial expertise to the subsidiary when there are no HCNs ready to fill the positions. In addition, the expatriate assignment is used by MNEs as a career development process for managers. Thus, the MNE has significant economic reasons for using expatriates. When one calculates the potential **direct costs of expatriate failure**, the amount of the investment increases. The MNE makes a major investment in selecting employees for placement in its subsidiaries, and training programs are another IHRM element used to protect that investment.

Predeparture Training

It should be noted that predeparture training programs do not focus on the technical ability of the expatriate unless there are new technical or managerial skills necessary for the assignment, for example, the introduction of new technology. Because one of the major causes of expatriate failure is the dissatisfaction of or the lack of adjustment by the employee's spouse, partner, or family, the inclusion of these people in predeparture training is very important. To assist the adjustment of the expatriate and his or her family to a new culture, predeparture training typically includes training in cultural awareness, language, and practical matters regarding daily living in the new culture. Most MNEs will also include preliminary visits as a part of predeparture training.

Another element in predeparture training that is highly recommended is **repatriation** training. Formal repatriation is the process that occurs as the expatriate and family return to their homeland. However, recent research and literature has indicated that the repatriation process should begin before the person leaves the home country. The expatriate may find on return that the situation that was expected in the home country (e.g., a promotion to a new position) is not available; and thus, the expatriate will seek other employment. This problem of losing expatriates during the repatriation process has been well documented in the literature (Black, 2000; Feldman & Tompson, 1993; Poe, 2000; Solomon, 1995). There is considerable discussion in the recent literature on the design and implementation of repatriation programs that suggests that companies need to begin repatriation training prior to the expatriate leaving the home country—in predeparture training—rather than waiting for the return of the expatriate (Briscoe & Schuler, 2004; Dowling et al., 2013; Evans, Pucik, & Barsoux, 2002), and most companies consider repatriation part of the career development program of the MNE.

Training in cultural awareness, language, and practical matters regarding daily living in the new culture constitutes the predeparture training that the expatriate and family will attend. It is important to recall that expatriate selection is a two-way street. The expatriate still has the right to decline the assignment. Thus, the predeparture training both informs and attracts, which are the two purposes of training. A large number of topics can be included in predeparture training. The topics listed in Table 13.1 make up possible content for the predeparture program. Note that this list could change depending on the host and parent countries involved.

TABLE 13.1 ■ Topics for Predeparture Training
1. Cultural values and religions
2. Websites for country information
3. Country history, recommended readings, videos,* and achievements in the country
4. Classical literature describing the country's history, its folkways, and heroes and heroines
5. Information about other HCN expatriates in the country
6. Information on job opportunities for spouses and partners
7. Descriptions of the educational facilities and opportunities for families
8. Current news about the country, particularly its relationship to the parent country
9. Traditional family roles of father, mother, and children
10. Locations for shopping and shopping hours
11. Dominant language of country; extent of bilingualism in country
12. Nonverbal gestures and their meanings
13. Political structure, particularly as it affects the operation of the MNE
14. Descriptions of currency, temperature variations, transportation, hours of business
15. Sightseeing, including historic, artistic, and important cultural locations that would appeal to all the family

Note: This is a very general list, which will vary from country to country.

*Videos, Web-based, and even app-based training may be made available to expatriates and their families.

Transfer of Training

The idea that the predeparture training program could change as a function of the two countries involved has been recognized by scholars, and several models have been proposed to provide guidelines on predeparture training programs (Mendenhall, Dunbar, & Oddou, 1987; Tung, 1981, 1998). These researchers argue that predeparture training should not be viewed as "one size fits all" but rather that the training design and program should be contingent on other factors in the expatriate assignment. According to Tung (1981, 1998), the two factors that most affect predeparture training design are (1) the dissimilarity between the expatriate's native country and the host culture—low to high—and (2) the expected amount of interaction between the expatriate and members of the host country—low to high. Based on an analysis of these two factors, Black and Mendenhall (1989) argue that the design of the training program can then vary on three dimensions: (1) the training methods used, (2) the level of training rigor, and (3) the duration of the training program. For example, if both the dissimilarity between the expatriate's native country and the host culture and the expected amount of interaction between the expatriate and members of the host country are quite high, then the predeparture training should be rigorous, and the length of training should be 1 to 2 months. In this situation, the training methods would attempt to immerse the expatriate in the host country's culture through assessment centers, simulations, sensitivity training, and extensive language training. As mentioned earlier, the use of the HRIS to track and analyze the success or failure of these training programs will enable the MNE to make more effective decisions about expatriates and their training in the future.

Performance Appraisal in MNEs

Performance appraisal is an important process for documenting the performance of employees, determining areas for development, deciding on pay increases and promotional opportunities, and giving employees the opportunity to express their views (Von Glinow, Drost, & Teagarden, 2002). The type of performance appraisal conducted and its content depend on the specific job requirements and personal attributes of the person being appraised (Schuler, Budhwar, & Florkowski, 2002). This is particularly true when we compare the appraisal of expatriates with that of HCN and TCN employees. The section in Chapter 12 on performance evaluation and performance planning covers a number of HRIS applications that could be used for performance appraisal in an MNE. Naturally, the inclusion of plants with a diverse employee population in multiple countries creates considerable complexity, particularly when the results of the appraisals are being used to move managers from country to country. However, most vendors of HRIS products have packaged software applications available that can be modified for local conditions in each specific country.

Appraising Expatriate Performance

Important considerations in the appraisal of an expatriate's performance are who should conduct the appraisal and what performance criteria are specific to the expatriate's situation (Snell et al., 2016). The first question is who should complete the performance appraisal. Typically, the performance of employees is appraised by their supervisors. Expatriate managers are geographically distanced from their parent-country supervisors, and, as a result, supervisors who are located in the parent country cannot observe the day-to-day activities of these employees (Dowling et al., 2013). Therefore, managers of expatriates tend to base their evaluations of the person on the objective criteria used for other employees in similar positions located in the parent country. A potential problem with this type of assessment is that the parent-country manager does not have direct information or observational data about the more subjective performance criteria, such as the expatriate manager's leadership skills or performance within the context of the subsidiary (Borman & Motowidlo, 1993). Moreover, the supervisor located in the parent country may not be aware of culturally bound biases that constrain the job performance of the expatriate manager.

Because of these complexities, it may be most appropriate to obtain multiple ratings of the expatriate's performance through the use of a 360° feedback system (Dowling et al., 2013). Ratings of the expatriate manager's performance could be garnered from his or her superiors, peers, and subordinates in the expatriate assignment, as well as from the expatriate himself or herself. This would provide a clearer picture of the expatriate's total job performance. In fact, in a study of 58 U.S. multinational firms, Gregersen, Hite, and Black (1996) found that 81% of the companies used more than one rater when assessing the job performance of expatriate employees. Evidently, HRIS with culturally consistent user interfaces and well-designed privacy, security, and useful outputs may go a long way to guarantee acceptance and create an equalitarian organizational culture.

Managing International Compensation

The management of compensation[3] in an MNE is one of the most complex but critically important functions of the IHRM department. Its complexity comes from having a mix of PCNs, HCNs, and TCNs within one company and, thus, having to handle wage, salary, and benefits information that differs across countries. As a result, the IHRM compensation manager must be aware of differences in taxation, labor laws affecting compensation and benefits, currency fluctuations, and cost-of-living differences within and between countries where the MNE has a presence. The criticality of compensation and benefits management by the IHRM rests, in part, on the effects that salary and benefits have on employee motivation. In spite of differences across countries regarding the motivational factors in the workplace, money seems to be consistently at the top of the list.

The other reason for the critical importance of compensation management in subsidiaries is its link to the strategy of the MNE. To help us understand some of the important elements and dynamics of compensation in an MNE, this section will cover (1) the objectives of international compensation, (2) the components of international compensation, and (3) two approaches to international compensation.

The Objectives of International Compensation Policy

Actually, the objectives of a compensation policy in an MNE are similar to those in a domestic company. It has been fairly well established in the management research literature that compensation administration is closely related to the strategy of the firm. For example, if the company has forecasted increased sales in the next year and thus has determined a need for new employees with specialized skills, it may be necessary to pay above the labor market's "going salary rate" in order to get the best available individuals. This necessity would be especially true when information from the labor market indicates that there is a shortage of people in a particular country having the skills needed for the target job—for example, computer programmers. Similarly, when the labor market statistics indicate that there is an abundance of people with the skills necessary for a specific job, it would be recommended that the compensation level match the labor market values.

As in a domestic firm, the *first objective* for an MNE is to align its compensation administration with the strategy of the firm. Of course, compared with the domestic firm, this alignment is much more complex for the MNE. It requires the MNE to have accurate and up-to-date labor market compensation information for all the countries in which it has a presence. This requirement is one of the most powerful advantages of having an HRIS with labor market information for the IHRM department. Labor market statistics, such as average compensation as well as forecasted shortages and surpluses for jobs, are available for most countries and can be stored in the HRIS. The applications in the computer software that produce analyses of these data would be quite similar to those described in Chapter 12. However, it should be clear that the reports generated from the HRIS would be significantly more complex in an MNE, since multiple countries would be involved.

The *second objective* of compensation administration in an MNE, as in a domestic firm, is to affect employee motivation in several ways. It must motivate employees to (1) join the firm, (2) be productive while members of the firm, and (3) stay with the firm. Employee motivation, then, is an important objective of an MNE's international compensation policy, which is complicated, since multiple cultures are involved. Although most cultures see monetary rewards as motivational, there are clear differences across world cultures in terms of the other factors that motivate employee behaviors. For example, the meaningfulness of the work may be very important in some cultures, whereas the opportunity for promotion would be most important in other cultures.

The *final objective* of compensation policy for an MNE is that it must be perceived as fair by the employees. This notion of fairness or equity has been shown to be a powerful motivator of human behavior (Colquitt, Conlon, Wesson, Porter, & Ng, 2001), and it may be the most important objective of an international compensation policy. Given the mix of employees from different companies (PCNs, HCNs, TCNs), *perceived or real* differences in wages or benefits between groups of employees could lead to considerable dissatisfaction among the less privileged groups and consequently affect the retention of employees. Easily understandable user interfaces in compensation-related HR information systems should be essential for organizations interested in increasing transparency in and satisfaction with pay packages designed to support the company's strategy.

The Components of International Compensation

The components of an international compensation system are very similar to those of a domestic program. The major components are a base salary and a set of benefits. However, extra pay premiums would be much more complex for an MNE. For example, there are foreign-service or hardship premia for expatriates, whether they are from the parent or a third country. Other premiums could be based on the "risk level" of the assignment in the country. Although most domestic companies give cost-of-living allowances (COLAs) based on where one works (e.g., rural vs. urban locations), MNEs must also use between- and within-country COLAs to have an equitable and attractive compensation system. These considerations, along with the other compensation issues discussed, make managing the compensation system a "living nightmare" for the IHRM department. Having the employee, country, and compensation/benefits data in an HRIS means that IHRM professionals have the ability to access important information quickly for making both policy and operational decisions about compensation in an MNE.

Two Approaches to International Compensation

The IHRM textbooks mentioned earlier in this chapter (Briscoe & Schuler, 2004; Dowling et al., 2013; Evans et al., 2002) all discuss two approaches to international compensation—the **going-rate** and the **balance-sheet approaches**. In the going-rate or **host-country approach** (Snell et al., 2016), the base salary for international employees is tied to the salary levels in the host country. For example, an expatriate would earn pay that is comparable with the salaries of employees in the host country. Thus, the compensation levels for employees would depend on wage surveys of (1) local nationals (HCNs), (2) expatriates of the same nationality, and (3) expatriates of all nationalities (Dowling et al., 2013). For low-pay countries, the base pay and benefits could be supplemented with additional payments. It should be obvious that HRIS applications for compensation based on the going rate would be useful for establishing initial compensation levels, particularly for expatriates. Having this database would also be quite useful for handling complaints by any MNE employee regarding the equity of his or her compensation. Computer-based compensation applications are available from the major providers of software platforms such as Oracle or SAP.

The second approach to compensation policy, the balance-sheet approach, has as its goal the maintenance of a home-country living standard plus a financial inducement for accepting an international assignment. As Dowling et al. (2013) note, "The home-country pay and benefits are the foundation of this approach; adjustments to home package to balance additional expenditure in the host country and financial incentives (expatriate/hardship premium) are added to make the package attractive." Although this approach would appear to be more attractive to the expatriate, it has a disadvantage for the IHRM department—it can be very complex to administer. Software applications and reports from an HRIS can assist in untangling these objectives, and probably perceived inequalities, but IHRM professional and line managers are still required to explain these programs to employees.

In sum, compensation is probably the most difficult and complex of the HR programs to implement and administer in an MNE. However, it is critically important to the equity exchange (or psychological contract) between the company and its employees; in consequence, it is likely to affect employee motivation. Interactions between employees and their immediate supervisors in a domestic enterprise or an MNE regarding compensation have the greatest impact on motivation of the employees. Having an HRIS produce the needed data and information on the equity of compensation among employees is a tremendous boon to employee relations.

HRIS APPLICATIONS IN IHRM

Introduction

It should be apparent from the previous sections of this chapter that HRM in an MNE is significantly more complex than in a domestic firm. As business becomes more global, ignoring its international aspects would be foolish. Among the challenges facing these companies last century were lack of sources for and the slow speed of transmission of important HR information for effective management decisions. However, with the current technologies and applications, difficulties in executing the basic HR functions of planning, recruiting, selecting, training, and managing performance in MNEs have been reduced through more sophisticated and better integrated HRIS.

Mason (2009) suggests that the successful implementation of a HRIS depends on three factors: (1) choosing the right vendor for technology, (2) choosing the right platform for HRIS implementation, and (3) ensuring a smooth company rollout. Johnson and Gueutal (2011) also suggest that "using external vendors is generally more cost effective and often will provide a more complete HR solution" (p. 2); they go on to compare choosing an "integrated solution" that supports multiple HR subfunctions with "best-of-breed solutions" in which organizations work with several vendors to supply the best available HRIS solution for each of their functional areas. Ruël and Bondarouk (2012) also note that e-HRM trends may help discern the extent to which HR practices are converging (or diverging) across nations.

Specific HRIS applications for MNEs have been noted previously, mostly in concert with software platforms such as Oracle and SAP. These two platforms have all HR applications needed for a global corporation. Not only are these the only software providers available for software applications in the IHRM field, but they are also good starting points for the student interested in examining the variety of software that can be used in an HRIS. Thus, this last section of this chapter will focus on broader issues in the application and use of an HRIS in IHRM. Problems and potential solutions will be examined and discussed briefly under three topics: (1) organizational structure for effectiveness, (2) IHRM–HRIS administrative issues, and (3) HRIS applications in MNEs.

Organizational Structure for Effectiveness

The issue of the *most effective* structure for the operation of an HRIS in an MNE has been a "moving target." The most common advice regarding the management of an MNE has been to "**think global, act local.**" This advice applies to the total management process of an MNE—its strategy, operations, finance, marketing, and HR—and has been followed religiously for many years in international management. However, Beaman (2008) has provided arguments for a different approach, at least in terms of the development and use of an HRIS in international organizations. As she states,

> I maintain that we have been going about globalization the wrong way. The slogan, "Think Global, Act Local" . . . is completely the inverse of what we should be doing with our HRIT [synonym for HRIS] organizations. Rather, it is only by first "thinking locally" to truly understand the needs of our local business communities, and then "acting globally" to seamlessly knit together diverse business functions and systems into a holistic, global approach that we can build an effective, efficient and competitive organization. (p. 6)

A well-established piece of advice in the management literature has been that "structure does not drive success—people do." So to build an organizational structure for an HRIS in an MNE, we should consider Beaman's very reasonable suggestion.

IHRM–HRIS Administrative Issues

Service-Oriented Architecture (SOA)

It may be repetitive, but it is important to reexamine some of the HRIS approaches covered in Chapter 8 in terms of HRIS applications in an MNE. These applications can be much more useful in an international firm than in a domestic one. One of the most important approaches for handling administrative issues in an MNE is the use of a service-oriented architecture (SOA). As discussed in Chapter 8, an SOA "is a paradigm for organizing and utilizing distributed [computing] capabilities that may be under the control of different ownership domains . . . providing a uniform means to offer, discover, interact with and use capabilities to produce desired [business] effects" (OASIS, 2006, p. 8). SOA is focused on providing a service for a function that is well-defined, self-contained, and context and platform independent, a function that adds value to the organization's business purpose rather than simply being focused on the technology itself. In effect, SOA is a collection of internal and external services that can communicate with each other by point-to-point data exchange or through coordination among different services to achieve a business purpose. As a result, an SOA can combine multiple business functions from different organizational departments, for example, production, marketing, and HR, that have similar electronic transactions (such as change of address or salary level) into a central procession unit. SOAs were created when it was discovered that the various departments of organizations (marketing, finance, operations, R&D, and HR) were storing the same basic information on employees. Creating an SOA was a way to use the IT capabilities of an organization more efficiently.

Outsourcing, Offshoring, and Insourcing

MNEs were the first organizations to outsource many of their jobs that required low levels of skills (e.g., call centers). Outsourcing in HR had been done for years, for example, using ADP Payroll Services (www.adp.com) for payroll administration. However, the HR departments in the 1990s were looking to outsource other programs (recruiting and selection) to supposedly save money for their operations. Thus, using the Internet for outsourcing HR programs became a reality (Gueutal & Stone, 2005; Walker, 2001). Most of these approaches failed for a variety of reasons; the major one had to do with the privacy and confidentiality of employees' personal data. Still, because of the tremendous financial benefits if the MNE could use outsourcing or offshoring, these practices continued. Another major problem, however, was that many companies outsourced or offshored HR functions that were a critical part of the primary business of the organization, for example, talent management. Thus, many companies reverted to insourcing certain business processes, particularly those in the HR department.

HRIS Applications in MNEs

As discussed in this chapter, most of the HRIS applications available for a domestic company can be used for MNEs. However, some modifications are necessary due to the complexity of the database in an MNE. In today's global environment, access to data from any physical location in the world is increasingly important. Teams of employees may be stationed in Thailand, India, and the United States. As covered in Chapter 2, two issues arise when data are shared across wide geographic locations. These are (1) managing the day and time of a transaction and (2) determining where to store the various components of the business application, DBMS, and database.

As part of a global information system design, organizations have chosen to break their business applications and DBMS into components, often called "tiers." More detail on tiers was covered in Chapter 3. Traditional client-server architectures broke an application into two tiers, typically with the **user interface** and some business logic on the user's computer, such as a PC (the client), and the database and mainstream parts of the application stored on a server. In today's global environment with high-speed data networks, **N-tier architectures** exist, with databases and applications being distributed among many different computers around the world. So if, for example, you are in an Internet café in Bangkok trying to get information about your benefit election, the hosting computer may be in London and the data may be located on a computer in Chicago. In sum, computer networks are created that provide instant access to these operational data, allowing real-time decision-making capabilities regardless of one's physical location.

A centralized database allows a company to confine its data to a single location and, therefore, to more easily control data integrity, updating, backup, queries, and access. A company with many locations and telecommuters, however, must develop a communications infrastructure to facilitate data sharing over a wide geographical area. The advent of the Internet and a standardized communication protocol made the centralized database structures and geographically dispersed data sharing feasible.

The database structures and system architectures we have discussed would be very useful to a multinational enterprise. Consider the differences between a compensation database for a domestic corporation operating in a single labor market and for an MNE. The multinational's compensation database would include labor market data for all countries in which the MNE has a presence, for example. Also, a great number of the modifications to an HRIS in an MNE would be driven by the different labor laws and regulations of the various host countries. As noted, there is software available for IHRM, but the use of this software demands that the database be accurate and timely. Being able to create and access reports based on employee data, and do it quickly, requires that the data be accurate and up to date—an axiom that has been emphasized throughout this book.

Summary

Globalization is a reality. Twenty-five years ago, it was the reality primarily for major corporations of the caliber of General Electric (GE) or IBM. Now, it has become increasingly important for midsize firms—the fastest-growing group in all countries. This chapter has examined the implications of this globalization on the HRM function in MNEs and has documented the explosion of the HRM function into a separate field, IHRM. How IHRM has become increasingly complex by expanding on the traditional HR functions of selection, training, and compensation was also covered. The complexity of having diversity of employees (PCNs, HCNs, and TCNs) and of contending with the varying laws

and practices of host countries dictated that MNEs abandon the paper-and-pencil system for computer technology.

The advantages of having employee information stored, manipulated, and reported using computer technology were discussed relative to the use of these capabilities in multiple IHRM programs. However, some of the more critical information that an HRIS can store, analyze, and produce reports on is contained in the cultural and legal profiles of countries. This information is valuable in all the activities and programs of the IHRM department and significantly influences the management of the many parts of an MNE.

Key Terms

balance-sheet approach 353
cross-cultural suitability 346
cultural environment of
    countries 344
cultural norm 343
culture shock 344
direct costs of expatriate
    failure 348
European Union
    (EU) 339
expatriate 344
expatriate failure 345
global corporation 337
globalization of business 335

going-rate approach 353
host-country approach 353
host-country nationals
    (HCNs) 341
International Association
    for Human Resource
    Information Management
    (IHRIM) 339
international corporation 337
multinational corporation 337
multinational enterprises
    (MNEs) 340
N-tier architectures 356
national culture 345

North American Free
    Trade Agreement
    (NAFTA) 336
parent-country nationals
    (PCNs) 341
predeparture training 348
repatriation 349
"think global, act local" 354
third-country nationals
    (TCNs) 341
transfer of training 348
transnational
    corporation 338
user interface 355

Discussion Questions

1. Describe the differences between domestic and international HRM.

2. What are the different types of organizational forms that corporations use for international operations?

3. What are the three types of employees who work in MNEs? Explain how an HCN could change to become a TCN in an MNE.

4. Describe the staffing process in an MNE. How does it differ from that of a domestic-only corporation?

5. What are the main causes of expatriate failure?

6. Describe a training program for expatriates. In what ways do HRIS help improve their effectiveness and efficiency? Why is it recommended that the family of the expatriate also receive training?

7. Is there a best method for completing performance appraisals for each of the three different types of employees in an MNE? If so, describe the ways in which an HRIS may help.

8. What are the main objectives of an international compensation plan? Would an "integrated solution" or a "best-of-breed" solution make more sense for a large multinational corporation? Do you believe that your answer would be different for a mid-sized company in the same industry? Explain your answer.

9. What are the modifications necessary for using HRIS software applications that are designed for domestic companies in an MNE?

Case Study: Global Issues in a Multinational Company

A large MNE in the cookware industry was having difficulties maintaining its market share due to a number of mergers among other competing firms in the industry. The MNE, with corporate headquarters in Canada, had production plants in 15 countries and a company presence in a total of 29 countries. Although the firm had a number of competitors, its product was considered as having the highest quality—the Mercedes of cookware. The firm was family owned and founded in 1937. The most pressing problem was how the firm could stay competitive in the marketplace and stop decreases in sales. Naturally, it was highly desirable to increase sales beyond annual averages, but first, the firm had to change something to stabilize its place in the market.

Examining the problem, the CEO and the corporate board, consisting of all the corporate vice presidents as well as the CEOs of all the international locations, concluded that it was necessary to reduce operating costs by 5% to 6% to remain competitive. Thus, it was decided to determine if these cost savings could be achieved in operations, raw materials, finances, or HR.

The MNE managers examined the latest production technology in their industry. The firm discovered that its technology was fairly current, and the few technological changes available would only help decrease costs by less than 1%. However, these modifications to their current technology were very expensive and did not appear to have a favorable return on investment (ROI).

Trying to obtain better financing was nearly impossible, since the MNE had very favorable financing currently. The same was true for raw materials, since a decision to use cheaper materials would greatly reduce the quality of the company's products.

As a result, the management of the MNE asked the IHRM department for some suggestions as to how personnel costs could be trimmed. However, there was one constraint established by tradition in the company. The MNE had never had a layoff of employees in its history, and the CEO refused to use this option to reduce personnel costs. One of the complicating factors was the different labor legislation as well as the very different cultures in the 29 countries in which the MNE did business.

Case Study Questions

1. How would you approach a solution to this problem for the MNE?

2. Assuming that reducing personnel costs is the best and probably only way to reduce overall corporate costs, what specific programs would you suggest to reduce costs? Why?

3. How would an HRIS for the MNE aid in finding HR programs to help solve this problem? What would be the most important data to access in the HRIS for the units and divisions of the MNE to determine feasible HR programs?

4. Are the problems of reducing personnel costs for an MNE different from those for a domestic-only company? Explain.

HR METRICS AND WORKFORCE ANALYTICS

Kevin D. Carlson and Michael J. Kavanagh

EDITORS' NOTE

The capacity to effectively manage an organization's workforce is limited by the type and quality of data available to managers. Better information provides a strong foundation for better understanding how HR can support the strategic direction of organizations. However, data alone are not the answer. As illustrated in this chapter, the best organizations will not simply collect more data. Instead, they will leverage data to solve key business problems. Rather than starting with the data, organizations should start with an HR or organizational problem or opportunity and determine what data are necessary to most effectively solve the problem or take advantage of the opportunity. Ultimately, workforce analytics and Big Data are only as effective as the problems they help the organization solve. This chapter offers a brief history of the efforts involved in the development of HR metrics and workforce analytics and of how these efforts have been enhanced by the advent of integrated HRIS. From benchmarking to operational experiments, the HRIS field is rapidly evolving on many fronts. These advances are changing how HR metrics and analytics are used in organizations and, subsequently, their impact on organization effectiveness.

CHAPTER OBJECTIVES

After completing this chapter, you should be able to

- Discuss why the objective of analytics efforts needs to be improving decisions and why doing so is critical to generating return on investment

- Discuss how a decision-based view of HR can be used to identify important workforce analyses that can drive improved value in almost any organization.

- Discuss the roles that activities such as data mining, predictive analytics, and operational experiments play in increasing organizational effectiveness

- Discuss the differences between analytics used to assess efficiency, operational effectiveness, and organizational realignment, and offer examples of each

- Discuss why the information from HR metrics and workforce analytics may fail to generate value for an organization

- Describe what factors managers should consider when building workforce analytics capability in an organization

HRIS IN ACTION

When Dan Hilbert arrived as Manager of Employment Services at Valero Energy, he wasn't quite sure what he wanted or needed to do. Coming from a background in operations, he was used to having information about the effectiveness of all current operations; yet, as he quickly learned, these data were not available for HR operations and programs, nor were there systems in place to generate them. He recognized the potential value of having even simple descriptive statistics about the organization's people and its operations to highlight potential opportunities and how changes in these values could signal potential problems. However, since these data were not currently available or easily developed, he created a small team, consisting of one HR staff member who could help get access to data from the organization's current systems and a graduate student with a statistical background, who was hired as a part-time employee. The team's assignment was to collect data about the human capital in the organization to learn more about the organization and its people, which Dan was now charged with supporting.

The team's analysis highlighted a unique characteristic of the Valero workforce: all its refinery managers were at least 55 years old.

This meant that these managers, each with long tenure in one of the most critical positions for assuring operating success, would be eligible to retire in fewer than 10 years. Further, given that these managers had all joined the company at roughly the same time and had held these refinery manager positions for many years, the promotion pipeline for succession to this position was limited. In other words, promising managers who had joined the organization at lower managerial positions decided to leave the company when it was clear that upward opportunities were limited.

When Hilbert presented the results of this analysis and his conclusions to senior managers, they were shocked. No one had considered the issue of the aging of refinery managers, and, likely, management would not have become aware of the situation until the refinery managers began to retire. By then, it would have been too late to develop internal replacements. Interestingly, as Valero's success increased and the stock price increased, the retirement age lowered, compounding the problem. The pipeline of trained managers capable of filling these positions internally would not have been sufficient to meet the demand created by the mass retirements, and the time to train them as refinery managers was lengthy. Here, the computation of relatively simple metrics and analytics provided new insights on the retirement status of employees. These data allowed management to engage in the training and development needed to build internal bench strength for this critical position prior to these managers retiring, likely saving the refiner millions in salary expense and reduced refinery performance.

INTRODUCTION

I have found that the largest single difference between a great HR department and an average one is the use of metrics . . . bar none, there is nothing you can do to improve yours and your department's performance that exceeds the impact of using metrics.

—John Sullivan (2003)

Human resources (HR) metrics and **workforce analytics** are hot topics in organizations of all sizes. Interest is rising, and organizations are reaching out to learn more about useful metrics and analytics and how they can use them to improve organizational effectiveness. Although the use of HR metrics and workforce analytics is not new, various factors are driving increased interest. An important driver is the widespread implementation of integrated HRIS and the greater availability of information from third-party sources. Today's HRIS builds on the capabilities of faster and more capable computers, improved connectivity through organizational networks and the Internet, and the availability of user-friendly analytics software. These changes have fundamentally altered the dynamics of human capital assessment in organizations, driving the marginal cost of assessment lower, while providing the potential for near real-time analysis and distribution of information. These factors, combined with recent and growing interest in evidence-based management, account for the rapidly growing interest in HR metrics and workforce analytics.

A BRIEF HISTORY OF HR METRICS AND ANALYTICS

Systematic work on the development of measures to capture the effectiveness of an organization's employees can be traced as far back as the days of scientific management (Taylor, 1911) and industrial and organizational psychology (Munsterberg, 1913). Methods of quantitative analysis and its use in decision making were developed during the buildup of both men and materiel leading up to and during World War II. Further study and development occurred during the great postwar industrial expansion in the United States that continued into the 1970s. Many of the HR metrics used today were first considered and developed during this period (e.g., Hawk, 1967).

Widespread assessment of HR metrics did not occur until the pioneering work of Dr. Jac Fitz-enz and the early benchmarking work he conducted through the Saratoga Institute. In 1984, Fitz-enz published *How to Measure Human Resources Management,* currently in its third edition (Fitz-enz, 2002), which is still a highly valued overview of many HR metrics and the formulas used to calculate them. A set of 30 metrics was developed through the joint efforts of the Saratoga Institute and the American Society for Personnel Administration (ASPA), the forerunner of the current Society for Human Resource Management (SHRM). These metrics are listed in Table 14.1. Initially, HR metrics were primarily used to measure or audit aspects of HR programs and activities as described by Cascio (1987) and Fitz-enz (2002). Next, metrics began to be used to measure HR effectiveness. SHRM

TABLE 14.1   ■   Measures in the Saratoga Institute/SHRM Human Resources Effectiveness Report
Revenue per Employee
Expense per Employee
Compensation as a Percentage of Revenue
Compensation as a Percentage of Expense
Benefit Cost as a Percentage of Revenue
Benefit Cost as a Percentage of Expense
Benefit Cost as a Percentage of Compensation
Retiree Benefit Cost per Retiree
Retiree Benefit Cost as a Percentage of Expense
Hires as a Percentage of Total Employees
Cost of Hire
Time to Fill Jobs
Time to Start Jobs
HR Department Expense as a Percentage of Company Expense
HR Headcount Ratio—HR Employees: Company Employees
HR Department Expense per Company Employee
Supervisory Compensation Percentage
Workers' Compensation Cost as a Percentage of Expense
Workers' Compensation Cost per Employee
Workers' Compensation Cost per Claim
Absence Rate
Involuntary Separation
Voluntary Separation
Voluntary Separation by Length of Service
Ratio of Offers Made to Acceptances

Source: Adapted from Fitz-Enz, J. (1995) How to Measure Human Resources Management, 2nd Edition. New York, NY: *McGraw-Hill, Inc.*

has identified several metrics that organizations can use in this way. These metrics comprise the HR Metrics Toolbox seen in Table 14.2 (SHRM, 2010). For example, cost per hire, which can be noted as cost per hire (CPH), equals the sum of external costs (recruiting) and internal costs (training new employees) divided by the total number of starts in the time period of interest (SHRM, 2010). There are also more detailed approaches for the measuring and benchmarking of employees' behaviors such as turnover, as well as for creating HR metrics for programs such as employee assistance and work-life programs (Cascio, 2000).

TABLE 14.2 ■ HR Metrics Toolkit (2010)		
HR Metrics		
Absence rate	{(No. of days absent in mo.) / [(Ave. no. of employees during mo.) × (No. of workdays)]} × 100	Measures absenteeism. Determines if your company has an absenteeism problem. Analyzes why and how to address the issue. Analyzes further for effectiveness of attendance policy and effectiveness of management in applying policy. See Hollmann (2002).
Cost per hire	(Advertising + Agency fees + Employee referrals + Travel cost of applicants and staff + Relocation costs + Recruiter pay and benefits) / No. of hires	Costs involved with a new hire. Use *EMA/Cost per Hire Staffing Metrics Survey* as a benchmark for your organization (Kluttz, 2003). Can be used as a measurement to show any substantial improvements to savings in recruitment/retention costs. Determines what your recruiting function can do to increase savings/reduce costs, etc.
Health care costs per employee	Total cost of health care / Total employees	Per-capita cost of employee benefits. Indicates cost of health care per employee. For benefit data from the Bureau of Labor Statistics (BLS), see BLS's publications titled *Employer Costs Trends* (BLS, 2020).
HR expense factor	HR expense / Total operating expense	HR expenses in relation to the total operating expenses of the organization. In addition, determines if expenditures exceeded, met, or fell below budget. Analyzes HR practices that contributed to savings, if any.
Human capital ROI	{Revenue – [Operating expense – (Compensation cost + Benefit cost)]} / (Compensation cost + Benefit cost)	ROI ratio for employees. Did organization get a return on its investment? Analyzes causes of positive/negative ROI metric. Uses analysis as an opportunity to optimize investment with HR practices such as recruitment, motivation, training, and development. Evaluates whether HR practices have a causal relationship in positive changes to improving metric.

(Continued)

TABLE 14.2 ■ (Continued)

HR Metrics		
Human capital value added	{Revenue – [Operating Expense – (Compensation cost + Benefit Cost)]} / Total no. of FTE	Value of workforce's knowledge, skill, and performance. This measurement illustrates how employees add value to an organization.
Prorating merit increases	(No. of mos. worked / No. of mos. under the current increase policy) × Increase in percentage the person would otherwise be entitled to	The basic steps to calculate an employee's pay increase appropriate to the period of time worked.
Revenue factor	Revenue / Total no. of FTE	Benchmark to indicate effectiveness of company and to show employees as capital rather than as an expense. Human capital can be viewed as an investment.
Time to fill	Total days elapsed to fill requisitions / No. hired	Number of days from which job requisition was approved to new hire start date. How efficient/productive is recruiting function? This is also a process measurement. See *EMA/ Cost per Hire Staffing Metrics Survey* for more information.
Training investment factor	Total training cost / Headcount	Training cost per employee. Analyzes training function further for effectiveness of training (e.g., Has productivity increased as a result of acquiring new skills and knowledge? Have accidents decreased?). If not, evaluate the causes.
Training (ROI)	(Total benefit – Total costs) × 100	The total financial gain/benefit an organization realizes from a specific training program less the total direct and indirect costs incurred to develop, produce, and deliver the training program (see white paper Four Steps to Computing *Training ROI* [Lilly, 2001] for more information on this topic).
Turnover costs	Total of the costs of separation + vacancy + replacement + training	The separation, vacancy, replacement, and training costs resulting from employee turnover. This formula can be used to calculate the turnover cost for one position, a class code, a division, or the entire organization. *Exit interviews* (Drake & Robb, 2002) are useful tools in determining why employees are leaving your organization (see white paper *Employee Turnover Hurts Small and Large Company Profitability* [Galbreath, 2000] for more information on this topic). Implements retention efforts. Evaluates whether HR practices are having a causal relationship in positive changes to improving cost of turnover.

Turnover rate (monthly)	(No. of separations during mo. / Avg. no. of employees during mo.) × 100	Calculates and compares metric with national average, using business and legal reports at www.bls.gov/jlt/home.htm. This measures the rate at which employees leave a company. Is there a trend? Has metric increased/decreased? Analyzes what has caused increase/decrease to metric.
		Determines what an organization can do to improve retention efforts. Evaluates whether HR practices have a causal relationship in positive changes to improving metric. (See white paper titled *Employee Turnover: Analyzing Employee Movement Out of the Organization* [Ofsanko & Napier, 1990].)
Turnover rate (annual)	[(No. of employees exiting the job / Avg. actual no. of employees during the period) × 12] / No. of mos. in period	Calculates and compares metric with national average, using business and legal reports at www.bls.gov/jlt/home.htm. This measures the rate at which employees leave a company. Is there a trend? Has metric increased/decreased? Analyze what has caused increase/decrease to metric. Determines what organization can do to improve retention efforts. Evaluates whether HR practices have a causal relationship in positive changes to improving metric. (See white paper titled *Employee Turnover: Analyzing Employee Movement Out of the Organization* [Ofsanko & Napier, 1990].)
Vacancy costs	Total of the costs of temporary workers + independent contractors + other outsourcing + overtime – wages and benefits not paid for vacant position(s)	The cost of having work completed that would have been performed by the former employee or employees less the wages and benefits that would have been paid to the vacant position(s). This formula may be used to calculate the vacancy cost for one position, a group, a division, or the entire organization.
Vacancy rate	(Total no. of vacant positions as of today / Total no. of positions as of today) × 100	Measures the organization's vacancy rates resulting from employee turnover. This formula can be used to calculate the vacancy rate for one position, a class code, a division, or the entire organization.
Workers' compensation cost per employee	Total WC cost for year / Average no. of employees	Analyzes and compares (e.g., Year 1 to Year 2, etc.) on a regular basis. You can also analyze workers' compensation further to determine trends in types of injuries, injuries by department, jobs, and so forth. HR practices such as safety training, disability management, and incentives can reduce costs. Use metric as benchmark to show causal relationship between HR practices and reduced workers' compensation costs.
Workers' compensation incident rate	(No. of injuries and/or illnesses per 100 FTE / Total hours worked by all employees during the calendar year) × 200,000	The "incident rate" is the number of injuries and/or illnesses per 100 full-time workers. 200,000 is the base for 100 FTE workers (working 40 hours/week, 50 weeks/year.) The calculated rate can be modified depending on the nature of the injuries and/or illnesses. For example, if you wished to determine the lost workday case rate, you would include only the cases that involved days away from work.

(*Continued*)

TABLE 14.2 ■ (Continued)		
HR Metrics		
Workers' compensation severity rate	(No. of days away from work per 100 FTE / Total hours worked by all employees during the calendar year) × 200,000	The "severity rate" is the number of days away from work per 100 FTE. To calculate the severity rate, replace the number of injuries and/or illnesses per 100 FTE from the incident rate calculation with the number of days away from work per 100 FTE. More information is available regarding the types of injuries, incident rates, and comparison with other SIC codes at www.bls.gov/iif/oshdef.htm#incidence.
Yield ratio	Percentage of applicants from a recruitment source that make it to the next stage of the selection process (e.g., 100 resumes received, 50 found acceptable = 50% yield)	A comparison of the number of applicants at one stage of the recruiting process with the number at the next stage. (*Note:* Success ratio is the proportion of selected applicants who are later judged as being successful on the job.)

Source: Adapted from Fitz-Enz, J. (1995) How to Measure Human Resources Management, 2nd Edition. New York, NY: McGraw-Hill, Inc.

Kaplan and Norton's (1996) introduction of the **balanced scorecard** further refined managers' thinking about metrics. The balanced scorecard recognizes the limitations of organizations' heavy reliance on financial indicators of performance. Such measures focus on what has already happened rather than providing managers information about what *will* happen. Balanced scorecards focus on developing leading indicators of performance from several important perspectives, including customer satisfaction, process effectiveness, and employee development, as well as financial performance. In addition, the thinking required to develop balanced scorecards help managers identify causal sequences was believed to lead to critical organizational outcomes.

About the same time, Huselid's (1995) work on high-performance work systems demonstrated that the systematic management of human resources was associated with significant differences in organizational effectiveness. This work provided evidence that human resource management did indeed have strategic potential. Becker, Huselid, and Ulrich (2001) helped bring these ideas together in the HR scorecard, which highlights how the alignment of HR activities with both corporate strategy and activity improve organizational outcomes.

LIMITATIONS OF HISTORICAL METRICS

Unfortunately, although the computing, communications, and software infrastructure supporting HR metrics and analytics has undergone dramatic change since the late 1990s, the metrics themselves have not. Organizations are currently capable of capturing data on a wide range of electronically supported HR processes, extracting, analyzing, and then distributing that information in real time to managers throughout the organization. However, many popular and current HR metrics were developed before current computing capabilities existed. As a result, the metrics organizations utilized were primarily a function of what data most organizations could easily and inexpensively gather before the computerization of basic HR transactions. A quick perusal of the metrics listed in Table 14.1 highlights the early emphasis on readily available data, most of which came from accounting systems.

Consequently, these metrics emphasize costs or easily calculated counts (e.g., head count, turnover) that often serve as proxies for costs. Every managerial decision, though, has cost and benefits consequences, whether we recognize them or not. As a result, when metrics and analytics systems only provide information about costs, they are of limited value to managers. If managers are only provided information about costs, with little or no information about benefits, costs are likely to become the primary driver of managerial decisions. This perpetuates the still-common perception of HR as a "cost center." Thus, the most effective metrics will focus on the benefits derived from a managerial decision as well as its costs. This allows firms to calculate an estimated return on investment (ROI) for a decision.

Second, several HR metrics use operational data aggregated to the organization level. As such, these metrics offer limited information that could be used to identify and diagnose within-organization differences. This has driven interest in the development of interactive reporting portals that allow managers to drill down to lower-level details in aggregate data. Organizational turnover rates, for example, can be heavily influenced by the turnover rate in the organization's dominant job category or its largest units, masking particularly high or low turnover rates for jobs or units with fewer incumbents.

Finally, early metrics focused on data captured after events had occurred. The resulting "feedback" metrics slowed responses to problems or opportunities. Feedback metrics can be effectively used to signal problems, but they are suboptimal as a primary source of data because they do not support real-time remedial action to minimize any negative effects.

CONTEMPORARY HR METRICS AND WORKFORCE ANALYTICS

Understanding Workforce Analytics Practices

"Workforce analytics" has become an umbrella term that encompasses an expanding range of evolving activities and processes. A sampling of categories of contemporary workforce analytics practices is introduced in the paragraphs that follow.

HR Metrics

HR metrics are data (numbers) that reflect some descriptive detail about given processes or outcomes, for example, success in recruiting new employees. In the domain of human resources, these often reflect attributes of the organization's HR programs and activities or related outcomes such as the number of applicants attracted, turnover rate, headcount, or the cost of conducting training programs.

A common question that analytics practitioners ask is "what metrics should we be tracking?" Although it is tempting to look to what metrics other organizations are tracking, the HR metrics an individual organization tracks and reports to managers are best determined by the challenges that specific organization is facing and the needs of its managers and employees. Having data about common metrics across organizations can aid benchmarking efforts. However, organizations are best served if the specific metrics tracked and the specific calculations used to create those metrics are customized to the specific needs of organization decision makers.

Workforce Analytics

Workforce analytics refer to strategies for combining data elements into metrics and for examining changes in metrics or the magnitude of relationships among them. Such analyses can inform managers about the current or changing state of human capital in an organization in ways that impact their decisions. Understanding what opportunities and problems managers face can suggest relevant analyses that can support better decisions. These analyses then determine what metrics the organization needs, what data elements are relevant and need to be captured, and how these data elements should be combined.

Benchmarking

Benchmarking is a method of creating useful comparisons between or within organizations. The Saratoga Institute was the first systematic effort to develop information on standard HR metrics to inform managers about differences in HR outcomes among major organizations. Benchmarking can be used to draw comparisons about human capital outcomes or the nature of cost of an HR practice. Benchmarking data are useful in that they provide insights into an organization's relative standing or insight into levels of outcomes that might be possible.

However, a challenge for benchmarking HR metrics is that an organization's human resource practices and the use of its HR staff reflect current challenges facing that organization. These challenges and resulting HR structures differ across and within organizations. Although most organizations have an HR department, the specific functions performed by these departments vary widely across organizations. Consequently, direct comparisons of external benchmarks of HR metric data to one's own organization may not provide realistic evidence of relative standing nor provide guidelines for either goal setting or forecasting the potential effectiveness of the remedial actions an organization might undertake.

Data Mining and "Big" Data

Interest in mining human capital data has been on the rise since the implementation of integrated HRIS and digitized HRM processes. **Data mining** refers to efforts to identify patterns that exist within data and that may identify unrecognized causal mechanisms that can be used to enhance decision making. To identify these causal mechanisms, data mining uses correlation and multiple regression methods to identify patterns of relationships in extremely large datasets. An example would be the identification of a correlation between employee characteristics and job satisfaction or employee turnover. Current interest in **big data** reflects efforts to extract insights from extremely large datasets created by many transaction systems. Often these datasets can be many terabytes (2^{10} gigabytes) or more. Many Web-based applications and transaction sites, like those generated by Amazon.com, Google, and many social media sites generate large numbers of transactions. Mining these very large data sets can uncover patterns that provide additional insights for managers about customer preferences or process characteristics that managers can use to drive greater sales, higher customer satisfaction, and reduce costs. In many cases, this process involves analyses of quantitative data as well as qualitative analysis of unformatted text.

It is suggested that big data is characterized by volume, variety, velocity, and veracity. It offers **volume** because it provides large amounts of data on which analyses can be based. In most cases, data sets as large as several hundred or thousand instances are sufficient to identify useful trends, although there are instances in which very large volumes of data may permit additional insights. Big data offers **variety** through access to a wider range of data elements. New insights may be generated by incorporating new types of data into analyses that were previously not available to the organization. A caution here, though, is that organizations tend to conduct these analyses independent of the existing data that managers currently use to make decisions. Social media, for instance, can be mined to identify characteristics of applicants who may be high performers, but the more important question is whether these data provide incremental validity for selecting employees beyond the practices organizations are currently using to make hiring decisions. **Velocity** refers to the speed at which data can be generated. Velocity is the big data characteristic most likely to consistently create value for organizations. In big data, data are generated at much faster velocities, resulting in organizations being able to generate relatively large samples of data on which to conduct analyses very quickly (in some cases, in a matter of hours), which can dramatically shorten decision cycles. Finally, big data must have veracity. **Veracity** refers to the quality of the data collected by the organizations. HR is plagued by inconsistencies and inaccuracies, and these problems must be fixed in order for planning and prediction to be meaningful (Vorhauser-Smith, 2014). When these problems are fixed for structured data, HR will then be able to embrace the wealth of value found in the relatively unstructured data present in market and social data.

There are two caveats when using data mining in human capital. One is that data mining can uncover spurious or nonsensical relationships (e.g., older employees have longer tenures; taller employees have higher leadership scores). This problem exists for data mining in all domains, not just in human capital. Data mining can identify relationships among variables in data, but it cannot determine whether those relationships are meaningful or whether they are causal, a requirement if an organization wants to try to create interventions based on relationships identified through data mining. A second important caveat is that data mining captures relationships that exist in previous patterns of relationship. If that data comes from a system in which systemic discrimination has existed, it is quite possible that the relationships and algorithms produced using data mining might further this discrimination even though the data used would not appear to be overtly discriminatory.

Predictive Analyses

Predictive analysis involves the creation of models of organizational systems that can be used to predict what will happen at some point in the future. Often this involves efforts to predict future outcomes for current organizational systems. It can also involve predicting how changes in the environment, like wage rates or unemployment levels, will influence key outcomes or predicting the consequences of planned organizational interventions. Predictive analysis attempts to use analytics to make organizational planning more proactive by integrating data on the direction and magnitude of future internal and external actions so that decision makers can act to enhance positive effects or mitigate negative ones. Predictive analysis includes a range of tools from trend analysis (estimating the future based on what has happened in the past) to more sophisticated models that might estimate the likelihood for individual employees to leave the organization. Efforts to develop balanced scorecards are examples of elementary predictive systems. They involve identifying leading indicators of important organizational outcomes and the nature of the influences and processes expected to determine those outcomes. Engaging in efforts to test the assumptions in these models over time can lead to enhancements in the quality of the models' underlying predictive analyses, either by identifying additional leading indicators or by better specifying the nature of the relationships between predictors and outcomes.

Artificial Intelligence and Machine Learning

Artificial intelligence refers to methods used to automate or enhance aspects of human decision making. In these systems, human decision makers and data mining are combined to create models of common decisions that may be replicated hundreds or thousands of times in organizations. Data about correct and incorrect decisions and factors related to decisions made are fed into various analysis models based on multiple regression and related technologies to identify data elements and decision rules that lead to the greatest number of correct decisions. Such systems can greatly exceed the effectiveness of human decision makers in two ways. First, computer algorithms can process the relevant data elements, contributing to a decision much more quickly than can be done by humans. Second, a computer-based algorithm always applies the optimum decision rule, which human decision makers, who often substitute their own judgment in making decisions, do not. Although the artificial intelligence of science fiction envisions substituting computers for human judgment in tasks with uncertain inputs and ambiguous decision rules, that capability does not exist today. But in circumstances in which decision rules are unambiguous, artificial intelligence can greatly enhance the effectiveness of decision making, freeing up human decision makers to spend more time in decision contexts that are more ambiguous and uncertain, where humans are comparatively more effective.

Machine learning involves the use of algorithms that can examine large bodies of moderately structured or unstructured data to learn relationships among data elements that can be useful to improving decision making. Machine learning is a set of emerging tools that can self-generate hierarchical patterns of abstraction within broad domains to help make sense of extremely large volumes of data. These systems ultimately may have the potential to work independently, but as is more common today, these systems work jointly with human decision makers to determine what variables or data structures are most relevant for improving decision making. These systems can rely on large volumes of structured and unstructured data about users or customers to attempt to understand and anticipate customer needs or to assist decision makers who may not possess deep systematic understandings of fields or problem domains that are new to them.

Modeling and Optimization

Modeling and optimization refer to efforts to create highly accurate models of key organizational systems. If data mining reflects initial attempts by the organization to understand the system of influences driving organizational outcomes, modeling represents a more complete and accurate understanding of the system of relationships and interrelationships among variables affecting outcomes. Accurate models can be used to estimate the input required to generate given levels of output, estimate the joint effects of environmental change or organizational action, and generate sophisticated hypotheses about the effects of new or untested interventions. **Workforce modeling** is a modeling application that attempts to understand how an organization's human capital needs would change as a function of some expected change in the organization's environment. This change may be a shift in the demand for the organization's product, entry into a new market, divestiture of one of the organization's businesses, or a pending acquisition of or merger with another organization. This process builds on and enhances a human resource planning (HRP) program, which is covered in more detail in Chapter 9.

Operational Experiments

The evidence-based management movement argues that managers should base their decisions on data drawn from the organization and evidence about the actual functioning of its systems in lieu of personal philosophies or untested models and assumptions about "how things work." One of the most effective methods for developing the evidence on which to base decisions is through **operational experiments** conducted within the organization. Ayres (2007) describes how Google uses operational experiments to test the effectiveness of the ad words used on its Web site. Rather than simply relying on intuition or "expert judgment" about which ad wording is more effective, it creates an experiment. It configures its site to alternate the presentation of competing ad text to visitors to its site and then tracks the number of "click-throughs" on the ad during a given time period. Given the large number of daily hits, Google can get objective data on the effectiveness of the various ads in a relatively short time and then adopt the ad wording demonstrated to be most effective.

HR METRICS, WORKFORCE ANALYTICS, AND ORGANIZATIONAL EFFECTIVENESS

Greater access to data can enhance managers' ability to improve human capital management. However, despite reporting more metrics with greater frequency to a wider group of managers, many HR professionals who generate HR reports question whether these efforts have had a significant impact on organization effectiveness. Often, these individuals report frustration with their inability to get managers to (a) tell them what information they need, (b) read or use the HR metrics data included in existing reports, or (c) even acknowledge receipt of the reports. These perceptions point to fundamental challenges and opportunities to improve the impact of workforce analytics efforts.

A Common and Troublesome View

Many managers perceive the increased interest in metrics and analytics as simply a mandate to compute and report more metrics. The assumption behind this perception is that assessing and reporting HR metrics results in better organizational performance. But it is not clear that generating and reporting more HR metrics will necessarily result in better individual, unit, or organizational performance. In fact, these links are not well established.

Further, a common misperception is that the objective of workforce analytics is to extract value from HR data. In this approach, the process starts with the HR data, and the objective is to use that data to create metrics. These metrics can then be combined in various analyses that can then be reported to managers, who use the information in these analyses to drive decision making. This view was dominant in the development of many metrics and analytics. However, if one starts with the data, it is not clear which data elements are relevant, nor is there a rational basis for guiding how available variables should be combined into metrics or how those metrics should contribute to analytics. This approach has two common and predictable outcomes. First, individuals tasked with developing and reporting HR metrics in organizations struggle to determine which metrics to report and how those metrics should be calculated. Second, as a result of the first outcome, these organizations subsequently report large numbers of metrics—because there is no a priori basis for choosing which are likely to be more useful—and the vast majority of these metrics ultimately have little or no impact on decision making and, therefore, offer no return to the organization.

A more effective approach is to start with the problems or opportunities faced by the organization and develop an understanding of what information is likely to be useful to support managers' decisions. An understanding of the problem to be addressed permits organizations to determine effectively the analysis that is most likely to be useful for improving decision making and organizational effectiveness. These analyses then determine which metrics are useful, which specific data elements are needed for those metrics, and how the data elements need to be combined to create the metrics. The difference between a "data first" versus a "problem first" approach is dramatic. The latter has more focus; analyses are targeted at specific managerial decisions, increasing the likelihood that the analysis will impact decision making while simultaneously reducing costs, because fewer metrics need to be calculated and reported.

Maximizing the Impact of Workforce Analytics Efforts

A fundamental problem for many of the currently popular HR metrics is that they do not provide a clear impact on important managerial decisions. An emphasis on improving managerial decisions changes the dynamics driving analytics efforts; that is, it raises the bar. It is not simply good enough to "do" metrics and analytics. These activities need to be approached in a way that increases the possibility that access to the information from these efforts will change managerial decisions, making them more effective.

More effective workforce analytics efforts will also attend to both the potential contributions and costs of analyses. Each workforce analysis effort has a potential return on investment; therefore, those individuals in organizations responsible for managing workforce analytics efforts need to recognize and attend to the potential return-on-investment dynamics of workforce analytics efforts. The challenge is to identify the analyses that provide managers with the information they need to make better decisions regarding the acquisition and deployment of an organization's human capital.

HR metrics and workforce analytics comprise an information system, and information systems can only have an impact on organizations if, as a result of the information they receive, managers make different and better decisions than they would have without that information. No information system, including HR metrics and analytics, generates any return on the investment unless managers change their decision behavior for the better. It is not good enough for analyses to confirm decisions that managers were already going to make. Although managers may feel better, the organization is no better off than it would have been otherwise. If managers do not make different and better decisions as a result of the information reported to them, the time and effort expended in conducting and reporting HR metrics and analytics is wasted.

If managers must make different or better decisions, they can do so in three different ways. First and most common, managers can make a different (and better) decision than the one they would have made before they received the results of the analysis. Second, managers can make the same decision they would have made before receiving the information, but they can make that decision sooner. Making the decision sooner can accentuate the benefits to the organization. Third, managers can choose not to make a new decision when one is not required. In some instances, managers can misinterpret data, confusing random variability with systematic changes, and conclude a change in practice is needed, when in fact it is not. Intervening when a system is under control generally results in a reduction rather than an enhancement of outcomes. The use of control charts is a good example of a decision support tool that can help managers recognize earlier when a process is heading out of control, allowing them to intervene sooner, but that also helps managers differentiate between normal variation in outcomes that are inherent in a process and systematic change in the system that requires intervention.

Triage in Evaluating Workforce Analysis Opportunities

There are many ways that workforce analytics can be focused in organizations. However, it is important to recognize that although many analyses may require roughly the same amount of analyst time and effort, not all opportunities to apply workforce analytics in an organization offer the same potential return on investment. In fact, the potential returns to investments in workforce analyses can vary dramatically. In large organizations that are just introducing workforce analysis, there are likely to be many analysis opportunities that can generate returns of hundreds or thousands of dollars. But there will be opportunities that can return hundreds of thousands or millions of dollars for the same analyst effort. Organizations that want to generate greater impact from their investments in analytics need to develop the capacity and discipline to recognize large analytics opportunities and focus their analysis there.

SO WHERE ARE THE BEST WORKFORCE ANALYTICS OPPORTUNITIES LIKELY TO BE FOUND?

One approach to isolating better opportunities is to focus on the right workforce analytics domains. Broadly, workforce analytics efforts fit into one of three categories: HR process efficiency, operational effectiveness, and strategic realignment. Each represents a separate domain in which organizations can and do conduct workforce analytics.

HR Process Efficiency

Currently, a substantial amount of workforce analysis and reporting addresses HR **administrative process efficiency.** These metrics focus on how well the HR department (and/or the broader organization) accomplishes critical HRM processes that support organizational effectiveness. Metrics in this area might include cost per hire, days to fill positions, percentage of performance reviews completed on time, and HR department costs as a percentage of total costs or as a percentage of sales. In many cases, base-level proficiency in **HR process efficiency analytics** is viewed as necessary to create credibility for HRM managers within an organization. However, in many cases, how well HR processes are executed has only limited potential to impact organization effectiveness. How well HR processes are executed is important but often less critical than assuring that the organization has the right processes in place to support the organization's objectives.

Operational Effectiveness

Operational effectiveness analyses focus on organizational process improvement. Here, the objective is to identify opportunities to improve operational outcomes through improved human capital interventions. Often, this requires analysts to utilize the technical competence of the HR professionals. For example, this could include using analyses to help managers determine whether changes to recruiting, selection, employee deployment, training, job design, employee motivation or engagement, development, or retention could help managers more effectively accomplish their objectives. These outcomes are outside of HR; they are the business units' operational metrics (i.e., percentage of on-time deliveries, operational downtime, lost-time accidents, units sold, or cost per unit). Analysts in these instances play a consultative role in helping identify opportunities to use HR interventions to improve the operational effectiveness of other units of the organization.

Strategic Realignment

Strategic realignment involves the set of activities most commonly known today as human resources planning (HRP; for more detail, see Chapter 9). These planning efforts focus on both long-term plans to ensure replacement of the labor power needed to operate as an organization and planning for needed strategic changes in the organization. Boeing, for example, engages in several efforts to ensure that it will have sufficient numbers of engineers available to staff operations in future years as the company faces the approaching retirement of a large portion of its engineering workforce. Strategic realignment also extends the use of HRM analytics to planning for new situations and circumstances. New situations and circumstances occur when an organization undergoes a strategic change in direction, such as through merger, acquisition, divestiture, or entry into new geographic or product markets. The ability of the HR department to estimate the future demand for and supply of needed human capital is largely driven by changes in organizational strategy, and this ability to forecast these future needs is crucial to the survival of the organization.

In sum, all three areas of expertise are important, but the emphasis of workforce analytics in organizations is shifting from HR process efficiency to operational effectiveness, and with that shift, organizations increase the potential impact of workforce analysis on organizational outcomes. HR managers must first be able to demonstrate their capacity to use metrics and analytics to manage their own operations well, and only then will others be more likely to listen to their recommendations. HR managers and professionals must also work closely with their business partners in operational departments to help improve their capability to achieve their desired outcomes. Using workforce analytics to improve strategic realignment is less developed in most organizations than analyses in the other two domains, but ultimately, these analyses, when done well, may have the greatest potential effect on an organization's bottom line.

Starting With the End in Mind

A key to generating impactful workforce analyses is to begin by identifying big problems or opportunities. An effective approach to surfacing potential problems is to identify, through either existing data or discussions with managers, those areas of greatest challenge or opportunity in the organization. Once these areas of opportunity are identified, the next step is to identify the organizational outcome associated with that opportunity; understanding what outcome variable would change if the organization was to solve the problem or capture the opportunity. Example outcome variables might be sales, levels of scrap, on-time shipments, etc. The second step is to represent that outcome using numbers. This set will be easier if the organization has existing metrics. If not, raw data may need to be collected, and the appropriate metric combining that data may need to be developed. Third, if possible, we would like to attach dollar values to differences in the values of these outcomes. Sales are already in a dollar metric, but the value of on-time shipments may require some additional thinking to develop an understanding of how it impacts revenue or costs.

These data are critical when triaging analytic opportunities. Triage is the process of examining available analytics opportunities to determine which should receive priority. By examining data on the level and distribution of existing outcome data, it is possible to identify where there may be opportunities to raise the average outcome (and by how much) or shift the distribution of outcomes (e.g., eliminate low outliers) and from these data estimate how much the organization might gain from tackling each analytics opportunity. It is important to remember that many workforce analytics projects will likely consume roughly the same amount of analyst time. But the potential differences in benefits will differ dramatically across potential projects. Thus, the potential benefits rather than the likely cost of conducting the analysis is likely to be more critical in triage decisions. Organizations should encourage analysts to spend their time on projects with very large opportunities. This is also important because not every analysis will completely solve the problem. But capturing only half of the value from a $5 million opportunity will still substantively benefit an organization.

Once an analyst understands the important outcomes, the focus then shifts to (1) understanding the factors that influence those outcomes and (2) identifying available intervention options and their costs. The system of factors that influence outcomes of interest (e.g., a downturn in the economy on sales) and the types of available interventions and their effects (e.g., changing a sales incentive system) are not always well understood in organizations. Many organizational systems have multiple sources of influence, and many organizational processes are actually sequential systems of intermediate outcomes. Each outcome may be subject to several influences, and each outcome is likely the result of a process into which managers can intervene. These sequential processes can often be depicted as shown in Figure 14.1. Here interventions or influences in early outcomes create new starting points for downstream processes, which can be further impacted by subsequent influences and decisions. In many cases, it is often useful to determine whether a chosen outcome is an intermediate outcome or the ultimate outcome of a process. A quick test is to ask yourself why you care about this outcome. If the answer is that it directly leads to increases in revenue, reductions in cost, or some combination thereof, you may have an ultimate outcome. If not, it is important that the analyst continue to ask *why* questions until the ultimate outcome can be identified.

This process is particularly important in workforce analytics because human resource interventions (i.e., changes in practice) almost never directly change an ultimate outcome. In most cases, the objective of the intervention is to cause some change in employee behavior (i.e., their actions and/or decisions) that impacts an outcome, which many sequentially influence one or more additional intermediate outcomes before impacting the ultimate outcome. An important challenge to human resource managers and business partners is attempting to understand these sequences. Frequently, the exact sequence of expected effects of many human resource management interventions are not known. This can lead to the following caricature of human resource interventions: We engage in Intervention X, which will improve intermediate outcome Y, and "then a miracle occurs" and we become more profitable. Limits in this understanding can lead to incorrect decisions about appropriate interventions and can

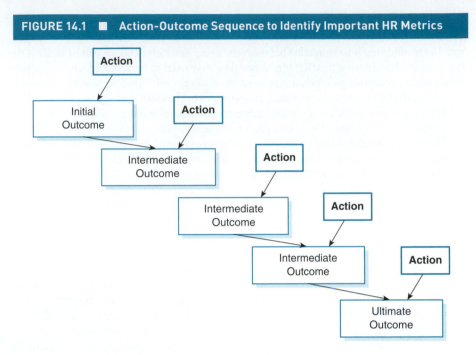

FIGURE 14.1   ■   Action–Outcome Sequence to Identify Important HR Metrics

result in managers not getting the outcomes they expect. In those instances, analysts should work with managers to surface the assumptions associated with the causal sequences expected from interventions so that the validity of these hypotheses can be tested.

AN EXAMPLE ANALYSIS: THE CASE OF STAFFING

Up to this point, the chapter has focused on the role of metrics and workforce analytics to support HR and employee-related decisions. In addition, it discusses how to best develop them and where they can most effectively support the organization. At this point in the chapter, we focus on a specific context in which metrics and analytics can be applied, walking the reader through an example of their use in support of the staffing function.

Carlson and Connerley (2003) discuss how staffing can be framed as a sequence of decisions rather than a sequence of processes. Their Staffing Cycle Framework highlights a sequence of seven high-level decisions that occur in staffing every position in an organization. These decisions, listed in Table 14.3, cover the time period from the initial intent of individuals and organizations to enter into employment relationships through the matching processes associated with making and accepting job offers to the decision by individuals or organizations to end these employment relationships. In staffing, these decisions are not seen as joint hiring decisions but as a sequence of decisions in which control shifts between job seekers and the organization. In Table 14.3, the following decision events (D1, D3, D5, and D7) are controlled by job seekers, which decision events (D2, D4, and D6) are controlled by organization decision makers. When they are not in a control of a decision, the job seeker or organization decision making acts as an influencer of those decisions.

TABLE 14.3 ■	Seven Core Decisions in the Staffing Cycle (Carlson & Connerley, 2003)
Decision Event	**Description**
D1	The job seeker's decision to enter the workforce (to begin actively seeking employment). In the United States, just over half of the population is a part of the workforce (employed or actively seeking employment).
D2	The organization's decision to create a position that it wants to hire an individual to fill. A key aspect of this decision is the organization's decision about how the job will be designed, compensated, incentivized, located, and supervised. In many cases, these decisions can substantially impact the success of subsequent staffing outcomes.
D3	The job seeker's decision to apply for the organization's position. In the United States, applicants must make an affirmative decision to seek a specific position within an organization. Carlson, Connerley, and Mecham (2002) argue that this decision is likely the most critical in staffing, as it determines who can potentially be hired. Influencing better-quality recruits to apply increases the potential impact of the cycle (achieving a high-quality hire). If high-quality applicants do not apply, they cannot be hired, and no subsequent action in the staffing cycle can replace this lost potential value. Recruiting is efforts by the organization to influence these job seekers' decisions.
D4	The organization's decision to extend an individual a job offer. This is the domain of selection. Organizations increase value by using more valid and cost-effective selection procedures.
D5	The job seeker's decision to accept a job offer. While we can offer individuals positions, not all of them may accept them. Top candidates who fail to accept job offers represent lost value; the value of that loss is determined by the difference in the potential to contribute to the organization between the top individuals that do not accept offers and the lesser-rated candidate who eventually accepts.
D6	The organization's decision to retain an employee. Framed in the negative, this is the organization's decision to dismiss an employee, or involuntary turnover. This may happen if the organization no longer needs the position (the opposite of D2) or the individual is unable to perform in the position that is acceptable to the organization. This decision in framed in the positive to acknowledge that the organization's evaluation of the individual is ongoing throughout their employment.
D7	The job seeker's decision to remain in a position. Framed in the negative, this is a person's decision to leave a position (but not necessarily the organization), or voluntary turnover. Retention programs are efforts by organizations to influence these decisions.

Source: Adapted from Kevin D. Carlson and Mary L. Connerley, (2003). The staffing cycles framework: Viewing staffing as a system of decision events. In *Journal of Management*, 29(1) p 51–78.

This framework is useful for guiding workforce analytics efforts in staffing because it identifies key intermediate outcomes in the sequence of staffing decisions that can be evaluated and helps identify the critical component processes (and roles of the key players) in influencing these outcomes. For example, consider the outcomes of decisions D3, D4, and D5.

Evaluating Recruitment Effectiveness (D3)

D3 is the decision by job seekers to apply for a position. The outcome of this decision is the creation of an applicant pool. Applicant pools have attributes that can be used to determine how good the outcome of D3 is for the organization. Traditionally, this is often evaluated by examining the number of applicants attracted. Having enough applicants to ensure that the position can be filled is an important outcome of recruitment. But not only does the organization want the process to result in a hire, it wants to hire an employee who, through their work, will be able to maximize value contributed to the organization. Thus, not only does the organization want to attract applicants, but it wants to attract high-quality applicants. Further, because every applicant that applies will require at least some amount of expense to process their application and candidacy, the organization does not want large numbers of low-quality applicants. Table 14.4 offers an example of a workforce analysis that provides insight into the quality of recruitment outcomes for a position in an organization. This analysis includes information about the number of applicants attracted for each job requisition and an estimate of their quality (e.g., capacity to contribute in this job).

These data highlight substantial differences in recruitment outcomes across requisition IDs and show that the number of applicants attracted to a job listing (requisition) may not be strongly associated with the number of high-quality applicants in the pool. For instance, Requisition 22473 resulted in the most applicants ($n = 319$), but generated slightly fewer high-quality applicants and substantially more low-quality applicants than requisitions 23549, 27158, or 27160. These types of data can be used to guide decisions regarding

TABLE 14.4 ■ Analysis of Quality of Applicants Attracted by Requisition ID

Req_ID/ SCORE	<10	10s	20s	30s	40s	50s	60s	70s	80s	90s	100s	110s	Total Apps
22473		37		52	73	68	27	32	21	8	1		319
23473	32	8	16	5	5	26	80	63	6				241
27453	22	7	2	4	3	23	69	30	1				161
25106	17	3	2	2	1	10	50	27	5				117
23549					1	9	19	38	29	15	3		114
27158						8	18	37	28	16	3		110
27160								32	59	19			110
32159						8	18	14	6	1	2		49
30060		9		2	1	8	11	9	4				44

recruiting processes, particularly with respect to how organizations might alter the content of their recruiting messages and channels to alter the distribution of quality scores in future requisitions. For instance, an organization may seek to replicate the recruiting outcomes, like those for 27158, or even improve upon these results. Carlson, Connerley, and Mecham (2002) offer guidance for helping organizations that currently do not generate quality scores for all applicants to do so.

Evaluating the Effectiveness of Job Offer Decisions (D4)

D4 is the organization's decision regarding who among those who have applied will receive job offers. As noted, the outcomes of D3 represent the starting point for D4 selection processes. Consequently, the outcomes of D3 have downstream effects on the outcomes of selection decisions. The objective of selection is to identify the applicants who will be the best performers; however, because the selection activities have costs, the objective is to optimize selection decisions in light of these costs. We know from selection research that an optimal set of selection devices can be identified for any job (though that optimal set will not guarantee perfect selection decisions). To maximize selection validity (i.e., making the most correct hiring decisions), the strategy that maximizes validity is to administer all useful selection devices to all applicants and then aggregate scores optimally across these devices. Offers should then be made first to those individuals with the highest scores.

Although this approach maximizes validity, it also maximizes cost. Therefore, organizations seek methods to find an optimal combination of validity and cost. One common approach is the use of multiple-hurdle selection systems. In multiple-hurdle selection, organizations administer one or a few devices at a time to applicants, identify high scorers (and dismiss low scorers), then administer the next device, retain high scorers, and so on until all useful devices have been used. This minimizes costs because not every device is administered to every applicant. However, validity is lost because not every device is equally valid, so individuals who score high on some devices may not score high on others. Consequently, applicants that may ultimately be top performers get dismissed during the process. This is further exacerbated by the incentive to use lower-cost devices early in the sequence when there are lots of applicants to process. However, lower-cost selection devices also typically have lower validity, which increases the likelihood of losing high-quality applicants early in the process.

The objective of workforce analysis in support of selection decisions is to help organizations first understand and then improve the validity of their selection practices. Validity refers to the association between scores on a predictor (selection device) and future job performance. The validity of a selection practice is typically evaluated by examining how individuals' scores on the selection device (i.e., a resume review, standardized test, interview, etc.) correlate with future job performance scores. Consider, for example, a situation in which the predictor and future job performance are correlated $r_{xy} = .50$ (Figure 14.2).

Figure 14.2 uses an oval to represent where within the plot area the greatest density of points will occur with a correlation of $r_{xy} = .50$. The horizontal and vertical lines divide the X and Y axes respectively into low versus high scores on the predictor and low versus high scores on the outcome, with high scores being to the right or above the lines respectively. In Figure 14.2, the intersection of these horizontal and vertical lines divides the area in the diagram in to four quadrants. Quadrant I represents people who scored high on the predictor and were hired and who were also high performers on the job. Quadrant III represents people who did not score well on the predictor and, therefore, where not hired but would

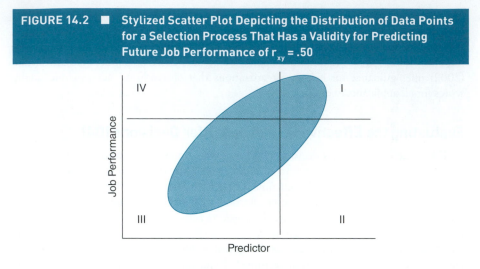

FIGURE 14.2 ■ Stylized Scatter Plot Depicting the Distribution of Data Points for a Selection Process That Has a Validity for Predicting Future Job Performance of $r_{xy} = .50$

have been poor performers had they been hired. Thus, Quadrants I and III represent correct hiring decisions. Quadrant II represents individuals who scored well on predictor but will not be high performers on the job; these are false positives. Quadrant IV represents people who do not score well on the predictor and were not hired, but, had they been hired, would have been high performers; these are false negatives. Both Quadrant II and IV represent hiring mistakes. The proportion of hiring mistakes here is indicated by the proportion of the area in blue that falls in Quadrants II and IV. Higher selection validity results in a tightening of the distribution of points, reducing the number of instances falling in Quadrants II and IV.

To evaluate selection device validity, the organization requires data on the correlation between applicant scores on selection devices and their future job performance. As readers may recognize, organizations are unlikely to hire all individuals in an applicant pool, so the organization will not have performance scores for all applicants. There are several imperfect solutions to this challenge. First, organizations can examine the magnitudes of relationships between predictor scores and outcomes for the data they do have (i.e., job performance for hires only). This can be a potential solution when the organization hires large numbers of individuals for a given position. Second, organizations can choose to rely on selection devices that have been developed by outside organizations for which large-scale validation studies have been conducted. Here evidence of validity generalization can be used to estimate the validity of devices for positions in a given organization. Schmidt and Hunter (1998) provide evidence of the validity of several common selection devices. Although methods for estimating the validity of selection devices may yield imperfect results, organizations should not be dissuaded from developing the best data they can to help improve the validity of selection procedures.

Evaluating Job Acceptance Performance (D5)

Finally, organizations want to maximize acceptance rates of applicants. Job acceptance performance refers to the extent to which the organization can influence its preferred candidates to acceptance of job offers. In our staffing example, an outcome of D4 is a list of individuals to whom the organization is willing to make job offers. If all preferred candidates accept the offers extended, job acceptance performance is maximized. Often, that is not the case. A traditional means of assessing job acceptance is through a yield ratio, the ratio of offers accepted to offers extended. For example, an organization that extends five job offers for a specific position and has three of them accepted would have a yield ratio of .60 or 60%. Organizations seek to maximize yield ratios.

A yield ratio does have limitations though. Specifically, yield ratios assume that every job offer that is accepted and, likewise, every job offer that is declined has the same impact on the organization. That is rarely true. Not everyone who is extended an offer is necessarily expected to produce the same on-the-job performance. Further, if the organization has a given number of positions to fill, failing to gain acceptance of an offer often means that an offer will need to be extended to the next-higher-scoring applicant pool that, by definition, is perceived to have lower potential. The difference in performance potential between the first-choice applicant and the person who eventually accepts the offer reflects the loss that occurs by not gaining an acceptance from the preferred candidate.

The magnitude of the opportunity that exists for improving job acceptance results is gauged by the number of individuals who do not accept offers and the difference in job performance potential between initial offerees and the individuals that ultimately accept positions. If an organization experiences few instances of rejected offers or recruits sufficient numbers of highly rated applicants such that there is little difference in performance potential between original offerees and accepters, then there may not be opportunities to substantively improve job acceptance practices. On the other hand, if job acceptance results are poor and poor recruiting results in few high-scoring applicants, then improving job acceptance results may be an important opportunity for the organization.

The following example illustrates these effects. The data in Table 14.5 represent applicant scores for the top 10 applicants for a position for two different job requisitions. The three top-scoring individuals from each applicant pool will receive offers. Now consider the following scenarios. First, assume that the top applicant in each pool does not accept their offers, while Candidates 2 and 3 do. In response to the nonacceptance, the organization offers the fourth-best candidate who then accepts. The amount of regret in each case can be initially scaled by the difference in applicant scores between the nonaccepting

TABLE 14.5 ■ Job Acceptance Performance Analysis		
Score Range	**Pool 1 Applicant Scores**	**Pool 2 Applicant Scores**
110–120		110
100–110	108, 107, 105, 102	102
90–100	99, 96, 95, 92, 90	93
80–90	87	85, 81
70–80		79, 76, 73
60–70		67, 65
50–60		

top-scoring applicant and fourth best applicant who accepts. In Pool 1, the presence of several high-scoring applicants results in a modest loss of six points (i.e., [1st – 4th] 108 – 102). In Pool 2, which has the highest-overall-scoring applicant, the smaller number of top scoring applicants results in a more substantial loss of 25 points (i.e., [1st – 4th] 110 – 85).

Consider the alternate scenario in which job acceptance performance is worse, resulting such that the first-, second-, and fourth-best applicants do not accept offers, but the third, fifth, and sixth do. In Pool 1, this results in a loss of 20 points (i.e., [1st – 4th] 108 –102 + ([2nd – 5th] 107 – 99) + ([4th – 6th] 102 – 96) = 20). However, in Pool 2, the result is a more substantial loss of 52 points (i.e., [1st – 4th] 110 – 85 + [2nd – 5th] 102 – 81 + [4th – 6th] 85 – 79).

Analyses like these can be useful for every organization. Ideally, organizations would attempt to estimate more precise value of differences in scores in dollar increments, though in many cases, this may not currently be feasible for at least some positions in every organization. But the value of working toward such estimates is easily seen in these examples, particularly when gauging the amount of investment an organization should be willing to make to intervene to capture opportunities of different magnitudes. But even in the absence of dollar-valued estimates of score differences, these analyses can be very useful. They provide guidance that is more conceptually correct than commonly used alternative metrics, and score differences are directionally correct and the magnitudes have at least ordinal interpretations—bigger differences in scores represent bigger opportunities for improvement.

Assessing the Financial Impact of Staffing Decisions: Utility Analysis

Thus far, the staffing analyses that have been described examine changes in intermediate staffing outcomes, such as increases in applicant quality, increased acceptance rates of first-choice job offerees, and retention of high-performing employees. Although improving these outcomes is important, these metrics do not provide an outcome that is readily interpreted in dollars that can be directly compared to changes in costs. Estimating the contribution of better performance on intermediate outcomes to organizations can be challenging. Boudreau's (1989) discussion of utility analysis provides an initial step toward estimating the value of the greater contributions of better employees to organization effectiveness. Utility analysis requires three pieces of information. The first is an estimate of where applicants fall in the distribution of potential employee performances. They can be estimated imperfectly by the relative location of an applicant's quality score in the distribution of all applicant quality scores. The second is an estimate of how imperfect the estimate of applicant quality is likely to be. This is provided by the estimate of the validity of the selection procedure. The third piece of information is an estimate of the value of differences in job performance. Jobs that have high autonomy, in which individuals have greater capacity to determine what they will do and how it will be done, have greater potential for increasing the variability in outcome. Done well, those decisions create the potential for high outcomes, but done poorly, there is also the potential for very poor outcomes. Low-autonomy positions tend to produce more consistent results. High responsibility increases the potential impact of each decision, perhaps because it involves more dollars or impacts more people, further increasing the difference in the value of high versus low performance. These can be estimated by subject matter experts, or in the absence of these data, a rough estimate can be develop using salary data as shown in what follows.

In utility analysis, differences in the value of better employees can be determined by estimating the difference between the location of two employees in the distribution of all employees. This can be done by calculating a standardized difference in applicant scores (i.e., ΔZ = [Score of Applicant 1 – Score of Applicant 2] / Standard deviation of applicant scores). If standardized differences are calculated, the value of these differences can be estimated if we know the difference in contribution we might expected for a one-standard-deviation difference in job performance. In utility analysis, this is known as the standard deviation of job performance in dollars (SD_y). This value will vary across jobs according to a number of factors, including the amount of autonomy and responsibility assigned to the job. In the absence of more specific information, an initial estimate of SD_y can be developed by multiplying .4 times salary. So for a job with a salary of $50,000, this approach would yield an estimate of SD_y = $20,000. Given these input differences, an initial rough estimate of differences in job performance could be estimated using the following formula:

$$Utility = \Delta Z \times r_{xy} \times SD_y$$

Therefore, for two applicants with scores of 110 and 90 for a device for which the standard deviation of applicant scores is SD = 20, a selection device with validity of r_{xy} = .50, and who are applicants for a managerial position with an annual salary of $50,000, an estimate of the difference in job performance per year would be calculated as follows:

$$Utility = (110 – 90)/20 \times .50 \times (.40 \times \$50,000) = \$10,000$$

Thus, when triaging selection analysis opportunities, greater opportunity comes from (a) high volume of hires, (b) low validity of current selection processes, and (c) the value of the standard deviation of performance for a given position. These data can then be evaluated in conjunction with data on the validity and cost of various alternative selection processes. Thus, workforce analytics can be used to put a tangible cost or benefit value to the hiring decision based upon the score on a selection device.

BUILDING A WORKFORCE ANALYTICS FUNCTION

Getting Started

When undertaking a metrics and analytics effort, the first question the organization needs to answer is, what problems in the organization are worth solving or what opportunities for enhancing organizational effectiveness exist? Organizations are awash in opportunities for increasing effectiveness. Choosing to spend time on projects with a greater potential return to the company makes good business sense. Given that most organizations' capabilities in HR metrics and analytics may not be well developed at this point, focusing on a limited number of potentially high-payback opportunities may be the best strategy as organizations develop their workforce analytics capability.

Understanding *Why*

Management scholars have theories of how organizations work. Most organizational members have their own personal theories regarding how their companies work. These theories provide a framework for identifying potentially important information, focusing attention on environmental stimuli, and strengthening the capacity to identify the tactics that can be used to solve problems. However, choices for outcome measures to assess are often based on personal theories about how things work in the organization, theories that may not reflect reality. For example, company employees often identify intermediate outcomes, such as implementation of flexible work hours (flex time) or changes in supervisors, as outcomes of interest. Intermediate outcomes are those that are more immediate indicators of things that employees believe lead to more important outcomes, for example, changes in the two previous intermediate outcomes leading to a "much happier" workplace. However, in some cases, the intermediate outcomes may not be the best ones on which to focus. This situation occurs when changes in decisions impact intermediate outcomes but do not have the expected impact on the ultimate or distal outcomes.

An important test of the appropriateness of intermediate outcomes is the *why* test. When one considers a potential outcome variable, it is useful to ask why the organization is interested in that specific outcome. If the answer is because it impacts some other variable that influences an important outcome, then care must be taken to ensure that changing the intermediate (or proximal) outcome also impacts the distal outcome. Organizational factors such as pay and working conditions that have influence through their effects on intermediate variables are reasonable targets for assessment, particularly if we understand the subsequent impact these factors have on ultimate, distal, and more important outcomes. Often, changing factors such as pay and working conditions will impact intermediate outcomes but may not produce any effect on the ultimate outcome of company profitability. Therefore, when analyzing intermediate outcomes, it is important to determine whether the intermediate outcome is limiting the performance of the ultimate outcome.

Employee turnover of valued employees, for example, is often identified as an important organizational outcome due to the costs associated with it (Cascio, 2000). It is among the most frequently assessed and reported HR metrics in organizations. Most managers agree that excessive turnover is a significant problem. High levels of turnover are disruptive to operations and can cause organizations to lose the critical expertise and capabilities of employees that leave. The answer to *why* turnover is important is that it disrupts operations and leads to potential loss of knowledge and important skill sets. But in many cases, it is not clear whether the departure of specific employees actually results in decreasing profits. In some cases, a departing employee is replaced by a stronger performer, which will enhance profits. At a minimum, asking why helps highlight the potential causal sequence through which these intermediate variable effects are expected to have their influence. These analyses can highlight which metrics are likely to be more critical and provide a framework for understanding how change in these metrics should be interpreted. Building the capacity to understand the causal sequences through which interventions have their effects is an important capability for an organization's workforce analysts.

Putting HR Metrics and Analytics Data in Context

Reporting HR metrics data alone is ineffective in leading to improvement in managerial decision making. Data points representing important organizational outcomes become useful when the decision maker can attach some meaning to them. Often data will need to be placed in context. For example, knowing that an organization's turnover level for newly hired management trainees is 13% is more meaningful when it can be placed in the context of the organization's previous turnover history for this position. Is turnover rising or falling for this position, and if so, how quickly? Reporting trend information for metrics is one way to provide the context that gives meaning to the data, thus creating useful information.

Benchmarking is a second means to putting data in context. Data on metrics from other organizations in the same industry can provide information that offers insight into an organization's performance relative to its peers. However, not all companies are organized in the same way. As a result, and particularly for HR metrics, how the HRM function is structured in an organization can have a significant impact on the value of HR efficiency metrics. A department with a more centralized structure of HR functions typically has lower efficiency metrics than HR departments structured such that more of the responsibility for HR processes and activities exists in operating units. As a result, HR benchmarking data need to be considered in the context of how the organization has structured the HR function. Senior management needs to ensure that the HRM function is supporting organizational effectiveness. Then the HR organization can be structured in order to maximize HRM effectiveness in supporting organizational objectives. HR effectiveness measures can then be maximized within the context of that structure. For these reasons, internal rather than external benchmarking will often provide more appropriate data for establishing operational objectives for the HR efficiency benchmarks. Although external data are useful, care needs to be taken to understand how HR functions and activities are structured in the organizations providing this data.

Reporting What We Find

Reporting metrics incorporate decisions about (a) what metrics will be reported; (b) how these metrics will be packaged; and (c) how, (d) when, and (e) to whom they should be reported. Effort has focused on attempting to identify what metrics an organization should use. However, trying to identify what metrics should be reported without considering an organization's problems and opportunities misses the reasons for the metrics. How metrics should be reported focuses on depicting metrics for decision makers so that the "message" relevant to them has a greater probability of being understood.

How questions deal with choosing between distributing metrics to decision makers using e-mail or creating opportunities for decision makers to extract metrics as needed. This latter approach can be done by posting the metrics on company Web sites.

When questions deal with the timing and frequency of metrics reports. In some cases, reporting is currently done annually, quarterly, or monthly. Some organizations are also considering the possibility of real-time updating for some metrics.

To whom questions address who receives metrics data. To date, it is most common for metrics and analytics to be reported first to senior executives. However, there is a growing recognition that managers at lower levels of the organization may be able to make more immediate use of the information contained in these data in order to assist in tactical, operational decisions.

HR metrics and workforce analytics information can be reported in several ways. Generally, a combination of "push" and "pull" means of communication will work for most organizations. Push communications channels, such as e-mail, actively push information and analyses to the attention of managers. These channels are used for information that is time critical or that the manager is unaware of. **Push systems** are excellent for getting information to decision makers. However, sending irrelevant or poorly timed information through push systems can contribute to information overload and reduce managers' sensitivity to messages. As a result, they may only skim the information sent through push systems or, even worse, not attend to it at all.

Pull systems are ways of making information available to managers so that they can access any of it at a point in time when it will be most useful for their decision making. Examples include (1) posting HR metrics and analytics analyses and reports on internal company Web sites, (2) offering access to searchable information repositories, or (3) providing access to analytics tools as examples. These pull methods avoid the e-mail clutter associated with push systems, but pull systems can be ineffective because managers may not know what information is available or when or where to look for the information.

How frequently data are analyzed and reported is also an important consideration. The existence of an integrated HRIS, faster computing capabilities, more effective software, and advanced internal communication systems creates the capability to analyze and report information in real time for managers. How frequently data are reported and how narrowly data are packaged are also critical to supporting effective decision making. Creating reporting cycles that are too long risks losing opportunities to make changes in operations on the basis of the reported information. Aggregating too much data from subunits to higher-level units can result in the problem of causing differences between operating units, departments, or functions to be buried in the aggregated averages for the higher unit. This information for managers' work units must be available to support decision making.

HR Dashboards

A common form of reporting HR analytics data is in the form of a dashboard. **Dashboards** reflect efforts to align real-time analysis of organizational and HR processes as well as an increased capacity to aggregate organizational data. Dashboards also contain business unit analyses to permit managers to drill down to examine metrics on several levels within the organization. The dashboard allows users to maintain a current snapshot of key HR metrics. In discussions with individuals who construct metrics and analytics reports, we hear a common concern: These individuals wonder *whether anyone pays any attention* to the reports they produce. Often, they send reports to managers and receive no feedback of any kind. Often those who do get positive feedback are HR professionals who embed an interpretation of what the data they mean for the organization and the decision maker. Reporting data in context is a key component of their success stories.

Being consultative is an important skill that workforce analysts need to develop. For individuals conducting metrics and analytics work, paying attention to the capabilities and needs of the targeted audience is critically important. The information reported must be relevant to the issues facing the managers who receive it. Further, simply providing numbers to managers is unlikely to be of much use to them until they can understand the meaning of the information for their decision situations. Consequently, the HR analyst must report the numbers but also provide an interpretation of what the data mean for the manager's decision situation. Some HR analysts argue that the interpretation of analyses is the central message that needs to speak to managers, which, in turn, is then supported by the data. When packaging a metrics analysis, then, we must understand the needs of the recipients and fit the data to the information needs of the decision maker.

USEFUL THINGS TO REMEMBER ABOUT HR METRICS AND ANALYTICS

Don't "Do Metrics"

The *primary objective* of developing capabilities in HR metrics and workforce analytics is *to increase organizational effectiveness*. It is not simply to generate a static menu of HR metrics reports. Simply conducting the analysis and developing reports are activities, and activities raise costs. Developing HR metrics and workforce analytics to be used by managers and professionals must involve a return on the organization's investment. The real test of the value of HR metrics and workforce analytics is whether managers who have access to the information provided by these analyses make different and better decisions.

Bigger Is Not Always Better

Bigger is not always better. Small metrics and analytics projects have several advantages over the multimillion-dollar implementation projects that include integrated prepackaged analytics systems. First, they cost less and require fewer resources in terms of time and materials. Second, they are less visible during the initial start-up while the project team is learning through trial and error. These two aspects provide the project team with opportunities to focus on critical HR metrics while giving them the flexibility to work through the necessary trials and errors.

Avoid the Temptation to Measure Everything Aggressively

Not every HR function, process, or metric that can be analyzed should be. Successful efforts will focus on those things, at a given point in time, that are most likely to have the greatest impact on managerial decision making. The intensity of an assessment project should be matched to how much opportunity it offers for improvements, and the project itself should be focused on factors, processes, and functions related to those things that are likely to have the greatest impact on organization effectiveness.

HR Metrics and Analytics Is a Journey—Not a Destination

Because the focus is on identifying and responding to opportunities and problems, useful and effective HR metrics and workforce analytics projects will change over time. Markets for both products and labor will change, as will organizational processes. These changes will require adjustments in the ideal size, skill requirements, and deployment of an organization's human capital. If organizations are successful in solving operational problems or capturing opportunities, the focus for managers naturally shifts to other problems or new opportunities. These problems are unlikely to require the same analytics and therefore may depend on identifying new metrics.

Be Willing to Learn

Organizations that have an HR metrics and analytics function will develop a bias for experimentation to try out new HR activities, programs, or processes. One consequence of organizational life is the ongoing opportunity to recognize that there may be a better way to do things than your current approach. This point is true not only for the organization's operational processes but also for its metrics and analytics efforts. The organization should develop a metrics and analytics "laboratory" in which the HRM professionals can experiment with new analyses and test existing assumptions about the requirements of the organization's current systems. This examination can foster new approaches and allow new metrics and analytics to be created.

Workforce Analytics and the Future

The development of useful and effective workforce analytics is likely to be viewed in the future as a very significant source of competitive advantage. We now have the tools and the computing infrastructure to handle these projects that can help us understand organizations and support effective organizational functioning. By using effective approaches to workforce analytics, decision makers will acquire the ability to more effectively manage and improve HR programs and processes as well as to improve the effectiveness of HRIS use. Using this acquired ability, managerial decision makers may be able to modify entire employment systems to manage the company's human capital more effectively. Bintliff-Ritchie (2006) notes the following managerial benefits of metrics for organizations:

- Operational reporting is more efficient and cost-effective because the data from individual applications is integrated and accessed through a single solution.

- Graphically rich information is available to the people who need to make decisions and show metric-based results.

- Human resources practices and investments can be optimized to meet enterprise performance goals.

As a result, organizations that make investments in internal human capital assessment resulting in useful HR metrics and workforce analytics will become less willing to share their knowledge with other organizations in their industry. Benchmarking, which has been a staple of HR metrics and workforce analytics for almost three decades, will become more difficult to access and develop as organizations recognize the competitive value of these capabilities.

Summary

The central focus of this chapter was to define workforce analytics and discuss how and when it can contribute to improving organizational effectiveness. Workforce analysis activities provide no return on the organization's investment unless managers make different and more effective decisions as a result of the information provided by metrics and analytics reports. Therefore, focusing the development of workforce analytics around organizationally important problems and opportunities is likely to increase the possibility of significant returns for the organization.

This chapter also highlights the wide range of activities that fall within the domain of workforce analytics. Although classic metrics still have value, new software offers tremendous opportunities to change both the metrics and types of analyses organizations undertake. We can expect the types of metrics organizations use in the future to change as the needs of decision makers change, and as these analyses continue to work toward effectively balancing the benefit and cost consequences of decisions (see Chapter 6). Components of this continued evolution of metrics and analytics capabilities are driven by increased use of both push and pull reporting systems, more extensive use of predictive analytics and operational experiments, and the development of organizational expertise in metrics and analytics capabilities. As these skills mature, organizations will be able to move beyond simple analyses of HR efficiency metrics to a greater emphasis on operational effectiveness and organizational realignment analyses, which will further enhance the value of workforce analysis systems.

Key Terms

administrative process efficiency 373

artificial intelligence 370

balanced scorecard 366

benchmarking 368

big data 368

dashboards 386

data mining 368

HR metrics 367

HR process efficiency analytics 373

machine learning 370

operational effectiveness 374

operational experiments 371

predictive analysis 369

pull systems 386

push systems 386

reporting metrics 385

strategic realignment 374

variety 369

velocity 369

veracity 369

volume 369

workforce analytics 368

workforce modeling 370

Discussion Questions

1. What factors have led to increased organizational interest in HR metrics and workforce analytics?

2. When might the information from numeric information systems such as HR metrics and workforce analytics *not* generate any return on investment (ROI)?

3. What are some of the limitations of the traditional HR metrics?

4. Discuss the historical role of HR benchmarking and its strengths and weaknesses as part of a metrics and analytics program in organizations today.

5. What roles might more recent analysis activities, such as data mining, predictive statistical analyses, and operational experiments, play in increasing organizational effectiveness?

6. What differences exist between metrics and analytics that focus on HR efficiency, operational effectiveness, and organizational realignment? Offer examples of each.

7. Describe which characteristics of HR metrics and workforce analytics are likely to result in greater return on investment and organizational impact.

Case Study: Regional Hospital

Regional Hospital is a 500-bed hospital and several associated clinics in a major East Coast metropolitan area. It has been an aggressive adopter of computing technologies in efforts to decrease costs and improve operational efficiencies. A critical challenge facing the hospital is meeting its ongoing challenges to staff the hospital and allied clinics effectively, given the ongoing shortage of nurses; uncertainty in health care legislation; emphasis on shortening hospital stays to reduce costs, which causes the daily census (numbers of patients in various departments) to vary dramatically from day to day and shift to shift; the continued aging of the population in its primary care area; and the unending competition for employees with key skill sets. Employee expenses represent more than 80% of the overall costs of operation for the hospital, so identifying ways to match optimal skills and numbers of employees to the appropriate shifts is critical to achieving consistent success. However, individual shift managers struggle to make effective staffing decisions, resulting in consistent overstaffing or understaffing of shifts and departments. These staffing problems potentially increase the high costs of varied levels of patient care and satisfaction and potentially increase the risk that staff turnover may escalate because of dissatisfaction with the continuing inability of managers to match staffing needs to demand.

Company managers recognize the potential that HR metrics and analytics might have for their organization, and they have come to you for help. They are hearing from their peers in other hospitals that metrics can help in this area but are not quite sure where to start. They are looking for you to offer guidance on how to do HR metrics and workforce analytics.

Case Study Questions

1. Do you believe that a program of HR metrics and workforce analytics might be useful in Regional Hospital? If so, why?

2. What opportunities do you see regarding *where* and *how* metrics and analytics might be applied in this organization?

3. Identify three analyses and associated metrics you think might be useful for Regional Hospital to consider.

4. How might Regional Hospital utilize benchmarking as a part of its metrics and analytics effort, if at all?

5. What advice would you offer to the managers at Regional Hospital about developing a program of HR metrics and workforce analytics?

6. What potential problems might occur in the establishment of an HR metrics and workforce analytics program for Regional Hospital managers about which you would want to alert them prior to beginning this project?

15

HRIS PRIVACY AND SECURITY

Humayun Zafar and Dianna L. Stone

EDITORS' NOTE

This chapter expands on the information security and privacy issues in HRIS described in Chapter 3 (system considerations) and Chapter 10 (HR administration). Many organizations mistakenly believe that the biggest threat to information security is from outside. This chapter explains the importance of employee information privacy, the threats to employee privacy, and the varying privacy protections afforded employees by laws. In addition, the chapter reviews information security, focusing on the technical and behavioral practices of strong information security practices. It also highlights how present and past employees can pose a greater threat to employee privacy than outsiders in the light of the emergence of collaborative and convergent technologies. Finally, the chapter describes the importance, legal aspects, and best practices in maintaining and promoting safe information-handling procedures.

CHAPTER OBJECTIVES

After completing this chapter, you should be able to:

- Describe the importance of information security and privacy in today's technology-intensive and information-driven economy
- Describe the important components of and threats to information security
- List the legal requirements pertaining to information security and privacy
- Discuss best practices in safe information-handling procedures

HRIS IN ACTION

Human resource (HR) departments around the world, and especially the United States, have become a major target for attackers. In 2018, the Internal Revenue Service (IRS) issued a warning to HR professionals specifying the risk that phishing posed. It highlighted how certain phishing attacks seeking W-2 forms had victimized "hundreds of organizations and thousands of employees." Even though HR professionals and employees had undergone security training, the attackers were still successful, since they were able to better disguise their HR breach efforts. They examined the writing styles of executives on LinkedIn and Facebook and were able to create authentic-looking phishing emails that most employees assumed were coming from a legitimate source. Even cloud-based payroll systems are not immune from these attacks. We predict that the future threat vector in this arena will only increase.

INTRODUCTION

We should treat personal electronic data with the same care and respect as weapons-grade plutonium—it is dangerous, long-lasting, and once it has leaked, there's no getting it back.

—Cory Doctorow

Information privacy and security are particularly important issues for HRIS because unlike many other organizational systems, an HRIS includes a great deal of confidential data about employees, such as Social Security numbers, medical data, bank account data, salaries, domestic partner benefits, employment test scores, and performance evaluations (DeSanctis, 1986; Kovach & Cathcart, 1999). These data are highly marketable on the dark web. The earlier scenario highlights how hackers can use techniques from phishing to posing as company executives asking for internal documents (a form of phishing also known as whaling) to exploit a system. To counter these threats, organizations have to follow safe computing protocols. Most organizations have moved away from using systems that are based on what the information security industry refers to as "knowledge-based authentication": things people know—and that can be stolen—such as an individual's password. In fact, the majority of the Internet relies on only an e-mail and password. A solution is to use two-factor authentication (2FA), which combines "something you know" with "something you have." For example, in addition to a username and password combination, the user will need to have something with them, such as a physical token. In the future, biometrics and artificial intelligence (AI) may also help. But because these threats will continue, it is critical for organizations to understand and pay close attention to what employee data is collected, stored, manipulated, used, and distributed—when, why, and by whom. Organizations also need to carefully consider the internal and external threats to this data and develop strong information security plans and procedures to protect this data and comply with legislative mandates. Past breaches (e.g., the

Anthem Healthcare breach in 2015) have shown that major companies have been negligent in ensuring confidentiality of data by not encrypting key data.

Ensuring secure systems is much more complex than it was 30 years ago. Consider that most computers at that time were mainframes that were secured in a central physical location, with very few HR staff having access to them. If an HR staff member had access to the mainframe, it was through "dumb" terminals with limited functionalities, and access was easily restricted through physical access and passwords. Due to this closed environment, there was little threat of **security breaches** or vulnerabilities being exploited. During those days, information security was considered to be a process that was composed mostly of physical security and simple document classification schemes. Physical theft of equipment, espionage, and sabotage were considered the primary threats. However, starting in the 1990s as computer networks became more common, threats to information security became more involved due to the presence of enterprisewide systems.

There is a growing concern about the extent to which these systems permit users (both inside and outside of the organization) to access a wide array of personal information about employees. As a result, employees may perceive that if these data are accessed by others, the information contained in their employment files may embarrass them or result in negative outcomes (e.g., denial of promotion or challenging job assignment). Recent research suggests that this concern may be well founded. For example, one report indicated that more than 500 million organizational records have been breached since 2005, and there has been a rise in the theft of employment data (Privacy Rights Clearinghouse, 2010). For instance, in 2010, a hard drive was stolen from AMR Corporation, the parent company of American Airlines. The hard drive included names, Social Security numbers, health records, and bank account data for many current employees, retirees, and former employees. As a result, some employees and retirees experienced identity theft. Given these problems, AMR took important steps to implement information security practices to secure the confidentiality of all employee records (Privacy Rights Clearinghouse, 2010). In addition, in 2010, ADP notified its clients that tax and salary data of employees was stolen (Pagliery, 2016).

In view of the growing concern about identity theft and the security of employment information in HRISs, a number of states (e.g., AK, CA, FL, HI, IL, LA, MO, NY, SC, WA) passed privacy laws requiring organizations to adopt reasonable security practices to prevent unauthorized access to personal data (Privacy Protections in State Constitutions, 2012). Despite these new laws, results of surveys revealed that 43% of businesses stated that they did not put any new security solutions in place to prevent the inadvertent release or access to employee data, and almost half did not change any internal policies to ensure that data were secure (Ponemon, 2012). The cost of these data breaches can be large. The average cost of a data breach has increased to almost $4 million per firm, and the average cost incurred for each stolen or lost record containing sensitive and confidential information has increased to $158 (Ponemon, 2016).

Software vendors such as Oracle are aware of the potential for security breaches and offer multiple security models (e.g., Standard HRIS Security and Security Groups Enabled Security) that enable an administrator to set up HRIS security specifically for an organization. This means that the software allows companies to determine the kind of data access and responsibility each employee has. For example, an HR manager will have higher privileges and access to data than an employee in sales or even an employee in human resources. This would allow him or her to access a wide array of employee data. On the other hand, a sales manager would need limited data for each employee (e.g., performance-based records for their subordinates) and thus would have less access to employee data. As the importance of HRIS privacy and security continues to grow in salience to organizations, it provides an interesting avenue for new employment opportunities. A typical entry-level HRIS analyst position now requires knowledge of implementing secure HR information systems.

Therefore, this chapter elaborates on various aspects of HRIS privacy and security. The next few sections consider (a) practices that may affect individuals' perceptions of invasion of privacy, (b) the components of information security, and (c) the implications for developing fair information management policies. After this, the chapter elaborates on some of the key security threats faced by organizations and the policies that organizations need to implement to ensure HRIS privacy and security. Before concluding, we explain contingency planning and its three components.

We discuss privacy issues first because security systems are typically designed to protect employee privacy and ensure that employment information is not subject to unauthorized access. We also look at privacy through a global lens, because almost all data are now shared across international boundaries. This is particularly important due to changes in the regulatory environment such as the European General Data Protection Regulation.

EMPLOYEE PRIVACY IN A GLOBAL ENVIRONMENT

Given the widespread use of the Internet, recent polls have shown that 61% of the American public are increasingly concerned about the protection of their personal privacy (Raine, 2018). Americans are not the only ones concerned with privacy, and many people around the world worry about online privacy. For example, recent surveys indicated that 65% of Internet users in Latin America, 63% of those in the Middle East and Africa, 54% of users in Asia and the Pacific, and 35% of those in Europe are apprehensive about their online privacy (Statista, 2019). Thus, approximately 109 nations have passed laws to protect the privacy of their citizens (Greenleaf, 2015), and a partial list of those nations with privacy laws is noted in Table 15.1. A complete list of countries can be found in Greenleaf (2015).

TABLE 15.1 ■ Example Privacy Laws in Various Countries

Country	Law	Date
Angola	Da Protecção de Dados Pessoais	2011
Argentina	Personal Data Protection Act	2000
Canada	Personal Information Protection and Electronics Document Act	2000
European Union	The European Union Data Protection Directive	1998
Germany	Bundesdatenschutzgesetz	2001
Japan	Personal Information Protection Act	2003
Mexico	Ley Federal de Protección de Datos Personales en Posesión de los Particulares	2010
New Zealand	The Privacy Act	1993
South Korea	Personal Information Protection Act	2011
United Kingdom	Computer Misuse Act	1998

In view of the large number of countries that have passed privacy laws, we believe that these legal restrictions have important implications for the design and development of HRIS and the establishment of privacy policies in organizations. Employers need to be aware of national and international privacy laws when designing and using HRIS to collect, store, use, and disseminate data about applicants and employees. In view of these privacy concerns and laws, the primary purpose of this section of the chapter is to review the privacy laws around the world and consider the specific laws in the European Union and the United States (U.S.). We begin by discussing the worldwide privacy laws, then present the European data laws, and finally the federal and state privacy laws in the U.S.

Worldwide Privacy Laws

To date, more than 109 nations have passed laws to protect the privacy of their citizens (Greenleaf, 2015). Interestingly, researchers have argued that laws are indirect indices of individuals' privacy values and norms, and they contend people in individualistic nations (e.g., Europe, U.S.) are often more concerned about privacy than those in collective countries (e.g., Asia, South America; Stone, Krueger, & Takach, 2017). The primary reason for this is that individualists often value independence, freedom, autonomy, and self-reliance, and control over personal information enables them to maintain their autonomy and freedom (Markus & Kitayama 1991a, 1991b; Stone-Romero et al., 2003). However, those in collective nations typically use the group as the unit of analysis in social relationships and value interdependence, security, and personalized relationships (Markus & Kitayama 1991a, 1991b; Triandis, 1994). As a result, they are often less concerned about individual privacy and sharing personal information with others than individualists because it helps them cultivate personal relationships (Stone et al., 2017). Therefore, researchers predicted that individualistic countries would be more likely to pass privacy laws than collective countries.

However, a review of the nations in Table 15.1 revealed that this prediction may not be correct, and many Asian countries that are considered collective have now passed privacy laws, even though privacy has not always been a key part of their values and norms. For instance, Hong Kong, Taiwan, Singapore, Japan, Macao, and Thailand have each passed privacy laws. Further, many Western, individualistic nations have also passed laws designed to protect privacy (e.g., the United Kingdom, Australia, U.S.). More than 50% of European countries now have laws to protect individual privacy. Given the passage of these laws, it can be argued that privacy is now a widespread global value, and it can be expected that additional nations will pass privacy laws in the near future. In view of these laws, organizations that conduct business across national boundaries should review their data collection, data dissemination practices, and HRIS to ensure that they comply with worldwide privacy laws.

It merits emphasis that the European Union has one of the most stringent regulations regarding privacy, and it has important implications for how European, multinational or transnational businesses process data (General Data Protection Regulation, 2018). Therefore, we provide a brief overview of the European General Data Protection Regulation and its consequences for the development of HRIS in multinational corporations.

European General Data Protection Regulation

In 2018, the European Union passed a data privacy protection law titled the **General Data Protection Regulation (GDPR)** that superseded the 1995 European Data Protection

Directive (1995). The new law applies to all EU organizations that collect, store, or disseminate personal information about individuals residing in the EU (including non–EU citizens) and any organization outside the EU that offers goods and services to EU citizens and processes information about them. The GDPR expands the privacy rights of individuals, sets requirements for organizational data processing, and places limits on how data can be processed or transferred across national borders. A brief review of each of these rights and requirements is considered, but it should be noted that we only provide a subset of the requirements because they are extensive.

A. The GDPR extends the rights of individuals (data subjects), and requires that organizations:

- Establish a governance structure and keep detailed records for data processing with roles and responsibilities

- Document data protection policies and procedures

- Implement appropriate measures to secure personal data

B. Enhances the privacy rights of individuals and requires that data subjects have:

- The right to be informed about the collection, storage, and release of data

- The right to access their data

- The right to ensure that the data are accurate, and rectify or erase data that are inaccurate

C. Requires that organizations comply with the following data processing principles. They must:

- Collect data only for specific legitimate purposes

- Limit data collection to that which is relevant and necessary

- Ensure data are accurate and kept up to date

- Store data only as long as is necessary.

D. Sets guidelines for the lawful processing of information. Data can only be processed:

- If the data subject has given his/her consent

- To meet contractual or legal obligations

- For legitimate interests of the organization

E. Requires that organizations comply with stricter rules for obtaining consent.

- Consent must be freely given, specific, informed, and unambiguous.

- Consent can be withdrawn at any time.

- Organizations must be able to show evidence of consent.

F. Specifies that data controllers and processors must implement technical and organizational measures designed to ensure the safety of data.

- Data protection must be considered at the design stage of any new process, system, or technology.

- A data protection impact assessment is an integral part of privacy by design.

G. Places limits on the transfer of personal data outside of the EU.

H. Requires organizations to report a breach of security leading to unauthorized disclosure, access, or transmission of data.

I. Requires organizations to appoint a data protection officer to oversee compliance with the law.

The GDPR is very comprehensive and indicates that organizations within the EU or those that do business in the EU will have to establish clear and specific privacy protection policies and practices that comply with the law. These policies will definitely affect the design and development of HRIS and expand applicants' and employees' privacy rights. For example, applicants or employees will have to give their consent before data are collected for a HRIS, stored in it, or released by the organization. They will also have to be given access to their data and provided with the opportunity to rectify or erase data that are inaccurate. Organizations will have to limit the transfer of data across national boundaries and provide applicants or employees with information about any breaches of their personal data. Many of these practices are already used by organizations in the U.S. and other countries, but any organization that sells products or services in the EU will have to become familiar with the regulation and implement the principles in it.

Privacy Laws in the United States

Although the Bill of Rights in the U.S. guarantees individuals the right to privacy, there is no overarching federal privacy law that places restrictions on the collection, use, or dissemination of data about private-sector job applicants or employees. However, there is a federal Privacy Act (1974) that protects the privacy of federal government employees, and there are other federal and state laws that restrict the collection and dissemination of employment data. Thus, we review the federal and state laws that affect the collection, use, and release of applicant and employee data in the sections that follow.

Data Collection About Applicants and Employees

Federal Laws. As noted, there is no overarching privacy law that places limits on the collection of information in the private-sector employment process. However, a number of related federal laws prohibit the collection of specific types of information about individuals. For example, the Americans with Disabilities Act (ADA; 1990) indicates that employers cannot collect data about disabilities in the employment process and must store information about disabilities separate from other files. Similarly, the Genetic Information Nondiscrimination Act of 2008 prohibits the collection of genetic data about applicants or employees.

Likewise, civil rights laws indicate that it is inadvisable for employers to collect data about individuals' age, race, ethnicity, gender, national origin, pregnancy, religion, or other protected information because they may be used as the basis for lawsuits regarding unfair discrimination. If employers collect these data, they will have to show that the information was not used to make employment decisions, and that is often difficult to do. Further, the Equal Employment Opportunity Commission (EEOC) specifies that employers should not collect data about arrests, criminal convictions, or credit that may result in a disparate impact against protected groups (e.g., racial minorities). Even though there is no omnibus privacy act at the federal level, a number of states have passed laws that place restrictions on the types of information that can be collected about individuals in the employment process.

State Laws. As noted, many states have passed laws that place limits on the collection of personal data about applicants and employees (e.g., CA, WI, NY).[1] Thus, we provide a cursory review of the types of state laws that restrict the collection of particular types of data in the employment process. It merits noting that this review is not meant to be comprehensive. For instance, many states place limits on the collection of credit reports in the hiring process (e.g., CA, NC, VT) because these reports are likely to have an adverse impact on racial and ethnic minorities who often have lower levels of socioeconomic status and poorer credit than their white counterparts. Similarly, a number of states have passed laws restricting the collection of data on applicants' arrests that do not lead to convictions (e.g., CA, TX, RI) because these types of data may have an adverse impact on ethnic and racial minorities. Other states restrict the collection of data on criminal convictions that are not directly job related or have been sealed or expunged (e.g., KS, MA, MO, NY). Further, many states place restrictions on the collection, use, and disclosure of Social Security numbers (SSNs) in the employment process (e.g., CA, NY, MN; Wugmeister & Taylor, 2008). Thus, we recommend that SSNs should not be used as employee identifiers or identifiers in a HRIS.

Collection of data in social media sites. The Internet and social media sites contain a lot of personal and lifestyle data about applicants and employees. As a result, employers have started reviewing applicants' websites or social media sites in order to gather lifestyle data or information about their personal background that may have a negative impact on job performance (Lukaszewski & Johnson, 2018). Given that these sites contain a great deal of sensitive information (e.g., sexual orientation, alcohol use, domestic partners), applicants have set privacy controls to prevent employers from accessing the data. However, some employers began asking applicants for their IDs and passwords so that they could review the sites. Applicants' complained that this practice was an invasion of privacy, so a number of states passed laws that prohibit employers from asking applicants or employees for IDs and passwords for these accounts (e.g., AR, CA, CO, IL, LA, MD, MI). More information on the use of social media to support human resources is found in Chapter 16.

In view of the federal and state laws that place restrictions on the collection of data in the employment process, we recommend that employers review their paper and online applications to ensure that protected data are not included as questions on them (e.g., arrests, credit data, or criminal conviction data, race, age, etc.). They should also ensure that HRIS do not use SSNs as employee identifiers or display SSNs on any reports generated by a HRIS. Although there are no federal or state laws that prevent employers from reviewing the Internet or social media sites for applicant information, we believe that they should set policies that place limits on the review of social media and websites. In particular, employers should only collect information from these sites that are job related, and they should not ask applicants or employees to disclose IDs or passwords for these sites.

Disclosure of Applicant or Employee Data

In view of the widespread use of HRIS, employees are increasingly apprehensive about identity theft and the security of their personal data stored by organizations. This may be justifiable, because there are numerous examples of organizations that have had their employee data hacked and disclosed to third parties. One of the major breaches of applicant and employee information was at the U.S. Office of Personnel Management, where more than 22 million records were stolen (Levine & Date, 2015). As a result, there are federal and state laws in the U.S. that prevent employers from releasing personal identifiable data to third parties.

Federal law. In order to prohibit the disclosure of personal applicant or employee information, the Privacy Act of 2005 was passed. It prevents employers from selling or disclosing personal identifiable information (e.g., Social Security number, driver's license number, birth date) about individuals to a commercial entity or non-affiliated third party. This act also requires organizations to protect sensitive data stored in HRIS including data about race, ethnicity, membership in unions, medical data, sexual orientation, domestic partnerships, etc.

Apart from the Privacy Act, other federal laws place restrictions on the release of personal information about applicants or employees. For example, the Americans with Disabilities Act (ADA 1990) and Family Medical Leave Act (FMLA) require that any information obtained by an employer about an employee's medical condition should be maintained in separate files and treated in a confidential manner. Employers may only disclose the information to (a) supervisors when they need to be informed about a medical condition to accommodate working conditions, (b) safety personnel who need the information for emergency treatment, and (c) government officials for compliance investigations. In addition, the Health Insurance Portability and Accountability Act (HIPAA) protects data collected by employer-sponsored health plans, and health providers cannot disclose individually identifiable health information without a HIPAA authorization from the patient or participant in the health plan. There are a few exceptions to HIPAA including request for data by law enforcement and the courts.

State laws. All states have passed laws that require employers to notify employees if any of their computerized personal information has been breached (Lazzarotti, Gavejian, & Atrakchi, 2018). However, there is great inconsistency in what these laws require of organizations.

The **U.S. Fair Labor Standards Act of 1938** requires employers to maintain basic information on all employees, including Social Security numbers, address, gender, occupation, pay, and hours worked. However, the increased use of HRISs to store these data has prompted concerns about the degree to which these systems have the potential to invade personal privacy. Information privacy has been defined as the "degree to which individuals have control over the collection, storage, access, and release of personal data" (E. F. Stone & Stone, 1990). Given the growing concerns about the privacy of information in HRIS, we consider some practices that may be perceived as invasive of privacy in the sections that follow. In particular, we discuss concerns about (a) unauthorized access to information, (b) unauthorized disclosure of information, (c) data accuracy issues, and (d) stigmatization of individuals.

Unauthorized Access to Information

One reason employees are concerned about the storage of data in an HRIS is that they fear that these systems may allow **unauthorized access** to their private information (D. L. Stone, Stone-Romero, & Lukaszewski, 2003). For example, employees may perceive that if users have access to their Social Security numbers or bank data, they will experience identity theft. In fact, some reports indicate that identity theft is the primary consequence of the breach of HRIS data (Privacy Rights Clearinghouse, 2010). Similarly, if unauthorized users have access to medical data or domestic partner benefits, then employees feel that they will experience embarrassment or loss of job opportunities (e.g., promotions, pay raises, challenging job assignments).

Interestingly, results of some survey research suggested that these concerns may be justifiable. For instance, one study found that 34% of companies collect and store medical and prescription drug information about employees (Society for Human Resource Management [SHRM] & West Group, 2000). In addition, the findings of the same study indicated that employee information is often released to insurance companies and future employers. Furthermore, even though there are laws that restrict the use of health data in the employment process (e.g., Americans with Disabilities Act [ADA], 1990; Health Insurance Portability and Accountability Act [HIPAA]), some employees have been terminated when employers discover they are using prescription drugs for hypertension, diabetes, or pain control (Personnel Policy Service, 2013). For instance, in one case, an organization established a policy requiring that employees report all drugs present in the body and prohibited the use of legal prescription drugs unless approved by a supervisor (e.g., *Roe v. Cheyenne Mountain Conference Resort*, 1997). Not surprisingly, the court ruled that requiring employees to report their legal prescription drug use was an invasion of privacy and in violation of ADA.

Some research also indicated that employees were more likely to perceive an HRIS as invasive of privacy when they were unable to control access to their personal data, and information was accessed by users outside the organization rather than those inside the organization (Eddy, Stone-Romero, & Stone, 1999). Results of other research revealed that the use of an HRIS was perceived as invasive of privacy when (a) supervisors were able to access information in employee records, (b) the same data were used for employment rather than HR planning decisions, and (c) the employees did not have the ability to check the accuracy of the data before decisions were made (Eddy et al., 1999). Furthermore, findings of another study showed that employees were more likely to perceive that their privacy had been invaded when medical data were collected and stored in an HRIS, and they were required to use a Web-based HRIS to enter personal data than when they were able to reveal the data to HR professionals (Lukaszewski, Stone, & Stone-Romero, 2008).

It merits noting that HIPAA requires that medical data should be stored separately from other employment data, but some HRISs still include medical or health data in employment records. For instance, HIPAA allows a great deal of medical information to be stored in employee records (e.g., data from drug tests, Family Medical Leave Act certifications, OSHA, workers' compensation, and sick leave). Similarly, Affirmative Action data (e.g., race, ethnicity, gender, age, self-reported disability status), which are collected for EEO-1 reports, are not always separated from employment data in these systems. As a result, applicants and employees may be concerned that sensitive data will be accessed by decision makers and used unfairly against them in the employment process. At present, there are very few legal restrictions on access to data in an HRIS. Therefore, we believe that organizations concerned with protecting employee privacy may want to utilize sound security practices to limit the degree to which unauthorized individuals have access to employee data.

Unauthorized Disclosure of Information

Another concern about the use of HRIS is that employees may perceive that these systems allow for the **unauthorized disclosure** of information about them to others (D. L. Stone et al., 2003). For example, research by Linowes (2000) revealed that 70% of employers regularly disclose employment data to creditors, 47% give information to landlords, and 19% disclose employee data to charitable organizations. In addition, some reports indicated that organizations regularly sell data collected on recruiting websites (D. Stone, Lukaszewski, & Isenhour, 2005). Furthermore, 60% of employers do not inform applicants or employees when they disclose information within or outside the organization (Society for Human Resources Management & West Group, 2000).

Thus, the use of an HRIS may make it much easier to disseminate personal information internally and externally to the organization, and there are currently few restrictions on the release of employee data in private-sector organizations. However, the disclosure of employee data may result in negative outcomes for employees if data collected for one purpose (e.g., performance appraisals) are used for other purposes (e.g., decisions about an apartment lease or credit). As a result, employees may be understandably concerned that HRISs facilitate the unauthorized release of personal information, and we believe that organizations should develop policies that limit the unauthorized disclosure of employee information.

Data Accuracy Problems

Employees are also troubled about **data accuracy** because HRISs may contain inaccurate or outdated information about them. Not surprisingly, individuals are often unaware that data in these systems are inaccurate, and many organizations do not give them the opportunity to review or correct data stored in an HRIS. For example, studies show that data from background checks, credit checks, or social media are often inaccurate and become permanent records in an HRIS (Society for Human Resource Management & West Group, 2000). In addition, survey results indicate that 73% of participants had errors in their background data that resulted in the loss of job opportunities (Society for Human Resource Management & West Group, 2000).

We believe that inaccurate data in HRISs are especially problematic because they may stigmatize individuals unfairly and result in denial of job outcomes (e.g., termination, loss of promotions or training opportunities). For instance, an executive at Hilton Hotels was terminated shortly after he was hired when data in his background check incorrectly noted that he had been convicted of a misdemeanor and served 6 months in jail (*Socorro vs. IMI Data Search and Hilton Hotels*, 2003).

Hilton hired a firm, IMI Data, to conduct the background check but did not check the accuracy of its findings. Socorro was not informed of the background check, but his managing director asked if he had ever been convicted of a crime or spent 6 months in jail. Socorro replied truthfully that he had not. Although the data about Socorro's conviction and jail sentence were incorrect, Hilton terminated Socorro for falsifying information on his job application. After Socorro's termination, Hilton told third parties that Socorro was fired because he lied on his application and that he was a convict who had spent 6six months in jail. Subsequently, he had a great deal of difficulty securing new employment because of the false and defamatory statements made by Hilton. Socorro did finally secure new employment, but at a substantially lower rate of compensation than the Hilton position.

It is clear from this example that the storage and use of inaccurate data in an HRIS may have a negative effect on both organizations and individuals. For example, when data in these systems are inaccurate, organizations may make erroneous decisions regarding employees and fail to hire or promote highly qualified individuals. In addition, employees may be unfairly denied job outcomes and opportunities to experience gratifying careers. As a result, employees are likely to perceive that HRISs are invasive of privacy if the data stored in them are inaccurate or outdated.

In support of these arguments, Linowes (2000) found that 72% of private-sector organizations do not allow employees to review their employment records for inaccurate data, and 24% do not give them the opportunity to correct their records. In addition, research by Stone, Lukaszewski, and Stone-Romero (2001) found that individuals were more likely to perceive that their privacy had been invaded when they were not able to check the accuracy of data in an HRIS than when they were allowed to check the accuracy of data. Thus, employee concerns about the degree to which inaccurate data may unfairly stigmatize them or affect their outcomes in organizations appear quite justified.

Stigmatization Problems

Employees are often uneasy about the use of HRISs, especially when they feel that networked data may lead to them being **stigmatized** or deeply discredited in the employment process (D. L. Stone & Stone-Romero, 1998). For example, HRISs often provide for the permanent storage of employee data (e.g., performance appraisals, credit scores, employment test scores) that are used to make employment decisions over time. For example, an employee who had below-average performance ratings very early in his or her career may have difficulty purging these data from an HRIS, and the data may negatively affect subsequent decisions about him or her. As a result, the employee's advancement and career development opportunities may be negatively affected by data that have no bearing on his or her present-day job performance.

Use of Data in Social Network Websites

Recently, organizations have started collecting and using data about applicants and employees from social network websites (SNWs; e.g., Facebook, LinkedIn, Twitter; Black, Johnson, Takach, & Stone, 2012; Roth, Bobko, Van Iddekinge, & Thatcher, 2012). For instance, organizations now use SNWs to collect information about job applicants' lifestyle, family background, friends, sexual orientation, religion, political affiliation, and personal interests. Estimates indicate that between 20% and 40% of employers now scan SNWs to gather data about job applicants (Framingham, 2008; Zeidner, 2007), and 75% of recruiters are currently required to do online research on applicants before making hiring decisions (Preston, 2011).

One consequence of the organizational use of SNWs data is that individuals are likely to perceive that the data in these systems will unfairly stigmatize them and result in the loss of job opportunities (D. L. Stone & Stone-Romero, 1998). For example, a recent court case (e.g., *Snyder v. Millersville University*, cited in Narisi, 2009) indicated that a student-teacher was terminated from a teaching position when a picture was posted of her on MySpace as a "drunken pirate." It merits noting that there was no evidence that she was drinking alcohol or drunk. Her students found the picture and reported it to school administrators and the university, who terminated her student teaching because they thought she would be a poor role model for the students. When she sued, the court ruled in favor of the university, indicating that she did not have the right to any free speech that might damage her employer's reputation (Narisi, 2009). As a consequence, data in SNWs may be used without an individual's knowledge and may result in termination or loss of other employment opportunities. Although the collection of data from an SNW is not illegal, there is a growing concern that the collection of information from these sites may erroneously stigmatize employees and result in an invasion of their rights to privacy.

Lack of Privacy Protection Policies

Despite the widespread use of HRISs and growing concerns about the (a) unauthorized access, (b) unauthorized release, (c) data accuracy, and (d) use of data to stigmatize employees, many companies have not established fair information management policies to control the use and release of employee information (Linowes, 2000). For instance, a study by Linowes (2000) found that 42% of companies do not have privacy protection policies, and the same number has not designated an executive-level person to be responsible for privacy and security of employment records. When no policies exist, the person in charge, whether a manager or record clerk, decides for himself or herself what and when sensitive personal information is released to others. Thus, we believe that one strategy for decreasing employees' perceptions of invasion of privacy is to develop fair information management policies with respect to the collection, storage, use, and dissemination of data in an HRIS. These policies will be discussed in greater detail in a section that follows. Prior to considering these policies, we will consider the important issue of information security and the components of information security systems in protecting employee information and privacy.

Given the federal and state laws in the U.S. that place restrictions on the disclosure of data, we recommend that employers set policies about the disclosure of information stored in HRIS and ensure that they gain permission from data subjects before they are released inside or outside the organization. They also need to establish privacy policies and clearly communicate those policies to all applicants or employees of the organization.

COMPONENTS OF INFORMATION SECURITY

Brief Evolution of Security Models

As noted, information security is particularly important for an HRIS because of the high degree of automation in these systems and the wealth of private employee data being stored. **Information security** has traditionally been defined as the protection afforded to an automated information system in order to attain the applicable objectives of preserving the confidentiality, integrity, and availability (CIA) of information system resources (Stallings & Brown, 2008). However, the complexity of the networked environment in which HR data is captured, stored, and utilized means that personnel transactions and information processing are increasingly more vulnerable to security threats and risks than ever before. Therefore, the traditional CIA model of information security does not suffice. The National Security Telecommunications and Information Systems Security Committee (NSTISSC) security model, also known as the **McCumber Cube** (see Figure 15.1), provides a more detailed perspective on security.

The McCumber Cube provides a graphical representation of the architectural approach widely used in information security. The McCumber Cube is more granular than the CIA classification because it examines not only the characteristics of the information to be protected but also the context of the information state. The cube allows an analyst to identify the information flows within an HRIS, view it for important security-relevant factors, and then map the findings to the cube. The cube has three dimensions. If extrapolated, the three dimensions of each axis become a $3 \times 3 \times 3$ cube, with 27 cells representing areas that must be addressed to secure a modern-day information system (Whitman & Mattord,

FIGURE 15.1 ■ The McCumber Cube

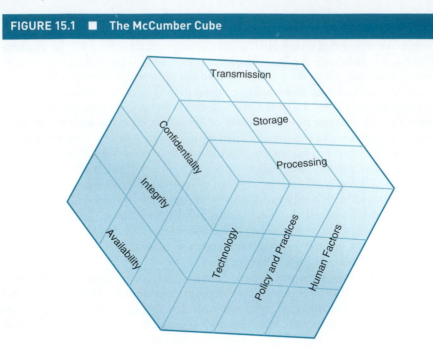

Source: Pohlman, M. B. (2008). Oracle identity management: Governance, risk, and compliance architecture (3 ed.). Originally by John McCumber, National Security Telecommunications and Information Systems Security Committee (NSTISSC).

2011). To ensure system security, each of the 27 areas must be properly addressed during the development and implementation of security processes and policies for the HRIS. The three dimensions and their attributes are categorized as follows:

- **Desired Information Goals**—Ensure that data is kept confidential, has not been manipulated, and is available to those who are authorized to access it.

  - Confidentiality assures that private data is kept safe from unauthorized individuals. It is critical for maintaining the privacy of the employees' personal data.

  - Integrity assures that data and programs are created and modified in a specified and authorized manner. It is important to assure the integrity of both the data and the system.

  - Availability assures that systems work and service are provided promptly to those who are authorized to use them.

- **State of Information**—Identify the state in which data is currently residing.

  - Storage is an inactive state of data that is waiting to be accessed.

  - Processing is a state in which data is being actively examined or modified.

  - Transmission is a state in which data is moving.

- **Countermeasures**—Identify mechanisms that can be used to protect data.

    ○ Technology is the use of hardware and software to limit threats to data.

    ○ Policy and practices is the use of procedures that mitigate risk or eliminate the possibility of threats.

    ○ Human factors revolve around giving each consumer of data the knowledge of how to identify and handle threats.

As an example of the use of the McCumber Cube, consider a 2005 data breach suffered by Ameriprise Financial in which data from more than 200,000 clients were stolen off an unencrypted laptop (Dash, 2006). Ameriprise needed to preempt the data needed to be encrypted (countermeasure) even when it was stored (state of information) and not just when it was being transmitted. This would have ensured confidentiality (desired information goal) of data. This is something that mirrors the issue faced by Anthem as previously mentioned. A critical point to consider is that regardless of whether encryption exists, at certain points data, may be visible and accessible. To counter these threats, HR departments need to recognize the value of data that is stored and the reasons it would be valuable to a hacker. In addition to protecting data at-rest and in-motion, HR should examine and deploy techniques that augment encryption and add variability to the process. Doing this would add an additional layer of difficulty and cost for the hacker.

As another example, consider the intersection between the technology countermeasure, the integrity goal, and the storage state. In other words, how do we use technology to ensure that our stored HR data maintains its integrity? One way to do this would be to develop a system for detecting host intrusion (intrusion at the individual workstation level), which protects the integrity of information by alerting the security administrators to the potential modification of a critical file. This is very pertinent to HRIS. An HRIS specialist is asked to perform group data updates and export the results to his or her immediate supervisor for verification. The results are encrypted, and a hash (an algorithm used to ensure that data remains secure and accurate) is computed and then uploaded to a server via secure FTP, which only specific employees have access to. This example covers multiple cells. For example, only specific employees are allowed access to specific information (*Confidentiality*), and the data is encrypted (*Technology*) before being stored (*Storage*). Also, since a hash is computed after it is encrypted, it ensures that information may not be changed outside of proper processes (*Integrity*). Data is transmitted via secure FTP, thereby maintaining security (*Transmission*). The use of secure transmission protocols is a matter of organizational policy (*Policy*). The examples touch on only a couple of the 27 possible cells in the McCumber Cube. Organizations need to consider the implications of all dimensions and attributes in this cube when designing an HRIS to get a more detailed and accurate representation of threats faced and countermeasures that need to be implemented.

Security Threats

What kind of threats are our organizational security practices protecting us from? In security, it is important to "know your enemy." You have to understand your vulnerabilities. If you do not know what the threat vector (attack method) is, you cannot plan to defend yourself. The following are common security threats:

- Threat Sources

  - *Human error:* When an HRIS is not well designed, developed, and maintained and employees are not adequately trained, there is a high potential threat of security breaches. Research suggests that human errors, such as incorrectly entered data or accidental destruction of existing data, constitute security threats to the availability, accessibility, and integrity of information. The Ameriprise Financial example shows that an error on the part of an employee can potentially expose private employee or customer data.

  - *Disgruntled employees and ex-employees:* One of the concerns overlooked by HR managers is that **disgruntled employees** may damage information. This is commonly referred to as an insider threat. Employees and ex-employees are dangerous, since they have extensive knowledge of systems, have the credentials needed to access sensitive parts of systems, often know how to avoid detection, and can benefit from the trust that usually is accorded to an organization's employees (Boyle & Panko, 2013).

  - *Other "internal" attackers:* Many businesses hire contract workers, who work for the organization for a short period. Contract workers, sometimes referred to as third-party vendors, usually gain temporary access to various critical areas of an organization. This creates risks almost identical to those created by employees.

  - *External hackers:* Another significant threat is the penetration of organizational computer systems by hackers. A **hacker** is defined as someone who accesses a computer or computer network unlawfully. Such attacks, often termed "intrusions" (Austin & Darby, 2003), can be particularly dangerous, because once the hacker has successfully bypassed the network security, he or she is free to damage, manipulate, or simply steal data at will.

  - *Natural disasters:* Typical forms of natural disasters are floods, earthquakes, fires, and lightning strikes, which destroy or disrupt computing facilities and information flow. As noted earlier in the chapter, physical threats such as this were once considered the main threats to computing resources. Although they are now less visible and do not pose the daily risks that these other security threats pose, each must be nonetheless considered when developing security practices.

- Types of Threats

  - *Misuse of computer systems:* One of the predominant internal security threats is employees' unauthorized access to or use of information, particularly when it is confidential and sensitive.

  - *Extortion:* The perpetrator tries to obtain monetary benefits or other goods by threatening to take actions that would be against the victim's interest.

  - *Theft:* The value of information can be much higher than the price of hardware and software. With contemporary advances in technological developments, a relatively small computer chip (e.g., a USB device) can easily store more than 100 GB of data. For example, the State of Hawaii's HR department had medical records stolen when offices of two doctors servicing workers' compensation claims were burglarized (Mangieri, 2013).

○ *Computer-based fraud:* There is growing evidence that computer-based fraud is widespread. More than 90% of companies have been affected by computer-based fraud, such as data processing or data entry routines that are modified (Garg, Curtis, & Halper, 2003).

○ *Cyber-terrorism:* **Cyber-terrorism** is the leveraging of an information system that is intended to intimidate or cause physical, real-world harm or severe disruption of a system's infrastructure (Austin & Darby, 2003; Hinde, 2003). In one such scenario, a person with high-level computer and network skills (e.g., a hacker) is hired to break into a specific computer or computer network to steal or delete data and information. Cyber-terrorists often send a threatening e-mail stating that they will release some confidential information, exploit a security leak, or launch an attack that could harm a company's systems or networks.

○ *Cyber-espionage:* As more and more information is available via networked technologies, cyber-espionage has come up as a legitimate threat to corporate networks. It entails the use of dangerous and offensive intelligence measures in the cyber realm.

○ *Phishing:* Victims usually receive e-mail messages that appear to come from an authentic source with which the victim does business. The official appearance of the message and the website often fool victims into giving out confidential information. According to Gartner, the estimated annual cost of **phishing** is around $2 billion (Moore & Clayton, 2007).

○ *Denial-of-service:* A **denial-of-service (DoS)** attempts to make a service unavailable for legitimate users by flooding it with attach packets. The server that is hosting that service is then unable to handle the large number of requests, thereby shutting it down. The financial services sector has been hit particularly hard by this type of attack. For example, Bank of America and JP Morgan Chase have both experienced outages on their public websites due to DoS attacks (Holland, 2012).

● Software Threats

○ *Malware:* **Malware** is a catch-all term for any form of "malicious software". The primary purpose of malware is to infiltrate a user's machine without his/her knowledge. Examples of malware include viruses, worms, spyware, Trojans, and ransomware.

○ *Viruses:* A **computer virus** is a type of malware that works by inserting a copy of itself onto a computer or device (e.g., smartphone) and then becoming part of another program. It can attach itself to files without the user's knowledge and duplicate itself by executing infected files. When successful, a virus can alter data, erase or damage data, create a nuisance, or inflict other damage (Panko, 2003). In a period of 5 hours in 2000, the "I love you" e-mail virus infected millions of computers, causing damages estimated at $10 billion (Abreu, 2001).

○ *Worms:* **Worms** are in some ways similar to viruses since they can replicate themselves. However, unlike viruses that require the spreading of an infected file, worms such as Code Red, Slammer, and MyDoom can spread by themselves without attaching to files (Panko, 2003).

○ *Spyware:* **Spyware** is software installed on an unknowing user's computer that gathers information about the user's activities on the Web (keystrokes, websites visited, etc.) and transmits it to third parties such as advertisers or attackers (Stafford & Urbaczewski, 2004). Problems associated with spyware include potential privacy invasion, appropriation of personal information, and interference with the user's computer operation (Stafford & Urbaczewski, 2004).

○ *Trojan:* A **Trojan** is another type of malware that usually hides inside e-mail attachments or files and infects a user's computer when attachments are opened or programs are executed. Trojans are named after the Trojan horse of Greek mythology in that they appear to be something positive but are in reality doing something malicious. Unlike viruses and worms, Trojans do not reproduce by infecting other files, nor do they self-replicate. Instead, they must be opened on a computer by a user. Some Trojans can work as spyware, while others can display a login or install screen and collect personal data such as usernames and passwords or other forms of identification, such as bank account or credit card numbers. They can also copy files, delete files, uninstall applications using remote access programs on the computers, and format disks without alerting the victim. One type of Trojan horse is a **rootkit**. A rootkit takes over a root (administrator) account and uses its privileges to hide itself. Most rootkits find their way into a system through installation or updating of application software, such as a word-processing program. Rootkits have the capability to modify the behavior of the application so that they can escape detection and do what they were written to do. Therefore, rootkits are seldom caught by ordinary antivirus programs, and rootkit detection programs have to be designed to detect a specific rootkit.

○ *Ransomware:* **Ransomware** is equivalent to a kidnapper's ransom note. In most circumstances it involves locking and denying of access to a system or files until a ransom is paid to the hacker. The best strategy to deal with ransomware includes preventive and recovery measures. Systems need to be kept up to date through regular system patches. It is also important for an organization to prioritize network security. Deploying antimalware applications in those cases can contribute to the end goal. Finally, it is also necessary to incorporate well-rehearsed backup and recovery processes. It is imperative that there is an up-to-date system backup kept off site.

INFORMATION POLICY AND MANAGEMENT

As you can see from this discussion, it is important that organizations have policies and procedures in place to protect employee data. There are two mechanisms through which this can occur: fair information management policies and strong security practices. We believe, as do others (e.g., Privacy Protection Study Commission, 1977; D. L. Stone & Stone-Romero, 1998) that one way to decrease individuals' perceptions of invasion of privacy is to establish fair information management policies for controlling data in HRIS. These policies and organizational strategies for ensuring information security will be considered in the sections that follow.

Fair Information Management Policies

To date, there has been legislation restricting the collection, storage, use, and dissemination of employee information in the public sector (e.g., Privacy Act of 1974), but there is no comprehensive federal legislation on employee information privacy in private-sector organizations. However, one state, California, has recently passed a law that protects the privacy of employee records in private-sector organizations (Privacy Protection in State Constitutions, 2012). Space limitations preclude a complete review of all employment-related privacy laws, but we suggest that interested readers see the Privacy Rights Clearinghouse at https://privacyrights.org/categories/background-checks for a complete review of all federal and state laws. In addition, multinational organizations should also consider the privacy practices in the countries in which they operate. The challenge for organizations is that every country takes a different perspective on protecting employee information privacy, and your organization will need to be familiar with all the applicable laws in each country in which you operate. A sample of interactional laws protecting employee privacy across the globe is found in Table 15.1.

Even though there are few laws governing the storage, use, and dissemination of information in HRIS, organizations may decrease the degree to which employees perceive that HRIS invades their privacy by establishing fair information management policies and practices. For example, in 1977, the Privacy Protection Study Commission recommended that private-sector organizations proactively establish policies for managing employee information to protect individuals' perceived or actual rights to privacy. For instance, they recommended that organizations limit the collection of information to data which are job related, control unauthorized access to information in HRIS, adopt reasonable procedures for assuring that data are accurate and timely, and limit external disclosures of data without employees' consent. A complete review of these recommendations is provided in Table 15.2.

We believe that the use of these fair information policies and practices may lessen many of the concerns that applicants and employees have about the collection, storage, use, and dissemination of data in an HRIS. However, it is imperative that all users review and clearly understand these policies before HRISs are implemented in organizations.

Effective Information Security Policies

The second way that organizations need to protect employee data is through their security practices. Bruce Schneier once stated that "security is a process, not a product" (Schneier, 2000). This statement alludes to the nature of information security. That is, information security is not predominantly a technical issue; it is more of a management issue. It is easy to see why at times there is a major focus on technology. Technology is visible, and there are many things that we can say about security technologies. Management can seem more abstract. There are fewer general principles to discuss, and most of these cannot be put into practice without well-defined and complex processes (Boyle & Panko, 2013). But the management issues are actually often complex and focused both on behavioral information policies and on the technical practices.

TABLE 15.2 ■ Fair Information Management Policies and Practices Based, in Part, on Privacy Protection Study Commission Recommendations (1977)	
Organizational Practice	**Policy Recommendation**
Collection of Employee Data	Limit the collection of information on individual employees, applicants, and former employees to that which is relevant to jobs or specific employment decisions.
Inform Employees About Uses of Data	Inform employees, applicants, and former employees about the uses made of their information and types of records maintained.
Ensure Accuracy of Data	Adopt reasonable procedures to ensure the accuracy, timeliness, and completeness of employment information.
Allow for Correction of Data	Permit employees to see, copy, correct, and amend records maintained about them.
Unauthorized Access to Data	Limit the internal and external use of records maintained about employees, applicants, and former employees. Data are available to users on a "need to know only" basis.
Unauthorized Release of Data	Limit external disclosures of information kept on employees, applicants, and former employees. Require that employees, applicants, and former employees provide authorization for the release of personal information or requests for verification of information.
Ensure That Employees Are Aware of and Understand Fair Information Management Policies	Provide employees with training about fair information management policies to ensure they understand them. Require that employees provide written acknowledgments that they understand these policies.

This lends credence to importance of effective security policies. Security policies identify valuable assets, provide a reference to review when conflicts pertaining to security arise, outline personal responsibility, help prevent unaccounted-for events, outline incident response responsibilities, and outline an organization's response to legal, regulatory, and standards of due care.

For effective implementation of security, organizations usually follow established security standards such as **ISO/IEC 27000** series. This series focuses on areas such as access control, security management, good practices, and protection of health-related information. Almost all aspects of the ISO/IEC 27000 series mesh with HRISs. For example, it is standard practice to require HR employees to change their passwords on a quarterly basis to achieve optimal access control. It is also a generally good practice to verify that all HRIS users are properly trained in the secure use and handling of equipment, data, and software. Many breaches occur when users are not consciously aware of what they are doing. Unconscious behavior can defeat the best efforts of security experts, meaning all of the security protocols in the world are powerless in the face of a stressed-out worker. According to Microsoft's Security Intelligence report, 44.8% of vulnerabilities result from user action such as clicking a link or being tricked into installing malware (Microsoft, 2011).

Several best practices have been proposed to ensure that employee data is secured and employee privacy is protected (Canavan, 2003; David, 2002; Tansley & Watson, 2000). These include the following:

- Adopt a comprehensive information security and privacy policy.

- Store sensitive personal data in a secure HRIS and provide appropriate encryption.

- Dispose of documents properly or restore persistent storage equipment.

- Build document destruction capabilities into the office infrastructure.

- Implement and continuously update technical (firewalls, antivirus, antispyware, etc.) and nontechnical (security education, training, and awareness) measures.

- When using social media, make sure that an employee does not post anything that will leak sensitive information about a company. Tools such as www .SecureMySocial.com provide measures that can prevent that.

- Conduct privacy "walk-throughs" and make spot checks on proper information handling.

Although there is no question that all organizations need to be aware of HRIS security issues and best practices, global organizations need to be particularly diligent. An organization may face specific laws regarding storage, transmission, and transfer of data based on the areas in which it operates. This may limit the flow of employee data across borders and may make the HRIS more complex or may require the organization to adopt different HRIS in different countries.

Contingency Planning

As highlighted already in this chapter, any company, regardless of size, is under threat from attackers. It is not a question of "if" but "when" a company may be breached. Therefore, it is imperative that organizations have comprehensive contingency planning (CP) set in place. The National Institute of Standards and Technology (NIST) delves deeper into the area of contingency planning for systems in general.[2] Contingency planning involves preparing for, detecting, and reacting to, and recovering from an unexpected event that threatens various resources and assets in an organization. Contingency planning consists of three key areas: incident response (IR), disaster recovery (DR), and business continuity (BC).

Incident Response (IR)

IR consists of a detailed set of processes and procedures that commence when an incident is detected. To be prepared for this stage, planners need to develop and document the procedures that must be performed during the incident and immediately after the incident has ended. Examples of procedures that may be performed before the incident include data backup scheduling, training schedules, testing plans, and business continuity plans. Once an incident has been contained, the recovery process can be initiated. This would include a damage assessment, addressing safeguards that may have failed, restoring data from backups, and even restoring confidence of stakeholders. Finally, it is important to note that if an incident violates civil or criminal law, it is the organization's responsibility to notify the proper law enforcement agencies.

Disaster Recovery (DR)

DR relates to the preparation for and recovery from a disaster, whether natural or man-made. The key role of a DR plan is to reestablish operations at the location where the organization is usually located. It is imperative that organizations understand that they must not only plan for natural disasters, or for that matter mock tests are enough. At times even backed up data may not be enough. For an effective DR plan organizations need to ensure that the DR planning and preparation processes are treated as a continuous task. It is important to have a multitude of backups and contingencies, and that mock tests are carried out at scheduled and unscheduled intervals.

Business Continuity (BC)

BC planning ensures that critical business functions can continue in a disaster. This segment of CP is activated and executed concurrently with the DR planning phase. A key area of this phase is that it relies on identification of critical business functions and the resources needed to support them. Usually this phase involves use of at least one of three different types of backup sites: hot sites, warm sites, or cold sites. A hot site is an exact replica of the current HRIS data, with all systems configured and waiting only for the last backups. This site can often be brought online within a very short time frame. Due to this reason it is also the most expensive approach in the DR process. A warm site has a reasonable set of equipment present to start the recovery process. Finally, cold sites are a little more than configured space. Everything required to restore service needs to be procured and delivered. Of the three options, this (cold site) is the least expensive.

As previously mentioned, it is important to test various plans. Contingency planning requires that as well. Various techniques can be used: desk check, structured walk-through, simulation, parallel testing, and even full interruption testing. Each of these techniques, while important, is beyond the scope of our discussion. Interested readers should review the work of Gordon (2015)[3] for more information on this topic. Results from these tests need to be carefully looked at, since they provide an avenue for iterative improvement. Constant evaluation and improvement will lead an organization toward an improved outcome.

Summary

Although it is clear that HRISs have numerous benefits in organizations, this chapter considers some recent issues associated with their use, including employee privacy and information security. In particular, the chapter considers (a) practices that may affect individuals' perceptions of invasion of privacy, (b) the components of information security, (c) the security threats faced by organizations, and (d) the implications for developing fair information management policies and security practices. Throughout the chapter, we argued that organizations should take proactive steps to develop fair information management policies that can be used to protect individual privacy and implement information security practices and policies that safeguard employment data. This needs to be coupled with effective contingency planning strategies to provide a more holistic level of HRIS security.

Key Terms

computer virus 407
countermeasures 405
cyber-terrorism 407
data accuracy 401
denial-of-service (DoS) 407
desired information goals 404
disgruntled employees 406
General Data Protection
   Regulation (GDPR) 395

hacker 406
information security 403
ISO/IEC 27000 410
malware 407
McCumber Cube 403
phishing 407
ransomware 408
rootkit 408
security breaches 393

spyware 408
state of information 404
stigmatized 402
Trojan 408
unauthorized access 399
unauthorized disclosure 400
U.S. Fair Labor Standards
   Act of 1938 399
worms 408

Discussion Questions

1. Why are information security and privacy important considerations in the design, development, and maintenance of an HRIS?

2. List and discuss the major information security and privacy threats to organizations.

3. What are the important goals and considerations of information security?

4. Identify the important legal provisions governing information security and privacy in your country.

5. What is the role of HR professionals in information security and privacy management?

6. What are some of the best practices to manage information security and privacy in terms of procedural, technical, and physical controls?

7. How might social media platforms (e.g., Facebook, LinkedIn, and Twitter) help hackers gain access to personal information or systems?

Case Study: Practical Applications of an Information Privacy Plan

XYZ University is a medium-sized tertiary education provider in the state of Queensland, Australia. In undertaking its normal business of teaching, learning, and research, the university collects, stores, and uses "personal information," that is, anything that identifies a person's identity.

With respect to students, this information may include, among other things, records relating to admission, enrollment, course attendance, assessment, and grades; medical records; details of student fees, fines, levies, and payments, including bank details; tax file numbers and declaration forms; student personal history files; qualifications information; completed questionnaire and survey forms; records relating to personal welfare, health, equity, counseling, student and graduate employment, or other support matters; records relating to academic references; and records relating to discipline matters.

The bulk of this information is retained in the student management information systems and in the file registry. Academic and administrative staff, at various levels, have access to these records only as required to carry out their duties. Portions of the information held in university student records are disclosed outside the university to various agencies, such as the Australian Taxation Office; the Department of Education, Employment and Workplace Relations; other universities; consultant student services providers; the Department of Immigration and Citizenship; and overseas sponsorship agencies.

The university has a well-documented information privacy policy in accordance with the community standard for the collection, storage, use, and disclosure of personal information by public agencies in Queensland. The policy relies on the 11 principles developed in the Commonwealth Privacy Act of 1988. These principles broadly state the following:

- Personal information is collected and used only for a lawful purpose that is directly related to the collector's function.

- Before the information is collected, the individual concerned should be made aware of the purpose, whether it is required by law, and to whom the information will be passed on.

- Files containing personal information should be held securely and protected against loss; unauthorized access, use, modification, or disclosure; or any other misuse.

- Personal information can only be disclosed to another person or agency if the person

concerned is aware of it and has consented and the disclosure is authorized or required by law.

- Personal information should not be used without taking reasonable steps to ensure that it is accurate, up to date, and complete.

Presented next are three scenarios in which you need to decide how to apply the privacy policy and principles. The following scenarios were sourced from the Griffith University Privacy Plan (https://www.griffith.edu.au/about-griffith/corporate-governance/plans-publications/griffith-university-privacy-plan). As you consider the following three scenarios, use these principles to help you answer the case study questions.

Scenario 1

Roger, a photocopier technician, has been asked to repair an office photocopier that just broke down while someone was copying a grievance matter against an employee of the agency. The officer who was copying the file takes the opportunity to grab a cup of coffee and leaves Roger in the photocopy room while the photocopier cools down. While waiting, Roger flips through the file and realizes that the person against whom the grievance was made lives on the same street as he does.

Scenario 2

Tom telephones a student at home about attending a misconduct hearing. The student is not at home; however, the student's partner, Christine, answers the phone. She states that she knows all about the misconduct hearing but asks for clarification of the allegations. When pressed, Tom provides further details. Tom feels comfortable about providing this information to Christine because she is the student's partner, and she has already told Tom that she knows all about her partner's misconduct hearing.

Scenario 3

Brad works in a student administration center, and Janet is a student. They know each other, as they used to attend the same high school. Occasionally, they get together at the university to have coffee and chat about mutual friends. Brad knows that Janet's birthday is coming up because Janet happened to mention that she'll be another year older in the near future. Brad decides to access the student information system to find out Janet's date of birth and home address. A few weeks later, Janet receives a birthday card from Brad sent to her home address.

Case Study Questions

With regard to the above scenarios, you need to decide

1. what information privacy principles (IPPs) have been breached,

2. how, and

3. what you would do to address the situation.

THE ROLE OF SOCIAL MEDIA IN HR

Stephanie L. Black and Andrew F. Johnson

EDITORS' NOTE

To remain competitive in today's global environment, organizations are constantly looking for more efficient and effective means of acquiring and maintaining a highly qualified workforce. To do this, organizations are increasingly turning to Web 2.0 tools—such as wikis, social tagging, blogging, microblogging—and social networking sites—such as Facebook, LinkedIn, Instagram, and Twitter. These tools have become valuable resources for organizations seeking to communicate organizational culture, to share information to attract top talent, and to provide potential job applicants with information about jobs, careers, and organizational culture. It is crucial that those studying HRIS gain a good understanding of the use of social media in the workforce and its ramifications for organizations, employers, and employees. In this chapter, the author outlines the major social networking tools globally, how they are being used by organizations in several different areas of the organization, as well as risks posed by the use of these tools, especially in the selection process.

CHAPTER OBJECTIVES

After completing this chapter, you should be able to:

- Possess a general understanding of how the Internet and particularly social media is being used in human resources for recruitment, selection, and training.

- Understand some of the current social media tools and how they are being used.

- Understand the use of social media around the globe.

- Discuss the value of using social media within organizations as well as some of the potential drawbacks.

- Discuss the policies and training needed when using social media.

- Explain some of the legal implications of using social media within organizations.

- Implement social media policies within human resource departments and organizations that incorporate good business practices.

HRIS IN ACTION

The Problem

Jeff Bloom, chief talent officer of estate.ly, was facing a challenge. For the first time in twenty years, they had fallen off *Fortune*'s "Best Companies to Work For." In addition, his workforce was aging, and he was having a hard time attracting newer and younger talent, especially millennials and Gen Z. But he was frustrated. He just could not figure out how to reach this new generation and to maintain and enhance the great workplace that estate.ly was known for. Things were falling apart, and he knew it.

Jeff picked up his cell and called Tanya, the company's chief brand officer, told her about his concerns, and tried to schedule a meeting. Tanya thought to herself, "Finally, he's open to listening about how social media can support HR more fully!" But she didn't say that out loud. Instead, she replied, "From everything you just told me, I don't think that things are as bad as you think. From what I'm hearing, I think that the biggest issue we may be facing is that we aren't branding our organization and our people effectively to younger employees. Would you be comfortable if I bring three or four of my more recently hired employees to the meeting?" Jeff indicated that would be fine, and they scheduled a meeting for the next week.

The Meeting

Jeff was at a loss to what to do, but Tanya had a plan. She started the meeting by introducing the newly hired employees, Nadia and Rachel. Tanya then discussed how estate.ly was using social media to market properties, to engage customers, and to develop relationships. "We can do the same for HR. Social media is a great tool for reaching potential employees, connecting current employees, and extending the corporate brand." She recommended the following:

1. Develop a corporate *Facebook* careers page to advertise career events, provide advice on getting a job, tell people about estate.ly and what it's like to work for us. And we can link to job openings directly from here. Nadia quickly pointed out that "Facebook is not really as popular with my generation, Gen Z. What other tools are you thinking about?

2. Use *LinkedIn* to build professional relationships and networks. LinkedIn is an excellent tool for reaching professionals in our industry. We already have a large network of clients on LinkedIn, and because LinkedIn is designed to link business professionals, we can tell them our culture and what it is

(Continued)

(Continued)

like to work for us. LinkedIn will probably connect us to a different audience than Facebook.

3. *Twitter* is a great way to advertise and communicate our culture and value. We can share our latest job openings here and can "live tweet" any events that prospective employees might find interesting.

4. *Instagram* provides an excellent way of presenting visuals about our core values, our culture, and our company. Rachel chimed in, "It's true: a picture can be worth a thousand words, and besides, I'm a lot more likely to pay attention to Instagram than Facebook."

5. Finally, *YouTube* is a great place for employee testimonials regarding what it is like to work for estate.ly. We could even present "a day in the life" of an employee. This can really enhance the message or brand we want to communicate to those who may work for us.

Tanya finished, by noting that "these are just some of the tools we're using today. Who knows what will come next. We need to regularly assess our tools and make changes as needed. In addition, in China, we're using a whole different set of tools, but that's a conversation for another day."

The Future

To put it mildly, Jeff was shocked at the potential for social media. He still wasn't completely sure how to use each of these tools, but he could clearly see the promise of using them in recruitment. He even could see how these tools could help connect our current employees. But could it help him make better employee hiring decisions? What were the risks of using social media? Lots of questions arose, but finally he had direction and an idea of how to rebuild estate.ly's brand. Hopefully, in a few more years, the company will be back on *Fortune*'s Best Companies to Work For list.

INTRODUCTION

We don't have a choice on whether we do social media; the question is how well we do it.

—Erik Qualman

Social media are Internet-based platforms based on Web 2.0 technologies that allow users to generate and exchange content (Kaplan & Haenlein, 2010). Whereas Web 1.0 is a "readable" information portal that has allowed users to receive information without the opportunity to respond via posts or comments, Web 2.0 is a "writable" platform that facilitates interaction between users and sites in a continuous and collaborative manner and promotes participation and information sharing (Laroche, Habibi, Richard, & Sankaranarayanan, 2012). Web 2.0 technologies emphasize tools and platforms that enable users to tag, comment, modify, augment, and rank. Users can also create online communities such as websites and blogs in order to share information, ideas, personal messages, videos, and other content. Some examples of Web 2.0 tools are Facebook, LinkedIn, Instagram, YouTube, and Wikis.

By using Web 2.0 tools, organizations can build and maintain social media public pages to promote their social network salience, increase interest in their organizations, and build relationships online (Parveen, Jaafar, & Ainin, 2016).

Although many organizations first started using social media for consumer marketing and branding, with the adoption of more technology-driven human resource practices, organizations have rapidly integrated social media tools for attraction, selection, recruitment, and engagement purposes both within and outside the organization. Social media offers organizations many new possibilities for building their employment brand, expanding their network, targeting their audience, and attracting employees that fit with their company's culture and core values. Also, with the increased competition for human capital, many companies have been forced to expand their traditional local and regional searches for talent to a more national or global pool of applicants. Social media sites such as LinkedIn offer HR managers the ability to connect and communicate with a larger and more diverse group of candidates. This can be particularly valuable when the job market is competitive and some positions are difficult to fill. Social media may also provide an efficient method for applicants to self-screen and to determine if they are a good fit for the position and organization. Further, social media is an excellent way to reach passive candidates, individuals who may not be currently looking for a position but could be potential future applicants.

Many organizations have begun to leverage social media as a cost-effective means of targeting a wider recruiting audience and to gather more information than provided in traditional resumes and cover letters (Brown & Vaughn, 2011; Hull, 2011). With advancement in technologies, HR managers have the ability to use social networks to gather personal as well as professional information about the applicant to help ensure the applicant is a good fit for the organization.

Organizational adoption of social media is increasing, with organizations increasingly spending more than $4.6 billion annually on this technology in support of recruiting and selection (Young, Brown, Keitt, Owayang, Kopolowitz, & Shey, 2008). One survey shows that approximately 84% of organizations are using **social media websites (SMWs)** regularly as a recruitment source, and an additional 9% are planning on adopting SMWs in the near future (SHRM, 2017). In fact, social media and social recruiting software were the No. 1 planned technology investment of 2017. Many organizations contended that social media marketing would be one of the most demanded HR skills by 2020, along with data analysis and predicative modeling (CareerArc, 2019).

In addition to recruiting and selection, organizations are using social media for employee performance development, monitoring key performance metrics, and organizational workflow. A study by CareerBuilder indicates that up to 48% of employers are using social media to monitor their employees, and 43% use it to connect with their employees and help promote retention (CareerBuilder, 2018). Social media has also become an effective tool to more readily disseminate work-related content (Verhoeven, Tench, Zerfass, Moreno, & Verčič, 2012), connect employees, (Schultz, Utz, & Goritz, 2011), distribute information about the organization, and improve many organizational processes (Treem & Leonardi, 2012).

Social media has become influential in almost all areas of employment (Gregory, Meade, & Thompson, 2013) and is a valued tool for employee attraction, selection, and engagement. Therefore, with organizations' increased usage of social media as a recruitment and selection tool, and as a way to improve **employee engagement**, this chapter seeks to provide a broad overview of how social media is being used within HR and to explain some of the positive and negative externalities with its usage.

GLOBAL SOCIAL MEDIA PLATFORM USE

In 2019, an estimated 3.48 billion individuals regularly accessed social media, a 9% increase from 2018 (Hootsuite, 2019), and 9 out of 10 of those users were using mobile devices to access social media (2018 Global Digital Report). Traditionally, the more-developed countries have had higher internet penetration and more social media usage. However, as of 2018, with the expansion of the Internet across the globe and the rapid adoption of affordable mobile smart phones and data plans, social media usage increased. Table 16.1 gives an example of some of the various levels of Internet penetration per country, the average daily usage rates, and the average time spent on mobile phones.

TABLE 16.1 ■ Internet Usage			
Country	Internet Penetration	Daily Internet Usage (hrs)	Daily Mobile Use (hrs)
Australia	87%	5:04	1:48
Brazil	70%	9:29	4:45
Canada	91%	5:51	2:07
China	57%	5:52	3:19
France	92%	4:38	1:25
Germany	96%	4:37	1:30
India	41%	7:47	3:43
Italy	92%	6:04	2:27
Japan	94%	3:45	1:25
Mexico	67%	8:01	3:50
Russia	76%	6:29	2:21
Saudi Arabia	89%	6:44	3:35
South Korea	95%	5:14	2:24
Spain	93%	5:18	2:11
Sweden	96%	5:56	2:11
Switzerland	95%	4:58	1:54
Turkey	72%	7:15	1:54
United Kingdom	95%	5:46	2:09
U.A.E.	99%	7:54	2:09
United States	95%	6:31	2:09
Global Median	57%	6:42	3:14

Source: Hootsuite, 2019; Pew Research 2019; Statista 2019

Social media penetration and usage also vary across the globe. Please refer to Table 16.2 to see the penetration rate per country, the average social media usage, the average number of social media accounts per person, and the statistics on how many individuals are currently using social media at work.

There are also some differences in the types of SMWs and tools used in various countries. According to a recent Pew Research Center survey (2019), the social media landscape in the U.S. is "defined by a mix of long-standing trends and newly emerging narratives." Americans have shown a strong preference for Facebook, LinkedIn, Pinterest, and YouTube.

TABLE 16.2 ■ Social Media Use				
Country	Social Media Penetration	Daily Social Media Usage (hrs)	Avg # of Acts Per Person	Individual Use of Social Media at Work
Australia	72%	1:31	6.10	13%
Brazil	66%	3:34	9.40	29%
Canada	67%	1:47	6.80	14%
China	71%	1:57	9.00	24%
France	58%	1:17	5.80	10%
Germany	46%	1:04	5.10	10%
India	23%	2:32	12.00	32%
Italy	59%	1:51	7.40	11%
Japan	61%	:36	3.70	6%
Mexico	67%	3:12	10.30	29%
Russia	49%	2:16	7.00	14%
Saudi Arabia	68%	2:50	9.30	22%
South Korea	85%	2:50	6.30	8%
Spain	60%	1:09	7.90	19%
Sweden	72%	1:39	7.10	16%
Switzerland	51%	1:16	6.60	20%
Turkey	63%	2:46	9.70	26%
United Kingdom	67%	1:50	7.10	13%
U.A.E.	99%	2:59	10.10	32%
United States	70%	2:04	7.10	14%
Global Median	45%	2:16	8.90	24%

Source: Hootsuite, 2019; Pew Research 2019; Statista 2019

However, younger Americans, those between the ages of 18 and 24, are embracing a variety of other platforms and using them more frequently. Among this age group, 78% use Snapchat, and the majority of these users visit the platform multiple times per day. Similarly, estimates show this group also uses Instagram (71%) and Twitter (45%; Pew Research, 2018a). Table 16.3 shows estimated global usage rates for some of the more common social media sites.

Although Facebook is currently the most popular social media site globally, many other sites are popular in specific countries. Table 16.4 shows current active user rates among various social media and messaging platforms that are currently popular across the globe.

TABLE 16.3 ■ Global Usage of Social Media Sites					
Country	Facebook	Instagram	LinkedIn	Twitter	Snapchat
Australia	76%	46%	56%	12%	30%
Brazil	75%	40%	23%	5%	6%
Canada	71%	40%	53%	17%	24%
China	20%	0.30%	4.00%	0.10%	-
France	74%	31%	33%	10%	34%
Germany	44%	27%	13%	5%	15%
India	29%	7%	6%	1%	1%
Italy	59%	36%	24%	4%	5%
Japan	22%	24%	2%	34%	1%
Mexico	85%	22%	13%	7%	11%
Russia	11%	30%	7%	2%	5%
Saudi Arabia	57%	49%	14%	43%	52%
South Korea	37%	29%	6%	10%	-
Spain	60%	37%	29%	15%	9%
Sweden	77%	58%	43%	14%	41%
Switzerland	51%	34%	38%	10%	22%
Turkey	66%	58%	12%	14%	10%
United Kingdom	71%	42%	51%	24%	30%
U.A.E.	82%	44%	50%	27%	24%
United States	76%	44%	59%	17%	%
Global Median	35%	15%	11%	4%	5%

Source: Hootsuite, 2019; Pew Research 2019; Statista 2019

TABLE 16.4 ■ Social Platforms: Active Monthly User Accounts (January 2019)

Social Media	Accounts (000)	Messenger	Accounts (000)
Facebook	2,271	WhatsApp	1,500
YouTube	1,900	FB Messenger	1,300
Instagram	1,000	Weixin/WeChat	1,083
Ozone	531	QQ	803
Douyin/TikTok	500	Skype	300
Sina Weibo	446	Snapchat	287
Reddit	330		
Twitter	326		
Douban	320		
LinkedIn	303		
Baidu Teiba	300		

Source: Hootsuite, 2019

Over the past few years, Brazil has experienced rapid growth in Internet and social media usage (Statista, 2015a; 2015b) and represents the largest Internet market in Latin America, with over 149 million users (Statista, 2019). Brazilians exhibit similar social media preferences to the U.S. with their strong use of Facebook, Twitter, and LinkedIn. However, most social media users in Brazil are younger, with 90% of social media users between the ages of 15 and 32. Brazil is currently the third-largest market for Facebook in the world after India and the U.S. (Internet World Stats, 2019). Brazil also has more than 18 million Twitter users, making Brazil the sixth-largest user base for Twitter. YouTube is also very popular with an estimated 79% of Brazilian Internet users (Internet World Stats, 2019). Other popular platforms include Orkut, WhatsApp, LinkedIn, Tumblr, and Skype (Internet World Stats, 2019).

India has experienced the second-highest growth in social media use (31%) after Saudi Arabia (32%; Global Digital Report, 2018). India currently has approximately 250 million SMW users and is expected to have more than 660 million users by 2023 (Statista, 2019), with a majority accessing the Internet over a mobile device rather than a computer (Velayanikal, 2016). The most popular SMW platforms in India are Facebook (30% market penetration), YouTube, (30%), WhatsApp (28%), Twitter (18%), and LinkedIn (15%; Statista, 2017).

Russia, which has the largest Internet population in Europe (109.6 million users), experienced 15% growth in Internet users in 2018 (Hootsuite, 2019). The most active social media platforms (including messaging apps) in Russia are: YouTube, VK, WhatsApp, and Instagram. More than twice as many Russians (83%) reported using the homegrown VK (also known as VKontakte) as Facebook (39%; Yorgan, 2019). VK is similar to Facebook but also has a file-sharing platform on which users can upload video and audio files. Another popular site, OK, tends to be used by individuals to connect with former classmates and friends (Smith, 2016). Both OK and VK are trying to take advantage of Russia's expanding "mobile-first" culture (Watson, 2016).

China is currently the world's largest social network market with approximately 674 million social media users in 2018 (Statista, 2019). However, their market differs significantly from the rest of the world, primarily due to the Chinese government's Internet censorship (informally called the "Great Firewall of China"). The Chinese government has blocked direct access to many of the popular social media sites such as Facebook, Twitter, and YouTube, which has led to SMW such as WeChat (similar to Facebook but with more features), Sina Weibo (similar to Twitter), Tencent Q (Instant Messaging App), Yoku Tudo (similar to YouTube), Baidu Tieba (a search engine forum), Ahihu (like Quora), Douban (a lifestyle discussion platform), and others. In China, most companies recruit through personal networks and social network sites. International companies face challenges with recruiting when entering Chinese markets if they do not have employees fluent in Chinese and have not yet developed local networks.

WeChat is currently the most popular platform in China with 1.132 billion users as of the second quarter of 2019 (Tencent, 2019). WeChat was developed by Tencent and is considered to be an all-in-one messaging app (Dragon Social, 2019). This platform allows families, work colleagues, and others to communicate via their mobile devices. A unique aspect of WeChat is that it allows up to 500 participants in a single group chat. In fact, many individuals use WeChat rather than email to conduct business. Business professionals can use WeChat QR (quick response) to exchange business contact information rather than exchanging business cards. The app is popular among Chinese for shopping online, paying bills, scheduling appointments, having food delivered, and booking taxis. Users are able to do almost everything they need within the app, which has made it the most popular social media in China. WeChat offers far more than most all of the Western messaging apps. In terms of comparison, it would be like combining Facebook, WhatsApp, Google News, Tinder, and Pinterest. It also enables users to access 10 million third-party apps called WeChat mini-programs (Dragon Social, 2019).

Multinational corporations can benefit from cost savings by utilizing social media for recruitment. For example, multinational corporations seeking to attract international candidates typically experience high costs associated with third-party recruiting, but social media enables organizations to reach a large global pool of candidates while avoiding third-party recruiting fees. Organizational use of social media sites can also reduce expenses associated with recruiting such as transportation, hotels, meals, and other expenses (Chapman & Webster, 2003). With the advancement of technology and social media platforms, applicants can upload their job application online from even a phone and hold a video conference with an HR manager from another part of the world in just a few clicks.

Around the world, many applicants are also embracing SMW tools at work. A global study by Adecco (2014) showed that approximately 49% of job seekers are using social media to distribute their resumés online, 29% are contacted by a recruiter thru social media, and 9% receive a job offer. This same study showed that geographically, Western Europe is currently the most effective in terms of the matching of job seekers with open positions thru the use of social media (Adecco, 2014).

With the improvements in technology and development of more live features, an increasing number of businesses are incorporating social media to interact with followers, applicants, and employees. Although platforms change in popularity, social media continues to grow globally about 9% year on year (Global Digital Report, 2019) and is considered a valuable resource for many organizations as well as applicants. "While the reasons for use may vary, the numbers of users, the length of time users spend on sites, and the global reach of social platforms explains why social media content is much more valued than ever before" (O'Brien, 2019).

SOCIAL MEDIA AND HR PRACTICES

Organizational Recruitment and Selection

Social media websites are now ubiquitous among organizations, as they allow recruiters to source, contact, and screen both active and passive job applicants. Through the use of **social network websites (SNWs)** such as Facebook, Twitter, and LinkedIn, organizations have been able to build their employment brand with prospective job applicants, expand their network of applicants, better target them, and better attract employees who fit with the company culture and core values. SMWs provide readily available information that allows for targeting of potential candidates with specific job skills. SMWs provide organizations with a potentially more effective tool for evaluating candidates than traditional HR selection means (Brown & Vaughn, 2011) at a significantly lower cost for recruitment (Anderson, 2003; Brady, Thompson, Wuensch, & Gorssnickle, 2003; Hull, 2011). As such, organizations are using social media platforms to collect the maximum amount of information possible on each applicant. This is done to maximize dependable role behavior, avoid negligent hiring lawsuits, and screen out applicants who might be untrustworthy or basically a poor hire for the company (Roth, Bobko, Van Inddekinge, & Thatcher, 2016). Industry research found that social media ranked fourth in terms of quality of applicants, behind referrals, internal transfers, and direct sourcing but before a company's own career site (Jobvite, 2014). This approach to recruitment is "creating a new technical world order where job applicants are found and evaluated by their merits and contributions, rather than how well they sell themselves in an interview" (Meister, 2014, p.1).

Organizations are also using online software, social networks, and other platforms to conduct what is now called "**social recruiting**" (Wauters, 2011). The large global audience on social network sites, such as Facebook, provides many easily accessible opportunities for organizations to utilize for recruitment and selection purposes. For example, a recent study shows that up to 51% of employers are currently screening applicants' social network content, and a high percentage of these organizations have rejected applicants based on reviewing material they found online (Grasz, 2014). In addition, with 77% of employees connected to co-workers via social media (O'Connor, Schmidt, & Drouin, 2016), organizations are using these networks to encourage employee referrals to find new qualified candidates.

As companies compete to attract and retain talented workers, and especially those with specialized skills, developing an effective recruiting strategy is a key concern for organizations. Thus, many of these companies are developing "**social media playbooks**" as they strategically manage their social media plans to engage employees, get referrals from their employees on potential candidates, and recruit talented employees. For example, in the United States, UPS uses Facebook, Twitter, and LinkedIn, to post job openings and promote relevant information about the company and its culture (Zielinski, 2012). Internationally, the Hard Rock Café solely used Facebook as a recruiting source to hire 120 employees for a new restaurant in Florence, Italy (Colao, 2012).

The extensive amount of information available on social media sites has made SNWs a good venue for organizations to learn more about potential hires, and organizations are increasingly using the Internet as a resource to select new employees. In fact, many consider SNWs a better measure of a person's true job performance potential, because recruiters are able to evaluate the applicant under different criteria outside of the traditional interview setting and obtain different applicant information than provided by a résumé, application, skills assessment, interview, personality inventories, and drug tests (Black & Johnson, 2012).

According to Kluemper and Rosen (2009), the broad characteristics shown on SNWS may "be more practical than assessing more narrow aspects of **social networking profiles** that may be unavailable and/or inconsistent for a large segment of the profiles" (p. 571). In addition to listing profile information, SNWs typically provide a list of the user's friends, interest groups, and special interests. The information also conveys the applicant's behavior and interactions in a unique light and in a context that is not necessarily focused on career advancement. Some research indicates that the individual's information on SNWs may actually be a more accurate reflection of the person's attributes than standard selection methods because they may reflect an individual's "maximal" work performance rather than the "typical" performance (Sackett, 2007).

Organizations are also more readily using SMWs to search for **passive job seekers** (SHRM, 2016). Passive job seekers are currently employed individuals who are not actively considering other employment but who might be of interest to the organization. Similar to benefits of Web recruiting, organizations can potentially increase the quantity and quality of their applicant pool by examining potential applicant profiles on Twitter, Facebook, and/or LinkedIn and then contacting those who are perceived as qualified for a position. Not surprisingly, approximately 66% of LinkedIn's revenue stems from its Talent Solutions division (Reuters, 2015), where recruiters purchase premium features to search for and access potential applicant profiles. SMWs may also be used to recruit active applicants, especially at the full-time, entry-level rank and even hourly or part-time positions (Colao, 2012). For example, a variety of organizations—from the United States Army to Aon—use Facebook and LinkedIn to post job openings. Other organizations (e.g., Kroger) use Facebook and Twitter to promote job openings (Robb, 2014).

Popular Recruitment Sites

Many organizations are recruiting employees via social media by actively managing their social media presence and using recruitment tools to attract applicants. Candidates often view a company's website and then turn next to a company's social network sites such as Facebook, Twitter, and Instagram to learn more about the company. Having a social media presence through a mixed-media feed of frequently posted status updates can help promote an organization's online credibility. Organizations wanting to attract younger employees are well served by using social media, as 73% of Millennials found their last position through a social media platform (CareerProfiles, 2019).

Presently, LinkedIn is among the most popular professional **social networking** sites used by organizations. LinkedIn allows organizations access the world's largest professional network on the Internet with more than 645 million registered users (LinkedIn, 2019). Research indicates that 89% of all recruiters reported having screened applicants on LinkedIn or chosen not to hire someone based on their online content (Akiode, 2013). For organizations, LinkedIn provides an abundance of information about the qualifications of various jobseekers, and organizations can effectively use LinkedIn to leverage their own networks (and those of their employees) in order to find potential candidates. In addition, LinkedIn allows organizations to create company profiles as well as set up information feeds for those who would like to follow them and be contacted about new job postings (Heathfield, 2015). LinkedIn also offers organizations a fee-based solution, which enables HR managers to more readily find potential job candidates that best fit the qualifications of the job they want to fill.

Facebook is another frequently used tool in recruitment. Among SNWs, Facebook has the largest audience, with more than 1.59 billion monthly active users (Facebook, 2019). Organizations have several options when using Facebook. They can target a general audience through a free job post in the Facebook Marketplace, or they can target a specific group of individuals by demographics with a Facebook advertisement. With a paid ad, organizations may pay per click (how many people clicked on the job posting), pay per impression (how many people potentially viewed the ad), and budget how much they want to spend. Moreover, they have the option of advertising the job posting on a continuous basis or for a fixed time.

Twitter is also effective for increasing exposure and communicating with groups of individuals who want to follow organizations. As such, many organizations have created job channels on Twitter to communicate with and attract new talent (Heathfield, 2015). According to their website, "Twitter is a simple tool that helps connect businesses more meaningfully with the right audience at the right time" (Twitter, 2016). With more than 321 million monthly active users as of 2018 (Statista, 2019), Twitter enables HR managers to broadcast announcements more efficiently to large groups at the same time, which can reduce costs and increase exposure. Many companies use Twitter to engage with job seekers, post job listings, and advertise career events but also to market the company to individuals looking for a great place to work. According to Westfall (2016), 78% of *Fortune* 500 recruiting tweets contain hashtags—most commonly with branded terms related to job opportunities (46%). In addition, 35% of *Fortune* 500 companies have a recruiting-specific Twitter handle, which they use to tweet one to three times per day (64%; Westfall, 2016). Twitter has a large user base under the age of 30 and is particularly useful when targeting applicants between 18 and 35 years of age (Westfall, 2016).

Training and Development

As organizations compete in a global market, they need to develop and enhance employee skills. Social media tools can assist organizations in multiple ways such as informing teams separated by geographic distance, time, culture, and organizational boundaries. Companies can use social media tools to communicate changes in company policies or organizational structures as well as to teach new job skills. Organizations can also utilize SMW tools to support e-learning, which offers delivery advantages and more flexibility to learners. Social media offers organizations the ability to share practices, promote information and educational material, and share opinions, views, and comments, embodying them in training programs and individual courses. For example, Facebook can be used to create an open or closed group to deliver content, and Twitter can be used in e-learning to connect learning communities or create smaller classrooms to inform employees on a specific topic or event, share highlights, make statements, or upload pictures.

Organizations can also use social media tools to assess metadata about the type of employees it has, as well as their knowledge, skills, and abilities. For instance, Avaya used collaborative tags to identify organizational experts and integrated these data into a communication system (John & Seligmann, 2006). Organizations can also use SMW sites to promote communication and enable their workers to expand their networks and social capital (Ferron, Frassoni, Massa, Napolitano, & Setti, 2010). SMWs can also be used to share information related to the status of ongoing organizational activities or to encourage inter-organizational communication (Zhao & Rosson, 2009). The use of social media allows individuals to develop weak network ties and create a more robust organizational network (DiMicco et al., 2008). These associations can help workers gain access to others in the company, which reduces the role of gatekeepers who traditionally control access to these individuals (Ehrlich & Shami, 2010). Employees using social media, particularly those in less powerful organizational positions, may be able to use the ease of associations to garner social resources that can be beneficial to the employee as well as the organization (Young et al., 2008).

Internal Communication and Engagement

According to a recent Gallup Poll (Harter, 2018), 16.5% of the American workforce feels actively disconnected, or not engaged, at work. Lack of engagement at work can lead to higher absenteeism, higher turnover, and lower firm performance. With many employees feeling isolated by their business function or geographic location, organizations are increasingly using SMW for employee engagement. With approximately 60 million U.S. workers using social media to discuss employment-related issues (Hawley, 2014), if used appropriately, social media can be a productive platform to improve employee engagement, helping users to collaborate with others, share ideas, and solve issues.

SMW can support employee engagement in a number of ways. First, it can improve internal communications, improve the exchange of ideas, and increase feelings of inclusion (Ruggs, Speights, & Walker, 2013). In addition, SMW have been shown to be effective in channeling employees' opinions (Miles & Mangold, 2014), gathering information (Fuller et al., 2006; Moqbel, Nevo, & Kock, 2013), and conveying competence (Ollier-Malaterre, Rothbard, & Berg, 2013). Social media tools can also be used to communicate with employees about the corporate culture, expected work behaviors, and other matters (Dreher, 2014; van Zoonen & zan der Meer, 2015).

Many organizations are actively using social media to increase employee engagement. For example, L'Oreal, a cosmetic company, believes that people will have greater trust in information about what it is like to work for a company when it comes from their peers on social media rather than from the company (Simpson, 2015). Therefore, they use various social tools and tagging (e.g., hashtags) to get their employees to talk about their work lives on personal social media sites to show organizational transparency, promote corporate values, and build brand awareness. They also have one hashtag, #LorealCommunity, which employees use to convey corporate culture and talk about their co-workers.

CONCERNS OVER SOCIAL MEDIA

The previous section discussed how social media is or can be effectively used to support HR functions. However, the use of SNW does not come without risks. Some organizations have experienced problems with social media, such as the dissemination of inappropriate posts and decreased employee productivity (Landers & Callan, 2014). In some instances, organizations have been forced to take disciplinary action and have even terminated employees due to inappropriate social media usage. An example of such dismissal can be seen in one case in which the employee was fired for posting something the company considered a violation of HIPPA privacy laws (Katarsky, 2010). In another example, an employee was terminated for posting work-related information on social media, even though it was positive information about the organization (Galli, 2014).

Research indicates that 36% of employees utilize social media while at work, even when it is explicitly against company policy (O'Conner et al., 2016). The unsanctioned and or inappropriate use of SMWs at work presents new problems for organizations due to the amount of time spent on social media as well as negative postings that may impair brand management, hurt company morale, or cause other issues. In addition, a number of potential legal issues may arise as a result of using SMWs. These issues are further discussed in the following sections.

Legal Issues in Social Media

Few protections provide blanket coverage for social media users in the United States, but the legal landscape in the U.S. is shifting to address the rapid changes brought about by social media. Protections tend to be based on laws that existed prior to the widespread use of social media and have been adapted through practice and interpretation to cover online activity (Sánchez Abril, Levin, & Del Riego, 2012). Some states have enacted protections specifically to bolster online privacy for citizens.

Much of the legal landscape that organizations navigate concerns HR functions. For instance, the California state constitution ensures that employees have a reasonable expectation of privacy when they are not at work (Genova, 2009). Nonwork activities of employees have protection from employers' disciplinary actions in a small number of states, including California, New York, Colorado, and North Dakota (Genova, 2009). Although these specific protections cover only a minority of U.S. citizens, they are representative of the patchwork of legal protections that create compliance challenges for organizations. These challenges are due more to idiosyncrasies across state laws than to the depth of guaranteed protections.

Given the current state of employee and consumer protections on social media, organizations have significant latitude in using social media for a range of activities including marketing, recruitment, and customer engagement. Typically, laws that are applicable to offline business activities are also applicable to the activity when conducted online. Practices that are deceptive or violate the rights of an employee are prohibited under law (Civil Rights Act of 1964; Genova, 2008). For instance, just as a firm may not discriminate based on protected classes during an in-person interview, the firm may not use information from social media to discriminate. It is extremely important that hiring managers not discriminate based on information obtained from social media, as this infringes upon Title VII (Johnson et al., 2019).

Social media does represent an additional means for gaining information on applicants that is not of a protected nature and thus may be used in the hiring process (Elzweig, Roberto, & Johnson, 2017). Organizations should be aware of the ethical challenges and reputational risks that may accompany the use of online information. Just over half of U.S. states have passed laws that prohibit employers from requiring the login information and password from an applicant for their social media accounts. Similarly, states have prohibited organizations from "mandatory friending" requirements for job applicants (Johnson et al., 2019).

Certain professions and industries face unique challenges when using social media to promote their business or for personal use. Attorneys face ethical dilemmas in the connections they make online (e.g., with judges) and face compliance issues in advertising online (Lackey & Minta, 2012). Also, the health care industry must ensure that any social media information is in compliance with protections covered by the Health Insurance Portability and Accountability Act of 1996 (Hader & Brown, 2010). In addition, different countries around the world have widely differing perceptions and laws regarding privacy (see Chapter 13 for more information on global privacy policies).

Corporate Social Media Policies

In an effort to address employee usage of social media, many companies have implemented social media policies to protect their professional reputations as well as proprietary information from exposure (O'Connor et al., 2016). In creating policies, organizations need to ensure they do not infringe upon the legally protected rights of their employees. According to Section 7 of the National Labor Relations Act (NLRA), organizations cannot restrict employees' right to communicate with co-workers about working terms and conditions. Depending on the type of work-related matter employees discuss via social media, their communications may be considered protected concerted activity and within the employees' right to debate (Schmidt & O'Connor, 2015). As such, many organizations have included nondisparagement clauses. These policies can range from requiring employees to not make disparaging remarks about the company to not being allowed to identify that they are employed by the company, and, in extreme cases, completely banning employees from posting anything organizationally related (Gordon & Argento, 2014). Nevertheless, it is important to understand that private-sector companies that place heavy restrictions and all-out bans on their employees run the same risk of violating Section 7 of the NLRA (Schmidt & O'Connor, 2015). Therefore, it is recommended that organizations use legal counsel to assist them with determining their organizational policies and ensuring that they do not violate federal laws. The National Labor Relations Board (NLRB) suggests that all employees be trained on social media usage and given social media policies with guidelines and clear examples of permitted and banned behaviors and how the organization's policy will be applied (Schmidt & O'Connor, 2015). Five examples of noteworthy social media policies can be seen at https://blog.hubspot.com/blog/tabid/6307/bid/29441/5-noteworthy-examples-of-corporate-social-media-policies.aspx.

Organizations also need to ensure that they provide adequate training for their employees. Although the majority of organizations (80%) have a social media policy (Rubenstien, 2014), it is not clear that companies have provided their employees with training on the policy and whether the employees are even aware of policy specifics (O'Connor et al., 2016). The limited research available suggests that many employees are not well informed on company policies regarding social media. For example, one study showed that only 31% of participants indicated their company had a social media policy, 34% indicated that their company did not have a social media policy, and 35% reported that they did not know if their company had a social media policy (O'Connor et al., 2016). Another global study by Adecco (2014) showed that among HR professionals who use social media for recruitment purposes, only 30% had attended training courses organized by their company. This same study also showed that 61% of HR respondents either did not receive guidelines for the use of social media or were unaware that these guidelines existed. These results indicate that more training and better communication must be implemented to inform employees and ensure that organizational policies are followed.

Recruitment and Selection

As noted, a majority of organizations are utilizing SNW as part of their recruitment and selection strategies. Organizations should exercise caution when using them because of potential legal issues associated with their use and the inability to verify with confidence the profile information on these sites. As previously noted, by viewing SNW profiles, recruiters may be discriminating—intentionally or unintentionally—against applicants belonging to a protected class. For example, a profile picture can reveal the applicant's gender, perceived age, ethnicity, and/or disability, all of which are not allowed to be used as part of a hiring decision. Organizations that view and judge applicant profiles on SMWs likely increase the probability of engaging in disparate treatment (i.e., intentional discrimination) and may even lead to disparate impact (i.e., unintentional discrimination; see Davison, Maraist, & Bing, 2011), leaving the organization susceptible to litigation. In fact, some organizations have faced legal issues when using social media for recruitment purposes. One study by Williams, Schaffer, and Ellis (2013) showed that the selection tools used by companies included material that had violations of the Fourth-Fifths Rules, administrative inconsistencies, personal bias problems, lack of documentation, unfair recruiting source issues, quota or unlawful affirmative action policies, unfair recruiting source, failure to provide accommodations, and other legal complications.

Validity of SMWs in Selection

Another concern for HR decision makers is the fact that organizations may be unable to infer—with relative validity—the qualifications, personality, and/or integrity-related information on an applicant's profile when using SNWs. Presently, there is relatively little evidence that shows employers are making valid inferences about applicants' job performance based on their social networking data (Kluemper, Rosen, & Mossholder, 2012; Roth et al., 2016), and research suggests that the spread of false information through social media can have negative ramifications for organizations and employees (Black, Stone, & Johnson, 2015).

One of the more difficult aspects when using social media is understanding the context in which the social media content was originally shared (SHRM, 2014) and determining if the source is credible. There is significant variability in terms of the content and information available across applicants, which creates issues for employers. For example, when employers view an individual's social media presence, they need to understand that they may not be looking at the entire conversation, history, or other factors. Where an individual places his or her professional content may also vary, because the average Internet user utilizes five different social media platforms (Bennett, 2014). Some applicants may not use the particular SNW that the employer may use for screening purposes; others may limit access to their account. In addition, some job applicants may not have SNW accounts or may not be active online users, which can lead to incomplete and inconsistent information regarding the individual's knowledge, skills, and abilities (KSAs; Johnson & Gueutal, 2014). Finally, an organization may be accessing an individual's personal site, such as Facebook, where the individual posts primarily to friends and family, while not accessing the candidate's professional site, such as LinkedIn, where he or she presents his or her professional attributes. Each of these can cause inconsistencies in the information collected, create undue bias, and lead to incorrect conclusions. In turn, it can create errors in the selection process, increasing the probability of selecting the wrong applicant for the job (i.e., type I error).

For this reason, it is important that organizations have a policy in place for notifying applicants of the use of this data as well as one that provides them with an opportunity to correct erroneous information. The lack of commonly accepted standards for SMW evaluations also increases the likelihood that different raters will apply different standards in evaluating various candidates (Johnson & Gueutal, 2014). Organizations need to be cognizant of these issues and create a work flow process that ensures that the validity of social networking sites data is established before they are used in the selection process (Brown & Vaughn, 2011; Davison, Maraist, & Bing, 2011; Lucero, Allen, & Elzweig, 2013; Roth et al., 2016). At present, there is limited research about the best method to determine credible and professional social networking site content to use for recruiting and selection efforts, which presents complications for an organization. It is important that organizations develop consistent and accurate methods of utilizing social media and the information it provides to ensure that they are evaluating the correct applicant and appropriate content and making better and more informed hiring decisions (Black et al., 2015). Without consistent and valid assessment measures in place, organizations may inadvertently expose themselves to liability. For this reason, we agree with scholars who have argued against the use of SMW in hiring decisions (Johnson & Gueutal, 2014) until its validity can be better understood.

Privacy Concerns

Many HR decision makers are using social networking sites to review and gather information about candidates' off-duty behavior, lifestyle, friends, religion, and political affiliations (Gross & Acquisti, 2005). This also poses legal concerns for organizations and can lead to applicant perceptions that their privacy was invaded (Gross & Acquisti, 2005; Tabibi, 2012). One reason for this is that posts on social networking sites are intended by the user for family and friends rather than for the organization. These personal data are often considered to be private by the applicant, and they believe that it is inappropriate for the organization to view them (Tabibi, 2012). In addition, social networking data are primarily focused on off-duty behavior such as romantic relationships, and this type of information is not usually perceived as job relevant. A third reason is that some data found on social networking sites could reveal stigmatizing information (e.g., alcohol or drug use, disability, sexual orientation), which could unduly stigmatize the applicant (Black et al., 2015). Other information that is not of a protected nature but potentially stigmatizing, such as political ideology, may also be considered in employment decisions (Roth et al., 2019).

From the perspective of the job applicant, many individuals have expressed concern about how organizations are reviewing their social networking data, giving employers access to data (e.g., photographs) that may reveal their protected class (e.g., race, disability status, age; Brown & Vaughn, 2011). According to one survey, 69% of American adults considered that employer access to social media was not acceptable and was an invasion of privacy (Rasmussen, 2012). Moreover, research showed that when applicants perceived that their privacy was invaded, they exhibited a negative attraction to the organization (Madigan & Macan, 2005), were less inclined to recommend the organization to others (Smither, Reilly, Millsap, Pearlman, & Stoffey, 1993), less likely to accept the job offer (Madera, 2012; Stone & Kotch, 1989), and less likely to remain with the organization (Hausknecht, Day, & Thomas, 2004). Also, when organizations invade an applicant's or employee's privacy, they may gain the reputation of violating individuals' rights. This in turn may negatively affect their ability to hire the most talented employees. Although the labor market will ultimately affect applicants' job acceptance rates, those who believe that their rights have been violated may be less likely to be as committed to the organization (Black et al., 2015). Given the shortage of skilled labor, especially for particular jobs (e.g., software engineer, nurse, machinist; Stone, Lukaszewski, Stone-Romero, & Johnson, 2013), organizations need to be cognizant of an applicant's or employee's privacy perceptions of organizational access to his or her social network data. For more information regarding the security and privacy of applicant and employee data, see Chapter 15.

Diversity Concerns

As more organizations use technology and implement SMW tools, they also must consider the risk of adverse impact. Some research has shown that individuals from lower socioeconomic backgrounds are less likely to have Internet access and use of computers and that some socioeconomic and demographic differences exist with organizations' use of e-selection (Kuhn & Skuterud, 2000; McManus & Ferguson, 2003). Although there are not significant differences by racial or ethnic groups or by gender among social media usage, there are socioeconomic differences (Pew Research Center, 2015); those with more education are consistently more likely to use social media. Presently, adoption rates for social media are at 79% among college graduates, 74% among those with some college education, and 64% for those with a high school diploma or less (Pew Research Center, 2019). In addition, 78% of households with higher incomes use social media, but only 68% of those in the lowest-income households use social media (a gap that has recently narrowed; Pew Research Center, 2019). There also are notable differences in usage by age; for example, ages 18 to 29 are most likely users of social media (90%; Pew Research Center, 2019). In contrast, those over the age of 65 are the least likely to use social media (40%; Pew Research Center, 2019).

Researchers contend that individuals belonging to traditionally marginalized groups may be at a disadvantage in the talent acquisition process when social media is used (Ruggs, Walker, Blanchard, & Gur, 2016). Although many young applicants and people of color may use social media, they tend to have smaller network structures, and individuals with larger network structures tend to have access to more opportunities (McDonald, 2011). Thus, somewhat counterintuitively, older and educated males may actually have an advantage when SMW are used for talent acquisition.

Thus, as social media tools become more commonplace, organizations need to be aware of how these tools may have a differential impact (Johnson & Gueutal, 2014). Organizations may unduly bias minority job applicants who tend to have lower-status networks than white males with less social capital (McDonald, 2011). Also, the use of SMW in the attraction and selection process may lead to legal issues related to discrimination to the extent that demographic information that is currently protected might be used by the organization that influences the screening and selection of new employees (Davison, Maraist, Hamilton, & Bing, 2012). These practices may also lead to disparate impact, as accessibility differences due to socioeconomic status may systematically disadvantage some groups to a greater extent than they do others (Davison et al., 2012).

To mitigate this risk, organizations can track who is engaging in their SMW during the attraction and selection process, collect the demographic data, and use the data to examine the relation between the proportion of people of color who engage with their organization and those who apply for jobs and examine the percentage of those hired to see if there are any discrepancies. Moreover, if SMW profiles are to be used in the screening process, training should be done within the organization to make HR decision makers aware of implicit biases in an effort to reduce bias (Devine, Forscher, Austin, & Cox, 2012) and encourage a more diverse workforce.

GUIDELINES FOR CORPORATE SOCIAL MEDIA POLICIES

Organizations are increasingly adopting policies for employees regarding their social media usage both during work hours and personal time. Specifically, these guidelines seek to limit employees' activities on social media, particularly if those activities might be considered an official view of the company. This approach mirrors the advice given to many job applicants to set their privacy settings high, minimize social media usage, and avoid creating any content that might be viewed negatively by prospective employers (Black & Johnson, 2012; Lam, 2016; Roberts & Roach, 2009). Although the approach may work for some organizations, blanket restriction of social media may not be conducive for specific organizations or specific positions. Social media policies should reflect the two-way interaction prevalent across Web 2.0 technologies. Organizations with strong online presence such as in marketing, sales, or customer service need to implement online policies that are geared toward their business model.

Consider, for example, the social media policy developed by Dell Computers. Dell Computers introduced a social media policy in 2018 that is straightforward yet seeks to be comprehensive. The five points are: (1) Be Nice, Have Fun, and Connect; (2) Protect Information; (3) Be Transparent and Disclose; (4) Follow the Law, Follow the Code of Conduct; and (5) Be Responsible. The statement is available online in 16 languages to improve accessibility for all stakeholders.[1] As with a vision or mission statement, it is important that employees are not just provided a document stating the social media policy but provided with training and insight on how to implement the policy in their daily work. Putting resources behind a statement also signals to employees and other stakeholders that the policy carries importance. For instance, Dell has a dedicated team to respond to any issues related to social media and a 24/7 Social Media Listening Command Center to monitor communications about Dell Computers across 11 languages (Dave, 2011). We recommend that employees should (a) be aware of their corporate social media policy and (b) if there is not one, work to establish one.

Although many positions within organizations do not require a robust knowledge of social media, there is an increasing need for social media talent. This creates challenges for employers and employees alike. Dell Computer acknowledges this need for talent by encouraging interested employees to take the Social Media Principles course offered by the company (https://www.dell.com/learn/us/en/uscorp1/corp-comm/social-media-policy). Ultimately, organizations must strike a balance between restrictiveness and openness in their policies. Policies that are too restrictive may fail to acknowledge the importance of social media in the workplace and more broadly to society.

Federal and State Guidelines

Corporate social media policies must also be consistent with federal and state laws. The most critical law is the Privacy Act of 1974. This act governs the collection, storage, and use of employee data in federal agencies in the United States and prohibits the disclosure of personnel information to third parties without an individual's consent. However, there is currently no similar federal protection for private-sector employees, and among the states, privacy laws differ. This inconsistent application of privacy laws has led to several state laws that limit the degree to which organizations can request social network site passwords or ask applicants to log into their accounts (Tabibi, 2012). To date, 26 states have enacted laws that apply to employers' access to social media accounts of their employees (NCSL, 2019). Also, in 2016, the Uniform Law Commission approved the Employee and Student Online Privacy Act to address employers' access to employees or prospective employees' social media and other online accounts accessed via username and password as well as other credentials of authentication (NCSL, 2019).

Other states either have legislation in the process of being passed or are considering legislating similar employer restrictions. For example, states such as New Jersey have passed laws prohibiting employers from seeking access to "a person's account," such as a "friends-only" account at Facebook. They also have banned "**shoulder surfing**," which refers to organizations making an employee access his/her personal account while managers watch and review material on the individual's social media page. The law also does not allow organizations to require an applicant or employee to change the privacy settings on a restricted account to a less-restrictive setting so that the employer can access it or by forcing the employee to accept an employer's "friend" request. The law also prohibits an employer from retaliating or discriminating against a job applicant or employee for refusing to provide log-in information to the employer or discriminating if the employee reports violations of this law to the authorities (Claypoole, 2014). Similar privacy laws also have been enacted in Europe and other nations, with laws such as the European Data Act (Levinson, 2010). A complete review of the U.S. and international privacy laws and legal cases can be seen in the work of Lucero et al. (2013), Levinson (2010), and Sprague (2009).

Despite these laws, organizations are still allowed to review social media pages, which typically are available to the general public. Also, employees or job applicants may voluntarily provide access to their social media accounts or may choose to "friend" work associates, including their supervisors. Taking advantage of these voluntary actions does not violate any of the new social media forced-access laws (Claypoole, 2014). Nevertheless, because of the increased trend toward protecting personal online accounts and communications, organizations should develop fair information policies to protect job applicants' privacy. For example, organizations should consider documenting how they obtain any social media information regarding employees or job applicants. These policies are discussed in the following section.

RESEARCH-BASED TIPS FOR THE USE OF SOCIAL MEDIA IN HR

In order to successfully utilize social media, organizations need to be proactive in the development of their social media processes and strive to stay current on the legal environment, the validity of the content used, and best practices. By proactively managing their use of social media platforms and implementing proper protocols, HR managers can stay connected with their target audience and be more successful in attracting and selecting a talented workforce (Black, Washington, & Schmidt, 2016). Based upon the research conducted to date, we present five recommendations for organizations that will help improve their social media policies:

1. *Be proactive in establishing social media policies and stay current on fair information policies regarding the use of SMW data.*

For example, organizations may want to appoint a qualified individual or individuals to monitor social media and technology applications, assist the organization in setting new social media goals, and provide feedback regarding the most appropriate social media platforms (Black et al., 2015). In addition, it is critical that HR managers stay well informed of changes at the state, federal, and international levels. Therefore, it is recommended that organizations retain legal counsel to keep abreast of new rulings as they arise and to stay current on legislation regarding social media use in order to ensure compliance.

2. *Implement measures to keep current on SMW technology adoption to ensure that the organization is using SMW technologies that are most popular in the locations in which the organization operates.*

Organizations may want to appoint a qualified individual(s) to monitor social media and technology applications to assist the organization in setting new goals, providing feedback on current usage, implementing new technology, and utilizing the most appropriate social media platforms (Black et al., 2015). In addition, because organizations tend to adopt technology more slowly than society does (Jobvite, 2014), it is important that organizations become more agile and adaptable in their use of SMWs and incorporate those that best fit their needs. One way to do this is by contracting with an outside entity to provide analytics on current trends and overall social media effectiveness.

3. *If a decision is made to use SMW in recruitment and selection, determine what type of information is relevant and valid, and ensure that collection methods do not collect data about characteristics protected by law.*

4. *Be active in establishing privacy policies for the HR decision makers, employees, and job applicants.*

It is important to note that the authors of this chapter and others (Johnson & Gueutal, 2014) are currently not in favor of the use of SMW as part of the selection process (due to concerns about the validity of SMW information, applicant privacy, and the potential for adverse impact). If an organization decides to use social media for these purposes, certain steps should be taken. First, use SNWs that are professionally rather than socially oriented (e.g., LinkedIn). These types of sites are more likely to contain job-relevant information than social-oriented websites. Second, verify that decision makers are using proper screening methods to ensure that they are not screening the wrong applicant and making recommendations based on false information. Third, consider having individuals not involved in the selection decision-making process screen the SMW for relevant data to ensure that data about protected classes are not shared with decision makers. Fourth, be active in establishing privacy policies for the HR decision makers, employees, and job applicants. Organizations need to implement fair information policies to increase individuals' perceived control over information and decrease their negative reactions to these practices. For instance, organizational policies might provide advance notice to applicants that SMW data will be collected during the selection process. In practice, employers could provide a disclosure form to applicants requesting a release of information and specifically refer to a company's policy regarding access to SMW (Black et al., 2016).

5. *Determine the level of employee involvement in developing and promoting social media policies, what the organization will state on social media sites, and how the information will be disseminated.*

Different levels of management should participate in the development of an organizationwide social media policy. In addition, they should help determine when new policies and initiatives will be implemented, how the content will be made readily available to share, and how it will be monitored. The organization needs to provide proper training to employees to help reinforce these corporate goals and initiatives.

Summary

Social media has become an integral part of society. It also has created new challenges for organizations, as they are now faced with integrating this technology within their organizational structure, particularly HR. In order to be competitive in the pursuit of talent and skilled labor, organizations must be agile in adapting to these new technologies and readily incorporate them into their social media practices. In addition, organizations must proactively establish fair information policies that address the use of SMW information as part of their overall Internet usage policy. Moreover, they must work to implement new tools that will enable them to better communicate with and train their employees, collect data to better inform hiring decisions, attract a new and more diverse workforce, and create a more engaged and connected workforce.

Key Terms

employee engagement 419

passive job seeker 426

shoulder surfing 435

social media 418

social media playbooks 425

social media websites 419

social network websites (SNWs) 425

social networking 426

social networking profiles 426

social recruiting 425

Discussion Questions

1. What are some of the advantages and disadvantages to using social media tools in the recruitment process?

2. Understanding the legal ramifications, what types of policies should organizations implement when using social media tools for recruitment?

3. How can a company enact policies that protect the rights of applicants while also ensuring that the company is protected from negligent hiring?

4. To what extent should a company use social media as a tool to screen candidates?

THE FUTURE OF HRIS

Emerging Trends in HRM and IT

Richard D. Johnson and Kevin Carlson

EDITORS' NOTE

In Chapter 1, the history of HRM was discussed along with its eventual merging with the field of IT, thus creating a new field of study and managerial practice—human resource information systems (HRIS). This book has provided information on the development and implementation of an HRIS. Most of the HRIS development and sophistication began in the United States, but these systems have spread rapidly throughout the industrialized countries of the world. The question to be answered here is where the field of HRIS is going in the future. This chapter will discuss some of these trends and provide our thoughts on where the HRIS field will be moving in the next few years.

CHAPTER OBJECTIVES

After completing this chapter, you should be able to

- Discuss the short-term future trends in HRM

- Discuss the long-term future challenges for HRM and tactics to handle them

- Explain the impact of future trends in IT/IS and workforce technologies on the improved operation of an HRIS and HRM programs

- Understand how HR and IT/IS are combining for future HRIS business applications

INTRODUCTION

The best way to predict the future is to invent it.

—Alan Kay

There is no doubt that technology has radically altered the world of work. Today, one can work anytime and anywhere, using any device—possibilities that have globalized the workplace and given it a 24/7 work cycle. Beyond the early advantages through automating HR processes, technology enables HR processes to be more integrated than ever with other corporate functions (e.g., payroll, finance, supply chain, marketing, etc.) in the pursuit of organizational success. Although HR has evolved from an administrative to a strategic focus, transactional activities, such as HR administration, legal compliance, and benefits management, still consume a major portion of HR resources. With the increasing focus on strategic HRM and developments in technology, HR professionals are deploying innovative technology solutions to address their core challenges, such as talent management and workforce metrics and analytics (Haines & Lafleur, 2008). Multinational enterprises are leveraging HRIS to align their information technology, processes, and people to replicate their HR policies and practices across global operations (Morris et al., 2009). Some enterprises also use HRIS for effective disaster planning and recovery during various crises, such as terrorist attacks and natural disasters (Hurley-Hanson & Giannantonio, 2008).

Although organizations have done an excellent job automating basic HR functions and reducing staff, organizations continue to question the strategic value of these changes. This does not mean that an HRIS fails to provide organizational value but instead that the value gained to date, as noted in many of the chapters in this book, has come through efficiencies gained through the automation and evolution of HR processes. To a great extent, HRM processes in organizations remain siloed, and so the potential inherent in being able to strategically align manipulate entire HRM systems has only begun to emerge. In addition, it is important to remember that technology is only an enabling tool and not a solution or panacea for HR-related problems. It is now largely up to HR professionals to exploit technology's potential fully by taking it to the next level of transformational impact. And we're just getting started! The future of eHRM will be driven by changes in both HRM and HRIS. In this chapter, we briefly touch on the trends affecting each.

FUTURE TRENDS IN HRM

In general, forecasting the future is quite difficult and even more so in HRM. Although one can examine past trends and extrapolate to the future, there can be unexpected contingencies, such as the financial crisis of 2008–2009, that impact HR processes. Also, changes in laws, directives, and guidelines from governmental agencies can strongly affect the future of HRM and HRIS. To examine any future trends in the HR field, one must look within and between countries, since labor laws differ from country to country and, thus, could have a significant impact on any new developments in HRM for that country (see Chapter 13). Although this chapter focuses on trends that are affecting HRM in the United States, it is important to remember that many of these trends will also be true for other countries, although they may differ somewhat in terms of specifics. We briefly discuss five trends that will impact HR in the coming years.

Health and Wellness

The cost of healthcare is a growing concern for organizations, with recent estimates suggesting that healthcare accounts for nearly 8% of an organization's operating costs (Society for Human Resource Management [SHRM], 2016). To address these concerns, organizations are turning to wellness initiatives, others are reconsidering what health plans to offer, and most are passing increased costs on to their employees. For example, companies are providing gym memberships, personal trainers, nutrition programs, smoking-cessation programs, and stress-reduction programs. In addition, they are turning to technology to help them manage healthcare costs. In support of this goal, nearly 20% of organizations are collecting health data from employees' wearable devices (Rowland, December 16, 2019). For example, Indiana University Health used a fitness tracker to encourage a healthier lifestyle. They found that more than 35% of their workforce used the fitness tracker, and more than 90% of these employees were motivated to continue the healthy changes (Wright, 2015). In addition, research suggests that nearly 20% of employers are now collecting health data from employees' wearable devices (Rowland, December 16, 2019).

Another major challenge facing organization is the uncertainty surrounding healthcare. From the passage of the Patient Protection and Affordable Care Act (i.e., "Obamacare") to the new administration's desire to repeal Obamacare, organizations are finding it challenging to navigate the new environment of employee benefits. For example, some organizations offer multiple health plans, some of which are available only to highly compensated employees. The Affordable Care Act makes some provisions of these plans illegal if they are not available to lower-compensated employees as well. In addition, organizations must consider the penalty costs of not offering health care to employees and the makeup of their workforce (e.g., full-time, part-time, contingent) as they determine how to best comply with the new law and to best provide plans that serve their employees. Some firms chose to cut employees' hours, downsize, and encourage low-income employees to sign up for Medicaid, and some offered higher deductible plans (Shane, 2014). Some companies moved to a defined contribution healthcare plan (Sammer & Miller, 2013). Finally, because of the increased regulatory and compliance requirements of the Affordable Care Act, companies are having to adopt new and upgraded software to support their reporting and compliance requirements. However, the current administration has eliminated a core component of the Affordable Care Act, the "individual mandate," or requirement for all individuals to either have a healthcare plan or pay a tax. This is just one example of how politics is creating new realities for organizations as they assess and deliver employee benefits. It is safe to say that health care issues will take up a lot of human resource professionals' time during the next 5 years.

People Analytics

HR is under increasing pressure to show that its policies and practices add value to the firm. To address these pressures, HR is increasingly turning to the use of business intelligence to support complex metrics. Although that is covered in greater detail in Chapter 7, we also briefly discuss analytics here because their use will only continue to grow. Many organizations already have basic reporting capabilities, but they are increasingly looking to incorporate more sophisticated metrics to better support HR programs. For example, organizations are using analytics in recruitment, one goal of which is increasing consistency and eliminating human biases in the hiring process. Deloitte reports that approximately 30% of firms they surveyed are beginning to feel comfortable moving into analytics (Fleck, 2016).

How important are metrics and analytics becoming to HR? Consider that each year, SHRM brings together a panel of experts to address the most important upcoming concerns facing HR, and one of the panels is specifically focused on metrics and analytics. Data analytics brings "decision-making tools such as environmental scanning, scenario-based planning, hypothesis formulation, and testing and organizational development tools . . . to improve workforce management decisions" (Clark & Schramm, 2012, p. 7). HR will need to develop metrics for both static descriptive statistics to "benchmark" HR progress and programs as well as dynamic measures that assess the effectiveness and progress of HR programs that change over time. In addition, HR will need to convince the C-suite of the importance of these tools. In a recent industry survey, less than 40% of executives had high confidence in the organizations use of analytics and metrics (Mauer, 2018).

Despite the growth in the use of metrics and analytics, it is critical that managers not lose track of the fact that a tool like "machine learning produces facts, rather than conclusions" (Cappelli, 2015, p. 5). Managers and employees make decisions and come to conclusions based upon the data. The risk for organizations is that as we continue to embrace more sophisticated analytics, managers and employees will understand less and less about how the data are analyzed and recommendations are presented. Ultimately, managers may assume that the system output represents a conclusion rather than facts for supporting a decision and place decision-making authority on the system rather than their own judgment. For this reason, HR professionals will need to better understand the capabilities and limitations of people analytics and the software supporting it to truly leverage analytics most effectively.

Demographic Workforce Changes

The workforce in the United States is undergoing a dramatic transformation on multiple fronts. First, it is becoming more diverse. More women and people of color are entering the workforce than ever before. For example, nearly 60% of working-age women are now in the workforce compared to only 40% in 1970 (Bureau of Labor Statistics, 2019). Also contributing to the diversity of the workforce is the growth in the Hispanic American (Hispanics) population in the United States. Currently, Hispanics comprise 18% of the population (U.S. Census Bureau, 2019), are the fastest-growing ethnic group, and are expected to comprise nearly 30% by 2060 (Colby & Ortman, 2015).

Second, there is a major demographic shift occurring in the workforce. As recently as a decade ago, we expected that large numbers of baby boomers would retire from the workforce. More recent data, though, suggests that baby boomers are postponing retirement. Data from the Bureau of Labor Statistics suggest that those over 65 years old will be the fastest-growing segment of the U.S. workforce, and those 75 and older will grow by more than 86% by 2024 (Toossi & Torpey, 2017)! This means that organizations will have a workforce that has much greater age diversity than they are typically used to managing.

What does this mean for human resources in the coming years? Although there are positive aspects to this changing age demographic, there will also be challenges for organizations. Having a workforce that has large ethnic, cultural, and age diversity brings tremendous opportunities for creativity, innovation, and market growth for organizations. But it can also bring challenges for human resources. HR will need to rethink recruiting and retention strategies in light of these changes. Employment factors that are attractive to a married 60-year-old male may be very different from those are attractive to a 24-year-old

Hispanic female. In addition, there are several critical technological factors that may come into play with a diverse workforce. For example, as briefly discussed in Chapter 10, there are several issues with respect to people of color, computer use, and adverse impact.

Second, with multiple generations working together, there will be varied experiences, comfort, and experience with technology. This contributes to a workforce that has diverse expectations regarding the use of technology at work and opinions on how to balance personal and work data. For example, college students are 3 times more likely to consume news from social media than a print newspaper (Head, Wihbey, Metaxis, MacMillian, & Cohen, 2018). In contrast, nearly 60% of those over 65 read a physical newspaper (Pew Research Center, 2012). Ultimately, organizations that can most effectively leverage the potential of their workforce diversity will be most successful. As noted by Cascio (2013, p. 14), "Workforce diversity is not just a competitive advantage. Today it's a competitive necessity."

Employee Engagement

Another major challenge facing organizations is employee engagement and retention. Engagement reflects the extent to which employees are emotionally connected and committed to the organization. Research has found that most employees are *NOT* engaged at work; some estimates suggest that as few as 13% of employees are engaged at work (Crabtree, 2013). Lack of engagement is estimated to cost organizations more than half a trillion dollars in lost productivity annually (Sorenson & Garman, 2013). Not surprisingly, organizations are very concerned about how to connect employees and increase their engagement at work. Organizations are increasingly turning to technology to improve engagement. Tools such as social media, groupware, gamified mobile apps, and recognition software are all being utilized to improve employee connections and engagement. Organizations are also using technology to push short surveys to regularly assess the pulse of employees' engagement (Boese, 2015). These surveys help organizations better understand the "why" behind engagement instead of simply the level of engagement. Thus, rather than waiting for employees to complete an annual engagement and satisfaction survey, organizations are better able to respond in a timelier fashion to engagement issues. Whatever approach an organization chooses to utilize in support of engagement, those studying HRIS cannot underestimate the importance of employee engagement and the extent to which HR will be involved in improving it.

Growing Complexity of Legal Compliance

One of the most important themes for HR will be the growing governmental and agency compliance requirements. Human resources has always been affected by legal compliance, but many would say that the pace of regulations continues to grow. For example, the EEOC continues to develop additional guidelines, and states continue to pass additional regulations on issues as varied as hiring practices and workplace safety. In addition, the recent negotiations due to the recent "fiscal cliff" has resulted in a change in the Social Security tax rates for all employees and the raising of taxes for high-earning employees. Human resources will need to be prepared to implement these changes, and additional changes are likely to occur in the coming years. For example, new federal and state guidelines such as the Lilly Ledbetter Fair Pay Act, new overtime regulations for salaried employees, new guidelines regarding the use of criminal records in hiring decisions, and broader interpretations of marriage are all having significant impacts on how organizations are making

HR decisions. In addition, consider the comments from SHRM's expert panel (Clark & Schramm, 2012):

1. Firms will increasingly focus on evidence-based hiring to ensure that they remain compliant with federal and state laws as well as EEOC guidelines.

2. Globalization means that labor law will be increasingly affected by trade agreements and global labor standards.

3. Organizations will need to be more actively aware of their compliance environment, as the National Labor Relations Board and the Department of Labor are becoming more active in making new rules and attempting to reverse prior decisions.

What will HR departments need to do in response to these changing laws and compliance guidelines? Essentially, they will need to have the information to support adjustments to the way that HR operates. But they will also have to ensure that the HRIS applications they are using can handle these changes. Fortunately, there are HRIS applications that assess the legal risk level in terms of unfair discrimination based on race, age, and gender. Results from these analyses can identify the departments where there could be legal problems in complying with laws and legal guidelines. This would enable the company to be proactive in resolving these problems before litigation.

Virtualization of Work

A final trend in HRM on which we briefly touch is the virtualization of work. No longer are employees confined by physical or temporal space. Employees can conduct work anywhere and at any time. "The **virtual workspace** can be defined as an environment where employees work away from company premises and communicate with their respective workplaces via telephone or computer devices" (Lockwood, 2010, p. 1). For example, one of the authors has recently taught a class in which a student was part of a virtual team. His team consisted of six members on four continents, none of whom had physically met. Together, they were responsible for ensuring that a global corporation's database systems were "constantly up" and free of errors. They had to coordinate global schedules to hold monthly meetings to ensure that the team was meeting targets and schedules. Yet they had to do this while never working in the same physical space. In addition, companies are allowing employees to develop more flexible arrangements for working in the office or at home (e.g., telecommuting). Approximately 25% of employees currently telecommute in one form or another, and nearly all employees desire to telecommute at some point (Global Workplace Analytics, 2016). Managing in this geographically dispersed environment creates challenges in leadership, in the effectiveness of communication, in technology, and in procedures for conducting virtual meetings and ensuring appropriate HR management. Given the growing use of telecommuting and virtual teams, organizations will increasingly need to be aware of the benefits and pitfalls of managing employees in the virtual workplace.

FUTURE TRENDS IN HRIS

As noted earlier in the book, technology has long had an impact on organizational and HR functioning. As such, it is impossible to talk about the future of HR without talking about the future of technology. The implementation of technology can influence HR practices, which in turn can drive the use of new technology within HR, which will then drive the creation of new HR practices. This ongoing relationship means that over time, HR and HRIS mutually influence the development of each other. Although early technology focused on the automation of HR processes, reduced expenses, and better service, the future of HRIS will be focused on social and mobile technologies that empower both employers and employees to deploy, share, and use their knowledge for the common benefit of their company. In this section, we briefly discuss the changes in technology that will have a large impact on the HRIS and the delivery of HR functionality.

Artificial Intelligence

Artificial intelligence refers to a set of tools that perform tasks that would typically require human intelligence to complete. Artificial intelligence can augment the productivity of human decision makers, dramatically altering business practices and disrupting and likely improving the speed and accuracy of HRM processes and decision making. In every domain in which it has been applied, artificial intelligence has changed the nature of work for staff and managers alike. Artificial intelligence has dramatically improved the effectiveness of existing practices but also allowed the creation of new products and services that could not be produced cost effectively without applying artificial intelligence.

The origins of AI can be traced to the 1950s, but only recently has AI evolved to the point that it is seen as valuable to human resources. For example, SHRM has identified AI as one of its top technology trends and as a key driver of HRM in the future (Wright, 2017). In addition, in a recent survey, 50% of HR executives indicated that they believe that AI can transform HR practices and roles (IBM, 2017). AI can also lead to substantial savings; IBM estimated that AI-enabled HR processes saved them more than $100 million in 2018 (Lewis, 2019)

There are several ways that AI can facilitate improved HR and people outcomes. First, AI can provide **cognitive insights** that facilitate decision making. Using algorithms and machine learning, AI can interpret vast amounts of data, looking for hidden patterns not previously identified. For example, AI has helped assess the link between job characteristics and employee satisfaction (Tian & Pu, 2008). In addition, IBM suggests that its AI-enabled tools can predict who will leave the organization with 95% accuracy (Rosenbaum, 2019).

Second, AI can enhance **business process automation (BPA)** by providing cognitive capabilities within automated software processes. AI-enabled process automation utilizes software algorithms to implement decisions with little human intervention. For example, DBS Bank created an AI recruitment bot that screened potential wealth-planning managers. The use of this bot reduced screening time from 32 minutes to 8 minutes, improved application completion rates to nearly 100%, and allowed recruiters to spend more time commutating culture and values of DBS Bank with applicants. In addition, the National Aeronautics and Space Administration (NASA) found that the use of AI enhanced HR processes allowed them to complete 86% of HR tasks without human intervention (Davenport & Ronanki, 2018). Another potential application of AI-enabled BPA is in employee benefits. Researchers have found that expert systems can replicate decisions of benefits experts (Sturman et al., 1996), and AI-enabled BPA could be designed to not only recommend a set of benefits from which employees can choose but would choose these benefits for employees and automatically sign them up.

Finally, using intelligent agents and chatbots, AI can support **cognitive engagement**. With cognitive engagement, the software can retrieve and share knowledge from an HR knowledge base with employees, applicants, or retirees through natural and human-like social interaction. One of the reasons for deploying chatbots in organizations is to handle the ever-increasing number of employee and customer requests for information. This is especially true in recruiting. More than 40% of applicants never hear back from a company after applying, which can be frustrating and can reduce the likelihood that they will accept a job if offered. Min (2018) suggests that chatbots can help with high-volume recruitment and the lack of connection felt by job candidates. Specifically, they can interact with candidates to provide organizational information, to answer basic questions, and to schedule interviews. In addition, Min suggests that nearly 70% of job candidates are comfortable with AI chatbots supporting scheduling and administrative tasks.

However, the use of AI does not come without risks or concerns. First, many people have been concerned that AI and its capacity to automate high-volume decisions will result in a dramatic reduction in employment. Some estimates of the percentage of jobs able to be automated out of existence by artificial intelligence run as high as 40% (Reisenger, 2019). This outcome was also predicted during the initial rollout of integrated HRIS and is unlikely to occur, because few jobs can be automated in their entirety. However, HR will need to consider the implications of AI on job design and staffing levels.

Second, managers and employees may assume that the results of AI-enabled insights produce more accurate and unbiased conclusions than those made by managers. However, companies have found that AI tools may have gender or ethnic bias due to previous organizational hiring and promotion patterns (Crawford, 2016; Dastin, 2018). For this reason, it is important for anyone utilizing AI-enabled processes to remember that AI is not a replacement for human decision making. Yes, well-defined decision-making processes can be automated, but many decisions are not well defined and are likely to require human intervention. AI is best thought of as a human decision-making enhancer—a tool to increase the effectiveness and productivity of human decision makers.

Therefore, as noted earlier, it is important for decision makers to remember that computers produce facts rather than making decisions and that decision makers should be able to understand and explain why specific decisions were made or conclusions reached.

Third, applicants and employees must trust the AI insights and recommendations if they are to utilize these systems effectively. Although research has shown that employees prefer to receive feedback from a computer (Earley, 1988), research also suggest that people may be less forgiving of errors in recommendations from a computer than from a human and less likely to trust the computer moving forward (Dietvorst, Simmons, & Massey, 2015).

Fourth, applicants have found AI-enabled digital interviews (e.g., one-way video interviews) "creepier and less personal" than two-way video interviews (Langer, König, & Krause, 2017). Finally, with the growth of AI that is social and designed to replicate human interaction (e.g., chatbots, intelligent agents, etc.), there is a risk that individuals will allow these systems to make a decision rather than serve as a decision-making support tool (Johnson, Marakas, & Palmer, 2006).

Blockchain

Originally gaining traction in the financial industry, organizations are increasingly considering how blockchain can improve HR outcomes. **Blockchain** is an encrypted, distributed digital ledger of public records. The blockchain is organized into individual blocks that are governed by the consensus of multiple parties (Avital, Beck, King, Rossi, & Teigland, 2016). One of the key characteristics of blockchain is that the data in the blockchain are immutable, or unchangeable, once entered and accepted by the system. Blockchain is already playing a very important role in the financial industry and is the backbone of cryptocurrencies such as Bitcoin. In addition, several governments are considering its use for managing data associated with land registries and medical records (Hyvärinen, Risius, & Friis, 2017). With respect to human resources, there are several potential areas in which blockchain may improve HR outcomes:

- Reduction of hiring risk—Blockchain may allow for a more stable and accurate verification process for validating employee credentials such as education, work history, or skills. In addition, since the data are more readily available, it can reduce the potential for applicants to make false statements on their applications or for missing data to affect hiring decisions.

- More robust employee data ownership—With a blockchain, an employee, especially those as part of the gig economy, may be able to "own" their own work history and performance and transport that from organization to organization.

- Smart contracts—Smart contracts are digital are software programs that digitally verify the fulfilment of a contract. With the rise of the gig economy, smart contracts allow for a more efficient and timely verification of contracts and more timely payments to gig workers.

- Compliance and auditing—With data already accurate and validated upon entering the blockchain, compliance and auditing can become more efficient, and HR can spend the time gained on more value-added activities.

However, not everything is positive. As noted earlier, the accuracy of data entering the blockchain will need to be agreed upon by all parties participating in the blockchain, which should improve accuracy. However, once bad data are entered into the system, the immutable nature of the system will make it even harder for individuals to correct data errors. This is particularly troubling for HR given the growing use of background and credit screenings done by organizations in both hiring and retention decisions. A recent FTC study found that 1 in 5 people have a material error in their credit reports (FTC, 2012), and errors in criminal background checks also occur regularly (Wells, 2008). With blockchain, data errors drawn from credit, criminal, and other databases may become institutionalized, and even more difficult for employees to challenge.

Bring Your Own Device

Technology is clearly affecting organizations, and mobile computing and "**bring your own device**" **(BYOD)** are important examples. The change is a dramatic departure from how organizations have previously managed their technological infrastructure and presents a challenge for organizational IT support. Previously, the most common arrangement by organizations was to manage a centralized and tightly controlled technological platform (e.g., IBM, HP, Dell, Windows, etc.), and anyone who wanted to use another platform (e.g., Mac, Linux, etc.) would potentially have problems receiving adequate support. However, today, employees are more likely to want to use their own personal devices (e.g., smartphones, tablets, and laptops) to work. More than 70% of employees have said that they want use their own personal devices at work. (Forrester, 2012), and in response, nearly 60% of organizations have some type of BYOD policy (Syntonic, 2016). In addition, research has found that BYOD is used more fully in higher-performing firms than in lower-performing firms (McConnell, 2016). For this reason, it is important that HR understand the implications of BYOD and develop policies consistent with organizational BYOD goals.

The move to mobile does create some interesting issues for employees and the organization. For example, how do you deal with the privacy issues associated with the storage and use of personal and work data on the same device? In addition, the complexity of managing network and data security dramatically increases when employees bring their personal devices into work, which means that organizations will need to rethink data and network security practices to support these devices. Companies must have formal BYOD policies regarding the use of these devices and who will pay for these devices. Cisco found that more than 70% of younger employees expected companies to pay for their mobile data plans if they used their personal device for work, but less than one-third of firms are doing this. Interestingly, though, the extent to which organizations will pay for subscriptions showed great variance by country, with companies in Mexico (72%), Brazil (61%), and China (58%) showing the greatest support (Cisco, 2011). However, some organizations are hesitant to pay for employee cell phones. In these cases, employees' personal phones should not be required to access company resources, and this should be clearly articulated in the BYOD plan.

Along with the growth in the use of mobile devices will be the growth in smartphone apps for HRIS. Most vendors already offer built-in apps where employees can use their mobile devices to access and connect to the corporate HRIS. In fact, most vendors now "assume" mobile and design their systems to support desktop, tablet, and smartphone interfaces. An example of a mobile app on the iPhone can be seen in Figure 17.1.

Mobile computing increases access to HR data. No longer are employees "chained" to their desks when working with HRIS data. For example, tablets can be used during the interview process to evaluate applicants in a real-time manner. Employees can fill out expense reports wherever they are located and can capture electronic images of receipts as they incur expenses. If a workers' compensation incident occurs, HR case managers can document issues at the scene of the event—taking photos of the situation for immediate storage in the database. In a BYOD world, as employees become more comfortable with using their personal devices at work, and as younger employees continue to lead, we expect there to be an expansion of organizational support for these devices.

Gamification

A second trend in HRIS is the gamification of business activities, especially those enabled by technology. It has been suggested that more than 70% of global companies will have gamified at least one business activity (Gartner, 2011) and that gamification will be an $11 billion market (Markets and Markets, 2016) in the next few years. **Gamification** is the use of game design elements in nongame contexts (Robson, Plangger, Kietzmann, McCarthy, & Pitt, 2015). For example, gaming elements can be designed into myriad business tasks such as onboarding, employee communication, knowledge sharing, and training. Gamification uses achievement levels and badges, rewards, and leaderboards to encourage friendly competition and is seen as a key way to drive employee engagement, productivity, compliance, learning, and health.

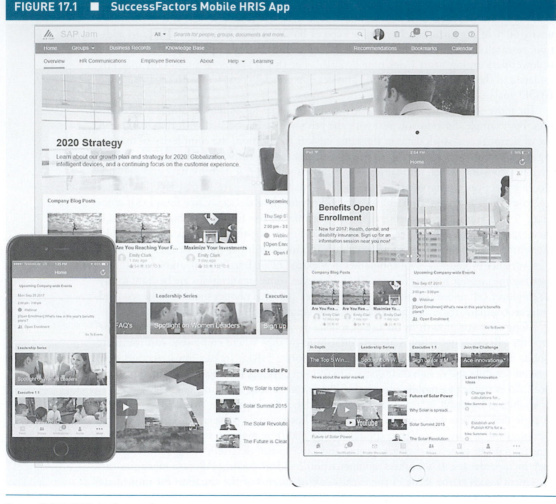

For example, companies are turning health activities into games, rewarding employees for engaging in activities such as exercising or eating healthily. In addition, firms are using gamification to help managers and employees gain insight about their performance. Cigna uses data from games to assess employee problem solving, quick thinking, and logic (Fleck, 2016). Novartis uses simulation games to train teams overseeing clinical trials (Robb, 2012). Finally, in a survey by TalentLMS, 83% of respondents who utilized gamified training were motivated during training compared to only 28% of employees who received non-gamified training (Apostolopoulos, 2019).

However, organizations should carefully assess the risks of gamification, as nearly 80% of gamified applications will not meet their stated goals (Gartner, 2012). Some employees may not like the competitive nature of games and the competition inherent in leaderboards. In addition, gamified activities run the risk of having the employees focus on the game activities and task rather than the business task at hand. Finally, poorly designed gamified activities can distract from the task and reduce engagement. To maximize the potential of gamified activities, here are some recommendations from Abshire (2013):

- Make games clear and simple
- Break long tasks into small, achievable, short-term goals
- Provide triggers to reinforce behaviors
- Address needs and desires of the employees
- Convert users into players
- Provide for social connections
- Create an overall unifying theme

There is no doubt that gamified applications in HR will continue to grow, and organizations will need to determine how to best integrate them into HR and organizational processes.

Web 2.0 and Social Networking

Web 2.0 refers to a second generation of Web-related services focusing on creativity, collaboration, and sharing. With Web 2.0, users not only access information but also generate, share, and distribute new content. Examples of Web 2.0 tools include:

- Social networking sites (e.g., Facebook, LinkedIn, Twitter)
- Wikis (collaborative, shared Web dictionaries that enable users to contribute to online knowledge repositories, documents, or discussions)
- Blogs (short for Web logs, i.e., personal or corporate online journals or diaries hosted on a website)
- Mash-ups (Web applications that combine data from multiple sources into a single location or application—e.g., pulling up a rental car booking site within an airline booking site)
- Podcasts (audio or video recordings)
- RSS (rich site summary/really simple syndication)—feeds that publish frequently updated sites such as blogs or news
- Personal websites
- Peer-to-peer networking (P2P)—file sharing (e.g., text, music, and videos)
- Collective intelligence (sharing knowledge to tap the expertise of a group)
- Web services (Web-enabled instant communication between users to update information or conduct transactions—e.g., a supplier and a retailer updating each other's inventory systems)

Web 2.0 has also encouraged businesses to promote user collaboration to share knowledge and to communicate with business partners, such as suppliers and outsourcing providers. With an emphasis on sharing, Web 2.0 can dramatically change the way in which employees communicate with each other and with customers. Using Web 2.0 will require the HR department to pay greater attention to the legal, ethical, and security implications of information exchange. Blogs are not only used to share information within the company and with external stakeholders but also to communicate organization culture and personality. Because organizational culture is based on the shared values of employees, informal communication such as this can help modify the company's culture, particularly during the development and implementation of a new HRIS.

But the most visible way that Web 2.0 is affecting HR is through its support of **social networking (SNW)**. Although we devote a full chapter to SNW in this book (Chapter 16), it is important for us to also note it as a trend in HRIS, because organizations are increasingly integrating these tools into their overall portfolios. In addition to tools such as Skype, LinkedIn, Twitter, and Facebook, organizations are increasingly embracing other social tools such as Pinterest, Instagram, YouTube, Periscope, and Snapchat into their SNW portfolios. In addition, they are developing their own tools to support internal networks based on the capabilities of the broader SNW tools. For example, Facebook at Work allows a company to leverage the capabilities of Facebook but to do so from within the corporate firewall. Skype for Business is a messaging, conferencing, and collaboration tool that connects organizational employees. Due to the growing use of social networking, HRIS vendors are developing applications within their product offerings to help support employee collaboration, onboarding, and learning. Figure 17.2 provides an illustration of how SAP Jam is designed to mimic such popular social tools as LinkedIn and Facebook to increase employee acceptance and reduce the employee learning curve.

But as briefly noted in Chapter 16, SNW is not static, and tools are always evolving. In fact, they evolve so quickly that organizations and society are not able to develop mechanisms to support and regulate these tools. For example, 25 states have recently passed legislation that limits an employer's ability to use and access applicant and employee accounts on tools such as Facebook. Due to the fluid legal state of the use of SNW and because of the relative novelty and complexity of using social networking tools, it is important that your organization have a specific organizational use policy. Although many firms have a dedicated person who manages the company's SNW strategy, more organizations typically rely on HR to develop and enforce the corporate SNW strategy. As such, HR leaders should stay abreast of the latest SNW tools and legislation.

Internet of Things

The **Internet of Things (IoT)** should also have a dramatic impact on the practice of human resources in the coming years. The IoT is a "worldwide network of interconnected objects uniquely addressable based on standard communication protocols" (Gubbi et al., 2013). Estimates suggest that by 2025, there will be 64 billion of these devices communicating over the Internet (Petrov, 2019).

With the IoT, technology is embedded into static objects such as roads and bridges, manufacturing equipment, medical devices, traffic controls, thermostats, clothing, watches, and more. These mobile and wearable devices are then embedded in a network

FIGURE 17.2 ■ SAP Jam

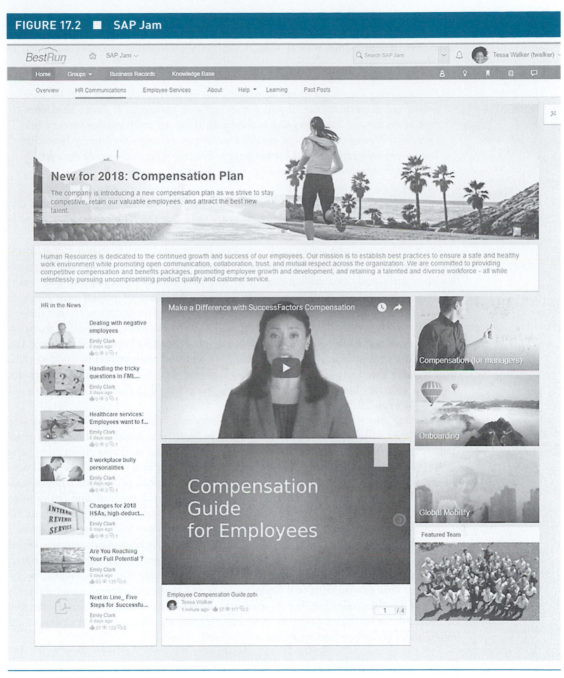

of IoT devices that interact through a device mesh to communicate, interact, share data, and analyze data throughout the globe. **Device mesh** is a connection of devices over a network in which each device has the potential to be connected to any other device on a network without human intervention. IoT allows for more efficient and real-time sharing of employee and productivity data and provides new opportunities for businesses, but it also brings with it risks. Consider the following example suggested by Zarrehparvar (2013):

> *I'm imagining I walk out of my front door with my device. My device locks the door behind me. It starts my car. It pays for my coffee at Starbucks. It knows that when I get in my car and I say I'm going to Starbucks, it has my order waiting for me when I get there. It recognizes that I'm late for a meeting and changes my meeting because it knows—by my location—that I'm not going to be at the office in time to be there for my video conference meeting and it changes it to a voice call.*

In this case, the devices make life more convenient for the wearer, but given that data are sent and received across the Internet, there are risks that this data can be intercepted by a third party.

With 10% of organizations already adopting IoT-enabled devices (Sierra-Cedar, 2015), research suggests IoT is already having an impact on business. Research has also suggested that there are already two million employees who may already be required to wear health and fitness devices (e.g., FitBit) that share data as a condition of employment (Gartner, 2015). Organizations thus must consider how to best deploy these devices so that they are positively received. Although it appears that a majority of employees are comfortable using wearable devices if it improves their performance, more than 40% surveyed indicated that they would not wear them (Cornerstone, 2013). In addition, with respect to using wearable devices for health, early indications are they can lead to better awareness of health and improved lifestyles, but it is hard to keep employees engaged in their use for more than 6 months (Stevens, 2015).

There are also several privacy and security concerns with the IoT. Wearable devices can share a lot of information about employees' performance, health, and other activities. Employees are right to be concerned about the risks associated with this information being intercepted. Consider, for example, data from a wearable device reveals that the CEO has a chronic or acute medical issue. This could negatively impact stock performance and hurt the firm's ability to compete. In addition, if an employee's personal, medical, and health information were compromised (or were entered incorrectly), he or she could be stigmatized. For example, if it was revealed that someone had AIDS, an employee might lose out on promotion or other opportunities. Imagine then if the data were incorrect and a promotion denied.

IoT is clearly going to have a dramatic impact on the practice of HR in the coming years, likely in ways we have yet to think of. As more and more data are collected, we can also expect that governments will begin to assess and make recommendations about the legality of this data collection. For these reasons, we recommend that before implementing any wearable or IoT based program, your organization should get employee consent and inform them about how and what data will be used.

Open-Source Software

As discussed throughout this text, traditionally, vendors developed software following a very structured approach. Software is often released in formal cycles, and in each cycle, new functionality is added and errors from previous releases are fixed. Each cycle, then, culminates with a release date. In addition, vendors will often stop supporting older releases as they place more resources in newer releases. The software developed in this way is copyrighted, and the source code is neither open nor available for others to enhance. This approach to software development has been criticized by some developers as increasing the cost of software, stifling innovation, and encouraging developers to make previous versions obsolete, thus requiring companies to upgrade.

In response to these concerns, some software developers have agreed to a different approach to the development of software called open source. In an open-source approach to software development, the developers make the source code available for anyone to see and to change. This means that other companies or developers can then expand on the product or easily develop complementary products. **Open-source software** also costs much less than traditional (or proprietary) software and is sometimes provided for free. Open-source products are available for a wide variety of organizational needs. Examples of open-source products include Linux (an operating system), Apache (a Web server that plays a central role in the operation of the Web), OpenOffice (a free alternative to Microsoft Office), and MySQL (a database product). The major risk facing organizations considering open-source adoption is the long-term viability of the product, as the continued success of these products depends on the continuing interest of the developers. But in many areas where needs are common across organizations, open-source products are finding strong support.

Open-source software should grow in importance for human resources in the near future. For example, many HR vendors such as Workday and Journeyx use open-source software in support of their product offerings. In addition, other companies are offering open-source software to support functions such as time and attendance (TimeTrex), benefits (Zenefits), and core HR (OrangeHRM, Apptivo). Central to these companies' business model is not the sale of the software itself but instead the customization and support services they provide. The business model thus changes from one of continual updates for profit to one of developing a long-term relationship with clients.

An Evolving Industry

As we will likely say in every revision of our book, the HRIS market continues to evolve. Markets and industries are cyclical. Innovations drive change and create new opportunities. In response to these opportunities, new companies emerge that specialize in new innovations. When ERP vendors first started introducing their products 20+ years ago, new opportunities arose for consultants, implementation partners, and other services surrounding their use. Over time, the markets consolidated and vendors merged, leaving a few dominant HR ERP vendors such as ADP, IBM, Oracle/PeopleSoft, SAP, and Ultimate Software. In the last decade, many of the changes in the vendor landscape were driven by cloud-based HR software. For example, SAP purchased SuccessFactors, Oracle purchased Taleo, and IBM purchased Kenexa. More recently, though, artificial intelligence, blockchain, and the Internet of Things are driving change in the vendor landscape (Table 17.1). For example, Infor purchased Predictix and Workday purchased Rallyteam to bolster their machine-learning capabilities. In addition, SAP has purchased several small AI firms to increase their expertise in machine learning and robotic process automation. We believe that the future of the industry and the vendor product offerings will be heavily influenced by these innovative small companies as they are integrated into vendor offerings. Therefore, it is important that you consider carefully a vendor's viability as you assess potential HR software options.

TABLE 17.1 ▪ Recent Acquisitions by HRIS Vendors			
Company	Acquisition	Year	Core Business
ADP	WorkMarket	2018	Workforce Management
	Celergo	2018	Global Payroll
Google	FitBit	2019	Health and Wellness
IBM	Red Hat	2018	Open-Source Software
	Agile 3 Solutions	2017	Information Security
	EZSource	2016	Data Visualization
infor	Birst	2017	Business Intelligence
	Predictix	2016	AI & Workforce Analytics
Kronos	Optimum Solutions	2019	Payroll, Time, & Attendance
	Digital Instinct	2017	Employee Scheduling
	EmLogis	2016	Employee Scheduling
Oracle	DataFox	2018	AI
	Iridize	2018	Employee Training & Onboarding
	Data Science	2018	Data Science
	SparklineData	2018	Analytics
SAP	Contextor	2018	AI
	Qualtrics	2018	Data Collection & Management
	Plat.One	2016	Internet of Things
Ultimate Software	PeopleDoc	2018	HR Documents and Onboarding
	Kanjoya	2016	AI & Analytics
Workday	Scout	2019	Procurement Management
	Trusted Key	2019	Blockchain
	Adaptive Insights	2018	Budgeting & Forecasting

Another example of the evolving landscape is the 2019 acquisition of Ultimate Software by a private equity firm (Hellman & Friedman) for approximately $11 Billion. Further, mergers and acquisitions are continuing in the consulting area surrounding cloud-based HR. For example, OmniPoint Consulting, a specialized firm focused on Workday implementations, was recently purchased by Aon-Hewitt to bolster its Workday offerings.

Evolving HRIS Technology Strategy

Along with the consolidation of the vendor and consultant landscape, organizations are reconsidering their HR delivery models. One of the challenges facing organizations is that many of them have historically chosen disparate best-of-breed approaches in which different vendors are added to current offerings, leading to a situation where organizations have added technology support for automating more HR processes (as discussed in Chapters 10–15). But this has created two issues for organizations. First, organizations are faced with managing the complexity of working with multiple vendors. Second, although organizations may have added a large amount of technology to their processes, they have realized that they have not really reflected as to whether these technologies are actually more effective in the delivery of HR services. Therefore, in the next few years, we believe that organizations will spend more time and effort assessing the most effective portfolio of HR technology, and many will likely consider moving to some type of consolidated technology platform.

HRIS Moves to Small Businesses

The last trend in HRIS that we focus on is the expanding options for small businesses. As recently as 5 years ago, the idea that a small business would be able to adopt a full-scale HR ERP would have seemed unlikely. However, these days, products are being made available at costs that make their attractiveness to small businesses high. One of the reasons for this change is the availability of cloud-based solutions. Companies no longer need the capital to invest in both hardware and software and the IT expertise to manage the HRIS. Now, much of the risk and expertise for managing the hardware and software are with the vendor. Therefore, small businesses are not only able to afford access to the software, but they are also not burdened by the technological overhead required to implement legacy systems. Now, no company is too small to have its employees supported by HR software.

Summary

As noted early in this chapter, forecasting the future is very difficult. One reason for this difficulty is that the field of HRIS is not just about what might become technically possible. It is, essentially, about systems that serve humans and human enterprise. Students focusing on understanding the field of HRIS must never forget the human issues involved in developing and implementing an HRIS. The field of HRIS continues to evolve, and it is important for those studying it not only to understand what is occurring today but also to look at the environmental and technological forces that will affect it in the coming years. If there is one central theme of our look toward the future, it is the importance of HR policies and programs matched with organizational change and technology; this alignment will have the greatest impact on the future success of HRIS and the organizations investing in these systems. Technology is not a substitute for managerial competence and employee discretionary behavior (Armstrong, 2005). It can only be a messenger, not a message. It is also impractical to expect information systems to supplant the soft functions of the HR department, such as an online electronic tutor replacing a good executive coach (Stanton & Coovert, 2004). In sum, technology is extremely important in the field of HRIS, but people are simply more important.

Key Terms

artificial intelligence 444

blockchain 445

bring your own device
(BYOD) 446

business process automation
(BPA) 444

cognitive engagement 445

cognitive insights 444

device mesh 451

gamification 447

Internet of Things (IoT) 450

open-source software 453

social networking websites
(SNW) 450

virtual workspace 443

Web 2.0 449

Discussion Questions

1. Looking 5 years into the future, how might the demographic diversity affect recruitment practices? How might it affect employee motivation and performance management?

2. Consider the future trends in HRM discussed in this chapter. Pick one of these trends and discuss how technology is central to its effective use.

3. Identify two risks of using artificial intelligence to support human resources. What can organizations do to overcome these risks?

4. List three ways blockchain can improve HR processes.

5. Discuss how people analytics might be enhanced by using AI.

6. Assume you are a small business that is considering adopting HRIS. What are the factors you would consider when implementing an HRIS? How might your needs differ from those of a large organization?

GLOSSARY

360° appraisal Any system in which employee performance is rated by managers, peers, subordinates, and (possibly) outsiders and the employee as well.

Ability test A standardized test of personal skills. Examples of ability tests include the Watson-Glaser Critical Thinking Appraisal that measures critical thinking skills, the Scholastic Aptitude Test (SAT), the Miller Analogies Test (MAT), and the Graduate Record Examination (GRE).

Acquiring talent The process through which an organization hires new employees.

Adaptable workforce A type of workforce in which employees are trained to complete multiple tasks and jobs and can effectively fill many different roles in the organization.

Adaptive learning platform A learning platform that utilizes artificial intelligence to adapt content and activities to the needs of the trainee.

Adaptive maintenance Type of system maintenance that focuses on changes to the software made necessary because of changes in the business or environment.

Administrative process efficiency This kind of HR efficiency refers to the capacity to conduct existing HRM processes accurately and on time while minimizing costs. Centralizing certain HRM processes, for example, recruiting new employees, offers process efficiency benefits.

Adverse impact Employment practices that are designed to have a neutral impact but have a negative impact on a protected class of employees.

Aesthetic features of a website The overall stylistic or innovative features of a website, such as contrasting colors, pictures, animation, and playfulness, that keep the user engaged while navigating through multiple Web pages.

Affirmative action plan (AAP) A written report detailing how an employer actively seeks to hire and promote

individuals in protected classes. For employers with government contracts totaling $50,000 or more, the Office of Federal Contract Compliance Programs (OFCCP) requires that an AAP be completed.

Age Discrimination in Employment Act (ADEA) The 1967 federal legislation prohibiting illegal discrimination in employment against individuals 40 years of age and older.

Alliance programs Partnerships between major HRIS vendors and small, independent vendors that allow organizations to implement fuller (or total) solutions for companies.

Americans with Disabilities Act (ADA) The 1990 federal legislation prohibiting illegal discrimination in employment against individuals with disabilities. A disability is defined as a physical or mental impairment that substantially limits one or more major life activities.

Analysis phase The phase in the systems development life cycle in which an organization's current capabilities are documented, new needs are identified, and the scope of an HRIS is determined.

Antidiscrimination laws Laws enacted to prohibit unfair hiring practices that discriminate against people in protected groups, such as women, racial/ethnic minorities, and older individuals.

Applicant-tracking system (ATS) A module in an HRIS that supports e-recruiting and the processing of applicants electronically.

Application service provider (ASP) A third-party firm that hosts and provides access to a bundle of one or more software application services from a central location to multiple clients via the Internet. Clients pay a subscription fee, which generally entails data management and software upgrades. ASPs are often considered a cost-effective way for organizations to manage their information requirements. Many learning management systems are ASP based; that is, access to applications is available through ASPs.

Acquiring talent The process through which an organization hires new employees.

Artificial intelligence A class of computer technologies that perform tasks commonly associated with human cognitive processing such as reasoning, intelligence, and learning from past experiences.

Asynchronous communication Two-way communication in which transmission does not take place in real time. Examples include e-mail or Internet discussion forums. It is useful for collaboration across different time zones.

Attraction or retention awards One-time rewards used to attract prospective employees or to persuade existing employees to remain with the organization.

Attributes Characteristics of an entity, for example, attributes of an employee entity may be employee ID, last name, first name, phone number, and e-mail address.

Average employee contribution (AEC) HR metric that is assessed as total gross profit divided by the number of employees or full-time equivalents in the firm.

Backsourcing The effort to bring functionality that had previously been outsourced back in-house.

Balance-sheet approach An approach for expatriate compensation that has as its goal the maintenance of a home-country living standard plus a financial inducement for accepting an international assignment.

Balanced scorecard A means of measuring strategic organizational performance that gives managers a chance to look at their company from the perspectives of stakeholders, including external customers, employees, and shareholders.

Bandwidth The rate and volume of data transfer, measured in bits per second.

Base pay The pay received by employees for doing their jobs, not taking into account overtime or bonuses. Base pay for some workers is stated in terms of pay per hour; for others, it is stated in terms of annual pay.

BCA guidelines A set of guidelines helping the benefit-cost analysis (BCA) team approach a BCA that provides them with an improved likelihood of making the best financial decision regarding an investment in an HRIS.

Benchmarking (also known as *best-practice benchmarking* or *process benchmarking*) A process used in management, and particularly in human resource management, to evaluate various aspects of the HR function, both activities and programs, usually within a firm's own market sector.

Benefit-cost analysis (BCA) The financial analysis of the benefits and costs of implementing a new or upgraded system. Important calculations include the break-even point, net present value, return on investment, and the benefit-cost ratio.

Benefit-cost ratio (BCR) A measurement that expresses the benefits of an HR project (e.g., implementation of an HRIS) as the numerator and the costs as the denominator; thus, values greater than 1 indicate a favorable ratio.

Benefit magnitude The size, or magnitude, of the benefits to be gained by implementing an HRIS.

Best of breed (BOB) An approach to acquiring HRIS capabilities in which the company will pick the best application to support each functional area of HR. Thus, the technology architecture combines the best-fit products from multiple vendors.

"Best-fit" approach to strategic HRM This is an approach to strategic HRM in which the organization adopts the practices that work most effectively for it rather than adopting industrywide best practices.

Best-fit learning event model A model of the conditions necessary for the most successful learning outcomes.

"Best-practice" approach to strategic HRM This is an approach to strategic HRM used by researchers in which organizations adopt industry-recognized best practices and use them in their organization.

Big data A collection of very large and complex data, created by transaction processing systems, which are mined for hidden patterns of relationships regarding customers or employees.

Blended learning As the term implies, it "blends" various approaches to learning and could incorporate, for instance, face-to-face, formal, informal, and online learning methods.

Blockchain An encrypted, distributed digital ledger of public records that is maintained across several computers linked in a peer-to-peer network.

Bloom's taxonomy A taxonomy of learning named after Benjamin Bloom that classifies levels of learning based upon the complexity and specificity of the training.

Bring your own device (BYOD) Workplace use of employee-owned technology devices such as smartphones and tablets.

Business intelligence (BI) A broad category of business applications focused on helping organizations and HR collect, store, and analyze data. BI applications include tools such as decision-support systems, query and reporting, statistical analysis, and data mining.

Business process automation A form of artificial intelligence that uses software algorithms to implement decisions with little human intervention.

Business process reengineering The analysis and redesign of work flow to improve an organization's efficiency and effectiveness.

Bureaucratic HRM Strategy An HRM strategy that focuses on organizing jobs and processes based on elaborate rules with a clear hierarchy.

"Caretaker" functions The early phase in the development of human resource management where HR was primarily involved in clerical record keeping of employees.

Change agent (also known as change leader) A person responsible for leading an organizational change or someone who is influential and can communicate and motivate others to accept a change by informal means.

Change equation formula A formula developed by David Gleicher that helps an organization assess its degree of readiness for change.

Change management A structured approach to changing the mindset and perceptions of individuals.

Chatbot A computer program that simulates conversations with humans.

Cloud computing The delivery of software functionality over the Internet in which HRIS functionality is delivered to companies via the Web. For the company, there is no hardware and software to install. It is a specific type of software as a service.

Cognitive engagement A form of artificial intelligence in which the software retrieves and shares knowledge from a knowledge base with employees, applicants, or retirees through natural and human-like social interaction.

Cognitive insights A form of artificial intelligence that utilizes algorithms and machine learning to interpret vast amounts of data, looking for hidden patterns not previously identified by decision makers in organizations.

Collaborative technologies Software and hardware, such as groupware (electronic meeting software), instant messaging, e-mail, and so on, that help groups (and trainees) communicate, interact, make decisions, and learn more effectively.

Commercial off-the-shelf (COTS) software Prewritten or developed software or hardware products that already exist for purchase.

Common attributes of talented individuals A set of skills common to higher-performing and more talented employees.

Computer virus A software program that inserts a copy of itself into another program and causes harm to a computer by altering data, erasing files, or other damage.

Computerized assessments Selection tests or batteries that are administered on a computer or over the Internet.

Configuration The use of tools within the software to adapt the look, feel, and functionality of software without writing any additional code.

Consolidated Omnibus Budget Reduction Act (COBRA) A federal statute governing health care. It is most well known as the statue that provided opportunities for employees to maintain insurance even if a qualifying event would cause them to lose the company-sponsored insurance.

Content information The degree to which the website hosts relevant information that the user deems valuable and informative in nature.

Context-level diagram The highest-level data flow diagram that contains the least amount of detail. It is used to represent the system, its boundaries, and the external entities that interact with the system.

Core competency A combination of some set of knowledge, skills, and abilities. Many industrial psychologists equate competencies with traits.

Corporate brand management Long-term talent management strategies also need to be linked to corporate strategy. One very important strategy that must be maintained despite the state of the marketplace is corporate brand management. It has been confirmed repeatedly that the best labor talent is linked to highly regarded corporations that have excellent brand images.

Corporate culture An organization's collective values, beliefs, experiences, and norms that shape the behavior of the group and the individuals within it.

Corrective feedback In performance management, information fed back to an employee pointing out the discrepancy between observed performance and a performance standard. The purpose is to solve any performance problem and increase performance level.

Corrective maintenance Type of system maintenance that focuses on fixing errors in the software.

Countermeasures Identification of mechanisms that can be used to protect data.

Cross-cultural suitability This term refers to an attribute of an expatriate. It could include language ability, cultural empathy, adaptability, and a positive attitude toward the assignment in the specific country being considered.

Cultural environment of countries A shared set of beliefs, customs, practices, and behaviors within a country.

Cultural norm A specific belief, attitude, or behavior that is defined as right or wrong, correct or incorrect, within a given culture in a country. Cultural norms are part of the cultural environment of a country.

Culture The shared beliefs, customs, social patterns, and values of a people, region, race, or religious group.

Culture shock The feeling of uneasiness and discomfort experienced when going from one culture to another, as well as the adjustment that occurs in a relatively short time when moving from one country to another.

Customization The modification of a software product to match specific organizational processes or needs.

Cyber-terrorism Politically motivated use of technology to do severe harm or disruption in society.

Dashboards A type of interface for reporting HR data that uses a visual, or graphical, representation of key HR data for view by managers.

Data accuracy The extent to which the value stored for an object is correct.

Data flow DFD (data flow diagram) component that represents the flow of data within the system. An arrow indicates the direction of flow, and the name of the flow indicates the type of data.

Data flow diagram (DFD) Graphical tool that represents the flow of data through a system and the various processes that manipulate or change the data.

Data migration The process of transferring employee data between storage types and computer systems or software applications.

Data mining The sophisticated statistical analysis of large datasets to identify recurring relationships and patterns. For example, data mining an employee database might reveal that most employees reside within a group of particular ZIP codes.

Data perspective A view of an HRIS that focuses on an analysis of what data the organization captures and uses and on the definitions and relationships of the data while ignoring how or where the data are used by the organization.

Data store A DFD (data flow diagram) component that represents the temporary or permanent storage of data within the system. A data store is represented by an open-ended rectangle in the data flow diagram.

Denial-of-service (DoS) A technique that attempts to make a computer, network, or service unavailable for legitimate users, often by flooding it with external communication requests.

Design phase The phase in the systems development life cycle in which the detailed specifications for the final system are laid out and final vendor evaluation and selection occurs.

Desired information goals Ensuring that data are kept confidential, have not been manipulated, and are available to those who are authorized to access it.

Developing leaders The process of preparing employees to become leaders.

Device mesh A network typology in which each device has the potential to be connected to any other device on the network without human intervention.

Direct benefits Benefits accruing from an information system that can be measured objectively in dollars.

Direct costs Costs associated with the implementation of a system that can be measured objectively in dollars.

Direct costs of expatriate failure These costs include the actual money spent on selecting and training, relocation costs for the expatriate (and family), and the salary of the expatriate.

Direct deposits The electronic transfer (or deposit) of a payment directly into an employee's bank account instead of issuing a paper check.

Direct estimation An approach to estimating indirect benefits of a new HRIS in which the analyst estimates the value of any indirect benefits of the HRIS.

Direct report The direct report is the employee whose job performance is being evaluated. At the broadest level, this definition of the performance would include any employee who fills the job position, that is, it describes the job performance expectations for any position in the organization.

Discrete HRO The outsourcing of only discrete, or selected, HR functions to third-party providers.

Disgruntled employees Employees who have grievances against an employer and who believe that these grievances cannot be resolved.

Distance learning The delivery of training over the Web; see also e-learning.

Diversity of the applicant pool The extent to which the applicant pool contains a variety of applicants from different ethnic/racial backgrounds, ages, and gender.

Dodd-Frank Wall Street Reform and Consumer Protection Act of 2010 A federal U.S. law that significantly strengthened the regulation of financial institutions and markets.

Domestic HRM The practice of human resources in organizations that only operate in one company.

Ease of use An individual's perception regarding the usability of a system.

Economic feasibility System feasibility assessment tool that focuses on the financial and economic benefits and costs that a new system would bring to the organization.

eHRM strategy An organization's strategy for deploying technology and infusing HR processes with that technology; will link to the broader HRM and organizational strategy.

E-learning A type of training in which trainees are often geographically distributed, communication and interaction occur via technology, and the training is provided in online repositories. Individuals can access the material via computers, kiosks, mobile devices, or other technology.

Electronic human resource management (eHRM) The implementation and delivery of HR functionality enabled by an HRIS that supports employees and their people-related decisions.

Employee data warehouse A centralized repository of a company's electronic data, specifically designed to facilitate reporting and analysis for decision making.

Employee engagement The extent to which an employee is emotionally connected and committed to an organization.

Employee participation and involvement Amount of time and effort an employee puts into the analysis, design, and implementation of a new HRIS.

Employee Retirement Income Security Act (ERISA) A federal U.S. law that established fiduciary standards governing private industry pension plans.

Employee self-service (ESS) A structural approach to HR administration through HR portals that provides a means for employees to access their personal information and HR services and information.

Employer Information Report EEO-1 A report required to be filed annually with the EEO that lists employee data categorized by job category, race/ethnicity, and gender.

Employment brand An organization's well-known values or distinctive image and culture (think Southwest Airlines or Apple). A company often sets itself apart from competitors by means of its employment brand.

Enterprise resource planning (ERP) software A set of integrated applications, or modules, that carry out the most common business functions, including human resources, general ledger, accounts payable, accounts receivable, order management, inventory control, and customer relationship management. ERP modules are integrated primarily through a common set of definitions and a common database.

Entity (data flow diagram) An external person, department, or agent that interacts with the system through receiving or sending data. An entity is represented as a square on the DFD (data flow diagram).

Entity (database) An object or thing of significance to an organization that has multiple characteristics of interest to the organization. For example, employees, dependents, managers, and health insurance plans are examples of entities in the human resources context.

Equal employment opportunity (EEO) The condition in which all individuals have an equal chance for employment, regardless of their race, color, religion, sex, age, disability, or national origin, as established in federal legislation and the U.S. Constitution and its amendments (13 and 14).

Equity Theory A work motivation theory based on the perceived fairness of the employee–employer exchange.

European Union (EU) An economic and political union of a number of European countries.

Evaluation The phase in needs analysis in which the data gathered are reviewed and assessed to create a clear picture of the current and desired states.

Exempt workers Not subject to the provisions of the Fair Labor Standards Act. See *nonexempt* workers.

Expatriate A parent-country national employee assigned to a subsidiary of a multinational enterprise in another country.

Expatriate failure The return of expatriates prior to the completion of their overseas assignments.

Experience Application Programming Interface (xAPI) A software specification (e.g., standard) in e-learning that allows learning content and learning systems to share data.

Exploration The phase during needs analysis in which the analyst gathers detailed data about current HR processes.

eXtensible Markup Language (XML) A markup language or set of rules for encoding an electronic document.

External labor market The supply of potential labor (e.g., potential employees) available to the organization outside of the organization.

Fair Labor Standards Act (FLSA) The 1938 federal legislation that established a minimum wage for hourly workers, set the rate of pay for overtime work beyond the defined workweek of 40 hours, prohibited oppressive child labor by restricting hours of work for children below 16 years, and listed hazardous occupations too dangerous for children.

Family and Medical Leave Act (FMLA) The federal legislation that requires organizations with 50 or more employees to provide up to 12 weeks of unpaid leave after childbirth or adoption, to care for a seriously ill family member, or for an employee's own serious illness.

Federal Insurance Contributions Act (FICA) A federal payroll tax that funds Medicare and Social Security.

Fidelity The degree to which a selection test accurately simulates a real business situation.

Firewall A device or set of devices that will permit or deny all computer traffic between computers with different security requirements based on a set of rules.

Flexible benefit plans Employee benefit plans that allow the employee to choose the benefits they want from a set of benefits provided by an employer.

Focus groups Diverse groups of organizational stakeholders that are brought together to provide data to analysts in support of the needs analysis of a new or upgraded HRIS.

Force-field analysis A procedure to understand the forces during any organizational change that focuses on the forces that drive or support a change in an HRIS and the forces that will inhibit the change.

Gamification The use of game design elements in non-game contexts.

Gap analysis An assessment of the differences between the current state of affairs in the organization and the desired future state.

Genetic Information Nondisclosure Act (GINA) A 2008 federal legislation that prohibits organizations from discriminating based on genetic information.

General Data Protection Regulation (GDPR) A privacy law in the European Union (EU) that protects the privacy rights of individuals residing in the EU and regulates organizational processing of personal information about individuals and places limits on how data can be processed or transferred across national borders.

Global corporation A form of business organization in which an international company locates operations in multiple countries and provides flexible and customized products for each country's market.

Globalization of business The process of integrating business operations and free flow of trade and competition across international borders.

Goal-setting theory A work motivation theory with the fundamental tenet that goals and intentions are responsible for human behavior on the job.

Going-rate approach An approach to expatriate compensation that ties the base salary for international employees to the salary levels in the host country. For example, an expatriate would earn pay that is comparable with that earned by employees in the host country.

Group-focused HRM strategy An HRM strategy that focuses on organizing and managing groups of highly skilled and specialized professionals.

Hacker An individual who accesses a computer or computer network unlawfully.

High-performance system An approach to managing employees that focuses more on empowerment, engagement, and autonomy of employees than on managing as a form of controlling employee behavior to ensure compliance.

Host-country approach A form of compensating an expatriate based upon the salary levels in the host country.

Host-country nationals (HCNs) Employees of the multinational enterprise who are citizens of a country in which a branch or subsidiary is located but where the organization's headquarters is located in a different country.

HR balanced scorecard An approach to measuring the value of the human resource function by identifying the key value-added HR activities that contribute to business goals, measuring them, and evaluating the effectiveness of HR through them.

HR metrics Measures used to evaluate the functioning of HR programs and as benchmarks for the total HRM department.

HR process efficiency analytics Analytics that focus on how efficiently HR functionality is being delivered; may support metrics such as cost per hire, days to fill positions, and HR department costs as a percentage of sales.

HR workforce scorecard See **HR balanced scorecard**.

HRIS functionality The number of programs or functions—such as recruiting, compensation, and job analysis—that are operational using the specific HRIS configuration, as well as the features of these programs that enhance their usability and capacity to affect outcomes.

HRIS vendor The developers of the software used to support HR processes.

Human capital This encompasses "the knowledge, skills, competencies and attributes embodied in individuals that facilitate the creation of personal, social and economic well-being" (OECD, 2001, p. 18).

Human capital management (HCM) Another term used for talent management.

Human resource information systems (HRIS) Systems used to acquire, store, manipulate, analyze, retrieve, and distribute information regarding an organization's human resources.

Human resource management (HRM) An integral part of the organizational system dealing with strategies, policies, and practices that aims to attract, develop, and retain high-quality intellectual capital.

Human resources outsourcing (HRO) Moving a company's human resource function outside the organization to an external company.

Human resources planning (HRP) A systematic approach to estimating the future needs of a company for human capital in terms of labor and supply.

Hypertext Markup Language (HTML) The predominant markup language for Web pages. It provides a means to describe the structure of text-based information in a document—by denoting certain text as links, headings, paragraphs, lists, and so on—and to supplement that text with interactive forms, embedded images, and other objects.

Implementation costs The costs associated with implementing a new HRIS.

Implementation phase The phase in the systems development life cycle in which an HRIS is built, tested, and readied for actual rollout.

Implementation team The team working with the project manager to complete the actual software implementation.

Incentive pay Compensation provided for some performance achievement. Unlike merit pay, it is not added to base pay but is a one-off reward that must be re-earned to be received again.

Indirect benefits The benefits associated with the implementation and use of a new HRIS that cannot be measured with certainty (also called intangible benefits). These can be factors such as improved HR reputation or employee morale.

Indirect costs The costs associated with the implementation and use of a new HRIS that cannot be measured with certainty (also called intangible costs). These can be factors such as lost employee productivity or a short-term loss of HR goodwill as employees learn to use the new system.

Indirect costs of expatriate failure Indirect costs are harder to quantify than direct costs, but they could include loss of market share in the country, negative reactions from the host-country government, and possible negative effects on local employee morale.

Individual development plan (IDP) A performance tool that helps facilitate employee performance and development to reach both short-term and long-term performance goals.

Individual retirement account (IRA) A type of retirement account that allows individuals to invest for retirement while providing tax benefits to investors.

Information According to the *Oxford English Dictionary*, information is the result of informing or giving form or shape to the mind. Information provides structure and meaning to abstract data and is of potential value to organizations.

Information and communication technology (ICT) A general term that describes those technologies that are used to communicate and to create, store, disseminate, and manage information. See also Information Technology (IT).

Information privacy A human value consisting of four elements that refer to human rights, namely, solitude, anonymity, intimacy, and reserve. Information privacy concerns come into play wherever personally identifiable information is collected, stored, and used.

Information security Ensuring the confidentiality, integrity, and availability of information.

Information technology (IT) The use of computers and computing technology to store, receive, transmit, and manipulate data.

Infrastructure as a service (IaaS) A software service that provides access to computing resources such as hardware, software, and servers.

Internal assessment A way of assessing indirect benefits that estimates them based upon current organizational metrics.

Internal rate of return (IRR) A capital budgeting metric that is the annualized effective compounded rate of return when the net present value of an investment is zero; it is an indicator of the efficiency of an investment.

International Association for Human Resource Information Management (IHRIM) The professional organization for specialists in both human resources and human resources technology.

International corporation A domestic corporation that expands its business (e.g., sales of products or services) into markets outside of its own country.

International human resource management (IHRM) The profession and practice of HRM within an international or global corporation.

Internet of Things (IoT) A network of objects with embedded sensors and other technology that allow the objects to collect and exchange data.

Internet-based training (IBT) Any Web-based training (WBT) or online learning or education.

Interview A meeting with an employee where an analyst will ask a series of questions about HR processes and needs.

ISO/IEC 27000 An internationally agreed-upon set of standards governing information security management.

IT architecture The basic hardware, software, and networking infrastructure of the organization.

Job analysis The process of systematically obtaining information about jobs by determining the duties, tasks, or activities of jobs, from which a set of KSA (knowledge, skills, and abilities) can be estimated.

Job description A written summary of the duties, tasks, responsibilities, and activities that define the working contract between the employee and the organization.

Job evaluation A rating or ranking system designed to create an internal hierarchy of job value. In many organizations, job evaluation results form the basis of the salary structure.

Kirkpatrick's evaluation taxonomy A four-level model for evaluating the effectiveness of learning; levels include employee reactions to training, employee learning, change in behavior, organizational results.

Knowledge management (KM) A process for identifying, creating, collecting, processing, distributing, and using knowledge.

Knowledge, skills, and abilities (KSAs) The requirements for each job in the organization. These provide the basis for HR planning and for the recruitment and selection of new employees.

Knowledge test A multiple-choice training posttest of knowledge of the tools, machines, and equipment used at a factory, designed to measure how well the new hire has learned essential job information taught in classroom training.

Kotter's eight-stage change model A model of organizational change developed by Dr. John Kotter that outlines eight steps that should be completed in order to manage change successfully and avoid the common pitfalls that have beset failed change programs.

Learner control The level of control trainees have over pace, content, and structure of the training itself.

Learning climate The organizational conditions within an organization that help promote the learning process and knowledge acquisition.

Learning content management system (LCMS) A software application that supports the creation, management, and implementation of training content.

Learning management system (LMS) Software application that supports the administrative aspects of the training, including scheduling, tracking, reporting, skills gap analysis, and resource allocation.

Learning organization A company that values, supports, and facilitates employee learning and development.

Learning, training, and development (LT&D) The HR function focused on improving the knowledge, skills, and performance of employees, groups, and the organization.

Legal and political feasibility A system feasibility assessment tool that focuses on the legal issues associated with the implementation of a new system and any political impacts that would emerge from its use.

Level 0 diagram The first-level DFD (data flow diagram) that outlines the major processes (functions) of the system, the basic sequence of these processes, the basic data stores, and the external entities that interact with the system.

Lewin's three-step change model One of the earliest key contributions to organizational change, Lewin's framework serves as a general model for understanding planned change.

Load balancing A technique in computer networking that spreads work between computers, network links, or CPUs in order to get optimal resource utilization from the network.

Logical design A phase in the SDLC (systems development life cycle) in which a new system is designed without regard to the technology (e.g., hardware, software, networking) in which it will be implemented.

Logical model A model of the system that graphically illustrates what the system does, independent of any technological architecture (e.g., hardware, software, networking).

Machine learning The application of artificial intelligence that allows systems to learn and improve from experience.

Maintenance phase The phase in the systems development life cycle in which the implemented HRIS is refined and updated to prolong its useful life, fix minor errors, and improve functionality.

Malware A broad term that refers to malicious software whose primary purpose is to infiltrate a user's machine without his/her knowledge. Examples of malware include viruses, worms, spyware, trojans, and ransomware.

Management information system (MIS) A type of information system designed to provide detailed data to aid managers in performing day-to-day activities.

Manager self-service (MSS) Within an HRIS, it is a portal that allows managers to access and manage employee and organizational data related to subordinates and to perform administrative tasks associated with managing these employees.

Market benchmarking A compensation practice designed to provide labor market rates for jobs in an organization. The labor markets may be local, regional, national, or global. The underlying rationale is that an organization should pay for a job roughly what other employers in the relevant market pay to attract and retain employees.

Market-oriented HRM strategy An HRM strategy that designs the personal structure around the need to react quickly to market and environmental developments; typically has fewer formalized relationships and rules than other HRM strategies.

McCumber Cube A graphical model, or framework, of the architectural approach used when establishing or evaluating organizational security measures.

Media richness A framework for explaining the extent to which a medium can communicate or reproduce information; focuses on a medium's ability to convey factors such as content, social cues, and feedback.

Mobile learning The delivery of training/learning over mobile devices.

Multinational corporation A company that has expanded production and distribution of products or services into multiple countries to capitalize on lower costs.

Multinational enterprise (MNE) Any organization that has a business presence in more than one country. A multinational enterprise is also called a multinational corporation.

Multiprocess HRO An approach to outsourcing HR administration, also known as *comprehensive* or *blended services outsourcing.* This approach involves outsourcing to niche, third-party providers all of one or more related HR functions, for example, recruitment and selection or defined and 401(k) retirement plan administration.

Multitenant A software environment that supports multiple customers on one server.

Nadler's congruence model An organizational performance model that is built on the view that organizations are systems and that only if there is congruence ("fit") between the various organizational subsystems can we expect optimal performance.

National culture The norms, behaviors, beliefs, and customs that exist within a nation.

Navigability (of a website) The overall ease with which a user can browse through multiple Web pages to locate topics of interest.

Needs analysis In the analysis of an HR system, the process by which an organization determines and documents its current and future system needs. These needs become the targets or goals that the new system will attempt to satisfy. See also **requirements definition.**

Needs analysis planning A stage in needs analysis that prepares the firm to investigate the current and new system.

Nonexempt workers Subject to the requirements of the Fair Labor Standards Act. Employers of nonexempt employees must pay them at least minimum wage, pay overtime of 1.5 times the base pay rate for every hour worked in one week in excess of 40 hours with 2.5 allowed for meals, keep track of hours worked, and file reports with the U.S. Labor Department demonstrating compliance.

North American Free Trade Agreement (NAFTA)

N-tier architectures The software and hardware configurations in which databases, applications, and other resources are distributed among many different computers around the world.

O*Net database A database containing job descriptions for a large number of jobs in a variety of industries. It is a good starting point for a job analysis project.

Observation The phase in needs analysis in which the analyst observes the current processes and systems.

Occupational Assessor® software Software developed and supported by the Economic Research Institute (ERI), which was founded in 1987 to provide compensation research to organizations and consultants in the form of published reports and survey software.

Occupational Safety and Health Act (OSHA) The 1970 law that authorizes the federal government to establish and enforce occupational safety and health standards for all places of employment affecting interstate commerce.

Office of Federal Contract Compliance Programs (OFCCP) An office of the U.S. Department of Labor that focuses on ensuring that organizations contracting with the federal government are in compliance with the relevant nondiscrimination laws and regulations.

Offshore ownership A form of offshoring in which the company moves operations overseas but retains ownership of the offshore operations in some form.

Offshoring An organization's use of groups outside of its home country (e.g., India, Ireland, or China for U.S. corporations) to provide services (e.g., HR call centers) to achieve strategic organizational goals.

Off-the-job training A formalized training program in which the training occurs outside of the employee's normal work context.

On-premise Installation and operation of software on the premises (or on site) of an organization.

Online recruiting (also known as *Web-based recruiting, Internet-based recruiting, cyber recruiting,* and *e-recruiting*) The use of the Internet in attracting job seekers to a company's job openings.

Online test The administration of a selection test over the Web.

On-the-job training Informal training conducted while an employee is doing her or his job.

Open-source software An approach to software development in which the developers make the source code available for anyone to view, adapt, or change.

Operating systems (OS) Software that manages the interaction between the computing hardware and software and provides services common to all applications.

Operational effectiveness Extent to which operational practices are of high quality and are designed around best practices.

Operational eHRM The use of eHRM to facilitate employees' tasks by making information easily available to them; supports transactional HRM activities.

Operational experiments One of the most effective methods for developing the evidence on which to base managerial decisions.

Operational feasibility System feasibility assessment tool that focuses on how well the new system will fit within the organization and can be used to consider issues such as development schedule, extent of organizational change, and user responses to the system.

Optical character recognition (OCR) The translation of images of handwritten or printed text into computer-editable text, usually by a scanner.

Organizational culture A concept defined as a complex set of shared beliefs, guiding values, behavioral norms, and basic assumptions acquired over time that shapes employees' thinking and behavior; they are part of the social fabric of the organization.

Organizational enhancement strategy An approach to justifying the purchase of HRIS software and systems that is based on identifying instances in which the addition of the functionality provided in the software has the capability to improve organization effectiveness by increasing revenues and/or reducing operating costs.

Organizational learning The process of creating, managing, and transferring knowledge in the organization.

Organizational strategy An organization's plans for achieving long-term goals and a competitive advantage over its competitors.

Organizational support The resources (e.g., tools, time allocation, and financial support) available to employees to pursue e-learning activities.

OSHA Form 300 Annual report required by OSHA in which an organization reports all work-related injuries and illnesses.

OSHA Form 300A A summary report that displays total illnesses and injuries that occurred during the year, which is posted for all employees to view.

OSHA Form 301 A supplement form to the OSHA Form 300 in which information is provided for each reportable injury and illness.

Outsourcing An organization's use of an outside group to provide services—from a few services (e.g., recruiting, compensation processing) up to a broad set of services (e.g., all HR functions)—to achieve strategic organizational goals.

Parent-country nationals (PCNs) Employees of the multinational organization (MNE) who are citizens of the country in which the parent, or headquarters, of the MNE is located.

Passive job seeker An individual who is currently employed but who is also open to considering other employment opportunities.

Patient Protection and Affordable Care Act A federal law passed in 2010 that focuses on the delivery and regulation of health care in the United States. It represents one of the most sweeping regulatory overhauls of health care in 50 years and has large implications for businesses.

Payback period A capital budgeting metric that calculates the number of years required for the flow of benefits returned by an investment to equal the cost of the investment.

Pension plans a retirement plan in which either the retiree receives a defined sum of money payed at a regular interval (e.g., defined benefit) or an employer makes a defined contribution to a retirement account (e.g., 401(k)).

Perceived usefulness The degree to which an individual believes that using a system will improve his or her performance.

Perfective maintenance Type of system maintenance that focuses on making small changes to the system to improve performance.

Performance appraisal A retrospective system noting how an employee has performed during a previous period. Performance appraisal data usually form the basis for merit pay.

Performance contract An agreed-upon performance standard by a manager and employee during the performance planning process.

Performance criterion An outcome, behavior, or competency used in the performance management (or appraisal) process. Performance criteria are the factors on which an employee's performance is rated.

Performance gaps Performance discrepancies between the current HR system, or HRIS, and the desired system.

Performance management A managerial process designed to improve employees' job performance. Performance management is broader than performance appraisal because it focuses on planning for performance, providing performance feedback to an employee, and rewarding changed job performance behavior.

Performance observation The observation of workplace performance by a manager or team leader; an employee may be "observed" and performance data captured through technology or through direct observation.

Performance planning A formal organizational process where managers and employees identify and discuss performance goals and standards for the next performance review cycle.

Perquisite A reward based on job status. In the past, these were usually reserved for executives (corporate jet, executive dining room, special parking), but now they are frequently used as performance rewards for other workers.

Personality test A type of selection test that captures an applicant's personality.

Phishing Attempting to acquire usernames, passwords, account information, or other personal information by appearing to look like an authentic source with which the victim does business.

Physical design A phase in the SDLC (systems development life cycle) in which a new system is designed with particular focus on how the hardware, software, networking, activities, and so on will be implemented.

Planning phase The phase in the systems development life cycle in which an organization reviews the existing technological and system capabilities and develops a general plan for adapting, upgrading, or changing these systems.

Platform as a service (PaaS) A software service that provides users a platform upon which they can design, test, and implement software applications.

Position analysis questionnaire (PAQ) A research-validated, structured/standardized job analysis tool consisting of 194 items that represent work behaviors, work conditions, and job characteristics.

Positive feedback Remarks made by a manager to a direct report concerning observed performance and designed to reinforce efforts leading to high performance.

Power test A type of test in which there is no designated time limit to create time pressure or in which the time limit is set such that most candidates will complete the test without working hastily.

Power user(s) The most demanding user(s) of HRIS who will use a large amount of the system functionality.

Predeparture training Training program for expatriates prior to taking an international position.

Predictive analysis A form of data analysis in which current and historical data are analyzed to make predictions about the future.

Preventative maintenance Type of system maintenance that focuses on maintaining the system to reduce the risk of a system failure or to extend the system's life.

Problem statement A well-defined and succinct description of the known symptoms and causes of problems with current HR operations and how the proposed system will address these problems.

Process A business function or activity through which data are created, manipulated, or transformed. A process is represented on a DFD (data flow diagram) by a square with rounded edges.

Process model A model that represents the key business processes or activities conducted by the organization.

Process perspective A perspective for analyzing an HRIS that focuses on the business processes and activities in which the organization engages and on how data flow through the HRIS.

Project champion An individual or group that has the authority and status to ensure appropriate resources are applied to a project.

Psychological contract Employees' beliefs about the reciprocal obligations and promises between them and their organizations.

Psychological safety A feeling that refers to mitigating the anxiety people feel whenever they are asked to do something different or new. People are concerned about losing their identities, looking dumb, and losing their effectiveness or self-esteem. This anxiety can be a significant restraining force to organizational change.

Pull systems Procedures of making information available to managers so that they can access any of it at a point in time when it will be most useful for their decision making.

Push systems Push communications channels, such as e-mail, actively push information and analyses to the attention of managers. These channels are used for information that is time critical or of which the manager is unaware. These are excellent for getting information to decision makers.

Questionnaire A paper or electronic set of questions produced to collect data from a large number of people.

Ransomware A form of malware that involves locking and access to a system or files until a ransom is paid to the hacker.

Rapid e-learning (REL) The delivery of tailor-made e-learning content swiftly and inexpensively to a large number of learners and the tracking of learning progress in order to stay abreast of rapidly changing knowledge and information needs.

Realistic culture preview A preview of what it is like to work for an organization that highlights cultural aspects of the company such as its philosophy, value systems, history, diversity, salary structure, and benefits.

Realistic job preview A preview of what it is like to work for an organization that shows applicants both the positive and negative attributes of a job.

Recognition award Any reward (whether cash or non-cash) with the primary purpose of celebrating the specific performance achievements of individuals or groups by publicly rewarding them.

Recruiting- and screening-oriented website A recruitment website that has the dual purpose of both encouraging a potential applicant to apply and engaging in initial candidate screening.

Recruitment An HR process whereby the organization attempts to identify and attract the most qualified and best people.

Reengineering See **Business process reengineering**

Refreezing The final phase in Lewin's change model, in which the new behaviors and processes are reinforced, institutionalized, and stabilized.

Relational eHRM The use of eHRM to support core HRM processes such as recruitment, selection, onboarding, etc.; supports traditional HRM activities.

Reliability The extent to which the system is available when needed, provides accurate and timely information, and is flexible enough to meet the needs of the trainees.

Repatriation The process that occurs as the expatriate and family return to their homeland. It is critically important that repatriation programs be established, since there is a readjustment (reverse culture shock) when individuals return to their home cultures.

Reporting The phase in needs analysis in which the final document is created that summarizes the needs analysis findings and presents recommendations for the design phase.

Reporting metrics A set of decisions made about what metrics to report, how to report them, and to whom they should be reported.

Request for proposal (RFP) A document that solicits potential consultants or vendors to submit proposals and bids for proposed work.

Requirements definition A document that lists and prioritizes each requirement the new system must meet.

Resistance to change Actions taken by individuals and groups to oppose a change when they perceive that the change is a threat to them.

Resource-based view A theory about organizations that suggests that the value of the firm is based upon its physical, organizational, and human capital.

Retaining talent Keeping current employees with the organization instead of them leaving for other opportunities.

Return on investment (ROI) A capital budgeting metric in which the flow of benefits that result from an investment is compared with the cost of the investment, usually in the form of a ratio, using the cost of the investment as the denominator. ROI is generally expressed as a percentage of the total benefits less total costs over the total costs, and it is usually determined by the following formula:

$$\frac{Total\ Benefits - Total\ Costs}{Total\ Costs} * 100$$

Risk avoidance strategy A strategy used by organizations as part or all of the justification for purchasing HRIS software. Risk mitigation results from the software allowing the organization to avoid potentially negative future events (e.g., a failed compliance audit, inability to generate data necessary to defend against a lawsuit).

Rootkit A type of virus that hides in the operating system and causes viruses to appear as necessary files.

Sarbanes-Oxley Act (SOX) A 2002 U.S. law that increased accounting and finance independence and reporting standards to better protect investors from fraudulent accounting activities.

Scientific management A management theory that focuses on the application of engineering and science principles to improve workflows and efficiency in production.

Scope creep Enlargement of original project scope.

Security breaches Illegal access to private data, services, networks, or devices by getting around security protections.

Selection procedures The tools used to help an organization choose among candidates or employees in a hiring or promotion decision.

Selection ratio The number of candidates who, based on the assessment, are chosen for the job divided by the number of candidates who are assessed.

Self-selection The choice of a potential applicant to apply or not to apply for a position.

Self-service portal See employee self-service.

Semantic level When considering the interoperability of systems, it is the level at which data share meanings across different applications.

Service-oriented architecture (SOA) A structure for organizing and utilizing distributed computing capabilities that may be under the control of different ownership domains.

Shared-service center (SSC) A technology-enabled centralized group designed to provide excellent service to internal customers at reduced costs.

Shared services A strategy in which one or more business functions of a firm are concentrated in a semiautonomous organization and managed like a business unit.

Short-term tactical strategy A time-limited talent management strategy in which the firm quickly adapts to a rapid change in market conditions.

Shoulder surfing With respect to social media, it is a request made by a manager or supervisor for an employee or applicant to provide the organization access to their social media accounts by entering their password.

Simplified employee pensions (SEPs) A defined contribution pension plan that allows a small business or self-employed individual to contribute a percentage of salary, tax free, to a retirement account.

Single tenant A software environment that supports only one customer on one server.

Social media A form of electronic communication through which users create online communities to share information, ideas, personal messages, and other content such as videos.

Social media playbooks The organization's plan to align social media initiatives (e.g., the *when, where,* and *how* of social media use) with the organization's strategy.

Social media websites (SMWs) Group of Web pages, usually containing hyperlinks to each other, made available by an individual or organization for the purpose of delivering information.

Social networking The use of online tools and websites to find and maintain relationships.

Social networking profiles Description of an individual's social characteristics (e.g., interests, expertise, professional and personal affiliations, geographic location, communication patterns and networks) that identify her or him on social media sites such as LinkedIn and Facebook.

Social networking websites Websites that allow people to create and manage content and connect with others. Some examples include Facebook, LinkedIn, Twitter, Instagram, and Pinterest.

Social recruiting The act of recruiting candidates using social media platforms.

Society for Human Resource Management (SHRM) The largest worldwide professional organization for HR practitioners and academics.

Software as a service (SaaS) An approach to the delivery and use of HR software in which the software is hosted remotely and accessed via a private or public (e.g., the Internet) network, and is often accessed using a Web browser. Instead of owning the hardware and software, the organization rents them. See also **cloud computing**.

Software testing The process of validating the accuracy and correctness of software code before it is implemented.

Sourcing partner organizations An external firm that partners with a company to provide some of its HR functionality, for example, recruitment or benefits management. Sourcing partners require certain information to complete these tasks, such as information about vacant positions, including position description, job specifications, desired candidate competencies, potential salary range, and contact information. The information provided is limited to specific searches for open jobs and is updated as needed.

Speeded test A type of selection that forces candidates to complete the test within an allotted time.

Spyware Software installed on a computer that gathers information about a user's activities on the Web and transmits it to third parties.

Stakeholders Those who have a direct interest or involvement in the implementation of an HRIS, or those who are affected by its implementation.

State of information The state in which data are currently residing. It can be in storage (data at rest, waiting to be accessed), in process (being actively examined or modified), or in transmission (data in motion).

Stigmatize To regard an individual negatively or with disapproval.

Strategic choices The choices a firm makes about how to organize itself, what markets to participate in, and what opportunities to pursue based upon its unique capabilities.

Strategic human resource management (strategic HRM) The strategic alignment of the HR management function with organizational goals. It aims to harness the potential of people as a key competitive advantage through the use of their creativity and innovation.

Strategic realignment The realignment of HR practices so that they are in alignment with overall corporate strategic goals.

Sustainable competitive advantage A way a firm achieves long-term competitive advantage in its market by having a resource that is valuable, rare, difficult to imitate, and does not have an easy substitute.

Synchronous communication "Real-time" or live communication using tools such as messenger services or videoconferencing.

Syntactical level When considering the interoperability of systems, it is the level at which different systems share the ability to interact and work with each other with respect to their programming languages.

System conversion The process of migrating from an old HRIS to a new HRIS.

Systems development life cycle (SDLC) A formal process through which a system is analyzed, redesigned, and implemented. The SDLC will include phases such as analysis/evaluation, design/improvement, development, implementation, and maintenance of the system.

Systems model of training and development A formal or planned approach to workforce training and development that helps organizations design more effective training; consists of four phases (identifying training needs, developing training initiatives, implementing training, evaluating training).

Talent management (TM) A strategic approach to the recruitment, selection, training, development, and management of employees, including the management of their performance and promotion, to meet the strategic objectives of a firm and thus improve the organization's competitiveness in the marketplace.

Talent management life cycle An integrated approach to managing talent that focuses on five key tasks: recruitment, selection, training, performance management, and succession planning.

Talent management system (TMS) An integrated software suite that comprises a range of HR activities such as applicant tracking, succession and career planning, performance management, compensation and benefits management, and learning management.

Technical feasibility A system feasibility assessment tool that focuses on the technical capability of the organization and the availability of the technology necessary to implement a new system.

Test security Protecting the security of selection tests so that the questions and answers do not become available to those taking the test.

"Think global, act local" The most common advice regarding the management of a multinational enterprise (MNE). This advice applies to the total management process of an MNE—its strategy, operations, finance, marketing, and HR—and has been followed religiously for many years in international management. Beaman has argued that this approach is completely the inverse of how we should be developing and managing our global HRIS projects.

Third-country nationals (TCNs) Employees of the multinational enterprise who are citizens of a country other than the parent or host country.

Three-tier architecture A computing architecture that distributes processing power across a machine that requests service (e.g., client) and two machines that provide data services (e.g., the database server) and application services (e.g., the application server).

Top management support Extent to which the executive managers of a firm (e.g., the C-suite) are willing to support and provide resources and authority necessary for project success.

Total HRO An outsourcing approach that involves having all or nearly all HR functions handled by one or more external vendors. All traditional HR administrative and functional activities would be managed through third-party vendors.

Traditional HR activities Activities that involve HR programs such as planning, recruiting, selection, training, compensation, and performance management.

Training complexity The level of information load, diversity, change, and interconnectedness required of learning tasks.

Training guidance Advice on how best to navigate and use e-learning tools.

Training needs analysis (TNA) The training activity that identifies any discrepancies between existing knowledge, skills, and abilities and those required in the future (e.g., the "gap").

Training transfer The transfer of competencies learned in training to the job.

Transfer of training See Training transfer.

Transaction cost theory The idea that organizations can choose to purchase the goods and services they need in the competitive marketplace or make those goods and services internally.

Transactional HR activities Routine, day-to-day activities of the HR department, such as record keeping, that are important but add little value to the competitive position of the organization.

Transformational eHRM The use of eHRM to facilitate strategic decision making and strategic change processes; supports transformational HR activities.

Transformational HR activities Those strategic-level activities tht focus on adding value to the organization—for example, cultural or organizational change, structural realignment, strategic redirection, and increasing innovation.

Transition The phase in Lewin's change model in which the change happens; also called *changing.*

Transnational corporation A type of multinational corporation that tailors business operations and HR management to the local culture.

Trojan A type of malware that hides inside e-mail attachments or files and infects a user's computer when it is opened and/or executed. Trojans are named after the Trojan horse of Greek mythology in that they appear to be something positive but are in reality doing something malicious.

Troubled Asset Relief Program (TARP) A U.S. government program that purchased financial assets of troubled companies with the goal of stabilizing the U.S. economy.

Two-tier (client-server) architecture The software and hardware configuration that divides a business application into two tiers, typically with the user interface and some business logic on the user's computer, such as a PC (the client), and the database and mainstream parts of the application stored on a server.

Unauthorized access To access employee (or other types) of data without permission or authority.

Unauthorized disclosure The disclosure of employee information to third parties without the permission of the employee.

Unfreezing The first step in Lewin's change model, in which the organization creates an awareness of the need for change and a desire to change in employees.

Uniformed Services Employment and Reemployment Rights Act (USERRA) A 1994 federal legislation that protects the civilian employment of active and reserve military personnel in the United States who are called to active duty.

Unproctored testing A form of selection testing in which the job candidate is tested online at a location and time convenient to them, and there is no proctoring of the exam by a test administrator.

U.S. Fair Labor Standards Act of 1938 A federal U.S. law that established the 40-hour work week, but it also required employers to maintain records of basic employee information.

Usability (of a website) The extent to which users are able to use a website effectively. Web usability is often viewed as being comprised of a number of dimensions, including navigability, content and display of information, aesthetics, and ease of use.

User acceptance The willingness of a user of a system to employ the new technology.

User documentation A description of how to interact with the HRIS. It should cover a variety of tasks such as data entry, using the system, and basic troubleshooting.

User interface The communication boundary between the hardware device (e.g., computer, PDA, kiosk) and the user of that hardware. It is the point at which the user interacts with the system, providing inputs and receiving information or feedback from the system.

Utility formula The value that a selection test provides for an organization; assessed as a formula that takes into account factors such as the validity of the test, the selection rate, and any change in performance that can be attributed to the test.

Validity coefficient A statistical correlation that indicates the correspondence between test scores and job performance or some other important work outcomes.

Variety The different forms of data collected by the organization and stored in the data warehouse.

Velocity The speed at which an organization captures data and stores it in the data warehouse.

Veracity Quality of the data collected by the organization and included in a data warehouse.

Virtual workspace A work environment in which the employees of a company work away from company premises and communicate with their respective workplaces via telephone or computer devices.

Volume In data warehousing, it refers to the amount of data that organizations collect and include in a data warehouse.

Web 1.0 The first generation of the Web, in which static web-pages are connected via hyperlinks.

Web 2.0 The second generation of the Web, which utilizes dynamic user-generated content, creativity, collaboration, and information sharing.

Web 3.0 An evolution of Web 2.0 that is based on a number of developments such as the semantic Web, open and mobile access, augmented reality, and intelligent applications.

Web-based training (WBT) Any training and learning that takes place via the World Wide Web.

Work simulation An in-basket exercise in which the examinee must examine a variety of types of information (correspondence, reports, and other information) and also interact with simulated coworkers, employees, or other business associates (whether computer simulated or role-played by actors over the telephone or in person). The examinee is evaluated on a variety of dimensions, from accuracy and the quality of decisions to work-related competencies, interpersonal skills, and other personal attributes.

Workforce analytics Strategies for combining data elements into metrics and for examining relationships or changes in HR metrics.

Workforce modeling A technique that attempts to understand how an organization's human capital needs would change as a function of some expected change in the organization's environment. This change might be a shift in the demand for the organization's product, entry into a new market, divestiture of one of the organization's businesses, or a pending acquisition of or merger with another organization.

Workforce Planning Systems (WPSs) HR software that helps organizations manage workforce planning.

Worms Stand-alone software programs that are meant to disrupt computer and network operations that can replicate themselves to spread. Unlike viruses that require the spreading of an infected file, worms can spread by themselves without attaching to files.

REFERENCES

Chapter 1

Becker, B. E., & Huselid, M. A. (2006). Strategic human resource management: Where do we go from here? *Journal of Management, 32*(6), 898–925.

Becker, B. E., Huselid, M. A., & Ulrich, D. (2001). *The HR scorecard: Linking people, strategy, and performance.* Boston: Harvard Business School Press.

Bussler, L., & Davis, E. (2001/2002). Information systems: The quiet revolution in human resource management. *Journal of Computer Information Systems, 42*(2), 17–20.

Cascio, W. F. (1984). *Costing human resources: The financial impact of behavior in organizations.* Boston: PWS-Kent.

Cascio, W. F. (2000). *Costing human resources: The financial impact of behavior in organizations* (4th ed.). Cincinnati, OH: South-Western College.

CedarCrestone. (2014). *CedarCrestone 2014–2015 HR systems survey: HR technologies, service delivery approaches, and metrics* (17th annual edition). Alpharetta, GA: CedarCrestone.

Cober, R. T., Brown, D. J., Blumental, A. J., Doverspike, D., and Levy, P. (2000). The quest for the qualified job surfer: It's time the public sector catches the wave, *Public Personnel Management 29*, 479–496.

Drucker, P. F., Dyson, E., Handy, C., Saffo, P., & Senge, P. M. (1997). Looking ahead: Implications of the present. *Harvard Business Review, 75*(5), 18–24.

Dulebohn, J. H., & Johnson, R. D. (2013). Human Resource Metrics and Decision Support: A Classification Framework. *Human Resource Management Review, 23,* 71–83.

Evans, W. R., & Davis, W. D. (2005). High-performance work systems and organizational performance: The mediating role of internal social structure. *Journal of Management, 31,* 758–775.

Fitz-enz, J. (1980). Quantifying the human resources function. *Personnel, 57*(3), 41–52.

Fitz-enz, J. (2000). *The ROI of human capital: Measuring the economic value of employee performance.* New York: AMACOM/American Management Association.

Fitz-enz, J. (2002). *How to measure human resource management* (3rd ed.). New York: McGraw-Hill.

Gherson, D., & Jackson, A. P. (2001). Web-based compensation planning. In A.J. Walker (Ed.) *Web-based human resources,* 83–95. New York: McGraw-Hill.

Gill, M. (2000). E-learning technology and strategy for organisations. In K. Fry (Ed.), *The business of e-learning: bringing your organization in the knowledge e-conomy.* University of Technology, Sydney.

Groysberg, B., & Connolly, K. (March 16, 2015). The 3 things CEOs worry about the most. *Harvard Business Review.* Retrieved from https://hbr.org/2015/03/the-3-things-ceos-worry-about-the-most

Gueutal, H. G., & Falbe, C. M. (2005). eHR: Trends in delivery methods. In H. G. Gueutal & D. L. Stone (Eds.), *The brave new world of eHR: Human resources management in* from *the digital age,* pp. 190–225.

Gueutal, H. G., & Stone, D. L. (2005). *The brave new world of eHR: Human resources management in the digital age.* San Francisco: Jossey-Bass.

Huselid, M. A., Becker, B. E., & Beatty, R. W. (2005). *The workforce scorecard: Managing human capital to execute strategy.* Boston: Harvard Business School Press.

Huselid, M. A., Jackson, S. E., & Schuler, R. S. (1997). Technical and strategic human resource management effectiveness as determinants of firm performance. *Academy of Management Journal, 40,* 171–188.

Johnson, R. D., Lukaszewski, K. M., & Stone, D. L. (2016). The evolution of the field of human resource information systems: Co-evolution of technology and HR processes. *Communications of the Association for Information Systems, 38,* 533–553.

Johnson, R. D., & Stone, D. L. (2019). Advantages and unintended consequences of using electronic human resource management (eHRM) processes. In R. Landers (Ed.). *Cambridge handbook of technology and employee behavior,* pp. 879–920.

Lawler, E. E., & Mohrman, S. A. (2003). HR as a strategic business partner: What does it take to make it happen? *Human Resource Planning, 26*(3), 15–29.

Lengnick-Hall, C. A., & Lengnick-Hall, M. L. (2006). HR, ERP, and knowledge for competitive advantage. *Human Resource Management, 45*(2), 179–194.

Ngai, E. W. T., & Wat, F. K. T. (2004). Human resource information systems: A review and empirical analysis. *Personnel Review, 35*(3), 297–314.

Porter, M. E. (1990). *The competitive advantage of nations.* Boston: Free Press.

Stone, D. L., & Lukaszewski, K. M. (2009). An expanded model of the factors affecting the acceptance and effectiveness of electronic human resource management systems. *Human Resource Management Review, 19,* 134–143.

Strohmeier, S. (2007). Research in e-HRM: Review and implications. *Human Resource Management Review, 17*(1), 19–37.

Ulrich, D., Younger, J., & Brockbank, W. (2008). The twenty-first-century HR organization. *Human Resource Management, 47*(4), 829–850.

Wright, P., McMahan, G., Snell, S., & Gerhart, B. (1998). *Strategic human resource management: Building human capital and organizational capacity* (technical report). Ithaca, NY: Cornell University.

Chapter 2

Adamson, L., & Zampetti, R. (2001). Web-based manager self-service. In A. J. Walker (Ed.), *Web-based human resources* (pp. 24–35). New York: McGraw-Hill.

Bedell, M. (2003a). Human resources information systems. In H. Bidgoli (Ed.), *The encyclopedia of information*

systems* (Vol. 2, pp. 537–549). Burlington, MA: Academic Press.

Bedell, M. (2003b). *An identification of the cost savings resulting from an HR information system implementation.* Paper presented at the meeting of the American Society of Business and Behavioral Sciences, Las Vegas, NV.

Fein, S. (2001). Preface. In A. J. Walker (Ed.), *Web-based human resources* (pp. vii–x). New York: McGraw-Hill.

Hendrickson, A. R. (2003). Human resource information systems: Backbone technology of contemporary human resources. *Journal of Labor Research, 24*(3), 381–394.

Jessup, L., & Valacich, J. (1999). Information systems foundations. In L. Jessup & J. Valacich (Eds.), *Que education & training* (pp. 4–10). Indianapolis, IN: Macmillan.

McManus, M. A., & Ferguson, M. W. (2003). Biodata, personality, and demographic differences of recruits from three sources. *International Journal of Selection and Assessment, 11,* 175–183.

Miller, M. S. (1998). Great expectations: Is your HRIS meeting them? *HR Focus, 75,* 1–2.

Rampton, G. M., Turnbull, J., & Doran, J. A. (1999). *Human resources management systems: A practical approach* (p. 142). Toronto, ON: Carswell.

Regan, E., & O'Conner, B. (2002). *End-user information systems: Implementing individual and work group technologies* (pp. 26–28, 368–369). Upper Saddle River, NJ: Prentice Hall.

Stone, D. L., Lukaszewski, K. M., & Isenhour, L. C. (2005). e-Recruiting: Online strategies for attracting talent. In H. B. Gueutal & D. L. Stone (Eds.), *The brave new world of eHR.* San Francisco: Jossey-Bass.

Walker, A. J. (2001). Best practices in HR technology. In A. J. Walker (Ed.), *Web-based human resources* (pp. 3–12). New York: McGraw-Hill.

Zampetti, R., & Adamson, L. (2001). Web-based employee self-service. In A. J. Walker (Ed.), *Web-based human resources* (pp. 15–23). New York: McGraw-Hill.

Zusman, R. R., & Landis, R. S. (2002). Applicant preferences for Web-based versus traditional job postings. *Computers in Human Behavior, 18,* 285–296.

Chapter 3

Harris, M. A., & Weistroffer, H. R. (2009). A new look at the relationship between user involvement in systems development and system success. *Communications of the Association for Information Systems, 24*(42), 739–756.

Kristie, M. L., Baird, M., & Duchesne, G. (2018). Using online meeting software to facilitate geographically dispersed focus groups for health workforce research. *Qualitative Health Research, 28*(10), 1621–1628. doi:10.1177/104973231878216

Smith, J. (2001, February/March). Knowledge transfer: The forgotten phase. IHRM.*link, 6,* 53.

Stewart, D. W., & Shamdasani, P. (2017). Online focus groups. *Journal of Advertising, 46*(1), 48–60. doi:10.1080/00913367.2016.1252288

Wu, J., & Marakas, G. (2006). The impact of operational user participation on perceived system implementation success: An empirical investigation. *Journal of Computer Information Systems, 46*(5), 127–140.

Chapter 4

Agarwal, R. (2000). Individual acceptance of information technologies. In R. W. Zmud (Ed.), *Framing the domains of IT management* (pp. 85–104). Cincinnati, OH: Pinnaflex Educational Resources.

Brynjolfsson, E., & Hitt, L. M. (1998). Beyond the productivity paradox. *Communications of the ACM, 41*(8), 49–55.

Collins, J. (2001). *Good to great: Why some companies make the leap . . . and others don't.* New York: HarperCollins.

Davis, F. D., & Venkatesh, V. (2004). Toward preprototype user acceptance testing of new information systems: Implications for software project management. *IEEE Transactions on Engineering Management, 51*(1), 31–46.

Dennis, A. R., Wixom, B. H., & Roth, R. M. (2006). *Systems analysis and design* (3rd ed.). Hoboken, NJ: John Wiley & Sons.

Hinojos, J. A., & Miller, M. (1998, July/August). Methodologies for selecting the right vendor. *Benefits & Compensation Solutions,* 38–42.

Kendall, K. E., & Kendall, J. E. (2008). *Systems analysis and design* (7th ed.). Upper Saddle River, NJ: Pearson.

Marakas, G. M. (2006). *Systems analysis and design: An active approach* (2nd ed.). New York: McGraw-Hill.

Patton, G. S. (1995). *War as I knew it.* Boston: Houghton Mifflin. (Original work published 1947)

Standish Group. (2004). *The chaos report.* Boston: Author.

Chapter 5

Abrahamson, E. (2004). *Change without pain.* Boston: Harvard Business School Press.

Anderson, B. (2010, March). Project leadership and the art of managing relationships. *T&D, 64*(3), 58–63.

Anderson, D., & Anderson, L. A. (2001). Beyond change management. Advanced strategies for today's transformational leaders. San Francisco: Jossey-Bass/Pfeiffer.

Anderson, D., & Anderson, L. (2010). *The change leader's roadmap: How to navigate your organization's transformation* (2e). San Francisco: Pfeiffer.

Anheier, N., & Doherty, S. (2001, October). *Employee self-service: Tips to ensure a successful implementation.* Retrieved from http://www.shrm.org/hrdisciplines/technology/Articles/Pages/CMS_000210.aspx

Armenakis, A. A., & Harris, S. G. (2002). Crafting a change message to create transformational readiness. *Journal of Organizational Change Management, 15*(2), 169–183.

Austin, D., Adkins, V., Fox, R., & Mency, Y. (2010). *HRMS implementation project: Communication plan.* Richmond, VA: Virginia Community College System.

Battilana, J., Gilmartin, M., Sengul, M., Pache, A., & Alexander, J. A. (2010). Leadership competencies for implementing planned organizational change. *The Leadership Quarterly, 21,* 422–438.

Baum, D. (2000). *Lightning in a bottle.* Chicago: Dearborn.

Beckhard, R., & Harris, R. (1987). *Organizational transitions: Managing complex change.* (2nd ed.). Reading, MA: Addison-Wesley.

Beer, M., & Nohria, N. (2000). Resolving the tension between theories E and O of change. In M. Beer &

N. Nohria (Eds.), *Breaking the code of change* (p. 1). Boston: Harvard Business School Press.

Benjamin, R., & Levinson, E. (1993, Summer). A framework for managing IT-enabled change. *Sloan Management Review, 34*(4), 23–33.

Bridges, W. (2003). *Managing transitions* (2nd ed.). Cambridge, MA: Perseus Books.

Browne, G. J., & Rogich, M. B. (2001). An empirical investigation of user requirements elicitation: Comparing the effectiveness of prompting techniques. *Journal of Management Information Systems, 17*(4), 223–249.

Burke, W. W. (2002). *Organizational change.* Thousand Oaks, CA: Sage.

Burke, W. W. (2008). *Organization change: Theory and practice.* Thousand Oaks, CA: Sage.

Burnes, B. (2004). Kurt Lewin and the planned approach to change: A re-appraisal. *Journal of Management Studies, 41*(6), 977–1002.

Cameron, E., & Green, M. (2004). *Making sense of change.* London: Kogan Page.

Ceriello, V.R. & Freeman, C. (1991). *Human resource management systems: Strategies, tactics, and techniques.* New York: Lexington Books.

Cotton, J. L. (1993). *Employee involvement: Methods for improving performance and work attitudes.* Thousand Oaks, CA: Sage.

Dannemiller, D., & Jacobs, R. W. (1992). Changing the way organizations change: A revolution of common sense. *The Journal of Applied Behavioral Science, 28*(4), 480–498.

Dawson, M. J., & Jones, M. L. (2003). Human change management: Herding cats. In PricewaterhouseCoopers (Ed.), *Risky business: The art and science of risk management* (pp. 21–25). New York: Author.

Duck, J. D. (2001). *The change monster.* New York: Crown Business.

Eccles, T. (1994). *Succeeding with change.* London: McGraw-Hill.

Gerstner, L. V. (2002). *Who says elephants can't dance? Inside IBM's historic turnaround.* New York: HarperCollins.

Graetz, F., & Smith, A. C. T. (2010). Managing organizational change: A philosophies of change approach. *Journal of Change Management, 1*(2), 135–154.

Greenberg, P., Fauscette, M., & Fletcher, S. (2000). *Special edition using PeopleSoft.* Indianapolis, IN: Que.

Harris, M. A., & Weistroffer, H. R. (2009). A new look at the relationship between user involvement in systems development and system success. *Communications of the Association for Information Systems, 24*(42), 739–756.

Henson, R. (1996). HRIMS for dummies: A practical guide to technology implementation in human resource information management system. *HR Focus, 73*(11), 3–5.

Herold, D. M., & Fedor, D. B. (2008). *Change the way you lead change: Leadership strategies that really work.* Stanford, CA: Stanford University Press.

Higgs, M., & Rowland, D. (2011). What does it take to implement change successfully? A study of the behaviours of successful change leaders. *Journal of Applied Behavioural Science, 47*(3), 309–355.

Johnson, R. D., & Marakas, G. M. (2000). The role of behavioral modeling in computer skills acquisition: Toward refinement of the model. Information Systems Research, *11*(4), 402–417.

Jones, M., & Price, L. (2004). Organizational knowledge sharing in ERP implementation: Lessons from industry. *Journal of Organizational and End User Computing, 16*(1), 21–40.

Kandel, A. (2007). The eight fatal flaws of *HR system implementations and how to avoid them* (SHRM HRTX Forum Library). Retrieved from http://www.shrm.org/hrtx/library_published/nonIC/CMS_006586.asp

Keener, D., & Fletcher, R. (2004, January). *Good planning, realistic scope and executive sponsorship important in HRIS projects.* Retrieved from http://www.shrm.org/hrdisciplines/technology/Articles/Pages/CMS_006631.aspx

Kirschner, E. M. (1997, November 3). In times of change, managers should forget noisemakers and focus on fence-sitters. *Chemical and Engineering News, 75*(44), 44–48.

Koch, C. (2002). Hershey's bittersweet lesson [Electronic version]. *CIO Magazine.* Retrieved from http://www.cio.com/article/31518

Kotter, J. P. (1996). *Leading change.* Boston: Harvard Business School Press.

Krigsman, M. (2012). The worldwide cost of IT failure (revisited): $3 trillion. Retrieved from http://www.zdnet .com/article/worldwide-cost-of-it-failure-revisited-3-trillion/ on June 22, 2016.

Lawler, E. E., & Worley, C. G. (2006). *Built to change.* San Francisco: Jossey-Bass.

Lemon, W. F., Bowitz, J., Burn, J., & Hackney, R. (2002). Information systems project failures: A comparative study of two countries. *Journal of Global Management, 10*(2), 28.

Lewin, K. (1946). Action research and minority problems. *Journal of Social Issues, 2,* 34–46.

Lorenzi, N. M., & Riley, R. T. (2000). Managing change: An overview. *Journal of the American Medical Informatics Association, 7*(2), 116–124.

Marakas, G. M., & Hornik, S. (1996). Passive resistance misuse: Overt support and covert recalcitrance in IS implementation. *European Journal of Information Systems, 5*(3), 208–219.

Mercer Delta Consulting. (2000). *Transition leadership: A guide to leading change initiatives.* Retrieved from http://www.biasca.com/archivos/for_downloading/ management_surveys/Mgmt_Change_and_Transition Leadership.pdf

Mercer Delta Consulting. (2003). *The congruence model.* Retrieved from http://www.mercerdelta.com/organizational_consulting/help_change_metrics.html

Miller, D. (2004). Building sustainable change capability. *Industrial and Commercial Training, 36*(1), 9–12.

Nadler, D. A. (1998). *Champions of change: How CEOs and their companies are mastering the skills of radical change.* San Francisco: Jossey-Bass.

Office of the Auditor General. (2005). *Performance audit* (Department of Administration, Report No. 05–02). Retrieved from http://www.auditorgen.state.az.us/ Reports/State_Agencies/Agencies/Administration_ Department_of/Performance/05–02/ 05–02.pdf

Paul, L. G. (2004, December 1). Time to change. *CIO Magazine, 18*(5), 78–86. Retrieved from http://www.cio .com/archive/120104/change.html

Potts, R., & LaMarsh, J. (2004). *Master change, maximize success.* San Francisco: Chronicle Books.

Rampton, G. M., Turnbull, I. J., & Doran, J. A. (1999). *Human resources management systems: A practical approach.* Scarborough, ON: Carswell.

Roberts, B. (1998, February). The new HRIS: Good deal or $6 million paperweight? *HR Magazine, 43,* 40–48.

Ruta, C. (2005). The application of change management theory to HR portal implementation in subsidiaries of multinational corporations. *Human Resource Management, 44*(1), 35–53.

Sabherwal, R., Jeyaraj, A., & Chowa, C. (2006). Information system success: Individual and organizational determinants. *Management Science, 52*(12), 1849–1864.

Schaffer, R. H., & McCreight, M. K. (2004). Build your own change model. *Business Horizons, 47*(3), 33–38.

Schein, E. H. (1996). Kurt Lewin's change theory in the field and in the classroom: Notes toward a model of managed learning. *Systems Practice, 9*(1), 27–47.

Schmidt, R., Lyytinen, K., Keil, M., and Cule, P. (2001). Identifying software project risks: An international Delphi study, *Journal of Management Information Systems, 17*(4), 5–36.

Thomas, A. B. (1988). Does leadership make a difference to organizational performance? *Administrative Science Quarterly, 33,* 388–400.

Twain, M. (2007). *Personal recollections of Joan of Arc.* Stilwell, KS: Digireads. (Original work published 1896)

Warhaftig, W. (2005). Flight to the future: Managing change in financial services for sustainable growth. *LIMRA International.* Retrieved from http://www.limra .com/abstracts/abstract.aspx? fid=5184

Walker, A. J. (1982). *HRIS development: A project team guide to building an effective personnel information system.* New York: Van Nostrand Reinhold.

Wexley, K.N. & Latham, G.P. (2002). *Developing and training human resources in organizations* (3rd ed). Upper Saddle River, NJ: Prentice Hall.

Williams, W. (2003). Why almost all organizational change efforts fail. *CEO Refresher.* Retrieved from http:// www.refresher.com/!wwfail.html

Chapter 6

Bondarouk, T., & Meijerink, J. (2010, August). *Implementation of an HR portal: Results of a qualitative study from a public sector organization.* Paper presented at the annual meeting of the Academy of Management, Montreal.

Boudreau, J. (1991). Utility analysis for decisions in human resource management. In M. D. Dunnette & L. M. Hough (Eds.), *Handbook of industrial and organizational psychology* (Vol. 2, pp. 621–752). Palo Alto, CA: Consulting Psychologists Press.

Cascio, W. F. (1987). *Costing human resources: The financial impact of behavior in organizations* (2nd ed.). Boston: Kent.

Cascio, W. F. (1991). *Costing human resources: The financial impact of behavior in organizations* (3rd ed.). Boston: Kent.

Cascio, W. F. (2000). *Costing human resources: The financial impact of behavior in organizations* (4th ed.). Boston: Kent.

Dery, K., Hall, R., & Wiblen, S. (2010, August). *HRISs and the constraint of human agency: The implications for HR skills.* Paper presented at the annual meeting of the Academy of Management, Montreal.

Dulebohn, J. (2010, August). *Assessing cross-functional teams in ERP/eHR implementation projects.* Paper presented at the annual meeting of the Academy of Management, Montreal.

Fitz-enz, J. (2001). *How to measure human resources management* (3rd ed.). New York: McGraw-Hill.

Grant, D., Newell, S., & Kavanagh, M. J. (2010, August). *Realizing the potential of an HRIS: Unintended consequences, human agency, and the HR function.* Symposium presented at the annual meeting of the Academy of Management, Montreal.

Howes, P. (2002, February/March). Calculating the ROI for an HRIS business plan. IHRIM.*link*, 12–15.

Kahneman, D., & Tversky, A. (1979). Prospect theory: An analysis of decisions under risk. *Econometrica, 47,* 313–327.

Kavanagh, M. J., Gueutal, H. G., & Tannenbaum, S. I. (1990). *Human resource information systems.* Boston: PWS-Kent.

Lemon, W. F., Bowitz, J., Burn, J., & Hackney, R. (2002). Information systems project failures: A comparative study of two countries. *Journal of Global Management, 10*(2), 28–39.

Mayberry, E. (2008). *How to build an HR business case* (SHRM White Paper). Alexandria, VA: Society for Human Resource Management.

Schmidt, F. L., & Hunter, J. E. (1983). Individual differences in productivity: An empirical test of estimates derived from studies of selection procedure utility. *Journal of Applied Psychology, 68,* 407–414.

Society of Human Resource Management (SHRM). (2010). *HR metrics toolkit.* Alexandria, VA: Author.

Standish Group. (2015). *Chaos Report 2015.* Boston: Author.

Tansley, C. (2010, August). *Project team branding on global human resources information systems projects.* Paper presented at the annual meeting of the Academy of Management, Montreal.

Chapter 7

Accenture. (2007). *Managing shared services change: Beyond communications and training.* New York: Author. Retrieved from http://www.accenture.com/us-en/Pages/insight-managing-shared-services-change-beyond-communications-training-summary.aspx

Anheier, N., & Doherty, S. (2001, October). *Employee self-service: Tips to ensure a successful implementation* (SHRM White Paper). Alexandria, VA: Society for Human Resource Management. Retrieved from http://www.shrm.org/hrdisciplines/technology/Articles/Pages/CMS_000210.aspx

Arveson, P. (1998). What is the balanced scorecard? *Balanced Scorecard Institute.* Retrieved from http://www.balancedscorecard.org/BSCResources/AbouttheBalancedScorecard/tabid/55/Default.aspx

Barney, J. (1991). Firm resources and sustained competitive advantage. *Journal of Management, 17,* 99–120.

Barney, J. (2001). Resource-based theories of competitive advantage: A 10-year retrospective on the resource-based view. *Journal of Management, 27,* 643–650.

Beaman, K. (Ed.). (2002). *Boundaryless HR: Human capital management in the global economy.* Austin, TX: IHRIM Press Book.

Beatty, R., Huselid, M., & Schneider, C. (2003). New HR metrics: Scoring on the business scorecard. *Organizational Dynamics, 32,* 107–121.

Becker, B., & Gerhart, B. (1996). The impact of human resource management on organizational performance: Progress and prospects. *Academy of Management Journal, 39,* 779–801.

Becker, B., Huselid, M., & Ulrich, D. (2001). *The HR scorecard: Linking people, strategy, and performance.* Boston: Harvard Business School Press.

Bender, J. (2001). HR service centers: The human element behind the technology. In A. J. Walker (Ed.), *Web-based human resources* (pp. 212–225). New York: McGraw-Hill.

Bennett-Alexander, D., & Hartman, L. (2018). *Employment law for business* (9th edition). McGraw-Hill.

Billingsley, K. (2007). *Playing tag: An RFID primer.* San Francisco: Pacific Research Institute. Retrieved from http://www.pacificresearch.org/docLib/20070706_RFID .pdf

Boglind, A., Hallsen, F., & Thilander, P. (2011). HR transformation and shared services. *Personnel Review, 40.5,* 570–588.

Boswell, W. (2006). Aligning employees with the organization's strategic objective: Out of "line of sight," out of mind. *International Journal of Human Resource Management, 17,* 1489–1511.

Briscoe, D. R., & Schuler, R. S. (2004). *International human resource management* (2nd ed.). New York: Routledge.

Campbell, S., & Mohun, V. (2007). *Mastering enterprise SOA with SAP Netweaver and my SAP.* Indianapolis, IN: Wiley & Sons.

CBR. (2007, May 29). Convergys wins $1bn Johnson & Johnson HR deal. *Computer Business Review.* Retrieved from http://www.cbronline.com/news/convergys_wins_1bn_johnson_johnson_hr_deal

CedarCrestone. (2012). *CedarCrestone 2012–2013 HR systems survey.* Alpharetta, GA: Author.

Ceriello, V. (1991). *Human resource management systems.* San Francisco: Jossey-Bass.

Chiamsiri, S., Bulusu, S., & Agarwal, M. (2005). Information technology offshore outsourcing in India: A human resource management perspective. *Research and Practice in Human Resource Management, 13,* 105–114.

Coase, R. (1937). The nature of the firm. *Economica, 4,* 386–405.

Cooke, F. (2006). Modeling an HR shared services center: Experience of an MNC in the United Kingdom. *Human Resource Management, 45,* 211–227.

Decoene, V., & Bruggerman, W. (2006). Strategic alignment and middle-level managers' motivation in a balanced scorecard setting. *International Journal of Operations & Production Management, 26,* 429–449.

Delmotte, J. (2008). HR outsourcing: Threat or opportunity. *Personnel Review, 37.5,* 543–563.

Dominguez, L. (2006). *The manager's step-by-step guide to outsourcing.* New York: McGraw-Hill.

Dowling, P. J., & Welch, D. E. (2005). *International human resource management: Managing people in a multinational context* (4th ed.). Mason, OH: Thomson/ South-Western.

EquaTerra. (2007). *Taking the pulse of today's human resources outsourcing market.* Retrieved May 18, 2007, from www.equaterra.com/KR/download.aspx?fnEqua-Terra-HRO-Buyer-Pulse-Results-April-2007.pdf

Erl, T. (2005). *Service-oriented architecture (SOA): Concepts, technology, and design.* New York: Prentice Hall PTR.

Esen, E. (2004). *SHRM human resource management outsourcing survey report.* Alexandria, VA: Society for Human Resource Management.

Everest Group. (2016). Benefits administration outsourcing (BAO) service providers' assessment. *Everest Group Peak Matrix.* Retrieved from https://research. everestgrp.com/wp-content/uploads/2016/06/ Benefits-Administration-Outsourcing-BAO-Service-Provider-Landscape-with-PEAK-Matrix-Assessment-2016-Global-Preview.pdf

Everest Research Institute. (2007). *Human resources outsourcing (HRO) market update: May 2007.* Retrieved from http://www.outsourcing-requests.com/common/sponsors/

60629/Human_Resources_Outsourcing_HRO_Market_Update.pdf

Fletcher, P. (2005). Personnel administration to business-driven human capital management. In H. Gueutal & D. Stone (Eds.), *The brave new world of eHR* (pp. 1–21). San Francisco: Jossey-Bass.

Florida, R. (2002). *The rise of the creative class: And how it's transforming work, leisure, community and everyday life.* New York: Basic Books.

Florida, R. (2005). *The flight of the creative class: The new global competition for talent.* New York: HarperCollins.

Goh, M., Prakash, S., & Yeo, R. (2007). Resource-based approach to IT in a shared services manufacturing firm. *Industrial Management & Data Systems, 107,* 251–270.

Greer, C., Youngblood, S., & Gray, D. (1999). Human resource management outsourcing: The make or buy decision. *The Academy of Management Executive, 13.3,* 85–96.

Gueutal, H., & Falbe, C. (2005). eHR trends in delivery methods. In H. Gueutal & D. Stone (Eds.), *The brave new world of eHR* (pp. 190–225). San Francisco: Jossey-Bass.

Gueutal, H., & Stone, D. (Eds.). (2005). *The brave new world of eHR.* San Francisco: Jossey-Bass.

Hatch, P. (2004). *Offshore outsourcing 2005 research: Preliminary findings and conclusions* (Ventoro Report, January 22, 2005, version). Retrieved from http://itonews.eu/files/f1222430088.pdf

Hersch, J. (1991). Equal employment opportunity law and firm profitability. *Journal of Human Resources, 26,* 139–153.

Hewitt. (2005). *A fresh look at the logic of HR outsourcing.* Lincolnshire, IL: Hewitt Associates LLC. Retrieved from http://www.outsourcing-requests.com/common/sponsors/54934/A_Fresh_Look_at_the_Logic_of_HR_Outsourcing.pdf

Hewitt. (2010). *HR outsourcing trends and insights 2009.* Lincolnshire, IL: Hewitt Associates LLC. Retrieved from http://www.aon.com/human-capital-consulting/thought-leadership/outsourcing/surveys_2009_outsourcing_trends.jsp

Kaplan, R., & Norton, D. (1992). The balanced scorecard: Measures that drive performance. *Harvard Business Review, 70,* 71–80.

Kaplan, R., & Norton, D. (1996). *The balanced scorecard: Translating strategy into action.* Boston: Harvard Business School Press.

Kaplan, R., & Norton, D. (2006). *Alignment: Using the balanced scorecard to create corporate synergies.* Boston: Harvard Business School Press.

Kavanagh, M., Gueutal, H., & Tannenbaum, S. (1990). *Human resource information systems: Development and application.* Boston: PWS.

Keebler, T. (2001). HR outsourcing in the Internet era. In A. Walker (Ed.), *Web-based human resources* (pp. 259–276). New York: McGraw-Hill.

KPMG Institutes. (2012). *3Q12 Global pulse survey.* Retrieved from http://kpmginstitutes.com/shared-services-outsourcing-institute/insights/2012/pdf/3Q12-sourcing-advisory-global-pulse-report.pdf

Lacity, M., & Willcocks, L. (2000). Relationships in IT outsourcing: A stakeholder perspective. In R. Zmud (Ed.), *Framing the domains of IT management: Projecting the future through the past* (pp. 355–384). Cincinnati, OH: Pinnaflex.

Lacity, M., & Willcocks, L. (2001). *Global information technology outsourcing: In search of business advantage* (1st ed.). West Sussex, England: Wiley.

Lawler, E. (2005). Making strategic partnership a reality. *Strategic HR Review, 4,* 3.

Lublinsky, B. (2007, May). Versioning in SOA. *Architecture Journal,* 11. Retrieved from http://msdn2.microsoft.com/en-us/arcjournal/bb491124.aspx

Lucenko, K. (1998, March). *Shared services: Achieving higher levels of performance* (The Conference Board Report R-1210-98-CH). New York: The Conference Board. Retrieved from http://www.conference-board.org/publications/publicationdetail.cfm?publicationid396

Marler, J. H., & Parry, E. (2016). Human resource management, strategic involvement and e-HRM technology. *International Journal of Human Resource Management, 19,* 2233–2253.

Marks, E., & Bell, M. (2006). *Service-oriented architecture: A business planning and implementation guide for business and technology.* Indianapolis, IN: Wiley.

Noe, R., Hollenbeck, J., Gerhart, B., & Wright, P. (2017). *Fundamentals of human resource management* (7th ed.). New York: McGraw-Hill.

O'Connell, S. (1995, June). Safety first: Computers to the rescue. *HR Magazine, 40*(6). Retrieved February 22, 2007, fromhttp://findarticles.com/p/articles/mi_m3495/is_n6_v40/ai_17191250

Organization for the Advancement of Structured Information Systems (OASIS). (2006). *OASIS reference model for service oriented architecture 1.0.* Burlington, MA: Author. Retrieved April 7, 2007, from www.oasis-open.org/committees/download.php/18486/pr-2changes.pdf

Osle, H., & Cooper, J. (2003). Structuring HR for maximum value. IHRIM.*link, 8,* 4.

Page, S. (2007). *The difference: How the power of diversity creates better groups, firms, schools, and societies.* Princeton, NJ: Princeton University Press.

Paskoff, S. M. (2003, September). *Around the world without the daze: Communicating international codes of conduct.* Paper presented at the fourth annual program on International Labor and Employment Law, Dallas, TX.

Phillips, T., Isenhour, L., & Stone, D. (2008). The potential for privacy violations in electronic human resource practices. In G. Martin, M. Reddington, & H. Alexander (Eds.), *Technology, outsourcing, and transforming HR* (pp. 193–230). Oxford: Butterworth Heinemann.

Pomerenke, P. (1998). Class action sexual harassment lawsuit: A study in crisis communication. *Human Resource Management, 37,* 207–219.

Powell, A. (2004). *Shared services and CRM* (Conference Board Technical Report E-0005-004RR). New York: The Conference Board. Retrieved from http://www.conference-board.org/publications/publicationdetail.cfm?publicationid=786

PricewaterhouseCoopers. (2006). *Key trends in human capital: A global perspective—2006.* Retrieved from http://www.pwchk.com/webmedia/doc/633077569676719728_hra_keytrends_mar06.pdf

PricewaterhouseCoopers. (2016). *Shared Services: Multiplying Success.* Retrieved from https://www.pwc.at/de/publikationen/financial-services/shared-services-multiplying-success.pdf

Procter & Gamble. (2011). Diversity and inclusion: Fulfilling our potential. Diversity and inclusion: Fulfilling our potential. Retrieved from http://www.pg.com/en_US/company/purpose_people/diversity_inclusion.shtml

Procter & Gamble. (2019). *Annual report.* Retrieved from https://www.pg.com/annualreport2019/index.html#/

Quinn, B., Cooke, R., & Kris, A. (2000). *Shared services: Mining for corporate gold.* London: Pearson Education.

Robinson, D., & Robinson, J. (2005). Strategic business partner: Aligning people strategies with business goals. New York: Berrett-Koehler.

Seth, M., & Sethi, D. (2011). Human resource outsourcing: Analysis based on literature review. *International Journal of Innovation, Management and Technology, 2.2,* 127–135,

Schwartz, E. (2003, December 8). Oracle launches HR-XML product: Will Microsoft Word follow? *InfoWorld .com.* Retrieved from http://www.infoworld.com/t/platforms/oracle-launches-hr-xml-product-390

SHRM. (2016). New EEO-1 form requires companies to report pay. Retrieved from https://www.shrm.org/resourcesandtools/legal-and-compliance/employment-law/pages/eeo-1-pay-data-.aspx

Sierra-Cedar. (2016). *Sierra-Cedar 2015–2016 HR systems survey.* Sierra-Cedar. Retrieved from http://www.sierra-cedar.com/research/publications/#toggle-id-1

Ulrich, D. (1997). *Human resource champions.* Boston: Harvard Business School Press.

U.S. Department of Labor. (2004). *OSHA instruction* (Directive No. CPL 02–00–135). Washington, DC: Author. Retrieved from http://www.osha.gov/pls/oshaweb/owadisp.show_document?p_table=DIRECTIVES&p_id=3205

U.S. Department of Labor. (2007). *Federal vs. state family and medical leave laws.* Washington, DC: Author. Retrieved from http://www.dol.gov/whd/state/fmla/index.htm

U.S. Department of Labor. (2011). OSHA quicktakes. Retrieved from https://www.osha.gov/as/opa/quicktakes/qt12152011.html

U.S. EEOC. (1964). *Title VII of the Civil Rights Act of 1964.* Washington, DC: Author. Retrieved from http://www.eeoc.gov/laws/statutes/titlevii.cfm

U.S. EEOC. (2018). *EEOC instruction booklet.* Washington, DC: Author. Retrieved from http://www.eeoc.gov/employers/eeo1survey/2007instructions.cfm

von Simson, E. (1990). The "centrally" decentralized IS organization. *Harvard Business Review, 68*(4), 158–162.

Walker, A. (1982). *HRIS development: A project team approach to building an effective personnel information system.* New York: Van Nostrand Reinhold.

Walker, A. (1993). *Handbook of human resource information systems.* New York: McGraw-Hill.

Walker, A. (Ed.). (2001). *Web-based human resources.* New York: McGraw-Hill.

Weatherly, L. (2005). HR outsourcing: Reaping strategic value for your organization. *SHRM Research Quarterly.* Retrieved from http://www.shrm.org/research/articles/articles/pages/0805rquart_essay.aspx

Williamson, I. O., Lepak, D. P., & King, J. (2003). The effect of company recruitment website orientation on individuals' perceptions of organizational attractiveness. *Journal of Vocational Behavior, 63*, 242–263.

Williamson, O. (1975). *Markets and hierarchies.* New York: Free Press.

Wright, P., McMahan, G., Snell, S., & Gerhart, B. (1998). *Strategic HRM: Building human capital and organizational capability* (Technical report). Ithaca, NY: Cornell University.

Chapter 8

Aral, S., Brynjolfsson, E., & Wu, L. (2012). Three-way complementarities: Performance pay, human resource analytics, and information technology. *Management Science, 58*(5), 913–931.

Bramham, J. (1994). *Human resource planning.* India: Universities Press.

Burrell, L. (2016). We just can't handle diversity. *Harvard Business Review, 94*(7/8), 70–74.

Cappelli, P. (1995). Rethinking employment. *British Journal of Industrial Relations, 33*, 563–602.

Cascio, W. F. (2016). *Managing human resources.* New York: McGraw-Hill.

CedarCrestone. (2012). *CedarCrestone 2012–2013 HR Systems Survey: HR Technologies, Deployment Approaches, Value, and Metrics* (15th ed.). Alpharetta, GA, Author.

Crawford, K. (2016). Artificial intelligence's white guy problem. Retrieved from https://www.cs.dartmouth.edu/~ccpalmer/teaching/cs89/Resources/Papers/AIs%20White%20Guy%20Problem%20-%20NYT.pdf

Dastin, J. (2018). Amazon scraps secret AI recruiting tool that showed bias against women. Retrieved from https://www.reuters.com/article/us-amazon-com-jobs-automation-insight-idUSKCN1MK08G

Economy, P. (2015). 11 Interesting hiring statistics you should know. *Inc.* Retrieved from https://www.inc.com/peter-economy/19-interesting-hiring-statistics-you-should-know.html

Ghorpade, J. V. (1988). *Job analysis.* Englewood Cliffs, NJ: Prentice-Hall.

Green, F. (1993). The impact of trade union membership on training in Britain. *Applied Economics, 25*(8), 1033–1043.

Kirkland, R. (2017). Focusing on what works for workplace diversity. Retrieved from https://www.mckinsey.com/featured-insights/gender-equality/focusing-on-what-works-for-workplace-diversity

Lockwood, N. (2006, June). Talent management: Driver for organizational success. *HR Magazine,* (SHRM White Paper). Alexandria, VA: Society for Human Resource Management.

Maurer, R. (2017). Employee referrals remain top source for hires. Retrieved from https://www.shrm.org/ResourcesAndTools/hr-topics/talent-acquisition/pages/employee-referrals-remains-top-source-hires.aspx

McKinsey and Company. (2001). *The war for talent.* New York: Author.

McCuiston, V. E., Wooldridge, B. R., & Pierce, C. K. (2004). Leading the diverse workforce: Profits, prospects and progress. *Leadership and Organization Development Journal, 25*, 73–92.

Morgeson, F. P., Brannick, M. T., & Levine, E. L. (2019). *Job and work analysis: Methods, research, and applications for human resource management* (3rd ed.). Thousand Oaks, CA: Sage Publications.

Naughton, K. (2006, October 30). The great Wal-Mart of China. *Newsweek, 148*, 1.

Noe, R., Hollenbeck, J., Gerhart, B., & Wright, P. (2010). *Fundamentals of human resource management.* New York: McGraw-Hill.

Peterson, T. O., & Taylor, S. D. (2004). When technology comes knocking: Using information technology to automate job descriptions. In J. W. Beard (Ed.), *Managing impressions with information technology* (pp. 73–93). Westport, CT: Praeger Publishers.

Reiter-Palmon, R., Brown, M., Sandall, D. L., Buboltz, C., & Nimps, T. (2006). Development of an O*NET web-based job analysis and its implementation in the U.S. Navy: Lessons learned. *Human Resource Management Review, 16*, 294–309.

SierraCedar. (2019). 2019–2020 HR Systems Survey (22nd ed.). Alpharetta, GA: Author.

Society for Human Resource Management (SHRM). (2010, September 21). SHRM poll identifies top HR challenges for next 10 years. *HR News.* (SHRM White Paper). Alexandria, VA: Society for Human Resource Management.

Stahl, G. K., Maznevski, M. L., Voigt, A., & Jonsen, K. (2010). Unraveling the effects of cultural diversity in teams: A meta-analysis of research on multicultural work groups. *Journal of International Business Studies, 41*(4), 690–709.

Trunick, P. (2006, January 1). Wal-Mart reinvents itself in China. *Logistics Today, 1.*

Whitman, T. S., & Hyde, A. C. (1978). HRIS: Systematically matching the right person to the right position. *Defense Management Journal, 14*(2), 28–34.

Chapter 9

Adverse.(2008).*Theadverseimpactofweb-basedhiringonminorities.* Retrieved from: http://freakonomics.com/2008/11/05/the-adverse-impact-of-web-based-hiring-on-minorities/

Allen, D. G., Mahto, R. V., & Otondo, R. F. (2007). Web-based recruitment: Effects of information, organizational brand, and attitudes toward a Web site on applicant attraction. *Journal of Applied Psychology, 92*, 1696–1708.

Baker, H. G. (1985). The unwritten contract: Job perceptions. *Personnel Journal, 64*, 36–41.

Barber, A. E., & Roehling, M. V. (1993). Job postings and the decision to interview: A verbal protocol analysis. *Journal of Applied Psychology, 78*, 845–856.

Becker, B., & Gerhart, B. (1996). The impact of human resource management on organizational performance: Progress and prospects. *Academy of Management Journal, 39*, 779–801.

Blum, M. L., & Naylor, J. C. (1968). *Industrial psychology: Its theoretical and social foundations* (rev. ed.). New York: Harper & Row.

Bouton, K. (2015). *Recruiting for cultural fit.* Retrieved from: https://hbr.org/2015/07/recruiting-for-cultural-fit

Braddy, P. W., Meade, A. W., & Kroustalis, C. M. (2008). Online recruiting: The effects of organizational familiarity, website usability, and website attractiveness on viewers' impressions of organizations. *Computers in Human Behavior, 24*, 2992–3001.

Braddy, P. W., Meade, A. W., Michael, J. J., & Fleenor, J. W. (2009). Internet recruiting: Effects of website content features on viewers' perceptions of organizational culture. *International Journal of Selection and Assessment, 17*, 19–34.

Breaugh, J. A., & Starke, M. (2000). Research on employee recruitment: So many studies, so many remaining questions. *Journal of Management, 26*, 405–434.

Bureau of Labor Statistics (BLS). (2019a). Number of job openings reached 7.1 million in August 2019. Retrieved September 15, 2019, from https://www.bls.gov/news.release/jolts.nr0.htm

Bureau of Labor Statistics (BLS). (2019b). Number of unemployed people decreased by 275,000 to 5.8 million in September 2019. Retrieved September 15, 2019, from https://www.bls.gov/opub/ted/2019/number-of-unemployed-people-decreased-by-275000-to-5-point-8-million-in-september-2019.h

Cable, D. M., Aiman-Smith, L., Mulvey, P. W., & Edwards, J. R. (2000). The sources of accuracy and job applicants' beliefs about organizational culture. *Academy of Management Journal, 43*, 1076–1085.

Cable, D. M., & Graham, M. E. (2000). The determinants of job seekers' reputation perceptions. *Journal of Organizational Behavior, 21*, 929–947.

Cable, D. M., & Yu, K. Y. T. (2006). Managing job seekers' organizational image beliefs: The role of media richness and media credibility. *Journal of Applied Psychology, 91*, 828–840.

Cappelli, P. (2001). Making the most of on-line recruiting. *Harvard Business Review, 79*, 139–146.

CareerArc. (2015). *2015 Employer branding study.* Retrieved from: https://d31kswug2i6wp2.cloudfront.net/marketo/content/careerarc-2015-employer-branding-study.pdf

Cascio, W. F. (2019). *Managing human resource: Productivity, quality of life, profits* (11th ed.). New York, NY: McGraw Hill.

Cascio, W. F., & Aguinis, H. (2011). *Applied psychology in personnel management* (7th ed.). Englewood Cliffs, NJ: Pearson.

Chapman, D. S., & Gödöllei, A. F. (2017). E-recruiting: Using technology to attract job applicants. In G. Hertel, D. L. Stone & R. D. Johnson (Eds.), *The Wiley Blackwell handbook of the psychology of the Internet at work* (pp. 213–233). Hoboken, NJ: John Wiley & Sons, LTD.

Chapman, D. S., & Webster, J. (2003). The use of technologies in the recruiting, screening, and selection processes for job candidates. *International Journal of Selection and Assessment, 11*, 113–120.

Chen, C., Lin, M., & Chen, C. (2012). Exploring the mechanisms of the relationship between website characteristics and organizational attraction. *The International Journal of Human Resource Management, 23*, 867–885.

Cober, R. T., Brown, D. J., Blumental, A. J., Doverspike, D., & Levy, P. (2000). The quest for the qualified job surfer: It's time the public sector catches the wave. *Public Personnel Management, 29*(4), 479–494.

Cober, R. T., Brown, D. J., Keeping, L. M., & Levy, P. E. (2004). Recruitment on the Net: How do organizational Web site characteristics influence applicant attraction? *Journal of Management, 30*, 623–646.

Cober, R. T., Brown, D. J., Levy, P. E., Keeping, L. M., & Cober, A. B. (2003). Organizational websites: Website content and style as determinants of organizational attraction. *International Journal of Selection and Assessment, 11*, 158–169.

Colao, J. J. (2012, September 12). *With Facebook, your recruitment pool is one billion people.* Retrieved from http://www.forbes.com/sites/jjcolao/2012/09/12/with-facebook-your-recruitment-pool-is-one-billion-people/

Daft, R. L., & Lengel, R. H. (1986). Organizational information requirements, media richness and structural design. *Management Science, 32*, 554–571.

Deloitte. (2017). *Culture, leadership and analytics matter more.* Retrieved from: https://www2.deloitte.com/au/en/pages/financial-services/articles/culture-leadership-analytics-matter-more.html

DelVecchio, D., Jarvis, C. B., Klink, R. R., & Dineen, B. R. (2007). Leveraging brand equity to attract human capital. *Marketing Letters, 18*(3), 149–164.

Deutsch, M. (2019). *What is ATS, and how does it work?* Retrieved from: https://www.topechelon.com/blog/owner-issues/what-exactly-is-an-applicant-tracking-system/

Dickter, D. N., Jockin, V., & Delany, T. (2017). The evolution of e-selection. In G. Hertel, D. L. Stone, & R. D. Johnson (Eds.), *The Wiley Blackwell handbook of the psychology of the Internet at work* (pp. 257–283). Hoboken, NJ: John Wiley & Sons, Ltd.

Dineen, B. R., Ash, S. R., & Noe, R. A. (2002). A web of applicant attraction: Person-organization fit in the context of Web-based recruitment. *Journal of Applied Psychology, 87*, 723–734.

Dineen, B. R., Ling, J., Ash, S. R., & DelVecchio, D. (2007). Aesthetic properties and message customization: Navigating the dark side of web recruitment. *Journal of Applied Psychology, 92*, 356–372.

Dineen, B. R., & Noe, R. A. (2009). Effects of customization on application decisions and applicant pool characteristics in a web-based recruitment context. *Journal of Applied Psychology, 94*, 224–234.

Farr, J. L., & Tippins, N. T. (Eds.). (2017). *Handbook of employee selection.* New York, NY: Routledge.

Fetzer, M., & Tuzinski, K. (Eds.). (2013). *Simulations for personnel selection.* New York, NY: Springer.

Fisher, C. (2017). *Ready for the robots: Survey says job candidates are mostly okay with AI apps in the application process.* Retrieved from: https://blog.allegisglobalsolutions.com/ready-for-the-robots-survey-says-job-candidates-are-mostly-okay-with-ai-apps-in-the-application-process

Galanaki, E. (2002). The decision to recruit online: A descriptive study. *Career Development International, 7*, 243–251.

Glassdoor. (2015). *50 HR & recruiting stats that make you think.* Retrieved from: https://www.glassdoor.com/employers/blog/50-hr-recruiting-stats-make-think/

Guenole, N., & Feinzig, S. (2018). *The business case for AI in HR.* Retrieved from: https://www.ibm.com/talent-management/ai-in-hr-business-case/

Guion, R. M. (1998). *Assessment, measurement, and prediction for personnel decisions.* Mahwah, NJ: Lawrence Erlbaum.

Guzzo, R. A., Fink, A. A., King, E., Tonidandel, S., & Landis, R. S. (2015). Big data recommendations for industrial-organizational psychology. *Industrial and Organizational Psychology: Perspectives on Science and Practice, 8*(4), 491–508.

Harrison, T., & Stone, D. L. (2018). Effects of organizational values and employee contact on e-recruiting. *Journal of Managerial Psychology, 33*(3), 311–324.

Heneman, H. G., Judge, T. A., & Kammeyer-Mueller. (2019). *Staffing organizations* (9th ed.). New York: McGraw-Hill.

Hoffman, D. L., & Novak, T. P. (1998). Bridging the racial divide on the internet. *Science, 280*(April 17), 390–391.

Hunter, J. E., & Schmidt, F. L. (1982). *Personnel selection programs based on cumulative knowledge.* Presentation at the PTC fall conference on validity generalization, Newport Beach, CA.

Ideal. (2019a). *AI for recruiting: A simple guide for HR professionals.* Retrieved from: https://ideal.com/resources/simple-ai-for-recruiting-guide/

Ideal. (2019b). *A how-to guide for using a recruitment.* Retrieved from: https://ideal.com/recruitment-chatbot/hatbot

IES. (2019). *e-Recruitment: Is it delivering?* Retrieved from: https://www.employment-studies.co.uk/report-summaries/report-summary-e-recruitment-it-delivering

International Testing Commission. (2006). Guidelines for computer-based and Internet-delivered testing. *International Journal of Testing, 6,* 143–172.

Jackson, L. A., Ervin, K. S., Gardner, P. D., & Schmitt, N. (2001). Gender and the Internet: Women communicating and men searching. *Sex Roles, 44,* 363–379.

Jackson, N. M. (2019). *3 clear advantages of online recruitment.* Retrieved from: https://www.adp.com/spark/articles/2018/12/three-clear-advantages-of-online-recruitment.aspx#

Jibe. (2014). *2014 talent acquisition survey.* Retrieved from: https://www.jibe.com/wp-content/uploads/2014/09/2014-Talent-Acquisition-Survey.pdf

Jobvite. (2014). *Jobvite job seekers nation study.* Retrieved from: http://web.jobvite.com/rs/jobvite/images/2014%20Job%20Seeker%20Survey.pdf

Jobvite. (2016). *Smartphone, dumb recruiting: Why mobile is a must.* Retrieved: https://www.jobvite.com/wp-content/uploads/2018/05/Smartphone-DumbRecruiting-eBook.pdf

Johnson, R. D., & Stone, D. L. (2019). Advantages and unintended consequences of using electronic human resource management (eHRM) processes. In R. Landis (ed.), *The Cambridge handbook of technology and employee behavior* (pp. 879–920). Cambridge, UK: Cambridge University Press.

Judge, T. A., & Cable, D. M. (1997). Applicant personality, organizational culture, and organizational attraction. *Personnel Psychology, 50,* 359–394.

Karat, J. (1997). Evolving the scope of user-centered design. *Communications of the ACM, 40,* 33–38.

Kaur, P. (2015). E-recruitment: A conceptual study. *International Journal of Applied Research, 1*(8), 78–82.

Kehoe, J. F., Dickter, D. N., Russell, D. P., & Sacco, J. M. (2005). e-Selection. In H. G. Guental & D. L. Stone (Eds.), *The brave new world of eHR* (pp. 54–103). San Francisco: Jossey-Bass.

Kim, K. H., Jeon, B. J., Jung, H. S., Lu, W., & Jones, J. (2011). Effective employment brand equity through sustainable competitive advantage, marketing strategy, and corporate image. *Journal of Business Research, 64*(11), 1207–1211.

Kristof-Brown, A. L., Zimmerman, R. D., & Johnson, E. C. (2005). Consequences of individuals' fit at work: A meta-analysis of person-job, person-organization, person-group, and person-supervisor fit. *Personnel Psychology, 58,* 281–342.

Kuhn, P., & Skuterud, M. (2000). Job search methods: Internet versus traditional. *Monthly Labor Review, 123,* 3–11.

Landers, RN., Fink, A. A., & Collmus, A. B. (2017). Using big data to enhance staffing: Vast untapped resources or tempting honeypot? In Farr, J. L., & Tippins, N. T. (Eds.) *Handbook of employee selection* (2nd ed., pp, 949–966). New York, NY: Routledge.

Lee, I. (2005). The evolution of e-recruiting: A content analysis of Fortune 100 career web sites. *Journal of Electronic Commerce in Organizations, 3*(3), 57–68.

LinkedIn. (2014). *The ultimate list of hiring statistics for hiring managers, HR professionals, and recruiters.* Retrieved from: https://business.linkedin.com/content/dam/business/talent-solutions/global/en_us/c/pdfs/Ultimate-List-of-Hiring-Stats-v02.04.pdf?src=aff-ref&veh=jobs_aff_ir_pid_10078_plc_Skimbit%20Ltd._adid_615074&trk=jobs_aff_ir_pid_10078_plc_Skimbit%20Ltd._adid_615074&clickid=WblWDUSHzxyJW%3A8xU-SAVSQkUknzvBThr26BTc0&irgwc=1

Love, L. F., & Singh, P. (2011). Workplace branding: Leveraging human resources management practices for competitive advantage through "Best Employer" surveys. *Journal of Business and Psychology, 26*(2), 175.

Lukaszewski, K. M., & Johnson, A.F. (2017). Social networking sites, search engines, and the employment process. In G. Hertel, D. L. Stone, & R. D. Johnson (Eds.), *The Wiley Blackwell handbook of the psychology of the Internet at work* (pp. 231–256). Hoboken, NJ: John Wiley & Sons, Ltd.

Lyons, B. D., & Marler, J. H. (2011). Got image? Examining organizational image in Web recruitment. *Journal of Managerial Psychology, 26*(1), 58–76.

MacMillan, D. (2007, May 7). The art of the online resume. *BusinessWeek,* 86. Retrieved from https://www.bloomberg.com/news/articles/2007-05-06/the-art-of-the-online-r-sum.

Maister, J. (2017). *5 ways end-to-end recruiting solutions reduce administrative burden.* Retrieved from: https://www.business2community.com/human-resources/5-ways-end-end-recruiting-solutions-reduce-administrative-burden-01954782

Mamedova, S., Pawlowski, E., & Hudson, L. (2018). A description of US adults who are not digitally literate. *Stats in Brief.* Washington DC: U.S. Department of Education.

Maurer, S. D., & Cook, D. P. (2011). Using company websites to e-recruit qualified applicants: A job marketing based review of theory-based research. *Computers in Human Behavior, 27,* 106–117.

McCourt-Mooney, M. (2000). Internet briefing: Recruitment and selection—R&D using the Internet—Part III. *Journal of Managerial Psychology, 15,* 737–740.

McDonagh, J. (2018). *10 employer branding statistics HR professionals need to know.* Retrieved from: https://www.business2community.com/human-resources/10-employer-branding-statistics-hr-professionals-need-know-02019303

McHugh, B. (2019). *Staffing tech 101: What is mobile recruiting?* Retrieved from: https://www.bullhorn.com/blog/2019/03/what-is-mobile-recruiting/

McManus, M. A., & Ferguson, M. W. (2003). Biodata, personality, and demographic differences of recruits from three sources. *International Journal of Selection and Assessment, 11,* 175–183.

Mead, A., & Drasgow, F. (1993). Equivalence of computerized and paper-and-pencil cognitive ability tests: A meta-analysis. *Psychological Bulletin, 114,* 449–458.

Mohamed, A. A., Orife, J. N., & Wibowo, K. (2002). The legality of key word search as a personnel selection tool. *Employee Relations, 24,* 516–522.

Monster. (2019). *Culture-based recruiting: Hire for the organization, not just the job.* Retrieved from: https://hiring.monster.ca/employer-resources/recruiting-strategies/strategic-workforce-planning/culture-based-recruiting-canada/

Morrison, E. W., & Robinson, S. L. (1997). When employees feel betrayed: A model of how psychological contract violation develops. *Academy of Management Review, 22,* 226–256.

Nielsen, J. (2000). *Designing Web usability.* Indianapolis, IN: New Riders.

Pande, S. (2011). E-recruitment creates order out of chaos at SAT Telecom: System cuts costs and improves efficiency. *Human Resource Management International Digest, 19,* 21–23.

Perrin, A., & Turner, E. (2019). *Smartphones help blacks, Hispanics bridge some—but not all—digital gaps with whites.* Retrieved from: https://www.pewresearch.org/

fact-tank/2019/08/20/smartphones-help-blacks-hispanics-bridge-some-but-not-all-digital-gaps-with-whites/

Pew Research Center. (2015). *Demographics of online job seekers.* Retrieved from: https://www.pewinternet.org/2015/11/19/searching-for-work-in-the-digital-era/pi_2015-11-19_internet-and-job-seeking_1-02/

Pollitt, D. (2005). E-recruitment gets the Nike tick of approval. *Human Resource Management International Digest, 13*(2), 33.

Potosky, D., & Bobko, P. (2004). Selection testing via the Internet: Practical considerations and exploratory empirical findings. *Personnel Psychology, 57,* 1003–1004.

PSI. (2016). *5 Tips for creating a realistic job preview that will reduce turnover.* Retrieved from: https://blog.psionline.com/talent/5-tips-for-creating-a-realistic-job-preview-that-will-reduce-turnover

PWC. (2017). *Artificial intelligences: A HR no-brainer.* Retrieved from https://www.pwc.nl/nl/assets/documents/artificial-intelligence-in-hr-a-no-brainer.pdf

Reed, K., Doty, H. D., & May, D. R. (2005). The impact of aging on self-efficacy and computer skill acquisition. *Journal of Managerial Issues, 17,* 212–228.

Reed Company. (2003). *The Reed Recruitment Index report.* Retrieved from http://www.onrec.com/content2/news.asp? ID=1981

Reiners, B. (2018). *Examples of stellar career pages.* Retrieved from https://builtin.com/recruiting/15-career-page-examples

Rossheim, J. (2019). *Make mobile recruiting part of your hiring strategy.* Retrieved from: https://hiring.monster.com/employer-resources/recruiting-strategies/talent-acquisition/mobile-recruiting/

Rousseau, D. M. (1990). New hire perceptions of their own and their employer's obligations: A study of psychological contracts. *Journal of Organizational Behavior, 11,* 389–400.

Rozelle, A. L., & Landis, R. S. (2002). An examination of the relationship between use of the Internet as a recruitment source and student attitudes. *Computers in Human Behavior, 18,* 593–604.

Russell, D. P. (2007). Recruiting and staffing in the electronic age: A research-based perspective. *Consulting Psychology Journal: Practice and Research, 59,* 91–101.

Saini, G. K., Rai, P., & Chaudhary, M. K. (2014). What do best employer surveys reveal about employer branding and intention to apply? *Journal of Brand Management, 21*(2), 95–111.

Schmidt, F. L., & Hunter, J. E. (1998). The validity and utility of selection methods in personnel psychology: Practical and theoretical implications of 85 years of research findings. *Psychological Bulletin, 124,* 262–274.

Schneider, B., Goldstein, H. W., & Smith, D. B. (1995). The ASA framework: An update. *Personnel Psychology, 48,* 747–773.

Selden, S., & Orenstein, J. (2011). Government e-recruiting web sites: The influence of e-recruitment content and usability on recruiting and hiring outcomes in US state governments. *International Journal of Selection and Assessment, 19,* 31–40.

Seminerio, M. (2001, April 24). E-recruiting takes next step. *eWeek, 18,* 16, 51–54.

Shields, J. (2018). *Top 500 resumes keywords: Examples for your job search.* Retrieved from: https://www.jobscan.co/blog/top-resume-keywords-boost-resume/

Smith, A. (2015). *Searching for work in a digital era.* Retrieved from: https://www.pewresearch.org/wp-content/uploads/sites/9/2015/11/PI_2015-11-19-Internet-and-Job-Seeking_FINAL.pdf

Society for Human Resource Management (SHRM). (2004). *Merging tests with applicant tracking systems.* Retrieved from http://www.shrm.org/hrdisciplines/staffingmanagement/articles/pages/cms_006199.aspx

Society for Human Resource Management (SHRM). (2016). *2016 human capital benchmarking report.* Retrieved from: https://www.shrm.org/hr-today/trends-and-forecasting/research-and-surveys/Documents/2016-Human-Capital-Report.pdf

Society for Human Resource Management (SHRM). (2017). *Using social media for talent acquisition.* Retrieved from: https://www.shrm.org/hr-today/trends-and-forecasting/research-and-surveys/pages/social-media-recruiting-screening-2015.aspx

Society for Industrial and Organizational Psychology (SIOP). (2018). *Principles for the validation and use of personnel selection procedures* (5th ed.). Bowling Green, OH.

Sokro, E. (2012). Impact of employer branding on employee attraction and retention. *European Journal of Business and Management, 4*(18), 164–173.

Starr, R. (2019). *41% of new hires found their positions at an online jobs board.* Retrieved from: https://smallbiztrends.com/2019/01/how-do-people-find-jobs.html

Stevens, L. (2007). *Where people are looking for jobs.* Retrieved from http://www.ere.net/2007/12/13/where-people-are-looking-for-jobs/

Stone, D. L., Lukaszewski, K. M., & Isenhour, L. C. (2005). e-Recruiting: Online strategies for attracting talent. In H. G. Gueutal & D. L. Stone (Eds.), *The brave new world of eHR* (pp. 22–53). San Francisco: Jossey-Bass.

Stone, D. L., Lukaszewski, K. M., Stone-Romero, E. F., & Johnson, T. L. (2013). Factors affecting the effectiveness and acceptance of electronic selection systems. *Human Resource Management Review, 23*(1), 50–70.

Stone, D. L., Stone-Romero, E. F., & Lukaszewski, K. (2003). The functional and dysfunctional consequences of human resource information technology for organizations and their employees. In D. L. Stone (Ed.), *Advances in human performance and cognitive engineering research* (pp. 37–68). Greenwich, CT: JAI Press.

Sullivan, J. (2013). *Why you can't get a job: Recruiting explained by the numbers.* Retrieved from: https://www.ere.net/why-you-cant-get-a-job-recruiting-explained-by-the-numbers/

Sylva, H., & Mol, S. T. (2009). E-recruitment: A study into applicant perceptions of an online application system. *International Journal of Selection and Assessment, 17*(3), 311–323.

Tippins, N. T. (2009). Internet alternatives to traditional proctored testing: Where are we now? *Industrial and Organizational Psychology, 2,* 2–10.

Tippins, N. T. (2015). Technology and assessment in selection. *Annual Review of Organizational Behavior, 2,* 551–582.

Tippins, N. T., Beaty, J., Drasgow, F., Gibson, W. M., Pearlman, K., Segall, D. O., & Shepherd, W. (2006). Unproctored Internet testing in employment settings. *Personnel Psychology, 59,* 189–225.

Uggerslev, K. L, Fassina, N. E., & Kraichy, D. (2012). Recruiting through the stages: A meta-analytic test of predictors of applicant attraction at different stages of the recruiting process. *Personnel Psychology, 65,* 597–660.

Ulrich, D. (2001). From e-business to e-HR. *International Human Resources Information Management Journal, 5,* 90–97.

U.S. Department of Labor. (1999). *Testing and assessment: An employer's guide to good practices.* Washington, DC: Author.

Verliden, N. (2019). *Why mobile recruitment is a must.* Retrieved from: https://www.digitalhrtech.com/why-mobile-recruitment-is-a-must/

Walker, H. J., Field, H. S., Giles, W. F., Armenakis, A. A., & Bernerth, J. B. (2009). Displaying employee testimonials on recruitment Web sites: Effects of communication media, employee race, and job seeker race on organizational attraction and information credibility. *Journal of Applied Psychology, 94,* 1354–1364.

Wanous, J. P. (1992). *Organizational entry.* Reading, MA: Addison-Wesley.

Weghoeft, M. (2018). *Four major difference between women and men in the job search.* Retrieved from: https://zocket.me/blog/gender-differences-in-job-search/

Westfall, B. (2017). *How job seekers use Glassdoor reviews.* Retrieved from: https://www.softwareadvice.com/resources/job-seekers-use-glassdoor-reviews/

Williamson, I. O., Lepak, D. P., & King, J. (2003). The effect of company recruitment Web site orientation on individuals' perceptions of organizational attractiveness. *Journal of Vocational Behavior, 63,* 242–263.

Wright, P. M., & Snell, S. A. (1998). Toward a unifying framework for exploring fit and flexibility in strategic human resource management. *Academy of Management Review, 23,* 756–772.

Zafar, H., & Stone, D. L. (2018). HRIS security and privacy. In M. Kavanagh & R. Johnson (Eds.), *Human resource information systems: Basics, applications, and future directions* (4th ed., pp. 422–443). Thousand Oaks, CA: Sage.

Zappe, J. (2016). *Your career site is your most important recruiting channel.* Retrieved from: https://www.ere.net/your-career-site-is-your-most-important-recruiting-channel/

Zielinski, D. (2012, August). Find social media's value: The platform's return on investment often eludes measurement. *HR Magazine, 57,* 53–55.

Zielinski, D. (2016). *Study: Most job seekers abandon online job applications.* Retrieved from: https://www.shrm.org/resourcesandtools/hr-topics/technology/pages/study-most-job-seekers-abandon-online-job-applications.aspx

Chapter 10

Alavi, M., & Leidner, D. E. (2001). Review: Knowledge management and knowledge management systems: Conceptual foundations and research issues. *MIS Quarterly 25*(1), 107–136.

Association for Talent Development. (2015). *The mobile landscape: Building toward anytime, anywhere learning.* Alexandria, VA: ATD.

Arbaugh, J. B. (2001). How instructor immediacy behaviors affect student satisfaction and learning in web-based courses. *Business Communication Quarterly, 64*(4), 42–54.

Arbaugh, J. B. (2002). Managing the on-line classroom: A study of technological and behavioral characteristics of web-based MBA courses. *Journal of High Technology Management Research, 13*(2), 203–223.

Arbaugh, J. B. (2004). Learning to learn online: A study of perceptual changes between multiple online course experiences. *The Internet and Higher Education, 7*(3), 169–182.

Arbaugh, J. B. (2014). System, scholar or students? Which most influences online MBA course effectiveness? *Journal of Computer Assisted Learning, 30*(4), 351–362.

Argote, L., Insko, C. A., & Yovetich, N., & Romero, A. A. (1995). Group learning curves: The effects of turnover and task complexity on group performance. *Journal of Applied Psychology, 25,* 512–529.

Argyris, C., & Schon, D. A. (1978). *Organization learning II: Theory, method and practice.* Reading, MA: Addison-Wesley.

Baldwin, T. T., & Ford, J. K. (1988). Transfer of training: A review and directions for future research. *Personnel Psychology, 41*(1), 63–105.

Barney, J. B., & Wright, P. M. (1998). On becoming a strategic partner: The role of human resources in gaining competitive advantage. *Human Resource Management, 37*(1), 31–46.

Bausch, S., Michel, A., & Sonntag, K. (2014). How gender influences the effect of age on self-efficacy and training success. *International Journal of Training and Development, 18*(3), 171–187.

Beaudoin M. (2013). The evolving role of the instructor in the digital age. In Y. Katz (Ed.), *Learning management systems and instructional design: Metrics, standards, and applications.* Hershey, PA: Inf. Sci.

Beckers, A. M., & Bsat, M. Z. (2002). A DSS classification model for research in HRIS. *Information Systems Management, 19*(3), 41–50.

Bell, B. S., & Kozlowski, S. W. J. (2002). Goal orientation and ability: Interactive effects on self-efficacy, performance, and knowledge. *Journal of Applied Psychology, 87*(3), 497–505.

Bersin, J. (2018). The learning experience platform (LXP) market expands. Retrieved from: https://joshbersin.com/2018/09/the-learning-experience-platform-lxp-market-expands/

Bloom, B. S., Engelhart, M., Furst, E. J., Hill, W., & Krathwohl, D. (1956). *Taxonomy of educational objectives: Vol. 1. The cognitive domain.* New York: McKay.

Bloom, B. S., Masia, B. B., & Krathwohl, D. (1964). *Taxonomy of educational objectives: Vol. 2. The affective domain.* New York: McKay.

Blume, B. D., Ford, J. K., Baldwin, T. T., & Huang, J. L. (2010). Transfer of training: A meta-analytic review. *Journal of Management, 36*(4), 1065–1105.

Bonadio, S. (2009). *HR field guide—5 tips to effective learning management.* Wayland, MA: Softscape.

Boydell, T. H. (1983). *A guide to the identification of training needs.* London: British Association for Commercial and Industrial Education.

Brinkerhoff, R. O. (2009). *The success case method: Find out quickly what's working and what's not* (2nd ed.). San Francisco, CA: Berrett-Koehler Publishers.

Brown, K. G. (2001). Using computers to deliver training: Which employees learn and why? *Personnel Psychology, 54*(2), 271–296.

Brown, K. G. (2005). An examination of the structure and nomological network of trainee reactions: A closer look at "smile sheets." *Journal of Applied Psychology, 90*(5), 991–1001.

Brown, K. G., & Charlier, S. D. (2013). An integrative model of e-learning use: Leveraging theory to understand and increase usage. *Human Resource Management Review, 23*(1), 37–49.

Burbach, R., & Dundon, T. (2005). The strategic potential of human resource information systems: Evidence from the Republic of Ireland. *International Employment Relations Review, 11*(1/2), 97–118.

Burnes, B. (2004). *Managing change: A strategic approach to organisational dynamics.* Harrow, UK: Prentice Hall/Financial Times.

Cellar, D. F., Stuhlmacher, A. F., Young, S. K., Fisher, D. M., Adair, C. K., et al. (2011). Trait goal orientation, self-regulation, and performance: A meta-analysis. *Journal of Business and Psychology, 26*(4), 467–483.

Chartered Institute of Personnel and Development. (2015). *Annual survey report: Learning and development 2015.* London, UK: CIPD.

Chien, T. (2012). Computer self-efficacy and factors influencing e-learning effectiveness. *European Journal of Training and Development, 36*(7), 670–686.

Chu, R. J. (2010). How family support and Internet self-efficacy influence the effects of e-learning among higher aged adults—analyses of gender and age differences. *Computers & Education, 55*, 255–264.

Colquitt, J. A., LePine, J. A., & Noe, R. A. (2000). Toward an integrative theory of training motivation: A meta-analytic path analysis of 20 years of research. *Journal of Applied Psychology, 85*(5), 678–707.

Collin, A. (2007). Learning and development. In J. Beardwell & T. Claydon (Eds.), *Human resource management: A contemporary approach* (5th ed., pp. 260–306). Harlow, UK: Prentice Hall, Financial Times.

Cummings, T. G., & Worley, C. G. (2009). *Organization development and change* (9th ed.). Cincinnati, OH: South-Western College Publishing.

Deloitte. (2018). *2019 Deloitte global human capital trends.* Deloitte Insights. Retrieved from: https://www2.deloitte.com/us/en/insights/focus/human-capital-trends.html

DeRouin, R., Fritzsche, B., & Salas, E. (2004). Optimizing e-learning: Research-based guidelines for learner-controlled training. *Human Resource Management, 43*(2&3), 147–162.

Dodd, C., Kirby, D., Seifert, T., & Sharpe, D. (2009). The impact of high school distance e-learning experience on rural students' university achievement and persistence. *Online Journal of Distance Learning Administration, 12*(1), 1–12.

Easterby-Smith, M. (1986). *Evaluation of management, training, and development.* Aldershot, UK: Gower.

Eom, S. B. (2011). Relationships among e-learning systems and e-learning outcomes: A path analysis model. *Human Systems Management, 30*, 229–241.

Ferdousi, B., & Levy, Y. (2010). Development and validation of a model to investigate the impact of individual factors on instructor's intentions to use e-learning systems. *Interdisciplinary Journal of E-Learning and Learning Objects, 6*, 1–21.

Fisher, S. L., & Ford, J. K. (1998). Differential effects of learner effort and goal orientation on two learning outcomes. *Personnel Psychology, 51*(2), 397–420.

Fisher, S. L., Wasserman, M., & Orvis, K. (2010). Trainee reactions to learner control: An important link in the e-learning equation. *International Journal of Training and Development, 14*(3), 198–210.

Fleming, N. D. (2001). *Teaching and learning styles: VARK strategies.* Christchurch, New Zealand: Author.

Fleming, N. D., & Mills, C. (1992). Not another inventory, rather a catalyst for reflection. *To Improve the Academy, 11*, 137–143.

Francona, K. (2001). Tips for increasing e-learning completion rates. *Workforce, 80*(10), 56.

Frauenheim, E. (2006). Talent management software is bundling up. *Workforce Management, 85*(19), 35.

Frauenheim, E. (2007). Your co-worker, your teacher: Collaborative technology speeds peer-peer learning. *Workforce Management, 86*(2), 19–23.

Fuller, R. M., Vician, C., & Brown, S. A. (2006). E-learning and individual characteristics: The role of computer anxiety and communication apprehension. *Journal of Computer Information Systems, 46*(4), 103–115.

Gagné, R. M. (1985). *The conditions of learning and theory of instruction* (4th ed.). New York: Holt, Rinehart & Winston.

Galy, E., Downey, C., & Johnson, J. (2011). The effect of using e-learning tools in online and campus-based classrooms on student performance. *Journal of Information Technology Education, 10*, 209–230.

Garavan, T. N., Carbery, R., O'Malley, G., & O'Donnell, D. (2010). Understanding participation in e-learning in organizations: A large scale empirical study of employees. *International Journal of Training and Development, 14*(3), 155–168.

Gascó, J. L., Llopis, J., & González, M. R. (2004). The use of information technology in training human resources: An e-learning case study. *Journal of European Industrial Training, 28*(5), 370–382.

Gibb, S. (2002). *Learning and development: Process, practices, and perspectives at work.* Basingstoke: Palgrave Macmillan.

Gold, A. H., & Arvind Malhotra, A. H. S. (2001). Knowledge management: An organizational capabilities perspective. *Journal of Management Information Systems, 18*(1), 185–214.

Granger, B., & Levine, E. (2010). The perplexing role of learner control in e-learning: Will learning and the transfer benefit suffer? *International Journal of Training and Development, 14*(3), 180–197.

Granger, B., & Levine, E. (2013). Complexity compromises learner-led e-learning, *T+D, 67*(4), 20.

Grant, R. M. (1996). Toward a knowledge-based theory of the firm. *Strategic Management Journal, 17*(10), 109–122.

Griffin, R. (2014). *Complete training evaluation: The comprehensive guide to measuring return on investment.* London: Kogan Page.

Gunnigle, P., Heraty, N., & Morley, M. (2017). *Human resource management in Ireland* (5th ed.). Dublin, Ireland: Gill & Macmillan.

Harrison, R. (2009). *Learning and development.* London: Chartered Institute of Personnel and Development.

Hashim, R., Ahmad, H., & Abdullah, C. Z. (2010). Antecedents of ICT attitudes of distance education students. *Turkish Online Journal of Educational Technology, 9*(1), 28–36.

Hatch, N. W., & Dyer, J. H. (2004). Human capital and learning as a source of sustainable competitive advantage. *Strategic Management Journal, 25*(12), 1155–1178.

Harvard, D., Taylor, K., & Eggleston Schwartz, M. (2018). Trends 2019: Adapting the training function to the complexity of today's business environment. *Training Industry Magazine, 12*(1), 24–30.

Hayashi, A., Chen, C. C., & Terase, H. (2005). Aligning IT skills training with online asynchronous learning multimedia technologies. *Information Systems Education Journal, 3*(26), 3–10.

Hayden, D. (2018). Evaluating learning and development. *Chartered Institute of Personnel and Development (CIPD).* Retrieved from https://www.cipd.co.uk/knowledge/fundamentals/people/development/evaluating-learning-factsheet#7075

Honey, P., & Mumford, A. (1992). *Manual of learning styles* (3rd ed.). London: Peter Honey.

Hornik, S., Saunders, C. S., Li, Y., Moskal, P. D., & Dzuiban, C. D. (2008). The impact of paradigm development and course level on performance in technology-mediated learning environments. *Informing Science: The International Journal of an Emerging Transdiscipline, 11*, 35–58.

Hurtz, G. M., & Williams, K. J. (2009). Attitudinal and motivational antecedents of participation in voluntary employee development activities. *Journal of Applied Psychology, 94*(3), 635–653.

Insala. (2014). *2014 employee career development survey report.* Dallas, TX: Author.

Islam, N. (2011). The determinants of the post-adoption satisfaction of educators with an e-learning system. *Journal of Information Systems Education, 22*(4), 319–330.

Janson, A., Söllner, M., & Leimeister, J. M. (in press). Ladders for learning: Is scaffolding the key to teaching problem solving in technology-mediated learning contexts? *Academy of Management Learning & Education.*

Johnson, R. D., & Brown, K. G. (2017). E-learning. In G. Hertel, D. Stone, R. Johnson, & J. Passmore (Eds.), *The Wiley handbook of the psychology of the Internet at work.* (pp. 369–400). Hoboken, NJ: Wiley & Sons.

Johnson, R. D., Gueutal, H., & Falbe, C. M. (2009). Technology, trainees, metacognitive activity and e-learning effectiveness. *Journal of Managerial Psychology, 24*(6), 545–566.

Johnson, R. D., Hornik, S., & Salas, E. (2008). An empirical examination of factors contributing to the creation of successful e-learning environments. *International Journal of Human-Computer Studies, 66*(5), 356–369.

Kaplan, R. S., & Norton, D. P. (1992). The balanced scorecard: Measures that drive performance. *Harvard Business Review, 70*(1), 71–79.

Kaplan, R. S., & Norton, D. P. (1993). Putting the balanced scorecard to work. *Harvard Business Review, 71*(5), 134–140.

Karim, M., & Behrend, T. (2014). Reexamining the nature of learner control: Dimensionality and effects on learning and training reactions. *Journal of Business and Psychology, 29*, 87–99.

Keebler, T. J., & Rhodes, D. W. (2002). e-HR: Becoming the "path of least resistance." *Employment Relations Today, 29*(2), 57–66.

Kickul, G., & Kickul, J. (2006). Closing the gap: Impact of student proactivity and learning goal orientation on e-learning outcomes. *International Journal on E-Learning, 5*(3), 361–372.

Kim, K., & Frick, T. W. (2011). Changes in student motivation during online learning. *Journal of Educational Computing Research, 44*(1), 1–23.

Kim, K., Trimi, S., Park, H., & Rhee, S. (2012). The impact of CMS quality on the outcomes of e-learning systems in education: An empirical study. *Decision Sciences Journal of Innovative Education, 10*(4), 575–587.

Kirkpatrick, D. L. (1960). Techniques for evaluating training programmes. *Journal of the American Society for Training and Development, 14*, 13–18, 25–32.

Kirkpatrick, D. L. (1994). *Evaluating training programs: The four levels*. San Francisco, CA: Berrett-Koehler.

Kirkpatrick, J. D., & Kayser Kirkpatrick, W. (2016). *Kirkpatrick's four levels of training evaluation*. Alexandria, VA: Association for Talent Development.

Kleitman, S., & Costa, D. S. J. (2014). The role of a novel formative assessment tool (Stats-mIQ) and individual differences in real-life academic performance. *Learning and Individual Differences, 29*, 150–161.

Knowles, M. S., Holton, E. F., III, & Swanson, R. A. (2005). *The adult learner: The definitive classic in adult education and human resource development* (6th ed.). San Diego: Elsevier.

Kodwani, A. D. (2017). Decoding training effectiveness: The role of organisational factors. *Journal of Workplace Learning, 29*(3), 200–216.

Kolb, D. A. (1984). *Experiential learning: Experience as a source of learning and development*. Englewood Cliffs, NJ: Prentice Hall.

Kovach, K. A., & Cathcart Jr, C. E. (1999). Human resource information systems (HRIS): Providing business with rapid data access, information exchange and strategic advantage. *Public Personnel Management, 28*(2), 275–282.

Kovach, K. A., Hughes, A. A., Fagan, P., & Maggitti, P. G. (2002). Administrative and strategic advantages of HRIS. *Employment Relations Today, 29*(2), 43–48.

Lance, C. E., Kavanagh, M. J., & Brink, K. E. (2002). Retraining climate as a predictor of retraining success and as a moderator of the relationship between cross-job retraining time estimates and time to proficiency in the new job. *Group and Organization Management, 27*, 294–317.

Liaw, S. (2008). Investigating students' perceived satisfaction, behavioral intention, and effectiveness of e-learning: A case study of the Blackboard system. *Computers & Education, 51*, 864–873.

Liaw, S., Huang, H. M., & Chen, G. D. (2007). Surveying instructor and learner attitudes toward e-learning. *Computers & Education, 49*(4), 1066–1080.

Marks, R. B., Sibley, S. D., & Arbaugh, J. B. (2005). A structural equation model of predictors for effective online learning. *Journal of Management Education, 29*(4), 531–563.

Mayo, A. (1998). Memory bankers. *People Management, 4*(2), 34–38.

Noe, R. A. (2002). *Employee training and development* (2nd ed.). New York: McGraw-Hill.

Noe, R. A. (2017). *Employee training and development* (7th ed.). New York: McGraw-Hill.

Noe, R. A., & Schmitt, N. (1986). The influence of trainee attitudes on training effectiveness: Test of a model. *Personnel Psychology, 39*(3), 497–523.

Nonaka, I., & Takeuchi, H. (1995). *The knowledge-creating company*. New York: Oxford University Press.

Nunes, J. M., McPherson, M. A., Annasingh, F., Bashir, I., & Patterson, D. C. (2009). The use of e-learning in the workplace: A systematic literature review. *Impact: Journal of Applied Research in Workplace E-learning, 1*(1), 97–112.

OECD. (2001). *The well-being of nations: The role of human and social capital*. Paris: OECD Publishing.

OECD. (2013). *Supporting investment in knowledge capital, growth and innovation*. Paris: OECD Publishing. https://dx.doi.org/10.1787/9789264193307-en

Orvis, K. A., Brusso, R. C., Fisher, S. L., & Wasserman, M. E. (2011). E-nabled for e-learning? The moderating role of personality in determining the optimal degree of learner control in an e-learning environment. *Human Performance, 24*, 60–78.

Orvis, K. A., Fisher, S. L., & Wasserman, M. E. (2009). Power to the people: Using learner control to improve trainee reactions and learning in web-based instructional environments. *Journal of Applied Psychology, 94*(4), 960.

Pappas, C. (2016). *6 LMS metrics elearning professionals should look for*. Retrieved from: https://elearningindustry.com/lms-metrics-elearning-professionals-should-look-for

Park, S., Sim, H., & Roh, H. (2010). The analysis of effectiveness on "transfer" through e-learning courses in industry and technology. *British Journal of Educational Technology, 41*(6), 32–34.

Pedler, M., Burgoyne, J., & Boydell, T. (1991). *The learning company: A strategy for sustainable development*. Maidenhead, UK: McGraw-Hill.

Pfeffer, J. (1996). *Competitive advantage through people: Unleashing the power of the work force*. Boston: Harvard Business School Press.

Pfeffer, J. (1998). *The human equation: Building profits by putting people first*. Boston: Harvard Business School Press.

Phillips, J. J. (1996a). How much is the training worth? *Training & Development, 50*(4), 20.

Phillips, J. J. (1996b). ROI: The search for best practices. *Training & Development, 50*(2), 42.

Phillips, J. J. (1996c). Was it the training? *Training & Development, 50*(3), 28.

Phillips, J. J. (2005). The value of human capital: Macro-level research. *Chief Learning Officer, 4*(10), 60–62.

Phillips, J. J. (2012). *Return on investment in training and performance improvement programs* (2nd ed.). London: Routledge.

Porter, M. (1990). *The competitive advantage of nations*. New York: Free Press.

Powell, M. (2019). *What is a learning management system? (2019 update)*. Retrieved from: https://www.docebo.com/blog/what-is-learning-management-system/

Prahalad, C. K., & Hamel, G. (1990). The core competencies of the corporation. *Harvard Business Review, 6*(3), 79–91.

Rouiller, J. Z., & Goldstein, I. L. (1993). The relationship between organizational transfer climate and positive transfer of training. *Human Resource Development Quarterly, 4*, 377–390.

Russ-Eft, D., & Preskill, H. (2005). In search of the Holy Grail: Return on investment evaluation in human resource development. *Advances in Developing Human Resources, 7*(1), 71–85.

Saadé, R., & Kira, D. (2009). Computer anxiety in e-learning: The effect of computer self-efficacy. *Journal of Information Technology Education, 8*, 178–191.

Sadler-Smith, E. (2009). *Learning and development for managers: Perspectives from research and practice*. Oxford, UK: Blackwell.

Saks, A. M., & Burke, L. A. (2012). An investigation into the relationship between training evaluation and the transfer of training. *International Journal of Training and Development, 16*(2), 118–127.

Salas, E., DeRouin, R. E., & Littrell, L. N. (2005). Research-based guidelines for designing distance learning. In H. G. Gueutal & D. L. Stone (Eds.), *The brave new world of eHR* (pp. 104–136). San Francisco: Jossey-Bass.

Salyers, V., Carter, L., Myers, S., & Barrett, P. (2014). The search for meaningful e-learning at Canadian universities: A multi-institutional research study. *International Review of Research in Open and Distance Learning, 15*(6), 313–337.

Santhanam, R., Sasidharan, S., & Webster, J. (2008). Using self-regulatory learning to enhance e-learning-based information technology training. *Information Systems Research, 19*(1), 26–47.

Sawang, S., Newton, C., & Jamieson, K. (2013). Increasing learners' satisfaction/intention to adopt more e-learning. *Education & Training, 55*(1), 83–105.

Senge, P. (1990). *The fifth discipline.* New York: Doubleday.

Sierra-Cedar. (2019). *The Sierra-Cedar 2019–2020 HR systems survey white paper—22nd annual edition.* Alpharetta: Sierra-Cedar.

Sitzmann, T., Bell, B. S., Kraiger, K., & Kanar, A. M. (2009). A multilevel analysis of the effect of prompting self-regulation in technology-delivered instruction. *Personnel Psychology, 62*, 697–734.

Sitzmann, T., Brown, K. G., Casper, W. J., Ely, K., & Zimmerman, R. D. (2008). A review and meta-analysis of the nomological network of trainee reactions. *Journal of Applied Psychology, 93*(2), 280–295.

Sitzmann, T., & Ely, K. (2011). A meta-analysis of self-regulated learning in work-related training and educational attainment: What we know and where we need to go. *Psychological Bulletin, 137*(3), 421–442.

Society for Human Resource Management. (2011). *Future Insights—The top trends for 2012 according to SHRM's HR subject matter expert panels.* Alexandria, VA: SHRM.

Soliman, F., & Spooner, K. (2000). Strategies for implementing knowledge management: Role of human resources management. *Journal of Knowledge Management, 4*(4), 337–345.

Stewart, J. (1999). *Employee development practice.* London: Financial Times/Pitman.

Sun, P., Tsai, R. J., Finger, G., Chen, Y., & Yeh, D. (2008). What drives a successful e-learning? An empirical investigation of the critical factors influencing learner satisfaction. *Computers & Education, 50*, 1183–1202.

Sweller, J. (1988). Cognitive load during problem solving: Effects on learning. *Cognitive Science, 12*, 257–285.

Torrance, M. (2016). What Is xAPI? *TD Magazine,* Monday, February 8, 2016. Retrieved from https://www.td.org/magazines/what-is-xapi

Tracey, J. B., Tannenbaum, S. I., & Kavanagh, M. J. (1995). Applying trained skills on the job: The importance of the work environment. *Journal of Applied Psychology, 80*, 239–252.

Training. (2014). *2014 Training industry report.* Minneapolis, MN: Lakewood Media Group, LLC.

Troshani, I., Jerram, C., & Rao Hill, S. (2011). Exploring the public sector adoption of HRIS. *Industrial Management & Data Systems, 111*(3), 470–488.

Velada, R., Caetano, A., Michel, J. W., Lyons, B. D., & Kavanagh, M. J. (2007, December). The effects of training design, individual characteristics, and work environment on transfer of training. *International Journal of Training and Development, 11*(4), 282–294.

Warr, P. B., Allan, C., & Birdi, K. (1999). Predicting three levels of learning outcomes. *Journal of Occupational and Organizational Psychology, 72*, 351–375.

Warr, P., Bird, M., & Rackham, N. (1970). *Evaluation of management training.* Aldershot, UK: Gower.

Webster, J., & Hackley, P. (1997). Teaching effectiveness in technology-mediated distance learning. *Academy of Management Journal, 40*(6), 1282–1309.

Welsh, E. T., Wanberg, C. R., Brown, K. G., & Simmering, M. J. (2003). E-learning: emerging uses, empirical results and future directions. *International Journal of Training and Development, 7*(4), 245–258.

Wright, P. M., Dunford, B. B., & Snell, S. A. (2001). Human resources and the resource based view of the firm. *Journal of Management, 27*(6), 701–720.

Yahya, S., & Goh, W.-K. (2002). Managing human resources toward achieving knowledge management. *Journal of Knowledge Management, 6*(5), 457–468.

Yang, Y., & Durrington, V. (2010). Investigation of students' perceptions of online course. *International Journal on E-Learning, 9*(3), 341–361.

Yanson, R., & Johnson, R. D. (2016). An empirical examination of e-learning design: The role of trainee socialization and complexity in short term training. *Computers & Education, 101*, 43–54.

Yukselturk, E., Ozekes, S., & Turel, Y. K. (2014). Predicting dropout student: An application of data mining methods in an online education program. *European Journal of Open, Distance and E-Learning, 17*(1), 119–133.

Chapter 11

Accenture. (2014). The future of HR: Five technology imperatives. Retrieved from: https://www.accenture.com/_acnmedia/accenture/conversion-assets/dotcom/documents/global/pdf/digital_1/accenture-oracle-hcm-ebook-future-of-hr-five-technology-imperatives.pdf

Adams, J. S. (1963). Toward an understanding of inequity. *Journal of Abnormal and Social Psychology, 67*, 422–436.

Adams, J. S. (1965). Inequity in social exchange. In L. Berkowitz (Ed.), *Advances in experimental social psychology*, 267–299. New York: Academic Press.

Ashley, D. (2006). Intuitive technologies increase employee adoption of human resource solutions. *Compensation & Benefits Review, 38*(1), 62–68.

Banks, C. G., & May, K. E. (1999). Performance management: The real glue in organizations. In A. I. Kraut & A. K. Korman (Eds.), *Evolving practices in human resource management: Responses to a changing world of work* (pp. 118–145). San Francisco: Jossey-Bass.

Bernardin, H. J., Hagan, C. M., Kane, J. S., & Villanova, P. (1998). Effective performance management: A focus on precision, customers, and situational constraints. In J. W. Smither (Ed.), *Performance appraisal: State of the art in practice* (pp. 3–48). San Francisco: Jossey-Bass.

Bing, J. W. (2004). Metrics for assessing human process on work teams. *IHRIM Journal, 8*(6), 26–31.

Brink, S., & McDonnell, S. (2003). e-Compensation. In *The e-merging technologies series go-to-guide* (pp. 4.1–4.18). Burlington, MA: IHRIM Press.

Ceccon, A. (2004). The real value statement: Aggregating pay and benefits on the Internet. *Compensation & Benefits Review, 36*(6), 53–58.

CedarCrestone. (2014). CedarCrestone 2013–2014 HR Systems Survey HR Technologies, Deployment Approaches, Value, and Metrics 16th Annual. Retrieved May 15, 2014, from http://www.cedarcrestone.com/media/whitepapers/CedarCrestone_2013-HRSS-HRTech-100713.pdf

Charles, E. W., Kurlander, P., & Savage, B. (2000). Tracking sales performance. *ACA News, 43*(3), 38–41.

Cocks, D. J., & Gould, D. (2001). Sales compensation: A new technology-enabled strategy. *Compensation & Benefits Review, 33*(1), 27–31.

Cohen, A. J., & Hall, M. E. (2005). Automating your performance and competency evaluation process. *WorldatWork Journal, 14*(3), 64–70.

Dawson, S. (1997). Leveraging an intranet for employee self-service: A Q & A with Unisys corporation. IHRIM. *link, 2*(3), 54–65.

Evans, E. M. (2001). Internet-age performance management: Lessons from high-performing organizations. In A. J. Walker (Ed.), *Web-based human resources: The technologies and trends that are transforming HR* (pp. 65–82). New York: McGraw-Hill.

Flowers, L. A., Tudor, T. R., & Trumble, R. R. (1997). Computer-assisted performance appraisal systems. *Journal of Compensation and Benefits, 12*(6), 34–35.

Forrer, S. E., & Leibowitz, Z. B. (1991). *Using computers in human resources: How to select and make the best use of automated HR systems*. San Francisco: Jossey-Bass.

Gale, S. F. (2002). How three companies merged HR and payroll. *Workforce, 81*(1), 64–67.

Gayeski, D. (2015). Will generation Z even care about HR technology? *Workforce Solution Review*, May, pp. 9–11.

Gillespie, P. (2017). Intuit: gig economy is 34% of US workforce. CNN Business. Retrieved from https://money.cnn.com/2017/05/24/news/economy/gig-economy-intuit/index.html

How HRIS can help with SOX compliance. (2005). *HR Focus, 82*(10), 7, 10.

Jones, S. D., & Schilling, D. J. (2000). *Measuring team performance: A step-by-step, customizable approach for managers, facilitators, and team leaders*. San Francisco: Jossey-Bass.

Keys, C. (2015). Creating a consumer-oriented HR platform for global communication. *Workforce Solution Review*, May, pp. 16–19.

König, C. (2015). HR technologies for the multi-generational workforce. *Workforce Solution Review*, May, pp. 20–23.

Koski, L. (2003). Executive/manager self-service: Stat Street Corporation's annual incentive program. *Compensation & Benefits Review, 35*(2), 21–25.

Locke, E. A., & Latham, G. P. (1984). *Goal setting: A motivational theory that works.* Englewood Cliffs, N. J.: Prentice Hall.

Locke, E. A., & Latham, G. P. (1990a). *A theory of goal-setting and task performance.* Englewood Cliffs, N. J.: Prentice Hall.

Locke, E. A., & Latham, G. P. (1990b). Work motivation and satisfaction: Light at the end of the tunnel. *Psychological Science, 1,* 240–246.

Locke, E. A., Shaw, K. M., Saari, L. M., & Latham, G. P. (1981). Goal-setting and task performance: 1969–1980. *Psychological Bulletin, 90,* 125–152.

Manyika, J., Lund, S., Chui, M., Bughin, J., Woetzel, J., Batra, P. and Ko, R. (2017). Jobs lost, jobs gained: workforce transitions in a time of automation. McKinsey & Company. Retrieved from https://www.mckinsey.com/~/media/mckinsey/featured%20insights/Future%20of%20Organizations/What%20the%20future%20of%20work%20will%20mean%20for%20jobs%20skills%20and%20wages/MGI-Jobs-Lost-Jobs-Gained-Report-December-6-2017.ashx

McCormack, J. (2004). Compliance tools: Technology can help HR stay on the right side of the law. *HR Magazine, 49*(3), 95–98.

Menefee, J. A. (2000). The value of pay data on the Web: Nominal or real? *Workspan, 43*(9), 25–28.

Metlife. (2019). The gig economy: opportunities, challenges, and employer strategies. Retrieved from https://www.metlife.com/content/dam/metlifecom/us/ebts/pdf/MetLife_EBTS-GigReport_2019.pdf

Meyer, G. (1998). 360 on the net: A computer toolkit for multirater performance feedback. *HR Magazine, 43*(11), 46–50.

Moynihan, J. J. (2000). HIPPA compliance offers human resource department savings. *Healthcare Financial Management, 54*(3), 82–83.

Perlmutter, A. L. (2002). Taking motivation and recognition online. *Compensation & Benefits Review, 34*(2), 70–74.

Robb, D. (2004). Marking time. *HR Magazine, 49*(7), 111–115.

Robert Half. (2018). What you should know about the latest in payroll technology. Retrieved from https://www.roberthalf.com/blog/salaries-and-skills/what-you-should-know-about-the-latest-in-payroll-technology

Rogers, A. (2018). How AI is humanizing people management. *Workforce Solution Review,* July–September, pp. 25–26.

Sherman, E. (2005). Use technology to stay in SOX compliance. *HR Magazine, 50*(5), 95–99.

Stegner, R., & Kofahl, B. (2004). Case study: Human performance improvement model at work. *IHRIM Journal, 8*(6), 18–20.

Stiffler, M. A. (2001). Incentive compensation and the Web. *Compensation & Benefits Review, 33*(1), 15–19.

Stone, D. L., Deadrick, D. L., Lukaszewski, K. M., & Johnson, R. (2015). The influence of technology on the future of human resource knowledge. *Human Resource Management Review, 23*(1), 216–231.

Teer, M. S. (1997). Surfing for benefits. IHRIM.*link, 2*(3), 66–74.

Thompson, D. (2018). AI, analytics, big data: the big three working together for payroll. American Payroll Association. Retrieved from https://www.americanpayroll.org/news-resources/apa-news/news-detail/2018/02/27/ai-analytics-big-data-the-big-three-working-together-for-payroll

Tobin, N. (2002). Can technology ease the pain of salary surveys? *Public Personnel Management, 31*(1), 65–77.

U.S. Department of Labor & U.S. Department of Justice. (1978). Uniform guidelines on employee selection procedures. (1978). *Federal Register, 43*(166), 38290–39309.

Van De Voort, D. M., & McDonnell, S. W. (2003). Computers and compensation. In W. A. Caldwell (Ed.), *The compensation guide* (pp. 21–32). Minneapolis, MN: Thomson/West.

Walker, A. J. (1987). *HRIS development: A project team guide to building an effective personnel information system.* New York: Van Nostrand Reinhold.

Weeks, B. (2000). Setting sales force compensation in the Internet age. *Compensation & Benefits Review, 32*(2), 25–42.

Wisskirchen, G., Biacabe, B. T., Bormann, U., Muntz, A., Niehaus, G., Soler, G. J., and von Brauchitsch, B. (2017). Artificial intelligence and robotics and their impact on the workplace. International Bar Association; Global Employment Institute. Retrieved from https://www.ibanet.org/Document/Default. aspx? DocumentUid=c06aa1a3-d355-4866-beda-9a3a8779ba6e

Wright, A. (2003). Tools for automating complex compensation programs. *Compensation & Benefits Review, 35*(6), 53–61.

Zafar, H. (2013). Human resource information systems: Information security concerns for organizations. *Human Resource Management Review, 23*(1), 105–113.

Zingheim, P. K., & Schuster, J. R. (2004). What's the next great pay and reward innovation? Business value, paying for skill, and the Internet! *IHRIM Journal, 8*(5), 47–50.

Zingheim, P. K., & Schuster, J. R. (2005). Evaluating human resource pay and reward computer and Web products. *Compensation & Benefits Review, 37*(5), 42–45.

Chapter 12

Alkhadher, O., Anderson, N., & Clarke, D. (1994). Computer-based testing: A review of recent developments in research and practice. *European Work and Organizational Psychologist, 4*(2), 169–189.

Beer, M., Spector, B. A., Lawrence, P. R., Mills, D. Q., & Walton, R. E. (1984). *Managing human assets*. Simon and Schuster.

Bondarouk, T. V. (2014). *Orchestrating the e-HRM symphony*. Universiteit Twente.

Bondarouk, T., & Furtmueller, E. (2012, July). Electronic human resource management: Four decades of empirical evidence. In *Academy of Management Proceedings* (Vol. 2012, No. 1, p. 15668). Briarcliff Manor, NY: Academy of Management.

Bondarouk, T., & Ruël, H. (2005). Does E-HRM contribute to HRM effectiveness? Results from a quantitative study in a Dutch ministry. In *4th International Conference of the Dutch HRM Network, Enschede, The Netherlands*.

Bondarouk, T. V., & Ruël, H. J. (2009). Electronic human resource management: Challenges in the digital era. *The International Journal of Human Resource Management, 20*(3), 505–514.

Bondarouk, T., & Ruël, H. (2013). The strategic value of e-HRM: Results from an exploratory study in a governmental organization. *The International Journal of Human Resource Management, 24*(2), 391–414.

Bondarouk, T., Schilling, D., & Ruël, H. (2016). eHRM adoption in emerging economies: The case of subsidiaries of multinational corporations in Indonesia. *Canadian Journal of Administrative Sciences/Revue Canadienne des Sciences de l'Administration, 33*(2), 124–137.

CedarCrestone. (2014). *CedarCrestone 2014–2015 HR systems survey: HR technologies, service delivery approaches, and metrics* (17th annual edition). Alpharetta, GA: Author.

Cober, R. T., Brown, D. J., Blumental, A. J., Doverspike, D., & Levy, P. (2000). The quest for the qualified job surfer: It's time the public sector catches the wave. *Public Personnel Management, 29*(4), 479–496.

Davis, F. D., Bagozzi, R. P., & Warshaw, P. R. (1989). User acceptance of computer technology: a comparison of two theoretical models. *Management Science, 35*(8), 982–1003.

Dulebohn, J. H., & Johnson, R. D. (2013). Human resource metrics and decision support: A classification framework. *Human Resource Management Review, 23*(1), 71–83.

EIU. (2019). The experience of work in Europe: The role of technology in productivity and engagement. Economist Intelligence Unit report. https://theexperienceofwork. economist.com/. Retrieved on 20-11-2019.

Gueutal, H. G., & Falbe, C. M. (2005). eHR: Trends in delivery methods. In H. G. Gueutal & D. L. Stone (Eds.), *The brave new world of eHR: Human resources management in the digital age*, 190–225.

Gueutal, H. G., Marler, J. H., & Falbe, C. M. (2007). Skill sets for the e-HR world. *IHRIM Journal, 11*(2), 9–15.

Haines, V. Y., & Petit, A. (1997). Conditions for successful human resource information systems. *Human Resource Management*. Published in Cooperation with the School of Business Administration, the University of Michigan, and in alliance with the Society of Human Resources Management, *36*(2), 261–275.

Johnson, R. D., Lukaszewski, K. M., & Stone, D. L. (2016a). The evolution of the field of human resource information systems: Co-evolution of technology and HR processes. *Communications of the Association for Information Systems*, *38*(1), 28.

Johnson, R. D., Lukaszewski, K. M., & Stone, D. L. (2016b). Introduction to the special issue on human resource information systems and human computer interaction. *AIS Transactions on Human–Computer Interaction*, *8*(4), 149–159.

Johnson, R. D., & Stone, D. L. (2019). Advantages and unintended consequences of using electronic human resource management (eHRM) processes. In R. Landers (Ed.), *Cambridge handbook of technology and employee behavior* (pp. 879–920). Cambridge, UK: Cambridge University Press.

Lengnick-Hall, M. L., & Moritz, S. (2003). The Impact of e-HR on the HRM function. *Journal of Labor Research*, *24*(3), 365–379.

Lepak, D. P., & Snell, S. A. (1998). Virtual HR: Strategic human resource management in the 21st century. *Human Resource Management Review*, *8*(3), 215–234.

Marler, J. H., & Parry, E. (2016). Human resource management, strategic involvement and e-HRM technology. *The International Journal of Human Resource Management*, 27, 2233–2253.

Orlikowski, W. J. (2010). Technology and organization: Contingency all the way down. *Research in the Sociology of Organizations*, *29*, 239–246.

Parry, E., & Tyson, S. (2011). Desired goals and actual outcomes of e-HRM. *Human Resource Management Journal*, *21*(3), 335–354.

Ruël, H., & Bondarouk, T. (2014). E-HRM research and practice: Facing the challenges ahead. In *Handbook of strategic e-Business management* (pp. 633–653). Berlin, Heidelberg: Springer.

Ruël, H., Bondarouk, T., & Looise, J. K. (2004). E-HRM: Innovation or irritation. An explorative empirical study in five large companies on web-based HRM. *Management Revue*, 364–380.

Shapiro, D. L., Von Glinow, M. A., & Xiao, Z. (2007). Toward polycontextually sensitive research methods. *Management and Organization Review*, *3*(1), 129–152.

Stone, D. L., Deadrick, D. L., Lukaszewski, K. M., & Johnson, R. (2015). The influence of technology on the future of human resource management. *Human Resource Management Review*, *25*(2), 216–231.

Strohmeier, S. (2007). Research in e-HRM: Review and implications. *Human Resource Management Review*, *17*(1), 19–37.

Ulrich, D. (1996). *Human resource champions: The next agenda for adding value and delivering results*. Harvard: Harvard Business Press.

Voermans, M., & Veldhoven, M. V. (2007). Attitude towards E-HRM: An empirical study at Philips. *Personnel Review*, *36*(6), 887–902.

Welsh, E. T., Wanberg, C. R., Brown, K. G., & Simmering, M. J. (2003). E-learning: Emerging uses, empirical results and future directions. *International Journal of Training and Development*, *7*(4), 245–258.

Chapter 13

Adler, N. J. (2002). *International dimensions of organizational behavior*. Cincinnati, OH: South-Western.

Adlung, I. C. (2010, March). The male-female salary gap. *Regional HR update: Europe, HRinsights*. New York: Jeitosa Group International.

Ark, B., Ozyildirim, A., & Levanon, G. (2015, November). *Global economic outlook 2016: Anticipating labor market tightness at times of slow global growth (CHRO Strategic Implications)*. (Report No. TBC-1595–Global-Economic-Outlook-2016-CHRO). New York: The Conference Board.

Bartlett, C., & Ghoshal, S. (1998). *Managing across borders: The transnational solution* (2nd ed.). Harvard Business School Press.

Batyski, H. (December 2007/January 2008). *Global HRIS: It's just a matter of turning it on, right?* IHRIM.*link*, *12*(8–6), 38–39.

Beaman, K. V. (2008). Think local, act globally: The collaborative transnational HRIT organization. IHRIM.*link*, *12*(6), 6, 10.

Beaman, K. V. (2011). *2011–2012 going global report: HCM trends in globalization.* New York: Jeitosa Group International.

Black, J. S. (2000, January/February). Coming home. *HR World,* 30–32.

Black, J. S., & Mendenhall, M. (1989). A practical but theory-based framework for selecting cross-cultural training methods. *Human Resource Management, 28*(4), 511–539.

Borman, W. C., & Motowidlo, S. J. (1993). Expanding the criterion domain to include elements of contextual performance. In N. Schmitt & W. C. Borman (Eds.), *Personnel selection in organizations* (pp. 71–98). San Francisco: Jossey-Bass.

Briscoe, D. R., & Schuler, R. S. (2004). *International human resource management* (2nd ed.). London: Routledge.

Colquitt, J. A., Conlon, D. E., Wesson, M. J., Porter, C., & Ng, K. Y. (2001). Justice at the millennium: A meta-analytic review of 25 years of organizational justice research. *Journal of Applied Psychology, 86*(3), 425–445.

Dowling, P., Festing, M., & Engle, A. D. (2013). *International human resource management.* (6th ed.). Boston, MA: CENGAGE.

Evans, P., Pucik, V., & Barsoux, J. (2002). *The global challenge: Frameworks for international human resource management.* New York: McGraw-Hill.

Feldman, D. C., & Tompson, H. B. (1993). Expatriation, repatriation, and domestic geographical relocation: An empirical investigation of adjustment to new job assignments. *Journal of International Business Studies, 24,* 507–529.

GLOBE Research Team. (2002). *Culture, leadership, and organizational practices: The GLOBE findings.* Thousand Oaks, CA: Sage.

GMAC Global Relocation Services & Windham International. (2002, October). *Global relocation trends 2002 survey report.* New York: Author.

Gregersen, H. B., Hite, J. M., & Black, J. S. (1996). Expatriate performance appraisal in U.S. multinational firms. *Journal of International Business Studies, 27,* 711–738.

Gueutal, H. G., & Stone, D. L. (Eds.). (2005). *The brave new world of e-HR.* San Francisco: Jossey-Bass.

Harzing, A.W, & Pinnington, A. (2014). *International human resource management.* Thousand Oaks, CA: Sage Publishing.

Hofstede, G. (1991). *Cultures and organizations.* New York: McGraw-Hill.

Johnson, R., & Gueutal, H. (2011). *Transforming HR through technology.* Alexandria, VA: Society for Human Resource Management (SHRM).

Mason, K. (2009). Streamlining HRMS for a global business. IHRIM.link, *13*(6), 34–35.

Mendenhall, M., Dunbar, E., & Oddou, G. (1987). Expatriate selection, training, and career-pathing: A review and critique. *Human Resource Management, 26,* 331–345.

Noe, R. A., Hollenbeck, J. R., Gerhart, B., & Wright, P. M. (2017). *Human resource management: Gaining a competitive advantage* (10th ed.). New York: McGraw-Hill Irwin.

Organizational Research Counselors. (2002, September). *Dual careers and international assignments survey.* Retrieved from *https://www.orc-netsafe.com/surveys/dual.cfm* (Name changed to ORC Worldwide in 2003 and to Mercer in 2010.)

Organization for the Advancement of Structured Information Systems (OASIS). (2006, May). *OASIS reference model for service oriented architecture 1.0.* Retrieved from http://www.oasis-open.org/committees/download.php/18486/pr-2changes.pdf

Özbilgin, M. F., Groutsis, D., & Harvey, W. S. (2014). *International human resource management.* Cambridge, UK: Cambridge University Press.

Poe, A. C. (2000, March). Focus on international HR: Welcome back. *HR Magazine,* 94–105.

Roberts, W. (2000, August). Going global. *HR Magazine, 45*(10).

Ruël, H. J. M., & Bondarouk, T. (2012). A cross-national perspective on the intersection between information technology and HRM. In C. Brewster & W. Mayrhofer (Eds.), *Handbook of research on comparative human resource management* (pp. 416–448). Cheltenham, UK: Edward Elgar Publishing.

Schuler, R., Budhwar, P. S., & Florkowski, G. W. (2002). International human resource management: Review and critique. *International School of Management Review, 4*(1), 41–70.

Schuler, R., & Tarique, I. (2007). International human resource management: A North American perspective, a thematic update, and suggestions for future research. *International Journal of Human Resource Management, 18,* 717–744.

Snell, S. A., Morris, S. S., & Bohlander, G. W. (2016). *Managing human resources* (17th ed.). Boston, MA: CENGAGE.

Society for Human Resource Management (SHRM). (2009). *Global diversity and inclusion: Perceptions, practices and attitudes.* Alexandria, VA: Author.

Solomon, C. M. (1995, January). Repatriation: Up, down, or out. *Personnel Journal,* 21–26.

Trompenaars, F. (1992). *The seven cultures of capitalism.* New York: Currency Doubleday.

Tung, R. (1981). Selecting and training of personnel for overseas assignments. *Columbia Journal of World Business, 16,* 68–78.

Tung, R. (1998). A contingency framework of selection and training of expatriates revisited. *Human Resource Management Review, 8*(1), 23–37.

U.S. Department of Labor. (2012). *International comparisons of hourly compensation costs for production workers in manufacturing.* Washington, DC: Bureau of Labor Statistics. Retrieved from http://www.bls.gov/news .release/pdf/ichcc.pdf

Von Glinow, M. A., Drost, E. A., & Teagarden, M. B. (2002). Converging on IHRM best practices: Lessons learned from a globally distributed consortium on theory and practice. *Human Resource Management, 41,* 123–140.

Walker, A. J. (Ed.). (2001). *Web-based human resources.* New York: McGraw-Hill.

World Bank. (2016). *GDP (current US$).* Retrieved from http://www.worldbank.org/en/about/contacts.

World Trade Organization. (2015). *International trade statistics 2015.* Retrieved from https://www.wto.org/ english/res_e/statis_e/its2015_e/its15_highlights_e .pdf.

Chapter 14

Ayres, I. (2007). *Super crunchers: Why thinking-by-numbers is the new way to be smart.* New York: Bantam.

BLS. (2020). Bureau of Labor Statistics Employer Cost Trends. Retrieved May 14, 2020 from https://www.bls .gov/ect/

Becker, B. E., Huselid, M. A., & Ulrich, D. (2001). *The HR scorecard: Linking people, strategy and performance.* Boston: Harvard Business School Press.

Bintliff-Ritchie, J. (2006). Finding hidden gold using business intelligence to mine workforce data. *IHRIM-link,* June/July, 12–15.

Boudreau, J. W. (1989). Selection utility analysis: A review and agenda for future research. In M. Smith & I. Robertson (Eds.), *Advances in personnel selection and assessment* (pp. 227–258). London: John Wiley and Sons, Ltd.

Carlson, K. D., & Connerley, M. L. (2003). The staffing cycles framework: Viewing staffing as a system of decision events. *Journal of Management, 29*(1), 51–78.

Carlson, K. D., Connerley, M. L., & Mecham, R. L., III. (2002). Recruitment evaluation: The case for assessing the quality of applicants attracted. *Personnel Psychology, 55*(2), 461–490.

Cascio, W. F. (1987). *Costing human resources: The financial impact of behavior in organizations* (2nd ed.). Boston: Kent.

Cascio, W. F. (2000). *Costing human resources: The financial impact of behavior in organizations* (4th ed.). Boston: Kent.

Drake, N., & Robb, I. (2002). *Exit interviews.* Alexandria, VA: SHRM White Paper.

Fitz-enz, J. (1995). *How to measure human resources management* (2nd ed.). New York, NY: McGraw-Hill, Inc.

Galbreath, R. (2002). *Employee turnover hurts small and large company profitability.* Alexandria, VA: SHRM White Paper.

Fitz-enz, J. (2002). *How to measure human resources management* (3rd ed.). New York: McGraw-Hill.

Hawk, R. H. (1967). *The recruitment function.* New York: The American Management Association.

Hollmann, R. W. (2002). Absenteeism: Analyzing work absences (SHRM White Paper). Retrieved February 16, 2008 from www.shrm.org/hrresources/whitepapers_published/CMS_000381.asp

Huselid, M. A. (1995). The impact of human resource management on turnover, productivity, and corporate performance. *Academy of Management Journal, 38,* 635–672.

Kaplan, R. S., & Norton, D. P. (1996). *The balanced scorecard: Translating strategy into action.* Boston: Harvard Business School Press.

Kluttz, L. (2003). *Employment Management Association cost per hire staffing metrics survey.* Alexandria, VA: SHRM Research Department.

Lilly, F. (2001). *Four steps to computing training ROI.* Alexandria, VA: SHRM White Paper.

Munsterberg, H. (1913). *Psychology and industrial efficiency.* Boston: Houghton Mifflin.

Ofsanko, F. J., & Napier, N. K. (1990). *Effective human resource management techniques: A handbook for practitioners.* Alexandria, VA: SHRM White Paper.

Schmidt, F. L., & Hunter, J. E. (1998). The validity and utility of selection methods in personnel psychology: Practical and theoretical implications of 85 years of research findings. *Psychological Bulletin, 124*(2), 262.

Society of Human Resource Management (SHRM). (2010). *HR metrics toolkit.* Alexandria, VA: Author.

Sullivan, J. (2003). *HR metrics: The world class way.* Peterborough, NH: Kennedy Information, Inc.

Taylor, F. (1911). *The principles of scientific management.* London: Harper Brothers.

Vorhauser-Smith, S. (2014, November 10). The little word behind big data in HR. *Forbes Magazine.*

Chapter 15

Abreu, E. (2001). *Computer virus costs reach $10.7 billion this year.* Retrieved from http://www.crn.com/news/channel-programs/18816957/computer-virus-costs-reach-10-7-billion-this-year.htm

Americans with Disabilities Act of 1990. ¶ 602 § 102.

Austin, R. D., & Darby, C. A. R. (2003). The myth of secure computing. *Harvard Business Review, 81*(6), 120–126.

Black, S. L., Johnson A. F., Takach S. E., & Stone, D. M. (2012, August). *Factors affecting applicants' reactions to the collection of data in social network websites.* Paper accepted at the meeting of the Academy of Management, Boston, MA.

Boyle, R., & Panko, R. (2013). *Corporate computer security* (3rd ed.). Upper Saddle River, NJ: Pearson.

Canavan, S. (2003). *An information security policy: A development guide for large and small companies.* Bethesda, MD: SANS Institute. Retrieved from http://www.sans.org/reading_room/whitepapers/policyissues/information-security-policy-development-guide-large-small-companies_1331

Dash, E. (2006). *Ameriprise says stolen laptop had data on 230,000 people.* Retrieved from http://www.nytimes.com/2006/01/26/business/26data.html

David, J. (2002). Policy enforcement in the workplace. *Computers and Security, 27*(6), 506–513.

DeSanctis, G. (1986). Human resource information systems: A current assessment. *MIS Quarterly, 10*(1), 15–27.

Eddy, E., Stone-Romero, E. F., & Stone, D. L. (1999). Effects of information management policies on reactions to human resource information systems: An integration of privacy and procedural justice perspectives. *Personnel Psychology, 52,* 335–358.

Fair Labor Standards Act of 1938 as amended 29 U.S.C. § 201 et seq.

Framingham, H. H. (2008). *Employers use social networks in the hiring process.* Retrieved from news.nsf/care/63C6E9BE6E9BE6AD920C C2574C90003ADDD

Garg, A., Curtis, J., & Halper, H. (2003). Quantifying the financial impact of IT security breaches. *Information Management & Computer Security, 11*(2), 74–83.

General Data Protection Regulation. (2018). Regulation (EU) 2016/679 of the European Parliament. Retrieved from https://op.europa.eu/en/publication-detail/-/publication/3e485e15-11bd-11e6-ba9a-01aa75ed71a1/language-en/format-xhtml

Greenleaf, G. (2015). Global data privacy laws 2015: 109 countries, with European laws now a minority. *133*

Privacy Laws & Business International Report. https://papers.ssrn.com/sol3/papers.cfm?abstract_id=2603529

Health Insurance Portability and Accountability Act of 1996, Public Law No. 104–191.

Hinde, S. (2003). Cyber-terrorism in context. *Computers & Security, 22*(3), 188–192.

Holland, S. (2012). *Bank group warns of heightened risk of cyber attacks.* Retrieved from http://www.nbcnews.com/technology/technolog/bank-group-warns-heightened-risk-cyber-attacks-1B5995458

Kovach, K., & Cathcart, C. (1999). Human resource information systems (HRIS): Providing business with rapid data access, information exchange and strategic advantage. *Public Personnel Management, 28*(2), 275–282.

Lazzarotti, J.J., Gavejian, J. C., & Atrakchi, M. (2018, April 9). State data breach notification laws: Overview of the patchwork. Retrieved from https://www.jacksonlewis.com/publication/state-data-breach-notification-laws-overview-patchwork

Levine, M. & Date, J. (2015). 22 million affected by OPM hack, officials say. ABC News. Retrieved from https://abcnews.go.com/US/exclusive-25-million-affected-opm-hack-sources/story?id=32332731

Linowes, D. F. (2000). *Many companies fail to protect confidential employee data.* Retrieved from http://epic.org/privacy/workplace/linowesPR.html

Lukaszewski, K. M., & Johnson, A. F. (2017). Social networking sites, search engines, and the employment process. In G. Hertel, D. L. Stone, & R. D. Johnson (Eds.), *The Wiley Blackwell handbook of the psychology of the Internet at work* (pp. 231–256). Hoboken, NJ: John Wiley & Sons.

Lukaszewski, K. M., Stone, D. L., & Stone-Romero, E. F. (2008). The effects of the ability to choose the type of human resources system on perceptions of invasion of privacy and system satisfaction. *Journal of Business and Psychology, 23*, 73–86.

Mangieri, G. (2013). *Security breaches by public agencies.* Retrieved from http://www.khon2.com/content/news/editorschoice/story/EXCLUSIVE-Security-breaches-by-public-agencies/bbXQ-zolp0SyzE1Cga7zuA.cspx

Markus, H. R., & Kitayama, S. (1991a). Culture and the self: Implications for cognition, emotion, and motivation. *Psychological Review, 98*(2), 224.

Markus, H. R., & Kitayama, S. (1991b). Cultural variation in the self-concept. In *The self: Interdisciplinary approaches* (pp. 18–48). New York: Springer.

Microsoft. (2011). *Microsoft security intelligence report.* Retrieved from http://www.microsoft.com/security/sir/default.aspx

Moore, T., & Clayton, R. (2007). *An empirical analysis of the current state of phishing attack and defence.* Paper presented at the Workshop on the Economics of Information Security.

Narisi, S. (2009). MySpace's "drunken pirate" gets fired, sues employer. *HR Tech News.* Retrieved from http://www.hrtechnews.com/myspaces-drunken-pirate-gets-fired-sues-employer/

Pagliery, J. (2016). Cyber thieves siphon tax forms from ADP payroll data. Retrieved from http://money.cnn.com/2016/05/03/technology/adp-w2-forms-stolen/

Panko, R. (2003). *Corporate computer and network security.* Upper Saddle River, NJ: Prentice-Hall, Inc.

Personnel Policy Service, Inc. (2013). *ADA and prescription drug use at work Q&A.* Retrieved from http://www.ppsupublishers.com/ez/html/121608txtb.html

Pohlman, M. B. (2008). *Oracle identity management: Governance, risk, and compliance architecture* (3rd ed.). Boca Raton, FL: Auerbach Publications.

Ponemon. (2012). *2012 business banking trust study.* Retrieved from http://info.guardiananalytics.com/rs/guardiananalytics/images/2012_Business_Banking_Trust_Study_Exec_Summary.pdf

Ponemon. (2016). *Ponemon cost of data breach study.* Retrieved from http://www-03.ibm.com/security/data-breach/

Preston, J. (2011, July 20). Social media history becomes a new job hurdle. *The New York Times.* Retrieved from http://www.nytimes.com/2011/07/21/technology/social-media-history-becomes-a-new-job-hurdle.html?pagewanted=all&_r=0

Privacy Act of 1974: Privacy act regulation. (2010). Lanham, United States. Retrieved from http://search.proquest.com/docview/758859747?accountid=7122

Privacy Protection Study Commission. (1977). *The report of the privacy protection study commission: Personal privacy in an information society.* Washington, DC: U.S. Government Printing Office.

Privacy Protections in State Constitutions. (2012). Retrieved from http://www.ncsl.org/issues-research/telecom/privacy-protections-in-state-constitutions.aspx

Privacy Rights Clearinghouse. (2010). *500 million sensitive records breached since 2005.* Retrieved from http://www.privacyrights.org/500-million-records-breached

Roe v. Cheyenne Mountain Conference Resort, 124 F.3d 1221 (10th Cir. 1997), the Tenth Circuit, Retrieved from http //.www.ppsupublishers.com/ez/html/121608txtb.

Raine, L. (2018). How Americans feel about social media and privacy. *Pew Research Center.* Retrieved from https://www.pewresearch.org/fact-tank/2018/03/27/americans-complicated-feelings-about-social-media-in-an-era-of-privacy-concerns/

Roth, P. L, Bobko, P., Van Iddekinge, C. H., & Thatcher, J. B. (2012). *Using social media information for staffing decisions: Some unchartered territory in validity research.* Symposium presented at the Academy of Management Conference, Boston, MA.

Schneier, B. (2000). Computer security: Will we ever learn. *Crypto-Gram Newsletter.* Retrieved from http://www.schneier.com/crypto-gram-0005.html

Society for Human Resource Management (SHRM) & West Group. (2000). *Workplace privacy survey.* Retrieved from http://www.shrm.org/surveys

Socorro v. IMI Data Search and Hilton Hotels. (2003). Retrieved from http://il.findacase.com/research/wfrm-DocViewer.aspx/xq/fac.20030428_0001388.NIL.htm/qx

Stafford, T., & Urbaczewski, A. (2004). Spyware: The ghost in the machine. *Communications of the Association for Information Systems, 14,* 291–306.

Stallings, W., & Brown, L. (2008). *Computer security: Principles and practice.* Upper Saddle River, NJ: Pearson Prentice Hall.

Statista. (2019). Share of internet users who are more concerned about their online privacy compared to a year ago as of February 2019, by region. Retrieved from https://www.statista.com/statistics/373338/global-opinion-concern-online-privacy/

Stone, D. L., Krueger, D., & Takach, S. (2017). Social issues associated with the Internet at work. *The Wiley Blackwell handbook of the psychology of the Internet at work* (pp. 423–447). Hoboken, NJ: John Wiley & Sons.

Stone, D., Lukaszewski, K., & Isenhour, L. (2005). E-recruiting: Online strategies for attracting talent. In H. G. Gueutal & D. Stone (Eds.), *The brave new world of eHR: Human resources management in the digital age* (pp. 22–53). San Francisco: Jossey-Bass.

Stone, D. L., Lukaszewski, K., & Stone-Romero, E. F. (2001, August). *Privacy and human resources information systems.* Paper presented at the Annual Meeting of the Society of Industrial and Organizational Psychology, San Diego, CA.

Stone, D. L., & Stone-Romero, E. F. (1998). A multiple stakeholder model of privacy in organizations. In M. Schminke (Ed.), *Managerial ethics: Morally managing people and processes* (pp. 35–60). Mahwah, NJ: Lawrence Erlbaum.

Stone, D. L, Stone-Romero, E. F., & Lukaszewski, K. (2003). The functional and dysfunctional consequences of human resource information technology for organizations and their employees. In D. Stone (Ed.), *Advances in human performance and cognitive engineering research* (pp. 37–68). New York: Elsevier.

Stone, E. F., & Stone, D. L. (1990). Privacy in organizations: Theoretical issues, research findings, and protection strategies. In K. M. Rowland & G. R. Ferris (Eds.), *Research in personnel and human resources management* (pp. 349–411). Greenwich, CT: JAI Press.

Stone-Romero, E. F., Stone, D. L., & Salas, E. (2003). The influence of culture on role conceptions and role behavior in organisations. *Applied Psychology, 52*(3), 328–362.

Tansley, C., & Watson, T. (2000). Strategic exchange in the development of human resource information systems (HRIS). *New Technology Work and Employment, 15*(2), 108–122.

Triandis, H. C. (1994). *Culture and social behavior.* New York: McGraw-Hill.

Whitman, M. E., & Mattord, H. J. (2011). *Principles of information security* (Vol. 4). Boston, MA: Course Technology.

Wugmeister, M., & Taylor, N. D. (2008). Six states now require Social Security number protection policies. Retrieved from https://www.jdsupra.com/post/documentViewer.aspx?fid=da627d01-2b49-4239-9852-26274f107e74

Zeidner, R. (2007). How deep can you probe? *HR Magazine, 52*(10), 57–62.

Chapter 16

Adecco. (2014). Social recruiting. A global study. *The Adecco Global Study*, pp. 1–62.

Akiode, S. (2013, June 19). [INFOGRAPHIC] The social recruiting pocket guide. Available from http://socialmeep.com/infographic-the-social-recruiting-pocket-guide/ [22 October 2015].

Anderson, N. (2003). Applicant and recruiter reactions to new technology in selection: A critical review and agenda for future research, *International Journal of Selection and Assessment, 11*(2–3), 121–136.

Bennet, S. (2014). *The average Internet user has 5 social media accounts*, Available from http://www.adweek.com/socialtimes/social-media-accounts/502588 [25 September 2015].

Black, S. L., & Johnson, A. F. (2012). Employers' use of social networking in the selection process. *Journal of Social Media in Society, 1*(1), 7–29.

Black, S. L., Stone, D. L., & Johnson, A. F. (2015). Use of social networking websites on applicants' privacy. *Employee Responsibilities and Rights Journal, 27*(2), 115–159.

Black, S. L., Washington, M. L., & Schmidt, G. B. (2016). How to stay current in social media to be competitive in recruitment and selection in social media in employee recruitment and selection. In R. N. Landers & G. B. Schmidt (Eds.), *Social media in employee selection and recruitment.* Cham, Switzerland: Springer.

Brady, P. W., Thompson, L. F., Wuensch, K. L., & Grossnickle, W. F. (2003). Internet recruiting. The effects of webpage design features. *Social Science Computer Review, 21*(3), 374–385.

Brown, V. R., & Vaughn, E. D. (2011). The writing on the (Facebook) wall: The use of social networking sites in hiring decisions. *Journal of Business and Psychology, 26*(2), 219–225.

CareerArc. (2019). Twenty-three stats on the future of recruitment- infographic. Retrieved June 20, 2019, from http://www.careerarc.com/blog/2017/04/future-of-recruiting-study-infographic/

CareerBuilder. (2018). More than half of employers have found content on social media that caused them NOT to hire a candidate. Retrieved from http://press.careerbuilder.com/2018-08-09-More-Than-Half-of-Employers-Have-Found-Content-on-Social-Media-That-Caused-Them-NOT-to-Hire-a-Candidate-According-to-Recent-CareerBuilder-Survey

CareerProfiles. (2019). 11 social media recruiting statistics to make you rethink your current strategies. Retrieved from https://www.careerprofiles.com/blog/social-media-recruitment-statistics-for-hiring/

Chapman, D. S., & Webster, J. (2003). The use of technologies in the recruiting, screening, and selection processes for job candidates. *International Journal of Selection and Assessment, 11*(2–3), 113–120.

Civil Rights Act of 1964 § 7, 42 U.S.C. §2000e et seq. (1964). Retrieved from the Equal Employment Opportunity Commission website: http://www.eeoc.gov/laws/statutes/titlevii.cfm.

Claypoole, T. F. (2014, Jan.). Privacy and social media. *Business Law Today*, pp. 1–4.

Colao, J. J. (2012, September 12). *With Facebook, your recruitment pool is one billion people.* Retrieved from http://www.forbes.com/sites/jjcolao/2012/09/12/with-facebook-your-recruitment-pool-is-one-billion-people/

Dave, R. (2011). How to engage in social media: A Dell perspective. *Dell Power Solutions.* http://i.dell.com/sites/content/business/solutions/power/en/Documents/ps1q11-20110266-socialmedia.pdf

Davison, H. K., Maraist, C., & Bing, M. N. (2011). Friend or foe? The promise and pitfalls of using social networking sites for HR decisions. *Journal of Business & Psychology, 26*(2), 153–159.

Davison, H., Maraist, C., Hamilton, R., & Bing, M. (2012). To screen or not to screen? Using the internet for selection decisions. *Employee Responsibilities and Rights Journal, 24*(1), 1–21. doi:10.1007/s10672-011-9178-y

Devine, P. G., Forscher, P. S., Austin, A. J., & Cox, W. T. L. (2012). Long-term reduction in implicit race bias: A prejudice habit-breaking intervention. *Journal of Experimental Social Psychology, 23*(1), 18–39.

DiMicco, J., Millen, D. R., Geyer, W., Dugan, C., Brownholtz, B., & Muller, M. (2008, November). Motivations for social networking at work. In *Proceedings of the 2008 ACM conference on computer-supported cooperative work* (pp. 711–720).

Dragon Social. (2019). 10 most popular social media sites in China (2019). Updated. Retrieved August 1, 2019, from https://www.dragonsocial.net/blog/social-media-in-china/#WeChat

Dreher, S. (2014). Social media and the world of work. *Corporate Communications: An International Journal, 19*(4), 344–356.

Ehrlich, K., & Shami, N. S. (2010). Microblogging inside and outside the workplace. *Proceedings of the Fourth International Conference on Weblogs and Social Media* (pp. 42–49). Menlo Park, CA: AAAI Press.

Elzweig, B., Roberto, K. J., & Johnson, A. F. (2017). Political ideology as a proxy for disparate impact discrimination. *Southern Law Journal, 27*(2), 277–292.

Facebook. (2019). About us. Available from https://newsroom.fb.com/company-info/

Ferron, M., Frassoni, M., Massa, P., Napolitano, M., & Setti, D. (2010). *An empirical analysis on social capital and Enterprise 2.0 participation in a research institute.* Proceedings of the 2010 International Conference on Advances in Social Networks Analysis and Mining (pp. 391–392). Los Alamitos, CA: IEEE Computer Society Press. doi:10.1109/asonam.2010.68

Fuller, J. B., Hester, K., Barnett, T., Frey, L., Relyea, C., & Beu, D. (2006). Perceived external prestige and internal respect: new insights into the organizational identification process. *Human Relations, 59*(6), 815–846.

Galli, T. (2014, December 19). Fired worker's fate focuses attention of social media policies. Retrieved from: http://www.wkow.com/story/27674626/2014/12/19/fired-workers-fate-focuses-attention-on-social-media-policies.

Genova, G. L. (2009). No place to play: Current employee privacy rights in social networking sites. *Business Communication Quarterly, 72*(1), 97–101.

Global Digital Report. (2018). We are social. Retrieved from https://digitalreport.wearesocial.com

Global Digital Report. (2019). We are social. Retrieved form https://wearesocial.com/global-digital-report-2019

Gordon, P., & Argento, Z. (2014). *NLRB's recent Triple Play decision tackles two critical social media issues for employers.* Littler.

Grasz, J. (2014). Number of employers passing on applicants due to social media post continues to rise, according to new CareerBuilder survey. Retrieved from http://www.carreerbuilder.com.

Gregory, C. K., Meade, A. W., & Thompson, L. F. (2013). Understanding internet recruitment via signaling theory and the elaboration likelihood model, *Computers in Human Behavior, 29*(5), 1949–1959.

Gross, R., & Acquisti, A. (2005, November). Information revelation and privacy in online social networks. In *Proceedings of the 2005 ACM workshop on Privacy in the electronic society*, 71–80.

Hader, A. L., & Brown, E. D. (2010). Legal briefs. Patient privacy and social media. *AANA Journal, 78*(4), 270–274.

Harter, J. (2018). Employee engagement on the rise in the U.S. Retrieved August 2, 2019, from https://news.gallup.com/poll/241649/employee-engagement-rise.aspx

Hausknecht, J. P., Day, D. V., & Thomas, S. C. (2004). Applicant reactions to selection procedures: An updated model and meta-analysis. *Personnel Psychology, 57*(3), 639–683.

Hawley, D. (2014, November 12). Why 60 million employees use social media to advocate for their companies. *Advertising Age.* Retrieved from: http://adage.com/article/digitalnext/60-million-employees-social-media-advocate/295823/

Heathfield, S. (2015). Use social media for recruiting, screening, and background checks? Available from http://humanresources.about.com/od/selectemployees/qt/why-use-social-media-for-recruiting-and-screening.htm [22 September 2015].

Hootsuite. (2019). The global state of digital in 2019 Report. Retrieved June 5, 2019, from https://hootsuite.com/pages/digital-in-2019

Hull, J. (2011). 50% reduction on recruitment costs: how social media became my best friend, *HR Magazine Online* 27 April 2011). Available from: http://www.hrmagazine.co.uk/hro/features/1019381/-reduction-recruitment-costs-social-media-friend. [15 March 2015].

Internet World Stats. (2019). Usage and population statistics. Retrieved August 1, 2019, from https://www.internetworldstats.com/top20.htm

Jobvite. (2014). *2014 Social recruiting survey.* Available from https://www.jobvite.com/.../2014/.../Jobvite_SocialRecruiting_Survey2014.pdf

John, A., & Seligmann, D. (2006). Collaborative tagging and expertise in the enterprise. *Proceedings of the 15th International Conference on World Wide Web.* New York: ACM. doi:10.1.1.134.296

Johnson, A. F., Lukaszewski, K. M., Isenhour, L. C., Murphy, S., Roberto, K. J., Schmidt, G. B., & Lievens, F. (2019). The use and collection of social media information and its impact on human resource management. In *Academy of Management Proceedings.* Briarcliff Manor, NY: Academy of Management.

Johnson, R. D., & Gueutal, H. G. (2014). E-selection in recruitment. Research-based tips for increasing effectiveness of e-selection: Part II. *Workforce Solutions Review.* 39–41.

Kaplan, A. M., & Haenlein, M. (2010). Users of the world, unite! The challenges and opportunities of social media. *Business Horizons, 53*(1), 59–68.

Katarsky, C. (2010, August 24). Nurse fired for HIPAA violation after discussing cop-killer patient: Was it fair? Retrieved from http://www.healthcarebusinesstech.com/nurse-fired-for-hipaa-violation-after-discussing-cop-killer-patient/.

Kuhn, P., & Skuterud, M. (2000). Job search methods: Internet versus traditional. *Monthly Labor Review, 123*(10), 3–11.

Kluemper, D. H., & Rosen, P. A. (2009). Future employment selection methods: Evaluating social networking web sites. *Journal of Managerial Psychology, 24*(6), 567–580.

Kluemper, D. H., Rosen, P. A., & Mossholder, K. W. (2012). Social networking websites, personality ratings and the organizational context: More than meets the eye? *Journal of Applied Psychology, 22*(2), 1143–1172.

Lackey Jr., M. E., & Minta, J. P. (2012). Lawyers and social media: The legal ethics of tweeting, Facebooking and blogging. *Touro L. Rev., 28*, 149.

Lam, H. (2016). Social media dilemmas in the employment context. *Employee Relations, 38*(3), 420–437.

Landers, R. N., & Callan, R. C. (2014). Validation of the beneficial and harmful work-related social media behavioral taxonomies: Development of the work-related social media questionnaire. *Social Science Computer Review, 32*(5), 628–646.

Laroche, M., Habibi, M. R., Richard, M. O., & Sankaranarayanan, R. (2012). The effects of social media based brand communities on brand community markers, value creation practices, brand trust and brand loyalty. *Computer Human Behavior, 28*(5), 1755–1767.

Levinson, M. (2010). Social networking ever more critical to job search success. *CIO Magazine.* Retrieved May 1, 2016, from http://www.cio.com/article/print/598151.

LinkedIn. (2019). About us. Retrieved from https://news.linkedin.com/about-us

Lucero, M. A., Allen, R. E., & Elzweig, B. (2013). Managing employee social networking: Evolving views from the National Labor Relations Board. *Employee Responsibilities and Rights Journal, 25*(3), 143–158.

Madera, J. M. (2012). Using social networking websites as a selection tool: The role of selection process fairness and job pursuit intentions. *International Journal of Hospitality Management, 31*(4), 1276–1282.

Madigan, J., & Macan, T. H. (2005). Improving applicant reactions by altering test administration. *Applied H.R.M. Research. 10*(2), 73–88.

McDonald, S. (2011). What's in the "old boys" network? Assessing social capital in gendered and racialized networks. *Social Networks, 33*(4), 317–330.

McManus, M. A., & Ferguson, M. W. (2003). Biodata, personality, and demographic differences of recruits from three sources. *International Journal of Selection and Assessment, 11*(2/3), 175–183.

Meister, J. (2014). 2014: The year social HR matters. *Forbes, 1*(6), 1.

Miles, S. J., & Mangold, W. G. (2014). Employee voice: Untapped resource or social media time bomb? *Business Horizons, 57*(3), 401–411.

Moqbel, M., Nevo, S., & Kock, N. (2013). Organizational members' use of social networking sites and job performance: An exploratory study. *Information Technology & People, 26*(3), 240–264.

National Conference of State Legislatures (NCSL). (2019). State social media privacy laws. http://www.ncsl.org/research/telecommunications-and-information-technology/state-laws-prohibiting-access-to-social-media-usernames-and-passwords.aspx

O'Brien, C. (2019). Social media use. What countries use it most & what are they using. Retrieved June 4, 2019, from https://digitalmarketinginstitute.com/en-us/blog/social-media-what-countries-use-it-most-and-what-are-they-using

O'Connor, K. W., Schmidt, G. B., & Drouin, M. (2016). Helping workers understand and follow social media policies. *Business Horizons*, *59*(2), 205–211.

Ollier-Malaterre, A., Rothbard, N. P., & Berg, J. M. (2013). When worlds collide in cyberspace: How boundary work in online social networks impacts professional relationships. *Academy of Management Review*, *38*(4), 645–669.

Parveen, F., Jaafar, N. I., & Ainin, S. (2016). Social media's impact on organizational performance and entrepreneurial orientation in organizations. *Management Decision*, *54*(9), 2208–2234.

Pew Research Center. (2015). Social media usage 2005–2015. Retrieved August, 5, 2019, from https://www.pewinternet.org/2015/10/08/social-networking-usage-2005-2015/

Pew Research Center. (2018a). Social media use in 2018. Retrieved August 6, 2019, from https://www.pewinternet.org/2018/03/01/social-media-use-in-2018/

Pew Research Center. (2018b). Social media use continues to rise in developing countries but plateaus across developed ones. Retrieved August 6, 2019, from https://www.pewresearch.org/global/2018/06/19/social-media-use-continues-to-rise-in-developing-countries-but-plateaus-across-developed-ones/

Pew Research Center. (2019). Social media fact sheet. https://www.pewinternet.org/fact-sheet/social-media/

Rasmussen. (2012). Rasmussen reports. Retrieved May 1, 2016, from http://www.rasmussenreports.com

Reuters. (2015, October 29). *LinkedIn shares leap on strong sales*. Retrieved from http://fortune.com/2015/10/29/linkedin-shares-leap-on-strong-sales/

Robb, D. (2014). HR technology how three companies went social with recruiting. Retrieved August 1, 2019, from https://www.shrm.org/hr-today/news/hr-magazine/pages/0914-social-media-recruiting.aspx

Roberts, S. J., & Roach, T. (2009). Social networking web sites and human resource personnel: Suggestions for job searches. *Business Communication Quarterly*, *72*(1), 110–114.

Roth, P. L., Bobko, P., Van Iddekinge, C. H., & Thatcher, J. B. (2016). Social media in employee-selection-related decisions: A research agenda for uncharted territory. *Journal of Management*, *42*(1), 1–30.

Roth, P. L., Thatcher, J. B., Bobko, P., Matthews, K. D., Ellingson, J. E., & Goldberg, C. B. (2019). Political affiliation and employment screening decisions: The role of similarity and identification processes. *Journal of Applied Psychology*. http://dx.doi.org/10.1037/apl0000422

Rubenstien, A. (2014, April 29). Employee misuse of social media on the rise, survey says. *Law 360*. Retrieved from: http://www.law360.com/articles/532775/employee-misuse-of-social-media-on-the-rise-survey-says

Ruggs, E. N., Speights, S., & Walker, S. S. (2013). Are you in or out? Employment discrimination in online and offline networks. *Industrial and Organizational Psychology*, *6*(4), 457–462.

Ruggs, E. N., Walker, S. S., Blanchard, A., & Gur, S. (2016). Online exclusion: Biases that may arise when using social media in talent acquisition. In *Social Media in Employee Selection and Recruitment* (pp. 289–305). Berlin: Springer International Publishing.

Sackett, P. R. (2007). Revisiting the origins of the typical-maximum performance distinction. *Human Performance*, *20*(3), 179–185.

Sánchez Abril, P., Levin, A., & Del Riego, A. (2012). Blurred boundaries: Social media privacy and the twenty-first-century employee. *American Business Law Journal*, *49*(1), 63–124.

Schmidt, G. B., & O'Connor, K. W. (2015). Fired for Facebook: Using NLRB guidance to craft appropriate social media policies. *Business Horizons*, *58*(5), 571–579.

Schultz, F., Utz, S., & Göritz, A. (2011). Is the medium the message? Perceptions of and reactions to crisis communication via Twitter, blogs and traditional media. *Public Relations Review*, *37*(1), 20–27.

SHRM. (2014). Using social media for talent acquisition—recruitment and screening. Retrieved April 23, 2016, at https://www.shrm.org/research/surveyfindings/pages/social-media-recruiting-screening-2015.aspx

SHRM. (2016). SHRM survey findings. Retrieved April 23, 2016, at https://www.shrm.org/research/surveyfindings/documents/shrm-social-media-recruiting-screening-2015.pdf

SHRM. (2017). Using social media for talent acquisition. Retrieved June 23, 2019, at https://www.shrm.org/hr-today/trends-and-forecasting/research-and-surveys/pages/social-media-recruiting-screening-2015.aspx

Simpson, J. (2015). How L'Oreal uses social media to increase employee engagement. Retrieved June 5, 2019, from https://econsultancy.com/how-l-oreal-uses-social-media-to-increase-employee-engagement/

Smith, B. (2016). The top 8 Russian social networks (and what makes them great). Retrieved from http://www.makeuseof.com/tag/top-8-russian-social-networks-makes-great/

Smither, J. W., Reilly, R. R., Millsap, R. E., Pearlman, K., & Stoffey, R. W. (1993). Applicant reactions to selection procedures. *Personnel Psychology, 46*(1), 49–77.

Sprague, R. (2009). International privacy laws: Rethinking information privacy in an age of online transparency. *Hofstra Labor and Employment Journal, 25*, 395–417.

Statista. (2015a, 2015b). Social network users in 2014 and 2018. Retrieved April, 2015, from http://www.statista.com

Statista. (2017). Reach of selected social networks in the United States as of February 2017, by age group. Retrieved https://www.statista.com/statistics/305245/us-social-network-penetration-age-group/

Statista. (2019). Social media—statistics & facts. Retrieved from https://www.statista.com/topics/1164/social-networks/

Stone, D. L., Lukaszewski, K. M., Stone-Romero, E. F., & Johnson, T. L. (2013). Factors affecting the effectiveness and acceptance of electronic selection systems. *Human Resource Management Review, 23*(1), 50–70.

Stone, D. L., & Kotch, D. A. (1989). Individuals' attitudes toward organizational drug testing policies and practices. *Journal of Applied Psychology, 74*(3), 518–521.

Tabibi, P. A. (2012). *Social media and the hiring process.* Mineola, NY: Meltzer, Lippe, Goldstein, and Breitstone LLP White Paper.

Tencent. (2019). Available from https://www.tencent.com/en-us/articles/15000801565777947.pdf

Treem, J. W., & Leonardi, P. M. (2012). Social media use in organization: Exploring the affordances of visibility editability persistence and association. *Communication Yearbook, 36*, 143–189.

Twitter. (2016). Retrieved from https://about.twitter.com/

van Zoonen, W., & van der Meer, T. (2015). The importance of source and credibility perception in times of crisis: Crisis communication in a socially mediated era. *Journal of Public Relations Research, 27*(5), 371–388.

Verhoeven, P., Tench, R., Zerfass, A., Moreno, A., & Verčič, D. (2012). How European PR practitioners handle digital and social media. *Public Relations Review, 38*(1), 162–164.

Velayanikal, M. (2016). How this language learning app got 100 million users without spending a dollar on marketing. *Tratto il giorno luglio* 25. Retrieved from https://www.techinasia.com/how-duolingo-got-110-million-users

Watson, E. (2016). Social media marketing in Russia (Part 1 of 2). Retrieved from https://www.motionpoint.com/blog/social-media-marketing-in-russia-part-1-of-2/

Wauters, R. (2011). Exclusive: Jobvite recruits $15 million in funding for social hiring application. Available from http://techcrunch.com/2011/05/17/exclusive-jobvite-recruits-15-million-in-funding-for-social-hiring-applications/

Westfall, B. (2016). How Fortune 500 companies engage talent on Twitter. *Software Advice.* Retrieved from http://www.softwareadvice.com/resources/hr-engage-talent-on-twitter/

Williams, K. Z., Schaffer, M. M., & Ellis, L. E. (2013). Legal risk in selection: An analysis of processes and tools. *Journal of Business and Psychology, 28*(4), 401–410.

Yorgan, A. (2019). 10 key statistics on social media usage in Russia (2019). Retrieved August 1, 2019, from https://russiansearchmarketing.com/10-key-statistics-social-media-usage-russia-2019/

Young, G. O., Brown, E. G., Keitt, T., Owyang, J. K., Koplowitz, R., & Shey, H. (2008, April 20). *Global Enterprise Web 2.0 market forecast: 2007 to 2013.* Retrieved from http://www.forrester.com/rb/research

Zhao, D., & Rosson, M. B. (2009, May). How and why people Twitter: the role that microblogging plays in informal communication at work. In *Proceedings of the ACM 2009 International Conference on Supporting Group W*(pp. 243–252). ACM.

Zielinski, D. (2012, August). Find social media's value: The platform's return on investment often eludes measurement. *HR Magazine, 57*, 53–55.

Chapter 17

Avital, M., Beck, R., King, J., Rossi, M., & Teigland, R. (2016). Jumping on the blockchain bandwagon: Lessons of the past and outlook to the future. *Proceedings of the Thirty Seventh International Conference on Information Systems*, Dublin.

Abshire, T. (2013). What do games have to do with a healthy workforce? *HR Focus,* February, 13–15.

Apostolopoulos, A. (2019). The 2019 Gamification at Work Survey. San Francisco: TalentLMS. Retrieved from https://www.talentlms.com/blog/gamification-survey-results/

Armstrong, G. (2005). Differentiation through people: How can HR move beyond business partner? *Human Resource Management, 44*(2), 195–199.

Boese, S. (May 6, 2015). The engagement solution. *Human Resource Executive*, 8.

Bureau of Labor Statistics. (2019). The Employment Situation—November 2019. Retrieved from https://www.bls.gov/news.release/pdf/empsit.pdf

Cappelli, P. (2015, July/August). Can machines ponder HR? *Human Resource Executive*, 5.

Cascio, W. F. (2013). *Managing human resources: Productivity, quality of work life, profits* (9th ed.). New York: McGraw-Hill.

Cisco. (2011). 2011 Cisco Connected World Technology Report. Retrieved from http://www.cisco.com/en/US/solutions/ns341/ns525/ns537/ns705/ns1120/2011-CCWTR-Chapter-3-All-Finding.pdf

Clark, M., & Schramm, J. (2012). *Future insights: The top trends according to SHRM's HR subject matter expert panels.* Alexandria, VA: Society for Human Resource Management, SHRM Research Department.

Colby, S. L., & Ortman, J. M. (2015). Projections of the Size and Composition of the U.S. Population: 2014 to 2060. U.S. Census Bureau, Washington, DC. Retrieved from https://www.census.gov/content/dam/Census/library/publications/2015/demo/p25-1143.pdf

Cornerstone. (2013). The State of Workplace Productivity Report. Retrieved January 30, 2016, from https://www.cornerstoneondemand.com/resources/research/state-of-workplace-productivity-2013

Crabtree, S. (2013). Worldwide, 13% of employees are engaged at work. Retrieved on September 3, 2016, from http://www.gallup.com/poll/165269/worldwide-employees-engaged-work.aspx#

Crawford, K. (2016). Artificial intelligence's white guy problem. Retrieved on May 12, 2019, from https://www.cs.dartmouth.edu/~ccpalmer/teaching/cs89/Resources/Papers/AIs%20White%20Guy%20Problem%20-%20NYT.pdf

Dastin, J. (2018). Amazon scraps secret AI recruiting tool that showed bias against women", Retrieved on May 5, 2019, from https://www.reuters.com/article/us-amazon-com-jobs-automation-insight-idUSKCN1MK08G

Davenport, T. H., & Ronanki, R. (2018). Artificial intelligence for the real world. *Harvard Business Review, 96*(1), 108–116.

Dietvorst, B. J., Simmons, J. P., & Massey, C. (2015). Algorithm aversion: People erroneously avoid algorithms after seeing them err. *Journal of Experimental Psychology: General, 144*(1), 114.

Earley, P. C. (1988). Computer-generated performance feedback in the magazine-subscription industry. *Organizational Behavior and Human Decision Processes, 41*(1), 50–64.

Fleck, C. (2016, June). An algorithm for success. *HR Magazine*, 130–135.

Forrester. (2012). The expanding role of mobility in the workplace. Retrieved from http://www.cisco.com/web/solutions/trends/unified_workspace/docs/Expanding_Role_of_Mobility_in_the_Workplace.pdf

FTC. (2012). Report to Congress Under Section 319 of the Fair and Accurate Credit Transactions Act of 2003. Retrieved from https://www.ftc.gov/sites/default/files/documents/reports/section-319-fair-and-accurate-credit-transactions-act-2003-fifth-interim-federal-trade-commission/130211factareport.pdf

Gartner. (2011). Gartner predicts over 70 percent of the global 2000 organizations will have at least one gamified application by 2014. Retrieved from http://www.gartner.com/it/page.jsp? id=1844115.

Gartner. (2012). Gartner says by 2014, 80 percent of current gamified applications will fail to meet business objectives, primarily due to poor design. Retrieved from http://www.gartner.com/it/page.jsp? id=2251015.

Gartner. (2015). Gartner reveals top predictions for IT organizations and users for 2016 and beyond. Retrieved from http://www.gartner.com/newsroom/id/3143718

Global Workforce Analytics. (2016). Latest telecommuting statistics. Retrieved on September 14, 2016, from http://globalworkplaceanalytics.com/telecommuting-statistics

Gubbi, J., Buyya, R., Marusic, S., & Palaniswami, M. (2013). Internet of Things (IoT): A vision, architectural elements, and future directions. *Future Generation Computer Systems, 29*(7), 1645–1660.

Haines, V. Y., & Lafleur, G. (2008). Information technology usage and human resource roles and effectiveness. *Human Resource Management, 47*(3), 525–540.

Head, A. J., Wihbey, J. Metaxas, P. T., MacMillan, M., & Cohen, D. (2018, October 16). *How students engage with News: Five takeaways for educators, journalists, and librarians.* Project Information Literacy Research Institute.

Hurley-Hanson, A. E., & Giannantonio, C. M. (2008). Human resource information systems in crises. *Proceedings of the Academy of Strategic Management, 7*(1), 23–27.

Hyvärinen, H., Risius, M., & Friis, G. (2017). A blockchain-based approach towards overcoming financial fraud in public sector services. *Business & Information Systems Engineering, 59*(6), 441–456.

IBM. (2017). *Extending expertise: How cognitive computing is transforming HR and the employee experience.* Armonk, NY: IBM.

Johnson, R. D., Marakas, G. M., & Palmer, J. W. (2006). Differential social attributions toward computing technology: An empirical investigation. *International Journal of Human-Computer Studies, 64*(5), 446–460.

Langer, M., König, C. J., & Krause, K. (2017). Examining digital interviews for personnel selection: Applicant reactions and interviewer ratings. *International Journal of Selection and Assessment, 25*(4), 371–382.

Lewis, N. (2019). *IBM transforms its approach to human resources with AI.* Alexandria, VA: Society for Human Resource Management.

Lockwood, N. R. (2010). *Successfully transitioning to a virtual organization: Challenges, impact and technology.* Alexandria, VA: Society for Human Resource Management, HR Content Program, SHRM Research.

Markets and Markets. (2016). Gamification market worth 11.10 billion USD by 2020. Retrieved from http://www.marketsandmarkets.com/PressReleases/gamification.asp

Mauer, R. (2018, March 23) The C-suite lacks confidence in HR data analytics. But why? Retrieved on October 4, 2019, from https://www.shrm.org/resourcesandtools/hr-topics/technology/pages/hr-data-analytics-trust-leaders-kpmg.aspx

McConnell, J. (2016, May 4). Tracking the trends in bringing our own devices to work. *Harvard Business Review.* Retrieved from https://hbr.org/2016/05/tracking-the-trends-in-bringing-our-own-devices-to-work

Min, J.-A. (2018). A how-to guide for using a recruitment chatbot. Retrieved from https://ideal.com/recruitment-chatbot/

Morris, S. S., Wright, P. M., Trevor, J., Stiles, P., Stahl, G. K., Snell, S., Paauwe, J., & Farndale, E. (2009). Global challenges to replicating HR: The role of people, processes and systems. *Human Resource Management, 48*(6), 973–995.

Petrov, C. (2019, March 22). Internet of Things statistics 2019 [The rise of IoT]. TechJury. Retrieved from https://techjury.net/stats-about/internet-of-things-statistics/

Pew Research Center. (2012). *The state of the news media 2012: An annual report on American journalism.* Retrieved from http://stateofthemedia.org/2012/newspapers-building-digital-revenues-proves-painfully-slow/newspapers-by-the-numbers/

Reisenger, D. (10 January, 2019) A.I. expert says automation could replace 40% of jobs in 15 years. *Fortune.* Retrieved from https://fortune.com/2019/01/10/automation-replace-jobs/

Robb, D. (2012). Let the games begin. *HR Magazine,* September 2012, 93–97.

Robson, Karen, Plangger, K., Kietzmann, J. H., McCarthy, I., & Pitt, L. (2015). Is it all a game? Understanding the principles of gamification. *Business Horizons, 58*(4), 411–420.

Rosenbaum, E. (2019). IBM artificial intelligence can predict with 95% accuracy which workers are about to quit their jobs. Retrieved on January 14, 2020, from https://www.cnbc.com/2019/04/03/ibm-ai-can-predict-with-95-percent-accuracy-which-employees-will-quit.html

Rowland, C. (December 16, 2019). With fitness trackers in the workplace, bosses can monitor your every step—and possibly more. *Washington Post.* Retrieved from https://www.washingtonpost.com/business/economy/with-fitness-trackers-in-the-workplace-bosses-can-monitor-your-every-step-and-possibly-more/2019/02/15/75ee0848-2a45-11e9-b011-d8500644dc98_story.html

Sammer, J., & Miller, S. (2013). Time for defined contribution health benefits? Retrieved on 9/12/16 from https://www.shrm.org/resourcesandtools/hr-topics/benefits/pages/defined-contribution-health-benefits.aspx.

Shane, S. (2014). How businesses are handling the Obamacare employer mandate. *Entrepreneur Magazine.* Retrieved on 9/12/16 from https://www.entrepreneur.com/article/239039.

Sierra-Cedar. (2015). CedarCrestone 2015–2016 HR systems survey: 18th annual edition: Innovation, insights, and strategy (18th annual ed.). Alpharetta, GA: Author.

Society for Human Resource Management (SHRM). (2016). *SHRM customized healthcare benchmarking report.* Alexandria, VA: Society for Human Resource Management.

Sorenson, S., & Garman, K. (2013). How to tackle U.S. employees' stagnating engagement. *Gallup Business Journal.* Retrieved on September 21, 2016, from http://www.gallup.com/businessjournal/162953/tackle-employees-stagnating-engagement.aspx

Stanton, J. M., & Coovert, M. D. (2004). Guest editors' note: Turbulent waters: The intersection of information technology and human resources. *Human Resource Management, 43*(2/3), 121–125.

Stevens, L. (2015). Fitness data, fad or frenzy. *Human Resource Executive.* December, 25–26.

Sturman, M. C., Hannon, J. M., & Milkovich, G. T. (1996). Computerized decision aids for flexible benefits decisions: The effects of an expert system and decision support system on employee intentions and satisfaction with benefits. *Personnel Psychology, 49*(4), 883–908.

Syntonic. (2016). BYOD usage in the enterprise. Retrieved from https://syntonic.com/wp-content/uploads/2016/09/Syntonic-2016-BYOD-Usage-in-the-Enterprise.pdf.

Tian, X., & Pu, Y. (2008). An artificial neural network approach to hotel employee satisfaction: The case of China. *Social Behavior and Personality: An International Journal, 36*(4), 467–482.

Toossi, M., & Torpey, E. (2017). *Older workers: Labor force trends and career options.* Washington, DC.: Bureau of Labor Statistics. Retrieved from https://www.bls.gov/careeroutlook/2017/article/older-workers.htm

U.S. Census Bureau. (2019). QuickFacts. Retrieved from https://www.census.gov/quickfacts/fact/table/US/PST045218

Wells, S. J. (2008). Ground rules on background checks. Retrieved from https://www.shrm.org/hr-today/news/hr-magazine/pages/2wells-development%20of%20industry%20standards.aspx

Wright, A. D. (2015). *How fitness trackers can boost employee wellness.* Alexandria, VA: Society for Human Resource Management.

Wright, A. (2017). *Top HR technology trends for 2018.* Alexandria, VA: Society for Human Resource Management

Zarrehparvar, M. (2013). Mobile is "the new IT": 5 reasons to spend more on enterprise mobility. Retrieved from http://venturebeat.com/2013/07/27/mobile-is-the-new-it-5-reasons-to-spend-more-on-enterprise-mobility/

ABOUT THE EDITORS

Richard D. Johnson received his PhD from the University of Maryland and is currently an Associate Professor at Washington State University. He has published more than 50 journal articles and book chapters on topics such as HRIS, computer self-efficacy, e-learning, the psychological impacts of computing, and the digital divide. His research has been published in outlets such as *Information Systems Research*, *Journal of the Association for Information Systems*, *International Journal of Human Computer Studies*, and *Human Resource Management Review*. Dr. Johnson is a past chair of AIS SIGHCI and is a senior editor at Data Base and an associate editor at AIS Transactions on Human-Computer Interaction. He is also an editor of the books *Human Resource Information Systems: Basics, Applications and Future Directions* and *The Wiley Blackwell Handbook of the Psychology of the Internet at Work*.

Kevin D. Carlson is Professor of Management and Associate Dean for Research and Faculty Affairs in the Pamplin College of Business at Virginia Tech. He has published research on a wide variety of topics related to the evaluation of individual, process, and organizational effectiveness. His work has been published in the *Journal of Applied Psychology*, *Personnel Psychology*, *Journal of Management*, and *Organizational Research Methods*. He is the 2016 recipient of the Robert McDonald Advancement of Organizational Research Methodology Award and past chair of the board of directors of the International Association for Human Resource Information Management (IHRIM). His current research addresses how to use HR metrics and workforce analytics to enhance organizational performance.

Michael J. Kavanagh is Professor Emeritus of Management at the State University of New York at Albany. He is past editor of *Group & Organization Management* and a fellow of the American Psychological Association, the American Psychological Society, the Society for Industrial and Organizational Psychology, and the Eastern Academy of Management. He has been involved in the HRIS field since 1982. He established the HRIS MBA program at the University at Albany in 1984 and has taught numerous courses in the field of HRIS. In 2006, he received the Award for Career Excellence from the International Association for Human Resource Information Management (IHRIM). He received his PhD in industrial/organizational psychology from Iowa State University in 1969.

ABOUT THE CONTRIBUTORS

Michael D. Bedell is Dean and Professor in the College of Business and Management at Northeastern Illinois University. He spent 15 years as a Professor of Management and M.B.A. Program Director at California State University, Bakersfield. He has worked in the banking industry as a TQM expert focused on improving service quality. He has also worked for Payless ShoeSource in corporate organizational development, and his responsibilities included developing and validating selection methods, implementing a PeopleSoft HRIS, and training merchandising teams. His research and consulting interests are centered on HRIS, HR metrics, and HR strategy, with a focus on small or family businesses. He is a member of numerous professional and academic organizations. He received his PhD in human resource management with a minor in operations management from Indiana University in 1996.

Stephanie L. Black is an assistant professor at Texas A&M University at San Antonio, Texas, in the department of management. She received her PhD at the University of Texas at San Antonio, Texas. She has worked in various industries for Fortune 500 companies as well as family businesses and start-up companies. She does consulting in the community with start-up companies and business development. Her research has been published in outlets such as the *Journal of Management, Journal of Business and Psychology, Journal of Small Business and Entrepreneurship, Employee Responsibilities and Rights Journal, Leadership*, and *Journal of Social Media in Society*. Her research interests focus on social media usage within organizations, entrepreneurship, and social networking.

Tanya Bondarouk is Professor of Human Resource Management and the head of the department of HRM at the University of Twente, the Netherlands. She also works as the associate editor for the *International Journal of Human Resource Management* and as the co-editor of the *Advanced Series in Management* (Emerald Publishers). She has been working on the research area of innovating HRM function, with the focus on electronic HRM, and has edited a number of special issues in international journals on this topic. Her main publications concern an integration of human resource management and social aspects of Information Technology Implementations and appear in the *International Journal of HRM, Personnel Review, European Journal of Management*, and *European Journal of Information Systems*. Her research covers both private and public sectors and deals with a variety of areas such as the implementation of e-HRM, management of HR-IT change, and HRM contribution to IT projects.

Ralf Burbach is the Assistant Head of School and Head of the Hospitality Management Discipline in the School of Hospitality Management and Tourism at the Technological University Dublin. Previously, he occupied the position of Campus Coordinator at Wexford Campus, Institute of Technology Carlow. Dr. Burbach has lectured in several higher education institutions in the Republic of Ireland. Prior to his academic career, Dr Burbach worked for 13 years in the hospitality industry and held managerial posts in Germany, the United Kingdom, and Ireland. His research interests include digital and electronic HRM, global talent management, international and comparative human resource management, HR metrics, international hospitality operations, and vocational and dual education systems. Dr. Burbach is the director of networking at the International Council on Hospitality Restaurant and Institutional Education (ICHRIE) and the immediate past president at European CHRIE. He is a chartered member of the Chartered Institute of Personnel and Development (CIPD) and a member of the Irish Hospitality Institute. In addition, Dr. Burbach serves on the Hospitality Careers Oversight Group for Ireland, an advisory body overseeing the development of human capital in hospitality and tourism.

Michael L. Canniff has been a computer science, management, and accounting information systems lecturer at University of the Pacific since 2003. He has received multiple grants and developed several new courses for MIS/AIS curriculum. He is also the CEO of PyanGo, which specializes in nonprofit accounting software and services. He has been a senior partner with Mercury Consulting, a leading cloud technology services company; vice president of development at Acuitrek, and director of development at PeopleSoft. Mike specializes in application integration between enterprise systems including human resource applications. He has more than 20 years of experience with all facets of software development.

Steven D. Charlier is an associate professor and chair of the Department of Management at Georgia Southern University. He holds degrees from the College of William and Mary (BBA/finance), the University of Denver (MIM/e-commerce), and the University of Iowa (PhD/management). Steve has held a variety of managerial positions in the information technology/consulting, automotive, and entertainment industries. He has been a certified project management professional (PMP) since 2003 and has consulted with several organizations, including various federal government agencies and nonprofit organizations. His research interests are focused on the modern work environment and include virtual teams, e-learning, leadership in a virtual world, and management education. His research has been published in *The Leadership Quarterly*, *Human Resource Management*, *Journal of Organizational Behavior*, *Academy of Management Learning & Education*, *Journal of Vocational Behavior*, and *Human Resource Management Review*. He is currently an associate editor for *Academy of Management Learning & Education* and *Human Resource Management*.

David N. Dickter is the director of interprofessional education research and strategic assessment at Western University of Health Sciences. He has been a consultant to *Fortune* 500 companies for the selection, assessment, and development of individuals at all levels. Previously, he was a senior manager in talent assessment at PSI and in the corporate organization effectiveness group at AT&T. His experience also includes personnel selection and research roles at Educational Testing Service and the United States Air Force. He has published and presented research and practical papers on selection and technology, turnover, decision making, and various other human resources topics. He received his PhD in industrial/organizational psychology from The Ohio State University.

James H. Dulebohn is professor of human resource management at Michigan State University's School of Human Resources and Labor Relations. His research interests include decision making, HRIS, compensation, leadership, and the application of neuroscience methods to examining organizationally relevant attitudes and behaviors. His articles have appeared in journals including the *Academy of Management Journal, Personnel Psychology, Journal of Applied Psychology, Journal of Management, Journal of Organizational Behavior, Journal of Risk and Insurance, Organizational Behavior and Human Decision Processes, Research in Higher Education*, and others. Prof. Dulebohn is also co-editor of the Research in Human Resource Management series published by Information Age Press. In 2017, he received *Journal of Management*'s Best Paper Award for the paper with the highest five-year impact. He has consulted and conducted research for a variety of organizations, including Avaya, Dow Chemical, Medtronic, Monsanto, Raytheon, Samsung, TIAA-CREF, State of Illinois, and State of Texas. He earned his PhD and master's degrees in human resource management from the University of Illinois at Urbana–Champaign.

Hadi El-Farr is currently the Director of the Professional Masters of Human Resource Management at the Department of Human Resource Management, School of Management and Labor Relations, Rutgers University–New Jersey. He has taught graduate and undergraduate courses in global HRM, strategic HRM, staffing, and organizational behavior and provided professional and executive training in artificial intelligence and its impact on HRM practices and HR functional excellence. Hadi completed his PhD in human resource management at the University of Leeds. His research interests focus on the role of HRM in supporting knowledge management within organizations and the impact of artificial intelligence on HR practices and the HR profession. Before academia, Hadi had several years of global and multi-industry professional experience. He is exposed to the American, European, Middle Eastern, and African markets and has worked in the management consulting, higher education, hotels and restaurants, trade, and retail industries.

Charles H. Fay is currently a professor of human resource management at the School of Management and Labor Relations, Rutgers University. He has taught undergraduate and graduate courses in rewards management, performance appraisal, HRIS, statistics, and labor economics. He has also taught rewards management, performance management, and HRIS in several executive and management education programs in the United States, Singapore, Malaysia, and Indonesia. His research focuses on rewards and performance management. He is the coauthor of several books, including *The Performance Imperative, New Strategies for Public Pay*, and *The Executive Handbook on Compensation*. He was a presidential appointee to the Federal Salary Commission and served as a consultant to the Bureau of Labor Statistics on the National Compensation Survey. He has earned certified compensation professional status from WorldatWork (formerly the American Compensation Association). He has served as an expert witness on compensation issues before the Presidential Emergency Board numerous times and testified before Congress on compensation and performance management issues. He has a PhD in management and organization behavior from the University of Washington.

Christopher J. Hartwell is an Assistant Professor of Management in the Jon M. Huntsman School of Business at Utah State University. His research focuses on employee selection, talent management, and the use of technology in organizations. He has published in high-quality academic journals such as *Journal of Applied Psychology, Journal of World*

Business, Personnel Psychology, and *Journal of Vocational Behavior*. Chris has held a variety of professional positions in the field of human resources and has been a certified human resources professional since 2001 through the Human Resource Certification Institute (PHR) and the Society for Human Resource Management (SHRM-CP). He received his PhD in organizational behavior and human resource management from the Krannert School of Management at Purdue University. He consults with organizations on various human resources topics, including recruitment and selection, inclusive diversity, onboarding, effective leadership, and developing successful organizational teams.

Linda C. Isenhour is currently a professor of management at Eastern Michigan University, where she develops and teaches courses in international human resource management, HRM, and HRIS. Her research interests include recruitment, cultural values, strategic human resource management, and human resource information systems. She has served as guest editor for editions of the *Journal of Managerial Psychology* and published articles and book chapters on HRM and technology, recruitment, HRM and cultural values, and HRM and privacy. In addition, she has presented scholarly papers to the Academy of Management, the Society of Industrial and Organizational Psychology, the Southern Management Association, and the Western Business and Management Association. A member of the Academy of Management, the Southern Management Association, and the Society for Human Resource Management, Dr. Isenhour has also earned certification as a Global Professional in Human Resources (GPHR) from HRCI and SHRM Senior Certified Professional (SHRM-SCP) from the Society for Human Resource Management.

Andrew F. Johnson received his PhD from The University of Texas at San Antonio in strategic management. He has been an assistant professor of management at Texas A&M University–Corpus Christi since 2015. He teaches courses in multinational management, strategic management, and a graduate-level course in business, government, and society. His primary areas of research are on the impact of social change on organizations. He has written articles on social media in the employment process, the role of politics within an organization, and corporate political activity. His articles have been published in *The Journal of Social Media in Society*, *Employee Responsibilities and Rights Journal*, *Journal of Management*, *Journal of Organizational Behavior*, *Human Resource Management Review*, and *Business & Society*. Prior to his academic appointment, he worked previously in state and local government.

Kimberly M. Lukaszewski is an associate professor of management at Wright State University. Her research is focused on electronic human resources, privacy, and diversity issues. Her work has been published in journals such as the *Human Resource Management Review*, the *Journal of Business and Psychology*, the *Journal of Business Issues*, the *Journal of the Academy of Business Education*, the *Business Journal of Hispanic Research*, and the *International Association for Human Resources Information Management Journal*. She has written various book chapters published in the *Handbook of Workplace Diversity*, *The Brave New World of eHR: Human Resources Management in the Digital Age*, *The Influence of Culture on Human Resource Management Processes and Practices*, *The Handbook of Human Resource Management Education*, and *Advances in Human Performance and Cognitive Engineering Research*. She received her MBA in HRIS and her PhD in organizational studies from the University at Albany.

Miguel R. Olivas-Luján is a Teaching Professor at The Pennsylvania State University and Associate Director of its Center for International Human Resources Studies (CIHRS). A former department chair and professor at Clarion University of Pennsylvania, his work is published in the *Journal of International Business Studies (JIBS)*, *International Journal of Human Resources Management (IJHRM)*, and others. Miguel has been recognized at both AOM and Eastern AOM, with several leadership or outstanding reviewer awards. A senior editor for the *Advanced Series in Management* (Emerald Publishing, UK), he has published more than 50 scientific articles, scholarly book chapters, and encyclopedic entries and served on editorial boards that include the *Journal of Managerial Issues* and the *Journal of Managerial Psychology*. He served as editor-in-chief for *The Business Journal of Hispanic Research*.

Lisa M. Plantamura is dean and professor, School of Professional Studies, and director of the MBA program at Centenary University in New Jersey. Previously, she was the co-founder and vice president of Operations and Development for *Professors on Demand*, and she spent more than 20 years in human resource information systems management positions, working in a variety of industries and as an independent consultant. She was a cofounder and director of the Human Resources Information Management Society and a director for IHRIM, from which she received the prestigious Summit Award for significant, long-term contributions to the association's advancement, as well as the Professional of Human Resources Information designation. She also served on the HRIM Foundation Board. Dr. Plantamura has a doctorate in organizational leadership and adult education, as well as an MBA, and has published several articles on HRIS topics. Her current areas of interest and research are in online teaching and learning.

Huub Ruël is a Professor in Global Talent Management and International Business Diplomacy at Hotelschool The Hague (The Netherlands; QS 2019 ranking no. 6 in the world) and a research affiliate at Twente University (The Netherlands; an FT100 university). He is one of the founding authors of e-HRM research publications, together with leading U.S. and European scholars, and he is one of the founding members of an international e-HRM/HRIS research community that organizes bi-annual international e-HRM research conferences. Huub Ruël published scholarly and practice-oriented articles in international journal, guest edited multiple special issues for international journals, and guest edited books on e-HRM/HRIS and international business diplomacy. Huub Ruël previously worked in Lebanon for the American University of Beirut, in Kuwait for the Kuwait-Maastricht School of Management in Kuwait City, and for Utrecht University (The Netherlands). Furthermore, he has a rich international teaching experience in places such as China, Finland, and Italy.

Dianna Stone received her PhD from Purdue University and is now a Research Professor at the University of New Mexico, a Visiting Professor at the University at Albany, and an Affiliate Professor at Virginia Tech. Her research focuses on diversity in organizations, cultural influences on human resource management, privacy, and electronic human resource management. Results of her research have been published in the *Journal of Applied Psychology*, *Personnel Psychology*, *Academy of Management Review*, *Organizational Behavior and Human Decision Processes*, and *Human Resource Management Review*. In 2005, she co-authored a book titled *The Brave New World of e HR: Human Resources Management in the Digital Age* with Hal Gueutal, and in 2018, she published a follow-up version of that book titled *The Brave New World of eHRM 2.0* with James Dulebohn. She is currently the editor of *Research in Human Resource Management* and a Fellow of the Society for Industrial Psychology, the American Psychological Association, and the Association for Psychological Science. Dr. Stone also received the Scholarly Achievement Award and the Sage Service Award from the Gender and Diversity Division of the Academy of Management and the Trailblazer Award from the PhD Project.

Humayun Zafar is a professor of information security and assurance at Kennesaw State University. He received his doctorate from the University of Texas at San Antonio and is a certified ethical hacker. His research interests include organizational security risk management, network security, and organizational performance. Some of his previous work has appeared in journals and conferences such as the *Communications of the Association for Information Systems, Information Resources Management Journal, Journal of Information Privacy and Security, AIS Transactions on Human Computer Interaction, Human Resource Management Review, International Journal of Information Management, Hawaii International Conference on System Sciences*, and *Americas Conference on Information Systems*.

NOTES

Chapter 1

1. The name of the company in the advertisement has been changed.

Chapter 3

1. Although most organizations no longer build full systems from scratch, many organizations find it necessary to customize their systems by building their own modules or apps. Thus, the same need and logic would apply to these small-scale changes.

Chapter 4

1. Interested readers are encouraged to read Ma and Liu (2004) for a thorough review of this research.

2. Note that this is the case from the vignette, plus added material.

Chapter 5

1. See Arizona Department of Administration, Human Resources website at http://www.hr.az.gov/HRIS/HRIS_About_Us.asp.

Chapter 6

1. Dollars are used as an example of currency throughout this chapter. Other currencies such as the euro, yen, or peso could be substituted for it as appropriate for each country or region.

2. The company name is fictitious to protect the confidentiality of the actual company.

3. The names of the company and employees are fictional to protect confidentiality.

4. See Chapter 9 for a discussion of some of these reports.

5. See Chapter 9.

Chapter 8

1. For more information on conducting a benefit-cost analysis, please see Chapter 14.

2. Ethical Bank is a pseudonym for a global bank that employees approximately 55,000 employees in more than 1,400 banks across 50 countries across the globe.

3. This chart was created with data drawn from SierraCedar (2019).

4. Please note this this is only a short summary of the use of SNSs in talent management. For more complete discussions, please see Chapters 9 and 16.

5. This chart was created with data drawn from SierraCedar (2019).

6. A full discussion of analytics is beyond the scope of this chapter. Interested readers can refer to Chapter 14 for a more detailed discussion of workforce analytics.

Chapter 10

1. The company's name must remain confidential.

2. The bold terms in this chapter are included in the list of key terms. These terms cannot and do not purport to provide an exhaustive list of HRIS T&D applications. However, they furnish explanations of the key concepts discussed in this chapter. More extensive e-learning glossaries are available on the Internet, for instance, from the Association for Talent Development, or ATD (https://www.td.org/Publications/Newsletters/Learning-Circuits/Glossary).

Chapter 12

1. Figure 12.1 communicates similar information as Figure 1.3. Readers are encouraged to look at both for an understanding of the role of HRIS and eHRM in organizations.

2. The full set of questions and concerns regarding privacy are beyond the scope of this chapter, but interested readers should look at Chapter 15 for more information on employee privacy concerns.

Chapter 13

1. The company and individual names used are fictitious.

2. This chapter cannot cover all the literature and issues in the field of IHRM. However, for the interested reader, there are excellent and comprehensive textbooks available on IHRM (Briscoe & Schuler, 2004; Dowling, Festing, & Engle, 2013; Harzing & Pinnington, 2014; Özbilgin, Groutsis, & Harvey, 2014).

3. In this chapter, compensation will refer to the entire wages, salaries, benefits, and extra allowances available in an MNE.

Chapter 16

1. https://www.dell.com/learn/us/en/uscorp1/corp-comm/social-media-policy.

INDEX

Note: Figures and Tables are indicated by 'f' and 't' following the page number.